PRINCIPLES OF

Microeconomics

FIRST EDITION

John E. Sayre
Capilano College

Alan J. Morris
Capilano College

McGraw-Hill Ryerson Limited

Toronto   New York   Auckland   Bogotá   Caracas
Lisbon   London   Madrid   Mexico   New Delhi
San Juan   Singapore   Sydney   Tokyo

PRINCIPLES OF MICROECONOMICS
First Edition

ISBN: 0-07-551685-3

1 2 3 4 5 6 7 8 9 10   BBM   5 4 3 2 1 0 9 8 7 6

Printed and bound in Canada

Care has been taken to trace ownership of copyright material contained in this text. The publishers will gladly take any information that will enable them to rectify any reference or credit in subsequent editions.

Senior Editor: Jennifer Mix
Supervising Editor: Margaret Henderson
Developmental Editor: Daphne Scriabin
Production Editor: Shirley Corriveau
Page Layout: Bookman Typesetting Co.
Typeface: New Century Schoolbook/Avant Garde
Cover & Text Design: Dianna Little
Cover Photo: Three Prisms in a Row © Tecmap/First Light
Printing & Binding: Best Book Manufacturers

Canadian Cataloguing in Publication Data
Sayre, John Edward, 1942-
    Principles of microeconomics

1st ed.
Includes index.
ISBN 0-07-551685-3

1. Microeconomics.   I. Morris, Alan J. (Alan James).
II. Title.

HB172.S38 1996   338.5   C95-931833-X

With love to my two daughters:
Alison and Meridith
(JES)

and

To the ones I love:
Wakako, Daniel and Christian
(AJM)

ABOUT THE AUTHORS

Alan Morris, though loathe to admit it, first worked as an accountant in England, where he became an Associate of the Chartered Institute of Secretaries and obtained his first degree in 1971 in Manchester, U.K. He subsequently obtained his Master's degree at Simon Fraser University, B.C. in 1973. He worked on his doctorate at Leicester University, U.K., and returned to work in business in Vancouver, B.C., until his appointment at Capilano College in 1988. He presently resides in North Vancouver with his wife and two sons and is an avid devotee of classical music, mountaineering, soccer and beer. He is not a past president of the Canadian Economics Association, nor was he ever a member of the Economic Council of Canada. To his knowledge, he has never been an advisor to the Canadian government.

John E. Sayre earned a B.S.B.A. at the University of Denver and an M.A. from Boston University. He began teaching principles of economics while in the Peace Corps in Malawi. He came to Vancouver to do Ph.D. studies at Simon Fraser University and ended up teaching at Capilano College for the next 28 years. As a balance to the rigours of economics, he enjoys reading popular accounts of the exciting developments in quantum physics, following the Blue Jays and listening to his extensive collection of Kitaro CDs.

CONTENTS IN BRIEF

CONTENTS

CHAPTER TWO Workbook   63

CHAPTER THREE Demand and Supply 2: Elaboration and Application   74

CHAPTER THREE Workbook   99

CHAPTER FOUR Elasticity 110

CHAPTER FOUR Workbook 136

CHAPTER FIVE Consumer Demand 147

CHAPTER TEN Monopoly 321

CHAPTER TEN Workbook 343

CHAPTER ELEVEN Monopolistic Competition and Oligopoly 356

CHAPTER THIRTEEN International Trade   440

CHAPTER THIRTEEN Workbook   461

CHAPTER FOURTEEN Towards a Political Economy   477

PREFACE

■ ■ ■ ■ ■ ■ ■

After teaching economics for many years, we are convinced that most economics textbooks are aimed more at other economists than at beginning students. Such books tend to be encyclopedic in scope and intimidating in appearance. It is small wonder that the average student emerges from an economics course feeling that the discipline really does earn its reputation of being daunting and unapproachable. Economics is challenging, but our experience is that it can also be intriguing and enjoyable. To help students see the discipline in this light, a textbook should be concise, without sacrificing either clarity or accepted standards of rigour, and it should be well written and well organized. To that end, we have tried to offer a creatively simplified approach to microeconomics without omitting any of the essentials.

In writing this text we attempted to stay focused on two guiding principles which come out of our experience as teachers. The first is that students are often unable to distinguish the fundamental principles of economics from current issues until they have had a thorough grounding in those principles. Second, we believe that students should learn fundamental principles which they can apply for a lifetime rather than concentrate on issues which in a few years will no longer be current. As a result, after much thought, we decided to keep discussion on current topics and issues to a minimum and leave it to the individual instructor to augment and elaborate in this area as necessary. In doing this, we do not mean to imply that issues are unimportant, and we know that students like to discuss them. However, the reward of a stimulating debate on issues must follow the work of learning what we believe to be time-honoured principles.

CONTENTS

The *Principles of Microeconomics* has not been divided into different sections since, in many ways, such a sectioning would be arbitrary and really of no great significance. After all, this is a very integrated subject and many important themes appear and reappear throughout the text.

Chapter 1 discusses some very important themes and sets the stage for a number of ideas which will be developed in detail later. For this reason, we have been careful not to intimidate the student with a barrage of new definitions and jargon. The chapter does, however, cover the essential aspects of the three fundamental questions facing all economies and looks at the ways in which different types of economies have tried to answer these questions. We look briefly at the language and methodology of economics and introduce the important concept of production possibilities.

Chapter 2 is an introduction to demand and supply. In all microeconomics textbooks this is a pivotal chapter, and it is vital that students get a good grip on this concept. We proceed through the various ideas as clearly as we can and introduce the concept of equilibrium as early as possible. Once this is done, we have found that students can then deal with the dynamics a little more easily.

Chapter 3 tries to broaden and deepen the students' grasp of the fundamental workings of the market. It looks at how the market adjusts to changing conditions and how it is prevented from functioning by the introduction of price controls. By "playing" with demand and supply curves, students are aided in their understanding of how abstraction can help to analyze many events in the real world of economics. Chapter 4 looks at elasticity, and without getting bogged down too much with formulae, shows how this tool can explain many happenings in the world and, just as importantly, how it can be used to dispel some currently held myths. Chapter 5 examines consumer behaviour by looking at the theory of marginal utility. Though often superseded by other theories, we believe that marginal utility is still able to shed a great deal of light on important aspects such as consumer surplus and price discrimination.

Chapter 6 is the first chapter to examine the behaviour of the firm. It gives a clear explanation of the different types of costs facing the firm and of the important distinction between the short run and the long run in economics. It then shows how the various cost curves are derived from production data. Chapter 7 looks at the long-run costs of the firm, introduces returns to scale and shows how economies and diseconomies of scale contribute to the structure of different industries.

Chapter 8 looks at perfectly competitive markets and shows how firms break even, how they are able to maximize economic profits, and why they are forced, at times, to temporarily shut down. Chapter 9 begins by looking at the long-run situation of both the competitive firm and the industry and then explains why, because of the benefits it can deliver to society, the competitive market is often regarded as a "perfect" market. The remainder of the chapter looks at some of the shortcomings of such markets. This is an important chapter because it brings together many of the themes from earlier chapters and lays the stage for the investigation of other market structures in subsequent chapters.

Chapter 10 is a reasonably straightforward look at monopoly markets and explains how they come into existence and why governments have been wary of their behaviour. It looks at the pros and cons of regulating monopolies and examines different ways in which this is done. The other forms of imperfect competition, monopolistic competition and oligopoly, are examined in Chapter 11. The discussion of oligopolies begins by reviving the classic Cournot model. In Chapter 12 we shift our attention from product to factor markets and give a broad but clear exposition of the markets for labour, natural resources, capital and entrepreneurial ability. Chapter 13 investigates international trade and introduces the theory of comparative advantage and looks at the pros and cons of free trade and at the effects of restricting trade.

Chapter 14 has a different flavour from the other chapters, and for this reason contains no study guide questions. In this chapter we look at the failure of government intervention and the failure of the discipline of economics to address some of the real issues facing people today. It looks at power and the way it has evolved over time, and at how a new group of knowledge workers might upset the present balance of power.

TEXTBOOK FEATURES

We have provided a number of features to help the student come to grips with the subject matter. Four different types of boxes are used throughout the book:

- **Glossary** boxes indicate the first use of any term which is part of the language of economics. The term itself is in bold print and the definition is given within the accompanying box. The page number of each box is supplied at the end of the chapter for quick and easy reference, and a complete glossary of terms is found at the end of the book.

- **Review** boxes contain very straightforward questions which cover the most basic material of each chapter. Students should be able to answer these questions directly from the text and must master these basics before they will be able to comprehend the more abstract concepts that are at the heart of economics.

- **Data** boxes identify material which is either general information or supplementary material which, hopefully, adds a little colour to the students' reading.

- **Study Guide Question** boxes have been integrated into the text and are scattered at important points throughout each chapter. Their purpose is to give students immediate feedback on how well they understand the more abstract concept(s) discussed. In doing this, we have tried to establish what we believe to be a minimum standard of comprehension which all students should strive to achieve. Students can check their own progress by comparing their answers with those in the Answer Key which is included with the book.

THE WORKBOOK FEATURES

We believe that answering questions and doing problems should be *part of the learning process*. For this reason we chose to integrate a complete **Workbook** within the text. Thus a workbook section, with pages screened in colour, immediately follows each chapter of the text. We specifically wrote the questions in the workbook to cover the material, but *only* the material, found in the text itself.

We have chosen a user-friendly design for the workbook sections and we hope this will encourage significant student participation. These sections therefore embrace a number of different types of tests.

Within each workbook section we begin with **Study Tips**, our suggestions to the students for managing the material in the chapter. Next, we reinforce the Review Questions and Glossary boxes from the text with a true/false section entitled **Are You Sure?** These questions obviously require students to make a choice, but if they choose false, they are required to explain why. The **Translations** section requires students to translate a graph or other mathematical material into words (or vice versa) or to translate words into a mathematical presentation. Next comes a series of multiple choice questions, entitled **Choose the Best**. These increase in difficulty and in number of optional answers offered as the student works through the twenty questions. The **What's Wrong?** section includes a paragraph of text in which students are asked to identify a few deliberately placed errors.

The most important part of each workbook section contains one or more **Key Problems** which students need to master. This problem encompasses the fundamental idea or ideas in the chapter. For those who have difficulty answering the Key Problem, we follow up by carefully working through the complete answer in the section called **Need a Hand?** Students are then given the opportunity to really test their understanding with an additional, very similar problem, called **More of the Same**. A number of shorter questions follow in a section imaginatively entitled **Other Problems**.

The answers to these different types of workbook questions, as well as answers to the Study Guide Questions found in the text itself, can be found in the **Answer Key** which is included with the text. We chose to provide the answers in this way so that the student can have the text open to the question page and the Key open to the answer at the same time.

The **Unanswered Questions** in the workbook section contain a number of short essay, analytical and numerical problems for which there are no answers in the Key. Instructors therefore have the option of using these questions for exams, out-of-class assignments, or other types of tests. The answers to the analytical and numerical questions are found in the *Instructor's Manual to accompany Principles of Microeconomics and Principles of Macroeconomics*.

SUPPLEMENTS FOR INSTRUCTORS

Instructor's Manual   There are three parts to each chapter of the *Instructor's Manual*. First is a brief overview of the chapter with some rationale for the topics included. Second is a description of how we think the material found in the chapter is best presented. Between the two of us, we have taught the micro principles course over two hundred times and we pass on helpful hints gained from this extensive experience to instructors who may not have been at it so long. More experienced instructors who have found a comfortable groove will simply ignore many of these suggestions.

The third part contains the answers to the analytical and numerical questions that appear in the Unanswered Questions section of the workbook. We have not included answers to the essay questions of this section because a basic answer can be directly found in the text and a more sophisticated answer would become rather subjective.

Testbank   Much effort went into writing the *Testbank to accompany Principles of Microeconomics* in order to ensure that the questions cover all topics in the textbook, but *only* those topics. Questions are written in plain English and in true question form to minimize any misunderstanding by students as to what is being asked. There are approximately one hundred questions per chapter. They come in the order of the topics covered in the chapter and include a mixture of both four- and-five-answer questions. In addition, certain clearly marked questions are repeats of multiple choice questions from the workbook section. This gives the instructor the option of including multiple choice questions on an exam that students have, or have not, seen before. A computerized version of the testbank is available free of charge to adopters of the textbook.

Annual Statistical Update Adopters of the text will also receive up-to-date national income statistics on disk annually.

Few things are more satisfying than witnessing a student's zest for learning. We hope that this textbook adds a little to this process.

ACKNOWLEDGEMENTS

The publication of *Principles of Microeconomics,* First Edition, brings to a close a six-year project in which we were helped by many people. Professor Emeritus Ken Strand and Professor Peter Kennedy, both of Simon Fraser University, and Larry Brown of Selkirk College read early drafts and gave us encouragement to continue. In addition, we wish to thank the following economists who participated in the formal review process:

Dale Box, University College of the Fraser Valley

Bill Gallivan, University College of Cape Breton

Cal Shaw, George Brown College

Frank Strain, Mount Allison University

Student assistants Marjike Nap and Carolus Chow helped with the nitty-gritty details of computer program learning and graphing.

We would like to acknowledge our colleagues in the Economics Department of Capilano College: Nigel Amon and Ken Moak for their encouragement, and Mina Nia and Mahak Yaseri for their work in the endless task of striving for accuracy and consistency in the workbook questions and answers. Numerous colleagues in other departments also gave us encouragement, and sometimes praise, which is greatly appreciated.

The administration at the college were very accommodating and supportive, while the staff of the computer services and social sciences division were always helpful and provided badly needed help when requested.

Shirley Corriveau's editing has been superb while Margaret Henderson and Daphne Scriabin at McGraw-Hill Ryerson have offered excellent professional skills.

We wish to acknowledge the patience, professionalism and continued faith shown in us by Jennifer Mix, our senior editor during most of the project. Her ability to ensure that things got done while remaining very human in the process is testimony to an exceptional person with many fine qualities.

We are particularly happy to recognize the endless hours of effort given by Clélie Rich in editing, providing graphics and offering friendly cajoling. She did her best to prevent us from being too academic and taught us to write and think much more clearly and, in the end, we hope, much more effectively. Clélie, more than anyone else, taught us that an idea is far more powerful and effective when expressed simply and clearly than when it is made to sound mysterious or overly important.

Finally, we wish to acknowledge the help and support of our families who patiently and good-humouredly took over many additional tasks in order to provide us with "free" time. We are deeply moved by this support, without which the text would never have been completed.

In the end of course, whatever errors or confusions remain are our responsibility.

The Economic Problem

What's ahead . . . In this first chapter we introduce you to the study of economics and hope to arouse your curiosity about this fascinating discipline. We first look at scarcity and choice, define economics, and examine three fundamental economic questions. We then take a brief look at different types of economies, discuss the methodology and language of economics, talk about the role of assumptions and make the distinction between macro- and microeconomics. Finally, we develop the idea of production possibilities to help you understand some of the fundamental choices facing all economies.

What might you expect from a course in economics? Well, it will not help you much with your personal finances and won't be directly helpful in your choice of the right stock to buy. But the study of economics will give you a broad understanding of how a modern market economy operates, and what the important things are within one. If you see yourself as a budding businessperson, the study of economics can offer some general insights that will be helpful. Yet you will not find specific tools or instructions. Economics is an academic discipline, not a self-help or how-to course. The common conception that economics is about money is only partly true. We study money, but more in the sense of what it is, and the effects of different central-bank money policies, than in the sense of how to make it. The study of economics may not help you to function better in the world in any specific sense, but it will probably help you to understand better how the world functions.

Microeconomic: actors make decisional allocation scarce resources

Scarcity, Choice and Technology

Economists put a great deal of emphasis on scarcity and the need to economize. Individual households face a scarcity of income and thus must budget expenditures. Most individuals also face a scarcity of time and must somehow decide where to spend time and where to conserve it. In the same sense, an economy as a whole has limited productive resources and must allocate those resources among competing uses.

factors of production: the productive resources that are available to an economy, categorized as land, labour, capital and enterprise.

Productive resources is a term that economists use interchangeably with the term **factors of production** or, sometimes, simply "inputs." Factors of production are traditionally divided into four categories: land, labour, capital and enterprise. Land is defined as anything natural such as fertile soil, deep harbours, good climate or minerals in the ground. Labour refers to any human endeavour ranging from that of a skilled naturopathic physician to that of a construction labourer. Capital is made up of the tools, equipment, factories and buildings used in the production process. Finally, enterprise is that very special human talent which is able to put abstract ideas into practical application.

Economists see such productive resources (the factors of production) as *scarce* in the sense that no economy has sufficient resources to be able to produce all of the goods and services that everyone wants. This is not to say that there aren't some people who would say that they have all that they want, but there are millions of people who possess a seemingly endless list of wants, and millions more like them waiting to be born. Since the economy cannot produce all that everyone wants, the resources available for production are scarce, and some kind of mechanism must be put into place to *choose* what will be produced and, thereby, by implication, what will not be produced. And this is why economics is sometimes called the *science of choice*.

The term *technology* means the process of using the factors of production, in one of an infinite variety of combinations, to create physical goods and services of an endless variety of types. The output of these goods and services give the citizens of an economy the ability to meet their wants and needs. In this sense, an economy that produces a large quantity of goods and services is more successful than one that is able to produce only a small quantity.

The success or failure of any economy depends a great deal on whether the individuals, firms and institutions within it can make the necessary choices in order to adapt to the technological and social changes that inevitably occur over time. For example, we have recently seen that economies that use an economic system which relies on individual choice and enterprise (Canada, the United States, Japan and Germany) continue to enjoy success while economies that relied on centrally controlled systems (Poland, Hungry and the U.S.S.R.) have faltered.

Another aspect of choice that economists consider important is that any society, much like an individual household, always has a choice between consumption now or in the future. A household could choose to consume less now and save more, enabling it to consume more in the future. Societies that consume less now can use scarce productive resources to build more capital goods with which to produce even more consumer goods and services *in the future*. We will return to this point later in this chapter.

Economics: A Definition

In the light of this discussion we can now venture a definition of economics:

> Economics is about the choices involved in the mobilization and allocation of scarce productive resources to produce goods and services which are directed towards satisfying the unlimited wants of people.

As we have already suggested, economics is also about how technology provides a context for the production of these goods and services which provides society with its ability to satisfy wants and needs.

Is Economics Relevant?

As we approach the twenty-first century, we find ourselves living in a society filled with a host of problems and a wide variety of issues that bombard us every day in the media and dominate many of our conversations. Will Quebec separate from the rest of Canada? Will governments try to deal with their budget deficits by reducing their spending, and will this drive up the cost of tuition? Are the threats to our environment too serious for us to adequately cope with them? What kinds of jobs will there be in the future, and will there be enough of them to meet the aspirations of our youth? Will cures for cancer and AIDS be found soon, and will Canada's health care system survive? Will this country's history of tolerance towards minorities continue, or will prejudice and hatred raise their ugly heads? Will a seemingly endless number of new special interest groups begin to tear at the fabric of our stable and democratic system of governance? Will we be able to continue to rely on conventional public services such as police and fire protection? Will productivity in Canada grow rapidly enough for Canadian firms to thrive in an increasingly globalized marketplace?

These questions are broad and diverse. Yet there is an economic dimension to every one of them. In fact, economics is one of the *most relevant* subjects that a student might study. Strangely, however, it does not have that reputation. There are a variety of reasons for this. One is that people often see economics as being too theoretical. However, let's remember that the most effective way to say something intelligent about nearly all the issues of the day is to use theory and abstraction. Another observation that students often make about the discipline of economics is that it seems too narrow in its focus. Yet a precise focus is sometimes needed to identify cause and effect.

Trying to understand economic theory can be challenging and certainly does not come easily, but the rewards, in terms of a better understanding of the world in which we live, are great. Economics is the study of ideas, and in a very real way this is the most important thing that a student can pursue. One of the most famous of twentieth-century economists, John Maynard Keynes, said:

> The ideas of economists, both when they are right and when they are wrong, are more powerful than is commonly understood. Sooner or later, it is ideas, not vested interests, which are dangerous for good or evil.[1]

The Three Fundamental Questions of Economics

A broad perspective on the discipline of economics can be obtained by focusing on what can be called the three fundamental questions of economics: what, how and for whom? That is, economics is about what gets produced, how it is produced, and who gets it.

What to Produce? Underlying the question of what should be produced is the previously mentioned reality of scarcity. Any society has only a fixed amount of resources

---

[1] John Maynard Keynes, *The General Theory* (1936).

at its disposal, and thus must have a system in place to make millions of decisions about production. For example, should 50 new military helicopters be produced or, instead, should the limited resources available be used to produce 10 new hospitals with (or without?) research facilities for the study of genetics? Should society exploit natural resources faster to create more jobs and more tax revenue, or slower to conserve these resources for the future? Should human effort, capital and land be directed toward more preschool day-care facilities so that women are not so tied to the home? Or, instead, should those same resources be directed toward increasing the number of graduate students studying science and technology so that the economy can win the competitive international race in the twenty-first century? Should scarce resources be devoted to persuading people to quit smoking, or should they be used to develop a less harmful form of tobacco?

No economist would claim to have the right answer to even one of these questions. That is no more the role of an economist than it is of any other member of society. What the economist can do, however, is to identify and measure both the benefits and the costs of any one answer — of any one choice.

Let's review what we have said so far. In the face of people's unlimited wants and society's limited productive resources, choice becomes a forced necessity. Because of these choices the decision to produce one thing means that some other thing will not be produced.

opportunity cost: the next best alternative that is given up as a result of making a particular choice.

This last point is so fundamental that economists have invented a special term to identify it — **opportunity cost**. For instance, suppose that the production of 50 new helicopters carries a price tag of $5 billion. In the conventional sense, that is their cost. However, economists would argue that it is equally valid, and more revealing, to measure the cost of the helicopters in terms of the 20 hospitals that can't be built because the helicopters were produced. Opportunity costs can thus be defined as what must be given up as a result of making a particular choice; in this case, the hospitals instead of the helicopters. In addition we should recognize that the $5 billion could be spent on other things besides hospitals — say, colleges and universities or mass transit systems. At this point society would presumedly choose what it considers to be its *next best* alternative. Thus our definition of opportunity costs needs to be modified to: the next best alternative that is given up as a result of making a particular choice.

The concept of opportunity cost can be applied not only at the level of the overall society but also at the individual level. For the individual, the constraint is not the limited quantity of productive resources but, instead, a limited amount of income. For example, you could think of the cost of going to two movies on the weekend as the sacrifice of one new CD. If you want to think of both of these choices (two movies or one CD) as each costing about $16, that is fine. But thinking of the one as costing the other is often more revealing. In general, your income will not allow you to have everything you may want, so you are forced to make choices about what you buy. And the cost of these choices can be measured in what must be given up as a result of making the choice. In the same sense, a society faces a similar set of choices imposed not by income but by a constraint on the quantity and quality of factors of production available.

How to Produce?   Let's move on to the second fundamental economic question that every society must somehow answer: what is the most appropriate technology to employ? We could reword this question by asking: how should we produce what we choose to produce?

For example, there are a variety of ways to produce ten kilometres of highway. At one extreme, a very labour-intensive method of production could be used involving rock crushed with hammers, roadbed carved from the landscape with shovels, and material moved in wheelbarrows. The capital equipment used in this method is very minimal. The labour used is enormous, and the time it will take is extensive. At the other extreme, a very capital-intensive method could be used involving large earth-moving and tarmac-laying machines, surveying equipment and relatively little but highly skilled labour. In between these two extremes are a large variety of capital/labour mixes that could also produce the new highway.

The answer to the question of how best to build the highway involves, among other things, knowing the prices of the various resources that might be used. This is because what underlies this whole discussion of how goods should be produced is the type of technology available. Remember that technology means the way the various factors of production are combined to obtain output. The most appropriate technology for a society to use (the best way to combine resources) depends on the relative prices of these resources. Thus, in the example above, the best way to build a highway depends on the price of labour and the price of capital as well as the productivity of each factor.

Let's assume that two countries have the same endowment of resources. Would this mean that the two countries would produce the same quantities and use the same mix of their resources in producing these quantities? Not necessarily. Say that the population of the country Alpha prefer alphas over betas and therefore choose to emphasize alpha goods production at the expense of beta goods production. Meanwhile, country Beta chooses the opposite emphasis. Let's assume that such preferences, and the related emphasis on production, has encouraged the development of technology that results in the price of alpha goods in Alpha being lower than those in Beta. Similarly, beta goods prices in Beta are lower for the same reason. The difference in the prices of the two goods would result in different prices for the resources being used to produce the two goods. The difference in the prices of the resources in the two countries would result in different mixes of the resources being used in production. Despite the fact that these two countries have the same endowment of resources, the difference in preferences between the two countries leads to different output mixes which result in different prices for two goods that are being produced. This, in turn, leads to differences in the prices of the (identical) resources in the two countries. The appropriate technology in Alpha, therefore, is different from the appropriate technology in Beta. As you can see, the simple question of how goods should be produced is more complicated than one might think at first glance. Yet, this is a question that every society must somehow answer.

For Whom?   We are now ready to move to the third fundamental economic question that every society must somehow answer: for whom? Here we ask: how should the total output of any society's economy be shared among its people? Should it involve an equal share for all, or should it, perhaps, be based on people's needs? Alternatively, should it be based on the contribution of each member of society? If so, how should this contribution be measured — in numbers of hours, or in skill level, or some other method? Further, who should define what is an important skill and which ones aren't very important?

Wrapped up in all this is the question of the ownership of resources and whether it is better that certain resources (like land and capital) be owned by society as a whole or by private individuals. In summary, the "for whom" question (as well as the "what" and "how" questions) cannot be adequately addressed unless we look at the society's attitude towards the private ownership of resources and the question of who has the power to make crucial decisions.

Thus, you can see that in addressing the for whom question, other questions about the fairness of income distribution, incentives and the ownership of resources all come into play. John Stuart Mill pointed out, nearly 150 years ago, that once an economy's goods are produced and the initial market distribution of income has occurred, society can intervene in any fashion that it wants to redistribute such income; i.e., there are no laws of distribution other than the ones that society wants to impose. Whether this observation by Mill gives enough consideration to the incentive for productive effort remains an open question to this day.

BOX 1.1
John Stuart Mill (1806–1873) is considered the last great economist of the classical school. His *Principles of Political Economy,* first published in 1848, was the leading textbook in economics for forty years. Raised by a strict disciplinarian father (James), John Stuart began to learn Greek at the age of three and calculus at twelve. He held a great faith in human progress, had a love of liberty and was an advocate of extended rights for women.

Thus, to a large extent, the way in which each of the three fundamental questions are answered by a society depends on how that society organizes itself. We will now turn to a discussion about this.

Types of Economies

Throughout history, humankind has coordinated its economies using some blend of the four Cs: cooperation, custom, command or competition. Thousands of years ago, members of small hunting and gathering groups undoubtedly relied on cooperation with each other in order to survive the dual threat of starvation and predators. They decided cooperatively what work needed to be done, how it was to be done, and who was to obtain what share of the produce. On the other hand, European feudal society in the Middle Ages was dominated by custom, which implied that sons followed the trade of their fathers and that traditional technology was regarded as superior to new ways of doing things. Serfs were required, by tradition, to share a portion of their produce with the feudal lord. Even today, in some societies, such as the San of the Kalahari Desert, a recent animal kill is divided among the members of the group in very precise ways dictated by tradition.

One need only think of an ancient civilization, such as Egypt 4,000 years ago, as an example of how society answered the three fundamental questions using the command method. There, most of the important economic questions were answered by the orders of those in power such as the pharaohs and members of the priesthood.

In this century, command has been the prevailing coordinating mechanism in fascist and communist regimes where a central committee (or presidium) makes most of the fundamental economic decisions.

Market societies, such as we see in most of the industrial countries around the globe today, did not begin to emerge until approximately 200 years ago. Here we find a large role played by competition while the roles of custom and cooperation have faded. Yet, in small ways we can still witness the role of custom. There are probably as many people in a typical movie theatre audience who use the restrooms as there are people who eat popcorn. However, the theatre charges for the popcorn but the use of the restrooms is free. Why? Because it is customary. The command aspect certainly appears in market societies in the form of government intervention in the economy and it is interesting to note that tradition and command totally replace use of competition within the family unit even in the most market-oriented societies.

Today's China is an example of a modern economy organized around a core of command, with custom and cooperation apparent, and competition on the horizon. Canada puts more emphasis on market and less on custom. To a large extent the essence of each of these different blends of the four Cs is found in the patterns of ownership and control of the factors of production. It is important to note that ownership of the factors doesn't always mean control over them. Land and capital was communally owned by the people in the former Soviet Union, but control of them was in the hands of a very few powerful party officials. Conversely, what we call capitalism today stresses the private ownership of the factors of production, but the law often places controls on how they are used.

The modern Canadian economy is referred to as a mixed economy since it comprises elements of the two dominant types: command and competition. In such an economy, incomes are earned through the payment of wages, interest, rents and profits to the private owners of the factors of production: labour, capital, land, and enterprise. The more valuable (in the sense of market value) the factor of production a person owns, the more income that individual receives. Thus the "for whom" question is answered by the distribution of ownership of the factors of production that the market considers valuable. Does the amount of income one earns have anything to do with hard work and productivity? Not always. A good, productive poet can work hard for a lifetime and still not receive much income. The what question in a modern market economy depends on the way that people choose to spend their income since it is this spending that makes up the demand for the various goods and services. The how question is answered by firms finding the most appropriate technology to produce their output, knowing that success brings profits and if they fail to do this they will not long be in business.

The Methodology and Language of Economics

Let's now turn to a brief discussion on the methodology used in economics. Earlier, we discussed the *concept* of opportunity cost. We used the word concept, but we could have conveyed the same meaning with the word *idea*. Concepts (or ideas) become the building blocks for the more general terms *theory* or *principle*. In building a theory, a concept is first identified as a hypothesis. Take, for example, the hypothesis that an increase in pay causes people to work longer hours. Combine this with the assumptions that this increase in pay is from employment income which comes on a regular basis and we can reach a conclusion such as: higher-income people work longer hours than lower-income people. This conclusion is then tested with empirical data gathered by observing actual events. On the basis of this test of data, the theory is accepted, revised or rejected.

In addition to terms like concept, principle and theory, you will also find that the discipline of economics has developed its own very specialized language. When we think about this, it really shouldn't be a surprise since every speciality, from sailing to the arts, from pottery to chemistry, has its own language. Such specialized language is, in fact, quite necessary in that the development and use of concepts, as well as the use of logic to draw conclusions, often requires language that is either not in general use or requires a more precise definition than is generally understood.

There may be times when the beginning student will think that economics is very abstract and theoretical. If this happens, try to remember that the purpose of theory is analogous to the purpose of a map — to compress a mass of detail down into a highly summarized, but manageable, form. Just as a map on the scale of 1:1 is useless, so too would be a theory that tries to explain every possible reality all at once. Good theories identify basic underlying relationships between crucial variables and have conclusions that point us in the right direction to answer important questions.

At some point in the past, you may have heard jokes about economists, such as, "What do you get when you put five economists in the same room? Six opinions." Economists do often disagree with each other. This is a natural by-product of a discipline which is part science and part art. It is also true, however, that there is wide agreement among economists on many questions, and this is remarkable given that economists ask a wide variety of questions, many of which do not get asked in other disciplines. For example, why do firms produce some goods internally and buy others in the market? Why do nations sometimes both export and import the same good? Why does society provide some things to children without charge (education) but not other things (food)?

In addition to asking sometimes profound questions economists also build theories to try to explain everyday observations that most people take for granted. Also you need to remember that all theories are built on a set of assumptions, and putting the same ideas together into a theory can lead to different conclusions if this is done using a different set of assumptions.

Alternatively, the same theory built on the same assumptions can lead to conclusions that can be seen, by different people, as good or bad depending on the importance that one gives to the different outcomes. For example, one could consider the North American Free Trade Agreement a good thing because it increases Canada's per capita income or a bad thing because it threatens Canada's sovereignty.

To help sort out the kind of thing that economists will probably agree on, and what they may well disagree on, we need to make the distinction between what is called a *positive statement* and a *normative one*. Positive statements are assertions about the world that can be tested by using empirical data. Normative statements are based on a value system of beliefs and cannot be tested by using empirical data.

An example of a positive statement would be: The quantity purchased of any commodity will rise if its price falls. There will be little or no disagreement among economists on the importance of this kind of statement, in that, all will agree that such a statement can be verified with data. An example of a normative statement is: Canadians should save more. Such a statement is normative because it implies a definite value judgement and it cannot be verified. This does not make such a statement unimportant, but it does mean that there is likely to be much more disagreement over it.

When building new theories and principles within the discipline, economists tend to work with positive ideas and statements and avoid the normative ones. None of this implies that economists should not enter the legitimate debate over controversial issues and policies, but they should be careful and use only sound economic principles in their thinking and then clearly identify the points at which they leave the positive behind and enter the world of normative judgement and advocacy.

The Role of Models

Imagine walking into the sales office of a condominium project under construction. Part of the sales presentation is a model of the entire project sitting on a table. You would have no trouble recognizing the model as a representation of what the building will eventually look like. This is true despite the fact that many of the details such as the elevators, furniture and appliances are absent from the model.

Economists also build models that try to give an understanding of the big picture. However, they cannot construct a physical representation as in the example of the building. Instead, the level of abstraction is even greater in that the model is all on paper and in the form of concepts, numbers and equations. The economist's model also ignores the details that really aren't that important. Constructing such models helps us to understand important relationships between variables. However, we need to remember that every model is an abstraction from reality. It doesn't intend to capture all possible details. In fact, it is often true that the more realistic we try to make our models, the more complex and thus the more confusing and distracting they become.

The Macro/Micro Distinction

macroeconomics: the study of the economy as a whole including the topics of unemployment, inflation, interest rate policy and the spending/taxation policies of government.

We now need to make the distinction between macro- and microeconomics. Many colleges and universities offer a separate course for each of these, but this is not always the case. **Macroeconomics** is the study of the economy as a whole and includes most of the topics a beginning student would expect to find in an economics course. These include unemployment, inflation, interest rates, tax and spending policies of government, and national income determination. **Microeconomics** focuses on the individual parts that make up the whole and include topics like supply and demand, the study of costs and the nature of market structures. This distinction can be described metaphorically as looking through different ends of a set of binoculars. In the first instance we see the big picture. In the second instance a very small part of that big picture appears in much more detail.

Study Guide

QUESTION 1.1

Below is a list of resources. Indicate whether the resource in question is land (N), labour (L), capital (K) or enterprise (E):
A) A bar-code scanner in a supermarket.
B) Fresh drinking water.
C) Copper deposits in a mine.
D) The work of a systems analyst.
E) The first application of CD-ROM technology to an economics textbook.
F) An office building.

microeconomics: the study of the specific parts that make the economy as a whole such as the supply and demand of goods, the costs of production and market structures.

QUESTION 1.2

Identify each of the following statements as positive or normative:
A) The government should reduce its budget deficit by cutting its spending.
B) If the price of apples rises, then the quantity of oranges bought will increase.
C) Monopolies tend to set prices higher than we would find in competitive markets.
D) The economic cost of cleaning up the environment is too high.
E) Higher-income Canadians should be willing to share their wealth with lower-income Canadians.

Review

BOX 1A
1. Identify the four *factors of production.*
2. What are the three fundamental questions in economics?
3. Define *opportunity costs.*
4. What are the four Cs that humankind has used to organize its communities?
5. What are the building blocks of a theory?
6. Distinguish between a positive statement and a normative one.
7. Distinguish between *macroeconomics* and *microeconomics.*

The Production Possibilities Curve

capital goods: those things that are used to aid in the production of other goods such as buildings, tools, equipment and machinery.

Let's now return to the point that every economy is faced with — the constraint of limited resources. To illustrate this constraint, imagine a society that produces only two categories of goods — capital goods and consumer goods. Economists define **capital goods** as the buildings, tools, machinery and equipment that are used to produce other goods. **Consumer goods** are those goods used by the consumer to satisfy their wants and needs. In our example we will use electric generators to represent capital goods and automobiles to represent consumer goods. Now, assume that the quantities of the two goods that this society is able to produce are those in Table 1.1 below.

consumer goods: goods used by consumers to satisfy their wants and needs.

TABLE 1.1 Production Possibilities for Generators and Automobiles

	Quantities Produced per Week in Thousands					
	A	**B**	**C**	**D**	**E**	**F**
Generators	0	2	4	6	8	10
Automobiles	20	19	17	14	9	0

production possibilities curve: a graphical representation of the various combinations of maximum output that can be produced.

The finite resources available to this economy allow it to produce up to a maximum of 10 generators per week, but this can be done only if no automobiles are produced. At the other extreme, up to a maximum of 20 automobiles per week can be produced, but only if no generators are produced. There are, of course, many other possible combinations in between these extremes, and Table 1.1 above identifies four of these.

We can take the data from Table 1.1 and use it to graph what is called a **production possibilities curve** which is a visual representation of the various outputs that can be produced. The production possibilities curve which appears in Figure 1.1 below is simply another way of presenting the data found in Table 1.1.

FIGURE 1.1 The Production Possibilities Curve I

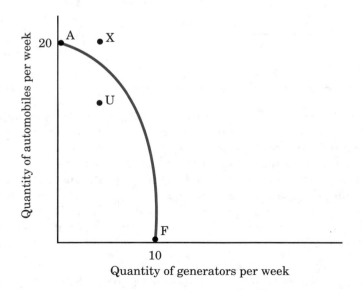

This society's limited resources allow for the production of a maximum of 20 automobiles if no generators are produced, as represented by point A. Moving down on the curve from point A, we find other combinations of fewer automobiles and more generators until we reach point F which is 10 generators and no automobiles. Point U indicates either the underemployment of resources, inefficiency in resource use or the use of inappropriate technology. Point X is unobtainable.

As mentioned above, this hypothetical economy can produce up to a weekly maximum of 20 automobiles if no generators are produced or 10 generators if no automobiles are produced. Next, we need to examine three assumptions which lie behind the data in Table 1.1 and its representation in Figure 1.1. The first is that maximum use of all of this economy's available resources is being achieved. Second, we assume that the resources are being used to maximum efficiency; and third, that the most appropriate technology available is being employed. As we will see a little later in this chapter, this last assumption does not necessarily always mean the most recent technology. If any one of these three assumptions do not hold, then the economy would be operating somewhere inside the production possibilities curve as illustrated by point U. On the other hand, point X represents an output of 20 automobiles and 5 generators which, given this economy's current resources, is unobtainable.

Next, let's address the actual shape of the curve. Why is it bowed out such that it is concave to the origin? We need to understand the implication of this particular shape. Figure 1.2 below will help.

FIGURE 1.2 Production Possibilities Curve II

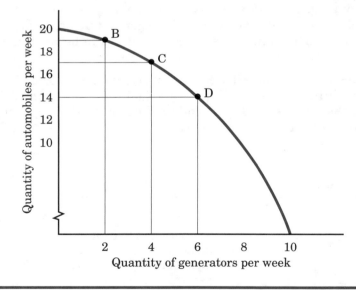

At point B, 2 generators and 19 automobiles are being produced. If society decided that it wanted 4 generators (point C) then 2 automobiles would have to be sacrificed to achieve the 2 additional generators. To increase generator production by yet another 2 would require a sacrifice of 3 automobiles (point D).

Assume that our hypothetical economy is currently producing 2 generators and 19 automobiles as illustrated by point B on the production possibilities curve. Then let's assume that the society decided that it really wants 4, not just 2 generators. Production decisions are made to reallocate some resources from automobile production to generator production. This is illustrated by point C. Note that here the opportunity costs of producing the 2 additional generators is 2 automobiles. That is to say, the additional 2 generators could only be obtained by reducing the output of automobiles from the original 19 to the new 17. This seems clear enough, but we are not done.

Next, assume that society decides to produce even more generators as illustrated by moving to point D (6 generators and 14 automobiles). This time the 2 additional generators cost 3 automobiles, which is more than the previous cost of 2.

We have just identified what economists call the **law of increasing costs**. This law states that as the production of any single item increases, the per unit cost of producing additional units of that item will rise. That is, as we move from B to C, an additional 2 generators costs 2 automobiles, while the move from C to D requires a sacrifice of 3 automobiles for the same additional 2 generators.

Let's look again at the movement from B to C. Here, the cost of 1 additional generator is 1 automobile, since 2 generators cost 2 automobiles. When moving from C to D, however, the cost of 1 additional generator rises to 1.5 automobiles (2 generators cost 3 automobiles). Thus, you can see that as the total production of generators is increased, the rising *per unit* cost of generators gives the production possibilities curve its bowed out shape.

But why does the per unit cost of generators increase, i.e., what is the reason behind the law of increasing costs? The answer is that not all resources are equally suitable for the production of different products. Our hypothetical society has a fixed amount of resources that are used to produce different combinations of both generators and automobiles. However, some of these resources would be better suited to producing generators while others would be better suited to producing automobiles. An increase in the production of generators would require that some of the resources currently producing automobiles would need to be reallocated to the production of generators. It is only reasonable to assume that those resources that are reallocated first are the ones that are relatively well suited to the production of generators, while those resources not so suited to the production of generators would continue to produce automobiles. After all this has taken place, if even *more* generators are to be produced, the only resources left to reallocate will be ones that are not very well suited for the production of generators. Therefore, a larger quantity of less well suited resources will have to be reallocated to obtain the desired increase in generator production. This will increase the per unit cost of generators and will require a larger sacrifice of automobile production for any given increase in generator production.

law of increasing costs: as the production level of any particular item increases, its per unit cost of production rises.

QUESTION 1.3

Below is a list of economic goods. You are to decide whether each is a consumer good (C), or a capital good (K), or possibly both, *depending* on the context in which it is used (D):

A) A jackhammer.
B) A carton of cigarettes.
C) An office building.
D) A toothbrush.
E) A hammer.
F) A farm tractor.

QUESTION 1.4
Given the following figure:

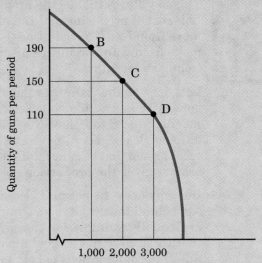

A) If the society produces 1,000 units of butter, how many guns can it produce?
B) Suppose that a society presently produces the combination shown as point B on the production possibilities curve; what is the cost of 1,000 additional units of butter?
C) Would the cost of 1,000 additional units of butter be greater, the same, or smaller as the society moves from point C to D compared to a move from point B to C?

Perhaps the way to really nail down this idea of increasing costs is to imagine yet another economy that produces only two products — leather shirts and leather moccasins. Assume that the leather and tools used to make both goods are exactly the same. Further, assume that all the people involved are clones of a long-deceased expert leather-maker and are therefore equally skilled. The production possibilities data for this economy are shown in Table 1.2.

TABLE 1.2 Production Possibilities for Shirts and Pairs of Moccasins

	Quantities Produced per Day					
	A	**B**	**C**	**D**	**E**	**F**
Shirts	20	16	12	8	4	0
Moccasins	0	8	16	24	32	40

From the data in Table 1.2, we see that 8 additional pairs of moccasins can, in all instances, be obtained by giving up 4 shirts, which is a ratio of 2 pairs of moccasins for 1 shirt. This can also be stated as 1 additional shirt costing 2 pairs of moccasins. Taking this data and plotting it as a production possibilities curve yields a straight line as can be seen in Figure 1.3.

Thus, we can see that a straight-line production possibilities curve is conceivable. The implications of a straight-line production possibilities curve

FIGURE 1.3 Production Possibilities Curve III

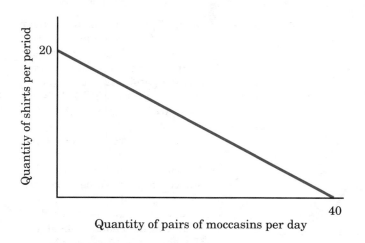

The opportunity cost of additional pairs of moccasins in terms of shirts sacrificed is constant, i.e., 4 additional shirts always costs 8 pairs of moccasins. This yields a straight-line production possibilities curve which, in this case, has a slope of 1/2 (i.e., 4/8).

is that the law of increasing costs does not apply. In fact, what we have above are constant costs — the cost of two pairs of moccasins is always one shirt.

Notice, however, what we had to assume in order to obtain such a result: homogeneous inputs to the production process — leather, identical tools and labour that is equally skilled — and the very similar outputs of leather shirts and moccasins. If resource inputs are not homogeneous, and if products are quite different, which is almost always the case, then we could not expect the production possibilities curve to be a straight line. Therefore, we would expect the law of increasing costs to prevail in the real world.

It is not difficult to find examples of this law. Thirty years ago, when there were very few air pollution controls in effect, the costs of obtaining a 10% reduction in air pollution was relatively cheap. Today when air pollution levels have been substantially reduced in many industries, an additional reduction of 10% would be much more costly because the most cost-effective reductions have already been made.

Or take another example. Assume that the infant mortality rate in a less-developed country is 55 out of every 100 births. The reduction of this level by five, (to 50 out of 100), could been achieved relatively cheaply — say, with a smallpox vaccination campaign that would require only a small quantity of additional resources. However, once the rate dropped to, say, 25 out of 100, then the resources required to gain an additional drop of five points, to 20 out of 100, would probably be enormous and the costs involved would be much greater. This is the law of increasing costs.

Earlier in the chapter we spoke of the important role that technology plays in economic performance. Technology is the application of human knowledge to satisfy the wants and needs of people. We can illustrate this importance with the production possibilities curve. The graphical effect of a technological improvement is an outward shift in the production possibilities curve. This is illustrated in Figure 1.4 on the next page where we use wheat and computers as the two goods being produced.

FIGURE 1.4 The Effect of Technological Change on the Production Possibilities Curve

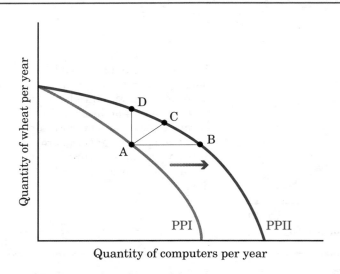

Start at point A, which is a point of efficient production on PPI. An improvement in technology in the computer industry shifts the production possibilities curve such that we now have PPII. This creates three possible results. First, the same quantity of wheat, and more computers, can now be produced as represented by point B. Alternatively, more of *both* wheat and computers can be produced as represented by point C. Point D represents the third possible result, which is more wheat and the same quantity of computers.

Let's start with the economy operating efficiently on the production possibilities curve PPI at point A. Now let's assume that a new technology becomes available which has application *only* in the computer industry. This is represented by a shift outwards in the curve, such that the new production possibilities curve becomes PPII. There are three possible results. First, the same quantity of wheat, but more computers, can be produced as represented by point B. Secondly, notice that more of *both* goods can also be produced as represented by point C. And third, this economy could now achieve an increase in the production of wheat if the same number of computers were produced (point D) despite the fact that this new technology could only be applied to the computer industry. This emphasizes the important role of technological change. It widens the choices (there's that word again) available to society and is often seen in a positive light. Alas, technological change also carries costs, and this is another subject that will receive our attention later.

An increase in the economy's stock of capital goods would have the same effect of shifting out the production possibilities curve. This is shown in Figure 1.5.

In this figure, Economy B places greater emphasis on the production of capital goods than does Economy A. This can be seen by comparing point B1 (50 units of capital goods) with point A1 (20 units of capital goods). This emphasis on capital goods production requires that there first be more savings in Economy B. Greater savings allows for greater production of capital goods which also means a lower production of consumer goods (40 units in Economy B compared to 73 in Economy A). While increased savings does mean fewer consumer goods now, the long-term result is the possibility of more consumer goods in the future. This is illustrated by the production possibilities curve shifting to the right more in the case of Economy B than in Economy A. After the increase in production possibilities, Economy B can continue producing 50 units of capital goods and 93 units of consumer goods. Economy A, by contrast, can produce only 80 units of consumer goods while maintaining capital goods production at the original 20 units. All of

FIGURE 1.5 Different Growth Rates for Two Economies

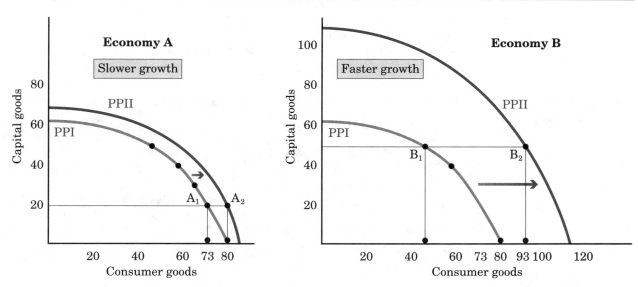

We begin with Economy A and Economy B being the same size as indicated by the same PPI curves. However, since Economy A chooses to emphasize the production of consumer goods (point A) while Economy B emphasizes the production of capital goods (point B), Economy B will grow faster. The result of this faster growth is that, over time, PPII shifts out more in the case of Economy B than it does in the case of Economy A.

QUESTION 1.5

Assume that a certain economy faces the following production possibilities:

	Quantities per Year			
	A	B	C	D
Grain	50	40	25	0
Tools	0	4	8	12

A) Draw a production possibilities curve (PPI) with tools on the horizontal and grain on the vertical axis.

Now assume new technology that can be used only in the tool industry is developed, which increases tool output by 50%.

B) Draw a new production possibilities (PPII) curve that reflects this new technology.

C) If this economy produced 12 units of tools per year, how many units of grain could be produced after introduction of the new technology?

this emphasizes the importance of savings in an economy, which is a central topic in the study of macroeconomics.

This completes your introduction to the study of economics. If there is only one thing that you retain from this chapter it should be the idea that society must continually make difficult choices about what, how and for whom to produce, and that these choices invariably involve costs. Perhaps the following story will help.

A sage of some bygone age said that there is no such thing as a free lunch. We can now make some sense out of this idea. Producing more of anything — a lunch, for example, since it involves the use of scarce resources — necessarily means producing less of something else. The lunch might be provided free to the people who eat it, but from the point of view of the society as a whole, it took scarce resources to produce it and therefore is not free.

BOX 1B
1. Define the term *capital good*.
2. Define the term *consumer good*.
3. What is a *production possibilities curve*?
4. Define the *law of increasing costs*.
5. What does a straight line production possibilities curve imply?
6. How would you shift the production possibilities curve if you wanted to illustrate technological change or the accumulation of more capital goods?

Chapter Highlights

This chapter begins by emphasizing that choice lies at the heart of economics. Individuals must choose how to spend their limited time and income and society must choose how to allocate the scarce resources available to the economy.

The chapter then defines economics and argues that it is, indeed, a very relevant subject to study. Next, the discussion of the what, how and for whom questions uncovers some of the contentious issues within economics, e.g., what is a fair distribution of income?

The discussion of the four Cs — cooperation, custom, command and competition — is done to emphasize the need of every society to have coordination mechanisms in place to help organize its economy.

Next, the chapter points out some aspects about the methodology used in economics and that the discipline has its own particular language. A brief discussion of the role of economic models and the definitions of macro- and microeconomics follows.

The chapter then develops the idea of production possibilities and brings out the law of increasing cost. This allows for the importance of choice to be reemphasized. The point that economic growth increases the choices available to society is illustrated graphically. The chapter closes by looking at a fundamental choice facing all societies — the choice of producing capital goods versus consumer goods. It points out that the way society answers this question not only impacts on the present but has very important implications for the future.

New Glossary Terms

Workbook

Study Tips

1.   Since this is your first chapter, you should not be overly concerned if it seemed to contain so much new terminology that it felt overwhelming. Mastering the principles of economics requires that you first learn the language of economics and the best way to do this is to use it over and over. Let this workbook help you do this. Conscientiously work through all of the questions before proceeding to the next chapter.

2.   Opportunity cost is one of the most important concepts in economics. As a start, make sure that you understand the basic idea that cost can be measured not just in dollars and cents but also in what has to be given up as a result of making a particular decision.

3.   This chapter introduces you to the use of graphs with the production possibilities curve. If you have any difficulty understanding graphs, you should practise with the simple PPC graphs until you become more comfortable using them because graphs are an integral part of economics.

4.   For many of you, economics will be one of the more difficult courses that you will encounter in your undergraduate studies. Yet, it can be mastered, and doing so can be very rewarding. You will probably be much more successful if you work a little on economics several times a week rather than have one long session a week. This way, you will gain mastery over the language more quickly through repetition and thereby gain confidence. You might consider buying a pack of 3 × 5 recipe cards and writing two or three definitions or simple ideas on each card. Carry several cards around with you so that you can glance at them several times a day. The authors found this technique helpful when, oh so many years ago, they started to learn the discipline.

Are You Sure?

Indicate whether the following statements are true or false. If false, indicate why they are false.

1.   Individual households face scarcity because of limited household income.

T or **F**   If false: _____

_____

_____

2.   An economy as a whole faces scarcity because of limited national income.
T or **F**   If false: _____

_____

_____

3.   The three fundamental questions in economics are what, how and how many.
T or **F**   If false: _____

_____

_____

4.   Opportunity cost is the value of the next best alternative that is given up as a result of making a particular choice.
T or **F**   If false: _____

_____

_____

5.   There are only three Cs that humankind has used to coordinate its economies: cooperation, custom and competition.
T or **F**   If false: _____

_____

_____

6.   Capital goods are those things that aid in the production of other goods and include buildings, tools, equipment and machinery.
T or **F**   If false: _____

_____

_____

7. A production possibility curve is a graphical representation of the various combinations of output that are wanted.
T or **F**   If false: _____

_____

_____

8. A straight-line production possibilities curve and the law of increasing costs are not consistent.
T or **F**   If false: _____

_____

_____

9. Technological improvement can be illustrated by a rightward shift in the production possibilities curve.
T or **F**   If false: _____

_____

_____

10. Macroeconomics focuses on the individual parts that make up the whole economy while microeconomics is a study of the economy as a whole.
T or **F**   If false: _____

_____

_____

Translations

Assume that a piece of land can produce either 600 bushels of corn and no soybeans or 300 bushels of soybeans and no corn. You may further assume that this corn/beans ratio of 2:1 is constant.

On the grid in Figure W1.1, draw a production possibilities curve for this piece of land. Indicate with the letters A and B an increase in bean production of 50 bushels and the cost of this increase using the same A and the letter C.

FIGURE W1.1

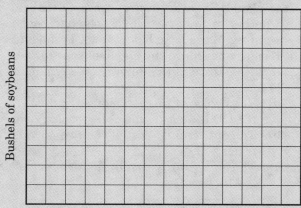

Bushels of soybeans

Bushels of corn

Choose the Best

1. The building blocks of a theory are:
   a) Concepts and mathematics.
   b) Concepts and ideas.

2. An economist's model comes in the form of:
   a) A physical representation of reality.
   b) Concepts, numbers and equations.

3. A decision to save more now means:
   a) Less consumption now and in the future.
   b) Less consumption now but more consumption in the future.

4. "Factors of production" is a term that can be used interchangeably with:
   a) Models.
   b) Consumer goods.
   c) Either resources or inputs.

5. What is the distinction between a positive and a normative statement?
   a) Positive statements are assertions that can be tested with data while normative statements are based on a value system of beliefs.
   b) Normative statements are assertions that can be tested with data while positive statements are based on a value system of beliefs.
   c) The distinction depends on the context in which each statement is used.

6. Meridith had only $16 to spend this last weekend. She was, at first, uncertain about whether to go to two movies she had been wanting to see or to buy a new CD she had recently heard. In the end she went to the movies. Which of the following statements is correct?
   a) The choice of the two movies and not the CD is an example of increasing costs.
   b) The opportunity cost of the two movies is one CD.
   c) The opportunity cost of the two movies is $16.

7. If two countries have the same technology and the same endowment of resources, would they use the same mix of resources in production?
   a) Yes, if the prices of the resources were the same.
   b) Yes, if the preferences for output were different in both countries.
   c) Yes, if the prices of the goods produced were different in both countries.

8. All of the following *except one* is a capital good. Which is the exception?
   a) An office building.
   b) A boiler in a pulp mill.
   c) The first application of CD-ROM technology to an economics textbook.
   d) An airport runway.

9. All of the following are positive statements *except one*. Which is the exception?
   a) The government must reduce its budget deficit.
   b) A decrease in price will lead to a larger quantity bought.
   c) Production is subject to the law of increasing cost.
   d) The degree of competition in our economy has been increasing in the last 10 years.

10. What are the factors of production?
    a) Land, labour, money and enterprise.
    b) Land, labour, money and capital.
    c) Land, labour, capital and enterprise.
    d) Competition, command, custom and cooperation.

11. J. S. Mill argued that:
    a) It is ideas, not vested interests, which are dangerous for good and evil.
    b) The distribution of money is dictated by the pattern of resource use.
    c) As technology changes, what gets produced also necessarily changes.
    d) Society can intervene in any fashion that it may wish to redistribute income.

In Figure W1.2 below is Mendork's production possibility curve for the only two goods that it produces — quirks and quarks. Refer to this figure to answer questions 12–17.

FIGURE W1.2

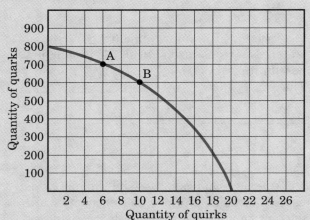

12. Refer to Figure W1.2 to answer this question. If this society chooses to produce 10 quirks, what is the maximum quantity of quarks it can produce?
    a) 500 quarks.
    b) 800 quarks.
    c) no quarks.
    d) 600 quarks.

13. Refer to Figure W1.2 to answer this question. What is the opportunity cost of producing 500 quarks?
    a) It is approximately 13 quirks.
    b) It is approximately 7 quirks.
    c) The opportunity cost of producing 500 quarks is greater than that of producing 400 quarks.
    d) The answer cannot be determined from the information given.

14. Refer to Figure W1.2 to answer this question. If Mendork's production is currently that indicated by point A, what is the cost of producing one more quirk (approximately)?
    a) 100 quarks.
    b) 50 quarks.
    c) 25 quarks.
    d) 200 quarks.
    e) 1 more quark.

15. Refer to Figure W1.2 to answer this question. What is the opportunity cost of one more quark as output changes from point B to A?
    a) 0.04 quirks.
    b) 4 quirks.
    c) 400 quirks.
    d) 1 quirk.
    e) 0.4 quirks.

16. Refer to Figure W1.2 to answer this question. If new technology increased the output of quirks by 50%, how many quirks could be produced if 600 quarks were produced?
    a) 18 quirks.
    b) 20 quirks.
    c) 15 quirks.
    d) 10 quirks.
    e) 0 quirks.

17. Refer to Figure W1.2 to answer this question. Which of the following statements is correct if Mendork is currently producing 500 quarks and 8 quirks?
    a) This society is using competition to coordinate its economic activities.
    b) This society is experiencing either unemployment or inefficiency.
    c) This economy is experiencing full employment.
    d) This society is not adequately answering the what question.
    e) This economy is growing quickly.

18. Which of the following statements describes the law of increasing costs?
    a) As the production level of any particular item decreases, its per unit cost of production rises.
    b) As the production level of any particular item increases, its per unit cost of production rises.

c) The prices of consumer goods always rise and never fall.
d) If you wait to make a purchase, you will pay a higher price.
e) The total cost of production rises as output goes up.

19. Which of the following statements is implied by a straight-line production possibilities curve?
    a) The law of increasing cost doesn't apply.
    b) The resources being used are homogeneous.
    c) The two goods being produced are very similar.
    d) The opportunity cost of both goods is constant.
    e) All of the above are correct.

20. Which of the following statements is correct for a society that emphasizes the production of capital goods over that of consumer goods?
    a) The society could enjoy the same quantity of capital goods and a larger quantity of consumer goods in the future.
    b) The society will have to save more now than a society that did not emphasize the production of capital goods.
    c) The society could enjoy the same quantity of consumer goods and a larger quantity of capital goods in the future.
    d) The society will grow faster than a society that emphasizes the production of consumer goods.
    e) All of the above are correct.

What's Wrong?

Can you spot the six errors in the following passage? (Ignore grammatical mistakes!)

Economics is about the choices involved in the allocation of the plentiful productive resources to produce goods and services which are directed toward satisfying the limited wants and needs of people. All societies must somehow answer the three fundamental questions of what, how and for whom. A society can coordinate its answers to these three questions using a blend of cooperation, custom, command and competition. The modern Canadian economy uses primarily competition and command while the former Soviet Union used primarily cooperation. One way to illustrate the what question is to ask how many resources an economy like Canada should devote to the production of capital goods and how many to the production of more factors of production. The how question involves the use of the most appropriate (newest) technology while the for whom question involves the distribution of income which results from natural economic laws.

Key Problem

Table W1.1 contains the production possibilities data for capital goods and consumer goods in the economy of Prudence.

TABLE W1.1

	A	B	C	D	E
Capital goods	0	3	6	9	12
Consumer goods	30	27	21	12	0

a) Use the grid in Figure W1.3 to draw the production possibilities curve for Prudence and label it PPI.

FIGURE W1.3

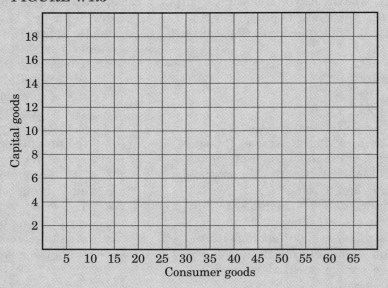

b) Is the production of 7 units of capital goods and 24 units of consumer goods possible?

Answer: _____.

c) Assuming the economy is producing combination D, how many units of consumer goods could be obtained if 3 less units of capital goods were produced?

Answer: _____.

d) Assuming the economy is producing combination D, what would be the opportunity cost of 3 more units of capital goods?

Answer: _____.

e) What law is illustrated by your answers to c) and d)?

Answer: _____.

f) Fill in Table W1.2 below assuming that, 10 years later, the output potential of capital goods has increased 50% while the output potential for consumers goods has risen by 12 for each of combinations A through D.

TABLE W1.2

	A	B	C	D	E
Capital goods					
Consumer goods					

g) Using the data from this table, draw in PPII in Figure W1.3.

h) Given the new table in f), how many units of consumer goods could be produced if 9 units of capital goods were produced? Label it point X.

Answer: _____.

i) Given the new PPII on Figure W1.3, approximately how many units of capital goods could be produced if 12 units of consumer goods were produced? Label it point Y.

Answer: _____.

j) Given PPII, is the combination of 13.5 units of capital goods and 24 units of consumer goods possible?

Answer: _____.

k) Given PPII, is the combination of 8 units of capital goods and 40 units of consumer goods possible?

Answer: _____.

l) Given PPII, what could you say about the economy of Prudence if 8 units of capital goods and 30 units of consumer goods were being produced?

Answer: _____

_____.

m) What are three possible reasons that would explain the shift from PPI to PPII?

Answer: _____

_____.

Need a Hand?

a) and g)   See Figure W1.4 on page 26.

b) **No**, since this combination lies outside PPI.

c) Three less units of capital goods would be 6, and this quantity of capital goods could be produced in combination with 21 units of consumer goods, which is a gain of **9 units** of consumer goods.

FIGURE W1.4 (completed Figure W1.3)

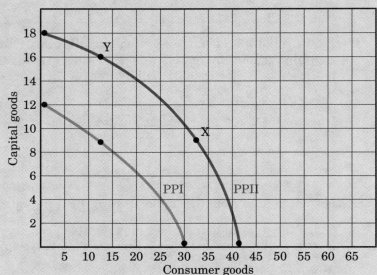

d) Three more units of capital goods would be 12, and if this quantity of capital goods were produced then 0 units of consumers goods are possible, i.e., the opportunity cost is **12** consumer goods.

e) The answers to c) and d) illustrate the law of increasing costs since increasing capital goods output from 9 to 12 units, costs 12 units of consumer goods while increasing capital goods output from 6 to 9 units cost only 9 units of consumer goods.

f)   **TABLE W1.3** (completed Table W1.2)

	A	B	C	D	E
Capital goods	0	4.5	9	13.5	18
Consumer goods	42	39	33	24	0

g) See Figure W1.4 above.

h) **33** units of consumer goods which is combination C in the table in f).

i) Approximately **16.5** units of capital goods which can be read directly from PPII on the graph in W1.4.

j) **Yes,** which can be verified from the table, i.e., it is the new combination D.

k) **No,** this combination is outside the PPII as can be seen on the graph in W1.4.

l) Since this combination is inside PPII, the economy must be: a) not using all of its resources, b) not using resources efficiently, or c) not using the appropriate technology.

m) **Technological change** could explain this shift, or since Prudence has emphasized the production of capital goods, then a rapid **accumulation of capital** could also explain it. The third reason could be that there is a larger quantity of other resources available.

More of the Same

Table W1.4 contains the production possibilities data for capital goods and consumer goods in the economy of Frivolous.

TABLE W1.4

	A	B	C	D	E
Capital goods	0	2	4	6	8
Consumer goods	20	19	16	10	0

a) Draw a PPI for Frivolous on Figure W1.5 below.

FIGURE W1.5

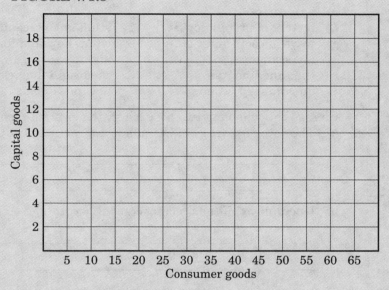

b) Assume that the people of Frivolous have decided to produce 2 units of capital goods and 19 units of consumer goods and indicate this combination with the letter B on the graph.

c) Assuming the economy is currently producing combination B, how many more units of consumer goods could be obtained if 2 less units of capital goods were produced?

d) Again starting from B, what would be the opportunity cost of 2 more units of capital goods?

e) What is the opportunity cost of the very first 2 units of capital goods? Of the last 2 units?

f) Make a table assuming that, 10 years later, the potential output of both capital and consumer goods increases by 25%.

g) Draw the data (from the table you constructed in f) on Figure W1.5 as PPII.

h) Given PPII, approximately how many units of consumer goods could be produced if 2 units of capital goods were produced?

i) Given PPII, approximately how many units of capital goods could be produce if 19 units of consumer goods were produced?

j) In this problem, the shift out of PPII was much less than it was for Prudence in Key Problem I. Why would this be if we assume that technological change and any increase in the quantity of resources in the two economies were similar?

Other Problems

1. Match the letters on the left with the blanks on the right.

   a) capital good
   b) consumer good
   c) land
   d) labour
   e) enterprise
   f) factors of production
   g) ways of coordinating an economy
   h) the fundamental questions in economics

   1. cooperation, custom, command and competition   _____
   2. the services of a brain surgeon   _____
   3. an apple   _____
   4. a satellite   _____
   5. land, labour, capital and enterprise   _____
   6. what, how and for whom   _____
   7. abundant clean water   _____
   8. the original marketing of a new power cell   _____

2. Change the following two positive statements into normative statements.
   a) The rate of savings in Canada is approximately 10% of national income.

   _____

   _____

   b) Unemployment has increased by 2 percentage points over the last year.

   _____

   _____

3. Change the following two normative statements into positive statements
   a) All students should take a course in economics.

   _____

   _____

   b) Economic growth is a desirable goal for a country.

   _____

   _____

4. Jennifer is planning how to spend a particularly wet Sunday and the choice is between watching video movies (each lasting 2 hours) or studying her economics textbook. She has 10 hours available to her. If she decides to study, she could read the following number of pages:

2 hours	80 pages
4 hours	130 pages
6 hours	160 pages
8 hours	175 pages
10 hours	180 pages

a) Given this information, draw Jennifer's production possibilities curve between movies watched and pages studied on the grid in Figure W1.6 below.

FIGURE W1.6

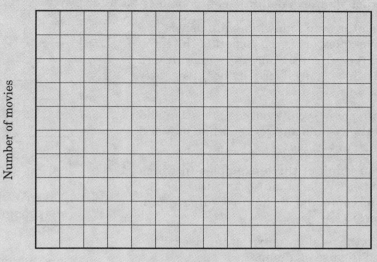

b) What happens to the opportunity cost of watching movies as more movies are watched?

_____

_____

c) Could Jennifer watch 3 movies and study 150 pages of her textbook?

_____

_____

d) If Jennifer has already watched 4 movies, what is the opportunity cost of watching the fifth movie?

_____

_____

Unanswered Questions

Short Essays

1. Identify and distinguish between the four factors of production and give two examples of each.

2. What does the term "technology" mean and how would you describe the effects of an increase in technology?

3. Why is economics sometimes described as the science of choice?

4. Comment on the following statement: "While society does have a choice about what types of goods to produce, it has no choice about the total quantity that can be produced."

5. Why do economists often disagree with one another?

6. Do you think the process of studying is subject to increasing opportunity costs?

Analytical Questions

1. Construct your own definition of economics.

2. Comment on the following statement: "The for whom question is the easiest of the three fundamental questions in economics to answer since it involves only positive statements."

3. Explain how a society based on custom and cooperation would answer the what, how and for whom questions.

4. Can you think of three examples in which contemporary Canadian society uses the element of command to help coordinate production?

5. Explain the analogy between the use of theory and the use of a map.

6. To what extent is the organization of the family based on the four Cs? What blend of the four Cs do you think is preferable and why?

Numerical Questions

1. Ken has just graduated from secondary school. His uncle has offered him a full-time job (40 hours a week) at his home improvement supply outlet at $10 an hour. Ken, however, has his heart set on going to university for four years to get a degree in engineering and, unfortunately, his uncle can't use him on a part-time basis. What is Ken's opportunity cost of getting a degree?

2. Kant Skatte is a professional player in the National Hockey League. Because he loved the game so much, Kant dropped out of high school and worked very hard to develop his physical strength and overcome his limitations. Eventually he made it to the majors. Estimate Kant's annual opportunity costs, in dollars, of continuing to play in the NHL.

3. Given the graph in Figure W1.7:
   a) What could explain the shift from PPI to PPII?

FIGURE W1.7

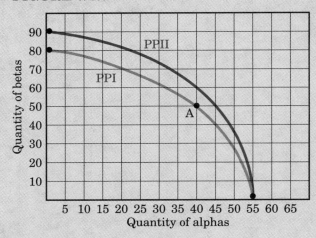

b) Given PPII, indicate with point B, the maximum quantity of betas that can now be produced if 40 alphas are produced.

c) Given PPII, indicate, with point C, the maximum quantity of alphas that can now be produced if 50 betas are produced.

d) Given point A, indicate, with point D, an increase in the production of both alphas and betas.

4. Pacifica produces only two goods, bats and balls. Only labour is required to produce both goods and the economy's labour force is fixed at 50 workers. Table W1.5 below indicates the amounts of bats and balls that can be produced daily with various quantities of labour.

TABLE W1.5

Number of Workers	Daily Production of Bats	Number of Workers	Daily Production of Balls
0	0	0	0
10	70	10	14
20	200	20	36
30	350	30	56
40	450	40	70
50	520	50	72

a) Draw a production possibilities curve for this economy assuming that labour is fully employed.

b) What is the opportunity cost of increasing the output of bats from 350 to 450 units a day? What is the opportunity cost of increasing the output of balls from 56 to 70 units per day?

c) Suppose that a central planning office dictates an output of 450 bats and 20 balls per day. Is this output combination possible?

d) Now assume that new technology is introduced in the production of balls so that *each worker* can produce 1/2 a ball more per day. Draw the new production possibilities curve. Is the central planning office's output goal in c) now possible?

CHAPTER **TWO**

■ ■ ■ ■ ■ ■ ■ ■ ━━━━━━━━━━━━━━━━━

Demand and Supply 1: An Introduction

What's ahead . . . This chapter introduces you to the fundamental economic ideas of demand and supply. It explains the distinction between individual and market demand and looks at the various reasons why consumers change their demand. We then take a look at things from the producer's point of view and explain what determines the amounts that they put on the market. Next we explain how markets are able to reconcile the wishes of the two groups and introduce the concept of equilibrium. Finally, we look at how the market price and the quantity traded adjusts to various changes.

If the average person were to think about the subject matter of economics, it is unlikely that she would immediately think of choice or costs, which was a principal topic of Chapter 1. More likely, she would think in terms of money or interest rates or demand and supply. Most people realize, without studying the topic, that demand and supply are central to economics. In our own ways, and as a result of our experiences in life, most of us feel that we know quite a lot about the subject. After all, who are better experts on the reaction of consumers to changes in the market than consumers themselves? However, as we will see shortly, the way that economists define and use the terms "demand" and "supply" differs from the everyday usage. To make matters worse, there doesn't seem to be a consensus among non-economists about their meanings. This is, of course, often the case with any language but it does lead to a great deal of confusion which can be illustrated in the following exchange:

Isn't it shocking that house prices have increased so much in the past year? It makes it very difficult for first-time buyers to get into the market.

Well, yes, but that's the law of demand. Presumably builders can get away with charging a higher price as long as people are willing to pay.

Are you suggesting that the demand for new houses has increased, then?

Must have done.

But surely, higher prices are going to lead to a lower demand. I thought that was the law of demand!

Well yes. But, don't you see, a lower demand will lead to lower prices.

And lower prices to a higher demand...

What's happening here? There obviously seems to be a degree of confusion, but what is causing it? Is it because neither of the speakers know what they are talking about? Well, that's a possibility, of course. But actually the root of the confusion surrounds that simple word "demand." As we shall see, demand is being used in two different ways and neither speaker is aware of this. It's probably clear to you already that economists are very fussy about defining and using economic terms correctly, and this is particularly true in a discussion about demand and supply. Demand doesn't simply mean what people want to buy, nor is supply just the amount being produced. Besides the problem of definitions, another source of confusion in the above discussion is a misunderstanding of cause and effect: is the price of houses the effect of changing demand, or its cause? Hopefully, this chapter will clear up some of the confusion and give us a basis on which to analyze and clarify some real practical problems. First, let us take a look at the concept of demand.

Demand

Individual Demand

demand: the quantities which consumers are willing and able to buy per period of time at various prices.

There are several dimensions to the term **demand**. First, economists use the word not in the sense of commanding or ordering but in the sense of wanting something. However, this want also involves the ability to buy it. In other words, it refers to both the *desire and the ability* to purchase a good or service. This means that although I may well have a desire for a new top-of-the-line Infiniti, I unfortunately don't have the ability to buy one and, therefore, don't have a demand for one.

Second, even though we know there are many factors which determine what products and what quantities a consumer purchases, economists would suggest that the price is usually the most important of these and for this reason they look at how consumers might react to a change in the price assuming that all other factors remain unchanged. The Latin phrase for this perspective is *ceteris paribus*, which literally means "all things being equal." However, it is usually interpreted by economists to mean "all things remaining the same." In other words, demand is the relationship between the price of a product and the quantities demanded, *ceteris paribus*.

demand schedule: a table showing the various quantities demanded per period of time at different prices.

Third, demand is a hypothetical construct which expresses this desire and ability to purchase, not at a single price, but over a *range of* hypothetical prices. Finally, demand is also a flow concept in that it measures quantities over a period of time. All of these aspects of demand are captured in Table 2.1 below which shows the **demand schedule** for an enthusiastic beer drinker named Tomiko.

TABLE 2.1 Individual Demand

Price per Case	Number of Cases per Week Quantity Demanded
$12	6
13	5
14	4
15	3
16	2
17	1
18	0

Once again, what we mean by demand is the entire relationship between the price and the quantities that people wish to purchase, and this relationship can be laid out in the form of a demand schedule. The above schedule shows the amounts per week that Tomiko is willing and able to purchase at the various prices shown. Note that there is an *inverse* relationship between the price and quantity. This simply means that at higher prices Tomiko would not be willing to buy as much as at lower prices. In other words, the higher the price, the lower the quantity demanded, and the lower the price, the higher the quantity demanded. Another, though less obvious, statement of this law of demand is to say that in order to induce Tomiko to buy a higher quantity of beer, the price must be lower. Tomiko's demand schedule is graphed in Figure 2.1 below.

FIGURE 2.1 Individual Demand Curve

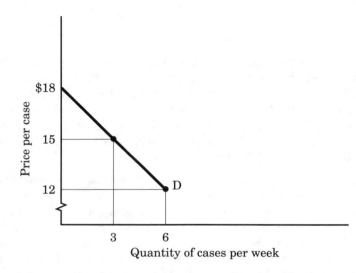

At a price of $12 per case, Tomiko is willing and able to buy 6 cases per week. At a higher price, $15 per case, the amount she is willing and able to buy falls to 3 cases. The higher the price, then, the lower the quantity demanded. (Note that the vertical axis contains a "broken" portion. In general, an axis is often broken in this manner whenever the information about, say, low prices, is either unavailable or unimportant.)

In Figure 2.1, at a price of $16, the quantity demanded by Tomiko is 2 cases per week while at a lower price of $12, she would be willing to buy 6 cases. The demand schedule therefore plots as a downward-sloping curve. (To economists, curves include straight lines!) You should note that when we use the terms "demand," or "demand schedule," or "demand curve," we are referring to a whole array of different prices and quantities.

It is very important for you to note that since price is part of what we call "demand," a change in the price cannot change the demand. Certainly it can affect the *amounts* we are willing to purchase and this we refer to as a **change in the quantity demanded.** This is illustrated in Figure 2.2.

> **change in the quantity demanded:** the change in quantity which results from a price change. It results in a movement along a demand curve.

A change in the quantity which is the result of a price change is called a change in the quantity demanded. Graphically, as we move down the demand curve, the quantity demanded increases; as we move up the demand curve, the quantity demanded decreases.

Why Is the Demand Curve Downward-Sloping?

There are a number of rationales for the proposition that people tend to buy more at lower rather than at higher prices. Most of us can confirm from our own personal experience that a lower price will induce us to buy more of a

FIGURE 2.2 Changes in the Quantity Demanded

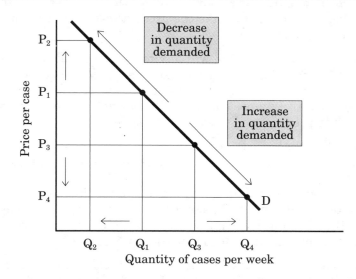

Whenever the price changes, there is a movement along the demand curve. An increase in the price from, say, P_1 to P_2, causes a decrease in the quantity demanded from Q_1 to Q_2. A decrease in the price from P_3 to P_4 leads to an increase in the quantity demanded from Q_3 to Q_4. Neither the demand, nor the demand curve, however, changes.

product or to buy something that we would not normally purchase. Witness the big crowds that are attracted to nothing more than the sign "SALE." In addition, most microeconomic research done over the years tends to confirm that the law of demand, and theories of consumer behaviour (such as the marginal utility theory which we shall study in Chapter 5), lend additional support to the idea.

Let's begin our exploration of the question of why people tend to buy more at lower prices. Remember that our demand for products is a combination of our desire and our ability to purchase. A lower price affects both of these. The lower the price of a product, the more income a person has left to purchase additional products. Let's explain this by assuming, for instance, that the price of beer in Table 2.1 was $15, and Tomiko was buying 4 cases per week, for a total expenditure of $60 per week. Next, let's say the price decreases to $12. Tomiko could, if she wished, buy the same quantity for an outlay of $48, thus saving a total of $12. It's almost as if Tomiko had had a pay raise of $12. In fact, in terms of its effect on Tomiko's pocketbook, it is exactly the same. Or, as economists would express it, her **real income** has increased. A decrease in price means that people can afford to buy more of a product (or more of other products) if they wish. This is referred to as the **income effect** of a price change, and it affects people's *ability* to purchase. This is because a lower price means a higher real income, and as a result people will tend to buy more of a product. (Conversely, an increase in the price would effectively reduce people's real income.)

In addition to this, a price change also affects people's *desire* to purchase. We are naturally driven to buy the cheaper of competing products such that the drop in the price of one of them increases our desire to substitute it for the now relatively more expensive product. For instance, if the price of wine were to drop (or for that matter, if the price of beer were to increase), then some beer drinkers might well switch to what they regard as a cheaper substitute. In general, this is saying that there are substitutes for most prod-

real income: income measured in terms of the amount of goods and services that it will buy. Real income will increase if either actual income increases or prices fall.

income effect: the effect which a price change has on real income, and therefore on the quantity demanded of a product.

substitution effect: the substitution of one product for another as a result of a change in their relative prices.

ucts, and people will tend to substitute the relatively expensive product with a relatively cheap one. This is called the **substitution effect**. On the other hand, a higher price tends to make the product less attractive to us than its substitutes, and so we buy less.

When the price of a product drops, we will buy more of it because we are *more able* (the income effect) and because we are *more willing* (the substitution effect). (There is a possible exception to this which we will look at in the next chapter.) Conversely, a price increase means we are less able and less willing to buy the product, and therefore we buy less.

The close relationship that exists between the price and the quantity demanded is so pervasive that it is often referred to as the *law of demand*.

Market Demand

market demand: the total demand for a product by all consumers.

Up to this point, we have focused on individual demand. Now we want to move to **market demand** (or total demand). Conceptually, this is easy enough to derive. By summing every individual's demand for a product, we are able to obtain the market demand. This is shown in Table 2.2 below.

Let's say we know not only Tomiko's demand but also the demands of three other friends in a small four-person economy. The market demand then is

TABLE 2.2 Deriving the Market Demand

Price per Case	Number of Cases per Week				
	Tomiko's Demand	Meridith's Demand	Abdi's Demand	Jan's Demand	Market Demand
$12	6	3	4	9	22
13	5	2	4	7	18
14	4	2	4	6	16
15	3	0	3	3	9
16	2	0	3	1	6
17	1	0	2	0	3
18	0	0	2	0	2

FIGURE 2.3 The Market Demand Curve

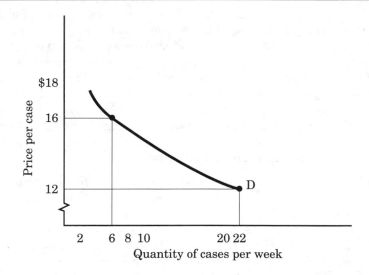

At a price of $12, the total or market quantity demanded equals 22 cases. As with individual demand, when the price increases to $16, then the quantity demanded will drop, in this case to 6. This is because at a higher price, each individual buys less and, in addition, there are fewer people who can afford to or are willing to buy any at all.

the horizontal summation of individual demands, which simply means that to find the quantities demanded at $12 we add the quantities demanded by each individual, i.e., 6 + 3 + 4 + 9 = 22. The same would be done for each price level. This particular market demand is graphed in Figure 2.3.

Note that, as with the individual demand curve, the market demand curve also slopes downward. This is because not only do people buy more as the price drops, but in addition more people buy. At a price of $18 in our example, only Abdi would buy any beer. As the price drops to $16, not only would Abdi buy beer, but so too would Tomiko and Jan. The price would need to drop to $14 to induce all four people to buy beer.

Finally, before we take a look at the supply side of things, note again that our demand schedule tells us only what people *might* buy; it tells us nothing about what they are actually buying because to know this, we also need to know the actual price. And to find out what the actual price of beer is we need to know ... yes, the supply.

QUESTION 2.1
Suppose that three people, Al, Bo and Cole each buys either a constant amount of milk or none depending on the price. However, Al refuses to pay more than $4 per container; Bo will not pay more than $5; and Cole will not pay more than $6. What will be the shape of their market demand curve?

Supply

Individual Supply

In many ways the formulation of supply is very similar to that of demand. Both measure hypothetical quantities at various prices, and both are flow concepts. However, we are now looking at things through the eyes of the producer, rather than the consumer. We will assume for the time being that the prime motive for the producer is to maximize profits, although we will examine this assumption in more detail in a later chapter. Certainly, as Adam Smith noted in *The Wealth of Nations*, few producers are in business to please consumers, nor of course, do consumers buy products to please producers. Both are motivated by self-interest.

supply: the quantities which producers are willing and able to sell per period of time at various prices.

The term **supply** refers to the quantities that suppliers are *willing and able* to make available to the market at various different prices. Table 2.3 shows a hypothetical **supply schedule** for Bobby the brewer.

supply schedule: a table showing the various quantities supplied per period of time at different prices.

TABLE 2.3 Individual Supply

Price per Case	Number of Cases per Week Quantity Supplied
$12	2
13	3
14	4
15	5
16	6
17	7
18	8

Data

BOX 2.1

Adam Smith (1723–1790) is generally regarded as the founding father of economics. In his brilliant work, *The Wealth of Nations*, Smith posed so many interesting questions and provided such illuminating answers that later economists often felt that they merely were picking at the scraps he left behind. He was born and brought up in Scotland and educated at Glasgow and Oxford. He later held the Chair of Moral Philosophy at Glasgow College for many years. He was a lifelong bachelor and had a kindly but absent-minded disposition. His main claim to fame is that he was the first scholar to analyze in a detailed and systematic manner the business of "getting and spending." In doing this, he gave useful social dignity to the professions of business and trading. Besides introducing the important idea of the *invisible hand*, which was his way of describing the coordinating mechanism of capitalism, he examined the division of labour, the role of government, the function of money, the advantages and disadvantages of free trade, what constitutes good and bad taxation, and many other things besides. For Smith, economic life was not merely a peripheral adventure of people but their central motivating force.

Note that there is a *direct* relationship between the price and the quantity supplied, which means that a higher price will induce Bobby to produce more. Remember that Bobby's reason for being in business is to make as much profit as possible. Suppose that Bobby was asked how much she will, hypothetically, be prepared to supply if the beer could be sold at $12 per case. Knowing what her costs are likely to be, she figures that she could make the most profit if she produces 2 cases. At a higher price, there is a likelihood of greater profits, and therefore she is willing to produce more. Also, as we shall see in Chapter 6, as firms produce more, often the cost per unit tends to rise and therefore the producer needs the incentive of a higher price in order to increase production. For the time being, however, we can rely on the proposition that a higher price means higher profits and therefore will lead to higher quantities produced. This is illustrated in Figure 2.4.

Joining together the individual points from the supply schedule gives us the upward-sloping supply curve shown above. You need to realize that, as with the term "demand," the term "supply" does not refer to a single price and quantity, but to the whole array of hypothetical price and quantity combinations that are contained in the supply schedule and illustrated by the supply curve.

change in the quantity supplied: the change in the amounts that will be produced as a result of a price change. This is shown as a movement along a supply curve.

Since price is part of what we mean by the term supply, a change in the price level cannot change the supply. A change in price does of course lead to a change in the quantity that a producer is willing and able to make available. Thus, the effect of a change in price we call a **change in the quantity supplied.** These changes are shown in Figure 2.5.

An increase in the price will lead to an *increase in the quantity supplied* and is illustrated as a movement up the supply curve; a decrease in the price, on the other hand, will cause a *decrease in the quantity supplied* which is illustrated as a movement down the supply curve.

FIGURE 2.4 Individual Supply Curve

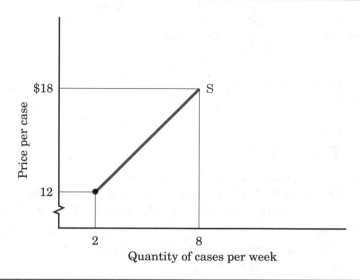

At a low price of $12, the most profitable output for Bobby is 2 cases. If the price increased, she would be willing and able to produce more, since she would be able to make greater profits. At $18, for instance, the quantity she would produce increases to 8 cases.

FIGURE 2.5 Changes in the Quantity Supplied

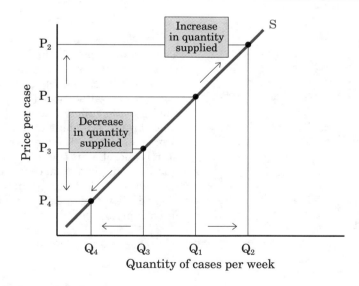

If the price changes, it will lead to a movement along the supply curve. An increase in the price from, say, P_1 to P_2 will cause an increase in the quantity supplied from Q_1 to Q_2. A decrease in the price from P_3 to P_4 will lead to a decrease in the quantity supplied from Q_3 to Q_4. The supply curve itself, however, does not change.

Market Supply

market supply: the total supply of a product offered by all producers.

As we did with the market demand, we could derive the **market supply** of a product by summing the supply of each and every individual supplier. A word of caution, however, is in order. We must make the necessary assumption that the producers are all producing a similar product, and consumers have no preference as to which supplier or product they use. Given this, it is possible to add together the individual supplies to derive the market supply. In our example, suppose that Bobby the brewer has three other competing brewers of similar size and with similar costs. The market supply of beer in this market would be as shown in Table 2.4.

TABLE 2.4 Deriving the Market Supply

| | Number of Cases per Week | | |
Price Per Case	Bobby's Supply	Supply of Other Brewers	Market Supply
$12	2	6	8
13	3	9	12
14	4	12	16
15	5	15	20
16	6	18	24
17	7	21	28
18	8	24	32

The total quantities supplied by the three other brewers is equal to the quantity that Bobby would supply at each price, multiplied by three. The fourth column, market supply, is the addition of every brewer's supply, i.e., the second column plus the third column.

The market supply of beer is illustrated in Figure 2.6 below.

FIGURE 2.6 The Market Supply

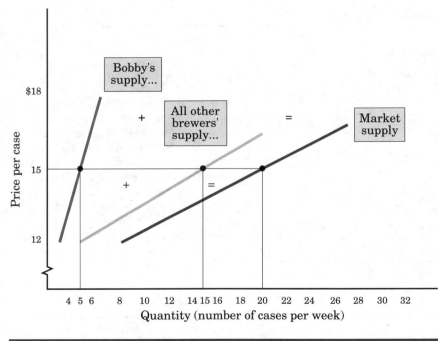

The market supply is the horizontal summation of each individual producer's supply curve. For instance, at a price of $15, Bobby would supply 5 cases; the other brewers combined would produce 15 cases. The market supply therefore is the total quantity supplied of 20 cases. To derive the market supply curve, we add the totals of each supplier at each price level.

The market supply curve is upward-sloping primarily for the same reason the individual supply curve is upward-sloping: because higher prices imply higher profits and will therefore induce a greater quantity supplied. There is an additional reason. In the example we have used, we assumed for simplicity's sake that the suppliers are of similar size and have similar costs. In reality that's unlikely: costs and size are likely to differ so that a price which generates a profit for one firm may mean a loss for another. As the price of a product increases, however, some firms that previously were unable to produce will now find that they can successfully operate at a profit. Thus, as the price of the product increases, currently operating firms will produce more. In addition, other firms not previously producing will enter the market and start to produce.

In summary then, a higher price which acts as a deterrent to consumers to buy more is an incentive for suppliers to produce more. Conversely, a lower price serves as an inducement to consumers to buy more but is a reason for suppliers to cut back their output.

The motives of consumers and producers are very divergent, the former wishing to obtain the lowest price possible, the latter wanting to sell at the highest. How can their wishes converge? How is trade possible in these circumstances? Well, if the question means: is it possible for *all* prospective consumers and suppliers to be satisfied, the answer must be no. If the question means, is it possible for *some* of these people to be satisfied, the answer will be, almost always, yes. Of course, this will require that they are able in some sense to meet and get together. A market enables them to do just that.

The Market

market: a mechanism to bring buyers and sellers together and to assist them in negotiating the exchange of products.

Most people are able to understand the terms market price and market demand but are not always clear as to what constitutes a **market**. Certainly the term includes those places which have a physical location, such as produce and fish markets. But, in broader terms, a market really refers to any exchange mechanism which brings buyers and sellers of a product together. There may be times when we feel that we need to inspect or get further on-the-spot information about a product before we buy it, and this is the purpose of the retail market. But there are other times where we possess sufficient information about a product or a producer that it's not necessary to actually see either of them before we purchase. This applies for instance if you wish to buy stocks and bonds or to buy from a mail-order catalogue. In such cases, a phone call is all that is required. Increasingly, in this modern age with the higher costs of in-person service and the greater availability of electronic communication, markets are becoming both wider and more accessible. The market for staple products such as copper or gold or rubber, for instance, is both worldwide and anonymous, in that the buyers and sellers seldom meet in person.

By a market then, we mean any environment in which buyers and sellers can communicate and which is relatively open without preference. When we talk of the market price then, we mean the price which is available to *all* buyers and sellers of a product; by market demand we mean the total quantities demanded; and market supply refers to the quantity made available by all suppliers.

Later in the text, you will encounter a variety of different types of markets, some of which work very well, and others which work poorly, if at all. The analysis in this chapter assumes that the market that we are looking at is very (economists call it "perfectly") competitive. We devote the whole of Chapter 8 to examining this type of market. For now, we need to mention that a perfectly competitive market is, among other things, one where there are many small producers, each selling an identical product. Given this caution, let's see how this market works.

Market Equilibrium

We now examine the point at which the wishes of buyers and sellers coincide by combining the market demand and supply for beer in Table 2.5.

TABLE 2.5 Market Supply and Demand

| Price per Case | Number of Cases per Week | | |
	Market Demand	Market Supply	Surplus (+)/ Shortage(−)
$12	22	8	−14
13	18	12	− 6
14	16	16	0
15	9	20	+11
16	6	24	+18
17	3	28	+25
18	2	32	+30

You can see from this table that there is only one price, $14, at which the wishes of consumers and producers coincide. Only when the price is $14 will the quantities demanded and supplied be equal. This price level is referred to as the **equilibrium price**. Equilibrium, in general, means that there is balance between opposing forces; here, those opposing forces are demand and supply. The word equilibrium also implies a condition of stability, so that if this stability is disturbed, there will be a tendency to return automatically to equilibrium. To understand this point, refer to Table 2.5 and notice that if the price were, say, $12, then the amount being demanded of 22 would exceed the amount being supplied of 8. At this price there is an excess demand, or more simply, a shortage of beer to the tune of 14 cases. This amount is shown in the last column and marked with a minus sign. In this situation there would be a lot of unhappy beer drinkers. Faced with the prospect of going beerless, many of them will be prepared to pay a higher price for their suds and will therefore bid the price up. As the price of beer starts to rise, the reaction of consumers and producers will differ. Some beer drinkers will not be able to afford the higher prices, and so the quantity demanded will drop. On the supply side of things, producers will be delighted with the higher price and will start to produce more, i.e., the quantity supplied will increase. Both of these tendencies will combine to reduce the shortage as the price goes up. Eventually, when the price has reached the equilibrium price of $14, the shortage will have disappeared and the price will no longer increase. Part of the law of demand suggests, then, that *shortages cause prices to rise*. This is illustrated in Figure 2.7.

equilibrium price: the price at which the quantity demanded equals the quantity supplied such that there is neither a surplus nor a shortage.

Now let's see, again using Table 2.5, what will happen if the price happens to be above equilibrium, at, say, $16 a case. At this price, the quantity demanded is 6 cases, and the quantity supplied is 24 cases. There is insufficient demand from the producers' point of view, or more simply, there is a surplus of 18 cases. This is shown in the last column of Table 2.5 as +18. This is not a stable situation, since firms cannot continue producing a product which they cannot sell. They will be forced to lower the price in an effort

FIGURE 2.7 How the Market Reacts to a Shortage

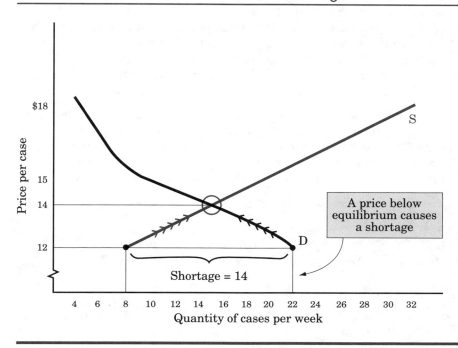

At a price of $12, the quantity supplied of 8 is far below the quantity demanded of 22. The horizontal distance between the two shows the amount of the shortage, which is 14. As a result of the shortage, competition between consumers will force up the price. As the price increases, the quantity demanded will drop, but the quantity supplied will rise until these two are equal at a quantity of 16.

to sell more. As the price starts to drop, two things happen concurrently. Consumers will be happy to consume more, or to use economic terms, there will be an increase in the quantity demanded. In Figure 2.8 below, note that

FIGURE 2.8 How the Market Reacts to Surpluses

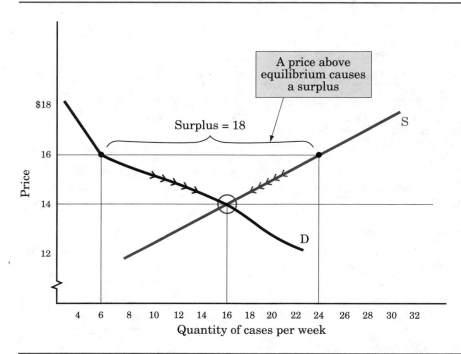

A price above equilibrium will produce a surplus. At $16, the quantity supplied of 24 exceeds the quantity demanded of 6. The horizontal distance of 18 represents the amount of the surplus. The surplus will result in producers dropping the price in an attempt to increase sales. As the price drops, the quantity demanded increases, while the quantity supplied falls.

as the price falls, the quantity demanded increases and this increase is depicted as a movement down the demand curve. At the same time, faced with a falling price, producers will be forced to cut back production. This is what we have called a decrease in the quantity supplied. In the same figure, this is shown as a movement along (down) the supply curve. The net result of this will be the eventual elimination of the surplus as the price moves toward equilibrium. In other words, *surpluses cause prices to fall*.

equilibrium quantity:
the quantity which prevails at the equilibrium price.

Only if the price is $14 will there be no surplus or shortage and the quantity produced will be equal to the quantity demanded. This is the equilibrium price. The quantity prevailing at the equilibrium price is known as the **equilibrium quantity**, in this case 16 cases. This equilibrium quantity is the quantity both demanded and supplied (since they are equal).

Study Guide

QUESTION 2.2
Can a change in the price of a product lead to a change in the demand? Can it lead to a change in supply? Explain.

QUESTION 2.3
The following table shows the demand and supply of eggs (in hundreds of thousands per day).

Price	Demand	Supply	Surplus/Shortage
$2.00	60	30	_____
2.25	58	33	_____
2.50	56	36	_____
2.75	54	39	_____
3.00	52	42	_____
3.25	50	45	_____
3.50	48	48	_____
3.75	46	51	_____
4.00	44	54	_____

A) What are the equilibrium price and equilibrium quantity?
B) Complete the surplus/shortage column. Using this column, explain why your answer in question A must be correct.
C) What would be the surplus/shortage at a price of $2.50? What would happen to the price and the quantity traded?
D) What would be the surplus/shortage at a price of $4.00? What would happen to the price and the quantity traded?

Review

BOX 2A
1. Define and explain the difference between the terms *demand* and *quantity demanded*.
2. What is a *demand schedule*?
3. Why is the demand curve downward-sloping?
4. *Income effect* means a higher price leads to a higher real income, which then leads to an increased quantity demanded. True or false?

> **BOX 2A** *(continued)*
> 5. *Substitution effect* means an increase in the price of product X leads people to buy less of it and more of competing goods instead. True or false?
> 6. Explain how the market demand curve can be derived.
> 7. What is the distinction between the *supply* and the *quantity supplied*?
> 8. Why are producers willing to produce more at a higher price than at a lower one?
> 9. What does the term *market supply* mean?
> 10. What is a *market*?
> 11. What do the terms: *equilibrium price* and *equilibrium quantity* mean?
> 12. Surpluses cause prices to increase; shortages cause them to fall. True or false?

Change in Demand

change in demand:
a change in the quantities demanded at every price, caused by a change in the determinants of demand.

Recall from the definition of demand that this concept refers to the *relationship* between various prices and quantities. In other words, both price and quantity make up what is known as demand. Thus, a change in price causes a change in the quantity demanded. That said, we must now ask: what are the other determinants, besides the price, that would influence how much of any particular product consumers will buy? Another way of looking at this is to ask: once equilibrium price and quantity have been established, what might disturb that equilibrium? The general answer to this question is a **change in demand**. Table 2.6 shows such a change in the demand for beer.

TABLE 2.6 An Increase in Demand

Price per Case of Beer	Number of Cases per Week Demand 1	Demand 2
$12	22	33
13	18	29
14	16	27
15	9	20
16	6	17
17	3	14
18	2	13

The original market demand, labelled Demand 1, is from Table 2.5, and was the demand that existed, let's say, last month. Demand 2 is the market demand for beer this month. There has been an increase in demand of 11 cases per week at each price. Or put another way, whatever the price, consumers are willing and able to consume an additional 11 cases. Thus, there has been an increase in the demand. Figure 2.9 on the following page graphically illustrates an increase in demand.

An increase in demand, then, means an increase in the quantities demanded at each price, i.e., a total increase in the demand schedule which is illustrated by a rightward shift in the demand curve. Similarly, a decrease in demand means a reduction in the quantities demanded at each price, i.e., a decrease in the demand schedule, and this is illustrated by a leftward shift in the demand curve.

FIGURE 2.9 An Increase in Demand

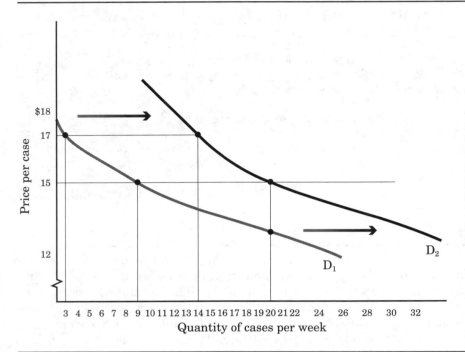

At each price, the quantities demanded have increased. In this example, the increase is by a constant amount of 11, thus producing a parallel shift in the demand curve, e.g., at $17, the quantity demanded has risen from 3 to 14, at $15, the quantity demanded has increased from 9 to 20 (by 11).

Determinants of a Change in Demand

Having illustrated what an increase in demand looks like, we now need to look at the factors which could bring about such a change. Some of these determinants of demand affect people's willingness to purchase, others affect their ability to purchase, and still others affect both. One factor that affects our willingness to purchase a product is our own particular *preference*. An increase in demand as shown in Table 2.6 could simply have been caused by a change in consumer preferences: consumers now prefer more beer.

There are a host of different things that could affect our preferences. Tastes change over time and are influenced by the weather, advertising, articles and reports in books and magazines, opinions of friends, special events and many other things. These things are difficult to measure, but we know that they affect demand and are often unpredictable. They can cause the demand for a product to either increase or decrease.

The second factor affecting the demand for a product is the *income* of consumers. This will affect their ability to consume. Generally speaking, you would expect that an increase in income leads most people to increase their purchases of most products, and a decrease in income generally causes a drop in the demand, i.e., there is a direct relationship between income and demand. Indeed for most products that we buy this is true and these products are called **normal products**. But it is certainly not true for all people and products. For instance, as the income of most people increase, they tend to buy less of such things as low-quality hamburger meats, packets of macaroni and cheese, cheap toilet rolls and so on. Instead, they start to substitute higher-quality and higher-priced articles which they could not previously afford. When income is low, we are forced to survive on lower-quality staple products that economists call **inferior products**. There is

normal products:
those products whose demand will increase as a result of an increase in income and will decrease as a result of a decrease in income.

inferior products:
those products whose demands will decrease as a result of an increase in income and will increase as a result of a decrease in income.

an inverse relationship between income and the demand for inferior products. As income levels go up, the demand goes down. It also means that as incomes fall, our demand for these inferior products will rise. In our beer example from Table 2.6, the increase in the market demand could have been caused by an increase in incomes in the community.

A third important determinant of demand is the *prices of related products*. A change in the price of related products will affect both people's willingness and their ability to purchase a particular good. Products are related if a change in the price of one causes a change in the demand for the other. For instance, if the price of Pepsi were to increase, a number of Pepsi drinkers might well switch over to Coke.

There are, in fact, two ways in which products may be related. They may be related as substitutes, or they may be related as complements. **Substitute** (or competitive) **products** are products which are sufficiently similar in the eyes of most consumers that price becomes the main distinguishing feature. Pepsi and Coke, therefore, are substitute products since an increase in the price of one will cause an increase in the demand for the other. The relationship between the price of a product and the demand for its substitute is, therefore, a direct one. It also means that if the price of a product falls, then the demand for its substitute will also fall, since many consumers are now buying the cheaper product.

Complementary products tend to be purchased together, and their demands are interrelated. Skis and ski boots are complementary products as are cars and gasoline or beer and pretzels. If the price of one product increases causing a decrease in the quantity demanded, then people will also purchase less of the complement. If the price of cameras were to increase so that people were buying fewer cameras, then we would also expect a decline in the demand for not only film but for other complementary products like lenses, tripods, carrying bags, and so on. There is, in this case, an inverse relationship between the price of a product and the demand for its complement which means that an increase in price of the one product leads to a decline in the demand for the complementary product. Similarly, a decrease in the price of a product will lead to an increase in the demand for a complement.

substitute products: those products which consumers see as interchangeable one for the other.

complementary products: products which tend to be purchased jointly and whose demands therefore are related.

QUESTION 2.4

The following table shows the initial weekly demand (D_1) and the new demand (D_2) for packets of pretzels (a bar snack).

Price	Demand (D_1)	Demand (D_2)
$2.00	10,000	11,000
2.50	9,800	10,800
3.00	9,600	10,600
3.50	9,400	10,400
4.00	9,200	10,200

To explain the change in demand from D_1 to D_2, what might have happened to the price of a complementary product, like beer? Alternatively, what might have happened to the price of a substitute product, like nuts?

A fourth determinant of demand is the *future expectations of consumers*. There are many ways that our feelings about the future influence our present behaviour. Future expected prices and incomes can affect our present demand for a product as does the prospect of a shortage. If consumers think that the price of their favourite beverage is likely to increase in the near future, they may well stock up in advance, just in case. The present demand for the product will therefore increase. Conversely, expected future price declines cause people to hold off their current purchases while awaiting the hoped-for lower prices.

In a similar fashion, an anticipated pay increase may cause some people to spend more now as they adjust to their expected higher standard of living. Similarly, it does seem likely that most people who fear a layoff or other cause of a drop in salary will cut down spending in advance of the fateful date. Finally, it should be added that the possibility of future shortages, caused for instance by an impending strike, often causes a mad rush to the stores by anxious customers trying to stock up in advance.

These four determinants of demand — preferences, income, prices of related products and future expectations — affect people's individual demand in varying degrees. If we shift our attention to the market demand, these four factors still apply. In addition, there are a few other factors that need to be mentioned. The *size of the market population* will affect the demand for all products. An increase in the size of the population, for example, will lead to an increase in the demand for most products in varying amounts. In addition, a *change in the distribution of incomes* will lead to an increase in the demand for some products, and a decrease in the demand for others, even though the total income has not changed. The same will also be true for the *age composition of the population*. An aging population will increase the demand for products which appeal to older people (Ann Murray CDs?), and decrease the demand for those which have appeal only to the young (Bon Jovi CDs?).

Notice that there is one factor *not* included in this list of determinants of demand, and that is supply. Economists are scrupulous in their attempts to separate the forces of demand and supply. Remember that the demand formulation is a hypothetical construct based on the quantities consumers are willing and able to purchase at various prices. There is an implied assumption that the consumer will be able to obtain these quantities, otherwise the demand schedule itself would not be relevant. In other words, when specifying the demand, we assume that the supply will be available, just as, when formulating supply, we make the assumption that there will be sufficient demand.

In summary, the determinants of demand are:

1. consumer preferences

2. consumer incomes

3. prices of related goods

4. expectations of future prices, incomes or availability

5. population size, income and age distribution

The Effects of an Increase in Demand

We have seen that the demand for any product is affected by many different factors. A change in any of these factors will cause a change in demand, and lead to a change in price and production levels. Let us first consider the effects of an increase in the demand for a product. In summary, any one of the following could cause such an increase in the market demand:

- a change in preferences toward the product
- an increase in incomes if the product is a normal product, or a decrease in incomes if the product is an inferior product
- an increase in the price of a substitute product
- a decrease in the price of a complementary product
- the expectation that future prices or incomes will be higher or that there will be a future shortage of the product
- an increase in the population or a change in its income or age distribution

Any of these changes could cause people to buy more of a product, regardless of its price. As an example, let us combine the data from Tables 2.5 and 2.6 into Table 2.7.

TABLE 2.7 The Effects on the Market of an Increase in Demand

Price per Case	Number of Cases per Week		
	Supply	Demand 1	Demand 2
$12	8	22	33
13	12	18	29
14	16	16	27
15	20	9	20
16	24	6	17
17	28	3	14
18	32	2	13

You can see that at the old demand (Demand 1) and supply, the equilibrium price was $14 and the quantity traded was 16 cases. Assume now that the demand for beer increases. Since consumers do not usually signal their intentions to producers in advance, producers are not aware that the demand has changed until they have evidence. The evidence will probably take the form of unsatisfied customers. At a price of $14 a case, the producers in total have produced 16 cases. At this price, the new demand is 27 cases. There is a shortage of 11 cases, and some customers are going to go home disappointed since there is not sufficient beer to satisfy all customers. The important question is: will these brewers now increase production to satisfy the higher demand? The surprising answer is no — at least not at the present price. Brewers are not in the business of satisfying customers, they are in the business of making profits. As the dean of economics, Adam Smith, wrote over 200 years ago:

> It is not from the benevolence of the butcher, the brewer, or the baker that we expect our dinner but from regard to their own self-interest.[1]

---

[1] Adam Smith, *Wealth of Nations* (Edwin Cannan edition, 1877), pp. 26–27.

You may object that unless firms are responsive to the demands of customers, they will soon go out of business. And you are right. But equally, a firm who is solely responsive to its customers will go out of business even faster. Look back at the supply schedule in Table 2.7. At a price of $14, the brewers said they are prepared to produce 16 cases. They are not prepared to produce 27 cases, the amount that consumers now want. Why is that? Because, presumably, they can make more profits producing 16 cases than they can producing 27 cases; otherwise they would have produced 27 in the first place. In fact, it may well be that if they produced 27 cases, they would end up making a loss. Does this mean therefore that the shortage of beer will persist? No, because we have earlier seen that *shortages drive prices up* until the shortage disappears and the new demand is equal to the supply. This will occur at a price of $15 where the demand and supply are equal at the equilibrium quantity of 20. This adjustment process can be seen in Figure 2.10 below.

FIGURE 2.10 Adjustment to an Increase in Demand

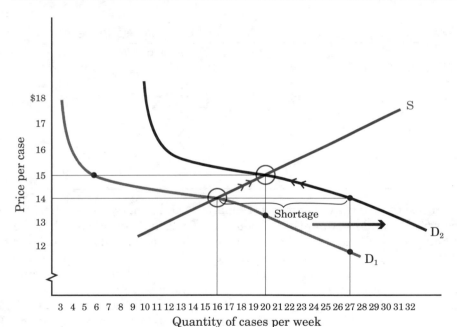

The increase in demand from D_1 to D_2 creates an immediate shortage of 11. This will cause an increase in the price of beer. The increase affects both the producers, who will now increase the quantity supplied, and consumers, who will reduce the quantity demanded. Eventually, the price will reach a new equilibrium at $15 where the equilibrium quantity is 20, and there is no longer a shortage.

You can see in the graph that at the old price of $14, the new quantity demanded exceeds the quantity supplied. This shortage causes the price to rise. As it does so, notice that the quantity of beer that producers make also rises, i.e., there will be an increase *in the quantity supplied*. Producers will produce more *not* because there is a shortage, but because the shortage causes a rise in price. Note also that the increase in price causes some customers to reduce their purchases of beer, i.e., there is a decrease *in the quantity demanded*. The price of beer will continue to increase as long as there is a shortage, and will stop as soon as the shortage disappears. This occurs when the price has increased to $15. At the new equilibrium price, the quantity demanded will again equal the quantity supplied but at a higher quantity traded of 20 cases. The increase in the demand therefore causes the price to increase and the quantity traded also to increase.

The Effects of a Decrease in Demand

Now let's see what happens when there is a decrease in demand. Remember that a decrease in demand cannot be caused by an increase in price but is caused by a change in any of the non-price determinants, such as:

- a decrease in the preferences for the product
- a decrease in incomes if the product is a normal product, or an increase in incomes if the product is an inferior product
- a decrease in the price of a substitute product
- an increase in the price of a complementary product
- the expectation that future prices or incomes will be lower or that there will be a future surplus of the product
- a decrease in the population or a change in its income or age distribution

A decrease in demand is shown in Table 2.8 and illustrated in Figure 2.11

TABLE 2.8 The Effects on the Market of a Decrease in Demand

Price per Case	Number of Cases per Week		
	Supply	Demand 1	Demand 2
$12	8	22	16
13	12	18	12
14	16	16	10
15	20	9	3
16	24	6	0
17	28	3	0
18	32	2	0

FIGURE 2.11 Adjustment to a Decrease in Demand

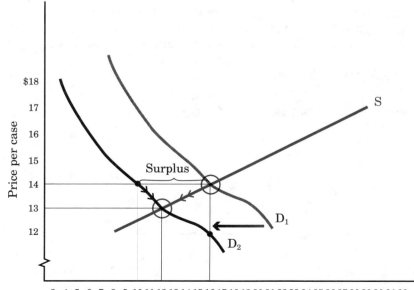

The drop in demand from D_1 to D_2 will cause an immediate surplus of 6, since the quantity supplied remains at 16, but the quantity demanded drops to 10. This surplus will cause the price to fall and, as it does, the quantity demanded will increase while the quantity supplied will fall. This process will continue until the surplus is eliminated. This occurs at a new equilibrium price of $13 and an equilibrium quantity of 12.

The initial equilibrium price is $14, and the quantity traded is 16. Assume that the demand now decreases to D_2 in the table and on the graph. At a price of $14, producers will continue to produce 16 cases; yet consumers now wish to purchase only 10 cases. A surplus is immediately created in the market. Mounting unsold inventories and more intensive competition between suppliers will eventually push down the price. Notice in Figure 2.11 that as the price decreases, the quantity supplied also starts to decrease and the quantity demanded begins to increase. Both of these factors will cause the surplus to disappear. The price will eventually drop to a new equilibrium of $13 where the demand and supply are equal at 12 cases. A decrease in demand will cause both the price and the quantity traded to fall.

QUESTION 2.5

What effect will the following changes have upon (i) the demand for; (ii) the price; and (iii) the quantity traded, of commercially brewed beer?

A) A new medical report praising the healthy effects of drinking beer (in moderation of course).
B) A big decrease in the price of home-brewing kits.
C) A rapid increase in population growth.
D) Talk of a possible future strike of brewery workers.
E) A possible future recession.

Determinants of a Change in Supply

change in supply:
a change in the quantities supplied at every price, caused by a change in the determinants of supply.

Let us again be clear about what we mean by supply: it is the relationship between the price of the product and the quantities producers are willing and able to supply. Price is part of what economists call supply. What we now need to figure out is what could cause a **change in supply**. What factors will cause producers to offer a different quantity on the market even though the price has not changed, i.e, what will cause a change in supply? We begin with Table 2.9 where an increase in supply is illustrated:

TABLE 2.9 An Increase in Supply

	Number of Cases per Week	
Price per Case of Beer	Supply 1	Supply 2
$12	8	14
13	12	18
14	16	22
15	20	26
16	24	30
17	28	34
18	32	38

For reasons we will soon investigate, suppliers are now willing to supply an extra 6 cases of beer at every possible price. This is illustrated in Figure 2.12.

An increase in supply causes the whole supply curve to shift right. (Be careful if you are tempted to describe it as a downward shift because then you

FIGURE 2.12 An Increase in Supply

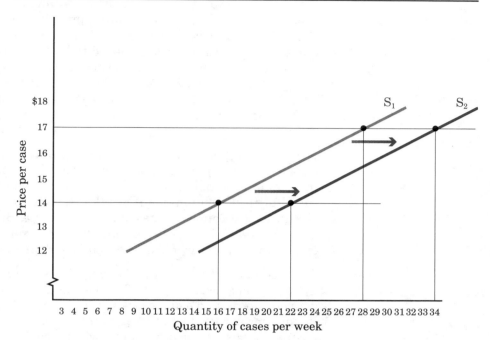

At each price, the quantities supplied have now increased, i.e., the supply curve has shifted right from S_1 to S_2. For example, at a price of $14, the original quantity was 16 and has now increased to 22. Similarly, at a price of $17, the quantity supplied has increased from 28 to 34. In this example, the quantities supplied have increased by 6 units at every price level, thus causing a parallel shift in the supply curve.

would be saying that as the supply goes up, the supply curve goes down, which could make things very confusing! Better to talk about a rightward shift.) This means that at each and every price, producers are now willing to produce more.

What could have happened in the brewers' world to make them wish to produce more even though the price is unchanged? Since we are assuming that the prime motivation for the supplier is profit, then something must have happened to make brewing more profitable, and it is this which is inducing a higher supply. Profit is no more than the difference between revenue and cost, and since the price is unchanged, then something must have affected the cost of producing beer. The first factor we will look at which might have decreased costs is the *price of productive resources*. For the brewer this includes the price of yeast, hops and malt and other ingredients, as well as the price that must be paid for the brewing vats and bottles and so on. If any of these should drop in price, then the cost for the brewer will fall and its profits will rise. Under these circumstances, since she is now making a bigger profit on each case of beer, she will be very willing to produce more. A fall in the price of productive resources will lead to an increase in supply. Conversely, an increase in the price of resources will cause a decrease in supply.

Another way of looking at the increase in supply as shown in Figure 2.12 is to say that, rather than firms being willing to produce more at a given price, they are willing to accept lower prices to produce any given quantity. For instance, previously, in order to induce the brewers to supply a total of 32 cases per week, the price needed to be $18. Now that the costs of production have dropped, these same brewers are able to make the same profits by producing the 32 cases at a lower price of between $16 and $17 (presumably, $16.50 per case). This is the same thing as saying that the brewers are now willing to produce the same quantities as before at lower prices. Again, this would produce a rightward shift in the supply curve.

It is often suggested that the availability of resources is a major determinant of the supply of a product. A bad grape harvest will obviously have an impact on the supply of wine. However, if you think about it, it's not really the difficulty in obtaining grapes that causes a decrease in the wine supply since most things can be obtained *at a price*. But there's the rub. A bad grape harvest will cause the price of grapes to increase, and it is this increase which will reduce the profitability and productivity of wine producers.

A second major determinant of supply is the *business taxes* that are levied by the various levels of government. They are similar to the other costs of doing business, and a decrease in them will lead firms to make higher profits and encourage them, therefore, to increase the supply; an increase in business taxes, on the other hand, will cause a decrease in supply.

A third determinant of supply is the *technology* used in production. An improvement in technology means nothing more than an improvement in the method of production. This will enable a firm to produce more with the same quantity of resources (or for that matter, to produce the same output with fewer resources). An improvement in technology will not affect the actual price of the resources, but, because more can now be done with less, it will lead to a fall in the cost of production. This means that an improvement in technology will lead to an increase in the supply. (We never consider the effects of a deterioration of technology since no rational producer would introduce it in the first place.)

The price of related products also affects the supply, just as it affected the demand. But here we must be careful, since we are looking at things from a producer's point of view and not a consumer's. In other words, what a producer regards as related will usually differ from a consumer's view of related. A fourth determinant of supply then is the *price of productively related products*. To a wheat farmer, for instance, the price of other grains like ryes and barley will be of great interest since the production of all grain crops are related in terms of production methods and equipment. A significant increase in the price of rye, for example, may well tempt the wheat farmer to grow rye in the future. In other words, an increase in the price of one product will cause a drop in the supply of products which are productively related. A decrease will have the opposite effect.

A fifth determinant of supply is the *future expectations of producers*. Again, this is analogous to the demand side of the market, but with a difference. While consumers will eagerly look forward to the drop in the price of products, producers view the same prospect with great anxiety. If a producer feels that the market is going to be depressed in the future and prices are likely to be lower, she may be inclined to change production now before the anticipated collapse. Lower expected future prices therefore tend to increase the present supply of a product. Higher expected future prices have the opposite effect and cause producers to hold off selling all of their present production in the hopes of making greater profits from the future higher prices.

Finally, the market supply will also be affected by the *number of suppliers*. An increase in the number of suppliers will cause an increase in the market supply, while a decrease in the number of suppliers will reduce the overall market supply.

Again, notice that one thing omitted from this list of supply determinants is any mention of demand. At the risk of repetition: firms are not in business to satisfy demand but to make profits. Simply because the demand for a product increases, does not mean that producers will immediately increase production to satisfy the higher demand. However, the higher demand will cause the price to increase, and it is this which induces firms to supply more, but this is termed an increase in the quantity supplied and *does not* imply an increase in the supply. This means that the supply curve is unchanged.

In summary, the determinants of market supply are:

1. prices of productive resources
2. business taxes
3. technology
4. prices of productively related products
5. future expectations of suppliers
6. number of suppliers

The Effects of an Increase in Supply

We have discussed six different factors which could affect the supply of a product. Let us recap what can cause an increase in supply:

- a decrease in the price of productive resources
- a decrease in business taxes or increase in subsidies
- an improvement in technology
- a decrease in the price of a productively related product
- the expectation of a decline in the future price of the product
- an increase in the number of suppliers

Let us see the effects of an increase in supply using the original demand for beer, and the increase in supply using Table 2.10 below.

TABLE 2.10 The Effect on the Market of an Increase in Supply

Price per Case of Beer	Number of Cases per Week		
	Demand 1	Supply 1	Supply 2
$12	22	8	14
13	18	12	18
14	16	16	22
15	9	20	26
16	6	24	30
17	3	28	34
18	2	32	38

At the original demand (Demand 1) and supply (Supply 1), the equilibrium price was $14 per case and the quantity traded was 16 cases. Assume that the supply now increases to Supply 2. At the present price of $14, there will be an immediate surplus of 6 cases. Before we look at the implications of this surplus, we ought to address a couple of possible qualms that some students might have. The first is this: won't customers take up this excess of beer? It is easy to see that, at this price, consumers have already given their response: they want to buy 16 cases, not 22 cases, or any other number. In other words, consumers are buying beer to satisfy their own tastes, not to satisfy the brewers. A second question is this: why would producers produce 22 cases knowing that the demand at this price is only 16 cases? The answer is, they don't know. Each producer knows the circumstances in her own brewery and knows that, until now, she has been able to sell everything she has produced. With the prospect of higher profits coming from, let's say, a decrease in costs, the brewer wants to produce more. If all producers do the same, there will be a surplus of beer. Figure 2.13 shows what will happen as a result of this surplus.

FIGURE 2.13 Adjustment to an Increase in Supply

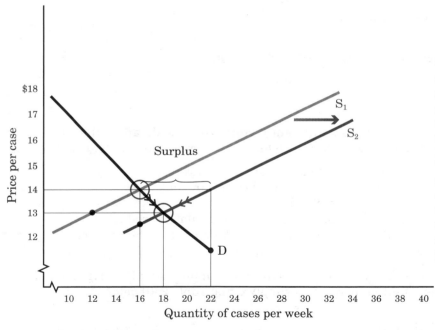

The increase in the supply has the immediate effect of causing a surplus since the demand has remained unchanged. In this figure, at a price of $14, the quantity supplied has increased from 16 to 22, causing a surplus of 6. This will cause the price to drop, and as it does, the quantity demanded increases and the quantity supplied decreases, until a new equilibrium is reached at a new equilibrium price of $13 and quantity of 18.

Faced with a surplus of beer, the market price will be forced down. As the price falls, the quantity demanded increases and the quantity supplied falls. Production increased initially, but because of the resulting drop in price, it is now dropping back slightly. The price will continue to drop until it reaches $13. Table 2.10 shows that, at this price, the demand and supply are now equal at 18 cases. The effect of the increase in supply, then, is a lower price and a higher quantity traded.

QUESTION 2.6

Suppose that the demand and supply for strawberries in a particular market are as follows (the quantities are in thousands of kilos per week):

Price	Demand	Supply 1	Supply 2
$4.00	140	60	_____
4.25	130	70	_____
4.50	120	80	_____
4.75	110	90	_____
5.00	100	100	_____
5.25	90	110	_____
5.50	80	120	_____

A) What are the present equilibrium price and equilibrium quantity? Graph the demand and supply curves, labelling them D_1 and S_1 and indicate equilibrium.

B) Suppose that the supply of strawberries were to increase by 50%. Show the new quantities in the S_2 column. What will be the new equilibrium price and quantity? Draw in S_2 on your graph and indicate the new equilibrium.

QUESTION 2.7

What effect will the following changes have on the supply, price and the quantity traded of wine?

A) A bad harvest in the grape industry results in a big decrease in the supply of grapes.

B) The number of wineries increases.

C) The sales tax on wine increases.

D) The introduction of a new fermentation method speeds up the time it takes for the wine to ferment.

E) The introduction of a government subsidy for each bottle of wine produced domestically.

F) The introduction by the government of a quota limiting the amount of foreign wine entering Canada.

G) There is a big increase in wages for the workers in the wine industry.

H) A big increase occurs in the prices of wine coolers (an industry which is similar in technology to the wine industry).

Final Words

We leave it to the student to confirm that a decrease in supply will cause a shortage which will eventually raise the price of the product. The net result will be a higher price *but* a lower quantity traded.

To complete this introduction to demand and supply let's use the following chart as a summary:

↑ Demand	→	shortage	→	↑ P	and	↑ Q traded
↓ Supply	→	shortage	→	↑ P	and	↓ Q traded

| ↓ Demand | → | surplus | → | ↓ P | and | ↓ Q traded |
| ↑ Supply | → | surplus | → | ↓ P | and | ↑ Q traded |

Note that when the demand changes, both the price and the quantity traded move in the same direction; when the supply changes, the quantity traded moves in the same direction, but the price moves in the opposite direction.

From this table you should confirm in your own mind that it is the supply of, and demand for, a product which determines its price, and not the price which determines supply and demand. A change in any of the factors which affects demand or supply will therefore lead to a change in the price. The price of a product *cannot* change *unless* there is a change in either the demand or the supply. It follows therefore that you cannot really analyze any problem which starts: "What happens if the price increases (decreases)...?" The reason for this, as the above chart makes clear, is an increase in the price of a product might be caused by either the demand increasing or by the supply decreasing. But in the case of an increase in the demand, the quantity traded also increases, whereas in the case of a decrease in the supply, the quantity traded falls. In the first case, we are talking about an expanding industry; in the second, we are looking at a contracting industry.

Data

BOX 2.2

Since the time of Adam Smith, economists have continually struggled to understand how prices are determined. Toward the end of the nineteenth century, they tended to group into one of two camps: those who believed that the cost of production was the main determinant; and those who believed that consumer demand was the main determinant. Demand, in turn, was determined by what the famous economist Alfred Marshall called the utility (or pleasure) derived from consumption. Marshall, writing at the end of that century, was the first to lucidly present a synthesis of the two views and suggest that neither demand nor supply alone can provide the answer. His famous analogy of the scissors says,

> We might as reasonably dispute whether it is the upper or the under blade of scissors that cuts a piece of paper, as whether value (price) is governed by utility or cost of production. It is true that when one blade is held still, and the cutting is effected by moving the other, we may say with careless brevity that the cutting is done by the second; but the statement is not strictly accurate, and is to be excused only so long as it claims to be merely a popular and not a strictly scientific account of what happens.[1]

---

[1] Alfred Marshall, *Principles of Economics*, 8th edition, p. 348.

The next chapter will develop the ideas of demand and supply further and will analyze a number of diverse problems. To close this chapter, let's try to figure out a simple exercise and make some final observations.

Looking back over the past decade or so, what has happened to the prices of home computers? Generally speaking, even ignoring the effects of inflation, they have decreased. And what about the quantity of computers that are bought and sold now compared with a decade ago? Definitely, it has increased. So, according to our little chart above, what could have produced this result in the marketplace? Well, there is only one thing that could lead to a decrease in price and an increase in the quantity traded, and that is an increase in supply. And what in the computer world over the past years could have caused an increase in supply? The answer must be an improvement in technology which has significantly reduced the costs of producing computers.

As we shall see in Chapter 3, not only is the market system an efficient way of preventing persistent surpluses and shortages, but it functions very well in rationing scarce goods, services and resources.

However, we should mention a number of themes which we will take up in Chapter 8. In the modern world, competitive markets are few and far between, since many markets are dominated by big corporations, big trade unions and consumer associations, and interfered with by governments. In addition, even when they are competitive, markets do not provide any guarantee that there will not be future periods of recession or inflation. Further, competitive markets cannot ensure that the right type or quantities of products are produced or that the distribution of incomes and wealth in a country are fair.

QUESTION 2.8

Below are various changes which occur in different markets. Explain what will happen to the equilibrium price and quantity and in each case state whether it is demand or supply which is affected.
A) An increase in income upon the market for an *inferior product*.
B) A decrease in the price of steel on the *automobile industry*.
C) A government subsidy given to operators of *day-care centres*.
D) A government subsidy given to parents who want their children to attend *day-care centres*.
E) A medical report suggesting that *wine* is very fattening.
F) A big decrease in the amount of Middle East oil exports on the *refined-oil market*.
G) An increase in the popularity of *antique furniture*.
H) An increase in the price of coffee on the *tea market*.

Finally, let's look back at the discussion which started this chapter and see if we can make sense of it. The one speaker started by stating that the price of houses has increased. (We presume he is talking about the market for existing, as well as new, homes.) Well, there are two major causes for a price increase: either the demand has increased (caused perhaps by lower interest rates or high immigration into the area?); or the supply has decreased (caused by higher building costs or perhaps the expectation by sellers that prices will be higher in the future?). In this particular conversation we are given no indication of the cause. However, the effects are going to be different. If housing prices increased because of a higher demand, you would expect to see a greater number of for-sale listings than usual; if they increased because of a lower supply, then the number of listings would be smaller than usual. It would be an easy enough job to figure out which. The rest of the conversation on the effects of a higher price is merely an exercise in confusion. Assuming that the present price is the equilibrium price then nothing further will happen — at least until there is another change in demand or supply. The next chapter will explore in detail some of the important applications of demand and supply. You will start to realize what a very important and versatile tool it is — but, like all tools, only if you use it properly (and clean it off after every use!).

BOX 2.3

It is important that the terms "demand" and "supply" are not confused with "purchases" and "sales." As we have seen in this chapter, demand and supply are not always equal. However, purchases and sales, since they are two sides of the same transaction, must always be equal. The following graph explains the differences in the terms.

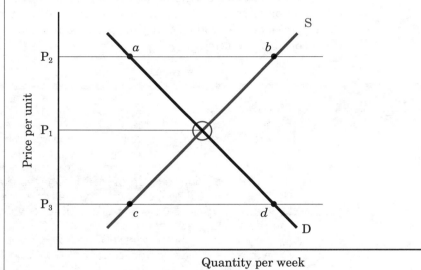

Quantity per week

P_1 is the equilibrium price, and at this price the quantity demanded and supplied are equal, i.e., this is the amount traded and is the same thing as the amount sold and purchased. If the price happened to be above equilibrium, however, at a price, say, P_2, then the quantity demanded is denoted by *a*, and the quantity supplied by *b*. Clearly, the two quantities are not equal. But how much is bought and sold at this price? The answer is quantity *a*. It really doesn't matter how much is being produced since, at this price, this is the maximum amount that consumers are willing to buy. The difference *ab* represents the amount unsold, or the surplus.

On the other hand, what is the effect of the price being below equilibrium? Suppose the price is P_3 where the quantity supplied (*c*) is less than the quantity demanded (*d*). This time, how much is being bought and sold? The answer must be quantity *c*. It doesn't matter how much consumers want to buy of this product if producers are only making quantity *c* available. In general, the amount bought and sold is always equal to the smaller of the quantity demanded or supplied.

BOX 2B
1. What are the four major determinants of individual demand?
2. Explain the difference between an *inferior* and a *normal* product.
3. What will happen to the price of a product if:
   a) the price of its substitute decreases?
   b) the price of its complement decreases?
4. Explain how future expectations can affect the behaviour of consumers.
5. What factors, aside from the determinants of individual demand, can affect the market demand?
6. Explain, step by step, how an *increase* in demand eventually affects both the price and the quantity traded.
7. Explain, step by step, how a *decrease* in demand eventually affects both the price and the quantity traded.
8. What are the six major determinants of the market supply?
9. Explain how the market adjusts to both an increase and a decrease in the supply of a product.
10. What can cause the price of a product to increase? What can cause it to decrease?

Chapter Highlights

This chapter is crucial to a good understanding of economics since demand and supply lie at the heart of almost all economic analysis. It begins by defining and illustrating the concept of individual demand, and looks at the important distinction between demand and the quantity demanded. It then explains why there is an inverse relationship between the price of a product and the quantity demanded. It does this by explaining the income and substitution effects of a price change. Next, the chapter examines the market demand and explains how it can be derived.

The supply side of the market is then investigated in a similar fashion to the demand. The chapter looks at individual supply, explains the difference between supply and the quantity supplied and why there is a direct relationship between the price and the quantity supplied. It then shows how the market supply can be derived.

Next, the demand and the supply are brought together by examining what is meant by a market. The important idea of equilibrium is introduced and defined in terms of both an equality between demand and supply and as the absence of a surplus or shortage. It then explains how a competitive market is able to eliminate such surpluses and shortages through changes in prices.

The rest of the chapter explains how changes in demand and supply can cause surpluses and shortages. It looks first at the five major factors which can cause a change in demand and explains how an increase in demand can come about and how it eventually causes an increase in the price of a product and in the quantity of output produced. Then, a decrease in demand is shown to produce a surplus which eventually leads to a decline in the price and in the output produced.

Next, the six major factors which can affect the supply are explained, after which, the effect of an increase in the supply is shown to produce an increase in the quantity produced but a decrease in the price of the product.

The chapter concludes by reiterating the important point that the price of a product is the result of the demand and supply and is not their cause. It shows how helpful demand/supply analysis can be in explaining market behaviour by taking a brief look at the computer market. Finally, the chapter mentions ways in which competitive markets can fail.

New Glossary Terms

Workbook

Study Tips

1. It is with this chapter that you will learn to appreciate the need for precision in the use of economic terms. For instance, the terms demand and supply have very clear definitions. "Demand" does *not* mean the amount a person wishes to buy or the amount she is buying. Demand is not a single quantity but a combination of different prices and quantities. Similarly, you cannot use the term "supply" synonymously with output, production or quantity supplied. It is *not* a single quantity but, again, a range of different quantities and prices.

2. If you have understood the first point, then this next one should make sense. A change in price cannot affect the demand, since price is already part of what we mean by demand. That doesn't mean that a change in price doesn't affect consumers; generally, people change the amounts they purchase as a result of a price change, but this is what we call a change in the quantities demanded and *not* a change in demand. Similarly a change in price leaves the supply unaffected. But it definitely affects the *quantity supplied*. These points are illustrated in the way that the demand and supply curves are affected. A change in price causes no change in the demand or supply curves but results in a movement *along* the curves. Only changes in other determinants, besides price, will cause a shift in the curves.

3. It is important for you to keep the concepts of demand and supply separate in your mind. A change in demand does *not* have any affect on the supply. This means that the supply curve will not shift when the demand curve changes. Similarly, you must disconnect the demand from the supply. A change in the supply has no impact on demand.

4. There really is no alternative to learning the factors which do affect the demand and supply. Memorize the five determinants of market demand and the six determinants of market supply. Note that with the exception of expectations of future price changes, the factors that affect demand have no impact on supply, and vice versa. If possible, try not to be too "cute" when trying to figure out the way in which various changes in determinants affect markets. It is possible to give a convoluted explanation why, for example, a change in the number of suppliers can affect preferences and, therefore, the demand of customers of that product. While remotely possible, the effect would be of minor significance. Instead use common sense and focus on the main effects. Remember that usually a change in one determinant will affect *only* the demand or the supply, seldom both.

5. Don't skip the basics in this chapter even if, at times, they might seem a little simple. For example, don't try to work out the effects of changes in demand or supply until you first have a good grasp of equilibrium.

6. Finally, the most important lesson that you can get from this chapter is that the price of a product is determined by both demand and supply. Price is the effect and not the cause. This means that the price cannot change in a free market unless there has been a change in either the demand or the supply.

Are You Sure?

Indicate whether the following statements are true or false. If false, indicate why they are false.

1. The term "demand" means the quantities that people would like to purchase at various different prices.
T or **F**   If false: _____

_____

_____

2. A change in the price of a product has no effect on the demand for that product.
T or **F**   If false: _____

_____

_____

3. An increase in the price of a product causes a decrease in the real income of consumers.
T or **F**   If false: _____

_____

_____

4. An increase in the price of a product leads to an increase in the supply.
T or **F**   If false: _____

_____

_____

5. Equilibrium price implies that everyone who would like to purchase a product is able to.
T or **F**   If false: _____

_____

_____

6. Surpluses drive prices up; shortages drive prices down.
T or **F**   If false: _____

_____

_____

7. An increase in incomes will lead to a decrease in the demand for an inferior product.
T or **F**   If false: _____

_____

_____

8. A decrease in the demand for a product will lead to a decrease in both the price and the quantity traded.
T or **F**   If false: _____

_____

_____

9. An increase in business taxes causes the supply curve to shift left.

T or **F**   If false: _____

_____

_____

10. A decrease in supply causes the price to fall and the quantity traded to increase.
T or **F**   If false: _____

_____

_____

Translations

Explain the possible cause and the effect of the movement from point A to point B in Figure W2.1.

FIGURE W2.1

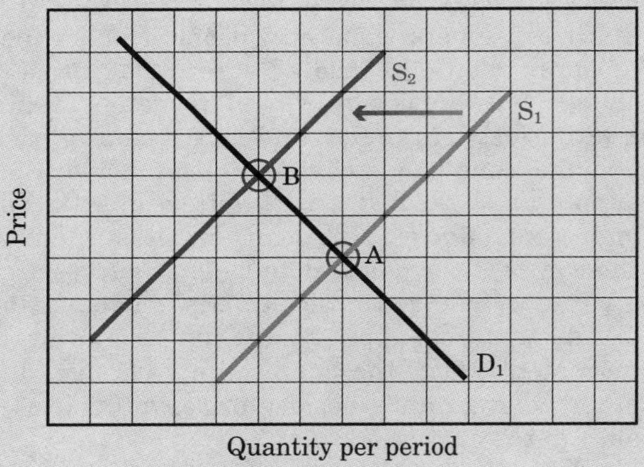

Quantity per period

Answer:

_____

_____

_____

_____

_____

_____

_____

Choose the Best

1. What does the term "demand" refer to?
   a) The amounts that consumers are either willing or able to purchase at various prices.
   b) The amounts that consumers are both willing and able to purchase at various prices.

2. What will a surplus of a product lead to?
   a) A reduction in supply.
   b) A reduction in price.

3. What is the effect of a decrease in the price of a product?
   a) It will increase consumers' real income while leaving their actual income unchanged.
   b) It will increase consumers' actual income while leaving their real income unchanged.

4. How will a change in income affect the demand for an inferior product?
   a) The demand will increase if the income of consumers increases.
   b) The demand will increase if the income of consumers decreases.
   c) The demand is not affected by consumer incomes.

5. Which of the following could cause an increase in the supply of wheat?
   a) A decrease in the price of oats.
   b) An imposition of a sales tax on wheat.
   c) An increase in the price of fertilizer.

6. What is the effect of an increase in the price of coffee?
   a) It will lead to an increase in the demand for tea.
   b) It will lead to a decrease in the demand for tea.
   c) It will have no effect on the tea market.

7. What is the slope of the demand curve?
   a) It is downward-sloping because when the price of a product falls, consumers are willing and able to buy more.
   b) It is upward-sloping because when the price of a product falls, consumers are willing and able to buy more.
   c) It is upward-sloping because when the price of a product increases, consumers are willing and able to buy more.

8. Which of the following factors will shift the demand curve left?
   a) An increase in the price of a substitute product.
   b) A decrease in the price of a complementary product.
   c) An increase in income if the product is an inferior product.
   d) The expectation that future prices of the product will be higher.

9. What is the effect of an increase in the price of a productive resource?
   a) It will cause a decrease in the supply of the product.
   b) It will cause an increase in the supply of the product.
   c) It will cause a decrease in the demand for the product.
   d) It will cause an increase in the demand for the product

10. What is the effect of a shortage?
   a) It will cause a decrease in the price leading to an increase in the quantity supplied and a decrease in the quantity demanded.
   b) It will cause a decrease in the price leading to a decrease in the quantity supplied and an increase in the quantity demanded.
   c) It will cause an increase in the price leading to an increase in the quantity supplied and a decrease in the quantity demanded.
   d) It will cause an increase in the price leading to a decrease in the quantity supplied and an increase in the quantity demanded.

11. In what way are Pepsi and Coca Cola related?
   a) They are substitute products.
   b) They are complementary products.
   c) They are inferior products.
   d) They are unrelated products.

12. A rightward shift in the supply curve for a product could be caused by all of the following *except one*. Which is the exception?
    a) The expectation by suppliers that the future price of the product will be higher.
    b) A decrease in the price of a productive resource used in its manufacture.
    c) A decrease in the price of a productively related product.
    d) A technological improvement in manufacturing methods.

13. What is the effect of a decrease in the supply of a product?
    a) It will cause an increase in both the price and the quantity traded.
    b) It will cause an increase in the price but a decrease in the quantity traded.
    c) It will cause a decrease in both the price and in the quantity traded.
    d) It will cause a decrease in the price but an increase in the quantity traded.

Table W2.1 depicts the market for mushrooms (in thousands of kilos per month). Use this table to answer questions 14 and 15 below.

TABLE W2.1

Price($)	2.50	3.00	3.50	4.00	4.50	5.00	5.50	6.00
Quantity demanded	64	62	60	58	56	54	52	50
Quantity supplied	40	44	48	52	56	60	64	68

14. Refer to Table W2.1 to answer this question. What are the values of equilibrium price and quantity traded?
    a) $3 and 52.
    b) $3 and 62.
    c) $4 and 58.
    d) $4.50 and 56.
    e) They cannot be determined from the data.

15. Refer to Table W2.1 to answer this question. What will happen if the price of the product is $3?
    a) There would be a surplus of 18 which would lead to a decrease in price.
    b) There would be a shortage of 18 which would lead to an increase in price.
    c) There would be a shortage of 18 which would lead to a decrease in price.
    d) There would be a surplus of 18 which would lead to an increase in price.
    e) There would be neither a surplus nor a shortage.

16. How will the demand and supply of a product be affected if people expect the future price of a product will be higher than at present?
    a) It will cause an increase in demand but a decrease in supply.
    b) It will cause an increase in both the demand and supply.
    c) It will cause a decrease in both the demand and supply.
    d) It will cause an increase in supply but will have no effect on demand.
    e) It will cause an increase in supply but a decrease in demand.

17. In what way are products A and B related if an increase in the price of product A leads to a decrease in the demand for product B?
    a) Product A must be a productive resource used in the manufacture of product B.
    b) Product B must be a productive resource used in the manufacture of product A.
    c) The two products must be complements.
    d) The two products must be substitutes.
    e) The two products must be inferior products.

Refer to Figure W2.2 to answer questions 18, 19 and 20.

FIGURE W2.2

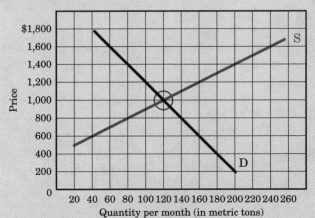

18. Refer to Figure W2.2 to answer this question. What will be the effect if the price is presently $1,200?
    a) There would be a surplus of 30.
    b) There would be a shortage of 30.
    c) 160 would be purchased.
    d) There would be a surplus of 60.
    e) The price will increase.

19. Refer to Figure W2.2 to answer this question. If the quantity presently traded is 80, what does this mean?
    a) Purchasers would be willing to pay an additional $600 for this quantity.
    b) The price must be above equilibrium.
    c) There must be a surplus of 30.
    d) There must be a shortage of 30.
    e) There must be a surplus of 60.

20. Refer to Figure W2.2 to answer this question. Suppose that initially the market was in equilibrium and demand increased by 60. What will be the new equilibrium as a result?
    a) A price of $1,000 and quantity traded of 120.
    b) A price of $1,000 and quantity traded of 160.
    c) A price of $1,200 and quantity traded of 160.
    d) A price of $1,400 and quantity traded of 160.
    e) A price of $1,400 and quantity traded of 240.

What's Wrong?

Can you spot the five errors in the following passage? (Ignore grammatical mistakes!)

When we say that the price of a product is determined by supply and demand, it is merely a shorthand way of saying that the price is affected by all those factors which affect the demand (price of the product, preferences, prices of related products, income, future expectations, and the size, age and income distribution of the population), and all those factors which affect the supply (prices of productive resources, consumer demand, changes in technology, business taxes, future expectations, prices of productively related products and the number of suppliers). A change in any one of these factors will change both the demand and the supply. The result of such a change will affect both the price and the quantity traded. An increase in business taxes, for example, will cause the price and the quantity traded to fall. On the other hand, a decrease in incomes will cause the demand to fall (assuming we are dealing with an inferior good).

Key Problem

Table W2.2 shows the market for wool (the quantities are in metric tons per year).

TABLE W2.2

Price ($)	100	200	300	400	500	600	700
Quantity demanded	10	9	8	7	6	5	4
Quantity supplied	1	3	5	7	9	11	13

a) Plot the demand and supply curves on Figure W2.3 which follows on the next page, and label them D_1 and S_1.

b) What are the values of equilibrium price and quantity? Mark the equilibrium as E_1 on the above graph.

   Equilibrium price: _____; equilibrium quantity: _____.

c) If the price of wool were $300, would there be a surplus or a shortage?

   (Surplus/shortage): _____ of: _____.

   Indicate the amount of the surplus or shortage on the graph.

FIGURE W2.3

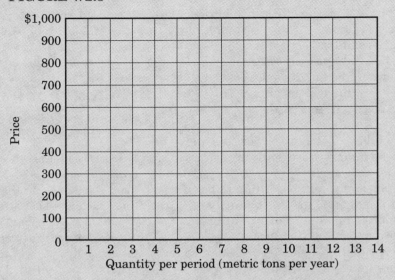

d) Suppose that the demand were to increase by 50%. Draw and label the new demand curve as D_2. What are the new values of equilibrium price and quantity? Mark the new equilibrium as E_2 on the graph.

Equilibrium price: _____; equilibrium quantity: _____.

e) Following the change in d), assume now that the supply decreases by 7 units. Draw and label the new supply curve as S_2. What are the new values of equilibrium price and quantity? Mark this new equilibrium as E_3.

Equilibrium price: _____; equilibrium quantity: _____.

Need a Hand?

a) and b) The plotting of the curves is reasonably straightforward, since they are both straight lines. (You know this from the table because the quantities change by a constant amount for each change in price). This being so, you don't really need to plot every single point. In fact just the first point (price $100, quantity demanded 10) and the last (price $700, quantity demanded 4) will be sufficient. Similarly with the supply curve. Drawn accurately, this should give an **equilibrium price of $400 and an equilibrium quantity of 7** as shown in Figure W2.4, and marked as E_1.

c) A price of $300 is below the equilibrium price of $400. Any price below equilibrium will produce a shortage because the quantity demanded will exceed the quantity supplied. The amount of the shortage is the distance between the curves. In this case it is **equal to 3**.

d) A 50% increase in the demand means that the demand curve shifts to the right but is not parallel to D_1. This is because the quantity demanded increases by different amounts for different prices. For instance, at a price of $100 the quantity increases by 5 to 15 (off our graph); at $200, the quantity increases by 4.5, from 9 to 13.5; at $300, the increase is 4, from 8 to 12 and so on. The new demand curve is plotted above as D_2, and the new equilibrium is where it intersects with S_1, at E_2. The **new equilibrium price is $500 and the new equilibrium quantity is 9**.

FIGURE W2.4 (completed Figure W2.3)

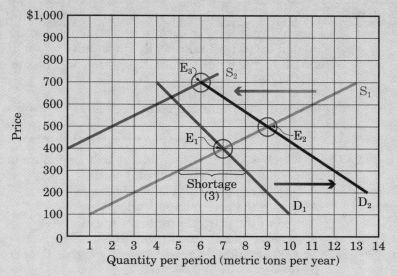

e) A reduction of the supply by 7 means that the supply curve shifts left and parallel to the old supply curve. Every point on the old supply curve moves to the left by 7 squares. This is plotted above as S_2. The intersection with the D_2 curve is marked as E_3 giving a new **equilibrium price of $700 and an equilibrium quantity of 6**.

More of the Same

Table W2.3 shows the market for olives (the quantities are in thousands of kilos per year).

TABLE W2.3

Price ($)	0	.50	1.00	1.50	2.00	2.50	3.00	3.50	4.00
Quantity demanded	5.5	5	4.5	4	3.5	3	2.5	2	1.5
Quantity supplied	1	2	3	4	5	6	7	8	9

a) Plot the demand and supply curves and label them D_1 and S_1.

b) What are the values of equilibrium price and quantity? Mark the equilibrium on the graph as E_1.

c) If the price of olives were $3.50, would there be a surplus or a shortage? How much? Mark the amount on the graph.

d) Suppose that the demand were to decrease by 3. Label the new demand curve, D_2. What are the new values of equilibrium price and quantity? Mark the new equilibrium on the graph as E_2.

e) Following the change in d), assume now that the supply decreases by 50%. Label the new supply curve S_2. What are the new values of equilibrium price and quantity? Mark the new equilibrium on the graph as E_3.

Other Problems

1. In a particular market, at a market price of $1 per kilo, there is a shortage of 60 kilos of avocados. For each 50 cents increase in the price, the quantity demanded drops by 5 kilos while the quantity supplied increases by 10 kilos. What will be the equilibrium price? What will be the surplus or shortage at a price of $4.50?

   Equilibrium price: _____.

   (surplus/shortage): _____ of: _____ kilos.

2. Circle which of the following factors will lead to an increase in the demand for cranberry juice (which is a normal good).
   a) A drop in the price of cranberries.
   b) A drop in the price of apple juice.
   c) A drop in the price of cranberry juice.
   d) A decrease in consumer incomes.
   e) The expectation by consumers that the price of cranberry juice is likely to increase.
   f) An improvement in the juicing process which lowers the costs of production of cranberry juice.

3. Circle which of the following factors will lead to a drop in the price of wine (a normal product which is regarded by consumers as a substitute for beer and a complement to cheese).
   a) A drop in the price of grapes.
   b) An increase in the price of beer.
   c) A drop in the wage costs in the brewery industry.
   d) A drop in the tax on wine but no change to beer taxes.
   e) A drop in the tax on beer but no change to the wine tax.

4. Consider the effects of each of the following events outlined in Table W2.4 on the market indicated. Indicate by placing a (+), (−), or (0) under the appropriate heading whether there will be an increase, decrease, or no change in demand (D), supply (S), equilibrium price (P), and quantity traded (Q).

TABLE W2.4

Market	Event	D	S	P	Q
a) Compact discs	A technological improvement reduces the cost of producing compact disc players.				
b) Butter	Medical evidence suggests that margarine causes migraines.				
c) Newspapers	Because of worldwide shortages, the price of pulp and paper increases dramatically.				
d) Generic toilet rolls	Consumer incomes rise significantly.				
e) Video rentals	Movie theatres halve their admission prices.				
f) Beef	World price of lamb increases.				

Unanswered Questions

Short Essays

1. Explain in terms of demand and supply analysis, why the price of maple syrup may be different in London, Ontario, compared with London, England.

2. Explain some of the factors which might reduce the price of movie theatre admission.

3. Explain what could cause a surplus and what could cause a shortage in a competitive market. How does the market eliminate them?

4. Explain the difference between a decrease in supply and a decrease in the quantity supplied.

5. What is the difference between "scarcity" and "shortage"?

6. Does the term "quantity demanded" mean the same thing as "quantity purchased"? Explain.

Analytical Questions

1. Given the graph of the market for a product shown in Figure W2.5:

   Explain each change in terms of a shift in the appropriate curve, or movement along a curve, and for each change give an example of what might have caused the change:

FIGURE W2.5

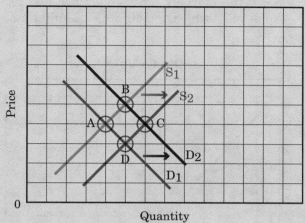

a) From point A to point B.
b) From point A to point D.
c) From point B to point C.
d) From point C to point D.

2. "The price of houses rises when the demand increases. The demand for houses decreases when the price increases." Are these two statements each correct? Are they contradictory? Explain.

3. Consider the effects of each of the following events on the market for beef in Canada. Indicate by placing a (+), (−), or (0) under the appropriate heading in Table W2.5 whether there will be an increase, decrease, or no change in demand, supply, equilibrium price, and quantity traded.

TABLE W2.5

Event	Demand	Supply	Quantity Price	Traded
a) Medical research indicates that cholesterol in beef is a major cause of heart attack.				
b) Improved cattle feeds reduce the cost of beef production.				
c) Chicken sales are banned due to an outbreak of chicken cholera.				
d) The price of pork increases because the government removes its subsidy to pork producers.				
e) A reduction in income taxes causes the incomes of Canadian consumers to rise sharply.				
f) The price of cattle feed rises due to a drought.				

4. The following two graphs in Figure W2.6 show the markets for orange juice and for apple juice, which are initially in equilibrium.

FIGURE W2.6

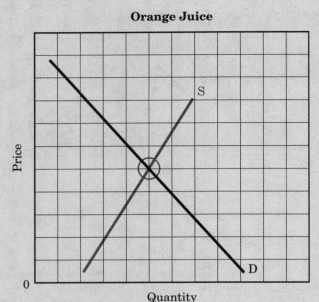

Orange Juice

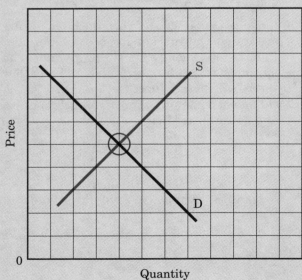

Apple Juice

Show what will happen to the prices and quantities traded of both products if a severe frost in Florida were to seriously damage the orange crop.

Numerical Questions

1. Table W2.6 shows the demand for and supply of a particular product.

TABLE W2.6

Price ($)	0	1	2	3	4	5	6	7	8	9	10
Demand	10	9	8	7	6	5	4	3	2	1	0
Supply	0	1	2	3	4	5	6	7	8	9	10
Shortage/ Surplus											

a) Complete the table, and then graph the demand and supply curves and label them D_1 and S_1. What is the equilibrium price and quantity?

b) Assume that the supply increases by 50%, i.e., the quantity increases by 50% at every price. Draw and label the new supply curve, S_2. What is the new equilibrium price and quantity?

c) Assume *instead* that the supply increases by 2 units at every price. Draw and label the new supply curve, S_3. What is the new equilibrium price and quantity?

d) Now assume that the demand increases by 2 units at every price. Draw and label the new demand curve, D_2. What is the new equilibrium price and quantity (D_2/S_3)?

2. Table W2.7 shows the demand for the upcoming concert to be given by the string quartet, Guns and Butter, at the new 3,000-capacity Saskatoon Auditorium.

TABLE W2.7

Price	Quantity Demanded
$10	8,000
15	7,000
20	6,000
25	5,000
30	4,000
35	3,000
40	2,000
45	1,000

a) Over what price range would there be a shortage of seats? Over what range would there be a surplus?

b) Suppose the promoters of the concert set the price at $25 per ticket. What will be the result?

c) In response to the great demand for the first concert, the promoters decide to add a second show open *only* to those who were unable to attend the first concert. What is the maximum price they could charge for this concert and still fill the auditorium?

3. Figure W2.7 shows the market for the new Guns and Butter compact disc, "Live at Saskatoon."
   a) Suppose that the CD producers put the disc on sale for $8 each. How much will be the surplus or shortage? How many will be sold?
   b) What is the maximum price at which the quantity actually sold in a) could have been sold?
   c) If the CD producers had actually put the CD on the market at the price mentioned in b), what would have been the resulting surplus/shortage?

FIGURE W2.7

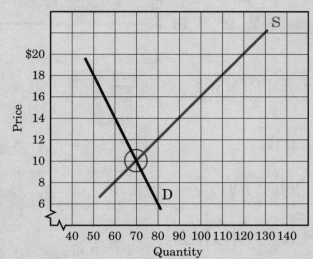

CHAPTER THREE

■ ■ ■ ■ ■ ■ ■

Demand and Supply 2: Elaboration and Application

W hat's ahead . . . We start this chapter by looking at circumstances which could cause simultaneous changes in demand and supply. We then ask how well markets operate and why governments often intervene. We next look at the reasons governments sometimes introduce various types of price controls and try to identify the costs and benefits of such intervention. Finally, we explore a number of variations of demand and supply and explain the situations which could cause the demand and supply to deviate from normal.

When we look at the way that markets operate, there is a great danger in believing that the laws of demand and supply are immutable scientific laws which are an integral part of the natural universe. Nothing could be further from the truth. As Oser and Brue wrote, commenting on the approach of the economist, Alfred Marshall,

> Economic laws are social laws — statements of tendencies, more or less certain, more or less definite.[1]

The collective behaviour of consumers and producers in the marketplace is a result of the society in which they live. Each society has its own history, economic structure and political structure. So, while the tools of demand and supply are versatile and powerful aids for economists, we must realize that they have certain limitations that we will look at in this chapter. The results which we obtain using demand and supply analysis demonstrate general tendencies which are only likely to occur under given circumstances. In the previous chapter we suggested that the price of a product is determined by demand and supply. This is only true under certain conditions. In many cases the price of the majority of products which we buy are set by the manufacturers and retailers and not by consumers and producers somehow coming together to form an agreement. Similarly, the government determines the price of a number of goods and services which it provides, and as we shall see later in this chapter, it also stipulates the minimum and maximum prices of a number of other products provided by the private sector.

---

[1] J. Oser and S. L. Brue, *The Evolution of Economic Thought*, 4th edition (New York: Harcourt Brace), p. 273.

Data

BOX 3.1

Alfred Marshall (1842–1924), was the son of a tyrannical father who was also a cashier at the Bank of England. His father wanted him to put away such frivolous pastimes as chess and mathematics and instead devote himself to higher pursuits. To this end, he decided that Alfred would train for the church. However, Alfred rebelled, and instead of taking up a scholarship to study divinity at Oxford, with the help of finance from an uncle, he studied mathematics, physics and later economics at Cambridge University. As later professor of economics at the same school, he influenced a whole generation of economists. His fame was sealed with the publication of his *Principles of Economics* in 1890. Marshall was a precise and painstaking scholar, and his book was the result of years of study and research. In this text, Marshall established himself as the intellectual leader of "neoclassical economics" and provided a synthesis of the classical ideas of Smith and Ricardo, with the new ideas of marginal analysis. Despite the fact that Marshall was an expert mathematician, he felt that mathematics should be regarded merely as a useful tool for economists rather than as the provider of fundamental economic truths. To Marshall, the "laws of demand" suggest what possible outcomes may result under certain circumstances. The results may be desirable but they are not imperative. Students of economics also owe a debt to Marshall for introducing graphical analysis into the discipline.

Under what circumstances do the forces of demand and supply determine the price of products? Strictly speaking, only in what economists term a "purely competitive market," a market in which there are no big dominant firms and no interference by the government. (Chapter 8 will look at this type of market in some detail.) It is important to be aware that competitive markets as we described in Chapter 2 only work well if they are truly competitive. The existence of bigness in the marketplace, whether it is in the form of big corporations, or big trade unions or big government detracts from the efficient working of the market. In essence, whenever there is a powerful participant or group of participants buying or selling in the market, the benefits of competition will be seriously reduced.

But does this also mean that if there are big firms operating they can then ignore the market and charge whatever prices they like? Well, from one point of view, yes they can — but only at their own peril. Figure 3.1 on the next page makes this clear.

This figure illustrates the market for a particular type of 4-wheel drive car. The demand curve, as usual, shows the market demand for this vehicle at various different prices. The supply curve shows the outputs which provide the greatest profit for the car manufacturer at each different selling price for the car. For information, the graph also shows what would be the equilibrium price. But this manufacturer can, if it wishes, charge any price it wants. Let's say it charges a price of $20,000, and produces 100,000 cars, since this is the quantity that will produce the greatest profit for the firm at this price.

FIGURE 3.1 An Overpriced Product

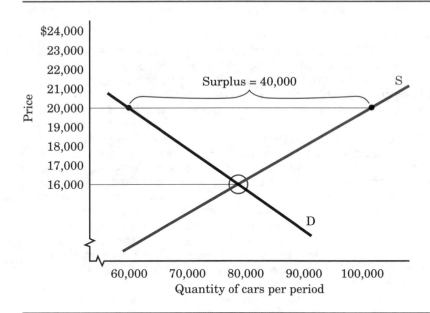

Although the car manufacturer can price its automobiles at whatever level it wishes, this graph shows that if it wants to sell *all* of its output of cars, then it must sell this particular model at a price of $16,000. If it over-prices it at, say, $20,000, the result will be a surplus of 40,000 unsold vehicles.

Unfortunately, the manufacturer will soon discover that consumers are not as excited about this vehicle as it had hoped. At a price of $20,000, they are only able to sell 60,000 units, leaving them with a surplus of 40,000. Obviously, they will eventually have no choice but to drop the price. The market can be a stern taskmaster.

What this example demonstrates is that even powerful producers (or for that matter, consumers or governments) must heed market forces since the market embodies the simple maxim that people cannot be forced to buy something they don't want. Similarly, producers cannot be forced to produce products which do not provide a sufficient profit.

In this chapter we will be looking at situations in which the market works well and other situations where the government feels the need to intervene and correct what it perceives are deficiencies in the market system. As we shall see, in some cases, markets do not always produce the right results for a number of reasons, but in other cases, interference by the government may do more harm than good. How well and how fairly markets operate is a central theme in microeconomics, and we shall be looking at this topic from various angles throughout this book. This chapter is a preliminary exploration into the efficacy of the market system and will help you to understand what powerful tools are provided by demand and supply analysis. First, however we need to dig a little deeper into these concepts.

Multiple Changes in Demand and Supply

In the last chapter, we looked at the causes of change in demand and supply and how they affect both the price and quantity traded of a product. However, in order to deepen our understanding, we need to be able to explain what will happen if *both* demand and supply change simultaneously since, of course, this may well happen in a dynamic, ever-changing economy.

In this next example, we look at the factor market rather than the product market, but the approach remains the same. In particular, let us examine possible changes in the supply of computer programmers. The supply of computer programmers is definitely increasing these days, since a career in computers is an attractive proposition for many students, and colleges and universities offer a wide range of computer courses. In addition, the demand for programmers by software companies as well as by business and government is forever increasing. Since both the demand and supply are increasing at the same time, what can we say about the salary of programmers and about future job opportunities in the industry? Figure 3.2 shows the effect of a simultaneous increase in both demand and supply.

FIGURE 3.2 The Demand for, and Supply of, Computer Programmers

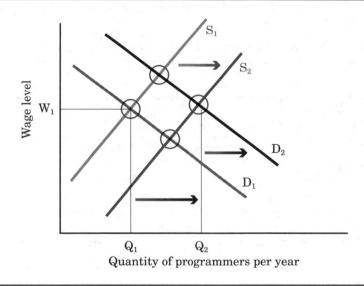

A simultaneous increase in both the demand for and supply of computer programmers will lead to an increase in the number of programmers employed, from Q_1 to Q_2. However it is uncertain what will happen to the wage level without knowing exactly how much they each increase.

We see that the result is a definite increase in the number of employed programmers from Q_1 to Q_2; however, the wage level seems not to have changed. In contrast, Figure 3.3A and 3.3B on the next page give different results.

In Figure 3.3A, the shift in the demand curve is greater than the shift in the supply curve, and since the demand increases more than the supply, the wage level increases from W_1 to W_2. Figure 3.3B shows, in contrast, a situation in which the supply increase exceeds the demand increase, resulting in a lower wage level. Both graphs show, as does the graph in Figure 3.2, that the number of programmers will increase, but what happens to the wage level depends on the comparative magnitude of the change in demand and supply. In other words, to find out what will happen to the wage level, we need to know the amounts by which demand and supply increase, otherwise the effect is inconclusive (or indeterminate, as economists say).

FIGURE 3.3 Simultaneous Increases in Demand and Supply and the Effect on Wages

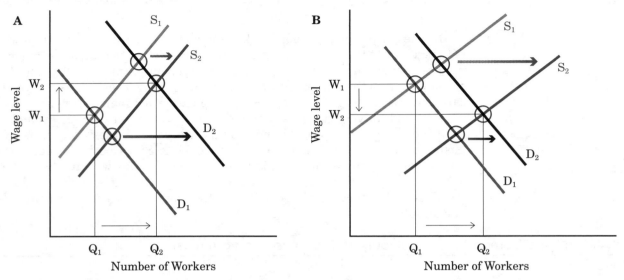

In Figure 3.3A, the increase in demand, from D_1 to D_2, is greater than the increase in supply, from S_1 to S_2. The result is an increase in the wage level, from W_1 to W_2. In Figure 3.3B, in contrast, the increase in the supply, from S_1 to S_2, exceeds the increase in demand, from D_1 to D_2. The result, in this case, is a drop in the wage level, from W_1 to W_2.

TABLE 3.1 Determinants of Demand and Supply

Determinants of Demand	Determinants of Supply
– consumer preferences	– prices of productive resources
– consumer incomes	– business taxes
– prices of related products	– technology
– expectations of future prices, incomes or availability	– prices of productively related products
– population size, income, and age distribution.	– future expectations of suppliers
	– number of suppliers

It is important to realize that there are many factors that can affect the demand and supply for a product. To refresh your memory on these determinants, Table 3.1 might be helpful.

Since there are many determinants, it is hardly surprising that in reality more than one will change at the same time. It is important, therefore, to be able to correctly identify whether the demand or supply has been affected, and in what manner.

Whenever multiple shifts are analyzed graphically the result will always be uncertain unless the amount of each change is known. Because of these indeterminate results, it's often a good idea to analyze the changes in terms of arrows rather than graphs. For instance, using the summary from Chapter 2, we know that an increase in demand and supply will produce the following results:

$$\uparrow D \quad \rightarrow \quad \uparrow P \quad \uparrow Q$$
$$\uparrow S \quad \rightarrow \quad \downarrow P \quad \uparrow Q$$

As you can see, both changes will tend to push up the quantity. However, the increase in demand will push the price up, whereas the increase in supply will push the price down. The net result on the price is therefore indeterminate. It therefore follows that:

$$\begin{array}{ll} \uparrow D & \Big\} \\ & \Big\} \\ \uparrow S & \Big\} \end{array} \quad \rightarrow \quad ?P \quad \uparrow Q$$

Similarly, we can analyze the effects of a decrease in demand and supply, as follows:

$$\begin{array}{lllll} \downarrow D & \Big\} & \rightarrow & \downarrow P & \downarrow Q \\ & \Big\} & & & \\ \downarrow S & \Big\} & \rightarrow & \underline{\uparrow P} & \underline{\downarrow Q} \\ & & & ?P & \downarrow Q \end{array}$$

In this case, the quantity will definitely decrease; the effect on the price, as in our last example, is indeterminate.

Next, let's look at what happens when the demand and supply move in opposite directions. Suppose that the demand for a product were to increase while, at the same time, the supply decreases — what effect would this have on the market? In terms of arrows, the result is clear, though as usual, indeterminate.

$$\begin{array}{lllll} \uparrow D & \Big\} & \rightarrow & \uparrow P & \uparrow Q \\ & \Big\} & & & \\ \downarrow S & \Big\} & \rightarrow & \underline{\uparrow P} & \underline{\downarrow Q} \\ & & & \uparrow P & ?Q \end{array}$$

It's the change in the quantity this time which is indeterminate; the price will definitely increase.

Finally, let's take a look at the last combination: a decrease in demand accompanied by an increase in supply:

$$\begin{array}{lllll} \downarrow D & \Big\} & \rightarrow & \downarrow P & \downarrow Q \\ & \Big\} & & & \\ \uparrow S & \Big\} & \rightarrow & \underline{\downarrow P} & \underline{\uparrow Q} \\ & & & \downarrow P & ?Q \end{array}$$

As in the previous case, the effect on the quantity is indeterminate; the price, however, will definitely decrease.

QUESTION 3.1

In each of the following cases, explain what effect the changes will have on the equilibrium price and quantity in the following markets:

Market	Change
A) Day-care Services	More mothers with small children are returning to the labour force; at the same time the government decides to introduce subsidies for day-care operators.

QUESTION 3.1 *(continued)*

B) Rubber Tires	The price of automobiles drop significantly; at the same time the price of rubber increases.
C) Marijuana	The government severely increases the penalties for both buying and selling marijuana.
D) Compact Discs	A new processing method significantly reduces the costs of producing CDs; at the same time, consumers are switching to high-resolution tapes which are cheaper and can be recorded on.
E) Beef	Vegetarianism increases as a result of medical reports extolling its health benefits; at the same time, tariff barriers on the importation of foreign beef are totally removed.

Returning to our market for computer programmers, we can now pose a practical problem that many students have to address: what are the prospects for a good job or a decent salary given the present trends? The answer depends to a great extent on the number of graduating students and the number of new jobs being created in industry. Suppose, in Figure 3.4, that the number of graduates exceeds the increased demand.

FIGURE 3.4 When the Increase in Supply Exceeds the Increase in Demand

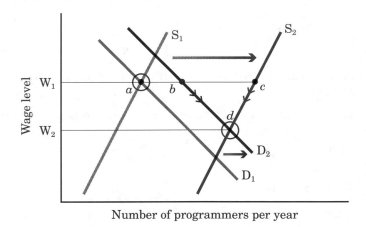

Number of programmers per year

The original wage is W_1, and the number of employed programmers is equal to a. The demand and supply now simultaneously increases, from D_1 to D_2 and from S_1 to S_2, respectively. As a result, the number of programmers wanting jobs (c) exceeds the number of jobs available (b). The result is a number of unemployed programmers indicated by the distance bc. As a result of this surplus of programmers, the wage will drop to W_2 and the new equilibrium number of programmers will be quantity d.

The initial wage level is W_1 and the quantity of programmers employed is shown as quantity a. Suppose that there is an increase in the demand from D_1 to D_2, and at the same time an increase in the supply from S_1 to S_2. The increase in the supply of programmers, however, exceeds the increase in the demand from industry. The number of new programmers wanted by industry is represented by the increased quantity b; the number of qualified programmers however has now increased to quantity c. There are a number of unemployed programmers (a surplus of programmers) in the amount bc. The competition among programmers for jobs may cause the wage level to eventually drop to a lower wage level, W_2. This lower wage level has eliminated the unemployed programmers, some of whom presumably gave up trying to find a job in computers and started looking for other types of work. The workings of the marketplace therefore does not ensure that everyone will be happy with the results. The number of employed programmers, however, has definitely increased from quantity *a* to the new equilibrium quantity *d*.

QUESTION 3.2
If the demand for a product were to decrease more than the supply decreases, will the result be a surplus or a shortage at the original equilibrium price? What will happen to the price level and the quantity traded as a result?

What this programmer example is designed to show is how competitive markets operate, and how, by changing the price (the wage level, in this case), surpluses and shortages are eliminated. Does this describe then how markets operate in Canada these days? Well...not entirely. Certainly, it's true that if the number of graduates exceeds the number of new jobs created, many of these graduates are going to be unemployed. The market's cure for this would be a reduction in wage levels. However, the market solution is not always the popular solution. Throughout the centuries, people have often attempted to circumvent or impede the workings of the market because they have either doubted the efficiency of the marketplace or not liked the results which it produces. The rest of the chapter investigates this interference.

How Well Do Markets Work?

Suppose that a devastating tsunami were to hit a major (coastal!) North American city resulting in the total destruction of one-half of its housing stock. Let's assume that this was a particularly benign tsunami in that nobody was actually killed; however, half the population find themselves without a place to live. The situation is illustrated in Figure 3.5 below.

FIGURE 3.5 Market Adjustment to a Decrease in Supply

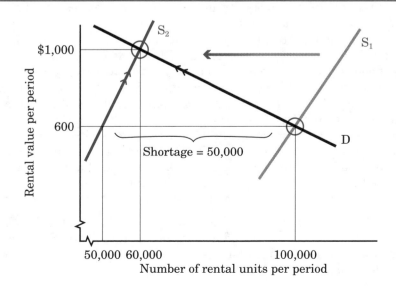

The initial equilibrium rental value was $600, and the number of rental units occupied was 100,000. A tsunami demolishes half the units, which is reflected in the supply curve shifting left from S_1 to S_2. With a shortage of 50,000 units, rents are forced up and in time a new equilibrium is reached at a rent of $1,000 and with 60,000 units now occupied.

Before the tsunami struck, the average rental value of housing stock (rented and owned, houses and apartments) was $600 per month and the number of occupied units was 100,000. The effect of the tsunami has been to reduce the supply of housing units to 50,000, leading to the current shortage of 50,000 units at the present rental value of $600. What we now want to look at is the way in which the market addresses changes in supply of this nature. The severe shortage of accommodation is definitely going to cause rents to increase appreciably as many families left homeless are only too willing to pay more than the present $600. As rents start to increase, the quantity supplied will also go up. How can this happen? Well, there are a variety of ways: many homeowners will be willing to rent out their basements; some shopkeepers may be willing to convert their shops into rented accommodation; many landlords and tenants will be very happy to subdivide their premises; at the low end of the accommodation scale, warehouses, stables, sheds and garages will become available — all at a price. As rents continue to skyrocket, the quantity demanded will fall as many people will simply be unable to afford the higher rents. Rents will continue to rise as long as there is a shortage and will stop when the market has eliminated that shortage.

This occurs in Figure 3.5 when the average value of accommodation has increased to the new equilibrium price of $1,000. At this figure, the number of units now occupied has increased to 60,000. But this is not the end of the story. This adjustment process probably occurs over a short period of time, maybe a few weeks. In the long run, more lasting change will come about in the market. The high value of rents and of property in general will encourage developers to start building more units. As new units are built, the supply of houses will increase, which we could have shown as a rightward shift in the supply curve. In time, as a result of the increased supply, the price of accommodation will drop, and the number of housing units on the market will increase. It could well be that eventually the number of units will return to 100,000 and the price of accommodation back to $600.

Now, consider the question that faces the government. Should it sit back and allow the market to cure the problem, or should it step in and effect its own cure? Certainly, the competitive market can eliminate shortages; the problem is that, since it works through economic incentives and disincentives on a voluntary basis, it may not always work fast enough for society's liking. In emergency situations, governments have the power to effect change far quicker than can the marketplace. In times of national disasters such as floods or earthquakes we expect that the government will step in immediately and take charge to alleviate suffering. Similarly in wartime, we take it for granted that a government would and should mobilize industry on behalf of the war effort. It generally will not leave it to market incentives to produce sufficient armaments or military personnel. In other words, we expect a government to conscript workers and factories because this is the fastest method of mobilizing resources. On the other hand, it is certainly possible that governments might intervene in situations where they should not, or use inappropriate methods in situations where they should.

Markets do not always adjust as quickly as we would like and this can be a problem. In addition, there is an additional problem which is that markets do not always produce equitable results as far as society or the government is concerned. Let's look at this aspect.

In our example of the tsunami, the market's short-run solution was to increase the price of accommodation. Suppose, admittedly an extreme scenario, that the destroyed houses were all in the richer section of the city; the houses in the poorer section were all left intact. As the price of accommodation starts to increase, there will be a number of tenants who will no longer be able to afford to rent their homes and will be evicted by their landlords who will gladly see them replaced by new tenants from the rich side of town. In time, we may well find that the rich now totally inhabit the poor side of town, and the former tenants are now homeless or forced to relocate. Notice in Figure 3.5, that when the price of accommodation reaches $1,000, there is no longer a shortage; this despite the fact that there are now only 60,000 units occupied compared to the 100,000 prior to the tsunami. There is technically no shortage of housing, despite the fact that 40,000 families have had their lives disrupted. (Remember that a shortage means insufficient supply at a particular price. There is sufficient supply at $1,000. The fact that many people cannot afford accommodation at $1,000 is a different point and is true of many products in our society).

In a sense, the marketplace, like justice, is blind. Resources and products are allocated according to the forces of demand and supply. Whether the results are desirable or not is not the concern of the market. The fact that most people cannot afford everything they would like is a fact of economic life. There are a number of things that are unavailable to most of us, from luxury yachts to summer cabins, from the latest CD-ROM computer to this year's model of car. The market allocates these products according to supply conditions, and according to people's desire *and ability* to purchase. The market does not allocate on the basis of who should or who should not get things. That is not the function of markets. However, most people believe that it is the job of governments to see that a certain amount of fairness prevails. Throughout history governments have attempted to correct what they perceive to be inequities in the marketplace. In addition, they often intervene where a competitive market just doesn't exist.

The problem here is not so much the goals of the government (which is obviously a matter of some debate), but the methods used to achieve those goals. It is these methods to which we now turn.

Review

BOX 3A
1. Explain why even a powerful producer has to pay attention to market forces.
2. What will be the effect on the equilibrium price and quantity of a product if the demand increases at the same time that the supply decreases? What would happen if the demand decreases and the supply increases?
3. Explain the effect on the price of the product if the demand increases more than the supply. What happens if the supply increases more than the demand?
4. Explain how a competitive market adjusts to a sudden decrease in supply.
5. Why are governments often forced to take charge of allocating goods and services in times of emergency?

Price Controls

price control: government regulation to set either a maximum or minimum price for a product.

A favourite method chosen by governments to correct what is seen by those in power as undesirable market prices is through the introduction of **price controls**. These are legally imposed minimum or maximum prices on various different types of privately produced goods and services. Failure to observe these controls usually carries fines or other punishments on the buyer or seller. A price ceiling is a maximum price for which a product can be sold; a price floor is a minimum price for which the product can be sold. In both cases, the government is establishing limits; it is not establishing a fixed price. Let's start by looking at price ceilings.

Price Ceilings

price ceiling: a government regulation stipulating the maximum price which can be charged for a product.

Suppose in our tsunami example, that under pressure, the government decides to introduce a **price ceiling**, i.e., a maximum price on rented accommodation so that more people will still be able to pay the rental rate. Figure 3.6 shows the effect of the introduction of such a price ceiling in our tsunami scenario.

rent control: a government regulation making it illegal to rent accommodation above a stipulated level.

This type of price ceiling is known as **rent control** and has been introduced in many cities around the world wherever market rents are felt to be too high, for whatever reason. Assume that the government sets the rent control price at the old rent of $600. (In reality, of course, there could be a number of different ceilings depending on the size of the accommodation, the number of bedrooms, and so on.) Landlords are not allowed to charge a higher rent, though they may charge lower, if they wish. The shortage of units at this rent is 50,000 and since rents are not allowed to increase, the shortage will remain. Without the rent controls, remember that in the short run higher rents would induce people to make more accommodation avail-

FIGURE 3.6 The Effect of a Price Ceiling on Rented Accommodation

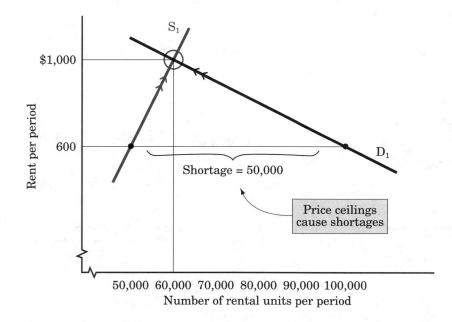

Suppose that the market rent is presently $1,000. The equilibrium number of rental units is 60,000. However, the government, believing the level of rents to be too high, introduces a price ceiling of $600. At this lower rent, the quantity demanded increases to 100,000 while the quantity supplied drops to 50,000, leaving a shortage of 50,000 units.

able. This will not happen now. But worse than this, since rents are not allowed to increase, there will be no inducement for developers to build more units in the future. In addition, unless the government periodically increases the controlled rents to compensate landlords for future cost increases, it's very likely that the future stock of rented accommodation will fall. This is because many landlords will not be able to make as good a profit as in alternative investments and will try to sell off the apartments, or perhaps convert them into condominiums, if they can, rather than rent them out. Or they may convert the accommodation into shops or warehouses or do what many landlords in New York City have done, which is simply to board up their properties and leave them empty since this alternative is more attractive than to rent out.

If all this is not bad enough, there is another serious problem with rent controls. If anyone gains from rent controls, it is those people who are presently renting since they are paying below-market rents. However, in this situation, landlords are in a very strong position because there are many people desperate to find accommodation. Because of this, single mothers, members of visible minorities or other disadvantaged groups will find themselves in a very vulnerable position since landlords can now pick and choose the types of tenants they want. This leads to a great deal of unfairness.

Another situation in which price ceilings are introduced is during national emergencies such as wartime. In World War II, most of the belligerent nations felt forced to introduce price controls. During wars, economies have to be mobilized for the war effort which means that productive resources are conscripted by the government away from their peacetime activities: certain factories are either taken over directly by the government or ordered to start producing armaments and other military requirements; workers are redirected into various different industries or directly into the military. The effect will be to reduce the amount of resources available to produce civilian goods and services. The result of this sudden reduction in the supply will be an increase in the prices of most civilian products, including the prices of most foodstuffs. Under these circumstances, the government may well feel politically obligated to introduce price ceilings so as to keep the price within the range of most people. The effect of price ceilings, any price ceiling, will be to cause a shortage as Figure 3.7 on the next page shows.

Assume that the graph illustrates the market for butter. The equilibrium price is $5 and the quantity being traded is 1,000 kilos per week. Unfortunately, the price is far higher than the peacetime price of $3 per kilo and so the government decides to establish a price ceiling for butter at this former price. This lower price is looked on very favourably by consumers and the quantity demanded rises to 1,200 kilos. For many farmers, however, the lower price spells disaster: a number of them are forced to cut back production, and some are forced out of the business of producing butter. At $3, the quantity supplied falls to 800 kilos. The price ceiling, therefore, has caused a shortage of 400 kilos of butter per week.

black market: an illegal market where products are bought and sold at a price above the government-imposed price ceiling.

Shortages generally, whether they are caused by price ceilings or not, often produce **black markets**. This means that some people, who can get their hands on those commodities which are in great demand, will be willing to risk the fines and penalties from breaking the law and will sell these items

FIGURE 3.7 The Effects of a Price Ceiling on Butter

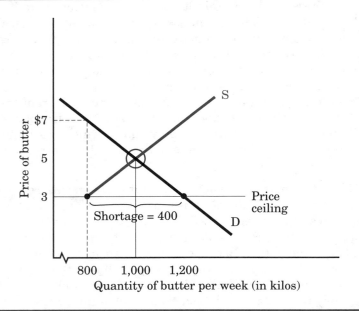

Suppose that the initial equilibrium price of butter is $5 and the equilibrium quantity being traded is 1,000 kilos per week. The government now introduces a price ceiling at the lower price of $3. The result of the price being set below equilibrium will be a shortage of 400 kilos since, at $3, the quantity demanded has increased to 1,200 while the quantity supplied has declined to 800 kilos. The dashed line shows the maximum (black market) price at which this smaller quantity could be sold. In this case, it is $7 per kilo.

above the price ceiling. Figure 3.7 shows that if black marketeers could get their hands on the total supply of 800 kilos they could sell it for as high as $7 per kilo.

QUESTION 3.3

The following table shows the demand for, and supply of, milk in a particular market (the quantities are in thousands of litres per day):

Price (per litre)	Demand	Supply
$0.80	60	42
0.90	56	44
1.00	52	46
1.10	48	48
1.20	44	50
1.30	40	52
1.40	36	54

A) Suppose that the government were to introduce an effective price ceiling which is 20 cents different from the present market equilibrium price. Would the result be a surplus or a shortage? Of what quantity?
B) If a black market were to develop as a result of the price ceiling, what would be the maximum black market price?

What the butter example above demonstrates is that if the market is not allowed to allocate goods and services in the normal manner, then someone or something else must perform that task. At the price ceiling of $3 per kilo, the supply of 800 kilos must somehow be allocated to consumers who are

producers' preference: an allocation system where sellers are allowed to determine the method of allocation on the basis of their own preferences.

rationing: a method of allocating products which are in short supply by the use of ration coupons issued by the government guaranteeing a certain quantity per family.

demanding 1,200 kilos. One way of allocating this short supply is on the basis of "first come, first served." But this is not a fair system since people who have time on their hands will be able to line up more easily than, say, a parent with young children to look after. Another method is to leave the allocation decision to **producers' preference**, i.e., leave it to the seller to decide which customers gets what amount of butter and which customers go without. Unfortunately, this method opens itself up to the possibility of favouritism, bribery and corruption. For instance, the seller may demand extra payments or services from a customer before selling, or may decide to sell only to favourites or refuse to sell to anyone he/she doesn't like and so on.

For this reason, governments are usually forced to undertake the allocation process themselves through the introduction of a **rationing** scheme. This means that butter, for instance, would be distributed equally between all families, each family being given ration coupons allowing it to purchase a specified quantity. In our example, each family would get ration coupons entitling it to 2/3 kilo of butter per week. (We are assuming that at $3 per kilo, there would be 1,200 families, each wanting to buy 1 kilo of butter. Each family's allocation would be, therefore, 800/1,200 or 2/3 kilo to each family.) Certainly this seems a much fairer method than allowing producers to decide on the allocation. But is it a fair system? On the surface it would seem so. But remember that people are being given an allowance of butter regardless of whether they would normally buy it or not. Imagine the plight of coffee drinkers and smokers if those two products were rationed (beer is not usually rationed in wartime — it's watered down instead). Their allowance would be the same as that of non-addicts. In contrast, the market normally takes intensity of desire into account, a rationing system does not. Given these circumstances, it's understandable that people might well trade away coupons they don't want for those they do. Since, however, bartering is a cumbersome exchange method, usually a market in ration coupons develops. This means that people will have to pay for extra coupons as well as paying for the product itself.

From this you can see that, with its faults, the market system usually works better than any alternative. Price ceilings are usually introduced when supplies of a product are limited and prices consequently are high. But ceilings only address one problem — high prices; and usually exacerbate the limited supply by causing it to shrink further. Many economists suggest that if the problem is affordability, then it might better be attacked by giving direct income relief to those in need rather than helping rich and poor alike by artificially depressing the price.

Study Guide

QUESTION 3.4
Given the demand and supply shown in Study Guide Question 3.3, suppose that the government were to impose a price ceiling of $1.20 per litre of milk. What impact would this have?

Let's now see what happens when the government introduces price controls, not to depress prices, but to increase them.

Price Floors

price floor: a government regulation stipulating the minimum price which can be charged for a product.

Figure 3.8 shows a market where the government feels that the price, rather than being too high, is in fact too low. It has therefore introduced a **price floor** above equilibrium. The price floor represents a minimum price: sellers can sell at a higher price if they wish; however, it is illegal to sell at a lower price.

It's obvious in this situation that by increasing the price above equilibrium, the government is assisting the producers and not the consumers. A higher price is going to mean a higher income for producers. Which type of producers would the government help in this way, and why? The answer is often farmers, because farming has always been regarded as a special type of industry. Agriculture is different from other types of production for a number of reasons. Firstly, unlike, say, manufacturing, the supply cannot be totally controlled by farmers. The size of the harvest in any one year is greatly determined by the weather. The harvest can fluctuate greatly from year to year and with it, the income of farmers. A second reason is that farmers produce a very basic and important commodity: food. Throughout history, countries have tried to ensure that they are not totally dependent on others for their foodstuffs. If they were so dependent, and the supply was interrupted because of war, civil unrest, drought or other disaster, then their position would become precarious. Finally, governments have often been reluctant to allow agricultural land to be traded freely in the marketplace. It's felt that this particular resource is very precious since once it is used for other purposes like a housing development or shopping mall, reconverting it back to farming is virtually impossible. For these reasons and others, governments in most countries have tried to protect and encourage their agricultural communities. One way of doing this is through a price floor on agricultural products, which will guarantee farmers a minimum price.

Figure 3.8 shows the immediate effect of a price floor: surpluses. The graph shows the market for wheat where the equilibrium price is $10 a bushel

FIGURE 3.8 The Effects of a Price Floor on the Wheat Market

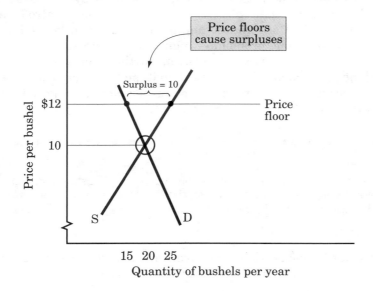

A price set above equilibrium will always produce a surplus. In this figure, the price floor of $12 causes a drop in the quantity demanded from the original 20 down to 15; it also causes the quantity supplied to increase from 20 to 25. Therefore, buyers want to purchase less, but sellers want to produce more. The result is a surplus of 10 million bushels.

and the quantity being traded is 20 (million) bushels. Suppose that the government now introduces a price floor of $12 a bushel. At this higher price, the quantity demanded drops to 15 bushels. The higher price will, on the other hand, induce present farmers to produce more and new wheat farms to start up. As a result, the quantity supplied increase to 25 bushels. Consequently, there is now a surplus of 10 bushels of wheat. This surplus belongs to the government, since by introducing the price floor it must take responsibility for any surplus thus created.

The problem for the government now is how to get rid of the surplus that a price floor will inevitably produce. A number of possibilities exist. If the surplus is storable, which is true of most grains, then it could be stored in grain elevators and used in the future when the supply may be lower. In this way, the grain elevators are being used as reservoirs, taking in grain whenever there is a surplus and releasing it whenever it is in short supply. If the agricultural surplus is perishable, as in the case of milk or eggs or produce, then the government may be able to convert it into other foodstuffs or freeze, dry or can it. But all such methods are likely to be expensive. Failing this, then, the government will have to dispose of the surplus. But, this is more difficult than it sounds. Selling it to other countries may not be feasible since, in order to do so, the price may have to be reduced. But this is forbidden by many international conventions and is termed **dumping**. Donating it to countries in need is similarly difficult, except in times of natural disasters, because doing so will undermine the receiving country's own agricultural industry or will disturb its present trading arrangements. The last option may be simply to destroy the surplus by burning it, burying it or literally dumping it in the ocean. Understandably, this last alternative is politically embarrassing to governments and is also unacceptable to many people.

dumping: the sale of a product abroad for a lower price than is being charged in the domestic market or for a price below the cost of production.

An alternative method, which has been tried by some governments, is to get farmers to stop producing a surplus! In other words, in our example from Figure 3.8, farmers would be asked to produce no more than 15 bushels so that no surplus results. The farmers, in compensation for voluntarily complying with this quota, would still get paid as though they had produced 25 bushels. In return for giving such a **subsidy**, the government no longer has the problem of trying to dispose of an embarrassing surplus.

subsidy: a payment made by the government to a firm (or others) which may be a lump-sum grant or may depend on the amount produced.

BOX 3.2

The governments of most countries in the world involve themselves in their agricultural sectors, the European Community more extensively than most. In Canada, there are more than 100 farm marketing boards regulating such produce as milk, eggs, wheat, peanuts, grains, poultry and so on. In total, they exercise control over more than 50% of total farm sales in Canada, and include such federal bodies as the Canadian Wheat Board, the Canada Livestock Feed Board, and the Canadian Dairy Commission. In addition, there are a number of provincial boards. Besides price floors, the other main methods of enhancing and stabilizing farm incomes are by way of quotas (which, by restricting output, increases the market price), and through subsidies granted to farmers (which gives them an additional sum of money for each unit of output produced).

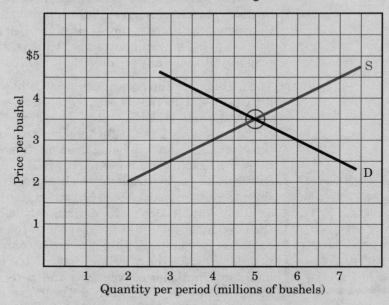

QUESTION 3.5
Given the market for corn described in the figure below:

A) In equilibrium, what is the total sales revenue being received by producers? Suppose that the government now imposes a price floor of $4 per kilo.
B) What quantity will now be demanded? What quantity will farmers produce? What quantity will be the government purchase?
C) How much will it cost the government to purchase the surplus?

It should be clear from this, that price floors in agriculture can lead to serious problems. Again, many economists would suggest that rather than interfering directly with the market, governments might be better advised to give direct income assistance to farmers since that is the problem they are trying to address.

The Minimum Wage

> **minimum wage:** the lowest rate of pay per hour for workers as laid down by government.

Finally, we will take a look at another type of price floor which is used in many countries; that of a minimum price for labour, or, in other words, a **minimum wage**. Minimum wage legislation is often introduced for the commendable reason of ensuring that all working people are guaranteed a minimum income. The goal is generally not criticized by economists; it is the method chosen by governments which is in question. Whenever the free workings of the marketplace are interfered with, a number of harmful side effects are usually produced. Let's look at the situation with the help of Figure 3.9.

This figure illustrates a particular labour market, one in which the equilibrium wage ($5 per hour in our graph) is considered by the government as too low. Suppose that the government therefore introduces minimum wage legislation forbidding the payment of any wage at a rate below $6 per hour. The following graph therefore describes a market where the going

FIGURE 3.9 Labour Markets and Minimum Wages

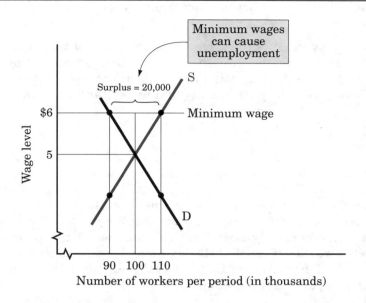

The imposition of a minimum wage of $6 means that firms will economize on the use of labour. In this figure, the quantity demanded will drop from the equilibrium quantity of 100,000 to 90,000. At the same time the higher wage will attract more people to want a job, i.e., the quantity supplied increases from 100,000 to 110,000. The result will be a surplus of workers of 20,000. In other words, more workers will be wanting jobs than there are jobs available, i.e., there will be 20,000 unemployed in this particular labour market.

wage is generally below the minimum wage, as for instance in fast-food restaurants, fruit picking and so on. These fairly low-skill occupations often attract disadvantaged members of society: the young, the old, the poorly educated, recent immigrants without sufficient language skills, etc. The effect, as we shall see, rather than helping these groups may well be to cause additional harm.

Figure 3.9 demonstrates the effect of a wage above equilibrium. The higher wage means that employers will be forced to economize on labour and will cut back on employment, i.e., the quantity demanded by firms falls from 100,000 to 90,000. At the same time, the now higher wage will attract more workers in this occupation and the quantity supplied increases to 110,000. The net result of this is that there will be a surplus of labour, or the same thing, unemployment to the tune of 20,000 workers. The 90,000 workers who have retained their jobs are obviously helped by the minimum wage legislation, though it is possible that they are required to work harder now that the number of employees has been reduced. But in our example, the legislation has resulted in an increase in unemployment, and it is this aspect of minimum wages which has been seriously criticized by some economists, who feel that the poor may be better assisted by providing direct income relief rather than by doing it indirectly through the marketplace. It is also highly likely that, since employers now have a big pool of unemployed workers from which to choose, some of them may be inclined to discriminate on the basis of gender, or race or religion or on other non-work-related grounds.

There are a number of supporters of minimum wage legislation, however, who consider that the benefits far exceed the costs. They suggest that it's not so much the case that many workers are paid low wages because they are unproductive, but they are unproductive because they are paid such low wages. If this is so, then the imposition of a minimum wage would actually increase productivity, and with it lead to an increase in the demand for labour by firms. This would consequently reduce the amount of unemployment.

Regardless of which version is the correct one, the point of this analysis is that all methods of allocation, whether done by the government or by the market impose costs. These costs are not always obvious. What economic analysis does is to help us identify and understand the nature of these costs.

Some Elaborations

A great deal of economic analysis and theorizing is the result of observations of the real world. However, much progress has been made as a result of economists abstracting from reality rather than merely reporting on it. In the context of demand and supply, economists are forever speculating on scenarios that do not obviously exist. They ask themselves the question: theoretically, what would happen if...? Having worked out the consequences of their analysis they often discover that in fact this exactly coincides with what happened in a particular situation.

What we want to do in the final section of this chapter is to look a little more closely at the shape and position of the demand and supply curves. In doing this we are exploring possibilities. But in this way, it may help to give you a deeper understanding of demand and supply.

Do All Demand Curves Slope Downward? The law of demand suggests that a lower price will produce a higher quantity demanded than will a higher price, but is this always true? Can the law of demand be broken? Figure 3.10, for instance, shows a vertical demand curve: is such a construct a figment of some economist's imagination, or can it really exist?

FIGURE 3.10 A Vertical Demand Curve

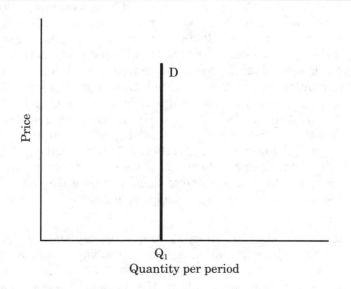

Whatever the price happens to be, the quantity demanded remains at Q_1. In this case, the price is irrelevant; this consumer does not react to a change in the price, since whether it drops or rises, he will buy the same quantity. Here, the price is not a determinant of how much is bought.

The demand curve in the above figure seems to suggest that for this particular consumer or in this particular market, the price of the product is irrelevant — the quantity remains the same regardless of the price. It says that no matter how high or how low the price, the quantity demanded remains constant. It would seem that this product is an "ultra" necessity, so that no matter how high the price goes, the same quantity would still be purchased. Perhaps it describes the demand for cigarettes by a smoker or for gasoline by a driver? But doesn't it seem ludicrous to suggest that they wouldn't reduce consumption a little if the price got astronomically high? Or for that matter that they wouldn't consume more if the price were zero? What about drugs then — either life-preserving drugs like insulin or life-taking drugs like cocaine? Isn't the demand for these products unlimited because people have to have them, irrespective of price? Consider the unfortunate fact that even though humans need to eat food to stay alive, many millions die of starvation throughout the world every year. Our demand in other words is limited by our income, i.e., by our ability to purchase. There is a maximum price for all of us, whether we are rich or poor. Therefore, although our demand for certain products may remain constant over a range of prices, eventually above a certain price, the quantity demanded will decrease which means that the demand curve must eventually slope backwards.

The next example seems even more perverse and totally contradicts the Law of Demand. Figure 3.11 shows an upward-sloping demand curve.

FIGURE 3.11 An Upward-Sloping Demand Curve

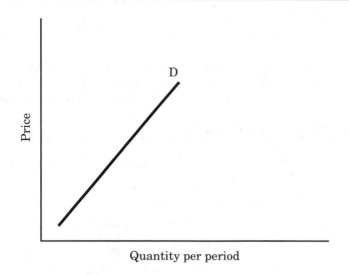

With this demand curve, the quantity demanded increases as the price increases: the lower the price, the lower the quantity demanded; the higher the price (without limit), the higher the quantity demanded. This direct relationship results in an upward-sloping demand curve.

This demand curve suggests that as the price increases, consumers purchase more. Surely, this is nonsensical? Well, certainly it is unlikely that the *whole* market would buy increasing quantities at increasing prices. However, it may be true for *certain individuals* over a limited range of prices. There are certain products whose values to some people are determined by their prices. The higher the price, the more attractive such products as jewellery, furs and perfumes may become for some people simply because the price is now higher. A higher price means that only an exclusive few people can now afford to buy such products. It is this exclusivity which makes such products attractive and invites these customers to "conspicuously consume," to use a phrase made popular by the iconoclastic American economist, Thorstein Veblen. But again, there is still a limit to this conspicuous consumption, and eventually at some high price one would imagine, even for the few individuals involved, the quantity demanded will start to fall so that the demand curve again becomes downward-sloping.

BOX 3.3

There is another explanation sometimes given for an upward-sloping demand curve which relates to what are termed *Giffen Goods*. In the nineteenth century, the economist Sir Robert Giffen, as the result of research he had done into the consumption of potatoes in Ireland following the 1856 famine, discovered an interesting paradox. As the price of potatoes rose, the consumption of potatoes actually increased, instead of falling. The reason for this is that purchases of potatoes in those days represented a big portion of the average working person's food budget. The increase in price meant a sharp drop in real incomes, which meant that for many families the price of meat for instance was out of reach. Instead of buying meat, they substituted even more potatoes, which at least guaranteed a full stomach. Not all economists, however, trust Giffen's data and do not believe that there is any evidence of an upward-sloping market demand curve.

Figure 3.12 below shows an even quirkier example. What product could this possibly describe? (Perhaps the demand for stair carpet!) It suggests that although the demand curve is generally downward-sloping, over a certain

FIGURE 3.12 An Individual's Demand for a Household Appliance

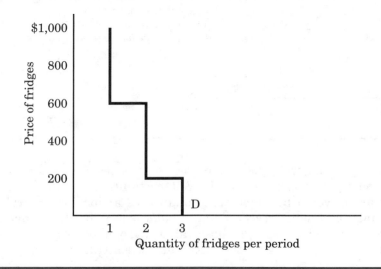

As far as this individual is concerned, if the price is above $600, she would only want to purchase 1 fridge. If the price is below $600, then she wants to purchase 2 fridges. But she could not be induced to buy more than 2 fridges unless the price drops to $200.

range of prices, from $1,000 to $600, the quantity demanded remains the same. Such a demand curve might describe the demand for household appliances like a refrigerator. Most people need only one fridge, though a sufficiently low price might induce them to buy a second fridge. However, over a very wide range of prices we are fairly indifferent to the price. The individual demand for many products might look like this demand. However, it's unlikely that the *market* demand curve would be anything other than a continuous downward-sloping demand curve, though it may not always plot as a straight line.

Economics is generally concerned with products that have a positive (above zero) price. Figure 3.13, in contrast, illustrates a market for a free good.

FIGURE 3.13 A Free Product

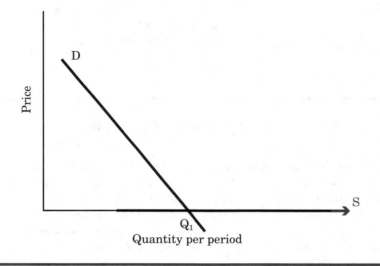

At a price of zero, the supply is unlimited, and irrespective of the demand, this must be a free good, i.e., demand plays no part in determining the price. However, the quantity demanded is still limited — in this case to a quantity Q_1.

The reason it is a free good is that the supply is so great that it does not require the inducement of a higher price in order to elicit a higher quantity. It might describe the supply of air perhaps or certain types of goods called public goods which we will be looking at in a later chapter. For these types of product, the equilibrium price is zero, and for that reason would not be worth a private company producing. Note however that the fact that the product is free does not imply that the quantity demanded is unlimited. There is a maximum quantity demanded for most things in life.

This next graph is straightforward, though the interpretation of the slope is a little more difficult. It describes the demand for water, for example. To obtain a small quantity of water (at a life-preserving quantity like quantity Q_1 in Figure 3.14), we would be prepared to pay a high price, like price P_1. At quantities higher than quantity Q_2, on the other hand, people are not prepared to pay more than a very low price like P_2. What price and quantity they are actually paying depends not only on the demand, of course, but also on the supply. In most countries the supply is usually fairly abundant as shown by the supply curve S_2 in the diagram, so that the price tends to be quite low. In desert areas of the world, on the other hand, the supply will be like S_1 in Figure 3.14 and will therefore result in a comparatively high

FIGURE 3.14 The Demand for Water

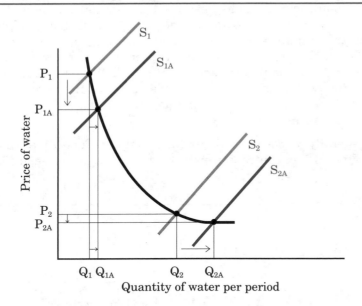

The effect on price of a change in supply depends very much on the shape of the demand curve. This figure depicts the demand curve for water which is very steep at low quantities, but quite flat at high quantities. If the present supply is S_1 giving a price of P_1 and a quantity of Q_1, then it requires only a small change in the supply to S_{1A} to bring about a big change in the price (though the quantity will not change greatly). On the other hand, if supply is abundant, as in curve S_2, then a change in supply (to S_{2A}) will not greatly affect the price (but will lead to a big change in the quantity).

price. In such places, even a small change in supply can have a great effect on the price.

This completes our look at various aspects of demand and supply. However, as you may have become aware in this chapter, demand and supply analysis can be used, and is used, in so many different situations that it would be presumptuous to suggest that this is the end of the discussion. The tool of demand/supply analysis is so powerful and its application so pervasive, that to an extent, much of economics is merely an elaboration and amplification of its basic principles.

QUESTION 3.6

A) Under what circumstances would an increase in supply have no effect on the price of a product?

B) Under what circumstances would it have no effect on the quantity traded of a product?

QUESTION 3.7

Below is the hypothetical demand for water in a particular country (price per 50 litres):

Price	$2	3	4	5	6	7	8	9	10	11	12	13	14
Demand	1,000	500	200	150	110	80	60	50	43	38	34	31	30

A) Suppose the present supply of 200 is cut by 50. What effect will it have on the price?

B) Suppose, instead, the present supply is 80, and it is now cut by 50. What effect will this have on the price?

Chapter Highlights

This chapter seeks to elaborate on the basic principles of demand and supply (discussed in Chapter 2) and apply those principles in a number of different situations. It is divided into three parts.

The first part of the chapter clarifies what is meant by competitive markets, and using a simple example in the automobile industry explains that the forces of demand and supply are still at work even in uncompetitive markets. It then tries to find out what might happen if both the demand and supply change at the same time. It shows how graphical analysis in these circumstances might be misleading, and that the resulting effect on either the price or quantity traded will be indeterminate, unless we have further knowledge of the magnitude of the changes. It then presents a simple schematic approach to analyzing the effects of multiple changes.

The second part of the chapter is centred on situations where governments often intervene in markets. It starts by looking at a scenario where a community is devastated by a natural disaster, in this case a tsunami, and explains what would happen if the market tried, unassisted, to repair the damage. It goes on to look at other, less obvious, areas where governments often intervene by way of instituting price controls. It looks at price ceilings, and shows that the result in both the case of rental housing and of markets for necessary products in wartime is the creation of shortages. It shows how governments try to cope with these shortages through rationing and how the shortages can lead to black markets and other inequities.

Another type of price control, a price floor, is then examined. The chapter first looks at the agricultural markets and explains the reasons why, in most countries, governments are involved in some type of regulation. It demonstrates that one of the undesired side effects of a price floor is the creation of surpluses. It argues that this result may also occur in those labour markets which are affected by minimum wage legislation, though in this case the surplus takes the form of unemployment.

The third and final part of the chapter is concerned with exploring various theoretical anomalies in markets. It looks at situations where, for instance, consumers may buy more rather than less at higher prices; where consumers are indifferent over wide ranges of price changes; and where the reaction of consumers is dependent on the amounts of a product they already possess.

New Glossary Terms

Workbook

Study Tips

1. In the first part of the chapter we take some of the principles from the last chapter and apply them to real world examples; while the second part deals with abstractions and may not necessarily describe a real life example. However, you need to become familiar with the process of abstraction. This simply means exploring various possibilities, e.g., what if the demand curve looked like this, or if the supply curve took this shape? In other words, don't be afraid of abstractions and don't always try to immediately find practical uses; they may not exist.

2. The chapter does not really introduce any new ideas; it simply extends the ideas developed in the last chapter. This means that even though the analysis, especially when we are dealing with multiple curve shifts, might seem forbidding at first, the principles behind things are ones you are familiar with.

3. Many students confuse the terms scarcity (or short supply) and shortage. Remember that all products and resources are "scarce" but the markets for them may well be in equilibrium in that the demand and supply are equal. A shortage, on the other hand, describes a disequilibrium situation where the quantity demanded exceeds the quantity supplied.

4. Remember that a price ceiling is a *maximum price* but is imposed *below* the equilibrium price and results in a *shortage*. On the other hand, a price floor is a *minimum* price but is imposed *above* the equilibrium price and results in a *surplus*.

Are You Sure?

Indicate whether the following statements are true or false. If false, indicate why they are false.

1. Economic laws are social laws — statements of tendencies, more or less certain, more or less definite.
T or **F**　If false: _____

_____

_____

2. If both the demand and the supply increase, it is impossible to say whether the price will rise or fall.
T or **F**　If false: _____

_____

_____

3. If the demand increases and the supply decreases, it is impossible to say what will happen to the price.
T or **F**　If false: _____

_____

_____

4. A shortage is caused by either a decrease in demand or an increase in supply.
T or **F**　If false: _____

_____

_____

5. A price floor, to be effective, must be set below the equilibrium price.
T or **F**　If false: _____

_____

_____

6. A price ceiling is a government regulation stipulating the maximum price which can be charged for a product.
T or **F**　If false: _____

_____

_____

7. Black markets and rationing schemes are often the result of the imposition of a price ceiling.
T or **F**　If false: _____

_____

8. Invariably, price floors cause shortages and price ceilings cause surpluses.
T or **F**   If false: _____

_____

_____

9. If the demand curve is vertical then an increase in supply will have no effect on the price.
T or **F**   If false: _____

_____

_____

10. Since water is a necessity, its demand is unlimited.
T or **F**   If false: _____

_____

_____

Translations

"Technological improvements over the last 10 years have so reduced the costs of producing compact disc players that, although they have greatly increased in popularity, the average price has dropped." Illustrate the changes in the compact disc market in Figure W3.1 below.

FIGURE W3.1

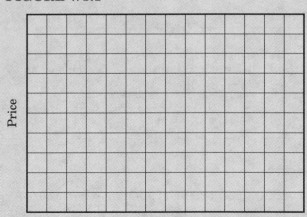

Price

Quantity per period

Choose the Best

1. A minimum wage is an example of a:
   a) Price floor.
   b) Price ceiling.

2. Rent control is an example of a:
   a) Price floor.
   b) Price ceiling.

3. Under what circumstances can a black market exist?
   a) When a price ceiling is imposed.
   b) When a price floor is imposed.

4. What will happen if both the demand for and supply of a product increase simultaneously?
   a) The effect on the price is indeterminate.
   b) The price will increase.
   c) The price will decrease.

5. What will happen if both the demand for and supply of a product decrease simultaneously?
   a) The effect on the price is indeterminate.
   b) The price will increase.
   c) The price will decrease.

6. What will happen if both the demand for and supply of a product increase simultaneously?
   a) The effect on the quantity traded is indeterminate.
   b) The quantity traded will increase.
   c) The quantity traded will decrease.

7. All of the following, *except one*, are examples of price ceilings. Which is the exception?
   a) Minimum wage legislation.
   b) Rent controls.
   c) Wartime price controls on the price of consumer necessities.

8. Which of the following type of firm would be most affected by minimum wage legislation?
   a) A company of management consultants.
   b) An airline company.
   c) A fast-food restaurant.
   d) A hospital.

9. Which of the following is an example of a price ceiling?
   a) Minimum wage legislation.

b) Dumping.

c) Rent controls.

d) Agricultural price supports.

10. What does a vertical demand curve suggest?

a) That producers are unable to adjust the quantity they produce.

b) That the price is not a determinant of the quantity demanded.

c) That consumers will not buy the product unless it is free.

d) That a change in supply has no effect on the price.

11. What is the term used to describe certain goods whose demand curve is upward-sloping?

a) Inferior goods.

b) Giffen goods.

c) Complementary goods.

d) Substitute goods.

Refer to Figure W3.2 when answering question 12.

FIGURE W3.2

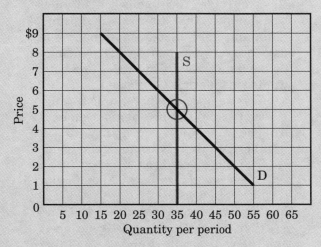

12. Refer to Figure W3.2 to answer this question. If this market is originally in equilibrium and demand increases by 10, what will be the new equilibrium price and quantity?

a) $3 and 45 units.

b) $5 and 35 units.

c) $5 and 45 units.

d) $7 and 35 units.

Refer to Figure W3.3 when answering questions 13 and 14.

FIGURE W3.3

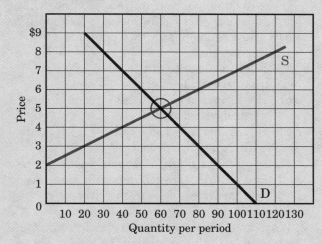

13. Refer to Figure W3.3 to answer this question. What would be the result if a price floor is set which is $2 different from the equilibrium price?

a) The price would be above equilibrium and a surplus of 60 would be produced.

b) The price would be below equilibrium and a shortage of 60 would be produced.

c) The price would be above equilibrium and a shortage of 60 would be produced.

d) The price would be below equilibrium and a surplus of 60 would be produced.

14. Refer to Figure W3.3 to answer this question. What would be the result if a price ceiling is set which is $2 different from the equilibrium price?

a) The price would be above equilibrium and a surplus of 60 would be produced.

b) The price would be below equilibrium and a shortage of 60 would be produced.

c) The price would be above equilibrium and a shortage of 60 would be produced.

d) The price would be below equilibrium and a surplus of 60 would be produced.

15. Under what circumstances would an increase in the supply of a product have no effect on the price?

a) If the demand curve is vertical.

b) If the supply curve is vertical.

c) If the demand curve is horizontal.

d) If both the demand and supply curves are vertical.

e) If the demand curve is upward-sloping.

16. If the demand curve is upward-sloping, what would be the effect of an increase in supply?
    a) An increase in supply would be impossible.
    b) It will reduce both the price and the quantity traded.
    c) It will increase both the price and the quantity traded.
    d) It will increase the quantity traded but will reduce the price.
    e) It might or might not increase the price and quantity traded depending on the comparative slopes of the curves.

17. Why is the market's allocation of products preferable to that of either the producers or of the government?
    a) Because it ensures that even the poor will be able to afford to buy everything.
    b) Because it ensures that only people who really need certain products will be able to afford them.
    c) Because it ensures that both demand and supply factors are taken into consideration.
    d) Because it will mean that scarce resources are available at low prices.
    e) Because it ensures that the income distribution of the population is ignored.

Table W3.1 describes the market for day-care workers in a particular city (quantity of workers in thousands). Refer to this table to answer questions 18, 19 and 20.

TABLE W3.1

Hourly wage ($)	5.00	5.50	6.00	6.50	7.00	7.50
Quantity demanded	17	16	15	14	13	12
Quantity supplied	13	14	15	16	17	18

18. Refer to Table W3.1 to answer this question. What are the implications if this market is in equilibrium?
    a) The wage rate would be $5 an hour and there would be 4,000 unemployed workers.

b) The wage rate would be $5.50 an hour and there would be 2,000 unemployed workers.

c) The wage rate would be $6 an hour and there would be no unemployed workers.

d) The wage rate would be $6.50 an hour and there would be 2,000 unemployed workers.

e) The wage rate would be $5 an hour and there would be 13,000 unemployed workers.

19. Refer to Table W3.1 to answer this question. What would happen if the government were to establish a minimum wage of $6.50 an hour?
    a) The wage would stay at $6 and there would be no unemployment.
    b) The equilibrium wage would rise to $6.50 and there would be no unemployment.
    c) The number employed would increase by 1,000.
    d) There would be 2,000 day-care workers unemployed.
    e) The day-care centres would have difficulty finding sufficient workers.

20. Refer to Table W3.1 to answer this question. Suppose that after the imposition of a minimum wage of $6.50, a number of new day-care centres opened up increasing the demand for workers by 4,000. In what way would this market be affected?
    a) The wage would increase to $7 and there would be no unemployment.
    b) The wage would remain at $6.50 but there would now be no unemployment.
    c) The wage would remain at $6.50 and there would now be 2,000 unemployed day-care workers.
    d) The wage would remain at $6.50 and there would now be 2,000 vacancies.
    e) The wage would drop to $5 and there would be no unemployment.

What's Wrong?

Can you spot the five errors in the following passage? (Ignore grammatical mistakes!)

Since the competitive market ignores demand and supply, the government often intervenes in certain markets by way of price controls. For instance, if the government considers the price to be too high in a certain market it may introduce a price ceiling. A price ceiling is the same thing as a minimum price. The problem with price ceilings, however, is that they cause surpluses. In other cases, when the government feels the price in the market is too low, it may introduce a price floor which is the same as a maximum price. One of the major problems with price floors is that they often lead to black markets.

Key Problem

Figure W3.4 depicts the market for rice in Concordia.

FIGURE W3.4

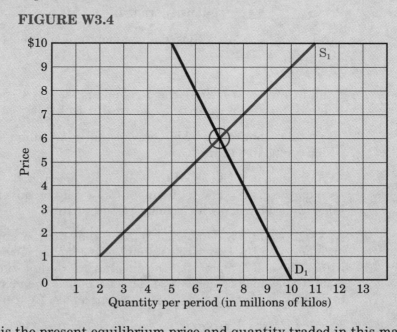

a) What is the present equilibrium price and quantity traded in this market?

Price: _____; quantity traded: _____.

b) How much, in total, are rice buyers paying for this quantity?

Total spending: _____.

c) Suppose that the government introduces a price floor of $8 per kilo. How much in total will rice buyers now be paying?

Total spending: _____.

d) As a result of the price floor, what will be the total amount of the surplus? What will be the dollar amount of this surplus? Who will be responsible for buying this surplus?

Surplus: _____ kilos of rice; dollar amount of surplus: $ _____;

is the responsibility of _____.

e) Suppose that after the imposition of the price floor, the demand in Concordia increases by 1.5 (million) kilos. Draw the new demand on Figure W3.4, and label it D_2. Now, how much in total will rice buyers be paying?

Price: _____; quantity traded: _____; total spending: _____.

f)   What will be the total amount of the new surplus? What will be the dollar amount of this surplus?

Surplus: _____ kilos of rice; dollar amount of surplus: $ _____.

g)   After the change in demand, what would happen if, as a result of a bad harvest, the supply now drops by 3 (million) kilos. Draw the new supply curve on Figure W3.4, and label it S_2. What will be the new price, the quantity traded, the total spending of buyers, the surplus and the dollar amount of the surplus?

Price: _____; quantity traded: _____; total spending: _____;

surplus: _____ kilos; dollar amount of surplus: $ _____.

Need a Hand?

a)   Equilibrium occurs where the demand and supply curves intersect which is at a **price of $6 and a quantity of 7 (million) kilos**.

b)   The total amount paid by buyers is equal to 7 million kilos times $6 each, which comes to **$42 million.**

c)   At a price now of $8 per kilo, the quantity demanded will drop to 6, as can be seen on the graph. The total amount now paid by buyers is equal to 6 million kilos times $8 each, which comes to **$48 million.**

d)   At $8, the quantity demanded is 6 and the quantity supplied is 9. The difference between the two is the amount of the surplus, which is equal to **3 million kilos**. The dollar amount of the surplus is 3 million times the new higher price floor of $8, which comes to **$24**. This surplus is the **responsibility of the government to buy** (and indirectly the citizens of Concordia).

e)   The new demand curve (D_2) is shown in Figure W3.5 below:

FIGURE W3.5 (completed Figure W3.4)

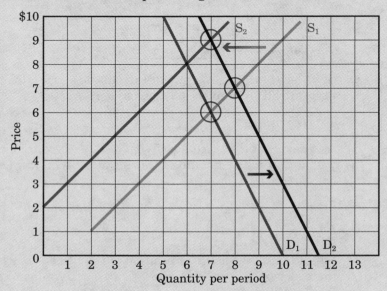

The demand curve shifts to the right by 1.5 million kilos (1 1/2 squares), so that it is parallel to the old demand curve. It now intersects the supply curve at a price of **$7**. However, this is below the price floor and is therefore irrelevant. **The price remains at the old level of $8**. The quantity now traded at $8, however, is different since it has now increased to **7.5 million kilos**. Total spending by buyers is equal to $8 times 7.5 million kilos, or **$60 million**.

f)   At a price of $8, the distance between the supply curve and the new demand curve is reduced to **1.5 million kilos**, the amount of the surplus. The dollar amount of this surplus is therefore **12 million**.

g)   The new supply curve (S2) is shown on Figure W3.5. It intersects demand curve D2, at a new price of **$9**. This will be the new market price since, although the rice cannot be sold below $8, it can certainly be sold at a price above it. At this new higher price, the quantity traded is **7 million kilos**, and the total spending is equal to $9 times 7 million, or **$63 million**. Since this is equilibrium, there is **no surplus** and the dollar amount of the surplus is **zero**.

More of the Same

Figure W3.6 depicts the market for potatoes in Discordia.

FIGURE W3.6

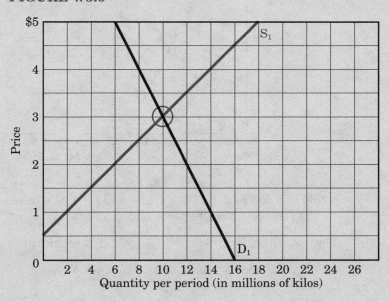

a)   What is the present equilibrium price and quantity traded in this market?

b)   How much in total are buyers paying for these potatoes?

c)   Suppose that the government introduces a price floor of $4 per kilo. How much in total will potato buyers now be paying?

d)   What will be the total amount of the surplus? What will be the dollar amount of this surplus? Who will be responsible for buying this surplus?

e)   Suppose that after the imposition of the price floor, the demand in Concordia increases by 3 (million) kilos. Draw the new demand curve on Figure W3.6 and label it D_2. Now, how much in total will potato buyers be paying?

f) What will be the total amount of the new surplus? What will be the dollar amount of this surplus?

g) After the change in demand, what would happen if, as a result of a bad harvest, the supply now drops by 3 (million) kilos. Draw the new supply curve on Figure W3.6 and label it S_2. What will be the new price, the quantity traded, the surplus and the dollar amount of the surplus?

Other Problems

1. Figure W3.7 shows the market for mandarin oranges in Cascadia for the month of November (in thousands of kilos).

    FIGURE W3.7

    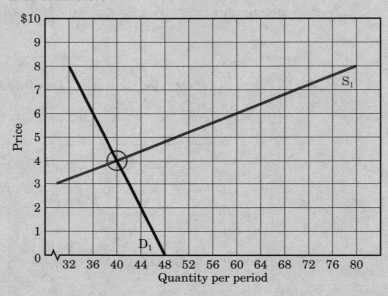

    Suppose that in December the supply of mandarin oranges increases by 20% while the demand doubles. Draw and label the new curves D_2 and S_2. What will be the new equilibrium price and quantity?

    New equilibrium price: _____; equilibrium quantity: _____.

2. Table W3.2 shows Cascadia's market for olive oil (in thousands of litres per month).

    TABLE W3.2

Price ($)	1	2	3	4	5	6	7	8
Quantity demanded	70	60	50	40	30	20	10	0
Quantity supplied	10	20	30	40	50	60	70	80

    Suppose that olive oil increases in popularity and Cascadia's buyers are willing to pay an additional $1 for each quantity demanded; at the same time, as the result of improved technology, oil producers are willing to accept $1 less for each quantity supplied. What will be the new equilibrium price and quantity?

    New equilibrium price: _____; equilibrium quantity: _____.

3. Suppose that a number of coincidental changes were to occur in the following markets. In each case, indicate what will happen to the price and quantity traded as a result. ($\uparrow$ = increase; $\downarrow$ = decrease; 0 = no change; ? = indeterminate.)

Changes affecting demand
1. incomes increase
2. price of substitute product increases

Changes affecting supply
A. price of input falls
B. price of productively related product increases

a) Assume that changes 1 and A occur, and the market is for an inferior product.

Equilibrium price: _____; equilibrium quantity: _____.

b) Assume that changes 1 and B occur, and the market is for a normal product.

Equilibrium price: _____; equilibrium quantity: _____.

c) Assume that changes 2 and A occur, and the market is for a normal product.

Equilibrium price: _____; equilibrium quantity: _____.

d) Assume that changes 2 and B occur, and the market is for a normal product.

Equilibrium price: _____; equilibrium quantity: _____.

4. Suppose that a number of coincidental changes were to occur in the following markets. In each case, indicate what will happen to the price and quantity traded as a result. ($\uparrow$ = increase; $\downarrow$ = decrease; 0 = no change; ? = indeterminate.)

Changes affecting demand
1. price of complementary product introduced
2. population increases

Changes affecting supply
A. technological improvement increases.
B. number of suppliers falls

a) Assume that changes 1 and A occur, and the market is for a normal product.

Equilibrium price: _____; equilibrium quantity: _____.

b) Assume that changes 1 and B occur, and the market is for a normal product.

Equilibrium price: _____; equilibrium quantity: _____.

c) Assume that changes 2 and A occur, and the market is for a normal product.

Equilibrium price: _____; equilibrium quantity: _____.

d) Assume that changes 2 and B occur, and the market is for a normal product.

Equilibrium price: _____; equilibrium quantity: _____.

Unanswered Questions

Short Essays

1. In what way are buyers' willingness and ability to purchase affected by a price change?

2. In what way are sellers' willingness and ability to produce affected by a price change?

3. If the government considers the price of a product too high for consumers, it could subsidize consumers rather than introduce a price ceiling. Discuss.

4. If the government considers the price of a product too low for producers, it could subsidize producers rather than introduce a price floor. Discuss.

5. Who gains and who loses from the imposition of rent controls?

6. Explain why the supply of rented accommodation tends to drop with the imposition of rent controls.

7. Discuss the pros and cons of minimum wage legislation.

Analytical Questions

1. Suppose that both the quantities demanded and supplied of an exclusive French perfume entitled "Eau de Biere" increased with its price. Would there be a surplus or a shortage of this perfume if it was priced above its equilibrium price? What would happen to its price as a result? Does your answer depend on the comparative slopes of the two curves?

2. As in the previous question, suppose that both the quantities demanded and supplied of an exclusive French perfume entitled "Eau de Biere" increased with its price. Imagine that the market price is at equilibrium, and both the demand and supply were to increase. What would happen to its price as a result? Does you answer depend on the comparative size of the increases? Explain. Does your answer depend on which of the two curves is steeper? Explain.

3. Explain clearly why a price ceiling imposed above the equilibrium price is as ineffective as a price floor imposed below the equilibrium price.

4. If the government were to impose a price ceiling on beer, what would happen to the demand for a substitute product like cider? What would happen to the demand for a complementary product like pretzels? Suppose that the government had instead imposed a price floor on beer. What effect would it have on the demands for cider and pretzels?

Numerical Questions

1. Table W3.3 shows the demand and supply per year for freezers in Antarctica. Graph and label the curves and find the equilibrium price. Explain this market verbally.

TABLE W3.3

Price	Quantities Demanded	Price	Quantities Supplied
$200	30	$500	0
300	20	600	10
400	10	700	20
500	0	800	30
600	0	900	40

2. Table W3.4 shows the market for kumquats in Canada.

TABLE W3.4

Price per Kilo	Quantities Demanded	Quantities Supplied
$0.50	100	10
1.00	95	20
1.50	90	30
2.00	85	40
2.50	80	50
3.00	75	60
3.50	70	70
4.00	65	80
4.50	60	90
5.00	55	100

a) What are the equilibrium values of price and quantity?

b) Suppose the government now imposes a price floor on kumquats which is $1 different from the present equilibrium price. What would be the resulting surplus/shortage?

c) Suppose the government instead imposes a price ceiling which is $1 different from the present equilibrium price. What would be the resulting surplus/shortage?

3. Figure W3.8 depicts the international market for the Canadian dollar (priced in terms of the U.S. dollar).

FIGURE W3.8

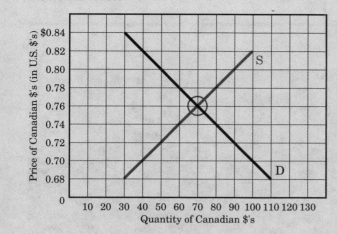

a) Assuming that the market is presently in equilibrium, suppose that the demand increased by $40 billion and the supply by $20 billion. What happens to the value of the Canadian dollar? How many Canadian dollars are now traded?

b) Suppose that the Bank of Canada had fixed the value of the Canadian dollar at its previous equilibrium level so that no one was allowed to trade Canadian dollars at any other price. What would be the surplus/shortage resulting from the increase in demand and supply mentioned in 3a?

4. Figure W3.9 depicts the market for rice in Estudia.

FIGURE W3.9

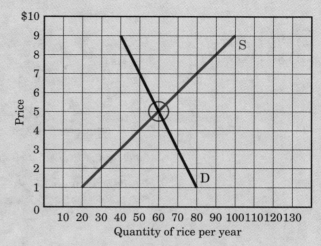

a) Suppose that, in an effort to boost the price of rice for its farmers, the government of Estudia introduces a quota which limits the total amount that farmers can produce to 50 million kilos per year. What is the maximum price at which this quantity could be sold?

b) What would be the result if this government decides, instead of using a quota, to introduce a price floor of $7 per kilo? What difference, if any, is there between the two schemes?

CHAPTER **FOUR**

■ ■ ■ ■ ■ ■ ■ ■

Elasticity

What's ahead . . . This chapter focuses on how consumers respond to a change in the price of any particular good. Such responsiveness is called price elasticity of demand. We begin by showing how the seller's total revenue is directly tied to elasticity. Next, we use the idea of elasticity to analyze four popular myths that are widely held by the general public. Finally, we see how elasticity is also used in the contexts of supply, income and interproduct comparisons.

total revenue: the total amount of income a firm receives from its sales; formally, it is price multiplied by the quantity of the product sold.

Chapter 2 introduced the law of demand and established the inverse relationship between price and quantity. Thus we know that a decrease in the price of, say, an airline ticket from Toronto to Montreal would result in a increase in the quantity of tickets sold. Obviously, this would be beneficial to consumers, but what we have not yet discussed is whether this would or would not be beneficial to the airline company selling the tickets. What is involved here is whether the airline would receive more or less total revenue as a result of selling more tickets at a lower price per ticket. **Total revenue** (TR), not to be confused with total profit, is simply the total dollar value of selling some quantity of an item at a certain price. Formally, it is:

$$TR = P \times Q$$

Here P stands for the price of the product and Q stands for the quantity sold. The effect of lowering price by itself will decrease total revenue. At the same time however, the lower price will result in the quantity sold going up and this will tend to increase total revenue. So what will be the net effect of these opposing pressures? The answer to this question depends on the concept economists call **price elasticity of demand**. The dictionary defines elasticity as "the state of being elastic or flexible" and our focus is on the flexibility of consumers' reactions to a change in price.

price elasticity of demand: the responsiveness of quantity demanded to a change in price.

Price Elasticity of Demand

Price elasticity of demand, which we will simply call elasticity for the time being, can also be defined as a measure of how much quantity demanded changes as a result of a change in price. The measurement of elasticity is obtained by taking the percentage change in quantity and dividing it by the percentage change in price. Note that we use percentage changes because price is expressed in dollars and quantity in units so that using just the absolute change in quantity divided by the absolute change in price would not work. Also, showing elasticity in percentage terms means that we can ignore the units in which the quantity is measured. Let's look at some hypothetical data, shown in Table 4.1.

TABLE 4.1 Demand for Airline Tickets I

Vancouver to Edmonton			Vancouver to Calgary		
Price	Quantity of Tickets	Total Revenue	Price	Quantity of Tickets	Total Revenue
$650	1,000	$650,000	$650	1,000	$650,000
550	1,100	605,000	550	1,250	687,500

Suppose the Vancouver to Edmonton ticket price is $650 and the quantity of tickets sold per day is 1,000. This would yield total revenue to the airline of $650,000 which is the $650 per ticket times 1,000 tickets. Next, assume that the price of a ticket falls to $550. As a result, the quantity of tickets sold rises to 1,100. Total revenue, however, actually *drops* to $605,000 ($550 × 1,100). In constrast, for the Vancouver to Calgary flight the same price change results in quantity rising from 1,000 to 1,250. As a result total revenue also *rises* to $687,500 ($550 × 1,250). From these examples we can conclude that the effect on total revenue can vary greatly depending on how quantity responds to a price change. It also means that one cannot predict the effect on total revenue of a price decrease without knowing how responsive the quantity demanded will be. This is what is meant by the concept of elasticity.

elasticity coefficient: a number that measures the responsiveness of quantity demanded to a change in price.

Let's use the same information in Table 4.1 to do some calculations of elasticity. To obtain what is called the **elasticity coefficient** we use the general equation mentioned above, where elasticity is symbolized by the Greek lower-case letter epsilon, the subscript P indicates that it is the price elasticity of demand that is being referred to and Δ means change in:

$$\in_\rho = \frac{\% \ \Delta \ \text{quantity}}{\% \ \Delta \ \text{price}}$$

To obtain the elasticity coefficient in the Vancouver to Edmonton example, we need to determine the percentage change in quantity as the quantity changes from the original 1,000 to the new 1,100. The absolute increase is 100 and we need to put this 100 over a base to get the percentage increase. This raises the question of whether that base should be the original 1,000 or the new 1,100. Since 100 ÷ 1,000 is 0.1 and 100 ÷ 1,100 is 0.09, it clearly does make a difference as to which base is chosen. To resolve this question we take the *average* of the original base and the new base which, in this case, is the average of 1,000 and 1,100 or 1,050. Thus, the percentage change in quantity is the absolute change of 100 divided by the average base of 1,050 multiplied by 100. (Using this approach ensures that we get the same result if the price goes down from $650 to $550 or up from $550 to $650.) This gives us the figure of 9.5% for the numerator in the above equation. Next we calculate the percentage change in price by dividing the absolute change of $100 by the average base, which is $600 (the sum of $650 + $550 ÷ 2) multiplied by 100 to get 16.7%. Actually, the technical answer is −16.7% but, with appropriate apologies to mathematicians, we simply ignore the negative sign. The reason economists do this is that price and quantity always move in opposite directions and thus *any* calculation of elasticity would result in a negative coefficient. We ignore the minus sign and use only the absolute value of the coefficient for simplicity of presentation. We can now obtain the elasticity coefficient:

$$\in_\rho = \frac{\% \, \Delta \, Q}{\% \, \Delta \, P} = \frac{9.5}{16.7} = 0.57$$

inelastic demand:
quantity demanded that
is not very responsive
to a change in price.

So, the Vancouver to Edmonton market has an elasticity coefficient of 0.57 which is less than 1 and is referred to as **inelastic demand**. This means that the quantity demanded is not very responsive to a price change. Specifically, a 1% change in price leads to only a 0.57% change in quantity. Note that because the demand is inelastic means that total revenue will fall as a result of the decrease in price. In Table 4.1 we saw that total revenue decreases from the original $650,000 to $605,000. We are now able to make our first generalization involving elasticity:

If demand is inelastic, and price falls, then total revenue will also fall.

Let's make the same calculation using the figures in the Vancouver to Calgary example. Here the absolute change in quantity is 250 which we put over the average base of 1,125 multiplied by 100 to get the result of 22.2% and this is the numerator for our equation. To obtain the denominator we put the absolute change in price, $100, over the average base of $600, just as we did above, multiplied by 100 to once again get 16.7%. Here the elasticity coefficient is:

$$\frac{22.2\%}{16.7\%} = 1.32$$

elastic demand:
quantity demanded
that is quite responsive
to a change in price.

The Vancouver to Calgary market, therefore, has an elasticity coefficient of 1.32 which is greater than 1 and is referred to as **elastic demand**. Here, the quantity demanded is much more responsive to a change in price. A 1% change in price leads to a 1.32% change in quantity demanded. Since the increase in quantity, which pushes total revenue up, is stronger than the decrease in price, which pushes total revenue down, we would expect that the net effect will be an increase in total revenue. This is what we have as total revenue increases from the original $650,000 to $687,500. We can now make our second generalization about elasticity:

If demand is elastic, and price falls, then total revenue will rise.

Study Guide

QUESTION 4.1
Below are three sets of prices and their related quantities. Calculate the elasticity coefficients for each set.

	Price	Quantity
Set I	$ 1.50	200
	2.00	100
Set II	120.00	1,600
	100.00	1,800
Set III	18.50	48
	22.50	40

Do we get the same kind of result if the price increases instead of decreases? Let's examine this by going to Table 4.2 in which we see price increasing from the original $650 to $750.

TABLE 4.2 Demand for Airline Tickets II

Vancouver to Edmonton			Vancouver to Calgary		
Price	Quantity	Total Revenue: C	Price	Quantity	Total Revenue: D
$650	1,000	$650,000	$650	1,000	$650,000
750	900	675,000	750	750	567,500

You should be able to verify that the elasticity coefficient in the Vancouver to Edmonton market is 0.74 and in the Vancouver to Calgary market is 2. These figures are different from the coefficients calculated previously, and there is a lesson in this. Moving up or down a demand curve results in the elasticity coefficient changing because the base changes. Note that the elasticity coefficient in the Vancouver to Edmonton example was 0.57 in the $550–$650 price range while it is 0.74 in the $650–$750 price range. This, despite the fact that the absolute change in price is $100 and the absolute change in quantity is 100 tickets in both cases. However, the two bases are not the same. The base quantity in the first instance is 1,050 but is only 950 in the second. Similarly, the base price is $600 in the first instance, but $700 in the second.

Study Guide

QUESTION 4.2

Below are two sets of prices and their related quantities. Calculate the elasticity coefficients for each set.

	Price	Quantity
Set I	$9	1
	8	2
Set II	2	8
	1	9

In each set the change in price is $1 and the change in quantity is 1 unit. Why aren't the coefficients the same?

Despite the difference in elasticity coefficients at different price ranges, one thing remains consistent: the Vancouver to Edmonton market is an example of inelastic demand and the Vancouver to Calgary market is an example of elastic demand. We saw earlier that if price *decreases* and demand is inelastic then total revenue would fall. Thus, we would expect the opposite, a rise in total revenue, if price were to *rise*, and this is exactly what we get as total revenue increases from $650,000 to $675,000.

Similarly, Table 4.1 indicated that if price *falls* and demand is elastic we would experience an increase in total revenue. Thus, we would expect that a price *rise* in combination with elastic demand would cause a decrease in total revenue, and this is exactly what happens in Table 4.2 as total revenue falls from $650,000 to $567,500.

Table 4.3 on the next page summarizes the effect of elasticity on total revenue as a result of a price change.

TABLE 4.3 Relationship between Price and Total Revenue

Elasticity Coefficient	Price	Total Revenue
inelastic (<1)	falls	falls
inelastic (<1)	rises	rises
elastic (>1)	falls	rises
elastic (>1)	rises	falls

We could also summarize the effects of a price change by saying that if the demand is inelastic, price and total revenue move in the same direction. If the demand is elastic, price and total revenue move in opposite directions.

Study Guide

QUESTION 4.3

What would happen to total revenue in each of the circumstances below:
A) $\epsilon > 1$ and price falls?
B) $\epsilon < 1$ and price rises?
C) $\epsilon < 1$ and price falls?
D) $\epsilon > 1$ and price rises?

QUESTION 4.4

Suppose that the price of four different products all increased by 20%. Given the elasticity coefficients shown below, what is the percentage change in the quantity of each product?
A) $\epsilon = 4$.
B) $\epsilon = 0.5$.
C) $\epsilon = 1$.
D) $\epsilon = 0$.

Determinants of Elasticity

Before we examine the determinants of elasticity, let's identify some commodities that typically have elastic demands and some that typically have inelastic demands (see Table 4.4).

TABLE 4.4 Examples of Products with Different Elasticities of Demand

Commodities That Have Elastic Demands	Commodities That Have Inelastic Demands
fresh tomatoes (4.60)	household electricity (.13)
movies (3.41)	eggs (.32)
lamb (2.65)	car repairs (.36)
restaurant meals (1.63)	food (.58)
china and tableware (1.54)	household appliances (.63)
automobiles (1.14)	tobacco (.86)

Source: H.S. Houthakker and Lester D. Taylor, *Consumer Demand in the United States* (Cambridge, Mass.: Harvard University Press, 1970).

A major determinant of elasticity is the *availability of close substitutes*. For example, almost any other vegetable is a substitute for tomatoes in most people's eyes. Home videos and other forms of entertainment are substitutes for movies while pork and beef are close substitutes for lamb. The substitute for a restaurant meal is to cook at home. Many households find that the substitute for furniture or china and tableware is to simply make do with less of what many consider to be non-essential items. Automobiles have the least elastic demand of those on our list because many people do not consider public transit or bicycling to be a close substitute. A clear conclusion comes out of all this:

> The more substitutes available for any particular commodity, the greater is the elasticity of demand for that commodity.

BOX 4.1

It is not uncommon for people to think of products as either luxuries or necessities. There is then a temptation to conclude that luxury products are elastic in demand while necessities must be inelastic. While there is undoubtedly validity in this rule of thumb we must be careful. To some, wine with a meal is an absolute necessity while to others it is a seldom-bought luxury. What is a bottle of brandy — a necessity for evening relaxation or a luxury used only in holiday times? What really matters when we are talking about the elasticity of demand is that normally we are looking at market elasticity, i.e., the preferences of the majority of people.

Let's now go through the list of commodities that have inelastic demands. Candles can be used as a substitute for electric light, but this is not an attractive option to most people. Eggs are an essential ingredient in baking and cooking. The only real substitutes for auto repairs is to repair the car yourself or to buy a new one, and both of these options are impractical most of the time. Food, as a category, has no substitutes. To the users of tobacco, this item involves an addiction to which there is simply no substitute. To most families, significant price swings in household appliances such as a hot water heater will not change the quantity demanded much.

Before leaving this discussion of the availability of substitutes we should note that a great deal depends on how the commodity in question is defined. The demand for food is an example of a broadly defined category and as such it is highly inelastic since there is no substitute for food. Yet the elasticity of demand for any one food item, such as green beans, is much more elastic since there are numerous close substitutes. As another example, the elasticity of demand for housing in general is quite low since all of us have to live somewhere whereas the elasticity of demand for home ownership is much greater since there is the alternative of renting.

A second determinant of elasticity is the *percentage of household income that is spent on the commodity*. In general we can say:

> The larger the percentage of one's income that is spent on a particular commodity, the more elastic is the demand for that commodity.

For this reason the elasticity of demand for a high-priced automobile or for a top-of-the-line stereo system will be high. On the other hand, the elasticity of demand for ordinary spices or hand soap will tend to be inelastic simply because the total percentage of a household's budget that is spent on such items is small.

The third determinant of elasticity involves the *amount of time that has elapsed since the price change*. The classic example here is that of gasoline. When the OPEC oil embargo of 1973 resulted in the halting of (most) oil shipments to North America, the price of gasoline increased four-fold in just 18 months. Measurements of elasticity made over this period of time indicated a very inelastic demand. This was because in the immediate aftermath of such a price shock very few close substitutes to gasoline were available. This fact became much less true as time wore on and a number of substitutes were developed. The most significant of these was the development and marketing of much more fuel-efficient automobiles that became increasingly popular in the later seventies. In addition, given enough time to adjust, people moved closer to their place of employment and the established patterns of driving long distances for a holiday or for a casual visit were changed. Subsequent measurements of the elasticity of demand for gasoline over a time period of 5 or 10 years after the price shock showed elasticity coefficients that were much higher than those taken in the first 18 months. All of this can lead us to conclude the following:

> The elasticity of demand tends to be greater, the longer the time period involved.

A Graphical Representation

What we need to do next is to take this concept of elasticity and give it graphical representation. We will start with Figure 4.1 below.

FIGURE 4.1 The Demand for Airline Tickets: Vancouver to Edmonton

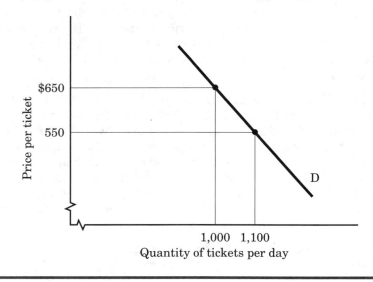

When the price of an airline ticket from Vancouver to Edmonton is $650, 1,000 tickets per day are sold. If the price falls to $550 then the quantity demanded rises to 1,100 tickets.

Using the data from Table 4.1 on page 111, Figure 4.1 shows that a price decrease of $100 in the Edmonton fare results in an increase in the quantity demanded of 100 tickets. You may recall that the elasticity coefficient in this case is 0.57. This indicates that demand is inelastic. This is reflected in the relatively steep demand curve in Figure 4.1. Contrast this demand curve with the one in Figure 4.2 on the next page.

FIGURE 4.2 The Demand for Airline Tickets: Vancouver to Calgary

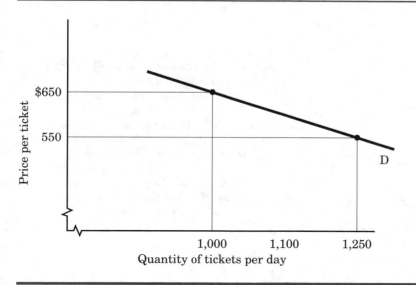

When the price of an airline ticket from Vancouver to Calgary is $650, 1,000 tickets per day are sold. If the price falls to $550, the quantity demanded rises to 1,250 tickets.

Here, using the Vancouver to Calgary data from Table 4.1, the demand curve plots out an increase of 250 tickets demanded as a result of a $100 decrease in price. This is an elastic demand. Notice that the demand curve is not as steep as was the one in Figure 4.1 but is, instead, relatively shallow. Does this mean that all demand curves that appear steep are inelastic and all that appear shallow are elastic — i.e., is there a relationship between the slope of the demand curve and elasticity?

We must be very careful here because the technical answer is no but the practical answer is maybe. To sort this out let us go to Figure 4.3 on page 118.

You may recall from high school math that the slope of any straight line is equal to the rise over run. Note in the demand curve in Figure 4.1 that an increase in price of $1 always results in a quantity decrease of 1. Thus the slope of the above demand curve is constant and equal to 1 (again the negative sign is ignored). Is elasticity also constant? Let's calculate the elasticity coefficient for a movement along the curve first for point *a* to *b* and then for point *c* to *d*. Movement *a* to *b* would yield a coefficient of:

$$\in_{\rho} = \frac{\% \, \Delta \, Q}{\% \, \Delta \, P} = \frac{2/2 \times 100}{2/8 \times 100} = \frac{100\%}{25\%} = 4$$

On the other hand, movement from point *c* to *d* would yield:

$$\in_{\rho} = \frac{2/8 \times 100}{2/2 \times 100} = \frac{25\%}{100\%} = 0.25$$

Quite clearly the elasticity coefficient is different at different points on the demand curve. Thus, it must be concluded that slope and elasticity are *not* the same thing.

FIGURE 4.3 A Constant-Slope Demand Curve

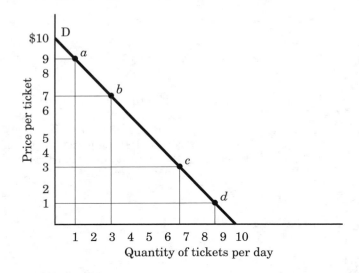

Both of the movements *a* to *b* and *c* to *d* involve a change in price of $2 and a change in quantity of 2 units. Yet, the elasticity coefficient for the *a* to *b* movement is much larger than that for the *c* to *d* movement. Since the slope of this demand curve is constant and the elasticity is not, we can conclude that slope and elasticity are not the same concepts.

QUESTION 4.5

Imagine that elasticity coefficients were recently measured in Canada over a period of one year for the following products. Indicate whether you think such a measurement would be elastic (>1) or inelastic (<1) demand.

A) Sugar   D) Restaurant meals
B) Gasoline   E) Women's hats
C) Ocean cruises F) Alcohol

There is more that we can learn from a simple demand curve such as that shown in Figure 4.3. Let's calculate, in Table 4.5, the total revenue associated with each price.

TABLE 4.5 Demand and Total Revenue Schedule

Price	Quantity	Total Revenue
$10	1	10
9	2	18
8	3	24
7	4	28
6	5	30
5	6	30
4	7	28
3	8	24
2	9	18
1	10	10

Notice how total revenue *rises* as price decreases from $10 to a price of $6. Since price is falling, and total revenue is rising, we know this means that demand must be elastic. Further, as price continues to fall from $5 to $1, total revenue *falls* indicating that demand is inelastic in this range of the demand curve. The price/quantity combinations of $5 and 6 units along with $6 and 5 units are also of particular interest because total revenue is the same $30, which is maximum revenue.

It is also evident that this $6/$5 price range is the midpoint of the demand curve. This is no coincidence. If total revenue ceases to rise as price falls, we can no longer be on the elastic portion of the demand curve. If total revenue has not yet begun to fall as price decreases, we cannot yet be on the inelastic portion of the demand curve. Thus, if demand is no longer >1 and not yet <1 then it can only be exactly equal to 1. From this we can conclude that the upper one-half of any straight-line demand curve is elastic and the lower one-half is inelastic while the midpoint is where we experience what is called **unitary elasticity**. This can be defined as the point where the percentage change in quantity is exactly equal to percentage change in price, and thus total revenue does not change.

unitary elasticity: where the elasticity coefficient is equal to one, i.e., where the percentage change in quantity is exactly equal to the percentage change in price.

We can now give a practical answer to the question that we asked above concerning the relationship between the slope of a demand curve and the elasticity. When we look at a shallow sloped demand curve as in Figure 4.4 below, what we are looking at is the upper half of what would be a much longer curve if it were extended all the way to the horizontal axis of the graph.

FIGURE 4.4 An Elastic and an Inelastic Demand Curve

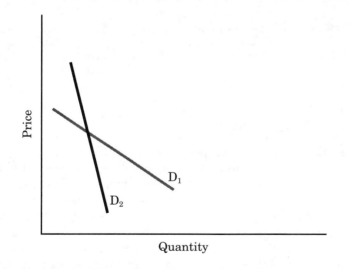

Demand curve D_1 is the elastic (upper) portion of a curve that could be extended downwards while D_2 is the inelastic (lower) portion of demand curve that could be extended upwards.

Since the upper half of any straight-line demand curve is the elastic portion, we can look at D_1 and say that it is an elastic demand curve even though we know that the lower half of the curve (most of which we do not see) is the inelastic portion. Similarly, when we look at D_2 we are looking at the lower portion of a much longer demand curve, and this lower portion is inelastic.

In summary, one can make some implications about elasticity from the appearance of a demand curve but we must remain aware that slope and elasticity are not the same thing.

QUESTION 4.6

Price	Quantity
1	18
2	16
3	14
4	12
5	10
6	8
7	6
8	4
9	2

A) Graph a demand curve using the data from the demand schedule above.

B) What is the slope of this demand curve?

C) How could you demonstrate that the elasticity of demand was not the same as the slope?

BOX 4A

1. How is *total revenue* calculated?
2. Write the formula used to calculate *price elasticity of demand*.
3. Distinguish between *inelastic* and *elastic* demand.
4. List the three determinants of elasticity.
5. Is it valid to say that the slope and the elasticity of a demand curve are the same things? Why or why not?
6. Define *unitary elasticity*.

Applications of Price Elasticity of Demand

Myth One: The Consumer Always Pays a Sales Tax

Sales taxes can take the form of a tax imposed by (federal or provincial) governments on a *specific* product such as alcohol, gasoline or a movie ticket (these are often referred to as excise taxes). Sales taxes can also take the form of a *general* tax on a wide category of goods as in the case of the GST. It is the seller who is, by law, responsible for collecting these taxes and actually sending the money to the government. But who really pays these taxes — the sellers or the consumers? Most people believe it is the consumer since they assume that the seller simply adds whatever amount the tax might be on to the price of the product and thus passes the tax on to the buyer. Is this correct?

We can use basic supply and demand analysis and the concept of elasticity of demand to answer this question. In Figure 4.5 we show the demand and supply curves, D_1 and S_1, for movie tickets before the imposition of an excise tax. The equilibrium price initially is $6 and the equilibrium quantity is 10 million tickets per month.

Now let's look at the effect on both equilibrium price and quantity of a $2 per ticket excise tax. The effect on the supply curve would be to shift it up by the same $2 which gives us the new supply curve S_t. The reason for this

FIGURE 4.5 The Effect of an Excise Tax on the Price and Quantity of Movie Tickets

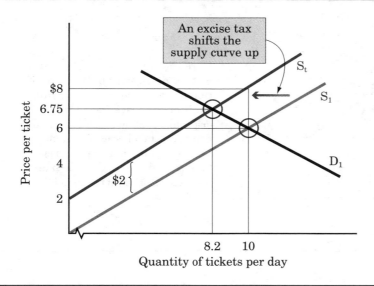

The effect of a $2 per ticket excise tax is to shift the supply curve up from S₁ to Sₜ. The result is that equilibrium price increases from $6 to $6.75 and equilibrium quantity decreases from 10 million to 8.2 million tickets per week.

is that it is the seller who must actually send payment to the government. Movie-house owners were previously willing to supply 10 million tickets per month at a price of $6. If they must now pay the government $2 for each ticket sold, they must collect $8 per ticket in order for them to continue to be willing to supply the same 10 million tickets. The same reasoning would apply to any price (not just $6) and so we get the supply shifting up by the amount of the tax — $2.

After the shift in the supply curve, we have a new equilibrium price of $6.75 and a new equilibrium quantity of 8.2 million tickets per month. Thus, the $2 per ticket excise tax increases equilibrium price from the original $6 to $6.75 and it is the consumer that pays an extra $0.75 (or 37.5% of the $2) and the seller must be paying $1.25 (or 62.5%).

But why does the price not simply increase from $6 to $8? The answer is that while movie-house owners will continue to supply 10 million seats per week just as they did before, moviegoers are simply not going to attend in the same numbers as they did before the price increase. The theatre owners will be forced to reduce the price until the number of empty seats is reduced. In our example, a new equilibrium will not occur until the price is reduced to $6.75.

But does the seller always pay the bigger part of an excise tax? Not at all. We got this particular result because we assumed that the demand for movie tickets is elastic and drew our demand curve accordingly. If demand was inelastic, we would have obtained a different result. We can see this in Figure 4.6 on the next page where D₁, S₁ and Sₜ are all exactly the same as they were in Figure 4.5 and the much more inelastic D₂ is added.

If the relevant demand curve is D₂ rather than D₁, then the equilibrium price, after the imposition of the tax, will be $7.50. In this case the consumer would be paying 75% of the excise tax ($1.50 of the $2) and the seller only 25% ($0.50).

FIGURE 4.6 The Effect of an Excise Tax on Two Different Demand Curves

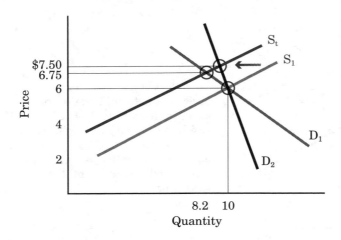

Here the supply curve shifts from S_1 to S_t as a result of the imposition of an excise tax. As a result, equilibrium price rises from the original $6. How much it rises depends on the elasticity of demand. In the case of D_1, the price rises to $6.75. In the case of the more inelastic D_2 the increase is $7.50.

We can generalize to say:

The more inelastic the demand for a product, the larger the percentage of an excise tax the consumer will pay.

Another way to look at this is that since there are few substitutes for products with inelastic demand, the higher price will not have a big effect on consumers as would be the case if demand was elastic, and they will be more willing to pay a higher price.

We will be able to expand this generalization somewhat later in this chapter after our discussion of supply elasticity.

QUESTION 4.7
Given the data below:

Price	Demand (D_1)	Supply (S_1)	Supply (tax)
$3	80	40	_____
$4	70	50	_____
$5	60	60	_____
$6	50	70	_____
$7	40	80	_____

A) What are equilibrium price and quantity assuming demand schedule D_1 and supply schedule S_1?
B) Fill in the blanks in the Supply (tax) column assuming that a $2 per unit excise tax was placed on this product.
C) What is the new equilibrium price and quantity after the imposition of the tax?
D) What proportion of the tax is paid by the consumer and what proportion is paid by the seller in this case?
E) Draw D_1, S_1 and S_t and verify your answers above.

Myth Two: Increasing the Tax on Products like Cigarettes and Alcohol Will Increase the Government's Tax Revenue

Most of you are probably aware that both the federal and the provincial governments apply very heavy excise taxes on tobacco and alcohol products. The reason for this is that these products have very inelastic demands. As we have seen, this means that the quantity purchased decreases by a smaller percentage than the price increases (because of a tax increase). Figure 4.7 below uses cigarettes to illustrate the effect of an increase in the per-pack tax rate on the governments' tax revenue.

FIGURE 4.7 The Effect of a Higher Cigarette Tax on Government Tax Revenues

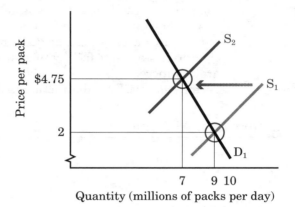

Assume that a $1 per-pack excise tax on cigarettes results in an equilibrium price of $2 and a quantity of 9 million packs per day. This results in government tax revenue of $9 million. Over a period of years the excise tax rose to $4 per pack which resulted in an equilibrium price of $4.75 per pack and an equilibrium quantity of 7 million. This gave governments $28 million in tax revenue ($4 per pack times 7 million packs).

Let's begin our analysis by assuming a $1 per-pack excise tax and an equilibrium price of $2 and a quantity of 9 million packs. The tax revenue of the government therefore is $9 million per day. Since the demand for cigarettes is inelastic we know that a rise in the tax on cigarettes, and thus in their price, would result in the quantity demanded falling proportionately less than the price increase so that the total tax revenue would rise. Revenue hungry governments in Canada used this fact extensively to raise their tax revenues by increasing the per-pack tax on cigarettes again and again throughout the 1970s and 1980s. Eventually, this excise tax reached, say, $4 per pack. Given the resulting higher price for cigarettes, some smokers tried to cut down on the amount they smoked, and others became non-smokers and so the quantity demanded dropped to, say, 7 million packs per day, but still tax revenues were up to $28 million per day ($4 per-pack tax times 7 million packs).

The lesson in all this is rather simple. Governments can put an excise tax on any product, and if that product has an inelastic demand, it will lead to an increase in their tax revenue. The other side of the coin is that putting an excise tax on so-called luxury products that have elastic demands won't raise much revenue because the effect of the tax on the quantity demanded will be significant. Thus, governments seldom try to tax things like luxury automobiles or yachts but instead stick to products which have inelastic demands such as cigarettes, alcohol and gasoline.

Continuing our story about cigarettes, governments sometimes discover, to their peril, that there is a limit to the price increases (caused by the tax increases) that consumers will tolerate. In the case of Canadian cigarettes many smokers continued to smoke even after many tax increases but they also began to look for alternatives. Eventually an alternative appeared. Canadian-made cigarettes which are exported to the United States are subject to much lower excise taxes and can be bought much cheaper in the U.S. Once the difference in the price of Canadian-made cigarettes in Canada compared to the U.S. became large enough, smuggled Canadian cigarettes began showing up back in Canada. Thus, while Canadians continued to consume more or less the same quantity of cigarettes, their purchases of legal cigarettes started to fall significantly while their purchases of smuggled cigarettes increased considerably. In effect, the demand for legal cigarettes became *elastic*. This distinction is illustrated in Figure 4.8.

FIGURE 4.8 The Demand for All Cigarettes and the Demand for Legal Cigarettes

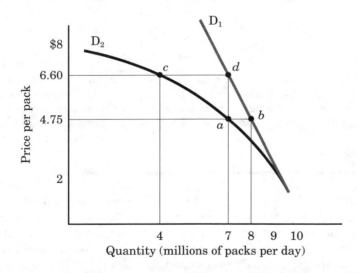

D_1 is the demand for all cigarettes while D_2 is the demand for legal cigarettes. At a price of $4.75 per pack, there was only minimal smuggling as represented by distance ab. However, tax increases slowly increased the price to $6.60 and led to an increase in the amount of smuggled cigarettes being purchased as represented by distance cd. The result was that the government was levying a higher tax on an increasingly diminishing quantity of legal cigarettes.

At lower prices there is no need to distinguish between the demand for cigarettes overall (D_1) and the demand for legal cigarettes (D_2). However, the continued increase in the price of cigarettes, due to the increase in the excise tax on cigarettes, created a divergence between the demand for all cigarettes and the demand for legal cigarettes. We saw that at $4.75 the quantity demanded of legal cigarettes was 7 million packs per day. This resulted in government tax revenues of $28 (7 million packs times $4 per pack). Then the excise tax rose again and the price was driven up to $6.60. At this point the difference between the $6.60 legal price in Canada and the price of Canadian cigarettes in the United States widened considerably. As a result, smuggling increased as represented by the distance cd on Figure 4.8. In addition, government tax revenues fell to $21 million a day (3.5 million packs times $6 per pack).

In the meantime more and more illegal cigarettes began to be openly sold in defiance of the law. Governments felt they had to do something to stem the tide of smuggled cigarettes. They had three options: put a tax of equal size on Canadian cigarettes exported to the U.S.; hire a small army of border police to enforce the anti-smuggling laws; or reduce the incentive to smuggle. Option one was rejected because the Canadian tobacco industry had made it clear that if the government took this action they would have no reason to continue to produce cigarettes in Canada and would therefore shift their operations out of the country. It was not at all clear that option two would work. That left option three, which was to reduce the incentive to smuggle by lowering the tax on cigarettes and therefore reducing the gap between the price of legal cigarettes and smuggled ones.

Some observers, using standard elasticity analysis, predicted that this would lower the tax revenue of government. Let's go to Figure 4.9 to examine what, in fact, really happened.

FIGURE 4.9 The Effect on Tax Revenue of an Excise Tax Reduction on Cigarettes

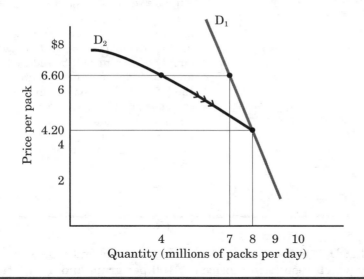

Reducing the excise tax decreased the price of cigarettes to approximately $4.20 and increased the quantity demanded to 8 million packs per day. At this price, the incentive to smuggle was greatly reduced so that cigarette smuggling was virtually eliminated. Thus, we assume that all of the 8 million packs per day sold were legal cigarettes. The government's tax revenue rose to $28 million ($3.50 times 8 million) which is higher than it was when the tax rate was $6 a pack.

Tax reductions reduced the excise tax to $3.50. This also reduced equilibrium price to $4.20 and increased equilibrium quantity to 8 million packs per day. The governments' tax revenue would then be $28 million per day up from the $21 million when the excise tax was at the higher $6 per pack.

We are able to make a rather unpredictable conclusion from all this. For years, governments were able to raise tax revenues by raising the tax rate on cigarettes, but they did it so often that smuggling became established with the result that tax revenues fell significantly. At this point the way to get revenues back up was not to increase the tax rates but, instead, to *lower* them.

Myth Three: A War on Drugs Will Reduce Crime

Most people feel that crime rates in our society are high, and seem to continue to rise year after year. Furthermore, the effects of crime appear to be spreading into the middle class of our society and are no longer confined to the underworld. The mood of the general public is becoming more intolerant of all this and some politicians are responding by calling for tougher laws against criminal activity. The criminal activity that often gets targeted in any get-tough-on-crime campaign is the selling of illegal drugs such as cocaine and heroin.

What is ignored in any such anti-crime policy is the fact that heroin and cocaine have highly inelastic price elasticities of demand. This has serious consequences when we consider that if the anti-crime policy is effective, the supply of illegal drugs will be reduced but not eliminated. This is illustrated in Figure 4.10 below.

FIGURE 4.10 The Cocaine Market

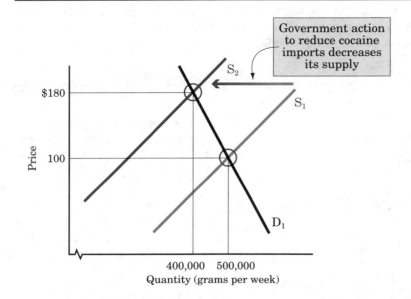

If D_1 and S_1 are the demand and supply curves for cocaine, the equilibrium price and quantity will be $100 per gram and 500,000 grams per week. One outcome of an effective campaign against the drug trade is that the supply of cocaine will be reduced and the supply curve will shift to the left as in S_2. This will greatly increase price (e.g., to $180) since, when demand is inelastic, a reduction in supply has a far greater impact on the price than on the quantity.

Let's assume that D_1 is the (inelastic) demand for cocaine and that S_1 is the original supply which results in a price of $100 per gram and a quantity traded of 500,000 grams per week. Next, let's assume that the government launches a campaign to crack down on drug imports with the result that the supply decreases, as illustrated by the curve shifting back to S_2. This causes the price of cocaine to rise to $180 per gram while the quantity demanded decreases to 400,000 grams per week.

What is important in all this is the amount that is spent by the consumers of cocaine in the two instances. When the price is $100 per gram, a total of $50 million per week is spent ($100 × 500,000) while $72 million is spent after the rise in price caused by the decrease in supply ($180 × 400,000). A large percentage of this money is obtained by the users of cocaine through various types of crime such as robberies, car thefts, muggings and hold-ups as well as white-collar crimes such as embezzlement. In our example, $22 million more per week is spent on cocaine than before the decrease in supply. We would have to conclude that it is highly likely that more crime will be committed to obtain these additional funds.

What we are left with is the seeming paradox that the anti-crime policy has, in fact, lead to an increase in the incidence of crime. This is perhaps an insight into why crime seems to continue to rise despite (or because of?) our anti-crime policies and the efforts of our police.

Myth Four: A Bumper Harvest is Good News for Farmers

A bumper harvest is one where crop yields per hectare are high and farmers are able to bring large quantities of what they grow to market. For example, a typical wheat farmer might harvest 25,000 bushels in a bumper year while an average harvest would be only 20,000 bushels. Wouldn't this be cause for celebration on the part of the farmer? The answer is no and the reason, again, involves the price elasticity of demand.

The elasticity of demand for some agricultural products is certainly elastic — tomatoes, lettuce and plums for example — since there are many close substitutes available. However, the elasticity of demand for the more basic commodities such as wheat is inelastic.

If we combine an inelastic demand with the fact that a bumper harvest would increase supply and shift the supply curve to the right and thus decrease price, the total revenue that would flow to the farmers as a group would decline. This is illustrated in Figure 4.11.

FIGURE 4.11 The Effect of a Bumper Harvest on the Wheat Market

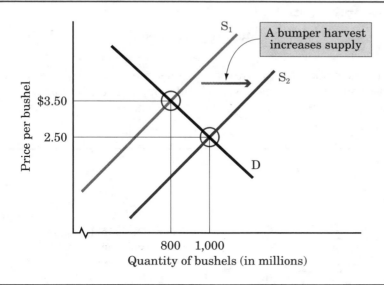

A bumper harvest increases the supply of wheat and shifts the supply curve from S_1 to S_2. Given the inelastic demand for wheat, the decrease in price is substantial and the total revenue going to farmers as a group decreases.

In Figure 4.11, we assume that the normal-year equilibrium price and quantity is $3.50 per bushel and 800 million bushels. This would give wheat farmers total revenue of $2,800,000,000. In the bumper-harvest year the supply curve shifts to the right and the new equilibrium price and quantity is $2.50 and 1,000 million bushels. This results in price dropping far more than the quantity increases so that the total revenue decreases to $2,500,000,000. The bumper harvest results in farmers losing $300,000,000 in revenue. This illustrates the old adage that farmers ask the gods for a poor harvest — for everyone except themselves.

Study Guide

QUESTION 4.8
Given the data below:

Demand (D_1) per Week	Price per Unit	Supply (S_1) per Week
2,000,000	$260	800,000
1,800,000	320	1,200,000
1,600,000	380	1,600,000
1,400,000	440	2,000,000
1,200,000	500	2,400,000

A) What is the equilibrium price and quantity?
B) What is the total expenditure at equilibrium?
C) If the supply was increased by 50% what would be the new equilibrium price and quantity?
D) What is the total expenditure at this new equilibrium?
E) What is the price elasticity of demand between these two equilibrium points?

Elasticity of Supply

supply elasticity: the change in the quantity supplied as a result of a change in price.

The concept of elasticity can be applied to supply as well as to demand. The definition of **supply elasticity** is:

$$\in_s = \frac{\% \, \Delta \text{ quantity supplied}}{\% \, \Delta \text{ price}}$$

As we did with the demand curve, we can make some generalizations about the elasticity of supply from the position and slope of the curve as seen in Figure 4.12.

FIGURE 4.12 Supply Elasticity

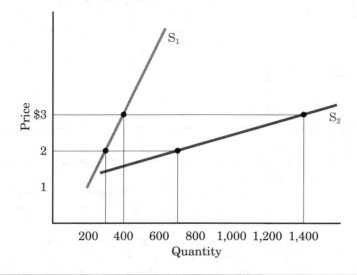

Supply curve S_1 is inelastic as can be seen from the fact that only a small quantity change results from the price increasing from $2 to $3. S_2, on the other hand, is an elastic supply curve since quantity doubles (from 700 to 1,400) as a result of the same price increase.

Here, we have two supply curves, S_1 and S_2, and a common price change from $2 to $3. In the case of supply curve S_1, the quantity supplied rises from 300 to 400, while in the case of supply curve S_2 the quantity supplied doubles from 700 to 1,400. We can therefore legitimately conclude that the supply elasticity of S_2 must be larger than that in S_1. This allows us to generalize that the supply elasticity of more shallow curves is greater than that of steeper curves, although we again caution that elasticity does change as we move along any supply curve, just as it did in the case of the demand curve. Given that producers would like to increase the quantity they supply as much as they can in response to an increase in price, what might explain the kind of difference in response indicated by S_1 and S_2? The first possible explanation involves the level of technology in use. If it is a sophisticated technology, such as one that requires complicated tool and die making, then S_1 is probably more representative. The use of a very simple technology, such as in cardboard carton production, would more likely be represented by S_2. Implied in this explanation, however, is an even more important determinant of supply elasticity, and that is the time frame involved.

QUESTION 4.9
Calculate the price elasticity of supply in the $2 to $3 range for both supply curves S_1 and S_2 in Figure 4.12.

Alfred Marshall recognized the importance of time in the determination of supply elasticity with his fish market example. In Figure 4.13A we see a

FIGURE 4.13 Supply Elasticity in Three Time Periods

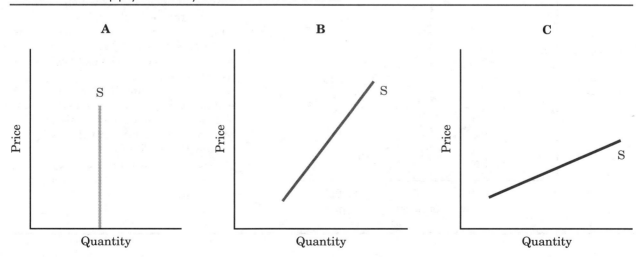

Supply is perfectly inelastic in A. Marshall called this the momentary market. In B, the short run, supply is still inelastic but not perfectly inelastic. In C, the long run, supply is elastic.

perfectly inelastic supply curve representing what Marshall called the momentary market period but is now usually referred to simply as the market period. As an example, he talked about the day's fish catch, in the quantity of Q_1, having been landed at the docks. This is all the fish that will be supplied until the next day (momentary supply) no matter how high the price might go. Marshall called the supply curve S_2 in Figure 4.13B the short-run supply curve, which is more elastic than S_1 and is reflective of the various responses that fishers might be able to make in the short run to a higher price. This might include putting on extra crew, staying out longer or repairing nets. The supply curve in Figure 4.13C is the long-run supply curve reflecting adjustments to higher price such as training additional crew and building more boats which could take a number of months or years to accomplish.

From Marshall's fish market example we can conclude that:

> The longer the time frame involved, the more elastic will be the supply curve.

Ticket Scalping An interesting application of supply elasticity involves the activity around any popular event, such as a playoff hockey game or a high-profile concert, where only a limited number of tickets are available for sale. In this case, the owners of the home team (or the promoters of the event) must set the price per ticket in advance trying to estimate, as best they can, what the demand for the event will be. Figure 4.14 below gives us three possible outcomes.

FIGURE 4.14 Perfectly Inelastic Supply

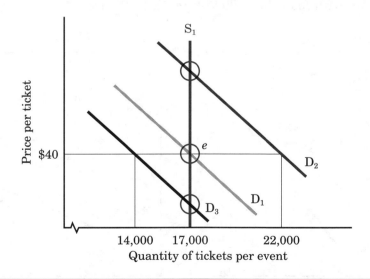

A concert hall or hockey rink has a fixed number of seats which gives us the perfectly inelastic supply curve S_1. Here, the price per seat is preset at $40. If demand turns out to be exactly as indicated by D_1 this $40 price will be equilibrium. If, however, demand turns out to be higher than anticipated (D_2) 5,000 people who wanted a ticket will have to do without. Finally, if demand proves to be that represented by D_3, there will be unsold seats for the event.

The fact that there is only a limited number of tickets for sale results in the supply curve being perfectly inelastic as reflected by S_1. Now assume that the price, which must be fixed before the tickets go on sale, is set at $40. If the demand for tickets to this event happens to be that represented by D_1 then we would have equilibrium with 17,000 tickets sold. If instead demand turns out to be higher as represented by D_2 the general public will wish to buy 5,000 more tickets than are available for sale. These are the circumstances of a shortage that ticket scalpers thrive on. Such individuals will get into the line to buy tickets as early as possible and then buy as many tickets as they can so that they can later resell them at a higher price. Whether such activity is or is not legal varies from province to province in Canada but undoubtedly goes on everywhere.

Does the activity of scalping tickets always pay off? The answer is clearly no if both the ticket-price setters, and the scalper overestimate the demand. This situation is represented by D_3 in Figure 4.14 above. Here 3,000 tickets will remain unsold and the scalper will have no option but to dump the $40 tickets at a greatly reduced price. This probably does not often happen however since there is evidence that event organizers prefer to set the official price a little below what they think they could sell at in order to reap the publicity that results when there are big line-ups for tickets. In any case it is clear that the phenomenon of a perfectly inelastic supply curve and a fixed preset price does generate some interesting twists in our analysis.

Study Guide

QUESTION 4.10
Leonard Cohen is scheduled to perform at Centennial Hall which seats 5,000. Ticket prices for this one-night concert are set at $50 each and go on sale two weeks in advance.
A) Draw a graph that includes both a supply and a demand curve which indicates the circumstances of many more than 5,000 people wanting a ticket.
B) Add to the same graph a curve which illustrates the fact that Cohen's agent announces a second concert on the night following the first one.
C) Is it possible that, after announcing the second concert, the $50 ticket price is an equilibrium price?

Income Elasticity

As we have seen, the concept of price elasticity of demand involves the responsiveness of the quantity demanded to a change in price. Another important idea is the responsiveness of quantity demanded to a change in income which is called **income elasticity** of demand. In the case of price elasticity, our measurement involves moving up or down on a single demand curve as illustrated in Figure 4.15A on page 132, while income elasticity involves the whole demand curve shifting since, as you recall from Chapter 2, a change in income causes a change in demand.

income elasticity: the responsiveness of quantity demanded to a given change in income.

The increase in the quantity demanded in Figure 4.15B is a result of the shift in the demand curve from D_1 to D_2, and the higher the income elasticity the greater will be this shift.

The mechanics of measurement of the coefficient of income elasticity are quite analogous to that of price elasticity:

$$\in_Y = \frac{\% \text{ change in quantity}}{\% \text{ change in income}}$$

FIGURE 4.15 Price Elasticity and Income Elasticity

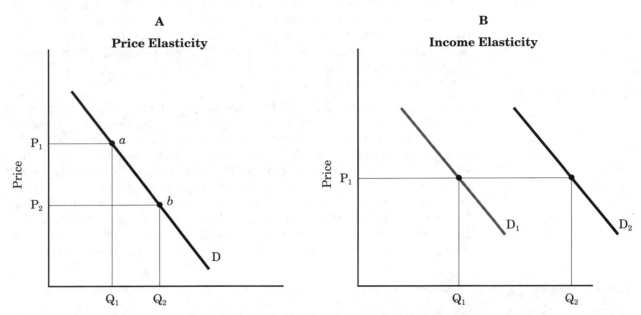

In 4.15A the movement along the demand curve from point *a* to point *b* involves the price elasticity of demand. In contrast, income elasticity of demand involves a shift in the demand curve such as D_1 to D_2 in 4.15B.

Once again, if this coefficient turns out to be greater than 1 the demand is said to be income elastic, and if it turns out to be less than 1 but greater than 0 we use the term income inelastic. Examples of products that tend to be income elastic are air travel, restaurant meals, hairstyling services and private swimming pools. Examples of products that tend to be income inelastic are tobacco, food, newspapers and telephone hook-ups (not long distance calling).

If these examples suggest to you that the distinction between products that are income elastic and income inelastic is one of luxuries and necessities, you are correct. Households with limited income tend to buy only necessities. If the household's income rises, almost all of that additional income would be spent on the luxuries that previously could not be purchased. An undeniable characteristic of a postindustrial economy is one where the percentage of total consumption on services rises while that of physical goods declines. This is a reflection of the fact that most people consider services such as travel, dining out, and hiring a gardener as little ways that they might give themselves a treat, and this kind of expenditure undoubtedly becomes a greater part of one's total expenditures as income rises.

Most products, be they income elastic or inelastic, have an income elasticity coefficient that is greater than zero and are therefore the normal products that were defined in Chapter 2. However, inferior goods do exist and here the quantity demanded of the product actually declines in response to an increase in income and, therefore, the income elasticity coefficient is negative. Staple foods such as rice, flour and cabbage are the most likely candidates for examples of inferior goods. Imagine a family so poor that rice is eaten three times a day. This family then experiences a rise in income. It is feasible that this family may in fact consume less rice (and greater quantities of more expensive foodstuffs) as a result. If the experience of this hypothetical family was typical of the families in society generally, rice would be an inferior good and conform to our definition of negative income elasticity.

QUESTION 4.11
Given the following data and assuming that the price of X and Y do not change:

Income	Quantity Demanded of X	Income	Quantity Demanded of Y
$10,000	200	$50,000	50
15,000	350	60,000	54

A) Calculate the income elasticity for products X and Y.
B) Are products X and Y both normal goods?

Cross-elasticity of Demand

cross-elasticity of demand: the responsiveness of the change in the quantity demanded of product A to a change in the price of product B.

Finally, in addition to price elasticity of demand, income elasticity and supply elasticity we also have the concept of **cross-elasticity of demand**. Here we are comparing the quantity response in one product, A, to a change in the price of another product, B. The formal definition is:

$$\in_{AB} = \frac{\% \, \Delta \text{ quantity demanded of product A}}{\% \, \Delta \text{ price of product B}}$$

Consider the two products, butter and margarine. An increase in the price of margarine will lead to an increase in the demand for butter as indicated in Table 4.6 below.

TABLE 4.6 Cross-elasticity of Margarine and Butter

Margarine		Butter	
Price	Quantity Demanded per Week (lbs.)	Price	Quantity Demanded per Week (lbs.)
$1.50	5,000	$3.00	1,000
2.10	3,200	3.00	2,000

Given the data in Table 4.6 it seems clear that the increase in the quantity demanded of butter is the result of the change in the price of margarine. The cross-elasticity of demand of butter for margarine therefore is:

$$\in_{AB} = \frac{\dfrac{+1,000}{1,500}}{\dfrac{+0.60}{1.80}} \times 100 = \frac{+67\%}{+33\%} = +2$$

When we are looking at cross-elasticity the sign of the coefficient is important. The fact that the coefficient is a positive number verifies that these two goods are substitutes and reinforces something that we learned in

Chapter 2, i.e., a rise in the price of a substitute product (margarine) will increase the demand of the product in question (butter).

It stands to reason that if substitute products have a positive cross-elasticity then complementary products will have a negative cross-elasticity. We can easily verify this. What would you expect to happen to the demand for film as a result of a price *decrease* in the price of cameras? Surely, it would *increase* and as a result the cross elasticity calculation between the two would have a negative sign as we would expect in the case of complementary products.

As we have seen, elasticity is a concept with wide application and one that extends our understanding of supply/demand analysis in many useful ways.

QUESTION 4.12
Given the following data:

Year	Income	Price of X	Quantity of X Demanded	Price of Y	Quantity of Y Demanded
1	$50,000	$200	80	$ 50	300
2	50,000	225	70	50	280
3	50,000	225	60	75	250
4	60,000	225	70	75	260
5	70,000	250	50	100	200

A) Calculate the price elasticity of demand for product X for years 1 and 2.
B) Calculate the income elasticity of product Y for years 3 and 4.
C) Calculate the cross-elasticity of demand of product X for Y for years 2 and 3.
D) Is it possible to calculate the price elasticity of demand for products X and Y between years 4 and 5?

BOX 4B
1. How would you show the effect of a new excise tax on a supply and demand graph?
2. If the government increases the excise tax on a product whose demand is inelastic, what would happen to tax revenues?
3. If the supply of a product decreases and its demand is inelastic, what happens to total expenditures on the product?
4. Define *elasticity of supply*. What determines the elasticity of supply?
5. What is the difference between Marshall's momentary market, short-run supply and his long-run supply?
6. What is unique about supply/demand analysis as it applies to an event such as a one-night concert by a well-known rock group?
7. Define *income elasticity*.
8. What is the difference between a *normal good* and an *inferior good*?
9. What is the formula for *cross-elasticity of demand*.

Chapter Highlights

This chapter examines the concept of elasticity by first focusing on the price elasticity of demand and emphasizing its relationship with the sellers' total revenue. It is stressed that the effect of a price change on the sellers' total revenue depends on whether the demand for the product is elastic or inelastic. This is followed by a discussion of the three primary determinants of the elasticity of demand for any given product which are the availability of close substitutes, the percentage of household income that is spent on the commodity and the amount of time that has elapsed since a price change.

The concept of elasticity is then presented in graphical terms and here it is stressed that the slope of a demand curve and its elasticity are not the same things.

Next comes a discussion of four myths that are designed to illustrate some applications of price elasticity of demand. These myths centre on the question of who pays a sales tax, the issue of the government taxing cigarettes, the effects of a war-on-drugs policy and the effect of a bumper harvest for farmers.

Supply elasticity is then introduced and the point is made that its primary determinant is the amount of time under consideration. Next is a ticket scalping example which is an application of the case of perfectly inelastic supply. The chapter concludes with a discussion of income elasticity and cross-elasticity of demand.

New Glossary Terms

Workbook

Study Tips

1. It may be helpful to think of elasticity as a concept that measures the responsiveness of one variable to a change in a related variable. As a way of summary, you can think of the most common application being the responsiveness of quantity demanded to a change in price, which is called price elasticity of demand or, simply, demand elasticity.

2. Bear in mind that the concept of elasticity can also be applied to the ways that a change in income or a change in the price of a related good affects the quantity demanded of a particular product. Similarly, it can be applied to the way a change in price affects quantity supplied. These applications are called income elasticity; cross-elasticity (of demand) and supply elasticity.

3. You must learn the formulas for calculating elasticities in the same way you learned your phone number — use them until they stick. The recipe card suggestion made earlier would really work here.

4. Since elasticity involves price and quantity, it also directly relates to a seller's total revenue. The effect of a price increase on total revenue will be to either increase or decrease it depending on elasticity. The same can be said for a price decrease. The exact relationships are, again, something you simply have to memorize.

5. The power of the concept of elasticity is illustrated in the analysis of the four myths presented in the chapter. If you follow the arguments in each of these, you can be reasonably assured that you have the basic idea in hand.

Are You Sure?

Indicate whether the following statements are true or false. If false, indicate why they are false.

1. A firm's total revenue is equal to price times demand.

T or **F**   If false: _____

_____

_____

2. The price elasticity of demand coefficient is, technically, always negative but for convenience economists ignore the minus sign.
T or **F**   If false: _____

_____

_____

3. If demand is inelastic, and price falls, then total revenue will rise.
T or **F**   If false: _____

_____

_____

4. If price rises and demand is elastic, the seller would experience an increase in total revenue.
T or **F**   If false: _____

_____

_____

5. If the elasticity coefficient is equal to one and the price rises then total revenue would also rise.
T or **F**   If false: _____

_____

_____

6. A primary determinant of demand elasticity is the number of complementary products available.
T or **F**   If false: _____

_____

_____

7. A straight-lined (constant-sloped) demand curve does not imply constant elasticity.
T or **F** If false: _____

_____

_____

8. Supply elasticity is measured by: percentage change in quantity supplied divided by percentage change in quantity demanded.
T or **F** If false: _____

_____

_____

9. If a calculation of cross-elasticity of demand is positive, we could conclude that the two products are substitutes.
T or **F** If false: _____

_____

_____

10. If income elasticity is positive, we could conclude that the product in question is an inferior good.
T or **F** If false: _____

_____

_____

Translations

Describe in words the demand curve illustrated in Figure W4.1. Include in your answer reference to elasticity and to the revenue of the seller(s).

_____

_____

_____

_____

_____

FIGURE W4.1

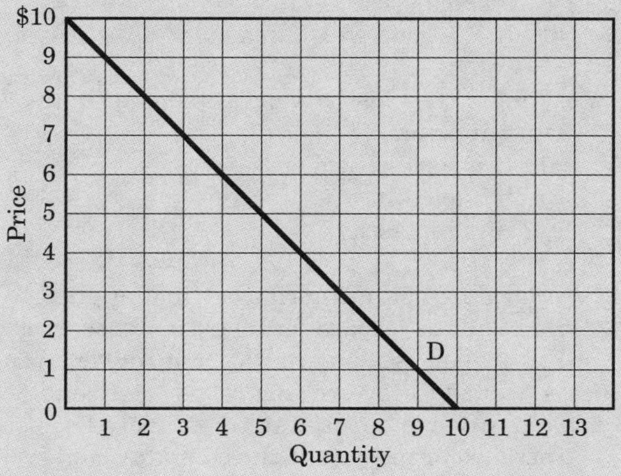

Choose the Best

1. What is the effect on total revenue if demand is elastic and price rises?
   a) Total revenue will fall.
   b) Total revenue will rise.

2. What is the effect of a rise in income on the quantity demanded of product A?
   a) It will rise if product A is an inferior good.
   b) It will rise if product A is a normal good.

3. How will the imposition of a sales tax shift the supply curve?
   a) The supply curve will shift to the left.
   b) The supply curve will shift to the right.

4. What is the supply curve for seats to a one-night concert in an auditorium?
   a) It is elastic.
   b) It is inelastic.
   c) It is perfectly inelastic.

5. What is the effect on tax revenue if the government increases the excise tax on a product which has an inelastic demand?
   a) It will rise.
   b) It will fall.
   c) It may rise or fall depending on the size of increase.

6. What is a normal good?
   a) It is a good whose income elasticity of demand is < 0.

b) It is a good whose demand will rise as income rises.

c) It is a good which has many substitutes.

7. What is the elasticity of Marshall's short-run supply curve?
   a) It is perfectly elastic.
   b) It is elastic.
   c) It is inelastic.

8. A local transit authority has just applied to its regulatory board for a fare increase on its rail-transit system arguing that the increase is needed to cover rising costs. A citizens committee is opposed to the proposed increase arguing that the company could increase its revenue by decreasing fares. Which of the statements below is correct?
   a) The company thinks that its demand is inelastic while the committee thinks it is elastic.
   b) The company thinks that its demand is elastic while the committee thinks it is inelastic.
   c) Both the company and the committee think that elasticity is unity.
   d) It is possible that both the company and the committee are correct.

9. Under which of the situations below will total revenue rise?
   a) If elasticity is >1 and price falls.
   b) If elasticity is >1 and price rises.
   c) If elasticity is <1 and price falls.
   d) If elasticity is = 1 and price falls.

10. What must have happened to the quantity demanded if the price elasticity of demand is 2 and the price increased by 10%?
    a) It must have increased 10%.
    b) It must have decreased 10%.
    c) It must have decreased 20%.
    d) It must have increased 20%.

11. If a product has many substitutes, which of the following statements is correct?
    a) Its income elasticity is high.
    b) It is likely that it is an inferior product.
    c) Its supply elasticity is high.
    d) Its price elasticity of demand is high.

12. What would be true if people spend a large percentage of their income on a particular product?
    a) The product would have a large number of substitutes.
    b) The elasticity of demand for the product would be high.
    c) The income elasticity for the product would be low.
    d) The elasticity of supply for the product would be low.

13. What would cause the elasticity of demand for a product to be high?
    a) A low percentage of income spent on the product.
    b) A small number of available substitutes.
    c) A high elasticity of supply for the product.
    d) A long time period used to measure elasticity.

14. What is the effect of imposing an excise tax on a product?
    a) It will shift both the supply and the demand curve for the product to the left.
    b) It will shift the supply curve for the product to the left.
    c) It will shift the supply curve for the product to the right.
    d) It will shift both the supply and the demand curve for the product to the right.
    e) It will shift the supply curve for the product to the left and the demand curve to the right.

15. Which of the following statements is correct if the government puts a $2 excise tax on a product and, as a result, price rises by $0.75?
    a) The sellers pay more of the tax than the buyers.
    b) The buyers pay more of the tax than the sellers.
    c) The government's tax revenue falls.
    d) The quantity demanded of the product falls by 37.5%.

16. What is the likely effect of the government reducing the supply of illegal drugs?
    a) The total amount spent on drugs will decrease.

b) The total amount spent on drugs will increase.

c) The quantity of drugs consumed will remain unchanged.

d) The demand for drugs will fall.

e) The demand for drugs will increase.

17. Which of the following circumstances will raise the total revenue of oat farmers?
    a) A bumper harvest combined with inelastic demand.
    b) A poor harvest combined with inelastic demand.
    c) A poor harvest combined with elastic demand.
    d) A bumper wheat and oat harvest combined with inelastic demands.
    e) A poor wheat and oat harvest combined with elastic demands.

Refer to Table W4.1 to answer questions 18, 19, and 20.

TABLE W4.1

Income	Quantity of K's Demanded	Quantity of L's Demanded	Quantity of M's Demanded
$50,000	200	40	80
60,000	260	50	85

18. Refer to Table W4.1 to answer this question. What is the income elasticity of product K?
    a) 1.5.
    b) 15.
    c) approximately 14.
    d) approximately 1.4.
    e) approximately 0.7.

19. Refer to Table W4.1 to answer this question. What is the income elasticity of product L?

a) Approximately 12.

b) Approximately 1.2.

c) Greater than the income elasticity of product K.

d) Approximately 0.8.

e) 8.

20. Refer to Table W4.1 to answer this question. Which of the following is correct about product M?
    a) It has an income elasticity of approximately 6.7.
    b) It has an income elasticity of approximately 0.2.
    c) It has an income elasticity of approximately 0.6.
    d) It is a normal good.
    e) It is an inferior good.

What's Wrong?

Can you spot the four errors in the following passage? (Ignore grammatical mistakes!)

The federal government was forced to increase the excise tax on cigarettes in the spring of 1994 because illegal smuggling of Canadian cigarettes from the U.S. into Canada became extensive. Since the demand for cigarettes is elastic, it seemed reasonable to assume that such a tax increase would raise the government's tax revenue. This is what did happen but the reason was because the incentive to smuggle was reduced and the quantity of legal cigarettes bought greatly increased. The reason why Canadian cigarettes could be smuggled in from the U.S. so cheaply was because the export tax on Canadian cigarettes was higher than the excise tax on domestically sold cigarettes. Anti-smoking groups argued that the resulting decrease in the price of cigarettes would dramatically increase the quantity of cigarettes consumed. We can conclude that they must have assumed that the demand for cigarettes is inelastic.

Key Problem

Assume that there is only one movie theatre and only one video rental outlet in a small mining town in northern Manitoba. The weekly demand, by all the townspeople, for movies and video rentals is given in Table W4.2 on the next page.

a) Fill in the total revenue columns.

b) What would be the most advantageous price for the sellers to charge?

Movie price: _____; video price: _____.

TABLE W4.2

Price of Movies	Quantity of Movies Demanded	Total Revenue	Price of Videos	Quantity of Videos Demanded	Total Revenue
$3	450	_____	$2.00	950	_____
4	400	_____	2.50	900	_____
5	350	_____	3.00	825	_____
6	300	_____	3.50	750	_____
7	250	_____	4.00	650	_____
8	200	_____	4.50	550	_____
9	150	_____	5.00	425	_____

c) What is the elasticity of demand for movies if the seller changes the price from $6 to $5 and what is the change in total revenue? What if the price changes from $6 to $7?

From $6 to $5: _____;   change in revenue: _____.

From $6 to $7: _____;   change in revenue: _____.

d) What conclusions can you draw from your answers in c)?

e) Suppose that the video store was charging the price which maximized revenue and then the city government imposed an excise tax on videos which resulted in the price of videos rising to $4.50. As a result, the demand for movies increased by 20 at each price. Would the movie seller want to charge the same price for movies?

Yes: _____.   No: _____.

f) Given the circumstances in e), what is the cross-elasticity of movies for videos? And what does this say about the relationship between the two products?

Elasticity: _____;   relationship: _____.

g) Referring back to the original data in Table W4.2, assume now that the average weekly earning of the townspeople rises from $500 to $550 and that, as a result, the demand for movies increases 20%. If the price being charged was $6, what would be the income elasticity of demand? And what does this suggest about the product, movies?

Elasticity: _____;   suggest: _____.

Need a Hand?

a) **TABLE W4.3** (completed Table W4.2)

Price of Movies	Quantity of Movies Demanded	Total Revenue	Price of Videos	Quantity of Videos Demanded	Total Revenue
$3	450	$1,350	$2.00	950	$1,900
4	400	1,600	2.50	900	2,250
5	350	1,750	3.00	825	2,475
6	300	1,800	3.50	750	2,625
7	250	1,750	4.00	650	2,600
8	200	1,600	4.50	550	2,475
9	150	1,350	5.00	425	2,125

b) The movie seller would want to charge **$6** and the video seller **$3.50** since these are the prices that would maximize the total revenue for each.

c) The elasticity of demand for the price change from $6 to $5 is:

$$\in_P = \frac{50/325 \times 100}{1/5.50 \times 100} = \frac{15.4}{18.2} = \textbf{0.85}$$

(325 is the average of 300 and 350 while $5.50 is the average of $5 and $6) The change in revenue is $1800 – $1750 = **$50**.

For the price change from $6 to $7 :

$$\in_P = \frac{50/275 \times 100}{1/6.50 \times 100} = \frac{18.2}{15.4} = \textbf{1.18}$$

The change in revenue is $1800 – $1750 = **–$50**.

d) For movie prices below $6, demand must be inelastic since reducing price decreases total revenue. For prices above $6, demand must be elastic since raising price also decreases total revenue. Therefore, $6 is the point of unity elasticity and the price that maximizes total revenue for the seller. Calculations of price changes for videos from $3.50 to $3.00 and from $3.50 to $4.00 would lead us to the same conclusion for videos.

e) **TABLE W4.4**

Price of Movies	(New) Quantity of Movies Demanded	Total Revenue
$3	470	$1,410
4	420	1,680
5	370	1,850
6	320	1,920
7	270	1,890
8	220	1,760
9	170	1,530

As can been seen from Table W4.4 above, total revenue is still maximized when price is $6 so the answer would be **Yes**.

f) At the $6 price for movies, the quantity demanded for movies rises from 300 to 320 as the price of videos increases from $3.50 to $4.50 so the cross-elasticity of movies for videos is:

$$\in_X = \frac{+20/310 \times 100}{+1/4 \times 100} = \frac{+6.4}{+25} = +0.26$$

Since the coefficient is positive, the 2 **products are substitutes**.

g) At the $6 price for movies, the quantity demanded for movies rises from 300 to 360 (by 20%) as incomes rise from 500 to 550 so the income elasticity for movies is:

$$\in_Y = \frac{+60/330 \times 100}{+50/525 \times 100} = \frac{+18.2}{+9.5} = +1.91$$

Since the coefficient is positive, **movies are a normal good** and, in addition, since it is greater than one, **movies are a luxury**.

More of the Same

The (weekly) local demand for mangos and pineapples is given in Table W4.5 below. The quantities are in thousands.

TABLE W4.5

Price of Mangos	Quantity of Mangos Demanded	Total Revenue	Price of Pineapples	Quantity of Pineapples Demanded	Total Revenue
$0.60	27	_____	$2.25	17	_____
0.70	24	_____	2.50	16	_____
0.80	21	_____	2.75	14	_____
0.90	18	_____	3.00	12	_____
1.00	15	_____	3.25	9	_____
1.10	12	_____	3.50	6	_____
1.20	9	_____	3.75	3	_____

a) Fill in the total revenue columns in the table above.

b) What would be the best prices for the sellers of mangos and pineapples?

c) What is the price elasticity of demand for mangos if price changes from $0.80 to $0.90 and what is the change in total revenue? From $0.80 to $0.60?

d) Given the total revenue data you calculated in b), what is the elasticity of demand for mangos if price changes from $0.80 to $0.70?

e) Assume that the prevailing price of pineapples rises from $2.50 to $3.50 and that, as a result, the demand for mangos increases by 50%. If the price of mangos was $0.80, what is the cross-elasticity of mangos for pineapples? What does the coefficient tell you?

f) Assume that average incomes rose by 10% and that, as a result, the demand for pineapples increased by 2 at every price level. If the price of pineapples was $3.50, what is the income elasticity of pineapples? What does the coefficient tell you?

Other Problems

1. Given the demand curve in Figure W4.2 below:

FIGURE W4.2

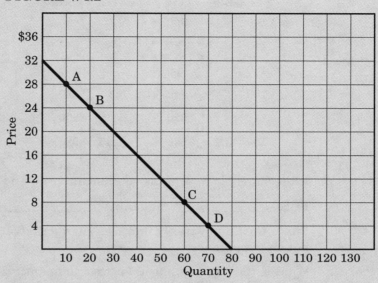

a) What can you say about the slope of the demand curve?

Answer: _____.

b) What is the elasticity of demand between points A and B, and between points C and D?

A and B: _____; C and D: _____.

c) At what price is the elasticity of demand equal to one?

Price: _____.

d) At what price would consumers spend the most on this product?

Price: _____.

e) Between what prices is demand inelastic?

Between: _____ and _____.

2. Fill in the blanks in Table W4.6 (each row is a different period).

TABLE W4.6

Income	Price of M	Quantity of M	Price of N	Quantity of N	Price $\in$ for M	Price $\in$ for N	Income $\in$ for M	Income $\in$ for N	Cross $\in$ of M for N
$50,000	2.50	100	20	800	X	X	X	X	X
50,000	2.80	90	20	800	_____	X	X	X	X
50,000	2.80	80	30	700	X	_____	X	X	_____
55,000	2.80	90	30	720	X	X	_____	_____	X

3. Given the data in Table W4.7:

    TABLE W4.7

Price	Demand	Supply (S$_1$)	Supply (tax)
$100	900	820	_____
110	880	840	_____
120	860	860	_____
130	840	880	_____
140	820	900	_____
150	800	920	_____

    a) If the supply is S$_1$, what is equilibrium price and quantity?

    Price: _____; quantity: _____.

    b) Fill in the Supply (tax) column assuming that a $20 per unit excise tax is put on the product.

    c) What is the new equilibrium price and quantity?

    Price: _____; quantity: _____.

    d) What portion of the $20 excise tax is paid by the seller and what portion is paid by the consumer?

    Paid by seller: _____; paid by consumer: _____.

4. Table W4.8 shows the demand for haircuts by pensioners and by other customers on an average weekday in the local hairdressing shop.

    TABLE W4.8

Price of Haircut	Quantity Demanded by Pensioners	Quantity Demanded by Other Customers
$20	1	9
18	4	10
16	7	11
14	10	12
12	13	13
10	16	14
8	19	15
6	22	16
4	25	17
2	28	18

    a) Between the prices of $16 and $20, which of the two demands is more elastic? Explain.

    _____

    _____

b) What is the price that would give the shop the greatest sales revenue?

Price: _____ .

Unanswered Questions

Short Essays

1. Give a definition of the price elasticity of demand and explain why the slope of a demand curve and the elasticity are not the same thing.

2. What is the relationship between the elasticity of demand and the revenue received by the sellers of the product?

3. Why is the elasticity of demand for carrots different from the elasticity of demand for cigarettes?

4. Why is the elasticity of demand for toothpicks different from the elasticity of demand for housing?

5. Under what conditions will the consumer pay all of the excise tax placed on a particular product?

6. What would happen if all of Canada's dairy farmers joined together and reduced the supply of milk by 50%?

Analytical Questions

1. The Dean of Arts at a large university recently said that she felt that the demand for post-secondary education must be very inelastic because enrollment has not decreased despite a doubling in tuition fees over the last ten years. Do you agree with the Dean? Why or why not?

2. Do you think there is a big difference between the price elasticity for kitchen stoves in the long run and in the short run? For paper towelling?

3. What do you think would have happened to the government's tax revenues if it had decided to spend the necessary dollars to stop cigarette smuggling in the spring of 1994 by using increased policing?

4. What would be the effects of a war on drugs that targeted drug users rather than drug suppliers?

5. The Vancouver Folk Music Festival is held each summer in a very large, fenced-in park which gives people ample room to wander from stage to stage or to go off and find a quiet spot for a picnic. In effect, the supply curve for admission to the festival is perfectly elastic. What is the best price of admission for the festival organizers to charge?

Numerical Questions

1. Draw a demand curve that illustrates zero quantity demanded at a price of $50 and a quantity demanded of 200 at a price zero. Calculate the price elasticity of demand if the price decreases from $50 to zero. Next, draw another demand curve that illustrates zero quantity demanded at a price of $200 and a quantity demanded of 50 at a price of zero. Calculate elasticity of demand if the price decreases from $200 to zero. What conclusion might you draw from this exercise?

2. Given the data in Table W4.9:

TABLE W4.9

Price	Demand	Supply (S1)	Supply (tax)
$50	660	420	_____
55	600	440	_____
60	540	460	_____
65	480	480	_____
70	420	500	_____
75	360	520	_____

a) What is the equilibrium price and quantity?
b) Fill in the Supply (tax) column assuming a $10 per unit excise tax is imposed on this product.
c) What is the new equilibrium price and quantity?

d) What portion of the $10 excise tax is paid by the seller and what portion is paid by the consumer?

3. Given the data in Table W4.10:

TABLE W4.10

Price	Demand
$44	920
45	900
46	880
47	860
48	840

a) At what price is the total expenditures by consumers at a maximum?

b) What is the price elasticity of demand at this price?

4. Given Figure W4.3:

FIGURE W4.3

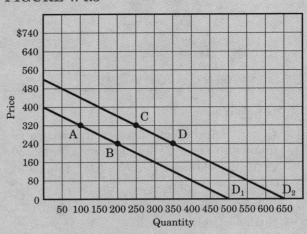

Is the elasticity of demand between A and B on D_1 greater or smaller than that between C and D on D_2? Explain.

CHAPTER **FIVE**

■ ■ ■ ■ ■ ■ ■ ►

Consumer Demand

> **W**hat's ahead . . . This chapter looks at the theory of consumer behaviour known as marginal utility theory. This helps us to better understand how the rational consumer allocates income towards the purchase of many different products. It also gives us a different perspective on the meaning of demand. We explain the idea of consumer surplus and look at attempts by producers to acquire this surplus through the practice of price discrimination.

You do not need to be a student of economics to appreciate that people's tastes differ: one man's meat is another man's poison. And even where people buy the same products we cannot be sure that they receive the same amount of satisfaction from them. Yet our formulation of an individual's demand is predicated on the basis that it measures, or is an indicator of, that person's desire as well as her ability to purchase. An increase in either would presumably cause her to purchase more. Measuring ability to purchase is easy enough: it can be gauged by that person's income and wealth. But how do we measure intensity of desire? Well, a number of economists in the latter part of the nineteenth century attempted to do just that and introduced the important new idea called the **margin**.

margin(al): the extra or additional unit.

The marginal revolution shifted the focus of economists away from totals, such as total profits or total costs or total utility, and toward the marginal, which means the extra or additional, profit or cost or utility. The English economist, Alfred Marshall, believed that concentrating on people's actions *at the margin* provided a better understanding of their behaviour. If we are trying to understand why a consumer buys one particular basket of goods rather than any other, it is more instructive conceptually to look at each purchase one at a time than trying to evaluate the total result of a morning's shopping. The basket of goods, after all, is the result of a number of individual decisions rather than being one single decision. Using this approach, Marshall developed the concept of marginal utility, and with it the important law of diminishing marginal utility. The theory of consumer behaviour which uses this concept is the focus of this chapter. Before we look at this, we should mention that the idea of the marginal is not always easy to grasp at a first acquaintance. It is definitely worth the effort, however, since it lies at the heart of so much economic analysis and is the basis of many of the ideas contained in later chapters.

Law of Diminishing Marginal Utility

Suppose that I wished to communicate to you the immense satisfaction which I get from my first beverage of the day. Of course, I could use words

utility: the satisfaction or pleasure derived from the consumption of a product.

like "greatly" or "fantastically" or even "indescribably" refreshing, but no words could accurately capture the degree of my pleasure, or **utility**, as economists call it. Suppose instead that I attempted to assign a number to indicate the amount of my utility, say, 100 utils. Does this communicate my pleasure any more accurately? Probably not, since you have no idea what a util is and we have no instrument with which to measure it. However, if I then tell you that the second beverage of the day gives me only 50 utils of pleasure, you have a very clear indication of how I rate these two drinks. On the other hand, my friend Anna might suggest that she gets 200 and 100 utils from her first two drinks. Since neither of us can objectively measure the amount of utility, we cannot conclude that she derives twice as much utility as I do. In other words, we cannot make interpersonal comparisons of utility. Nevertheless, we can still draw some interesting conclusions about consumer behaviour by pursuing this idea of utility.

For example, assume that a perspiring student enters her local watering hole after a particularly exhausting game of tennis and drinks a glass of her favourite refreshment. Assume that it is a non-alcoholic liquid so that she is able to keep score of the amount of pleasure (measured in utils) that she derives from successive drinks. Of course, this is her own subjective evaluation, which might change from day to day. It seems reasonable to suppose that the very first drink would give her the greatest satisfaction, and each drink afterwards would give less and less pleasure as shown in Table 5.1.

TABLE 5.1 Total and Marginal Utility

Quantity	Marginal Utility (MU)	Total Utility (TU)
1	120	120
2	90	210
3	65	275
4	45	320
5	25	345
6	23	368
7	10	378
8	4	382
9	0	382
10	−2	380

marginal utility: the amount of additional utility derived from the consumption of an extra unit of a product.

law of diminishing marginal utility: the amount of additional utility decreases as successive units of a product are consumed.

The column headed **marginal utility** shows the amount of pleasure or satisfaction, measured in utils, which this consumer derives from each unit consumed. It can be seen that this consumer derives decreasing marginal utility from each successive drink. Although each drink, at least until the ninth glass, gives this consumer positive marginal utility, each drink is less satisfying than the previous one. This is known as the **law of diminishing marginal utility.** It seems reasonable to suppose that this law is applicable to most of us most of the time. Our knowledge of life and our own personal experiences alone can validate the law of diminishing utility: more may be better, but additional units do not give the same degree of pleasure, and in time there will come a point where more becomes worse. For the consumer illustrated in Table 5.1 that comes with the 10th drink. Since the first unit gives us positive utility and the last one, negative utility, marginal utility must be declining with successive amounts.

The last column in Table 5.1 shows the total utility derived from consuming the various quantities. Total utility increases with the amount consumed, but the rate of increase slows down with increasing quantities. This is the same thing as saying that marginal utility diminishes. Table 5.1 is illustrated in Figure 5.1 below.

FIGURE 5.1 Total and Marginal Utilities

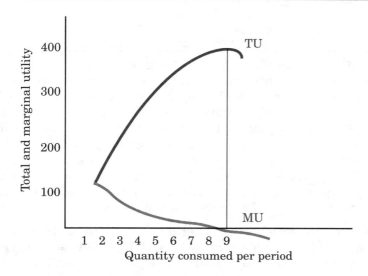

Total utility (TU) increases as more of this product is consumed — at least, up to the 9th unit. However, the rate at which it increases gets smaller and smaller, i.e., the slope of the total utility curve gets smaller (or the curve gets flatter). The slope of the TU curve is the same thing as the marginal utility. In other words, starting from a high of 120 utils when one unit is consumed, the MU declines with increased consumption until it eventually becomes 0 with the consumption of the 9th unit. Note that the TU curve is at a maximum when MU equals 0.

Before we start to develop this theory of utility a bit further, it is important for us to understand that, like most economic theories, we need to be careful to state the conditions under which it operates. First of all, we take it for granted that the consumers we are describing act rationally. By this, we mean that they will wish to consume more as long as total utility increases. This point bears repeating: a rational consumer will want to consume more so long as increased consumption adds to total satisfaction. The objective of the con-

QUESTION 5.1
Complete the following table of utilities:

Quantity	Total Utility (TU)	Marginal Utility (MU)
1	20	____
2	____	____
3	45	10
4	____	8
5	58	____
6	60	____
7	____	0
8	____	−5

sumer, it is assumed, is to maximize the pleasure derived from consumption, i.e., to maximize total utility. In addition, this idea of diminishing marginal utility makes sense only if we are considering a particular time period. If our drinker — whose name is Anna, by the way — were to consume the 10 drinks over 10 evenings then it's likely that her marginal utility would remain constant. Finally, as Marshall pointed out, certain products are indivisible so that a small quantity may be insufficient to meet certain special wants, i.e., three automobile tires would not give a great deal of utility without the fourth.

Optimal Purchasing Rule

From the information contained in Table 5.1, it is apparent that if Anna had unlimited income or if the refreshment were free, there would still be a limit to how much she would drink. She would never drink more than 9 colas, since no rational consumer would consume a unit which gives negative marginal utility. In other words, if we wanted to develop some rule of rational consumer behaviour, we might suggest that a person with unlimited income should consume every product to the point of satiation! The problem with this little rule is that it doesn't apply to any known consumer since all people, no matter how rich or poor, have limited incomes (not to mention limited time) and therefore have to make choices.

To derive a more relevant rule of consumer behaviour, let's suppose that Anna has a limited budget of $36 and has a choice of buying two products: cola or pizza slices, each costing $4. The utility of both products is shown in Table 5.2.

TABLE 5.2 Comparison of the Utilities of Cola and Pizzas

Glasses of Cola			Pizza Slices		
Quantity	Marginal Utility	Total Utility	Quantity	Marginal Utility	Total Utility
1	120	120	1	60	60
2	90	210	2	50	110
3	65	275	3	35	145
4	45	320	4	21	166
5	25	345	5	16	182
6	23	368	6	10	192
7	10	378	7	0	192
8	4	382	8	−5	187
9	0	382	9	−10	177
10	−2	380	10	−15	162

The question now is, how should Anna best allocate her evening's budget if she wishes to maximize her total utility? She certainly cannot consume to the points of maximum total utility of both products since that would cost her $36 for the 9 glasses of colas and $28 for 7 slices of pizza, for a total of $64 — more than her budget. We need to figure out (on her behalf) what combination of the two goods, costing $36, will produce the maximum total utility. One way to do this would be to work out every possible combination, given the $36 constraint, and see which particular combination maximizes utility. The procedure is a little tedious, but not particularly difficult, as Table 5.3 shows.

A glance at the last column of Table 5.3 shows that the best combination is 6 glasses of colas and 3 slices of pizza since this yields the maximum total utility of 513 utils.

TABLE 5.3 Utility Obtained from Combinations of Colas and Pizzas

Colas		Pizza Slices		Both
Quantity	Total Utility	Quantity	Total Utility	Total Utility
0	0	9	177	177
1	120	8	187	307
2	210	7	192	402
3	275	6	192	467
4	320	5	182	502
5	345	4	166	511
6	**368**	**3**	**145**	**513**
7	378	2	110	488
8	382	1	60	442
9	382	0	0	382

If we were to compare the two products from this student's point of view, we would tend to suggest, based on the evidence of Table 5.2, that she prefers colas to pizzas. However, this would be a misleading statement. The reason why this is so is that if we were to categorize products in terms of absolute favourites, then it would seem reasonable to spend all our incomes on our favourite products. We don't do this for one obvious reason: even our favourite products lose their attractiveness if we buy them to the exclusion of all other products. Translated into marginal utility theory, it suggests that we would buy a product until its marginal utility falls below that of some other product at which point we would switch purchases. There's a little more to it than that, but it does give us a more valuable insight into our spending behaviour and a better method of solving the previous budget problem. Instead of trying to decide in advance how Anna should spend her budget, let's look at choices one at a time i.e., marginally.

Suppose that, on entering the snack bar, Anna takes $4 from the $36 out of her purse, and walks up to the counter to place an order. What should she buy? Table 5.2 shows us that a cola looks more attractive since the marginal utility of the first cola exceeds that of the first slice of pizza. Having downed her drink, should she now buy her *second* cola or should she buy her *first* slice of pizza? Well, the colas still look more attractive since the MU is 90 compared with that of 60 from the first slice of pizza. Third purchase: another cola, the third, or the first pizza? Answer: another cola, since the MU of the *third* cola (65) still exceeds that of the *first* pizza (60). Not until the fourth purchase, do pizzas look as attractive as colas. The *first* slice of pizza now yields more utility than does the *fourth* cola. All of this means that since marginal utility declines with consumption, the comparative attractiveness of any two products depends on how much of each has been consumed. After 3 glasses of colas, pizzas now look more attractive to Anna. We continue in a similar fashion until Anna's $36 has been exhausted. This is shown in Table 5.4 on the next page.

At the end of the evening, Anna will then have purchased a total of 6 colas and 3 slices of pizza, and in doing so will have maximized her utility at 513 utils (Table 5.2 shows that 6 colas gives 368 utils and 3 pizza slices gives 145 utils). We have already seen from Table 5.3 that this combination will ensure maximum utility.

TABLE 5.4 Successive Purchase Choices

	Total Spent	Purchases of Colas	Purchases of Pizzas
First purchase	$ 4	1st cola	
Second purchase	8	2nd cola	
Third purchase	12	3rd cola	
Fourth purchase	16		1st pizza
Fifth purchase	20		2nd pizza
Sixth purchase	24	4th cola	
Seventh purchase	28		3rd pizza
Eighth purchase	32	5th cola	
Ninth purchase	36	6th cola	

From this knowledge, we could perhaps adopt a new optimal purchasing rule to the effect that in order to maximize utility, a consumer should allocate spending by comparing the marginal utility of each product and purchase the product which gives the greatest marginal utility. There is however a very serious defect with this rule. Suppose, for example, that I were to compare the marginal utilities of two following products, and, according to this rule, purchase the one which gives the greatest marginal utility, as follows:

1st bottle of beer: MU = 120 utils

1st Porsche car: MU = 10,000,000 utils

So, of course, I would buy the Porsche even though it's way outside my budget! Our purchasing rule obviously needs a little more refinement since we need to take the price of products into consideration. What we really need to compare to make a rational decision is the amount of utils per dollar spent. Or, expressing it more colloquially, we are trying to find out which product gives the most bang for the bucks! In terms of a formula, it is:

$$\text{MU per \$ spent} = \frac{\text{MU}}{\text{Price}}$$

Suppose that the price of a pizza happened to be $2. The MU per dollar spent for her first purchases of both colas and pizzas would then be equal for Anna and she would, therefore, be indifferent as to which she purchased:

$$\text{MU per \$ spent on 1st cola} = \frac{120}{4} = 30$$

$$\text{MU per \$ spent on 1st pizza} = \frac{60}{2} = 30$$

QUESTION 5.2

Given the following marginal utilities and prices, which product would a rational consumer choose?

	Apple	Beer	Ice Cream	Hot Dog
Marginal Utility	120	300	140	150
Price	$1.50	$4.00	$2.00	$3.00

What this suggests then is that a rational consumer would continue to purchase a product as long as its MU per dollar spent is greater than that of any other product. Of course, as the consumer increases the consumption of any given product its MU is going to fall so that some other product will then become a more attractive proposition. Let's return to the cola-pizza example and, in Table 5.5, assume that the management of the snack bar decides to increase the price of colas to $5 but leaves the price of pizzas unchanged at $4. Now how would she spend her budget of $36?

TABLE 5.5 Marginal Utility per Dollar Spent

	Colas			Pizza Slices	
Quantity	MU	Mu per Dollar (price = $5)	Quantity	MU	MU per Dollar (price = $4)
1	120	24	1	60	15
2	90	18	2	50	12.5
3	65	13	3	35	8.75
4	45	9	4	21	5.25
5	25	5	5	16	4
6	23	4.6	6	10	2.5
7	10	2	7	0	0
8	4	0.8	8		
9	0	0	9		

To figure out the optimal allocation of Anna's $36 budget, we will proceed as we did before, by looking at each separate purchase. To start with, each of the first two colas give a higher MU per dollar spent than does the first pizza slice (24 and 18 respectively, compared to 15 for the first pizza), and so these would be her first two purchases. The first pizza, however, does give a higher MU per dollar spent than does the third cola, and so she would at this point switch to a slice of pizza. We can continue in this fashion, purchase by purchase, and the result is summarized in Table 5.6.

TABLE 5.6 Choice of Colas and Pizzas, Purchase by Purchase

	Total spent	Purchases of Colas	Purchases of Pizzas
First purchase	$ 5	1st cola	
Second purchase	10	2nd cola	
Third purchase	14		1st pizza
Fourth purchase	19	3rd cola	
Fifth purchase	23		2nd pizza
Sixth purchase	28	4th cola	
Seventh purchase	32		3rd pizza
Eighth purchase	36		4th pizza

The best way for Anna to spend her $36 is to purchase 4 colas and 4 pizza slices. This would give her (check back to Table 5.2) a total utility of 486 (320 + 166) utils which is higher than could be produced by any other combination that could be purchased with $36. Note also the effect of this increase in the price of colas: the number of colas purchased dropped from 6 to 4 while the quantity of the related product, pizza slices, increased from 3 to 6. We will look at this aspect in more detail later.

This means that the optimal spending choice for the rational consumer is that he should purchase the product which yields the greatest marginal utility per dollar.

The procedure we have developed enables us to derive an **optimal purchasing rule**. It suggests that whenever the MU per dollar spent on a certain product, product A, is greater than some other product, product B, then we would buy and consume more of A. As this is done, of course, the MU per dollar spent on product A starts to decline, until we get to the point where other products, product B or product C become more attractive, i.e.:

$$\text{if } \frac{MU_A}{P_A} > \frac{MU_B}{P_B} \Rightarrow \text{consume more A}$$

$$\text{if } \frac{MU_A}{P_A} < \frac{MU_B}{P_B} \Rightarrow \text{consume more B}$$

Our conclusion then is that we should buy and consume products to the point at which the MU per dollar spent on each product is more or less equal for all products. The Optimal Purchasing Rule then is:

$$\frac{MU_A}{P_A} = \frac{MU_B}{P_B} = \ldots \frac{MU_Z}{P_Z}$$

If we didn't purchase products in this fashion, then we would be acting irrationally. For instance, suppose that the MU per dollar spent on the last apple we bought is 15 utils (and it doesn't matter if this is the 1st, 5th, or 100th apple) and an additional pear gives a MU per dollar spent of 25 utils, then we would gain 10 utils by giving up one apple and buying an additional pear instead.

> **optimal purchasing rule:** in order to maximize utility, a consumer should purchase the product which yields the greatest marginal utility per dollar spent.

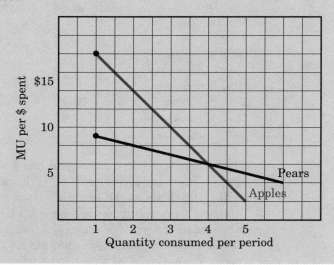

QUESTION 5.3

Given the following MU per dollar curves for apples and pears, how many of each would a rational consumer purchase if she could only afford nine purchases?

Applications of Marginal Utility Theory

Marginal utility theory, as esoteric as it might at first appear, does provide us with some interesting insights into consumer behaviour. It can explain some obvious, and some not so obvious, activities. For instance, it explains why none of us spend all our income on one single product. Even our favourite product is only a favourite *up to a point*. After consuming a certain quantity, its MU per dollar spent drops to the point where other things become our temporary favourites.

It is an interesting experiment to imagine how one would spend additional increments of income starting off, say, with a basic $100 per week, and increasing it by $100 each time. Let's say you did have only $100 per week, what would you spend the money on? Presumably, you would spend it on those things which have the greatest marginal utility for you; for most of us, this would mean using our money on food and shelter. Income would need to increase appreciably before any allocations are made for clothes, and be higher still before any entertainment dollars are spent.

The way in which we adjust our purchases to higher income levels is what is meant by the concept of income elasticity that we encountered in the last chapter. You can imagine that products with low income elasticities (water, food) will be highest in terms of priority and those products with high elasticities (airline travel, movies) will have a lower priority. Research has consistently demonstrated that poorer families spend by far the largest proportion of their incomes on the basic necessities like food and shelter (often well over 50%) whereas, richer families spend proportionately less (sometimes less than 30%).

A second intriguing aspect of marginal utility theory is trying to think of situations in which the law of diminishing marginal utility may not apply. The law is applicable to all products and all people but maybe not at all times. For example, it's certainly possible to think of certain things for which the MU seems to increase the more that is consumed. (Think of a CD of new music; it often takes repeated hearings before you get full enjoyment from it.) This may be true also of fine wines and paintings and so on. However, Marshall cautioned his readers that the idea of diminishing marginal utility only makes sense if the product is consumed over a reasonably short period of time.

BOX 5.1

In the nineteenth century, a German statistician named Ernst Engel did a survey among working people in England to find out how the average person's income was allocated to different forms of spending, and how this changed as income changed. He discovered that the percentage spent on food (though not the actual amount) tended to decline with increasing incomes, whereas the percentage spent on housing remained constant; the percentage spent on clothing remained the same or declined, and other items increased. These results (often graphed in the form of an Engels Curve) have been repeated in many other surveys over the years. In Canada, StatsCan publishes a periodical survey of consumer spending. The following table shows an extract from a recent survey:

FAMILY INCOME QUINTILE GROUP
Percentage of Total Consumption Spending

	All Classes	Lowest 20%	4th 20%	3rd 20%	2nd 20%	Top 20%
Food	19	24	20	19	19	17
Shelter	22	31	24	22	21	19
Clothing	8	6	7	8	8	11
Travel	18	11	17	18	19	20

The idea of diminishing marginal utility takes on another interesting twist when we look at another fascinating commodity: money. Is money also subject to the law of diminishing marginal utility? Does it mean that the more money you have, the less valuable additional amounts become for you? Since money is just one form of wealth, often the question is amended to ask: does the MU of wealth or income decline as more is obtained? For example, imagine a rich person and a poor person walking towards each other on the street and halfway between them lies a $10 bill. Which would gain the greater utility from its possession — the rich person, for whom it might be the hundred-thousandth $10 bill of the year, or the poor person, for whom it could be the difference between life and death? Intuition suggests that the MU of the poor person is likely to be far higher than the MU of the rich person, for whom the gain (or loss, for that matter) of $10 might well go unnoticed. Here, intuition seems to confirm the law of diminishing marginal utility even for the product, money. If this is so, some might argue that this is strong grounds for advocating a more equitable distribution of income and wealth since the gain in MU by the poor would greatly exceed the loss of MU by the rich so that overall utility (or social welfare) is increased.

Note that the above idea need not imply an equal distribution, but a more equitable or fair one. The idea would be to take from the rich and give to the poor as long as the MU of the former is smaller than the MU of the latter. This would continue until (figuratively) the screams of the rich person (who may no longer be rich) are equal to the whoops of joy coming from the poor person (who may no longer be quite so poor). It may well be that their MUs become equalized when the rich person now has an income reduced to $5,000 per week, while that of the poor person has been increased to

$500. However, you might protest such a scheme. After all, you may well ask: what is fair about a system that takes income from one person, who may have worked extremely hard to earn it, and gives it to another who may have done nothing to deserve it? The central question is less concerned with value judgements about who is, and who is not, deserving than with attempts by modern governments to maximize the overall well-being of their communities. It is most likely that those individuals with higher incomes (lower MU of money) tend to save more and receive, in turn, relatively more of their income from their investment sources. Governments have typically imposed higher taxes on this type of income, perhaps a de facto acceptance of the argument that these marginal income dollars yield lower MU for their recipients than the higher MU gained from labour by lower income earners.

There is another issue in this argument in that it rests on the assumption that we can compare utilities between people. In fact this is just not possible. We might well be inclined to believe that the rich person's MU is less than the poor person's, but there is simply no way of establishing this.

From all of this, however, we should not conclude that the theory of marginal utility is invalid or that it should be discarded. As we shall see, one of its most important uses is to give a strong underpinning to the law of demand, which is the topic of the next section.

QUESTION 5.4

The table below shows the total utility which two children, Jan and Dean, derive from various amounts of weekly allowance:

Amount of Weekly Allowance	Jan's Total Utility	Dean's Total Utility
$ 1	200	400
2	380	500
3	540	595
4	680	685
5	800	770
6	900	850
7	980	925
8	1,040	995
9	1,080	1,060
10	1,100	1,120

As their parent, you can afford to pay them only a total allowance of $10. How would you divide this amount between the two children so as to maximize their combined total utility? What will be the combined total utility?

Marginal Utility and the Demand Curve

We saw earlier in our cola-pizza example that marginal utility theory suggests that an increase in the price of one product leads to a decrease in the quantity purchased of that particular product while increasing the quantity purchased of the competitive product. We need to look at this aspect in more detail.

We mentioned at the outset that the units in which utility is measured cannot be objectively quantified and, in a sense, what units we use is of little importance. However, there is one particular measuring unit with which we are all familiar, and that is money. We could, if we wished, measure utility in dollars. For instance Akio could suggest that his first drink after a hard game of tennis gives him, say, $8 worth of utility; or another way of expressing it would be to say that, irrespective of its actual price he would be willing to pay $8 for it. Let's table Akio's utility for his favourite drink below in terms of dollar utility.

TABLE 5.7 Akio's Dollar Marginal Utility

Quantity Consumed	$MU
1	$8
2	5
3	4
4	3
5	2
6	1
7	0

Although they look similar, do not confuse our previous term, MU per dollar spent, which measures the number of utils obtained for each dollar spent, with $MU which is measuring utility itself in terms of dollars. Table 5.7 above suggests that Akio's $MU declines with increasing quantities; there's nothing particularly startling about this, it simply reflects the law of diminishing marginal utility. However, with this information we can work out exactly how much Akio would purchase at different prices. Suppose, for instance, that the price of his drink was $10 a bottle; how much would he purchase? The answer must be zero since even his first drink of the day is worth only $8 for him, so why would he pay $10 for some product which he rates at only $8? Similarly if the price was $9. What if the price is dropped to $8; now how many would he buy? The answer will be one, since he would surely pay $8 for something he felt was worth $8. However, he would not purchase a second drink since he only rates it at $5 which is less than the price. Let's continue to drop the price. Say the price is $7: now how many will he purchase? Presumably, he still wouldn't be prepared to buy more than one since the price is still higher than his valuation of the second drink. The same is true at $6. Not until the price drops to $5 would Akio be prepared to buy two drinks. Continuing to drop the price by $1 each time would produce the results in Table 5.8 below.

TABLE 5.8 Demand Curve, Derived

Price of Drinks	Quantity Demanded
$10	0
9	0
8	1
7	1
6	1
5	2
4	3
3	4
2	5
1	6

What this table spells out, of course, is Akio's demand schedule, which relates the quantities demanded at various different prices. This is graphed in Figure 5.2 below.

FIGURE 5.2 Marginal Utility and the Demand Curve

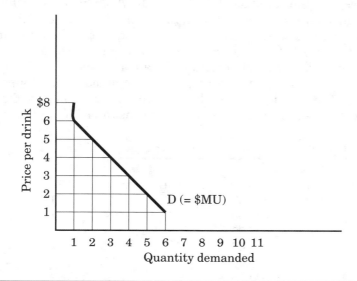

To induce Akio to buy one drink, the price cannot be higher than $8, since that is how much he values the first drink. To get him to buy a second drink, the price must drop to $5 because that is his evaluation of the second drink. If the price drops to $4, then Akio would be prepared to buy 3 drinks. The price must continue to drop in order to encourage Akio to buy more. His $MU curve is the same thing, then, as his demand curve.

The derivation of the demand curve in this manner, while not being particularly ingenious, does provide a very different perspective on demand. In a sense it shifts the emphasis away from the price and on to the quantity. Instead of asking the question: "How many would you buy at this price?", it asks, "What is the maximum price you would pay to buy this quantity?" From Akio's point of view, the price cannot be more than $8 in order to induce him to buy one drink. In order to get him to buy two drinks, the price of the second drink must drop to $5 simply because we know that the MU of his second drink will be lower. In other words, to induce people to buy increasing quantities of any product which they value less and less, the price must be lower. To get Akio to buy 6 drinks, the price must be as low as $1. In a sense it is the value of the last one purchased and not the total value of them all which determines how much is bought.

The fact that it is the marginal utility *of the last unit* purchased which determines the price you are prepared to pay for a product and the quantity you are buying is a very subtle idea, one which is difficult to grasp on first acquaintance. It does however provide a solution to the famous diamond-water paradox which was first introduced by Adam Smith in his *Wealth of Nations*.

Diamond-Water Paradox

Smith was interested in finding out what determines the value of products and realized that the rather elusive term "value" is used in two different contexts. It could mean what he termed "value in use" which is what we mean by utility, i.e., it is the amount of satisfaction which the individual derives on the basis of her individual evaluation. Alternatively, the word might mean what he termed "value in exchange." This is the value which the market places on the product, i.e., in exchange for other products (or for money). Most things that we buy have similar values in use and in exchange. However, there are a number of products like water which have a very high value in use but are worth almost nothing in exchange. Conversely, there are other products like diamonds which have a very high exchange value but quite low value in use. Smith tried, unsuccessfully, to resolve this seeming paradox. It took almost a century and the introduction of marginal utility theory before economists were able to provide a solution. In the following example instead of diamonds let us look at the contrast between water and another very precious commodity, oil. Suppose we are comparing the utilities derived from 50 litre drums of each. Table 5.9 presents the preferences of Karl, an average consumer:

TABLE 5.9 The Utilities of Water and Oil

Water			Oil		
Quantity	$MU	$TU	Quantity	$MU	$TU
1	$1,000	$1,000	1	$30	$30
2	500	1,500	2	29	59
3	200	1,700	3	28	87
4	100	1,800	4	27	114
5	50	1,850	5	26	140
6	25	1,875	6	25	165
7	10	1,885	7	24	189
8	5	1,890	8	23	212
9	2	1,892	9	22	234
10	1	1,893	10	21	255

The first thing that strikes one is how highly valuable water is when compared to oil. The total utility (value in use) far exceeds that of oil. Suppose that you literally had no water, how much would you be prepared to pay for it? Karl would pay almost anything — $1,000 for the first drum of water. This may be his whole income, but it would be worth spending it to stay alive. But notice how dramatically the MU drops. After 9 drums of water Karl not only has enough to drink, but enough to wash his clothes, his body and his house and still have plenty left over to water the garden and fill up the swimming pool. The value of a 10th drum of water is only $1. In contrast, though, note how gradually the MU of oil drops.

Now, suppose that Karl has a budget of $300 and the price of both oil and water is $25, how much of each would he purchase? You can see that his first $125 would be spent on 5 drums of water, but the next $125 would go on 5 drums of oil. Then he would buy one of each, for a total of 6 drums of water and 6 drums of oil. After spending $300 he values the oil and water equally despite the fact that 6 drums of water gives him a total $ utility of $1,875 compared to only $165 for oil — over 11 times as much. But the total utility is irrelevant when it comes to deciding on the next purchase and Smith's idea of value in exchange centres on the marginal and not the total utility. If Karl had another $100 to spend, you can see that he would buy only oil. Thus, we can see that the answer to Smith's paradox is that value in use is reflected in the *total utility* of a product whereas the value in exchange (the price) is determined by its *marginal utility*. And it is the marginal utility of a product which determines just how much of a product we will buy.

Consumer Surplus

Our water-oil paradox showed that the total value that a consumer derives from consuming products usually exceeds the total expenditure on them. Table 5.9 shows, for instance, that if the price of water is $25 a drum, Karl would consume 6 drums at a cost of $150. The total $ utility of those 6 drums, however, is $1,875. In dollar terms then, Karl obtains a bonus amounting to the difference of $1,725. This bonus is called the **consumer surplus.** The surplus is not a sum of money received, but is the additional satisfaction that we receive for free. It comes about from the fact that normally we can obtain as much or as little of a product as we want at a single constant price. Karl could obtain 1 drum or 5 drums or 100 drums and they would still have cost him $25 each. However, except for the last one he buys, every unit he buys is worth more than the price. He obtains a consumer surplus on each one, as the Table 5.10 shows.

> **consumer surplus:**
> the difference between the consumer's evaluation of a product and the price which is paid for it.

TABLE 5.10 Marginal and Total Consumer Surplus

Drums of Water	$MU	Price	Marginal Consumer Surplus	Total Consumer Surplus
First	$1,000	$25	$975	$ 975
Second	500	25	475	1,450
Third	200	25	175	1,625
Fourth	100	25	75	1,700
Fifth	50	25	25	1,725
Sixth	25	25	0	1,725

Study Guide

QUESTION 5.5
Given Akio's utility for beverages as shown in Table 5.7, if the price was $2, what quantity would he purchase and what would his total consumer surplus be as a result?

Since all of us derive consumer surplus from our purchases, we can illustrate the idea in terms of the market demand. Figure 5.3 on the next page shows the demand curve for CDs.

Suppose that the present price is $20 for this particular recording and that 60,000 CDs are being sold at this price. The demand curve tells us, though, that if the price had been $30, the quantity demanded would have been only 10,000 CDs; 10,000 people would have been prepared to pay $30 for this CD. The fact that they only have to pay $20 means that each of them obtains a consumer surplus of $10. If instead the price had been $28, then 20,000 people would have bought the CD. But we already know that 10,000 of those 20,000 would have paid $30; the other 10,000 weren't prepared to pay $30 but they are willing to pay $28. This latter group then are enjoying a consumer surplus of $8 each. If we continue this exercise down to the $20

FIGURE 5.3 Consumer Surplus, Graphically

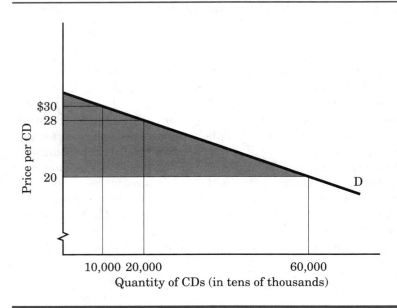

The demand curve shows the maximum price that could be charged at various different quantities, e.g., 10,000 CDs could be sold at a price of $30; 20,000 CDs could be sold at $28 each and so on. The demand curve, therefore, represents how much people would be willing to pay. Let's assume that the price is $20. The vertical distance between the price line and the demand curve represents the amount of consumer surplus at each quantity. The total area between the price line and the demand curve represents the total amount of consumer surplus for all quantities up to the present quantity.

price level, we will discover that the total consumer surplus is $300,000, as shown in Table 5.11.

TABLE 5.11 Calculating Consumer Surplus

Consumers	would have paid:	but only pay:	therefore get a consumer surplus of:	for a total consumer surplus of:
1st 10,000	$30	$20	$10	$100,000
2nd 10,000	28	20	8	80,000
3rd 10,000	26	20	6	60,000
4th 10,000	24	20	4	40,000
5th 10,000	22	20	2	20,000
6th 10,000	20	20	0	0
			Total Consumer Surplus	**$300,000**

This consumer surplus, then, can be represented by the triangular area above the price line as shown in Figure 5.3. A higher price will mean of course that consumers will be enjoying a smaller total consumer surplus; a lower price means a higher total consumer surplus from that product. In addition, Figure 5.4 shows that consumers enjoy a bigger consumer surplus from products with inelastic demands than from those which have elastic demands.

The idea that consumers derive a greater surplus from products with inelastic demands in fact conforms with our idea of what is meant by inelastic: i.e., that buyers are not particularly resistant to price changes presumably because they derive a greater benefit from the product than is represented in the price of the product. The benefit that most smokers get from

FIGURE 5.4 Consumer Surplus Varies with Elasticities

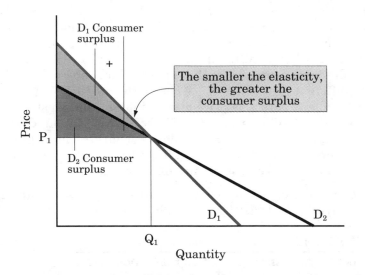

If the price is P_1, then the quantity purchased of each of the two products is quantity Q_1. At lower quantities, however, buyers of product 1 (demand curve 1) would have been prepared to pay higher prices than would buyers of product 2 (demand curve 2). The area between the price line and the demand curve represents the total amount of consumer surplus. The graph shows that this area is much greater in the case of the inelastic demand curve, D_1, than it is with the elastic demand curve, D_2.

cigarettes usually far exceeds even the very high prices they have to pay for them.

It is easy to see why producers would like to, if they could, capture this consumer's surplus for themselves. At the present price of $20 per CD, producers in our last example in Figure 5.3 are deriving an income of $60,000 \times \$20 = \$1,200,000$ from the sales. However as Table 5.11 shows consumers are enjoying an additional psychic benefit, or consumer surplus, of $300,000. This is a tempting amount of possible revenue for the seller of the product. Let us examine the ways in which sellers in general attempt to capture a portion, and sometimes all, of this consumer surplus.

One thing that sellers need to do in order to capture the consumer surplus is to first identify it; they need to know just how much individual consumers are prepared to pay for the product. One way of doing this is through an auction. Here, customers bid up the price to the point where (ideally from the sellers' point of view) the sole remaining customer is being forced to pay what she really thinks it is worth. A Dutch auction works even better from the seller's point of view and captures even more of the consumer surplus. Here, the auctioneer starts the bidding at a very high price which is then bid down by customers. In order to avoid missing out on a purchase, customers may well end up paying the maximum they are prepared to go. In addition, you will notice that if an auctioneer has four identical items to sell, he will sell them one at a time so as to get the maximum consumer surplus from each. Another way of capturing this consumer surplus is to recognize that consumers value the first item purchased far more than they do subsequent purchases. A seller of CDs then might charge $25 for a single CD, but sell 2 for $40 and 3 for $50 and so on. You might think of this as receiving a discount from bulk-buying, but alternatively you could look on it as having to pay a premium for short-buying!

Price Discrimination

price discrimination:
the selling of an
identical product at
a different price to
different customers
for reasons other
than cost.

A final example of the way in which producers attempt to capture this consumer surplus is through **price discrimination**. Price discrimination means that the same product, with the same costs of production, is being sold to different consumers at different prices. It recognizes the fact that consumers have different demands for the same product and are therefore prepared to pay different prices in order to obtain the product. As we shall see, in order for a seller to practise price discrimination, she must be able to recognize that there are different groups of buyers with different demand elasticities and somehow she must be able to separate those groups. Furthermore, if people are being charged different prices, then the seller must try to find a way of preventing resales of the product.

Suppose that you are the owner of a movie theatre and you estimate that the demand for movie visits is as shown in Table 5.12.

TABLE 5.12 Demand for Movie Tickets

Price of Admission	Number of Daily Visits
$8	200
6	250
4	300

Suppose that at present you are charging $8 admission and receiving a daily revenue of $1,600. Of course, you would like to increase your revenue by attracting more customers. However, you realize that there are a number of people who are not willing to pay $8 on a regular basis and the only way to attract them would be to reduce the price. The trouble is that if you do reduce the price, your total sales revenue will fall to $1,500 at $6 (i.e., $6 × 250) and to $1,200 at $4 ($4 × 300). This is because if you do reduce the price, you will have to reduce the price for everyone. Or do you? What you need to find out is: who are the people who are reluctant to pay $8 but would be willing to pay, say, $4? Included in this group are low-income people, many of whom would happily visit the theatre for $4 but are unable to afford a price of $8. However, you have no way of recognizing such people. But there are identifiable groups who are generally, though not always, poor. This includes young people and retired people. So what you would do is charge a lower price for these groups but continue the high price for your regular patrons. In this way, you can increase your revenue appreciably. Your regular 200 patrons continue to pay $8 and you attract an additional 100 patrons (300 total, less the 200 paying $8) each paying $4. Your total revenue increases by $400 per day as a result. On the surface, it looks as though you are offering discount prices to certain identifiable groups and, of course, that is how you would probably advertise it. The truth of the matter is that you are, in fact, charging a premium price to the other identifiable group (the relatively rich).

In order to practise price discrimination then, it is necessary to be able to identify groups of customers with different demands, to separate them from the others and to ensure that those obtaining the lower prices cannot resell the product. This is true of theatre admissions since a young person cannot resell the seat to an older person. For this reason, price discrimination is mostly practised with personal services rather than goods. Other examples of discrimination on the basis of *age* occurs in the area of transportation where in most countries and cities, pensioners and students travel at reduced fares on buses, trains and planes.

QUESTION 5.6

The following table shows the demand for haircuts on an average weekday in your hairdressing salon. Investigation of the demand has revealed to you that the demand from pensioners differs greatly from that of your other customers, as follows:

Price of Haircut	Quantity Demanded by Pensioners	Quantity Demanded by Other Customers
20	1	9
18	4	10
16	7	11
14	10	12
12	13	13
10	16	14
8	19	15
6	22	16
4	25	17
2	28	18

A) Which of the two demands is the more elastic? Why?
B) If you could only charge one price to all customers, which price would give you the greatest sales revenue?
C) Suppose, however, that you charged a different price for pensioners from that of your other customers. What prices would you charge each group in order to maximize your sales revenue?

Price discrimination is also practised on the basis of *time*. Suppose I own a coffee shop and I have no trouble attracting customers between 7 and 10 o'clock in the morning, the time when most people are desperate for coffee. However, business falls off considerably after that time. In order to attract more customers in the off-peak periods, I would have to drop my prices but why should I give everyone the benefit of lower prices when they are quite happy to pay my regular prices? The answer of course would be to have two-tiered prices: a higher price in peak periods than in off-peak periods. Again, this is a method practised by many transport companies and for many other businesses such as hairdressers and movie theatres which have times of the day or whole days where sales are sluggish. Similarly, many telephone and hydro companies have different rates at different times.

Another case where customers are charged different prices for the same item is with bulk-buying. This is discrimination on the basis of the *volume of purchases*. As we saw earlier, it is true that often if you wish to buy a single item of a product you may have to pay more than if you buy a dozen for instance. However, this is not necessarily price discrimination since the costs per unit in terms of packaging, storing and merchandising are often much higher for single items than for bulk. In a sense when you buy in bulk, the costs are lower per item for the seller, and as a result the savings are passed on to the buyers (as witness the success of warehouse-style stores opening up all over the country). However, it is certainly true that big customers often get charged lower fees for many services, such as banking and legal services, than is the case for small customers who only use these services infrequently or not extensively.

BOX 5B

1. In what way is marginal utility related to income elasticity?
2. Is it possible for marginal utility to increase with increased consumption of a product?
3. What does the term *dollar marginal utility* mean?
4. Explain the relationship between marginal utility and the demand for the product.
5. What did Adam Smith mean by the terms *value in use* and *value in exchange*? Explain with examples.
6. What is *consumer surplus*? What is the difference between marginal consumer surplus and total consumer surplus?
7. Which produces a greater total consumer surplus: products with elastic demands or products with inelastic demands? Why?
8. What does the term *price discrimination* mean? Give three examples of price discrimination.
9. What conditions must exist in order for price discrimination to be practised?
10. What are the different bases on which price discrimination is founded?

Chapter Highlights

Chapter 5 goes behind the demand curve and gives a logical explanation of consumer behaviour in terms of marginal utility theory. It begins by explaining the idea of the marginal and then looks at the important law of diminishing marginal utility. This law is nothing more than the statement that additional amounts of any product that a person consumes are likely to produce less and less satisfaction. Starting from this basic proposition, the idea of an optimal purchasing rule is developed. This rule suggests that if a consumer wants to allocate income so as to maximize utility, that person should spend each dollar on products which give the maximum marginal utility.

The rest of the chapter is concerned with showing how marginal utility theory can be put to work. First, it looks at a number of different applications beginning with how the theory can explain why different income groups allocate their income on different types of products. Next, it poses the intriguing question of whether money itself is subject to the law of diminishing returns and what effect this might have on various tax proposals. The next application of the theory was its most important as far as its popularizer, Alfred Marshall, was concerned. We see how the concept of marginal utility enables us to validate the law of demand. The chapter gives an illustration of how knowledge of a person's marginal utility enables us to derive that person's demand curve. It then explains, by way of Adam

Smith's famous diamond-water paradox, why some very important commodities are relatively cheap and why other less essential products are far more expensive. It shows the price we are prepared to pay for any article depends on our valuation of the last unit purchased, not on its average or total value to us.

The final part of the chapter explains the concept of consumer surplus and demonstrates that most consumers derive an extra benefit when they purchase more than one unit of a product at the same price, since they value the first unit far more than successive ones. From this concept, the chapter shows how producers attempt to capture this surplus by practising price discrimination which allows them to charge higher prices to those customers who value the product more highly than do other customers.

New Glossary Terms

Workbook

Study Tips

1. Do not be discouraged if on a first reading you become dismayed by the level of abstraction in this chapter. It may seem to you that all that economists do is to make the commonplace seem unnecessarily esoteric and complicated. But think of the level of abstraction that a physicist brings to her job. Imagine you are trying to find out how a five year old successfully negotiates a steep curve without falling off his bike. The boy might give you a very graphic, and comical description of his achievement. A physicist, on the other hand, is likely to enter into a serious and pedantic discourse involving factors like centrifugal force, the velocity of the bike, the weight of the child, angle of declension and so on. Both are describing the same phenomenon: the child's description is likely to be more interesting but the physicist's will be more illuminating and helpful in the long run — once you understand it. In a sense, this is what an economist is trying to do with the mundane tasks of buying and selling. She is not dealing in abstractions to make things incomprehensible, but, to make them eventually, more comprehensible.

2. If the above advice is not helpful and you are struggling with some of the ideas in this chapter, do not despair. And do not abandon economics! The remainder of the text can be fairly easily absorbed without much reference to the theory of consumer demand.

3. If, initially, you have difficulty grasping the optimal purchasing rule, try working through a number of problems. You may find, in this case, actually "doing" economics is preferable to simply reading it.

4. One of the most important lessons in this chapter is that it is the marginal and not the total utility which determines consumer behaviour. This simply means that asking a person to name his favourite product doesn't make sense except in context. In other words, my favourite product at any moment depends on how much of it I have recently consumed. If I have recently consumed very little, I am likely to rate it highly (it has a high marginal utility); if I have consumed a great deal, then I am not likely to rate it very high (its marginal utility is small) and will likely prefer other products.

5. Bear in mind that economic theories of consumer behaviour try to explain people's actions and do not try to figure out reasons behind that behaviour; that, after all, is the role of the psychologist. It is sufficient for economists to conclude that, faced with identical prices, a consumer who buys product A as opposed to product B does so because it possesses a higher marginal utility, i.e., because she prefers it. This is not a particularly profound observation. However, its implications are reasonably fruitful.

Are You Sure?

Indicate whether the following statements are true or false. If false, indicate why they are false.

1. The term "marginal" means the difference between averages.
T or **F**   If false: _____

_____

_____

2. Utility is defined as the satisfaction or pleasure derived from the consumption of a product.
T or **F**   If false: _____

_____

_____

3. Marginal utility is the additional utility derived from the consumption of one more unit of a product.
T or **F**   If false: _____

_____

_____

4. The law of diminishing marginal utility suggests that as successive units of a product are consumed, total utility eventually declines.

T or **F**   If false: _____

_____

_____

5. If the MU per dollar spent on product A is greater than on product B, then a rational consumer should consume more of product B to compensate.

T or **F**   If false: _____

_____

_____

6. It is the marginal utility of the *last* unit consumed which determines how much a consumer is prepared to pay for a product.

T or **F**   If false: _____

_____

_____

7. Consumer surplus is the additional amount that consumers have to pay if they really need a particular product.

T or **F**   If false: _____

_____

_____

8. The consumer surplus derived from products which have an inelastic demand is greater than that from products with an elastic demand.

T or **F**   If false: _____

_____

_____

9. Price discrimination is the practice of charging different prices for different products.

T or **F**   If false: _____

_____

_____

10. Price discrimination cannot be practised if consumers are able to resell the product.

T or **F**   If false: _____

_____

_____

Translations

Explain in words what the following expression means. What action on the part of the consumer would it lead to?

$$\frac{MU_A}{P_A} > \frac{MU_B}{P_B}$$

Answer:

_____

_____

_____

_____

_____

_____

Choose the Best

1. What is the correct expression for marginal utility?
   a) It is equal to total utility divided by quantity consumed.
   b) It is the change in total utility resulting from a change in the quantity consumed.

2. If total utility is falling then:
   a) marginal utility must be negative.
   b) marginal utility must also be falling.

3. When is total utility at a maximum?
   a) When marginal utility is maximum.
   b) When marginal utility is zero.

4. What does the diamond-water paradox refer to?
   a) The fact that water is far more plentiful than diamonds even though people need more diamonds.
   b) The fact that water is far more valuable than diamonds, yet its price tends to be far lower.
   c) The fact that although people don't necessarily want diamonds, they are prepared to pay a high price for them.

5. Which of the following is correct in reference to the law of diminishing marginal utility?
   a) The amount of additional utility decreases as successive units of a product are consumed.
   b) Marginal utility increases at first, but after some point starts to decline.
   c) Total utility declines at first, but after some point starts to increase.

6. Suppose that the price of a plate of sushi is $10 and Jan's marginal utility is 8 while Jin's marginal utility is 12. What can be deduced from this information?
   a) That Jin should buy the sushi but Jan should not.
   b) That Jin likes sushi better than does Jan.
   c) No deductions can be made from this information.

7. Which of the following is a correct statement of the optimal purchasing rule?
   a) $MU_A/MU_B = P_B/P_A$.
   b) $MU_A/P_A = MU_B/P_B$.
   c) $P_A/MU_A = P_B/MU_B$.

8. Which of the following products are likely to yield the greatest amount of consumer surplus?
   a) Water.
   b) Diamonds.
   c) Ice cream.
   d) A Persian carpet.

9. What will happen if $MU_A/P_A > MU_B/P_B$?
   a) The price of A will be forced to drop.
   b) The price of B will be forced to drop.
   c) The consumer will purchase more of product A.
   d) The consumer will purchase more of product B.

Refer to Table W5.1 when anwering questions 10 and 11.

TABLE W5.1

Quantity Consumed	Total Utility
1	30
2	55
3	75
4	90
5	100
6	105
7	105
8	100

10. Refer to Table W5.1 to answer this question. What is the marginal utility of the 5th unit?
   a) 10.
   b) 20.
   c) 100.
   d) Cannot be answered from this information.

11. Refer to Table W5.1 to answer this question. If the price of this product is $5, how many units should this consumer purchase?
   a) 4.
   b) 5.
   c) 6.
   d) Cannot be answered from this information.

12. In order for price discrimination to work, three conditions must be fulfilled. Which of the following is *not* one of those conditions.
   a) The seller must be able to identify and separate different groups of buyers.
   b) The different groups of buyers must have different elasticities of demand.
   c) The product must be a necessity.
   d) It must be impossible to resell the product.

Refer to Figure W5.1 to answer questions 13 and 14.

FIGURE W5.1

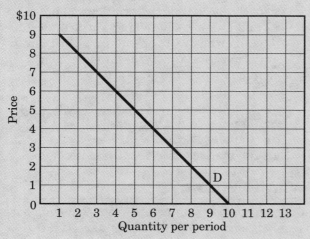

13. Refer to Figure W5.1 to answer this question. What is the value of total consumer surplus at a price of $5?
    a) $10.
    b) $12.
    c) $20.
    d) $35.

14. Refer to Figure W5.1 to answer this question. At what price is the total consumer surplus equal to $21?
    a) $3.
    b) $4.
    c) $5.
    d) $6.
    e) $9.

15. Suppose that Jon is purchasing the optimal amounts of apples and oranges. The marginal utility of the last apple is 8 and of the last orange is 6. If the price of an apple is $1, what must be the price of an orange?
    a) 50 cents.
    b) 75 cents.
    c) $1.33.
    d) $1.40.
    e) Cannot be determined from this information.

16. Suppose that, for a certain consumer, the marginal utility of product A is equal to 40 and its price is $42, while the marginal utility of product B is 30 and its price is $40. What conclusion can be inferred from this?
    a) This consumer should buy more of product A and less of product B.
    b) This consumer should buy more of product B and less of product A.
    c) This consumer should buy more of product B because it is cheaper.
    d) This consumer should buy neither product since the prices exceed the marginal utilities.
    e) This consumer should buy more of product B because it gives greater value for money.

Refer to Figure W5.2 to answer questions 17 and 18.

FIGURE W5.2

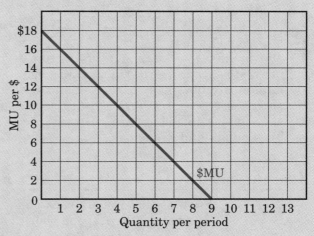

17. Refer to Figure W5.2 to answer this question. What is the maximum price that would be paid by this consumer, assuming that partial units cannot be purchased?
    a) $9.
    b) $10.
    c) $16.
    d) $18.
    e) Cannot be determined from this information.

18. Refer to Figure W5.2 to answer this question. At what quantity would this consumer maximize her total utility?
    a) 5.

b) 9.
c) 10.
d) 18.
e) Cannot be determined from this information.

Refer to Table W5.2 when answering questions 19 and 20.

TABLE W5.2

Quantity Consumed	MU Apples	MU Bananas
1	20	18
2	18	17
3	16	14
4	14	11
5	12	8
6	10	5
7	8	2
8	6	0

19. Refer to Table W5.2 to answer this question. Suppose that the price of both apples and bananas is $1 each and this consumer has $8 to spend. In order to maximize her total utility, how many of each should she purchase?
a) 3 apples and 5 bananas.
b) 4 apples and 4 bananas.

c) 5 apples and 3 bananas.
d) 8 apples.
e) 8 bananas.

20. Refer to Table W5.2 to answer this question. Suppose that the price of an apple is $2 and the price of a banana is $1 and this consumer has $8 to spend. In order to maximize her total utility, how many of each should she purchase?
a) 1 apple and 6 bananas.
b) 2 apples and 4 bananas.
c) 3 apples and 2 bananas.
d) 4 apples.
e) 8 bananas.

What's Wrong?

Can you spot the four errors in the following passage? (Ignore grammatical mistakes!).

Utility expresses the amount of usage that can be obtained from a product. As we consume more of any product, its total utility will decline. In addition, as successive units of any product are consumed, the amount of additional utility de-clines. This is known as the optimal purchasing rule. The optimal purchasing rule implies that the amount of utility per dollar spent on all products will be the same. It will also mean that the consumer will be de-riving the maximum total utility from each product.

Key Problem

Suppose that you are vacationing at a resort in the Caribbean and you are trying to determine how to spend your time and money on two particular activities, windsurfing and snorkelling which both cost $10 per hour. The marginal utility of the activities are shown in Table W5.3.

TABLE W5.3

No. of Hours	Windsurfing Marginal Utility	Windsurfing Total Utility	Snorkelling Marginal Utility	Snorkelling Total Utility
1	85	_____	100	_____
2	80	_____	90	_____
3	65	_____	75	_____
4	60	_____	70	_____
5	55	_____	50	_____

6	40	_____	25	_____
7	30	_____	20	_____
8	5	_____	10	_____

a) Complete the columns of total utilities.

b) Assume that you have a budget of $60. In order to maximize your total utility, how would you allocate your spending between the two activities? What is the resulting total utility?

$_____ (_____ hours) on windsurfing; and $_____

(_____ hours) on snorkelling. Total utility: _____ utils.

c) At the end of the day, you dig deep in your pocket and discover an extra $20. If you allocate this additional spending between the two activities so as to maximize your total utility, what will be the utility of the $80 spent?

$_____ (_____ hours) on windsurfing; and $ _____

(_____ hours) on snorkelling. Total utility: _____ utils.

d) Suppose that your utility from the two activities remains unchanged the next day, when you arrive with $80 in you pocket. Unfortunately, you discover that the hourly charge for snorkelling has increased to $15. How will you now allocate your expenditures in order to maximize your total utility, assuming that partial hours cannot be purchased? (Complete the columns in Table W5.4 marked "marginal utility per dollar spent" to assist you.)

TABLE W5.4

	Windsurfing			Snorkelling		
No. of Hours	Marginal Utility	Total Utility	Marginal Utility per Dollar Spent	Marginal Utility	Total Utility	Marginal Utility per Dollar Spent
1	85	_____	_____	100	_____	_____
2	80	_____	_____	90	_____	_____
3	65	_____	_____	75	_____	_____
4	60	_____	_____	70	_____	_____
5	55	_____	_____	50	_____	_____
6	40	_____	_____	25	_____	_____
7	30	_____	_____	20	_____	_____
8	5	_____	_____	10	_____	_____

$_____ (_____ hours) on windsurfing; and $_____

(_____ hours) on snorkelling. Total utility: _____ utils.

e) Show the effects of the price change on the two products on the graphs in Figure W5.3 below.

FIGURE W5.3

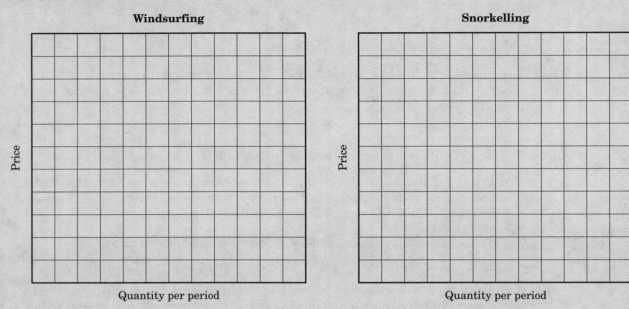

Windsurfing

Snorkelling

f) The next year you are vacationing at a resort in Buffalo and, with your utility unchanged, discover to your joy that windsurfing and snorkelling are free. How will you allocate your eight-hour day between the two activities in order, as usual, to maximize your total utility?

_____ hours on windsurfing; and _____ hours on snorkelling.

Total utility: _____ utils.

Need a Hand?

a) Since marginal utility is the utility derived from the consumption of each additional unit, the total utility is the accumulation of each unit's marginal utility, i.e., it is a running total. This gives the figures shown in Table W5.5.

TABLE W5.5 (completed Table W5.3)

No. of Hours	Windsurfing Marginal Utility	Windsurfing Total Utility	Snorkelling Marginal Utility	Snorkelling Total Utility
1	85	**85**	100	**100**
2	80	**165**	90	**190**
3	65	**230**	75	**265**
4	60	**290**	70	**335**
5	55	**345**	50	**385**
6	40	**385**	25	**410**
7	30	**415**	20	**430**
8	5	**420**	10	**440**

b) To find the best allocation, look at the marginal utility of each activity in turn. For instance, the 1st hour of snorkelling gives greater utility than the 1st hour of windsurfing (100 compared to 85), so you would choose that. Having spent an hour snorkelling, your choice is between a **2nd** hour of snorkelling or a **1st** hour of windsurfing. Again, snorkelling is preferable giving 90 utils compared to 85 for windsurfing. After two hours of snorkelling, you need to choose between a **3rd** hour of snorkelling or, again, your **1st** hour of windsurfing. Now, windsurfing is preferable since it is worth 85 utils compared to the 75 for the third hour of snorkelling. Continuing in a similar fashion will produce the following results:

> 1st hour: snorkelling 2nd hour: snorkelling
> 3rd hour: windsurfing 4th hour: windsurfing
> 5th hour: snorkelling 6th hour: snorkelling

Therefore, you would spend **2 hours and $20 on windsurfing and 4 hours and $40 on snorkelling.** Glancing at the table shows that 2 hours of windsurfing produces 165 utils and 4 hours of windsurfing gives 335 utils. The total therefore is **500 utils.**

c) The secret here is *not* to go back to the beginning. Since you have already worked out the first six hours of activities, continue from that point and work out the 7th and 8th hours. You have already spent 2 hours on windsurfing and 4 hours on snorkelling. The 7th hour is therefore either your 3rd hour of windsurfing or your 5th hour of snorkelling. The former is preferable since the marginal utility is 65 compared to the 50 for the 5th hour of snorkelling. Similarly, the 4th hour of windsurfing at 60 is better than the 5th hour of snorkelling of 50. The full eight hours is therefore summarized as:

> 1st hour: snorkelling 2nd hour: snorkelling
> 3rd hour: windsurfing 4th hour: windsurfing
> 5th hour: snorkelling 6th hour: snorkelling
> 7th hour: windsurfing 8th hour: windsurfing

Therefore, you would spend **4 hours and $40 on windsurfing, and 4 hours and $40 on snorkelling**. Glancing at the table shows that 4 hours of windsurfing produces 290 utils and 4 hours of snorkelling gives 335 utils. The total therefore is **625 utils.**

d) We are now dealing with two different prices for the activities, so in order to make them comparable we must calculate the MU per dollar spent on each. To do this we divide the column of MUs by the price of 10 for windsurfing and the column of MUs by the price of 15 for snorkelling. The result is as shown in Table W5.6.

TABLE W5.6 (completed Table W5.4)

	Windsurfing			Snorkelling		
No. of Hours	Margin Utility	Total Utility	MU per Dollar Spent	Marginal Utlity	Total Utility	MU per Dollar Spent
1	85	85	8.5	100	100	6.67
2	80	165	8.0	90	190	6.0
3	65	230	6.5	75	265	5.0
4	60	290	6.0	70	335	4.67
5	55	345	5.5	50	385	3.33
6	40	385	4.0	25	410	1.67
7	30	415	3.0	20	430	1.33
8	5	420	0.5	10	440	0.67

We use the same method as we did before: compare utilities (this time MU per dollar), purchase by purchase. Each of the first two hours of windsurfing gives greater MU per dollar than does the first hour of snorkelling, but the first hour of snorkelling is better than the third hour of windsurfing, and so on. This gives the following results.

1st hour: windsurfing   2nd hour: windsurfing
3rd hour: snorkelling   4th hour: windsurfing
5th hour: snorkelling (or windsurfing)   6th hour: windsurfing (or snorkelling)
7th hour: windsurfing

Therefore, you would spend **5 hours and $50 on windsurfing and 2 hours and $30 on snorkelling**. You could not afford an 8th hour since you have now exhausted your budget of $80. Glancing at the table shows that 5 hours of snorkelling produces 345 utils and 2 hours of windsurfing gives 190 utils. **The total therefore is 535 utils.**

e) The important point to remember is that a change in the price of a product (in this case, snorkelling) causes a movement *along* the demand curve and a *shift* in the demand curve of a substitute (windsurfing). This is illustrated in Figure W5.4.

FIGURE W5.4 (completed Figure W5.3)

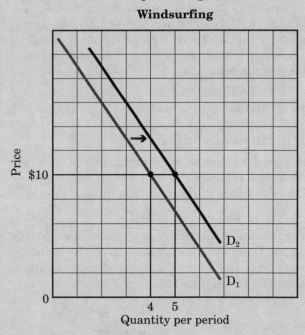

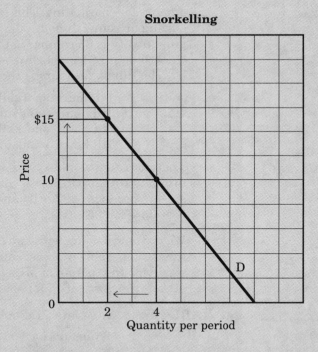

f) Although money is no longer a constraint, you still have a scarce resource: time. Since you cannot spend all of your time both windsurfing *and* snorkelling, you must allocate your *time* so as to maximize your total utility. The answer and the method are the same as in c). This time the prices of each activity are the same and equal to zero. Since we ignore prices, we need only compare MUs as we did in c). The answer then is that you would spend **4 hours on windsurfing, and 4 hours on snorkelling, and the total utility is therefore 625 utils.**

More of the Same

Suppose Jean spends recreation time and money on two leisure activities: tennis and fishing. The cost per hour of tennis (court fees) and fishing (boat rentals) are both $2. Table W5.7 shows the total utility that Jean derives from the two activities.

TABLE W5.7

	Fishing			Tennis	
No. of Hours	Total Utility	Marginal Utility	No. of Hours	Total Utility	Marginal Utility
1	31	_____	1	38	_____
2	60	_____	2	72	_____
3	87	_____	3	102	_____
4	111	_____	4	130	_____
5	131	_____	5	152	_____
6	149	_____	6	170	_____
7	161	_____	7	184	_____
8	167	_____	8	194	_____

a) Complete the columns of marginal utilities.

b) Assume that Jean has a budget of $8. In order to maximize her total utility, how would she allocate her spending between the two activities? What is the resulting total utility?

c) At the end of the day, Jean digs deep in her pocket and discovers an extra $4. If she allocates this additional spending between the two activities so as to maximize her total utility, what will be the final totals?

d) Suppose that Jean's utility from the two activities remains unchanged the next day, when she arrives with $12 in her pocket. To her pleasure, she discovers that the hourly charge for boat rentals has decreased to $1. How will she now allocate her expenditures in order to maximize her total utility?

e) Show the effects of the price change on the two products graphically.

Other Problems

1. a) Suppose that Daniel is willing to pay a maximum of $5 for his first slice of pizza. For each additional slice he would be prepared to pay up to 50 cents less. If Daniel could obtain the pizza for free, how many slices would he eat?

    Number of slices: _____

b) If the price of a slice of pizza happened to be $2, how many slices would he purchase (assuming his budget allowed it)? What would be his total consumer surplus as a result?

Number of slices: _____; consumer surplus $_____.

2. Figure W5.5 below depicts Christian's dollar marginal utility for ice creams and for giant chocolate cookies.

FIGURE W5.5

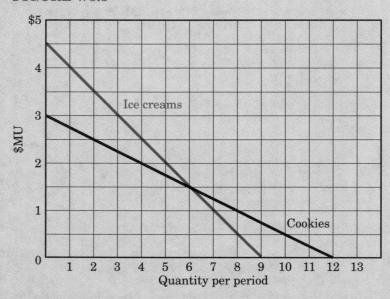

a) If Christian's budget only allowed him enough to make a total of 6 purchases, how many of each product would he buy?

_____ ice creams, and _____ cookies.

b) What if he found he could afford 10, how many of each product would he buy?

_____ ice creams, and _____ cookies.

3. a) Chika has determined the marginal utility that she derives from her earned income and from leisure. This is presented in Table W5.8 below. In her ideal world, where she could work as few or as many hours as she wished, how would she allocate her 16 waking hours (she does need to sleep)?

TABLE W5.8

Hours	Paid Employment MU	Leisure MU
1	100	80
2	90	75
3	80	70
4	70	65
5	60	60
6	50	55
7	40	50
8	30	45
9	20	40
10	10	35

_____ working hours, and _____ leisure hours.

b) Unfortunately, Chika begins to realize that unless she gets an education, she won't enjoy a high salary and therefore won't be able to afford more leisure time. She therefore decides to spend 6 hours each day studying. How much will she now devote between work and leisure?

_____ working hours, and _____ leisure hours.

4. Sam's drive-in movie theatre attracts two main groups of customers: teenagers and parents with young infants. The demand of the two groups is shown in Table W5.9.

TABLE W5.9

Admission Price ($)	Teenagers Quantity Demanded	Total Revenue ($)	Parents Quantity Demanded	Total Revenue ($)	Both Groups Total Revenue ($)
8	100	_____	0	_____	_____
7	150	_____	5	_____	_____
6	180	_____	15	_____	_____
5	200	_____	30	_____	_____
4	210	_____	55	_____	_____
3	215	_____	80	_____	_____
2	218	_____	100	_____	_____
1	220	_____	150	_____	_____

a) If Sam charges a single admission price, and wants to maximize his total revenue, what price should he charge, and what will be his total revenue?

Price: $_____; Total revenue: $_____.

b) Suppose, instead, that Sam is able to discriminate between the two groups and charge different prices to each. How much would he charge each, and what would be his total revenue now?

Price to teenagers: $_____; Price to parents: $_____;

Total revenue: $_____.

Unanswered Questions

Short Essays

1. What are total and marginal utility and how are they related? Explain the law of diminishing marginal utility.

2. Explain the optimal purchasing rule. In what way do you think it helps explain observed consumer behaviour?

3. Explain how the demand curve for the individual can be derived from knowledge of her marginal utility curve.

4.   What is meant by consumer surplus? How does it relate to the individual's demand curve, and to the market demand curve?

5.   How is consumer surplus related to the price elasticity of demand?

6.   What is price discrimination? What conditions are necessary for it to be practised? Give three examples and explain what the grounds are for the discrimination.

Analytical Questions

1.   If a nightclub charges a higher entrance fee after 10 p.m. than before, do you think that latecomers are being penalized or are early-comers being favoured?

2.   To what extent is time a factor when examining the law of diminishing utility? Why? Can you name products that might give increased rather then decreased marginal utility over time? Does this invalidate the law?

3.   If two people are both willing to pay the same price to watch a soccer game, does that imply that their marginal utilities are equal? Why or why not?

4.   Suppose that you are trying to decide on whether to play an hour of squash which will cost you $6, or instead go swimming for an hour at a cost of $4. The marginal utility of squash is 180 utils and swimming is 140 utils. Which is a better buy for you? What does the marginal utility of swimming need to be to make you indifferent between the two?

5.   Explain why a higher elasticity of demand results in a smaller consumer surplus. Under what circumstances would consumer surplus be zero?

6.   If you buy more than one unit of any product, you will always obtain some consumer surplus. Is this true? Why, or why not?

Numerical Questions

1.   Yoko has $14 to spend on lunch. Unfortunately, the deli doesn't have a very extensive menu: apples at $1 each, bagels at $2 each, and cappuccino at $3 each. Given her utility figures in Table W5.10, how should she allocate her $14?

TABLE W5.10

Quantity	Apples Total Utility	Bagels Total Utility	Cappuccino Total Utility
1	80	200	270
2	145	350	480
3	200	470	630
4	240	560	735
5	260	610	825
6	275	630	840

2.   Mina is wondering how to spend her $12 evening budget. She has decided she wants to watch videos and eat pizza. A movie rental and a pizza slice both cost $2. Her total utility for the two products is shown in Table W5.11, parts A and B.

TABLE W5.11

A Video Movies		B Pizza Slices	
No. of videos	Total Utility	No. of Slices	Total Utility
1	34	1	40
2	64	2	76
3	88	3	108
4	106	4	136
5	118	5	162
6	126	6	184

a)   How should she allocate her budget between the videos and pizzas to maximize her total utility?

b)   Suppose that the Pizza shop has a deal whereby you can buy a 6-slice pizza for the price of $10. How will she allocate her budget now?

3.   Akira's pleasure from eating sushi and drinking sake is shown in Table W5.12, parts A and B, which shows his marginal utility measured in terms of dollars, i.e., in $MUs.

TABLE W5.12

A Sushi		B Sake	
No. of Pieces	$MU	No. of Drinks	$MU
1	10	1	6
2	8	2	5
3	5	3	4.50
4	3	4	4
5	2	5	3.50
6	1	6	1
7	0.50	7	0
8	0	8	−2

a) Suppose Akira has a budget of $16 and the price of both sushi and sake are $2. How many of each will Akira consume so as to maximize his total utility? How much total utility will he derive? How much consumer surplus will he obtain from each product, and what will be the total consumer surplus?

b) Suppose Akira is not restricted to his $16 budget. How much of each will he buy, how much will his total dollar utility and his total consumer surplus be?

4. In Lumbolia, milk drinking is correlated to hair colouring (or is it vice versa?). The demand for milk of these three groups is shown in Table W5.13.

TABLE W5.13

Litres of Milk	Redheads	Brunettes	Blondes
Price ($)	Daily quantity	Daily quantity	Daily quantity
3	10	20	60
2.50	20	26	62
2	30	32	64
1.50	40	38	66
1	50	44	68
0.50	60	50	70

The country's milk is provided by a single dairy farmer.

a) What price should the farmer charge if he wishes to maximize his total sales revenue? What is the farmer's total revenue?

b) Suppose that the government of Lumbolia allows the dairy farmer to price discriminate on the basis of hair colour. If he wishes to maximize his total revenue, how much should he charge each group? What will be his total sales revenue now?

c) What is the price elasticity of demand for these three groups for a price change from $3 per litre to $2.50? What do you think is the connection between price discrimination and price elasticity?

CHAPTER SIX

■ ■ ■ ■ ■ ■ ■

The Costs of Production

What's ahead . . . In this chapter we look at the costs of production faced by a typical firm. An understanding of costs is necessary for us to be able to study market structure which comes in subsequent chapters. You will learn that a firm's productivity is closely linked to it costs. There are, in fact, several different types of costs that are discussed. These include total cost, average total cost, marginal cost, average variable cost and fixed cost.

We now need to shift our focus from supply/demand analysis to that of the business organization — what economists call the "firm."

We will be discussing the firm and its behaviour over the next five chapters. As a general introduction to the study of the firm consider some of the different types of decisions that the typical firm must make: What is the right product(s) to produce? What is the right level of production for now and how might this change in the future? What methods of distribution and marketing approaches are the most appropriate? And what is the right price to charge?

 Data

BOX 6.1

One of the truly intriguing questions in economics is: why do firms exist? Ronald Coase (1910–), a Nobel laureate who spent many years at the University of Chicago, offered an elegant answer in the late 1930s. Consider the situation where I want a new house. I could locate a lot and arrange to buy it; then hire someone to prepare the lot for construction; locate and hire someone to dig a hole for the basement; still someone else to prepare and pour the concrete foundation; others to frame the building after yet someone else has been found to design the structure; still others to do the roofing, plumbing, electrical and finishing work. At each stage I would have to seek bids, negotiate prices, product types and schedules and hope that everyone delivered on what they promised. All of this would take a lot of time and money — i.e., has *transactions costs*.

Alternately, I could simply buy a house that some firm has put onto the market. In putting a house up for sale, the firm has absorbed all the transactions costs and since they have produced dozens (hundreds) of houses, as well as the one I buy, they have been able to reduce the *per-house* transactions costs and that is why they exist — they are more efficient.

Out of this comes two fundamental questions that economist ask about the behaviour of firms. This first is why is price set by the firm at the level that it is and, second, why is production at the level that it is? In the process of answering these questions we will look (in Chapters 8–11) at what economists call market structure. But first we need to understand all that falls under the general topic called the *costs of production*.

Production is the activity of a business organization or firm using inputs in order to obtain output of some product. We see examples of production every day. For example, think of inputs like sand, gravel, cement, water, machines and labour which are used to produce the output concrete.

depreciation: the annual cost of any asset that is expected to be in use for more than one year.

Now, of course, the inputs used in production have to be paid for, and this payment becomes the firm's cost. When most students hear the word costs they think of the dollars and cents that are actually paid out by the firm. Many costs can be thought of in just this way, but this is by no means the whole story. For example, a firm may buy a machine for $200,000 that it expects to be able to use for eight years. What is the cost of this machine in the first year of its use? Surely, the answer is not the full $200,000. Instead, it could be thought of as the amount of the machine which is used up or worn out during that year. What is called **depreciation** is the annual amount of this wear. In this example, the cost of depreciation could be equal to, say, one-eighth of $200,000 or $25,000.

Explicit and Implicit Costs

Let's take another example involving costs. In the case of smaller firms of the mom and pop variety where the owners often contribute their own money and time to the firm. Is the contribution of money to the firm free? Should we consider the time put into the firm by its owners as having no costs? The answer to both questions is no, and this once again raises the concept of opportunity costs introduced in Chapter 1. Let's say that our hypothetical owners, Otto and Melissa, put $100,000, which they obtained from an inheritance, into their own soup and sandwich shop, the Moonlight Cafe. The costs to the firm, economists would argue, must include what this couple could have done with the $100,000 instead of putting it into their own business. One clear alternative would be to buy some mutual funds from which they could earn, let us say, 10% per year. Therefore, the cost to the firm of using this $100,000 is the sacrifice of the lost return of $10,000 per year. Similarly, we could ask what could Otto and Melissa do instead of putting 18 hours a day of work into their own business? Well, both of them could hire their labour out to someone else in a similar business who wanted the skills that our hypothetical couple possess. Let us assume that the going market wage for this type of labour (short-order cook and waiter) was $8 an hour. We should then assign a cost to the firm of this couple putting their time into the business of $144 a day. The important thing for you to note is that neither the $10,000 per year nor the $144 per day need necessarily be actually paid out by the firm, but each is a legitimate cost of doing business using the concept of opportunity cost. In other words, to an economist, there is a cost involved — even if no payment is made — if an activity involves the use of productive resources since those resources could have been used elsewhere.

Study Guide

QUESTION 6.1

Judy, who has two young daughters in day-care, is currently working as an activities facilitator at a nearby community centre. She is unhappy with her job, but the idea of not being able to work and having to stay home all day with the kids makes her even more unhappy. Therefore, she is contemplating returning to college for a two-year certificate in computer technology. Judy has collected the following facts:

a) college tuition per year	$860
b) two-year estimate for textbooks	1,200
c) cost for day-care per child per year	4,800
d) Judy's per month income (after taxes)	1,056
e) transportation to and from college per year	600
f) Judy's contribution to the household budget per month	656

What would be an economist's estimate of the cost for Judy to take the two-year program at the college?

explicit costs: costs that are actually paid out in money.

We can see that there are two distinct types of costs in our example of the Moonlight Cafe: **explicit costs** which are the costs which are paid to non-owners, e.g., wages to employees and payments to suppliers; and **implicit costs** which means the costs of using the owners' resources (whether or not any payment is made).

implicit costs: an opportunity cost that does not require an actual expenditure of cash.

Below, in Table 6.1, is a typical month's accounting of the business activity for the cafe.

TABLE 6.1 Profit and Loss Statement

Income:		
Cash Sales (including Sales Tax)		$14,445
Expenses:		
Rent	$ 900	
Chicken, Meat and Fish	2,700	
Vegetables and Fruit	1,850	
Rice and Pasta	1,200	
Sundries	1,000	
Insurance	100	
Business Licenses, etc.	50	
Tax Remittance	945	
Hired Labour	1,600	
Other	400	
Advertising	1,200	
Depreciation on Equipment	500	
Total Explicit Costs:		12,445
Accounting Profit:		2,000
Implicit Costs:		
Opportunity Costs of the $100,000 Put into Business	833	
Labour Put in by Owners (25 days)	3,600	
Total Implicit Costs:		4,433
Economic Loss:		(2,433)

Note that an accountant and an economist treat the depreciation on equipment calculation differently. Let's assume that the $500 depreciation expense is the maximum the tax laws allow in this particular year and, thus, is the figure used by the accountant. The economist would argue, however, that the actual cost of equipment this year is the decline in its market value which results from it being one year older. This might or might not be equal to $500, but for expediency we will assume that it is.

As you can see from Table 6.1, if we considered only direct out-of-pocket expenses (explicit costs) we would conclude that Otto and Melissa had made a profit of $2,000 in this month. In fact, this is the way that an accountant would report the month's activities because the tax authorities do not allow firms to claim implicit costs as deductible expenses. Economists, however, recognizing the concept of opportunity costs, argue that rather than making a $2,000 profit, the Moonlight Cafe in fact lost $2,433 in this month. Another way of looking at this is that if Otto and Melissa had put their money into a mutual fund and hired themselves out at the going market wage rate, they would have been $2,433 ahead for this month. However, they do enjoy the benefit of working for themselves which is attractive to many people. In addition, there is the prospect of better months in the future which Otto and Melissa will weigh before becoming too depressed about their business decisions.

Sunk Costs Have Zero Opportunity Costs

sunk costs: the historical costs of buying plant, machinery and equipment that is unrecoverable.

To better understand what the concept of cost means to an economist consider the following scenario. You are walking through the local mall and come upon the food fair section and decide to buy something to eat. At first, you can not decide between a taco platter for $4.99 or a soup and sandwich combo for the same price. You understand (from Chapter 1) that the opportunity cost of the one is the sacrifice you make by not buying the other, but there is more. Let's assume that you decide on the taco platter and sit down to enjoy your purchase. After a single bite you realize that you made the wrong choice and you really don't want to eat even another bite. What is the cost of leaving the platter uneaten and simply walking away? To an economist, the answer is zero because the $4.99 you spent on the taco platter is a **sunk cost**. A sunk cost is the historical cost of buying something that has no current resale value. Sunk costs are absolutely irrelevant to decision making. Even if a firm has spent millions of dollars on equipment, if that money has already been spent and the equipment has no resale value, then throwing it away has no cost.

Normal Profits and Economic Profits

normal profits: when revenue is just equal to all costs — explicit and implicit, i.e., an amount of profit necessary to keep the entrepreneur in business.

We need to say something about the different possible definitions of profit. If the Moonlight Cafe had made enough revenue just to cover both its explicit and implicit costs, is it right for the economist to say that Otto and Melissa have made zero profit while the accountant would say that they had made a profit? We can sort out this possible confusion by making a distinction between normal profit and economic profit. When a firm has enough revenue just to cover *all* costs (implicit and explicit) we say it is making **normal profits** only. That is to say, economists consider normal

economic profits: revenue over and above all costs including normal profits.

profits as a cost, and earning at least normal profits is considered a necessary part of doing business. Since accountants measure only the explicit costs then, to them, profit is merely the difference between total revenue and explicit costs. However, to the economist, **economic profit** is the difference between total revenue and all costs (both explicit and implicit). Would Otto and Melissa stay in business if, month after month, they made zero economic profits? They probably would since they are making normal profits.

QUESTION 6.2

Houton recently gave up his job, which paid $9.00 an hour (net of taxes), and opened a convenience store using $40,000 of his own money. He spent $30,000 on equipment and physical improvements to his leased space. The remaining $10,000 is in a chequing/savings account which pays only 3% interest since Houton felt that he could not risk tying it up in a one-year term deposit which would have paid 6%. Houton's accountant advises that a 20% depreciation rate on all assets is reasonable.

Based on the information above what are Houton's implicit costs for the first month of operations in which he worked 336 hours?

Total, Average and Marginal Product

It is clear that more production will involve higher costs and this output/cost relationship is one that we need to spend time on. First, however, we need to understand some basic relationships *within* the concept of production itself.

Common sense would lead one to think that if more inputs were added to the production process, more output would be obtained. Yet to leave things at that would skirt over some of the most important aspects of the production process.

short run: any period of time in which at least one input in the production process is fixed.

Not all inputs can be increased at the same time. For example, a farmer can add more variable inputs such as water and fertilizer to his fields this season, but he can not increase the size of his fields. Thus, we need to recognize that, within any given time period, some inputs will be fixed. This leads us to the very important point that as long as any one input is fixed, we are in what economists call the **short run**. This chapter will be entirely in the context of the short run. In the next chapter we will look at the long run where all inputs are variable.

Let's now look at some hypothetical data in Table 6.2 which, for simplicity's sake, assumes that there are only two inputs needed to produce grain which is our output. The first of these two inputs is land which we assume is a fixed size of 10 hectares and the second is labour which we will assume comes equipped with some fixed complement of seed, fertilizer, water and tools.

TABLE 6.2 Total Product Data

Units of Labour (L)	Total Product (TP) in bushels
0	0
1	8
2	20
3	45
4	75
5	100
6	120
7	130
8	135
9	135
10	130

total product: the total output of any productive process.

The right hand column in Table 6.2 indicates the output which is what economists call **total product** (TP). Here we see what happens to total product as we add successive units of labour (which is the variable input). What is important to notice about this data is that total product does not rise proportionately with the increase in labour. The explanation for this involves the use of a concept that economists call **marginal product** (MP) which is defined as the change in total product as a result of adding one more unit of input, which is, in this case, labour. Formally then, the marginal product of *labour* is:

marginal product: the increase in total product as a result of adding one more unit of input.

$$MP_L = \frac{\Delta TP}{\Delta L}$$

It is important for you not to confuse marginal product with **average product** (AP) which is nothing more than total product divided by the number of inputs. Average product is often called productivity per worker. Formally, the average product of *labour* is:

average product: total product (or total output) divided by the quantity of inputs used to produce that total.

$$AP_L = \frac{TP}{L}$$

Let's go to Table 6.3 to examine these new concepts in detail.

TABLE 6.3 Marginal and Average Product Data

Units of Labour	Total Product (TP)	Marginal Product (MP)	Average Productivity (AP)
0	0	—	—
1	8	8	8
2	20	12	10
3	45	25	15
4	75	30	18.8
5	100	25	20
6	120	20	20
7	130	10	18.6
8	135	5	16.9
9	135	0	15
10	130	−5	13

The data in the third column of Table 6.3 indicates that the marginal product of the first unit of production is 8 while that of the second production unit rises to 12. Why might the marginal product of labour rise? Does it mean that the second worker is more productive than the first? No, because we assume that each worker is equally productive. So what is the explanation? An analogy may help here. Can you imagine trying to build a fence by yourself? It could be done, but it would be slow and awkward. You would have to set each post temporarily and then step back to see if it was straight and then readjust it and step back again and so on and so on. Clearly, two people (each with tools and material) could build a fence at a rate that is more than twice as fast as one person. That is to say, the marginal product of the second person would be higher than that of the first person.

division of labour: the dividing of the production process into a series of specialized tasks, each done by a different worker.

Adam Smith referred to this phenomena as the **division of labour** in his famous example of the pin factory. Smith marvelled at the fact that a state-of-the-art factory in eighteenth-century England, which employed only ten workers, was able to produce 48,000 ordinary straight pins in a single day by dividing the process of pin-making into 10 distinct functions in which each worker performed but one task. The emphasis here is on the word process as distinct from the situation where each worker separately and independently would make a whole pin from start to finish which, in Smith's estimation, would result in the production of less than 1,000 pins in a day.

Data

BOX 6.2
Adam Smith saw five distinct reasons for the productive power of the division of labour:
a) the ability to fit the best person to the right job;
b) the increased dexterity achieved when the labourer makes a single operation his sole employment;
c) the time savings gained from not having to change tools;
d) the time savings gained which would otherwise be lost in moving from one operation to another (what we would today call assembly-line production);
e) the machine specialization that can be developed around specific, discrete operations.
It is this last aspect which is such a vital step in the industrial process. Without the division of labour, the extensive use of machines that has occurred over the last two centuries simply would not have been possible.

---

law of diminishing returns: as more of a variable input is added to a fixed input in the production process, the resulting increase in output will, at some point, begin to diminish.

We have now established that the marginal product of labour will, at first, increase as more labour is added to a production process. Next we need to ask the question: why, after a point, does marginal product decline? (We see this in Table 6.3 beginning with the addition of the fifth unit of labour.) The answer to this question involves one of the most important concepts in all of microeconomics: **the law of diminishing returns**. This law states that as more and more units of a variable resource (in this case, labour) are added to a production process, at some point, the resulting increase in output (MP) begins to decrease, assuming at least one other input (in this case, land) is fixed. A more accurate term would be the law of diminishing *marginal productivity* but we will stick with the more common law of diminishing returns.

The law of diminishing returns is a technological reality that must be valid; otherwise we could grow the world's food in a flowerpot by simply adding more and more variable inputs until production rose to the necessary level. We can't do this and the reason we can't is because of the law of diminishing returns.

We now need to make three points of clarification. First, while the fixed input in our example above happens to be land, it could have been *any* input — the only necessity for the law of diminishing returns to apply is that at least one input be fixed. Second, our example had only one variable input, labour, and we illustrated the law of diminishing returns by showing that the marginal product of labour declines. However, if there had been two variable inputs instead of one, both would have manifested diminishing returns. Finally, while our example is in the context of agriculture, the law of diminishing returns applies in all productive activities.

It is very important for you to note that even after the point of diminishing returns has been reached the total product *continues to rise*. However the *rate of increase* in the total product does begin to fall. Those of you who have taken calculus will recognize that marginal product is the first derivative of total product. Those of you who have not taken calculus need only realize that total product can continue to rise even though marginal product has started to decline.

Study Guide

QUESTION 6.3

Units of Labour	TP	MP_L	AP_L
0	0	—	—
1	80	___	___
2	170	___	___
3	___	80	___
4	310	___	___
5	___	___	70
7	370	___	___

Assuming that amount of capital is fixed:
A) Fill in the blanks in the table above.
B) Diminishing returns begin with the addition of which unit of labour?
C) The average product of labour is at a maximum when how many units of labour are used?
D) What is the value of marginal product when total product is at a maximum?

The data in Table 6.3 can also be put into graphical form. Let's go to Figure 6.1 on the next page to illustrate this.

You should note three things about this curve. First, total product rises quickly at first because of the advantages gained from the division of labour. Second, at the point of diminishing returns (with the use of the fifth

FIGURE 6.1 The Total Product Curve

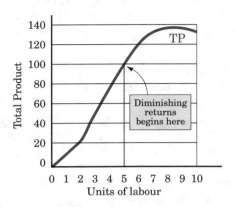

As more units of the variable input labour are used (up to nine units), total product rises, but the rate of increase slows with the use of the fifth unit of labour. This is the point of diminishing returns. Maximum total product of 135 is reached when 8 (or 9) units of labour are employed.

unit of labour) the rate of increase in the curve decreases. Third, the rise in total product continues despite having passed the point of diminishing returns.

Let us now turn to a discussion of average product. There is a marginal/average relationship reflected in the data in Table 6.3 that needs to be emphasized. All students intuitively know what this relationship is, but many are not aware that they do. Imagine that you are taking a course in which the grade is made up of ten quizzes worth 10 points each. You know that if you got 4 points on the first quiz and 6 points on the second quiz, your average quiz score is, at that point, 5. You also know that in order to raise your average test score you will have to get a mark on the third quiz that is above 5. The mark on the third quiz is the marginal mark, and if the marginal is above the average, the average will rise. If, however, your third test mark is less than 5, your average of all three quizzes would fall, i.e., if the marginal is below the average, the average will fall.

Let's take this marginal/average relationship and look back at the data in Table 6.3. Notice that the third, fourth and fifth units of labour all have a marginal product that is above the average product, and therefore, average product rises. The addition of the sixth unit of labour, which has a marginal product that is exactly the same as the previous average (20), results in the average product neither increasing nor decreasing, but remaining constant at 20. The seventh unit of labour has a marginal product of 10 which is below the average, and therefore, average product falls to 18.6. We can generalize as follows:

> Average product will rise if marginal product is above it and will fall if marginal product is below it.

Figure 6.2 illustrates this relationship graphically. In this figure, you can see that marginal product is at a maximum when four units of labour are used. Further, when marginal product equals average product, average product is at its maximum. This latter point of maximum average product occurs with the addition of the fifth unit of labour.

FIGURE 6.2 The Average Product and Marginal Product Curves

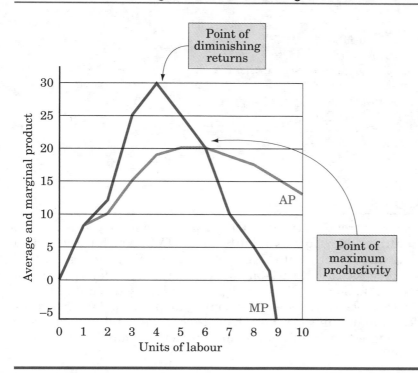

As long as the marginal product curve lies above the average product curve, the latter continues to rise. Similarly, if the marginal product curve is below the average product curve, the average declines. Finally, at the point where the marginal product curve intersects the average product curve, the average is at its maximum which is 20 bushels per unit of labour. Recall that total product is at a maximum when nine units of labour are being used which is where MP = 0.

We have now identified three maximums: of total product, which was achieved with the addition of the eight unit of labour; of marginal product, which was achieved with the addition of the fourth unit of labour; and of average product, which is at a maximum with the sixth unit of labour. So which is the most productive point? When economists use the term most productive or mention *highest productivity* they are referring to maximum average product.

A similar, but not identical, question is: what is the best output to produce? The answer is that we have no way of telling without knowledge of the costs of the inputs and the price of the output. We will leave discussion of the price of output for later and take up discussion of the costs of production next.

QUESTION 6.4

Given the data below, calculate both the MP_L and the AP_L for each unit of labour used.

Quantity of Labour	Total Output
1	400
2	1,000
3	1,500
4	1,800
5	1,900

Marginal and Variable Costs

total variable costs:
the total of all costs
that vary with the level
of output.

Table 6.4 below reproduces the first four columns from the previous table and adds a fifth column, **total variable costs** (TVC) which is the sum of all costs that vary directly with the level of output. Variable costs would normally include the cost of variable inputs such as materials, power and labour. However, in our simplified example, we have assumed that labour is the only variable cost. Suppose in our example that labour can be obtained for $100 per unit per day. The figures in the total variable costs column are then obtained by simply multiplying the number of units of labour by $100.

marginal costs: the
increase in total vari-
able costs as a result
of producing one more
unit of output.

The sixth column introduces the very important concept of the **marginal cost** (MC). Marginal cost is the increase in total variable cost as a result of producing the last unit of output. Ignore the seventh column for the moment.

TABLE 6.4 Cost Data for a Firm

Units of Labour	TP	AP	MP	TVC	MC	AVC
0	0	—	—	0	—	—
1	8	8	8	$100	$12.50	$12.50
2	20	10	12	200	8.33	10.00
3	45	15	25	300	4.00	6.67
4	75	18.8	30	400	3.33	5.33
5	100	20	25	500	4.00	5.00
6	120	20	20	600	5.00	5.00
7	130	18.6	10	700	10.00	5.38
8	135	16.9	5	800	20.00	5.93
9	135	15	0	900	∞	6.67
10	130	13	−5	1,000	∞	10.00

To obtain the value for marginal cost we need to remember that our definition of marginal cost involves the last *unit* of output produced. Therefore, we need to divide the $100 increase in total variable cost, which results from using one more unit of labour, by MP in order to find the cost of an additional *unit of output* produced. For example, when the first unit of labour is employed, the marginal cost is equal to $100 divided by 8 or $12.50 per unit produced.

Similarly, the second unit of labour increases total product by (has a marginal product of) 12 which, divided into the $100 that this input also costs, yields a marginal cost of $8.33. The third unit of labour has a marginal product of 25, and therefore the marginal cost of production when three inputs are employed is $4.00, and so on.

In summary, each unit of labour that is hired costs an identical $100. However, the amount of output which each unit produces (the marginal product) is different. The cost of producing additional units of output (the marginal cost) therefore will also vary.

We will see later in this, and in subsequent, chapters that this concept of marginal cost is at the centre of a great deal of microeconomics analysis.

The formal definition of marginal cost can be expressed as:

$$MC = \frac{\Delta \text{ TVC}}{\Delta \text{ output}} \text{ or } \frac{\Delta \text{ TVC}}{MP}$$

average variable cost: total variable cost divided by total output.

Let's now look at the seventh column of our data in Table 6.4. Here, we have **average variable costs** (AVC) which is simply the total variable costs divided by the total output. Formally, this is:

$$AVC = \frac{\text{TVC}}{\text{output}}$$

To illustrate this calculation assume that eight units of labour were being used which result in an output of 135 and total variable cost of $800. Dividing the $800 by 135 yields an average variable cost of (approximately) $5.93.

Study Guide

QUESTION 6.5

Units of Labour	Total Output	TVC	MC	AVC
0	—	—	—	—
1	100	____	____	____
2	220	____	____	____
3	320	____	____	____
4	400	____	____	____
5	460	____	____	____
6	480	1,200	____	____

A) Assuming that all units of labour cost the same, fill in the blanks in the table above.
B) When is marginal cost at a minimum?
C) What is the marginal product of labour when four units of labour are used?

We should point out that the same marginal/average relationship we discussed in reference to the marginal and average product also applies to the marginal/average costs relationship. Thus, just as the average product was

FIGURE 6.3 The Marginal Cost and Average Variable Cost Curves

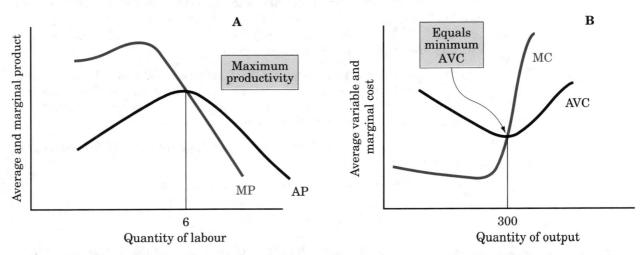

In 6.3A the MP curve intersects the AP curve at its maximum point when 6 units of labour are being used. In 6.3B the MC curve intersects the AVC curve at its minimum which occurs at an output of 300. This is the output that 6 units of labour can produce.

at a *maximum* when it was equal to marginal product, average variable cost will be at a *minimum* when it is equal to marginal cost. Figure 6.3 will help you understand this.

In Figure 6.3A you see the marginal product and average product curves. They are, roughly, two inverse-U shaped curves with the marginal product curve intersecting the average product curve at the latter's *maximum* point. This occurs when six units of labour are being used and is the firm's *most productive* point for this size of plant. Next, look at the graphing of the marginal cost and average variable cost curves in Figure 6.3B. What you see there are two U-shaped curves with marginal cost intersecting average variable cost at the latter's *minimum* point. This is at an output of 300 which is the output that six units of labour are able to produce. In short, when the average product of the variable *input* is at a maximum, the total *output* produced will result in the average variable cost being at its minimum. It is also true that the amount of labour used when marginal product is at a maximum will produce an output that results in marginal costs being at a minimum.

As mentioned above, this is not a coincidence. Average variable cost and marginal cost are mirror images of average product and marginal product. That is to say, variable costs of production are a reflection of productivity. This is what lies behind the observation that an increase in productivity is equivalent to a decrease in costs.

Earlier in this chapter we talked about how the advantages of the division of labour and the law of diminishing returns gave the marginal product curve its inverse-U shape. We can now apply these same ideas to costs and say that the marginal cost curve initially declines because of the production advantages gained by the division of labour and later rises as these advantages are outweighed by the law of diminishing returns. This is a basic law of production — as long as at least one input is fixed, an increase in output eventually mean a increase in both marginal and average costs.

Total Costs and Average Total Costs

total fixed cost: those costs that do not vary with the level of output.

We have established the fundamental relationship between productivity and costs. Our next step is to complete our discussion of costs by reminding ourselves that, in the short run, any production process involves at least one fixed factor, and we therefore need to add the concept of fixed cost to our analysis. **Total fixed costs**, in contrast to variable costs, do not vary with the level of output. Examples of fixed costs could be a long-term lease, a business license or an insurance policy.

We are now going to introduce a new set of figures which are those experienced by Rosemary who runs a small pottery business out of her home. Rosemary faces very low fixed costs because she is able to rent kiln time at the local school. Notice that the new data in Table 6.5 below (unlike Table 6.4) shows what happens to costs as we increase *output* one unit at a time rather than investigating the effects of increasing *inputs* one unit at a time. This will make our calculations much easier.

TABLE 6.5 The Complete Table of Costs

Output (per week)	TVC	AVC	MC	TFC	AFC	TC	ATC
0	—	—	—	$30	—	$ 30	—
1	$ 20	$20.00	$20	"	$30.00	50	$50.00
2	28	14.00	8	"	15.00	58	29.00
3	42	14.00	14	"	10.00	72	24.00
4	60	15.00	18	"	7.50	90	22.50
5	82	16.40	22	"	6.00	112	22.40
6	110	18.33	28	"	5.00	140	23.33
7	148	21.14	38	"	4.28	178	25.43
8	198	24.75	50	"	3.75	228	28.50

average fixed cost: total fixed cost divided by the quantity of output.

The first column is simply the output (or total product) per week of the large vases in which Rosemary specializes. Columns two, three, and four have been explained. The fifth column is the total fixed cost which, in this example, we assume to be $30. Next, we have **average fixed costs** (AFC) which are simply:

$$AFC = \frac{TFC}{output}$$

total cost: the sum of both total variable cost and total fixed cost.

Notice that average fixed cost declines continuously as output rises.

To obtain **total cost** (TC) we simply do a summation:

$$TC = TVC + TFC$$

average total cost: total cost divided by quantity of output.

Total cost rises continuously as output rises, and the *rate* of rise also begins to increase once diminishing returns set in.

Finally, **average total cost** (ATC) is:

$$ATC = \frac{TC}{output}$$

Also note that since we know that:

$$TC = TVC + TFC$$

it then follows that:

$$ATC = AVC + AFC$$

QUESTION 6.6
Fill in the blanks in the table below.

Output (per day)	TC	TVC	AVC	TFC	AFC	ATC	MC
0	$200	—	—	—	—	—	—
1	280	____	____	____	____	____	____
2	340	____	____	____	____	____	____
3	420	____	____	____	____	____	____
4	520	____	____	____	____	____	____
5	640	____	____	____	____	____	____
6	780	____	____	____	____	____	____

The relationship between marginal cost and average *variable* cost that we stressed earlier in this chapter also applies to the interaction between marginal cost and *average total* cost. As long as marginal cost is below average total cost, average total cost will fall (as it does for the first five units of output). But as soon as marginal cost rises above average total cost, the latter will begin to rise. Given this basic relationship, it is also true that the marginal cost curve will intersect the average total cost curve at the latter's minimum point. This can be seen at point *a* in Figure 6.4 below.

FIGURE 6.4 The MC, ATC, AVC and AFC Curves

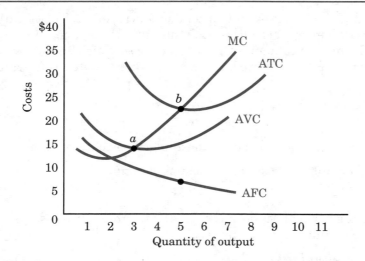

The U-shaped marginal cost curve intersects the average variable cost curve at its minimum point (*a*) which is an output of 3 units and a cost of $14. It also intersects the average total cost curve at its minimum point (*b*) which is 5 units and $22.40. The average fixed cost curve declines continuously.

Using this figure as a visual representation, let's pull things together. The U-shaped marginal cost curve reflects the advantages of the division of labour as it declines, and then, as it rises, the law of diminishing returns.

Second, marginal cost is initially below the average variable cost curve and the average total cost curve but then rises above each of these, which explains their basic U shape.

Third, the marginal cost curve intersects the average variable cost curve at its minimum point and the average total cost curve at its minimum point.

Finally, the average fixed cost curve continuously declines.

Let's now focus on point a, the minimum point of the average variable cost curve. This occurs at an output of three vases. Since the average variable cost curve is a mirror image of the average product curve we know that the average product curve must be at its maximum. Next, notice that the minimum point on the average total cost curve is at an output of five vases (point b). Comparing these two points enables us to emphasize that the most productive point, where average product is at a maximum, is not the lowest cost point, where average total cost is at a minimum. This is simply a reflection of the fact that fixed costs are part of average total costs, but they are not part of average variable costs.

Figure 6.5 is a graphing of the total cost (TC), total variable cost (TVC), and total fixed cost (TFC) curves.

The TVC curve starts at the origin because variable costs are zero when output is zero and rises slowly at first (reflecting declining average variable

FIGURE 6.5 The TC, TVC and TFC Curves

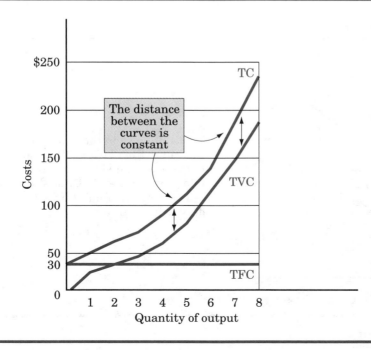

The total cost curve begins at $30 (the amount of fixed cost) and rises from there. The total variable cost curve starts at the origin since variable cost is zero when there is no output. The total fixed cost curve is horizontal, reflecting the fact that the fixed cost of $30 does not vary with output. The difference between the TC and TVC is this constant $30.

cost) but then more quickly later (reflecting rising average variable cost). The TC curve starts at $30 because total fixed costs are equal to this level even when output is zero. The TFC curve starts at the same $30 and does not vary with output.

Let's now ask how many vases per week would Rosemary want to produce? The lowest average total cost is achieved when she produces six a week. Would she ever choose to produce seven, eight or even more? We hope that you can see that the answer to this question depends on how much she gets for each vase when she sells them. Putting what we have now learned about costs together with revenue analysis, which will come later, will eventually allow us to get to an answer.

Shifts in Average and Marginal Costs

Our presentation of costs so far has been one in which average total, average variable and marginal costs change only as a result of a change in the level of output. Underlying this approach is the assumption that the price of all inputs remain unchanged. However, we need to recognize that input prices can change — even in the short run.

Recognizing this possibility is not difficult to deal with. In graphical terms, a decrease in the price of the variable input(s) would shift down the marginal, average variable and average total cost curves. We will isolate the average total and the marginal cost curves in Figure 6.6 below to illustrate such a shift.

In Figure 6.6 the marginal cost curve shifts down as a result of a decrease in the input price of the variable input such that the minimum point of the curve occurs at a lower dollar cost and at a higher level of output. There is also a corresponding shift in the average total cost curve. We have not

FIGURE 6.6 A Shift in the Marginal and Average Total Cost Curves

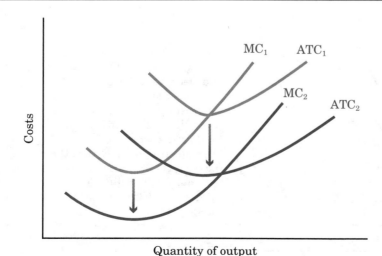

The shift down in the marginal cost curve from MC_1 to MC_2 and in the accompanying average total cost curve — ATC_1 to ATC_2 — is the result of input prices decreasing.

shown the average variable cost curve but, if we had, it too would shift down. The basic shape of the curves remains unchanged however since the law of diminishing returns still applies. Would the average fixed cost curve also shift down? Only if the price of the fixed input(s) decreased. Similarly, the curves would shift up if input prices increased.

Capacity Output and Excess Capacity

capacity output: that output where average total cost is at a minimum, also called the most economically efficient output for a given-sized plant.

Economists define the term **capacity output** (or most economically efficient output) as the output which results in minimum average total cost. This level of output does not, however, imply maximum physical capacity. This is because most production processes probably reach minimum average total cost at about 75–80% of physical capacity.

Would firms want to operate at an output level above this capacity? Perhaps in the short run they would if demand and prices were particularly high but almost certainly not in the long run as we will see in the next chapter.

Would firms ever want to operate at an output which is less than capacity output? No, they would not want to but firms are sometimes forced to reduce output because of market conditions. The consequences of this are illustrated in Figure 6.7.

FIGURE 6.7 A Firm Experiencing Excess Capacity

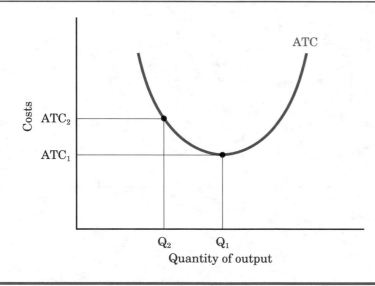

If market conditions force a firm to operate at output level Q_2 then its average total costs (ATC_2) will be higher than they would be if the firm operated at capacity (Q_1).

excess capacity: the situation where a firm's output is less than it would be under conditions of economic capacity.

In Figure 6.7 we assume that market conditions have forced this firm to reduce output so that it is now operating at Q_2 with average total costs of ATC_2 which are higher than they would be at capacity output (ATC_1). This is the situation that economists describe as **excess capacity** which is defined as the situation where a firm's output is less than capacity output. Excess capacity is inefficient in the sense that average total costs are not at a minimum. We will refer to this concept again in Chapter 11 in the context of different market structures.

QUESTION 6.7

Total Output	TC$_1$	MC$_1$	ATC$_1$	TC$_2$	MC$_2$	ATC$_2$
0	$150	—	—	—	—	—
10	175	___	___	___	___	___
25	200	___	___	___	___	___
35	225	___	___	___	___	___
40	250	___	___	___	___	___
40	275	___	___	___	___	___

Assuming that each output row represents one more (constant cost) input:
A) Fill in the blanks in the MC$_1$ and ATC$_1$ columns.
B) Assuming that the cost of the variable factor decreases by 20%, fill in the TC$_2$, MC$_2$ and ATC$_2$ columns.

QUESTION 6.8
Given the graph below:

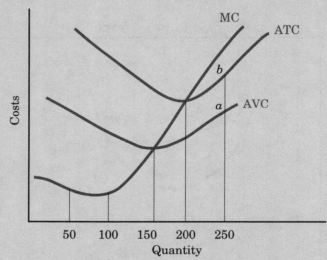

A) At what output is MP at a maximum?
B) At what output is AP at a maximum?
C) At what output is ATC at a minimum?
D) When output is 250, what does *ab* represent?

BOX 6B
1. Identify and define TVC, MC and AVC.
2. Write a mathematical expression for marginal cost and average variable cost.
3. What is the relationship between the AP/MP curves and the AVC/MC curves?
4. What are *fixed* costs?

BOX 6B *(continued)*
5. How would you calculate AFC?
6. Which curves are affected by an increase in the price of variable inputs? The price of fixed inputs?
7. What is *capacity output*?
8. What is *excess capacity*?

Chapter Highlights

This chapter signals a shift in emphasis from supply and demand analysis to that of the firm and its costs of production. It begins by discussing the many decisions that a firm must make and asks the fundamental question that economists ask about a firm's behaviour: why does it charge the price it does and produce the output that it does? The answers to this question involve the firm's costs of production and this is the primary focus of the chapter.

The distinction between explicit and implicit cost as well as normal and economic profits is made early in the chapter.

Next is the explanation of what lies behind a firm's costs which is seen to be the productivity of its inputs. This leads to the introduction and definition of marginal product, average product and total product. Total product is the economist's term for total output. Marginal product is the change in total product as a result of adding one more unit of factor input while average product is total product divided by the quantity of inputs used. The definition of the short run is then explained as the circumstances when at least one input is fixed. Out of this comes the ideas of the division of labour and the law of diminishing returns. These help to explain the shape of the marginal and average product curves and these concepts are illustrated graphically.

The chapter then relates this discussion of productivity to costs and introduces marginal cost, average variable cost and total variable cost. Marginal cost is the increase in total cost as a result of one more unit of output. Average total cost is total cost divided by the units of output produced and average variable cost is total variable cost divided by the units of output produced. Cost are a reflection of productivity and this fundamental point is illustrated in Figure 6.3.

The chapter then gives an explanation of shifts in the costs curves which result from a change in input prices or technological change. Finally, the chapter defines capacity output as the output where average total costs are at a minimum, and excess capacity as any output lower than that which achieves economic capacity.

New Glossary Terms

Workbook

Study Tips

1. There are many new terms and definitions for you to learn in this chapter — probably more than in any other chapter. None of the terms are complex, however, so you should be able to handle them if you simply learn a few at a time.

2. Students usually find the distinction between explicit costs and implicit costs quite straightforward but get a little puzzled over how these concepts tie in with normal and economic profits. Simply remember that if both explicit and implicit costs are being covered, then the firm is earning a normal profit. Revenues in excess of explicit and implicit costs result in economic profits.

3. Two of the more important concepts in the whole of microeconomics are the division of labour and the law of diminishing returns. They are used in this chapter to explain the relationship between the use of factors of production and their productivity. Once you understand marginal and average productivity you can understand marginal and average variable cost. This is crucial and is therefore, the focus of the Key Problem.

4. Adding fixed cost and average total cost to the analysis is quite straightforward. Once this is done, a graph like that found in Figure 6.4 can be constructed. Here is a prime example of the phrase "a picture is worth a thousand words."

5. Students should always remember that the amount of total cost at an output of zero is the total fixed cost that the firm faces.

6. We hear a great deal about the importance of firms' cutting their costs. Just what is meant by this phrase is ambiguous. A firm can always cut its total cost by reducing output and it might be able to decrease its average cost by increasing output. The only unambiguous way the phrase cutting costs makes sense is a reduction of marginal and average cost *at each level of output*. This is illustrated graphically by a downward shift in the two curves.

7. It may not be clear to you why the concepts of capacity output and excess capacity are introduced in this chapter. Don't worry about that now, the importance of these concepts will become more clear when we get to an analysis of market structure.

Are You Sure?

Indicate whether the following statements are true or false. If false, indicate why they are false.

1. Marginal cost will equal average variable cost when the latter is minimized.
T or **F**   If false: _____

_____

_____

2. Depreciation is the annual cost of any asset that is expected to be in use for more than one year.
T or **F**   If false: _____

_____

_____

3. Implicit costs are the amounts that are actually paid out in money.
T or **F**   If false: _____

_____

_____

4. Sunk costs are the historical costs of buying something that has no current resale value.
T or **F**   If false: _____

_____

_____

5. If a firm is making economic profits, then it must also be making normal profits.

T or **F**   If false: _____

_____

_____

6. The short run is any period of time in which at least two inputs are fixed.
T or **F**   If false: _____

_____

_____

7. Marginal product is the increase in total product as a result of adding one more unit of output.
T or **F**   If false: _____

_____

_____

8. Total product and total output are the same thing.
T or **F**   If false: _____

_____

_____

9. The division of labour is the dividing of the production process into a series of specialized tasks, each done by a different worker.
T or **F**   If false: _____

_____

_____

10. The law of diminishing returns applies in both the short run and the long run.
T or **F**   If false: _____

_____

_____

Translations

Explain the graph in Figure W6.1 in words.

FIGURE W6.1

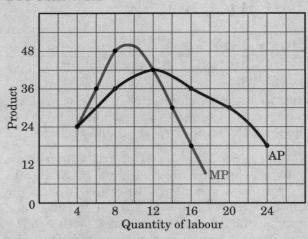

_____

_____

_____

_____

_____

_____

Choose the Best

1. Which of the following statements about the MP of a factor is correct?
    a) It may either rise or fall as more labour is used.
    b) It always falls as more labour is used.

2. Which of the following statements about marginal cost is correct?
    a) It is always below average costs.
    b) It can be either above or below average costs.

3. Which of the following statements is true about the average product of labour?
    a) It is equal to total output divided by the quantity of labour inputs used.
    b) It is equal to the increase in total output divided by the quantity of labour used.

4. Which of the statements below is true about the marginal product of capital?
   a) It is total output divided by the quantity of capital inputs used.
   b) It is the increase in total output resulting from the use of one more unit of capital.
   c) It is the increase in total output divided by the quantity of capital inputs used.

5. What is the value of the sum of the marginal costs of all of the units produced?
   a) Total cost.
   b) Average cost.
   c) Total variable cost.

6. What is average fixed cost?
   a) It is all the costs that do not vary with the level of output.
   b) It is total cost less total variable cost.
   c) It is total fixed cost divided by the level of output.

7. What is the sum of total variable costs and total fixed costs?
   a) It is equal to the sum of average product and marginal product.
   b) It is the sum of all marginal costs.
   c) It is total cost.

8. All the items below are explicit costs *except one*. Which is the exception?
   a) The weekly cost of a lease on a building.
   b) The total wages paid each week.
   c) The monthly hydro bill.
   d) The wages withdrawn by the owner each week.

9. Which of the following conditions is necessary in order to consider a cost a sunk cost?
   a) It must have occurred over six months ago.
   b) It must have occurred as a result of the purchase of a fixed asset.
   c) It must have occurred as a result of the purchase of a fixed asset and have no resale value.
   d) It must have occurred as a result of the purchase of a fixed asset and be fully paid for.

10. Which of the following statements is true about the division of labour?

a) It causes the marginal product of labour to increase but it has no effect on the average product of labour.
   b) It was first thought of by David Ricardo in his example of a hat factory.
   c) It is an idea that has little application in the real world.
   d) Its application results in both the marginal and average product of labour increasing.

11. What is significant about the level of output at which marginal product begins to decline?
    a) It is the point of maximum average product.
    b) It is the point of minimum average cost.
    c) It is the point at which the division of labour begins.
    d) It is the point at which diminishing returns begins.

12. What will happen to total product after the point of diminishing returns has been reached?
    a) It will continue to rise until marginal product becomes zero.
    b) It will continue to rise until marginal product begins to decline.
    c) It will begin to fall.
    d) It will start to rise for the first time.

13. What is the significance of the maximum point on the total product curve?
    a) It is the point where the increase in output begins to slow down.
    b) It is the point where diminishing returns sets in.
    c) It is the point of maximum marginal product.
    d) It is the point where marginal product becomes zero.

14. If marginal product is declining, which of the following statements is correct?
    a) Average product must be falling.
    b) Average product could be rising or falling.
    c) Marginal cost must be falling.
    d) Average variable cost must be rising.
    e) Average variable cost must be falling.

15. What do economists mean by the term, "the most productive output"?
    a) The output where total product is at a maximum.
    b) The output where average product is at a maximum.
    c) The output where marginal product is at a maximum.
    d) The output where marginal cost is at a minimum.
    e) The output where average total cost is at a minimum.

16. Which of the following statements regarding total fixed costs is correct?
    a) When total fixed costs are graphed, the curve will rise from the origin at a constant rate.
    b) When total fixed costs are graphed, the curve will be horizontal.
    c) Total fixed costs equal total variable costs less total average costs.
    d) Total fixed costs rise slowly at first, but then more quickly as output increases.
    e) Total fixed costs equal total marginal costs plus total variable costs.

17. If we assume that the level of output remains unchanged, which of the following could cause a decrease in average total, average variable and marginal costs?
    a) A decrease in the price of the variable factor.
    b) An increase in the price of the variable factor.
    c) An increase in the firm's capacity output.
    d) A decrease in the firm's capacity output.
    e) A decrease in the firm's fixed cost.

18. All of the following statements *except one* are correct. Which is the exception?
    a) If the marginal cost curve shifts down, then the average total cost curve will also shift down.
    b) If the marginal cost curve shifts down, then the average variable cost curve will also shift down.
    c) The average fixed cost curve will be unaffected by a shift in the marginal cost curve.

    d) If the marginal product curve shifts up then the marginal cost curve will shift up.
    e) If the marginal product curve shifts up then the average product curve will shift up.

19. How do economists define capacity output?
    a) The maximum physical output possible.
    b) The output that maximizes total cost.
    c) The output that maximizes total product.
    d) The output that minimizes marginal cost.
    e) The output that minimizes average total cost.

20. Which of the following statements would be true about a firm that is operating under conditions of excess capacity?
    a) The firm's average total cost would be at a minimum.
    b) The firm's average total cost would not be at a minimum.
    c) The firm's average total cost may or may not be at a minimum but the firm would not be at capacity output.
    d) The firm would not be at capacity output, but its average total cost would be at a minimum.
    e) The firm would need to reduce output to achieve minimum average total cost.

What's Wrong?

Can you spot the six errors in the following passage? (Ignore grammatical mistakes!)

The most important lesson in this chapter is the relationship between productivity and costs. Productivity involves the relationship between various factor inputs and their prices. In general, as output increases, total cost rises and this means that average variable and marginal cost are also rising. The excess capacity that the firm is experiencing will be eventually eliminated as output continues to rise. Total cost will then be minimized, and the firm will have found its capacity output. The most productive level of output is the point of maximum total product which must occur when marginal product is rising.

Key Problem

Last summer Daniel started the Custom Made Fencing Company which specializes in building fences to meet the specific needs of his customers. Since Daniel works out of his parents basement, uses an old pick-up, and only a few simple tools, his fixed costs are minimal. He measures the firm's output in terms of the number of feet per day of fence which is built. Experience has shown Daniel that different crew sizes can build fence as shown shown in Table W6.1.

TABLE W6.1

Number of Workers in Crew	TP_L (feet per day)	MP_L (feet per day)	AP_L (feet per day)
1	20	_____	_____
2	80	_____	_____
3	150	_____	_____
4	200	_____	_____
5	230	_____	_____
6	246	_____	_____

a) Fill in the marginal and average product of labour columns in the table above.

b) On the graph in Figure W6.2 below, draw the two curves.

FIGURE W6.2

c) Assuming that each worker costs $240 a day (wages and materials), fill in Table W6.2.

d) On the graph in Figure W6.3 below, draw the average variable and marginal cost curves.

TABLE W6.2

Number of Workers in Crew	TP (feet per day)	TVC (feet per day)	AVC (feet per day)	MC (feet per day)
1	20	_____	_____	_____
2	80	_____	_____	_____
3	150	_____	_____	_____
4	200	_____	_____	_____
5	230	_____	_____	_____
6	246	_____	_____	_____

FIGURE W6.3

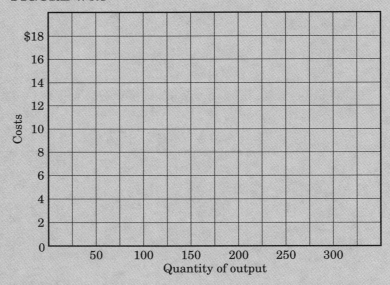

e) Looking back at Figure W6.2, determine how many workers are used to achieve maximum average product. (Remember that the definition of maximum AP is where it equals MP.)

Answer: _____.

f) What output can this number of workers produce?

Answer: _____.

g) Now from Figure W6.3, what is true at the output level you gave as your answer in f)?

Answer: _____.

h) Return to Figure W6.2 and, this time, determine how many workers are used to achieve maximum marginal product.

Answer: _____.

i) What output can this number of workers produce?

Answer: _____.

j) Look at Figure W6.3 again and determine what is true at the output level you gave as your answer in i).

Answer: _____.

k) What conclusion can you make from your answers in e) through j)?

_____

_____

_____

_____

_____

_____

_____

_____

_____

_____

_____

Need a Hand?

a)   **TABLE W6.3** (completed Table W6.1)

Number of Workers in Crew	TP_L (feet per day)	MP_L (feet per day)	AP_L (feet per day)
1	20	20	20
2	80	60	40
3	150	70	50
4	200	50	50
5	230	30	46
6	246	16	41

b) **FIGURE W6.4** (completed Figure W6.2)

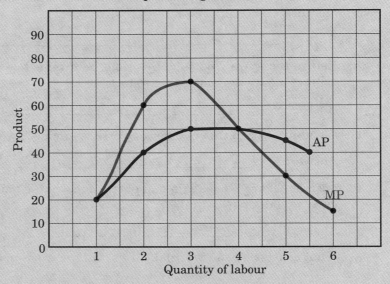

c) **TABLE W6.4** (completed Table W6.2)

Number of Workers in Crew	TP	TVC	AVC	MC
1	20	$240	$12.00	$12.00
2	80	480	6.00	4.00
3	150	720	4.80	3.43
4	200	960	4.80	4.80
5	230	1,200	5.22	8.00
6	246	1,440	5.85	15.00

d) **FIGURE W6.5** (completed Figure W6.3)

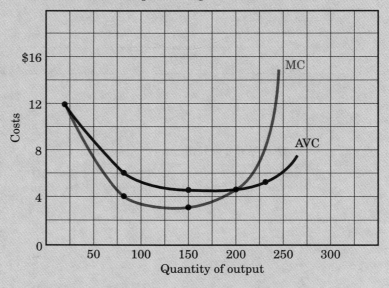

e) The answer, which is read from the graph, is **4** workers.

f) The answer, which is read from the table, is **200**.

g) We can see on the graph in Figure W6.3 that **minimum average variable cost** occurs when output is **200**.

h) The answer, which is read from the graph, is **3** workers.

i) The answer, which is read from the table, is **150**.

j) We can see on the graph in Figure W6.3 that **minimum marginal cost** occurs when output is **150**.

k) The conclusion is that maximum average product occurs using the same number of workers that are used to produce an output that minimizes average variable costs. Similarly, maximum marginal product occurs using the same number of workers that are used to produce an output that minimizes marginal costs.

More of the Same

Table W6.5 provides some data for the output of sugar beets (tons per year) in the agriculturally rich land of Nearvana.

TABLE W6.5

Quantity of Labour	Total Output	MP_L	AP_L
1	200	_____	_____
2	600	_____	_____
3	900	_____	_____
4	1,000	_____	_____
5	1,040	_____	_____

a) Fill in the marginal and average product of labour columns in the table above.

b) On the graph in Figure W6.6 below, draw the two curves.

FIGURE W6.6

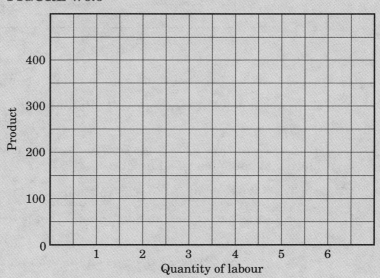

c) Assuming that each worker costs $160 a day (for wages and materials), fill in Table W6.6.

TABLE W6.6

Quantity of Labour	Total Output	TVC	AVC	MC
1	200	___	___	___
2	600	___	___	___
3	900	___	___	___
4	1,000	___	___	___
5	1,040	___	___	___

d) On the graph in Figure W6.7 below, draw the average variable and marginal cost curves.

e) Looking back at Figure W6.6, determine how many workers are used to achieve maximum average product?

FIGURE W6.7

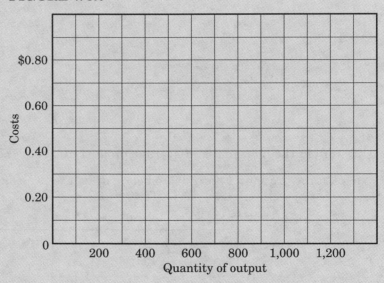

f) From Table W6.6, what output can this number of workers produce?

g) Now from Table W6.6, what is true at the output level you gave as your answer in f)?

h) Return to Figure W6.6 and, this time, determine how many workers are used to achieve maximum marginal product.

i) From Table W6.6, what output can this number of workers produce?

j) Look at Figure W6.7 again and determine what is true at the output level you gave as your answer in i).

k) Does this exercise verify the conclusion that you reached in Key Problem 1 k)?

Other Problems

1. David recently graduated with a B.A. in Economics and was offered a job with a large company which would have paid $36,000 per year. At about the same time David's grandfather died and left him an inheritance of $40,000. David decided to pass up the job, and using $30,000 from the inheritance, he purchased a tool rental business. (David put the other $10,000 into a savings account that pays 6% per year interest.) He put his full effort into the new business and in the first three months of operation he had revenues of $25,600 and total explicit costs of $12,400. What was David's economic profit/loss for the three months?

2. a) Complete Table W6.7 below.

TABLE W6.7

Output	TFC	TVC	TC	AFC	AVC	ATC	MC
0	$60	—	—	—	—	—	—
1	___	___	___	___	___	___	$45
2	___	___	$145	___	___	___	___
3	___	___	___	___	___	___	$35
4	___	___	___	___	___	___	$30
5	___	$185	___	___	___	___	___
6	___	___	___	___	___	___	$40
7	___	___	___	___	___	___	$45
8	___	$325	___	___	___	___	___
9	___	___	___	___	___	___	$65
10	___	___	$525	___	___	___	___

b) At what level of output is average product at a maximum?

Answer: _____.

c) What is average total cost at this output?

Answer: _____.

d) If fixed cost were to double, what would be the marginal cost of the fifth unit of output?

Answer: _____.

3. a) Fill in the blank columns in Table W6.8 assuming that the cost of variable inputs decreases by 50%.

TABLE W6.8

Output	TVC$_1$	TVC$_2$	AVC$_1$	AVC$_2$	MC$_1$	MC$_2$
1	$ 44	_____	$44.00	_____	$44.00	_____
2	64	_____	32.00	_____	20.00	_____
3	78	_____	26.00	_____	14.00	_____
4	88	_____	22.00	_____	10.00	_____
5	100	_____	20.00	_____	12.00	_____
6	120	_____	20.00	_____	20.00	_____
7	150	_____	21.42	_____	30.00	_____
8	200	_____	25.00	_____	50.00	_____

b) Draw AVC$_1$, MC$_1$, AVC$_2$ and MC$_2$ on the grid in Figure W6.8 below.

FIGURE W6.8

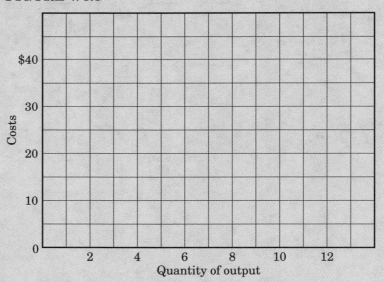

4. a) On Figure W6.9 on the next page, draw an ATC curve that has the following characteristics:
    – AVC is $30 and AFC is $20 when output is 10.
    – AVC declines $5 for every increase in output of 10, up to a output of 50.
    – Above output levels of 50, AVC rises $5 for every increase in output of 10.

    b) Between what output levels is the firm experiencing excess capacity?

    Answer: _____.

    c) Which output level is the most productive?

    Answer: _____.

FIGURE W6.9

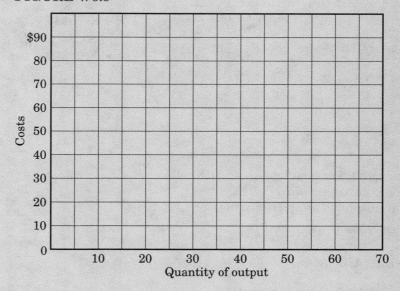

Unanswered Questions

Short Essays

1. To an economist, costs include profit. Discuss.

2. Comment on the following statement: "If a firm wants to cut costs, it must first increase productivity."

3. Explain the difference between an explicit cost and an implicit cost.

4. What is the most productive output level for a firm to produce? Why would it ever produce less than this output?

5. Comment on the following statement: "A decrease in the prices of factor inputs makes a firm more productive."

Analytical Questions

1. Suppose that the Innovative Cab Company announced that, henceforth, its rates within the downtown area of Vancouver would be half price on all sunny days. Is this pricing decision related to the firm's cost of production? Is it related to the opportunity costs of cab users?

2. It has been observed that all the members of peasant families in third world countries often work intensively on small pieces of land. What do you think the MP_L is in these cases? Is this rational?

3. Assume that you paid, in advance, $400 tuition for a course in microeconomics.
   a) What is the cost of sleeping in and missing one of the lectures?
   b) How would you answer a) if the tuition was $200?
   c) How would you answer a) if tuition was free?

4. What is the cost for the Toronto Maple Leafs to give a local boys club 50 free tickets to a hockey game? Does it matter for what game the tickets are offered?

5. Make a list of what you would consider to be the explicit costs of a college providing parking spaces for faculty and students on land that it owns. Is there an implicit cost in providing the spaces?

Numerical Questions

1. Christie Krunch raises carrots in the backyard of her home for her own consumption, and she just can't get enough of them. Christie has discovered that she can increase the yield of her carrot patch by adding bags of fertilizer (which she gets free from a neighbour who is a mushroom grower) as indicated in Table W6.9.

TABLE W6.9

Bags of Fertilizer Applied	Bushels of Carrots Produced
0	6
1	14
2	21
3	26
4	28
5	28

a) How many bags of fertilizer should Christie use on her carrot patch?

b) At what output is productivity maximized?

2. Given the data in Table W6.10:

TABLE W6.10

Quantity	Total Cost
0	$200
1	240
2	260
3	300
4	360
5	440
6	560

a) What is the level of fixed cost?

b) What is the marginal cost of the fifth unit produced?

c) What is the total variable cost of producing three units of output?

d) What is the average total cost of producing four units of output?

3. a) Complete Table W6.11 below.

TABLE W6.11

Number of Workers	Total Produce	Average Product	Marginal Product
0	0	—	—
1	1	___	___
2	3	___	___
3	___	2	___
4	___	___	4
5	15	___	___
6	___	3	___
7	___	___	2
8	21	___	___
9	___	___	−2

b) How many workers are being used when the point of diminishing returns first begins?

c) How many workers are being used when total product is at a maximum?

d) What is the most productive point?

4. Suppose the following data describes the cost data of a furniture manufacturer.

a) Complete Table W6.12 by assuming that labour costs $10 an hour.

b) Describe the shapes of the AFC, AVC, and ATC curves.

c) What is the most productive output? What are AVC and ATC at this quantity?

d) What is capacity output?

TABLE W6.12

Output of Tables	Total Hours	Average Hours per Table	Marginal Hours per Table	TVC ($)	AVC ($)	TFC ($)	TC ($)	ATC ($)	MC ($)
1	40	___	___	___	___	$600	___	___	___
2	70	___	___	___	___	___	___	___	___
3	90	___	___	___	___	___	___	___	___
4	120	___	___	___	___	___	___	___	___
5	160	___	___	___	___	___	___	___	___
6	210	___	___	___	___	___	___	___	___

CHAPTER SEVEN
■ ■ ■ ■ ■ ■ ■

Costs in the Long Run

What's ahead . . . In this chapter we continue the discussion of costs by shifting the focus from the short run to the long run. In making this shift, the concept of returns to scale and economies of scale are introduced and explored. We discuss the idea of the right size of firm and look at the concepts of excess capacity and minimum efficient scale.

long run: the circumstances in which all inputs are variable.

The discussion about the costs of production in the previous chapter was in the context of the short run, a period of time in which at least one factor of production is fixed. In contrast, economists define the **long run** as a period of time in which the producing firm has the option of varying all of its inputs. Put another way, in the long run there are no fixed factors.

There is a technique in perceiving the long run. You should recognize that at any one *point in time* the firm must always be in the short run. Imagine a factory manager as he steps out of his office onto the shop floor. Are any of the factor inputs used in production fixed? The answer is, of course. At least one input, and probably several, would be fixed — the square footage of the plant, or the number of machines or the quantity of some crucial raw material. Firms are always operating in the short run. Now, imagine our factory manager walking back into his office, and closing the door as he sits down to ask himself: where do we want to be in five years? As he proceeds to answer this question he is able to treat all inputs as variable. He is able to conceptualize the long run. It is in this sense that economists described the long run as a planning horizon. In short, all production processes operate in the short run. Therefore, diminishing returns are an unavoidable reality. In the long run, on the other hand, diminishing returns do not apply because there are no fixed factors.

long-run average cost curve: a graphical representation of the per unit costs of production in the long run.

We now need to elaborate on this very important short-run/long-run distinction by carefully developing the **long-run average cost curve** (LRAC). (Note that for the balance of this chapter we will use the term "average cost" to refer to the short run and "long-run average cost" for the long run.)

We will begin this process by imagining a firm, called Rising Sun Products Limited, which produces high-quality CDs and operates in a small-sized plant, which we shall call Plant I.

Further, we will assume that there are also three other plant sizes available to Rising Sun. Plant II which is exactly twice the size of Plant I; Plant III which is exactly three times the size of Plant I; and Plant IV which is exactly four times the size of Plant I.

Some short-run average (total) cost data is presented in Table 7.1 below.

TABLE 7.1 Rising Sun's Plant Size Alternatives

Output of CD's per Day	AC in Plant I	AC in Plant II	AC in Plant III	AC in Plant IV
100	$ 6.00	$ 7.00	7.50	$8.00
200	5.00	6.00	6.50	7.10
300	6.00	5.50	6.00	6.50
400	8.00	5.00	5.70	6.00
500	11.00	5.50	5.30	5.80
600	15.00	6.00	5.00	5.50
700	20.00	7.00	5.30	5.20
800	26.00	8.00	5.70	5.00
900	33.00	9.50	6.00	5.20
1,000	41.00	11.00	6.50	5.50

Remember from the previous chapter that the definition of economic capacity is that output at which average costs are at a minimum. From Table 7.1 we can see that economic capacity is achieved, using Plant I (Rising Sun's present plant), with an output of 200 CDs per day. However, Rising Sun's reputation for producing a quality product has been steadily growing within the industry, and it has had to increase production to 400 a day for the last couple of months just to meet customers' orders. The consequence of this strong demand, which the firm welcomes, is that its average costs have been running at $8 per unit which is far above the minimum average cost level of $5. Something has to be done. Rising Sun must either start refusing some customers' orders, which is undesirable; or raise prices which might have negative long-run consequences; or build a bigger plant which can handle the 400 per day output and still maintain minimum average total costs.

The decision is made to build a larger plant, but there is some debate among management about the size of the new plant. The options are, first, to go conservative and opt for Plant II which achieves minimum average total costs of $5 at the current output level of 400 units per day. The second option is to anticipate even more growth in the future and opt for Plant III, which would require an output of 600 units a day to achieve the desired minimum average total costs of $5. There are, however, two drawbacks associated with Plant III. The first is that it is more expensive to build, and the second is that if Plant III is chosen, the current rate of production of 400 per day would only lower its average costs to $5.70. Thus building Plant III would prove to be the right decision only if the future brings in further increases in orders to justify a production run that is higher than the current level. Since no one can predict the future with certainty, let's assume that a decision is made to stay conservative and build Plant II.

In time the new plant is ready, and Rising Sun is able to handle the runs of 400 units per day at a reduced average total cost of $5. But, of course, the story does not end here. Our firm's fortunes continue to grow, and sales rise to the point that production runs of 600 units a day are needed to keep up with commitments made to customers. As we can see in Table 7.1 (Plant

II column), this raises average cost to $6, and Rising Sun is again faced with a major decision about what is the correct plant size for its operations. Now it could upgrade to Plant III and reduce average costs (at current rates of output) to $5, or it could get really bold and build a new Plant IV in anticipation of even more growth in sales in the future. If it does this, it takes the risk that if sales in the future decline it could again face higher average costs.

As you can see, the long run involves planning which requires trying to anticipate the future and is, by its very nature, risky. Businesspeople do not always like taking risk, but doing so is often unavoidable.

Figure 7.1 below is a graphical presentation of the average total costs data from Table 7.1.

FIGURE 7.1 Average Total Costs of Production in Four Sizes of Plant

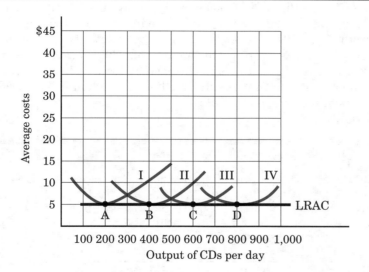

A, B, C and D are each points of minimum average total costs in four different sizes of plant.
By connecting these four points we obtain the long-run average cost curve.

Points A, B, C and D in Figure 7.1 identify the capacity output levels in each of the four plant sizes, i.e., where average costs are at a minimum. By connecting these four points, can we obtain a long-run average cost curve? Technically the answer is no if these four different-sized plants are the *only* options. This is because the LRAC curve would be the SRACI curve up to output 300 and the SRACII curve between outputs 300 and 500. However, if we assume that there are many other possible plant sizes there would exist many other SRAC curves that have not been shown. Each of these unseen cost curves would have a minimum point and connecting these many minimum points would give us something close to a horizontal LRAC curve as shown in Figure 7.1. Let's make this assumption and proceed with our focus remaining on the four mentioned plant sizes.

In its long-run planning, Rising Sun must choose one of these four points as its daily production target. Which of the four it chooses would, of course, depend on its estimates of its long-run production requirements, and that would depend on its estimates of its future sales. However, once a decision is made, be it Plant I, II, III, or IV, the firm finds itself on one of the four short-run average cost curves. That is, the firm finds itself in the short run where, above economic capacity, the average costs rise as output levels rise. Thus we say, once again, a firm can *plan* as if it is in the long run but it always *operates* in the short run.

Constant Returns to Scale

constant returns to scale: the situation where a firm's output increases in proportion to the increase in its inputs.

Let's return to Figure 7.1 and point out that the horizontal long-run average cost curve shown there is a reflection of the concept of **constant returns to scale**. This term is used only in the context of the long run and refers to the situation where output increases in exact proportion to an increase in inputs.

You will recall that in this example we assumed that Plant II was exactly twice as large as Plant I. If we also assume that the amount of labour and materials being used in Plant II is also exactly twice the quantity used in Plant I, and if we assume that the prices of these inputs do not change, the total cost of producing 400 units per day would be exactly twice the total costs of producing 200 units per day. This means that the average costs will be the same. You can verify that this is the case by looking back at Table 7.1. Such are the conditions that result in a horizontal long-run average cost curve, i.e., constant returns to scale.

QUESTION 7.1

Below are some cost data pertaining to Plant I. Complete the table. Suppose that Plant II is exactly twice the size of Plant I and uses (at capacity) twice the amount of labour and materials. Further, assume that the prices of these inputs are the same and that Plant II can produce 3,000 units of output at economic capacity.

Output	Average Total Cost	Total Cost
0	$ 0	$5,000
500	50	_____
1,000	45	_____
1,500	40	_____
2,000	45	_____
2,500	50	_____
3,000	65	_____
3,500	85	_____

A) At what output is economic capacity achieved in Plant I?
B) How much is total fixed cost in Plant I?
C) If plant sizes I and II are the only two possible plants, what is the shape of the long-run average cost curve?

Increasing Returns to Scale

To take our discussion of long-run costs one step further we introduce a new firm, Deep Sea Cement, which is currently producing 1,000 metres of concrete a day in Plant I. We will assume that the total cost of doing this is $40,000 which means that Deep Sea's average total cost of production is currently $40 a metre.

Next, let's assume that Deep Sea builds a larger Plant II in which both its inputs and its total cost exactly double. The crucial question at this stage is what will happen to its output level? Would output exactly double also, as it did in the case of Rising Sun? It could, of course, but it is also quite possible that Deep Sea's output will *more than* double, and these are the circumstances of **increasing returns to scale**. Increasing returns to scale exist if a doubling of inputs result in output more than doubling.

increasing returns to scale: the circumstances under which an increase in inputs of x% results in output increasing by more than x%.

Let's assume that as a result of doubling its inputs Deep Sea's output level increased from the original 1,000 metres up to 2,500 metres per day. Remember that costs have doubled from $40,000 to $80,000. If we divide the new output level of 2,500 metres into $80,000 we obtain a new per metre cost of $32, which is one point on Plant II's short-run average cost curve. This is well below the original $40 which is one point on Plant I's short-run average total cost curve. If we connect these two points, we see a portion of the long-run average cost curve and this (partial) curve will be downward-sloping. This leads us to the conclusion that when a firm experiences increasing returns to scale, per unit costs of production are lowered in the long run. Figure 7.2 below is a graphical illustration of the long-run average cost curve when increasing returns to scale are present.

FIGURE 7.2 Long-Run Average Costs under Conditions of Increasing Returns to Scale

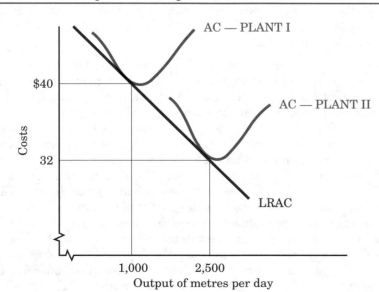

AC — Plant I and AC — Plant II are both short-run average cost curves. We have identified one point on each curve representing two output levels used in our example. Connecting these two points gives us a portion of the long-run average cost curve which declines as output rises.

Firms in industries that are characterized by assembly-line production of standardized products such as automobiles, television sets, refrigerators, or railway cars, are likely to experience declining long-run average cost. In these cases, such firms become formidable competitors because increased output means lower unit costs. As we will examine in much more detail in later chapters, this is the reason why these industries are often dominated by a few large firms.

Economies of Scale

economies of scale:
cost advantages that are achieved as a result of large-scale operations.

We now need to look at the reasons *why* the long-run average costs might decline as output increases. The explanation involves what economists call **economies of scale** which can be defined as cost advantages that are achieved by a larger scale of operations. There are both *technical economies of scale* and *pecuniary economies of scale*.

Technical economies of scale are very closely related to the advantages gained from the *division of labour* discussed in the previous chapter. In many contexts, production workers save time if they do not have to switch job functions during the day, or if they can develop special skills as a result of performing only one particular operation. Small plants also utilize the division of labour, but big plants are able to exploit it on a far greater scale. In addition to the use of the division of labour, large-scale production also encourages *management specialization*. Two examples of this, for instance, are that of a supervisor who is just as capable at handling 12 workers as 8, or an accounting department that does not grow in size despite a 30% increase in the output of the firm. Further, as a firm grows in size, rather than increase the number of general managers, it would make sense for it to hire specialized managers such as controllers, marketing managers, production managers and so on. A third type of technical specialization, *machine specialization*, is also possible. A classic example here is the use of robots on a expensive assembly line, something that would probably not be an option for a low-volume firm.

We have now established that technical economies of scale lead to decreasing long-run average cost — what we have already called increasing returns to scale. But our explanation of decreasing long-run average cost does not end here. As mentioned above, pecuniary economies of scale can exist. These come in four forms. The first involve the *cost of borrowing*. Large firms with large output often need, and are able, to borrow large sums of money, and the interest rate that they have to pay is often lower than the rate charged when smaller amounts are borrowed. Second, high-volume firms can *buy inputs in bulk* which also often means at a lower per unit price. In addition, their *bulk selling* lowers their per unit sales cost. Third, a large volume of output often means that previously wasted *by-products can be sold* — think of a fruit canning operation. Once volume is high enough, the firm is also able to sell canned fruit juice using what was previously a waste by-product. Fourth, large firms have advantages of pecuniary economies of scale in *marketing and advertising*. A thirty-second national television ad costs the high-volume firm no more than it does the lower-volume firm, but the per unit of output cost of the ad is much lower.

As a way of summary, let's return to the example of Rising Sun Products which experiences constant returns to scale. This means that there must have been no economies of scale present. However, in the case of Deep Sea Concrete, it enjoys increasing returns to scale which means that the long-run average cost curve is declining. The reason for these increasing returns is that economies of scale, be they technical or pecuniary, are present.

BOX 7A
1. Define the *long run*.
2. Identify and define the *LRAC curve*.
3. Explain what is meant by *economic capacity*.
4. What happens to average total costs as output rises above economic capacity output?
5. What is the shape of the long-run average cost curve under conditions of constant returns to scale?
6. Define *increasing returns to scale*.
7. What are *economies of scale*?
8. Distinguish between technical economies of scale and pecuniary economies of scale.

Decreasing Returns to Scale

decreasing returns to scale: the situation where an increase in inputs of x % results in output increasing by less than x %.

Decreasing returns to scale exist if a doubling of inputs results in output increasing by less than double. The presence of decreasing returns to scale means that long-run average cost increases as output levels increase. This is illustrated in Figure 7.3 where decreasing returns to scale are experienced for output levels above 4,000 units and result in a rising long-run average cost curve.

FIGURE 7.3 The LRAC Curve under Conditions of Decreasing Returns to Scale

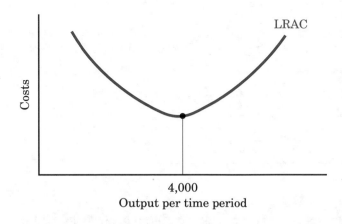

Decreasing returns to scale are present for all output levels above 4,000 units as indicated by the rising long-run average cost curve.

diseconomies of scale: bureaucratic inefficiencies in management that result in decreasing returns to scale.

What could cause such decreasing returns to scale? Since it is difficult to imagine how *pecuniary* **diseconomies of scale** could exist, we have to conclude that the only reason for decreasing returns to scale would be *technical* diseconomies of scale. Such technical diseconomies would most likely occur as a result of bureaucratic inefficiencies in management that all larger firms (as well as non-profit organizations and governments) experience. This is due to size and does not necessarily imply incompetence. The main reason for such diseconomies is that interpersonal communication passes through more channels and becomes subject to interpretation by many more people. Since the lines of communication increase exponentially with the number of personnel, the cost of communication can increase dramatically. Misinterpretation thus becomes more likely, especially if the information is complicated and technical in nature. Further, as the management organization within the firm becomes larger, the points of responsibility and decision making become blurred. If the problem of miscommunication and uncertain responsibility become serious enough, diseconomies of scale would occur.

If such technical diseconomies of scale outweighed the pecuniary economies of scale that might be present, then decreasing returns to scale would result and the long-run average cost curve would begin to rise.

Changes in Short- and Long-Run Costs

It is not only a change in the size of operation, however, that can affect the costs of production. We pointed out in Chapter 6 that if the price of a factor input decreases, short-run average cost would decrease which results in the average cost curve shifting down. Similarly, an increase in factor cost would cause the curve to shift up.

We can add to this by pointing out that a shift in the short-run average cost curve would result in a corresponding shift in the long-run average cost curve. Recall that the long-run average cost is derived from a family of short-run curves. If, for example, technological change results in one of these curves shifting down, then all of the short-run curves that make up the "family" will shift down and, thus, so too will the long-run average cost curve.

QUESTION 7.2

Assuming that the prices of all inputs remain fixed, in the following cases decide whether constant returns to scale or increasing returns to scale exist.

	Total Cost	Output
A:	$420,000	620
	840,000	1,240
B:	$ 80,000	40
	160,000	82
C:	$ 80,000	40
	120,000	61

QUESTION 7.3

Assume that a firm's total cost of producing an output of 600 units is currently $24,000. If total cost increases to $48,000 and the price of inputs and technology remain unchanged, explain what must happen to the quantity of output under conditions of:

A) Constant returns to scale.
B) Increasing returns to scale.
C) Decreasing returns to scale.

What Is the Right Size of Firm?

In the previous chapter, when we looked at a firm's operations in the short run, we pointed out that the most important question faced by the firm is: what is the best output level? The most important question in the long run is: what is the best size of firm? Can a firm be too small? Can it be too big? Our discussion of returns to scale allows us to answer questions like these. Figure 7.4 will help.

FIGURE 7.4 The Complete Long-Run Average Cost Curve

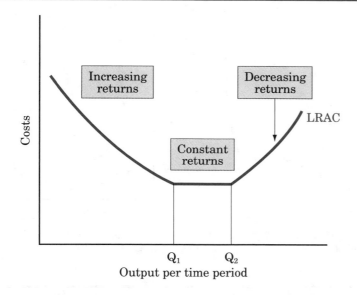

Increasing returns to scale exist for output levels up to Q_1. Constant returns to scale prevail for output levels between Q_1 and Q_2. Finally, decreasing returns to scale prevail for output levels above Q_2.

Firms in many industries are not subject to only constant, increasing or decreasing returns to scale. In fact, for many, there may be a combination of all three. Figure 7.4 illustrates a situation where increasing returns to scale exist for any output level up to quantity Q_1. Output levels that are greater than Q_1, but less than Q_2 are subject to constant returns to scale, and any output level above quantity Q_2 is subject to decreasing returns to scale.

If this long-run average cost curve were typical for a particular industry, we would conclude that any firm that has an output level below quantity Q_1 is probably too small. Output levels below Q_1 would put any firm at a cost disadvantage compared to its competitors. Similarly, we would also conclude that any firm whose output level was above quantity Q_2 was probably too big and could lower its average cost of production by scaling down the size of its operations.

Notice that the long-run average cost curve in Figure 7.4 has the same general U shape as the short-run average total cost curve found in the previous chapter. The similar shapes of the two curves are the result of quite different reasons however. In the case of the short-run average total cost curve, the reasons involve the division of labour and diminishing marginal productivity. The long-run average cost curve, on the other hand, takes on this shape because of increasing, constant and decreasing returns to scale.

Another way to view the issue of the right size of firm is to ask the rather significant question: is bigger better? We can now see that it really depends on the industry in question. Appropriately sized firms are able to take advantage of any increasing returns to scale that exist without becoming too big and experiencing decreasing returns to scale. Figure 7.5 below shows three possible LRAC curves for different industries each resulting in the appropriate-sized firm being different.

FIGURE 7.5 Three Possible LRAC Curves

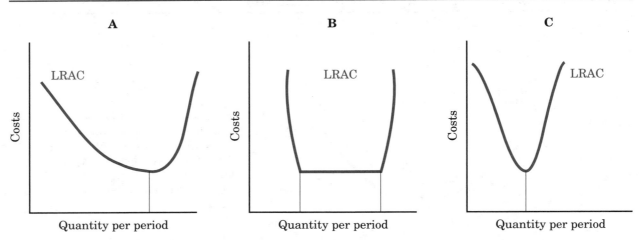

Given the LRAC curve in 7.5A above, the appropriate-sized firm would need to be large. In 7.5 B, a variety of firm sizes would be appropriate. However, the LRAC curve in 7.5C would indicate that small firms would be appropriate.

Figure 7.5A illustrates the case where a firm would have to be quite large to capture all of the economies of scale available. In 7.5B, we can imagine a variety of sized firms, all of whom are able to capture economies of scale. Figure 7.5C illustrates that relatively small firms would be appropriate.

In general, industries such as automobiles, pipelines, satellite data transmission, cable distributors, television transmission and petrochemicals are all ones in which a firm's output level needs to be quite large in order for increasing returns to scale to be fully realized. This is not the case in industries such as shoe retailing, vegetable growing, computer software, and real estate services where the typical firm can be quite small.

Can a Market Be Too Small?

Adam Smith observed, over two hundred years ago, that the division of labour was limited by the size of the market. Is it possible that a limited size of market can restrict the extent to which firms achieve increasing returns to scale. In Canada with its small population and, therefore, small market the answer is yes, at least for some industries.

minimum efficient scale: the smallest level of output at which a firm is able to minimize long-run average cost.

This leads us to the concept of **minimum efficient scale** (MES), which is the smallest level of output at which a firm is able to minimize long-run average costs. If a small market results in firms being unable to achieve minimum efficient scale, then inefficiency can become widespread throughout the industry. The Canadian economy has historically faced this problem. It is too small a market for firms in industries where the MES dictates that a large output is necessary to minimize average cost. As a result such firms are inefficient by world standards. This situation is illustrated in Figure 7.6.

FIGURE 7.6 Minimum Efficient Scale

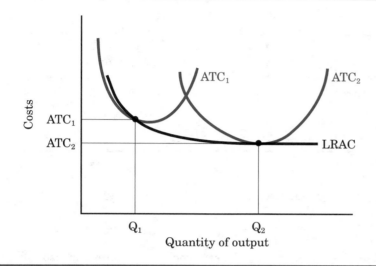

If a small market limits the firm's output to Q_1, then Plant ATC_1 is not able to achieve minimum efficient scale. A larger market that allowed an output of Q_2 and thus Plant ATC_2 would enable the firm to achieve its minimum efficient scale.

A small market may force a firm to limit its output to Q_1 and experience average total cost of ATC_1 as illustrated in Figure 7.6. This is above the level of minimum long-run average cost.

A larger market would allow the firm to build a larger plant, as represented by the ATC_2 curve, and achieve minimum long-run average costs.

Thus, we can see that Adam Smith was correct about his observation that the division of labour can be limited by the size of the market in both the short-run and the long-run sense. In the short run, a limited-sized market can force a firm to operate at an output which is less-than-capacity output. More significantly, a limited-sized market can prevent firms from building large-scale plants and capturing available economies of scale through increased output levels. This inability to increase output levels limits the firm's ability to gain all of the possible advantages of the division of labour.

BOX 7.1

Proponents of both the Free Trade Agreement with the U.S. and NAFTA argue that the failure to achieve minimum efficient scale by many Canadian firms will be addressed by opening up the U.S. and Mexican markets to Canadian firms. With such an enormous expansion in the size of the market, Canadian firms will be able to capture increasing returns to scale and achieve a minimum efficient scale of operation. The result will be that successful Canadian firms will not need to take a back seat to any firm in the world in terms of efficient production.

Concentration Ratios

> **concentration ratio:**
> a measurement of
> what percentage of
> an industry's total
> sales is controlled by
> the largest few firms.

An industry's **concentration ratio** measures the percentage of the industry's total sales that the largest few firms control. While this definition seems quite straightforward, the precise measurement of any concentration ratio is subject to a serious pitfall. Figure 7.7 below will help us understand why.

If the concentration ratio is based on the output of the largest three firms, then Figure 7.7 suggests that Industry B is more concentrated than Industry A. However, if the measurement is based on the five largest firms, we would reach the opposite conclusion. The point is that concentration ratios do suffer from the fact that a lot depends on how the measurement is defined. Another point is just how large a percentage of industry sales do these largest three or five firms have? An answer of 80% gives us quite a different picture of concentration than an answer of 30%.

FIGURE 7.7 Hypothetical Concentration Measures for Two Industries

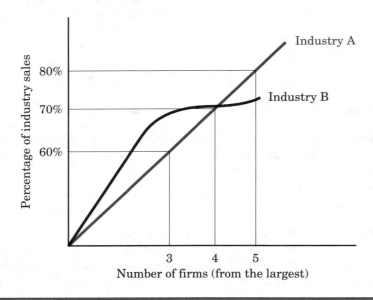

If a concentration ratio measured the output of only the largest three firms, Industry B would have the highest ratio. However, if the ratio was based on the largest five firms, then Industry A would have the higher ratio.

Nonetheless, there is no doubt that some industries are much more concentrated than others, and concentration ratios help to verify this. High concentration industries include those we mentioned above, such as pipelines and satellite data transmission, where large output levels are required to fully capture existing increasing returns to scale.

A general rule of thumb here is that if the firm is large enough to be a recognized household name — General Motors, Chemical Industries Limited (CIL), Air Canada, Johnson and Johnson, Boeing, Northern Telecom — then it is a firm that experiences substantial economies of scale and is in an industry with a relatively high concentration ratio. Similarly, we can deduce that industries that have relatively low concentration ratios must contain firms that do not experience economies of scale to any extensive degree and will tend to be small.

Are the Advantages of Economies of Scale Changing?

Let's consider what is probably the economist's favourite example of technical economies of scale. The cost of a pipeline is roughly proportional to its circumference — the larger the circumference, the more steel needed to build it. However, the carrying capacity of a pipeline is determined by its area, which means that larger pipelines have disproportionately increased capacity and thus lower per unit costs. For instance, a 12-inch-diameter pipe requires twice the steel of a 6-inch pipe but can carry four times the volume. This illustrates the classic relationship between bigger volume and lower long-run average cost.

However, the invention of the microchip raises the possibility that this classic relationship can, in many cases, be inverted. As technology advances, smaller and smaller computers can do what could previously only be done with a room-sized mainframe. Thus, unlike the pipeline, increased efficiency comes from *reductions* in the size of the means of production. This new concept, that smaller is better, fits well with emerging evidence that market demand for many products is shifting to one where producing customized output is the key to future success. More and more, consumers are demanding unique products that meet highly specialized needs. Thus, production must become much more flexible and its emphasis is shifting to customized products.

Next, consider that networks of small computers can quickly be expanded or scaled back. Thus firms can deploy *many* assembly lines, each one turning out a customized variant of the same basic product, rather than only *one* huge assembly line that stamps out a standardized product in massive volumes.

The fundamental question that gets raised by all of this is whether this new technology will alter the scale of the firm that uses it. In other words, as production becomes more customized, and computers become more sophisticated, will efficient production mean smaller firms? Are huge corporations finding it cheaper to farm out work to lower-cost specialists, rather than retain the bureaucratic organizational structure necessary to manage the entire process within a single operation?

Evidence to suggest such downsizing comes from the fact that small automotive-parts firms have been growing in the last decade, while large automobile manufactures have been laying off workers. This leads some economists to argue that as production becomes significantly more specialized and products more customized, we will see growth in the numbers of efficient small firms at the expense of giant firms.

Not all economists agree that this is the trend — pointing out that what can be done efficiently in a small firm can also be done in the corner of a General Motors plant. However, if the trend of smaller is better does prove valid, then a great deal will change and this chapter on long-run average cost and the related advantages of economies of scale will have to be rewritten.

Study Guide

QUESTION 7.4

A) Draw a short-run average total cost curve for Firm X on a graph and indicate an output level, Q1, that results in excess capacity.

B) If output was increased to achieve capacity output, would the firm necessarily also have achieved its minimum efficient scale?

BOX 7B
1. Define *decreasing returns to scale*.
2. What is the most likely cause of decreasing returns to scale?
3. In what sense might a firm be too small?
4. What does a *concentration ratio* measure?
5. In Canada, what is the likely cause of production being below MES?
6. Identify and define *minimum efficient scale*.

Chapter Highlights

This chapter opens by defining the long run as the circumstances in which all inputs are variable and identifies the long-run average cost curve. An example involving a firm called Rising Sun is then presented to illustrate constant returns to scale, which is defined as the situation where a firm's output increases in proportion to the increase in its inputs. Constant returns to scale imply a horizontal long-run average cost curve.

Next, the chapter defines increasing returns to scale as the circumstances under which increasing inputs by x% results in output increasing by more than x%. Then another example is used to lead into a discussion of economies of scale. This latter concept can take the form of either technical economies of scale, such as the division of labour, or management and machine specialization, or pecuniary economies of scale which come in four varieties including the ability to borrow, buy and sell in large quantities and to advertise on a large scale.

The possibility of decreasing returns to scale is then discussed. This is followed by a brief discussion of how changes in the costs of production can come about through technological change or a decrease in the prices of factor inputs that the firm buys.

The chapter then asks the question: what is the right size of firm? It is demonstrated that the answer to this question depends on the presence of constant, increasing or decreasing returns to scale. This leads to a discussion of the concept of the minimum efficient scale of operations in context of market size.

The chapter ends with a discussion of concentration ratios and by asking if the advantages of economies of scale are changing in our new information age.

New Glossary Terms

Workbook

Study Tips

1. Students who come to understand the law of diminishing returns often wonder what explains the often observed phenomenon of both rising output levels and falling prices for things like VCRs, computers or CD players. Surely, if the law of diminishing returns applies, then higher output would be associated with higher marginal and average costs and, therefore, higher prices. Yet, we actually see lower prices for these products. An understanding of the long run, where diminishing returns does not apply but increasing returns to scale often do, reconciles this apparent contradiction.

2. Many students are thrown by the word "pecuniary." It simply means: pertaining to money.

3. Students often think that the terms "increasing returns to scale" and "economies of scale" refer to the same phenomena. This is not quite correct. Increasing returns to scale refers to the increase in output which results from the increase in inputs associated with a larger plant size. The term economies of scale, on the other hand, includes both increasing returns to scale and also the pecuniary advantages that sometimes go with a larger scale of operations.

4. Remember that, for the sake of convenience, we often refer to average total cost in the short run as "average cost" and to average total costs in the long run as LRAC.

5. The value of graphical analysis to help one understand concepts is quite apparent in this chapter. Do take the time to draw the graphs in the questions where you are asked to and keep in mind the concept that is being illustrated. You will find yourself beginning to "think in graphs" as well as in words.

Are You Sure?

Indicate whether the following statements are true or false. If false, indicate why they are false.

1. The long run is the circumstance where at least one input is variable.

T or **F**   If false: _____

_____

_____

2. While a firm can plan for the long run, it must always operate in the short run.
T or **F**   If false: _____

_____

_____

3. Constant returns to scale is the situation where a firm's output increases by the same percentage as the increase in its inputs.
T or **F**   If false: _____

_____

_____

4. Increasing returns to scale is the situation where a firm's output increases by the same percentage as the increase in its inputs.
T or **F**   If false: _____

_____

_____

5. The long-run average cost curve declines continuously as output levels increase.
T or **F**   If false: _____

_____

_____

6. Labour, management and machine specialization are examples of pecuniary economies of scale.
T or **F**   If false: _____

_____

_____

7. Economies of scale are divided into those cost advantages which are technical and those which are pecuniary.
T or **F**   If false: _____

_____

_____

8. A firm's economic capacity and its most productive output level are the same.
T or **F**   If false: _____

_____

_____

9. Pecuniary diseconomies of scale probably do not exist.
T or **F**   If false: _____

_____

_____

10. The right size of firm is determined by the minimum point on its short-run average cost curve.
T or **F**   If false: _____

_____

_____

Translations

On Figure W7.1, draw and label the curves needed to illustrate the following passage (don't forget to label the axes too).

Sketch in a short-run average cost curve and label it ATCI. Also label its minimum point as output Q_3. Next, show an increase in output from Q_1 to Q_2 which results in excess capacity at both points. Now illustrate a larger-sized plant with ATCII which shows a lower minimum average total cost at a higher output level than is possible given ATCI. With the letter C and D show an increase in output from Q_4 to Q_5 on ATCII in which excess capacity is eliminated. Now, sketch in a LRAC curve which is just tangent to ATCI and II. This LRAC curve should illustrate that

increasing returns to scale are present for output levels up to Q_5.

FIGURE W7.1

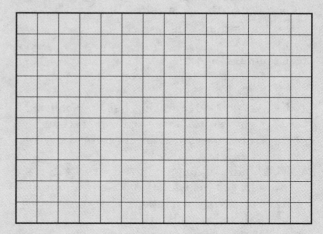

Choose the Best

1. Which of the following is correct in reference to the long run?
   a) All inputs are variable.
   b) Only one input is variable while all others are fixed.

2. If increasing returns to scale are present then:
   a) Economies of scale are also present.
   b) Economies of scale may or may not be present.

3. Which of the following statements is correct?
   a) A firm can operate in either the short run or the long run.
   b) While a firm can plan as if it is in the long run, it can operate only in the short run.

4. What is meant by the term "capacity output"?
   a) An output level where the firm is physically unable to increase output.
   b) The output level where average variable cost is at a minimum.
   c) The output level where average total cost is at a minimum.

5. Which of the following statements is correct if constant returns to scale are present?

a) A doubling of inputs will lead to output more than doubling.
b) A doubling of inputs will lead to output also doubling.
c) A doubling of output will lead to inputs more than doubling.

6. Economies of scale:
   a) Is another term for constant returns to scale.
   b) Are cost advantages that are achieved as a result of large-scale operations.
   c) Only come in pecuniary forms.

7. The ability of a person to supervise 12 workers just as well as 8 is an example of:
   a) The division of labour.
   b) Labour specialization.
   c) Management specialization.

8. All of the following, *except one*, are examples of pecuniary economies of scale. Which one is the exception?
   a) A lower interest rate paid on money borrowed.
   b) The ability to sell the by-products of production.
   c) The ability to use specialized inputs such as a robotic assembly line.
   d) The ability to obtain lower prices by buying in bulk.

9. The fact that a one-minute television commercial costs a high-volume firm no more than a low-volume firm is an example of which of the following?
   a) Increasing returns to scale.
   b) Pecuniary economies of scale.
   c) Technical economies of scale.
   d) Management specialization.

10. Which of the following is the most likely cause of diseconomies of scale?
    a) Increasing returns to scale.
    b) A small scale of operations and output.
    c) Low productivity.
    d) Bureaucracy.

11. Which of the following statements is correct if a firm's capacity output increases from 400 to 800 and its total costs rise from $60,000 to $110,000?
    a) The firm is experiencing constant returns to scale.
    b) The firm is experiencing decreasing returns to scale.
    c) Both the firm's short-run and long-run average costs must have decreased.
    d) The firm's long-run average cost must have decreased but its short-run average cost could have either decreased or increased.

12. Which of the following statements is correct when a firm builds a larger plant under the conditions of constant returns to scale?
    a) The capacity output of the larger plant has a lower average cost.
    b) The capacity output of the larger plant has the same average cost.
    c) Economies of scale are present.
    d) LRAC will decrease as output increases.

13. Which of the following statements is correct if a firm builds a larger plant and, at any particular output, its short-run average cost increases?
    a) Decreasing returns to scale must be present.
    b) Increasing returns to scale must be present.
    c) Constant returns to scale must be present.
    d) Decreasing, increasing and constant returns to scale are all possible.

14. Which of the following statements is correct if the appropriately sized firm is one with a large output.
    a) Constant returns to scale must begin at low levels of output.
    b) Increasing returns to scale must prevail until high levels of output are reached.
    c) Decreasing returns to scale must begin at low levels of output.
    d) Constant returns to scale must be absent.

15. What does the term "minimum efficient scale" mean?

a) The smallest level of output at which a firm is able to minimize both short-run and long-run average costs.

b) The smallest level of output at which a firm is able to minimize short-run marginal cost.

c) The smallest level of output at which a firm is able to minimize short-run average cost.

d) The smallest level of output at which a firm is able to minimize long-run marginal cost.

e) The smallest level of output at which a firm is able to minimize both short-run and long-run marginal cost.

16. Suppose a firm builds a larger plant and increases its output. Which of the following statements is correct?
    a) Its MES output must increase.
    b) Its MES output must decrease.
    c) It will be able to achieve its MES output only if it also achieves capacity output.
    d) Its short-run average cost curve for the original plant will have shifted down.
    e) Its long-run average costs must have increased.

17. Adam Smith's observed that the division of labour is limited by the size of the market. Which one of the following contradicts this statement?
    a) A limited-sized market can prevent firms from achieving capacity output.
    b) A limited-sized market can prevent firms from achieving their minimum efficient scale.
    c) A limited-sized market can prevent firms from achieving minimum short-run average cost.
    d) A limited-sized market can prevent firms from achieving minimum long-run average cost.
    e) A limited-sized market can prevent firms from achieving excess capacity.

18. Suppose that the concentration ratio of an industry is high. Which of the following statements would be correct?
    a) Increasing returns to scale are insignificant for the firms within the industry.

b) Increasing returns to scale are significant for the firms within the industry.

c) The industry will have many firms within it.

d) The firms within the industry will have all achieved their minimum efficient scale.

e) All the firms must be of a similar size.

Refer to Figure W7.2 to answer questions 19 and 20.

FIGURE W7.2

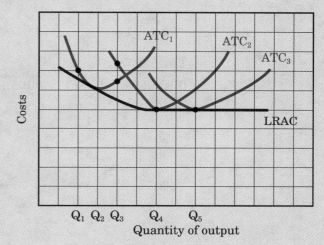

19. Refer to Figure W7.2 to answer this question. All of the following statements *except one* are correct. Which is the exception?
    a) Plant ATC_1 has excess capacity at output level Q_1.
    b) Output level Q_2 is capacity output for plant size 1.
    c) Output level Q_3 can be produced cheaper in plant 2 than in plant 1.
    d) Plant ATC_2 achieves minimum efficient scale.
    e) Increasing returns to scale are experienced when output is increased from Q_1 to Q_4.

20. Refer to Figure W7.2 to answer this question. All of the following statements *except one* are correct. Which is the exception?
    a) ATC 1, 2 and 3 are short-run average cost curves.
    b) The long-run average cost curve illustrates both increasing and constant returns to scale.

c) Constant returns to scale exist between outputs Q_4 and Q_5.

d) Increasing output from Q_1 to Q_3 would require that a larger plant be built.

e) Both the short run and the long run are illustrated in this graph.

What's Wrong?

Can you spot the four errors in the following passage? (Ignore grammatical mistakes!)

The fact that the world's food cannot be grown in a flowerpot can be explained by the law of diminishing returns to scale. On the other hand, the continuous fall in the prices of, say, computer hardware must reflect the fact that, as output increases, fixed costs decrease. This decrease in prices is a reflection of constant returns to scale which must mean that the output level needed for computer firms to gain minimum efficient scale must be small.

Key Problem

Table W7.1 below contains short-run cost data for five different plant sizes.

TABLE W7.1

Output	Plant I	Plant II	Plant III	PlantIV	Plant V
10	$ 8.00	$10.50	–	–	–
20	7.00	9.00	–	–	–
30	6.00	7.50	$10.00	–	–
40	6.50	6.00	8.00	–	–
50	7.50	5.00	6.50	$10.30	–
60	9.00	5.80	5.00	8.50	–
70	10.50	7.00	4.00	7.00	–
80	–	8.20	4.90	5.10	$6.50
90	–	10.00	6.00	4.00	6.00
100	–	–	7.80	4.30	5.40
110	–	–	8.50	5.60	5.00
120	–	–	–	7.70	5.30
130	–	–	–	10.00	6.00
140	–	–	–	–	7.10

a) On the grid in Figure W7.3, graph the short-run average cost curves for the five plants.

b) What is the best size of plant if output is:

    30?   Plant: _____.
    40?   _____.
    50?   _____.
    60?   _____.
    70?   _____.
    80?   _____.
    90?   _____.
    100?   _____.
    110?   _____.
    120?   _____.

c) Roughly sketch in the long-run average cost curve in Figure W7.3.

d) What plant size would the firm need to use in order to achieve minimum efficient scale (MES) of operations?

FIGURE W7.3

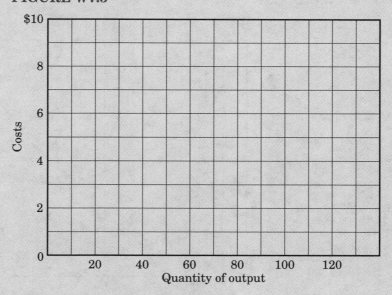

Answer: _____.

e) What is the output level that achieves MES?

Answer: _____.

f) If a firm is producing an output of 80 in plant size IV, does excess capacity exist?

Answer: _____.

g) What would be the capacity output level for plant size IV?

Answer: _____.

h) Given the LRAC curve in Figure W7.3, increasing returns to scale exist between what output levels?

Answer: _____.

i) Given the LRAC curve in Figure W7.3, constant returns to scale exist between what output levels?

Answer: _____.

j) Given the LRAC curve in Figure W7.3, decreasing returns to scale exist between what output levels?

Answer: _____.

k) If this firm's sales are limited to 50, we can say that the market is too small for what plant sizes.

Answer: _____.

Need a Hand?

a) and c)   **FIGURE W7.4** (completed Figure W7.3)

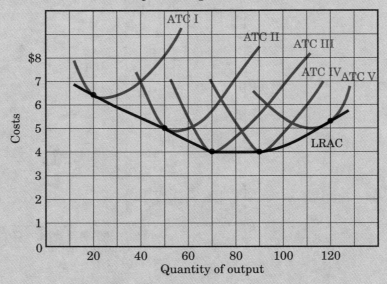

b) It is easiest to answer this question by referring to the data in Table W7.1, although the answers could also be read off the graph.

Output	Plant
30	I
40	II
50	II
60	III
70	III
80	III
90	IV
100	IV
110	V
120	V

d) Minimum efficient scale is the smallest level of output at which a firm is able to minimize long-run average cost. This is achieved in **plant size III**.

e) **70** is the output where minimum long-run average cost is achieved.

f) **Yes**, excess capacity exists because an output of 80 is below the output (90) at which minimum average cost of $4 is achieved.

g) **90** is capacity output where short-run average costs are minimized.

h) Between the outputs of **0 and 70**, where long-run average costs are declining.

i) Between the outputs of **70 and 90**, where long-run average costs are constant.

j) **Above the output of 90**, where long-run average costs are increasing.

k) In plant sizes **III, IV and V**, the short-run average costs are higher at an output of 50 than the minimum level of $5, which can be achieved in plant size II.

More of the Same

Table W7.2 below contains short-run cost data for five different plant sizes.

TABLE W7.2

Output	Plant I	Plant II	Plant III	Plant IV	Plant V
2	$0.50	$0.70	–	–	–
4	0.45	0.55	–	–	–
6	0.50	0.45	$0.65	–	–
8	0.60	0.40	0.50	–	–
10	0.75	0.45	0.40	$0.60	–
12	–	0.55	0.35	0.45	–
14	–	0.70	0.40	0.35	$0.60
16	–	–	0.50	0.30	0.45
18	–	–	0.65	0.35	0.35
20	–	–	–	0.45	0.30
22	–	–	–	0.60	0.35
24	–	–	–	–	0.45
26	–	–	–	–	0.60

a) On the grid in Figure W7.5, graph the short-run average cost curves for the five plants.

FIGURE W7.5

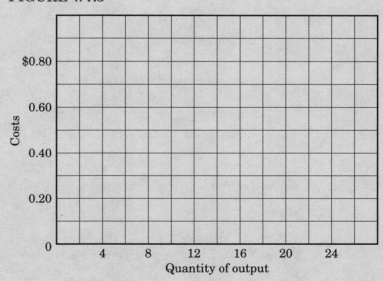

b) What is the best size of plant for each of the following output levels: 4, 6, 8, 10, 12, 14, 16, 18, 20, 22, 24?

c) Do a rough sketch of the long-run average cost curve in the graph above.

d) What plant size would the firm need to use in order to achieve minimum efficient scale of output?

e) What is the output level that achieves MES?

f) If the firm is producing an output level of 10 in plant size III, does excess capacity exist?

g) What would be the capacity output level for plant size II?

h) Given the LRAC curve in Figure W7.5, increasing returns to scale exist between what output levels?

i) Given the LRAC curve in Figure W7.5, at what output level do constant returns to scale begin?

j) Given the LRAC curve in Figure W7.5, is there any evidence of decreasing returns to scale?

k) What is the smallest level of sales that could exist in order for us to conclude that this firm is not constrained by a limited size of market?

Other Problems

1. The following is cost data for three different sized plants, I, II and III which are the only three plants possible.

TABLE W7.3

Output	ATCI	ATCII	ATCIII
100	$12	$15	$19
200	11	12	16
300	10	8	12
400	11	11	9
500	12	15	10

a) In what plant size is MES achieved?

Answer: _____.

b) What is the capacity output for plant size III?

Answer: _____.

c) What is the right-sized plant to produce an output of 400?

Answer: _____.

2. Figure W7.6 illustrates a series of short-run average cost curves numbered ATC_1 through ATC_5 which correspond to five different plant sizes.

a) What is true about output levels 200, 400, 600, 800 and 1,000?

Answer: _____.

b) What is the right-sized plant to produce an output of 900?

Answer: _____.

c) Between what output levels do increasing returns to scale prevail?

Answer: _____.

FIGURE W7.6

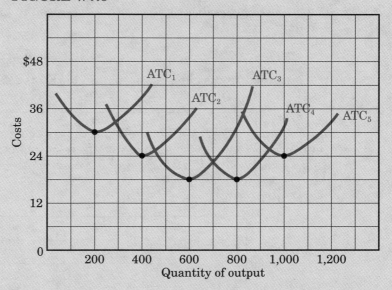

d) At what output levels do decreasing returns to scale prevail?

Answer: _____.

3. Figure W7.7 below illustrates a series of short-run average cost curves numbered ATC_1 through ATC_4 which correspond to the only four different automobile plant sizes possible.

FIGURE W7.7

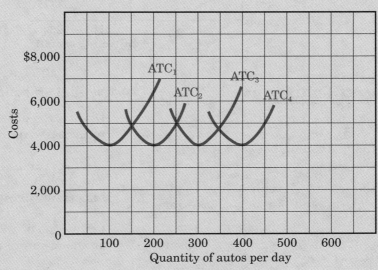

a) What can you say about returns to scale?

Answer: _____.

b) Are economies of scale present?

Answer: _____.

c) If it takes 40 workers and 100 units of capital to produce 200 automobiles a day, how much labour and capital is involved in producing 600 automobiles a day?

Answer: _____.

d) At what output is capacity output and MES the same?

Answer: _____.

4. On the graph in Figure W7.8, sketch in the cost curves necessary to illustrate a firm which faces a very small market size resulting in it being unable to achieve either capacity output or MES.

FIGURE W7.8

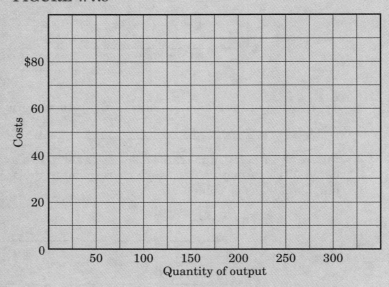

Unanswered Questions

Short Essays

1. Discuss the distinction between increasing returns to scale and economies of scale.

2. Discuss the effects of technological change on the short-run and the long-run average cost curves.

3. What does it mean to suggest that a firm is the "right size"?

4. Explain in what sense the domestic market in Canada might be too small.

5. The advantages of economies of scale are changing. Discuss this statement.

Analytical Questions

1. Discuss the difference between diminishing returns and decreasing returns to scale.

2. If a firm can never operate in the long run, why do economists consider the long run an important concept?

3. Is the idea of a right-sized firm a short-run or a long-run concept?

4. How does a firm's capacity output change if the price of a firm's variable inputs fall?

5. What could you say about an industry that has a concentration ratio of 100?

Numerical Questions

1. Assume that a firm's total cost of producing an output of 50 units an hour is currently $8,400. If the price of inputs and technology remain unchanged, and total costs increase to $16,800, what must happen to the quantity of output under conditions of:

   a) Constant returns to scale: _____.

   b) Increasing returns to scale: _____.

   c) Decreasing returns to scale: _____.

2. The following is cost data from three different-sized plants, 1, 2 and 3 which are the only three sizes possible.

TABLE W7.4

Output	ATC$_1$	ATC$_2$	ATC$_3$
50	$80	$ 95	$120
100	75	80	100
150	65	60	75
200	75	80	55
250	90	100	80

   a) What is capacity output for each of the three plants?

   b) At what output is minimum long-run average cost achieved?

   c) What is the right size of plant to produce an output of 150?

   d) What is the right size of plant to produce and output of 50?

3. Figure W7.9 illustrates a series of short-run average cost curves numbered ATC$_1$ through ATC$_6$ which correspond to six different plant sizes.

   a) Between what levels of output are increasing returns to scale present?

FIGURE W7.9

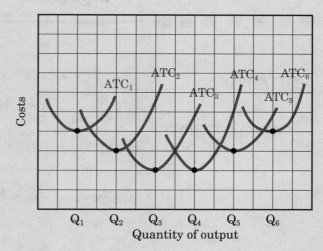

   b) What are the output levels where decreasing returns to scale are present?

   c) What is true about all six levels of output, Q$_1$ through Q$_6$?

   d) What is the best size of plant to produce the output represented by the quantity halfway between Q$_4$ and Q$_5$?

4. Draw four short-run average cost curves for plant sizes I through IV. Indicate the capacity output for plant I as l00 and the capacity output of II as twice that of I, and of III as three times that of I, and of IV as four times that of I. You are to assume that the quantity of inputs needed to produce the capacity output in II are less than twice those needed to produce output I. Similarly, the quantity of inputs needed to produce capacity output in III are less than 50% more than those needed to produce the output in II. Finally, the quantity of inputs needed to produce the output in IV are exactly 33 1/3% more than those needed in III. Now sketch in the long-run average cost curve. How does this curve illustrate both increasing and constant returns to scale?

CHAPTER EIGHT

Perfect Competition

What's ahead . . . In this chapter, we take our first look at market structures using the perfectly competitive model. After describing some examples of perfect competition, we look at the behaviour of the individual firm and how it decides on its production level and how profits are affected. We derive rules for determining the output level where the producer breaks even, where it will make the most profit, and when it might be advised to shut down operations. The rest of the chapter shows how the market and the individual producer react to changes in both demand and technology.

This, and the next four chapters, could collectively be called the theory of producer behaviour. We will focus our study on the quantities that firms produce and what determines the price of these quantities. The last two chapters provided us with a background for this focus in that the costs of production definitely have an effect on both the price of the product and how much firms will willingly produce. To be able to fully understand price and quantity determination though, we need to know a bit more about a product than just its costs. We need to know something about the product itself, about other firms in the industry, and about the customers and how many there are. In other words, we need to know more about the market in which the product is sold. Let us be careful about terminology before we go any further: an "industry" is the collective name for all the firms producing a similar product — the different firms in the industry may or may not know each other well, they may or may not be members of some sort of common association and they may or may not agree on various types of collective action. What they have in common is that they produce a similar product, usually using the same technology. A "market," on the other hand, is the place where producers and consumers come together. In other words, an industry is the name for a group of producers; a market is the name for both producers and consumers.

Characteristics of Different Markets

Economists see two main ways in which markets differ. One way is in terms of the type of product sold: do the producers sell an identical product or are there differences between one firm's product and that of other firms? The second difference is in terms of the numbers of buyers and sellers: is the market populated by many firms and consumers or conversely is it dominated by a few big players in the game? The degree of control that a single firm can exercise over the price of its products and the quantity it is able to sell depends very much on the amount of competition that exists between producers and on the relative power of producers and consumers. In addition, it also depends on the degree of difference that exists between its product and that of the competition. Table 8.1 shows the range of possible markets that exist. The type of market depends on the number of producers and whether the firms produce identical or differentiated products.

TABLE 8.1 Matrix of Markets

	Many Firms	Few Firms	One Single Firm
Identical product	Perfect competition	Undifferentiated oligopoly	Monopoly
Differentiated product	Monopolistic competition	Differentiated oligopoly	N.A.

perfect competition: a market in which all buyers and sellers are price takers.

As we shall see, the greater the number of firms and the more similar the products, then the more competitive the market will be. In later chapters we will be looking at other forms of competition; this chapter and the next will concentrate on the form known as **perfect competition**.

Perfect Competition

Features of Perfect Competition

Markets are said to be perfectly competitive when no single consumer or producer has any greater power or influence in the market than any other consumer or producer. Such a market can only perform well when no single producer or consumer can affect the price or the quantity produced. A competitive market, in other words, provides a level playing field where all participants are treated equally. This can only happen when four conditions are fulfilled. Firstly there must be *a large number of buyers and sellers* and all must be small in relation to the whole market. Since each producer is relatively small, then a decision by any particular producer to double its output (or to produce nothing at all) will not have much impact on the market. Similarly, whether or not any particular consumer increases or decreases her purchases will also have no perceptible effect on total sales. Also, a competitive market does not exist if there is any collusion between producers or between consumers since it is assumed that each person operates separately and independently. Nor is a market competitive if producers or consumers form co-operatives or associations which make decisions on behalf of their members. A competitive market therefore is one in which the buyers and sellers all act separately and independently, and each individual producer and consumer has so little market power that no single one of them can influence the price or materially affect the quantity exchanged. For each of them, the market price is a given.

The second feature of a perfectly competitive market is that it is a market where *there are no preferences shown*. This means that the consumer neither knows nor cares where she buys a particular product since, among other things, the producers all make an identical, or undifferentiable, product. Nor are there any other reasons why a particular producer would be preferred. Similarly, producers show no preference toward any particular consumer. For them, all consumers are equal.

The third defining feature of a competitive market is that *there should be easy entry and exit into the market* from the viewpoints of both producers and consumers. This is sometimes rephrased to say that there are no significant barriers to entry. For the prospective producer, this implies that it should be reasonably easy to set up in business: the producer does not require a great deal of financial capital, nor have to pay a membership fee, licence fee or any other type of entry fee; nor does the producer have to join any club or organization in order to trade. In this manner, existing firms in an industry have no advantage over newcomers. It also means that when there are extensive sunk costs, firms will be reluctant to both enter and leave an industry despite the fact that such costs are, by definition, irrecoverable. Irrespective of this, if market conditions turn sour, firms might hang on longer than is prudent simply in the hope that they may eventually be able to recover such sunk costs. Easy entry and exit also means that consumers too should not be required to belong to a particular organization or to possess particular attributes in order to buy a certain product.

The fourth and final feature of perfectly competitive markets is that *all producers have all the market information necessary to make rational production and purchasing decisions.* This condition is to ensure that no particular participant in the market has any advantage (or competitive edge) over the other participants. It means, for instance, that we don't have a situation where only a select few customers are aware of a particular sale going on in town, or where a firm introduces a superior technology which is unknown to other firms. In other words, if the knowledge is not equally shared, then some people will have an advantage over others, and unless there is equality in the marketplace, it is not perfectly competitive.

If these four conditions exist, the marketplace is said to be perfectly competitive. The result will be that the anonymous forces of demand and supply determine both the price of the product and the quantity which is traded. Conversely, if these conditions do not exist, then it will usually mean that one participant is stronger than the others and can therefore have some degree of influence over the price and quantity. We would expect that if markets are competitive then any change in the demand or supply conditions should affect the price, and since presumably demand and supply are almost always changing, we should expect to see the price change quite frequently. Prima facie evidence of a competitive market is provided, then, whenever the price in the market regularly changes. Conversely, if the price of a particular product seldom changes, then there is prima facie evidence that that market is *not* competitive. Let us try then to find some examples of competitive markets in our economy.

Examples of Perfectly Competitive Markets

In searching for examples of competitive markets, we should emphasize that the first condition does not require that every producer be small in size, but only *small in relation to the total market.* It is just as possible then to have some reasonably big competitive firms, as it is to have one single small monopolist. In respect to the second condition, that no preferences be shown, this immediately rules out examples like travel agents, hairdressers, gas stations and so on, since people do show preferences even though the difference between suppliers may seem small. Economists recognize that, from a chemist's point of view, a particular brand of gasoline is identical to some other brand, but if consumers show a preference for one over the other, then there is a difference between the two, even if it is only the name of the gasoline. Another important point to remember is that it is not the number of products that makes the market competitive but the number of individual producers. For example, there are upwards of a hundred different breakfast cereals on the market, but they are produced by just two or three giant firms, which makes it a very uncompetitive market.

Allowing for these caveats, are there good examples of competitive markets these days? Well, the closest we will come is a situation where the market is very big and the product is generic, say, for example, in the world markets for commodities like aluminum, zinc, cotton, rubber, oil, soybeans, and so on. The price of these products often changes hourly in response to changing conditions around the world and their current prices are published every day in the financial section of most newspapers. A Canadian producer of a particular commodity, however big it may be in Canada, is unlikely to have much impact on the world supply. In most respects, then, world markets for commodities are reasonably competitive. But what about inside Canada — are there any competitive markets domestically? The stock market is often cited as an example of a perfect market where the prices of products (stocks and bonds) often change minute by minute. However, on closer inspection it is far from competitive since the action of a single large buyer or seller can and does affect the price of stocks. This offends our criterion that no single buyer or seller can affect the price. As well, you do need to use the services of an agent or broker and pay a commission in order buy a particular stock, which means that there is not perfectly free access to the market.

At first glance, markets for agricultural products within Canada seem to provide a good example of fairly competitive markets. There are thousands of farmers of wheat and other grain crops, and, though some prairie farms are very big, they are insignificant in relation to the total market in Canada. In addition, the products are identical in that no one knows, or for that matter, cares, which particular farmer grew the wheat or the oats or the potatoes that they purchase. So, on the surface it would appear that agricultural markets are fairly competitive. However, as we saw in Chapter 3, the Canadian government has a great deal of involvement in agricultural markets through its establishment of various different marketing boards to regulate price and output levels. For this reason agriculture is not a good example of perfect competition in Canada. In truth, there are very few examples of competitive markets in the modern world compared to the eighteenth century when Adam Smith first wrote about market characteristics. In Smith's day, all producers were small, and the output of most producers was very similar to that of the competition. This, of course is no longer true. Given this fact, it is reasonable to ask why economists continue to talk about and analyze such a market structure if it has become non-existent. The answer is that economists use the construction of the perfectly competitive market structure as an "ideal structure." Then, once we have figured out how perfectly competitive markets work, we have a benchmark with which to judge and compare "real world" markets. If you think about it, in this sense, the economist is no different than the physicist who explains what will happen in ideal situations and then goes on to revise the conclusions for other circumstances. Galileo, for example, investigated the behaviour of falling bodies and concluded that they all fall at identical rates of acceleration *in a vacuum*. It is surprising that many people have learned this snippet of theory, forgetting that it is true only in the idealized situation of a vacuum. They will argue vigorously that a kilo bag of feathers and a kilo bag of lead, if thrown from a high building will both hit the ground at the same time! (They don't, as a matter of fact! A kilo bag of feathers is far bigger than a kilo of lead and encounters more air resistance.)

Finally, it should be said that the economist's definition of perfect competition differs greatly from the everyday understanding of competition. Most people, asked to give examples of "vigorous" competition, would cite Pepsi and Coca Cola or Reebok and Nike or the competition in the automobile industry. To economists, however, this is about as uncompetitive as you can get, since each of these producers is very powerful and exerts a great deal of influence in its own markets. To an economist, true competition exists between a wheat farmer in Alberta and another farmer whom she has never met in Manitoba, a thousand kilometres away.

The Competitive Industry and Firm

As we have seen, in perfectly competitive markets the individual producer (and consumer) has no control over the price at which the product is bought and sold. The price is determined by the collective action of thousands, if not millions, of separate individual participants in the market. The forces of demand and supply determine the price, and once established, it becomes a "take it or leave it" proposition for each individual. Using wheat farming as an example, and assuming no intervention from the government, this is illustrated in Figure 8.1.

FIGURE 8.1 The Competitive Industry and Firm

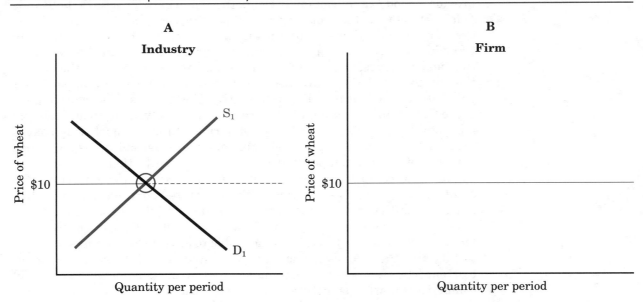

The market demand, D_1, shown in Figure 8.1A, is the total demand from the many buyers of wheat, and the supply of wheat, S_1, comes from thousands of individual farmers. The individual farm depicted in Figure 8.1B produces part of the supply, S1, but its contribution is such a small part that its actions have little impact on it. The market price of $10 applies to all buyers and sellers including this particular farm which can then sell as much or as little as it wishes at this price.

In Figure 8.1A, given the market demand and supply curves for wheat, the equilibrium price will be $10 a bushel. This is the market price and is the only price at which wheat will be bought and sold. From the individual farmer's point of view, shown in Figure 8.1B, the price will remain at $10 irrespective of how much or how little this farmer decides to produce. In a sense, to the farmer this price line represents the (perfectly elastic) demand curve for her wheat. She cannot sell the wheat for a higher price since nobody will buy it if they can purchase wheat elsewhere for $10; nor would she want to sell it at a lower price since she can sell as much as she wants at $10. She is very much at the mercy of the market, and should the demand for wheat increase, she will benefit from a higher price. On the other hand should more farmers be attracted to the wheat industry, the supply of wheat will increase, and the individual farmer will lose out because of the lower price. For the individual farmer, the only decision is to figure out what quantity will provide the greatest profit. Before we can do this, however we need to look a bit deeper at the possible sales revenue for the farmer.

Competition and Revenues

Suppose that the market price for wheat is presently $10 a bushel and our farmer, Farmer Blue, is trying to decide how much to produce. Table 8.2 shows what sales revenues she will receive for different quantities sold.

TABLE 8.2 Deriving Average and Marginal Revenue

Output (Q)	Price (P)	Total Revenue (TR)	Average Revenue (AR)	Marginal Revenue (MR)
0	$ 0	$ 0	$ 0	$ 0
1	10	10	10	10
2	10	20	10	10
3	10	30	10	10
4	10	40	10	10
5	10	50	10	10
6	10	60	10	10
7	10	70	10	10

average revenue: the amount of revenue received per unit sold. It will always equal the price of the product.

The total (sales) revenue which Farmer Blue receives depends on the quantity she sells and the price at which she sells it, i.e.,

$$\text{Total Revenue (TR)} = \text{Output (Q)} \times \text{Price (P)}$$

The **average revenue** that she receives per bushel is simply the total revenue divided by the quantity sold:

$$\text{Average Revenue (AR)} = \frac{\text{Total Revenue (TR)}}{\text{Output (Q)}}$$

marginal revenue: the extra revenue derived from the sale of one more unit.

Finally, the **marginal revenue** is defined as the additional total revenue derived from the sale of an additional unit:

$$\text{Marginal Revenue} = \frac{\Delta \text{ Total Revenue } (\Delta \text{ TR})}{\Delta \text{ Output } (\Delta \text{ Q})}$$

In Table 8.2 you can see that the price, average revenue and marginal revenue all equal $10. The equality of these three holds for all competitive firms. Stated in the form of an equation, Table 8.2 says that given a perfectly elastic demand curve:

$$\text{Price} = \text{Average Revenue} = \text{Marginal Revenue}$$

This says nothing more than that the average amount that Farmer Blue receives for selling a bushel of wheat is the price she sells it for, and this remains a constant $10. Similarly, the marginal revenue (how much she receives for selling an additional bushel) is also a constant $10, i.e., the price. Although this might all seem unnecessarily complicated, we shall soon see that the concept of the marginal lies at the heart of economic analysis. In addition, as we shall also see in later chapters, price and marginal revenue are not the same in other market situations.

Let us look at these variables graphically in Figure 8.2 below.

FIGURE 8.2 Revenue Curves

A: Total Revenue Curve

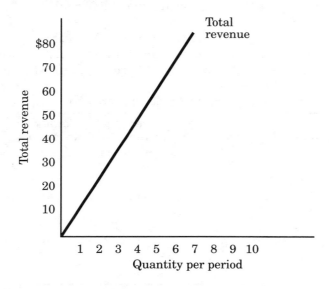

The total revenue curve is upward-sloping which means that the more wheat sold, the greater the total revenue. It also has a constant slope (it is a straight line) because each additional bushel sold increases the total revenue by the same amount, in this example, by $10.

B: Average and Marginal Revenue Curves

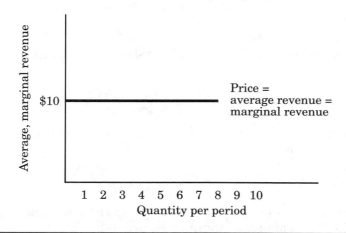

The average revenue, the marginal revenue and the price are all equal to $10 and all remain constant regardless of the quantity sold.

The total revenue curve is a straight, upward-sloping curve whose steepness depends on the marginal revenue (or price) of the product. The greater the price, the steeper will be the slope of the TR curve. The average and marginal revenue curves are the same as we already saw in Figure 8.1B and are independent of output, i.e., they are horizontal to the output axis and their values do not depend on the output level.

Price, Profit and Output under Perfect Competition

We have seen that the price at which the farmer can sell her wheat is a given; she has no control over it. Her only decision is to decide which output level will produce the maximum profit. (Economists generally assume this is the prime goal of the firm. Whether this is a legitimate assumption, and what other goals might be considered, is a discussion we will leave until Chapter 11.) Profit maximization depends on both the revenue and the costs of production. Table 8.3 repeats the revenue information from Table 8.2 and adds to it the costs of production on Farmer Blue's farm.

TABLE 8.3 Total Revenue, Cost and Profit for a Perfectly Competitive Producer

Output (Q)	Price (AR = MR)	Total Revenue (TR)	Total Cost (TC)	Total Profit (Tπ)
0	$10	$ 0	$12	$–12
1	10	10	17	–7
2	10	20	20	0
3	10	30	25	5
4	10	40	34	6
5	10	50	45	5
6	10	60	60	0
7	10	70	78	–8

Total profit is the difference between total revenue and total costs. The amount of profit — and we are talking about economic profit — varies with the output level. When Farmer Blue produces no wheat, she still has to contend with fixed costs of $12 and so would make a loss of $12 at zero output. If she produces an output of one bushel, she would still make a loss (of $7) though it is less than when she produces nothing at all. If she produces 2 bushels, she will just break even, i.e., her total costs and revenue are equal so that she makes zero profit. This level of output is referred to by economists as the **break-even output**. Remember though that economists regard a normal profit as being part of costs, so that although Farmer Blue is making zero economic profit when she produces 2 bushels, she is still making normal profit and would therefore remain a producer rather than go out of business. If she were to produce an output of more than 2 bushels she would be making not only normal profit, but also the economic profit shown in the table. She would make maximum economic profit of $6 at an output of 4 bushels. As Farmer Blue tries to increase production above an output of 4, her costs start to rise faster than the revenue so that the total profits start to decline. At an output of 6, she

break-even output: the level of output at which the sales revenue of the firm just covers fixed and variable costs including normal profit.

would again be breaking even and at higher outputs, she would start to encounter losses.

QUESTION 8.1
Suppose that the total fixed costs of the farmer depicted in Table 8.3 were to increase by $5. What would be the new level of break-even output and the profit-maximizing output?

A firm will maximize profit, therefore, when:

(Total Revenue – Total Cost) is greatest.

This idea is illustrated in Figure 8.3.

FIGURE 8.3 Total Revenue, Costs and Profits

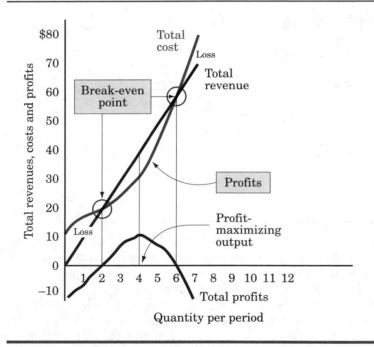

If Farmer Blue produces either 0 or 1 bushel, she will make an economic loss because the total costs will exceed the total revenue. The amount of loss is illustrated as the distance between the TR curve and the TC curve and is shown explicitly at the bottom in the total profit curve. At an output of 2 bushels, the two curves intersect, which implies zero profit, i.e., this is the break-even output. Any output between 2 and 6 will produce an economic profit since the TR curve lies above the TC curve. Maximum profits occur where the distance between the two curves is greatest — at an output of 4 bushels. The total profit curve is at a peak at this output. Outputs greater than 6 would result in a loss since the TR curve is below the TC curve.

Because of fixed costs, total costs are always higher than revenues at low output levels. The distance between the two curves shows the amount of profit or loss. Until break-even is reached at an output of 2 bushels, the total cost curve is above the total revenue curve and Farmer Blue would be making a loss and this is shown in the total profit curve. Break-even is where the two curves intersect, at outputs of 2 and 6 bushels, and where the total profit curve crosses the horizontal axis. At these two output levels, total profit is zero. At outputs above 6 bushels, Farmer Blue would be making a loss, but any output between 2 and 6 would produce a profit. Graphically, the greatest profit is realized when the gap between the two curves is greatest, and this occurs at an output of 4 bushels. This is shown explicitly in the total profit curve.

Study Guide

QUESTION 8.2
Given the following data, calculate the level of total profits at each output and plot the total revenue, total cost and profit curves. Indicate the break-even and profit-maximizing outputs:

Output (Q)	Price (P)	Total Costs (TC)
0	$50	$ 40
1	50	115
2	50	160
3	50	190
4	50	210
5	50	250
6	50	280
7	50	350
8	50	450

Returning to Farmer Blue, if the price of wheat increases, she will enjoy a higher total revenue at every price. This means that at every output level, total profit will be higher (or total losses lower). In addition, as Table 8.4A below shows, the range of outputs where she can make a profit is greater.

TABLE 8.4 Total Profit at Different Price Levels

Output (Q)	Total Costs (TC)	A Price = $12 Total Revenue (TR)	Total Profit (Tπ)	B Price =$8.50 Total Revenue (TR)	Total Profit (Tπ)
0	$12	$ 0	−$12	$ 0	−$12.00
1	17	12	−5	8.50	−8.50
2	20	24	4	17.00	−3.00
3	25	36	11	25.50	0.50
4	34	48	14	34.00	0.00
5	45	60	15	42.50	−2.50
6	60	72	12	51.00	−9.00
7	78	84	6	59.50	−18.50

If the price increases to $12, it is possible for her to make a profit at any output between 2 and 7, and the amount of profit is higher at every output level than when the price was $10. Her profit-maximizing output level is now at the higher level of 5. In contrast, a drop in the price of wheat to, say, $8.50 a bushel, as depicted in Table 8.4B means that the profitable output levels narrow — only an output of 3 bushels is profitable. The level of profit is also lower at every output, and the profit-maximizing output is reduced to an output of 3.

In summary, then, a higher price means a wider range of profitable outputs for the producer; it also means that the producer will increase production and achieve greater profit. In contrast, a lower price reduces the range of profitable outputs and results in lower production and smaller profit (or bigger losses) for the producers. Using the numbers from Table 8.4, these ideas are presented in Figure 8.4 on the next page.

FIGURE 8.4 The Effect on Production and Profits of a Change in Price

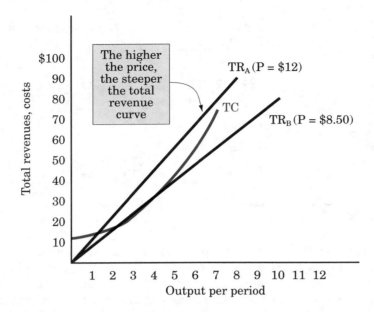

The higher the price,
the steeper the total
revenue curve

TR$_A$ (P = $12)

TC

TR$_B$ (P = $8.50)

The higher the price of wheat, the greater the total revenue at each output level. This will mean a steeper curve. The lower the price, the flatter the curve. At a price of $12, economic profits can be made at any output greater than 1 bushel. Profits are maximum at $15 at an output of 5. At a price of $8.50, an economic profit can be made only at a single output level of 3 bushels. Here, maximum profit is only $0.50.

QUESTION 8.3
Given the data in Table 8.4, calculate the break-even and profit-maximizing outputs if the price of wheat is $15 a bushel.

The Marginal Approach to Profitability

An alternative method of finding the maximum profit level for the producer is in terms of marginals. This marginal approach, though at first glance slightly more daunting than the total approach, is a far more revealing way of looking at profit and also highlights other interesting facets. Let us begin by looking at the average and marginal costs in graphical form, as shown in Figure 8.5.

The cost curves are the short-run costs of the firm that we looked at in Chapter 6. You may recall that the average cost curve is U-shaped due to labour specialization and diminishing returns, and it is an arithmetic relationship between the average and marginal costs that ensures that the two are equal when the average cost is at a minimum.

Let us now begin our analysis with a given price of P$_1$. You will notice that this price (or average revenue) line intersects the average total cost curve at point *a* and at point *b*. These are the break-even outputs that we saw in Figure 8.3. This must be so, since if at break-even outputs, total revenue equals total cost, then similarly it must be true that average revenue is equal to average cost. At outputs less than *a* and above *b*, average costs are higher than average revenue and so the firm would make a loss. Between those outputs, the firm can make a profit. But where is the point of profit maximization? At first glance, it would seem to be at the output where the

FIGURE 8.5 Average Revenue, Costs and Profits

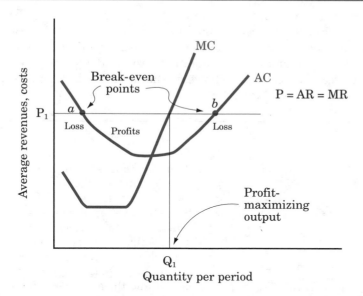

If the price is P_1, then at outputs below a and above b, the firm will incur losses. Outputs a and b are break-even outputs; here, the firm is making normal profits only. Between a and b, the firm will make economic profits. The profit-maximizing output occurs at Q_1 where the marginal revenue (= price) is equal to the marginal cost.

average costs are lowest, since here the difference between the two curves is greatest. However, this is the point of maximum *average* profit and we are looking for the point of maximum *total* profit. How do we find this output? This is where an understanding of the marginal cost comes in. The marginal cost represents the cost of each separate individual item produced. If the firm can sell each unit for more than its marginal cost, then it will do so.

If successive units are also profitable, then more should be produced. The firm should produce more and more units as long as the price (the marginal revenue) exceeds the marginal cost. Production should be extended up to the point where the last unit produced just breaks even, i.e., where its marginal cost exactly equals the marginal revenue. By the same token, a firm should not produce an item if its marginal cost exceeds the marginal revenue, since that would entail a loss on that item. In terms of Figure 8.5, for every unit of output produced up until output Q_1, the marginal revenue (price) exceeds the marginal cost. Each unit, therefore, is profitable. The amount of profit on each one (called its **marginal profit**) varies since the marginal cost is different for each unit produced. The Q_1-th unit, however, just breaks even. No matter, the costs include normal profit so that one is also worth producing. However, the firm should not produce more than Q_1 since for units of output in excess of this, the marginal cost exceeds the marginal revenue and would produce a loss (getting successively bigger) on each extra unit. The point of profit maximization therefore occurs where the marginal revenue is equal to the marginal cost. These ideas are important, so let us summarize them:

marginal profit: the additional economic profit from the production and sale of an extra unit of output.

If marginal revenue	>	marginal cost	→	produce more
If marginal cost	>	marginal revenue	→	produce less

And therefore, to maximize its total profit, the firm should increase production to the point where the marginal profit is zero, i.e., where:

average profit: the profit per unit produced, i.e., the total profit divided by the output.

marginal revenue = marginal cost

In Figure 8.6, we can illustrate the amount of total profit, by noting that the distance between the *average revenue* and the *average cost* indicates the **average profit**. At the profit maximizing output, Q_1, this is equal to the distance *cd*. If we multiply this amount by the quantity produced, Q_1, then we have the rectangular area $PcdAC_1$ which shows us the total profit at this output.

FIGURE 8.6 Average and Total Profits

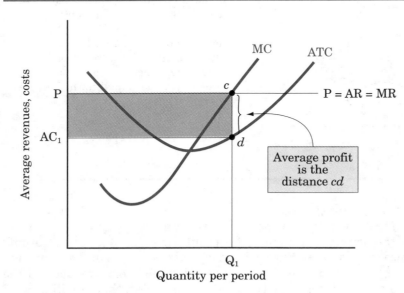

Average profit is the difference between the average revenue (or price) and the average cost. Since the average revenue is constant for the perfectly competitive firm, the average profit depends on the average cost. At an output of Q_1, the average cost is AC1 and the average profit is equal to the distance *cd*. The total profit is equal to the average profit times the quantity produced. This is represented graphically by the shaded area $PcdAC_1$.

Break-Even Price and Shutdown Price

break-even price: the price at which the firm makes only normal profits, i.e., makes zero economic profits.

If the demand for a product increases, then the price for the competitive firm will rise. You can perhaps work out for yourself in Figure 8.6, that the effect of an increased price will be that the intersection with the marginal cost curve will now occur at a higher level of output and will result in a higher profit for the firm. But what if the price should drop? Then, the firm will be forced to cut production and accept lower profit. What we now need to establish is the lowest level to which the price can fall before the firm is producing a loss. To find the answer to this, we need to realize that as long as the price is above the average (total) cost, the firm can be profitable. If it is below, then it does not matter where the firm produces, it will be making a loss. The **break-even price**, therefore, is the price which is just equal to the minimum average total cost curve as shown in Figure 8.7.

We can now state that any price above the break-even price P_{BE} in Figure 8.7 will enable the producer to make an economic profit (the greatest profit being made where the price equals the marginal cost), and any price below P_{BE} will result in a loss. But would a firm ever willingly produce at a loss? In many cases, the answer will be yes. In the *short run*, faced with a *price that is less than average total cost*, the competitive firm has only two choices: continue to produce, but at a loss; or temporarily shut down. In either case, the firm will continue to exist, hoping that the market will eventually pick up. (If it doesn't, in the *long run* it may have little choice but to shut down permanently). So if the price is below the break-even price, what should it do: produce or shut down? The answer will depend on whether the

FIGURE 8.7 Break-Even Price and Shutdown Price for the Competitive Firm

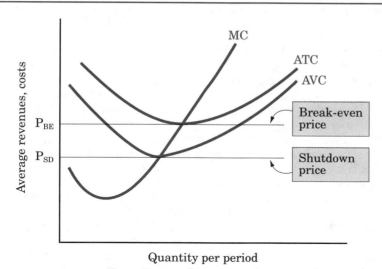

The break-even price (P_{BE}) is located at the point of minimum average (total) costs. If the price is above this level, the firm can make a profit; below this, it will make a loss. The shutdown price (P_{SD}) is located at the minimum of the average variable cost curve. If the price is above this, the firm will produce; below this, it will (temporarily) shut down.

loss from producing is bigger or smaller than the loss from shutting down. And what loss will be incurred if the firm decides to shut down? The amount of its total fixed costs. As long as the losses from production are less than its total fixed costs, then the firm would be advised to produce.

Suppose that the total fixed costs of a firm are $10,000 per week; then the worst loss that the firm can incur is $10,000 which will come from shutting down and producing zero. What this says, in terms of an operational rule, is that, since the firm can do little about its fixed costs as these costs have already been incurred, it should at least try to ensure that it can cover its variable costs such as the wages, materials and so on. If the firm is unable to cover even its variable costs let alone its fixed costs, then it would be foolish to produce at all. However, if it can at least cover the variable costs with a little surplus left over, then this surplus can help to pay for some of the fixed costs. All of this boils down to suggesting that the aim of the firm must always be to at least cover the variable costs, and if it cannot, then it should shut down. In Figure 8.6, this means that the **shutdown price** (P_{SD}) is located at the lowest point of the average variable cost curve. If price is above this level, then the firm will produce even if it entails a loss because it can more than cover its variable costs. And the best output to produce will be where the price is equal to the marginal cost. This will at least ensure the smallest loss. If the price falls below the shutdown price, then the firm should shut down temporarily and absorb the loss which will be equal to its total fixed costs.

shutdown price: the level of price which is just sufficient to cover a firm's variable costs.

Since some of these ideas can seem a little confusing on a first acquaintance, let's summarize what we have said so far:

- If, at some output level, price is greater than ATC, then the producer can make a profit. Maximum profit is achieved where MR (price) equals MC.
- If the price is below ATC at all levels of output, then the producer will make a loss. However, it is worth producing as long as the price is greater than the AVC. Minimum loss is achieved where MR (price) equals MC.
- If the price is lower than the minimum AVC, then the producer should temporarily shut down.

BOX 8.1

Far from being an esoteric topic which has no relevance in the business world, marginal costs and marginal profits play a very important part in determining prices and total profits for many major companies. For example, fixed costs are very high for most airlines. To fly a 747 plane from Toronto to Los Angeles is an expensive proposition, costing tens of thousands of dollars in terms of flight crew, fuel, insurance, landing fees and so on. The increased variable costs, i.e., the marginal costs per passenger, on the other hand are very low since they are comprised of a prepacked meal, perhaps a drink or two, the cost of cleaning a headset and a little more fuel because of the extra weight. Rather than cancel a flight, which it cannot do if it is a scheduled flight, it is entirely reasonable for an airline to offer seats below their full costs if it can at least cover the marginal costs. In other words, as long as the price is above the marginal costs, it will be worthwhile to take on one more passenger.

For a similar reason, many hotels charge room rates far below "total" costs during off-season periods, again on the basis that the important factor is the marginal cost per room and not its average total costs.

QUESTION 8.4

The following graph shows the costs of production for a perfectly competitive firm.

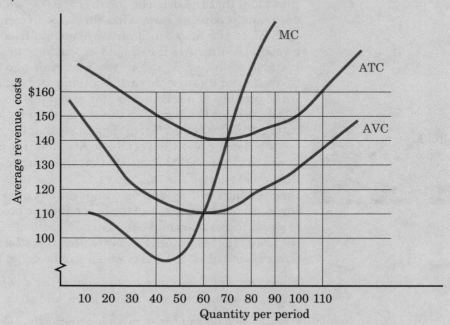

A) Where is the break-even price?

B) If the price is $120, what quantity will the firm produce? What will be its average profit/loss at this output? And what will be its total profit/loss?

QUESTION 8.4 *(continued)*
C) If the price is $150, what quantity will the firm produce? What will be its average profit/loss at this output? And what will be its total profit/loss?
D) What is the firm's shutdown price?

BOX 8A
1. What is the difference between an industry and a market?
2. What are the four main types of markets? In what ways do they differ?
3. What are the four main features of perfectly competitive markets? (For each feature, explain why its absence would make the market uncompetitive.)
4. Why do economists analyze perfectly competitive markets if such markets do not exist in the real world?
5. Why is the demand curve facing the perfectly competitive firm said to be perfectly elastic? Why is the price for the competitive firm a "take it, or leave it" proposition?
6. Define and explain the difference between average revenue and marginal revenue.
7. Using the total profit approach, explain the idea of break-even output and profit-maximizing output for the firm.
8. What is meant by the term *marginal profit*? What is the profit-maximizing rule when using the marginal approach? Explain what the rule means.
9. What is meant by the *break-even price*?
10. What is meant by the *shutdown price*?

The Firm's Supply Curve

Let us now put some flesh on these ideas by working through an example, and in doing so help to derive a supply curve for the firm. For a change of pace, let us look at some of the costs of an apple cider producer as shown in Table 8.5 below. Assume that the output is in quantity of 10-litre jars:

TABLE 8.5 Deriving the Firm's Supply Curve

Output (Q)	Total Costs (TC)	Marginal Costs (MC)	Average Variable Costs (AVC)	Average Total Costs (ATC)
0	$ 40	—	—	—
1	65	$25.00	$25.00	$65.00
2	85	20.00	22.50	42.50
3	100	15.00	20.00	33.33
4	120	20.00	20.00	30.00
5	145	25.00	21.00	29.00
6	180	35.00	23.33	30.00
7	225	45.00	26.43	32.14
8	280	55.00	30.00	35.00

First of all let us confirm some important benchmarks for this producer. The break-even price is $29, which coincides with the lowest average total cost. If the price is higher than this, he can make a profit; if it is lower, he will make a loss. The shutdown price is $20, which is the lowest average variable cost. If the price is between $20 and $29, the producer will make a loss but it is still worth producing; below $20, the producer should, at least temporarily, shut down operations. Given this basic information, let us figure out the supply curve for this producer, relating the quantities he would like to produce at various different prices.

Suppose that the price is $15. We have already decided he wouldn't produce at this price. By not producing at all, his loss will be equal to his total fixed costs of $40. Now let us see what happens at a price of, say, $25. We know he will make a loss at this price but let us confirm the best output and the size of the loss. To do this we look down the MC column. As long as the price which the cider producer receives can cover the cost of each additional unit, it will be worthwhile producing it. Bear in mind that the additional costs of producing each unit involve variable costs only. Given this, then, the first five units are definitely worthwhile. However, production of the sixth unit results in a marginal cost of $35, which exceeds the price of $25. The cider manufacturer should therefore produce only 5 units at a total cost of $145 and receive 5 × $25 = $125 in total revenue, thereby making a loss of $20. This is certainly preferable to the shutdown loss of $40.

Let's try a third price of $35. We know in advance that the producer should be able to make a profit at this price. Again the profit-maximizing output will be where the price is equal to the MC. Looking at Table 8.5, we can see that this occurs at an output of 6, where the MC is also $35. The total cost at this output is $180, and total revenue will be equal to 6 × $35 = $210. The profit therefore will be $30 ($210 − $180).

We could continue in similar fashion for other prices, say $45 and $55. The results are tabulated in Table 8.6.

TABLE 8.6 The Firm's Supply Curve

Price (P)	Output (Q)	Profit/Loss
$15	0	−$40
25	5	−20
35	6	+30
45	7	+90
55	8	+160

You can see from this table that the higher the price of the cider, the higher the chosen level of production and the more profitable is production. What this table does is relate the various quantities that the producer would produce at various different prices; in other words, this is the producer's supply curve. Since the producer will always equate the price with the MC, the supply curve of the firm is, in fact, identical to its MC curve as Figure 8.8 makes clear.

Because of the equality between the price and MC, *the supply curve for the firm is that portion of its MC curve which lies above its average variable cost curve.* As we noted before, if the price is lower than the minimum AVC, then the firm would simply not produce.

FIGURE 8.8 The Firm's Supply Curve

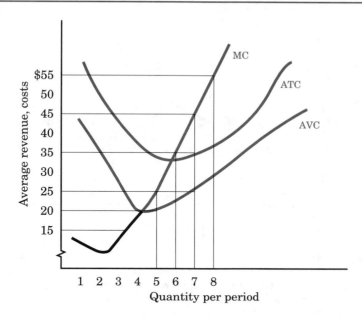

The profit-maximizing (or loss-minimizing) output occurs where the MR (or price) equals the MC. At a price of $55, profit maximization is at an output of 8; at $45, it is at an output of 7; at $35, an output of 6; at $25, it is at 5, and so on. These points all occur along the MC curve, which is therefore synonymous with the firm's supply curve, i.e., the MC curve is the supply curve. However, if the price is below $20, the firm could not cover its AVC. It would, therefore, be forced to shut down and produce zero. The supply curve is therefore not the whole of the MC curve, but that portion above the AVC curve.

Study Guide

QUESTION 8.5

Complete the following table of costs for a competitive firm, and derive and plot its supply curve at prices of $25, $35, $45, $55, $65 and $75:

Output	Total Costs	Marginal Costs	Total Variable Costs	Average Variable Costs
0	$ 50	—	—	—
1	90	___	___	___
2	110	___	___	___
3	140	___	___	___
4	180	___	___	___
5	230	___	___	___
6	290	___	___	___
7	360	___	___	___
8	440	___	___	___

The Industry Demand and Supply

The total supply of cider for the whole industry is derived by adding together the supply of each individual cider producer. For instance, if there were 9 other similar-sized producers in the industry, then the total supply would be equal to 10 times the quantities shown in Table 8.6. This is shown in Figure 8.9 on the next page.

FIGURE 8.9 Industry Supply and Market Equilibrium

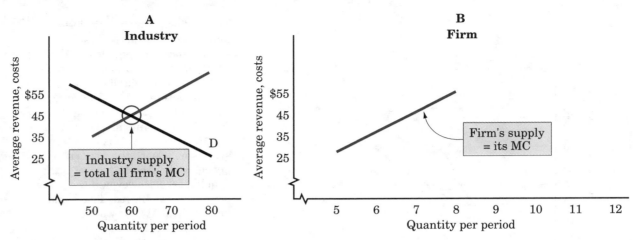

The supply of the firm shown in Figure 8.8B is based on Table 8.6. If the industry consists of 10 identical firms, the market supply would be that shown in Figure 8.8A. Given the demand curve shown in that figure, then the equilibrium quantity is 60 and the market equilibrium price will be $45. Figure 8.8B shows that at a price of $45, this average firm will produce 6 units, and since there are 10 firms in total, this confirms the industry output of 60.

The industry supply curve in Figure 8.9A is the summation of the supply curves of the 10 cider producers. Since each firm's supply curve is identical to its MC curve, then the industry supply curve is identical to the MC curve of the whole industry. Figure 8.9A also shows the market demand for cider. The equilibrium price for cider therefore is $35 per jar. This price is the same for each cider producer and we can see in Figure 8.9B that at this price, the average producer will produce an output of 6 jars. Table 8.9 confirms that at this output, the average firm will make a profit of $30. (The industry profit is therefore 10 × $30, or $300). In this way the fortunes of the industry and the individual firm are inextricably entwined. Let us pursue this further by seeing what happens when the demand for cider changes.

Long-Run Effects of an Increase in Demand

We now need to recall what is meant by the ideas of the short and long run from the perspective of both the firm and the industry. As we saw in Chapter 7, the short run for the firm is a period of time during which it can do nothing to affect the size of its premises: the capacity of the firm is therefore fixed. From the industry's point of view, the short run also means that the size of the industry is fixed, in that the number of firms in the industry is fixed, and as we said, the size of each firm is also fixed. From the firm's point of view, the long run is the amount of time it takes to change the size of its premises, while for the industry it is the amount of time it takes to enable present firms to quit or new firms to join the industry. In summary, the short run is a period of time in which the size of both the firm and industry is fixed; in the long run they are variable.

Let us now work through the effects of an increase in the demand for cider in both the short and long run. Suppose that new medical evidence suggests that cider reduces cholesterol levels in the body and the result of this information is a big increase in the demand for cider. From the industry point of view, the effect of this good news is an increase in the price of cider. This is shown in Figure 8.10A.

FIGURE 8.10 The Effects of an Increase in Demand on the Industry and Firm

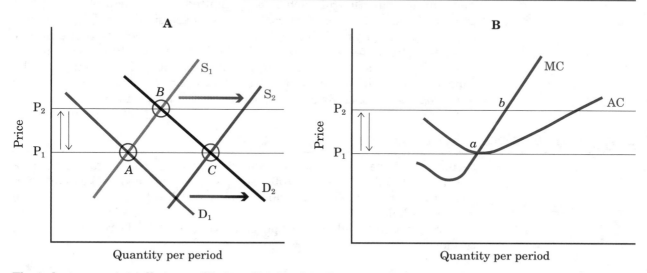

The industry was initially in equilibrium at point *A* in Figure 8.10A (D$_1$S$_1$), and at the equilibrium price P$_1$, the average firm was breaking even and producing an output of *a* in Figure 8.10B. As a result of the increase in the demand from D$_1$ to D$_2$, both the price and the industry output increases to point *B* in Figure 8.10A. The output increases because the higher price induces the average firm to produce more: to point *b* in Figure 8.10B. However, in the long run, new firms enter and the market supply increases from S$_1$ to S$_2$. As a result, the market price drops to point *C*. The average firm finds the price falling and reduces its output back to point *a* in Figure 8.10B.

Figure 8.10 illustrates why the increase in demand leads to an increase in price and an increase in the quantity produced. Suppose that the firm shown on the right is a representative cider producer and is presently breaking even, i.e., is making only normal profit. As the price of cider starts to rise, this firm as well as the other producers realize they can increase profit by increasing production. The increased production in the industry (from point *A* to *B* in Figure 8.10A) is the result of the present firms producing more (from point *a* to *b* in Figure 8.10B) with their present facilities. Each producer, who was previously making only normal profit, now finds itself making economic profit. This situation is unlikely to last indefinitely. New firms will be attracted by the high profit being made in the cider industry and will enter the industry, thus increasing the number of firms. This is shown by a shift in the supply curve from S$_1$ to S$_2$. The effect of the increased competition in the industry will be a fall in the price of cider and a new equilibrium being established at point *C* in Figure 8.10A. From the point of view of the older firms, the long-run drop in the price of cider will force a cutback in production and profit until they are back where they started at point *a* in Figure 8.10B. Although in the long run the price, profitability and production levels for the average firm are the same as they were previously, there is one big difference: the size of the industry is now much bigger and the increased industry production is the result of more firms being in the industry.

Besides the changes analyzed so far, there may well be an additional change to consider. The first effect of the increase in demand was an increase in price which stimulates firms to produce more. However, the maximum production of each firm is limited by the size of its present premises and by the fact that costs will increase significantly as the firm approaches its physical limits. If the average firm feels that the higher demand is likely to be maintained in the future it will have every incentive in the long run to increase the size of its facilities. In the long run, the capacity of the industry may increase *not only* because there are more firms *but also* because each firm is bigger than it was previously.

Long-Run Effects of a Decrease in Demand

As in the last example we will assume that, initially, the average cider producer is just making normal profit. Suppose that new medical evidence suggests that while cider may reduce cholesterol levels in the body, it also causes tooth decay and constipation. Faced with this new information, consumers drastically reduce their purchases of cider. The decrease in demand is shown in Figure 8.11 below.

FIGURE 8.11 The Effects of a Decrease in Demand on the Industry and Firm

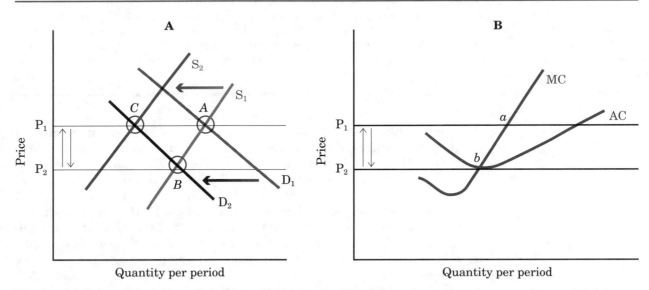

The drop in demand from D_1 to D_2 reduces the output level and the price, i.e., a movement from point A to point B in Figure 8.11A. The reason why output drops is because the average firm is forced to cut back production as the price falls. This is shown in the movement from a to b in Figure 8.11B. Since the average firm is now producing at a loss, in the long run some firms will be forced out of business. This is shown by a leftward shift in the supply curve from S_1 to S_2 in Figure 8.11A. This will cause the price to recover to point C. From the existing firm's point of view, the higher price will cause them to return to point a in Figure 8.11B, where they again will be breaking even.

The fall in demand will cause a drop in the price and quantity traded in the industry as shown in the movement from point *A* to point *B* in Figure 8.11A. This retraction is the result of changes that are forced on the average cider producer as shown in Figure 8.11B. Here, the drop in price causes a fall in profit and a fall in production from point *a* to *b*. The average firm is now being forced to produce at a loss. This is an untenable situation in the long run. There is a limit to how long firms can continue to incur losses. In the long run, some firms will be forced to close down permanently. The more inefficient ones with higher costs will presumably be forced out of business first. The effect of this exodus from the industry is shown as a decrease in the industry supply curve in Figure 8.11A. The supply curve shifts left from S_1 to S_2. The effect of this will be fewer firms serving the industry with the result that the price will be forced up until the bleeding within the industry stops. This will occur when the representative firm is no longer making a loss; that is to say, when the price level returns to its original level at point *C*. From the firm's viewpoint Figure 8.11B shows that as the price starts to recover, production and prices will follow suit so that eventually the firm is back at its previous production level at point *a*.

The representative firm in the long run is back where it started, having suffered lower production and profit in the meantime. However, in the long run the size of the industry has shrunk with the exit of a number of firms.

Long-Run Supply of the Industry

The analysis which we have just done on the long-run effects of a change in the demand for a product suggests that while it may have an impact on the size of the industry and on levels of production, it leaves the price level unchanged. This may or may not be true depending on whether or not changes in the industry size affect the costs of production. For instance, as the industry grows in size with the entrance of new firms, its demand for all sorts of resources, including labour, will similarly grow. The result may be that the price of these resources and therefore the costs of production for the representative firm may well increase as a result. If that happens then the marginal cost will be higher as the industry grows, and graphically, results in the marginal cost curve shifting upward. The result will mean a higher price being charged for the product. If costs of production do tend to rise as an industry expands, then it is known as an increasing-cost industry and its long-run supply curve will look like that in Figure 8.12A on the next page. If, on the other hand, costs of production were, for some reason to fall, as the industry expands in size, then we have a decreasing-cost industry and the resulting downward-sloping supply curve is illustrated in Figure 8.12B. Finally, the type of industry we have supposed so far — a constant-cost industry with a perfectly elastic long-run supply curve — is shown in Figure 8.12C.

But why would the costs change as an industry expands? The answer, as we suggested, lies in the effect that such an expansion has on the price of resources that a particular industry depends on. If the cider industry consumes a big proportion of all apples sold in the market, then it is likely that as the cider industry grows and with it the demand for apples, the price of apples and therefore the industry's own costs of production will start to rise.

FIGURE 8.12 Increasing-Cost, Decreasing-Cost and Constant-Cost Industries

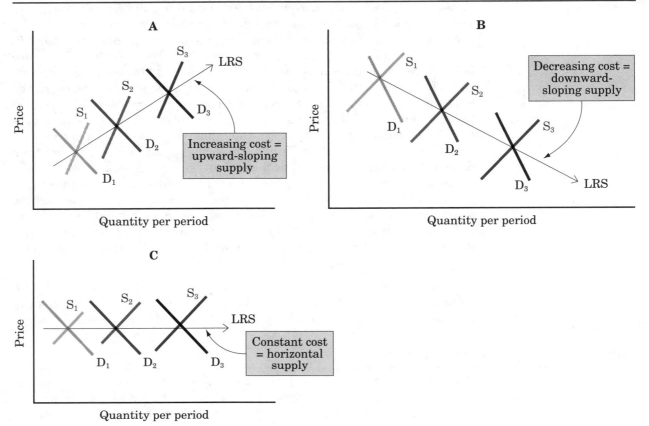

In all three cases, A, B, and C, the increase in demand from D_1 to D_2 to D_3 are all accompanied in the long run by increases in supply from S_1 to S_2 to S_3. If this expansion has no impact on the costs in the industry as in Figure 8.12C, then the increase in each case exactly matches the increase in demand. Thus, the price is unaffected with the result that the long-run supply curve is horizontal. In Figure 8.12A, the expansion in the industry is the same as in Figure 8.12C, *but* costs increase as the industry expands. This causes the short-run supply curve to shift back to the left a little so that the long-run supply curve is upward-sloping. With Figure 8.12B, as the industry expands, the costs of production falls so that the supply curve shifts a little further to the right each time resulting in a downward-sloping, long-run supply curve.

If that were the case, the cider industry would be regarded as an increasing-cost industry. The long-run supply curve in that case would be upward-sloping which means that an increase in the size of the industry is accompanied by an increase in the price of cider. If, on the other hand, the cider industry purchased only a very small fraction of the output of the apple industry (or if in general the cost of apples was only a tiny fraction of the total costs of producing cider), then the cider industry could grow without having any impact on apple prices. It would then be categorized as a constant-cost industry and its supply curve would be horizontal. But what about decreasing costs in the long run? This could happen if, say, the expansion of both the cider and apple industries caused the latter to start to enjoy economies of scale, it could then start to offer apples at a lower price to the cider industry. The cider industry would then be a decreasing-cost industry with a corresponding downward-sloping long-run supply curve.

Study Guide

QUESTION 8.6

Suppose that initially the market demand and supply for a product are as shown in the following table:

Price	Demand	Supply
$ 2	110	10
4	100	20
6	90	30
8	80	40
10	70	50
12	60	60
14	50	70
16	40	80
18	30	90

A) Plot the curves and label them D_1 and S_1. Identify the equilibrium price and quantity.

B) Suppose that the demand increases by 30 units at every price, and as a result new firms enter, causing the supply to increase by a similar 30 units. Label the new curves D_2 and S_2. Identify the new equilibrium.

C) Assume that as a result of the industry expansion the costs of production increase by $4 per unit. Label the new supply curve S_3. Identify the new equilibrium and draw in the industry's long-run supply curve.

In summary, we can see from these examples how dynamic, interrelated and self-adjusting are competitive markets. A change in demand gets translated into price changes, which affects production, profitability and the size of the industry. Needless to say, each of these changes will also affect employment and the purchase of resources, which in turn will bring about changes in the supplier, complementary and competing industries. Additionally, changes in costs and technology will also affect the profitability of firms and cause the exit or entry of firms, and with it, the price, production and profitability of the industry. In this way, perfectly competitive markets could be called perfectly sensitive markets since they respond quickly and efficiently to the smallest of changes. In addition, as Chapter 9 will show, they also produce a number of other significant benefits. But that chapter will also point out the ways in which a perfect market can fall down and fail to live up to its billing.

Review ?

BOX 8B

1. "A firm will continue to operate as long as its loss is no greater than its total fixed costs." Explain this statement.
2. What does the term *break-even price* mean?
3. "If the price is below a firm's ATC but above its AVC, the firm will still produce even though it makes a loss." Explain this statement.
4. Explain why the supply curve for the firm is that part of its MC curve which lies above its AVC curve.
5. Explain the effect on both the industry and the individual firm of an increase in the demand for a product.

BOX 8B *(continued)*

6. Explain how a decrease in demand affects both the industry and the average firm in the industry.
7. What is the long-run supply curve of the industry? How might it be upward-sloping? Downward-sloping? Horizontal?

Chapter Highlights

The chapter explains in detail how a firm operating in a perfectly competitive market would decide on its best output level and shows how the firm's profits varies with its output levels. It also goes on to describe the circumstances under which a firm might end up making a loss and when it may be wise to shut down operations. In the final section, it looks at the way whole industries grow and how they can also die.

The chapter begins by explaining the four characteristics which make markets perfectly competitive: a large number of buyers and sellers; the lack of preferences towards producers by buyers and vice versa; the ease of entry and exit; and well-informed producers and consumers. It explains why unregulated agricultural markets come closest to being perfectly competitive, and demonstrates why in such markets, the individual producer has no control over the price and becomes therefore a price taker.

The concepts of total, average and marginal revenues are then explained. Figure 8.3 shows that a producer will maximize total profits when she produces an output where the difference between total revenue and total costs is at its greatest. It then goes on to show that an increase in the price will both increase the size of profits and will also expand the range of profitable outputs, whereas a decrease in price will do the opposite.

The chapter then looks at the same ideas but in terms of the marginal and average costs and revenues and explains why total profits are maximized when the marginal revenue is equal to the marginal costs. It also explains why, as long as a firm is able to cover its variable costs, it is still worth producing, even though it may be at a loss, and why therefore it would be advised to temporarily shut down if it is unable to cover its variable costs.

After demonstrating why the firm's supply curve is the portion of its marginal cost curve above the average variable cost curve, the final section of the chapter looks at how the average firm and industry react to changes in demand. The analysis suggests that the increase in price and profits that result from an increase in demand leads to the entry of new firms into the industry which causes the price to drop and the profits of the average firm to return to normal. Similarly a decrease in demand produces a chain reaction of falling prices and profits which force some firms to leave the industry, causing the price to return to its previous level so that those remaining firms which were temporarily making losses will return to making normal profits. Finally, the chapter shows why in an increasing-cost industry the effect of an increase in demand might not be to return the price to its previous level but to cause it instead to increase, whereas in a decreasing-cost industry the effect is the opposite.

New Glossary Terms

Workbook

Study Tips

1.   Probably the most difficult part of this chapter, for most students, is the derivation of the firm's profit-maximizing output using the marginal approach. Remember, if all else fails, it is always possible to find this output level using the total approach, i.e., for each different price, compare the total revenue and total cost for every output level and see which gives the greatest profit. However, it is worth putting in effort to understand the marginal approach since it is a far easier and more revealing method.

2.   When looking at the marginal approach, bear in mind two things: first, the fixed costs play no part in the decision making since these costs have already been incurred. You only need to think of them as the limit to the firm's loss in the short run. The second thing to remember is that the marginal costs are variable costs and do not need to be incurred, since the firm is not obliged to incur them if it decides not to produce. Given these two facts, you can think of the production process as involving a number of separate, discreet decisions. The owner awakes each day to ask: shall we produce or not today? If not, the fixed costs will still have to be paid and that will be the total loss. On the other hand, producing just one unit produces both cost (the marginal cost) and revenue (the price). As long as the price exceeds the marginal cost, it pays to produce it since the excess will help go against the fixed costs. What about a second unit, or a third unit? Are they worthwhile? Yes, as long as the (same constant) price exceeds the marginal cost. That's how we derive the rule that a firm should produce as long as the price exceeds the marginal cost.

3.   Another point of confusion for many students is the idea of break-even. They wonder why a firm would ever produce if it is merely breaking even and not making profits. But the firm *is* making profits. It is making enough to keep the owners in business, i.e., it is making normal profits which economists include in, and regard as, a cost of production. However, at break even it is true that the firm will not be making

economic profits. These are an added bonus and are not necessary to the continued existence of the firm. A similar point of confusion, for some, involves the rule that a firm maximizes its profit by producing at an output where the price is equal to marginal cost. Some would ask: doesn't this mean that the firm is just breaking even? No, this is not so. While the firm does indeed break even on the *last* item it has produced, it has made profits on each unit up until that last one.

4.   Most students can accept the fact that it is often worthwhile for a firm to stay in business in the short run even though it might be operating at a loss since the alternative is closing down and possibly incurring even bigger losses. Yet despite this, they still feel that the rule should be that a firm must only cover its fixed costs to avoid shut down. This is not true. It does not matter whether the firm produces a little or a lot or whether it produces at all, fixed costs remain the same. What it does have control over are the variable costs. These costs must be covered since if they are not, the firm is in double trouble being unable to pay all of either the fixed or the variable costs. In this case, it would definitely be better not to produce at all. Therefore, the rule is: cover the variable costs; ignore the fixed costs.

Are You Sure?

Indicate whether the following statements are true or false. If false, indicate why they are false.

1.   In a perfectly competitive market, all buyers and sellers are price takers.
T or **F**   If false: _____

_____

_____

2.   Marginal revenue is the extra income a firm receives above break-even.
T or **F**   If false: _____

_____

_____

3. Profit maximization occurs at the output where marginal revenue equals zero.
T or F   If false: _____

_____

_____

4. A firm will not shut down in the short run as long as it is covering its variable costs.
T or F   If false: _____

_____

_____

5. In order to maximize its profits, a firm will produce an output where the marginal revenue equals the marginal cost.
T or F   If false: _____

_____

_____

6. A firm will maximize its profits at the output where the difference between its average revenue and average total cost is greatest.
T or F   If false: _____

_____

_____

7. The supply curve of the firm in perfect competition is that portion of the marginal cost curve above the average variable cost curve.
T or F   If false: _____

_____

_____

8. An increase in the demand for a product will cause many firms to leave the industry.
T or F   If false: _____

_____

_____

9. The long-run supply curve of an increasing cost industry is upward-sloping.
T or F   If false: _____

_____

_____

10. The reason why the long-run supply curve is upward- or downward-sloping is the result of changes in production costs that accompany any change in the size of the industry.
T or F   If false: _____

_____

_____

Translations

You are given the following cost and revenue data for a single, perfectly competitive firm. Sketch out the following curves on the graph in Figure W8.1: AVC, ATC, MC, MR, AR. Determine if the firm is making a profit or loss and indicate whether or not this firm is producing the optimal output, (i.e., should it produce more, or less, or none at all?) (*Hint:* The price can be determined after finding the quantity produced.)

Total revenue: $1,200; TFC: $300; ATC: $10; AVC: $7; MC: $15

FIGURE W8.1

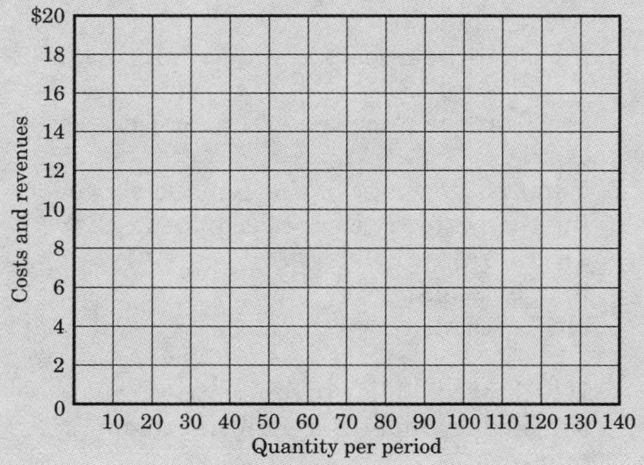

Choose the Best

1. What is the name of the type of market which is dominated by a few firms?
   a) Oligopoly.
   b) Monopolistic competition.

2. Which of the following refers to the perfectly competitive firm?
   a) It is a price maker.
   b) It is a price taker.

3. How is average revenue defined?
   a) It is the extra revenue derived from the sale of one more unit.
   b) It is the total revenue divided by the number of units sold.

4. What type of product is sold by the representative firm in a perfectly competitive market?
   a) The same as is sold by the other firms.
   b) A unique product.
   c) A product similar to that sold by the other firms.

5. What does break-even output mean?
   a) The output where the price is equal to the average revenue.
   b) The output where the price is equal to the marginal revenue.
   c) The output where the price is equal to the average total cost.

6. Which of the following conditions means that the competitive firm is maximizing its profits?
   a) That the price equals average revenue.
   b) That the price is equal to marginal revenue.
   c) That the price is equal to marginal cost.

7. What is the shape of the demand curve facing the perfectly competitive firm?
   a) Downward-sloping.
   b) Horizontal.
   c) Vertical.

8. Which of the following industries provides the best example of a perfectly competitive market?

a) Insurance.
b) Hairdressing.
c) Oil-refining.
d) Agriculture.

9. What will happen if firms exit from a perfectly competitive industry?
   a) The market demand curve will shift to the right.
   b) The market demand curve will shift to the left.
   c) The market supply curve will shift to the right.
   d) The market supply curve will shift to the left.

10. What action should a perfectly competitive firm take if, at its present output, MC is both increasing and is greater than the price and the price is greater than the average variable cost?
    a) It should shut down.
    b) It should increase its output.
    c) It should decrease its output.
    d) It should increase the price.

11. What long-run effect will a decrease in market demand have on a constant-cost industry?
    a) The price will stay the same and the number of firms in the industry will increase.
    b) The price will stay the same and the number of firms in the industry will decrease.
    c) The price will decrease and the number of firms in the industry will increase.
    d) The price will decrease and the number of firms in the industry will decrease.

12. What long-run effect will a decrease in market demand have on a decreasing-cost industry?
    a) The price will increase and the number of firms in the industry will increase.
    b) The price will increase and the number of firms in the industry will decrease.
    c) The price will decrease and the number of firms in the industry will increase.
    d) The price will decrease and the number of firms in the industry will decrease.

13. What is the correct interpretation of the perfectly competitive firm's supply curve?
    a) It is the same as its average variable cost curve.
    b) It is the same as its total variable cost curve.
    c) It is the same as that portion of its marginal cost curve which lies above the average variable cost curve.
    d) It is the same as that portion of its average variable cost curve which lies above the marginal cost curve.

Refer to Table W8.1 to answer questions 14, 15, 16, 17 and 18.

TABLE W8.1

Output	Total Costs
0	$10
1	15
2	18
3	20
4	23
5	28
6	38
7	50

14. Refer to Table W8.1 to answer this question. What is the value of the break-even price?
    a) $3.60.
    b) $5.
    c) $5.60.
    d) $18.
    e) $28.

15. Refer to Table W8.1 to answer this question. What is the value of the shutdown price?
    a) $3.25.
    b) $4.
    c) $5.75.
    d) $13
    e) $23

16. Refer to Table W8.1 to answer this question. What is the profit-maximizing output if the price is $3?
    a) 0.
    b) 3.
    c) 4.
    d) 5.
    e) 6

17. Refer to Table W8.1 to answer this question. What is the profit-maximizing output if the price is $10?
    a) 0.
    b) 3.
    c) 4.
    d) 5.
    e) 6.

18. Refer to Table W8.1 to answer this question. If the price is $10, what profit or loss will this producer earn?
    a) 0.
    b) −$4.40.
    c) +$4.40.
    d) +$22.
    e) +$32.

Refer to Figure W8.2 to answer questions 19 and 20.

FIGURE W8.2

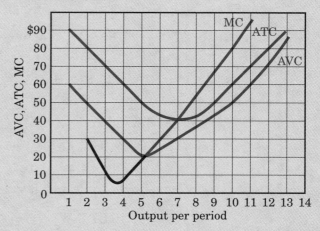

19. Refer to Figure W8.2 to answer this question. If the price of the product is $70, what is the profit-maximizing output, and what is the amount of economic profits?
    a) 7 and zero.
    b) 7 and $10.
    c) 7 and $70.
    d) 9 and $180.
    e) 11 and zero.

20. Refer to Figure W8.2 to answer this question. What are the values of the shutdown price and the break-even price?
    a) $10 and $20.
    b) $10 and $40.

c) $10 and $50.
d) $20 and $40.
e) Cannot be determined from this information.

What's Wrong?

Can you spot the four errors in the following passage? (Ignore grammatical mistakes!)

A perfectly competitive market is said to exist when: there are numerous small firms, all producing simi-lar but not identical products; where there is easy entrance and exit into the market; and where all the participants have perfect knowledge. Given these assumptions, the producers are said to be price makers. The optimal output for each firm is where the marginal cost is equal to the marginal revenue. This will ensure that the firm is either maximizing its profit or loss. In general, a perfectly competitive firm will continue to produce even though it is making a loss as long as it is able to cover its fixed costs.

Key Problem

Table W8.2 is the cost data for Farmer Blue, a barley farmer:

TABLE W8.2

Quantity	Total Cost ($)	Total Variable Cost ($)	Marginal Cost ($)	Average Total Cost ($)	Average Variable Cost ($)
0	6	—	—	—	—
1	____	____	4	____	____
2	____	____	2	____	____
3	____	____	4	____	____
4	____	____	6	____	____
5	____	____	8	____	____
6	____	____	10	____	____
7	____	____	12	____	____

a) Complete the table and graph the MC, AC and AVC curves on Figure W8.3.

FIGURE W8.3

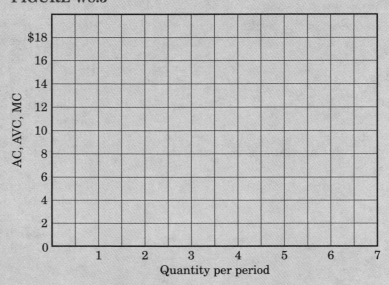

b) Given the prices shown in column 1 of Table W8.3, complete columns 2 and 3 indicating how much Farmer Blue would produce, and what profit or loss she would make.

TABLE W8.3

(1)	(2)	(3)	(4)	(5)	(6)
			Total Quantity Supplied 1	Total Quantity Demanded	Total Quantity Supplied 2
Price	Output	Profit (+)/ Loss (−)			
$ 2	_____	_____	_____	800	_____
4	_____	_____	_____	700	_____
6	_____	_____	_____	600	_____
8	_____	_____	_____	500	_____
10	_____	_____	_____	400	_____

c) Suppose that there are a total of 100 farms including and identical to Farmer Blue's in the barley market. Show the total supply in column 4.

d) If the market demand for barley is as shown in column 5, what will be the equilibrium price and quantity traded?

Price: _____; quantity traded: _____.

e) At the equilibrium price, what quantity will Farmer Blue produce and what will be her profit? Indicate the price and quantity on your graph. What will be the industry profit?

Quantity: _____; firm profit: _____; industry profit: _____.

f) As a result of your answer in e), will firms enter or leave this industry?

Answer: _____.

g) Suppose that in the long run, the number of firms increases by 50. Show the new totals in column 6 of the table. As a result, what will be the new equilibrium price? What quantity will Farmer Blue produce and what will be her profit? Again, indicate the new price and quantity on your graph. What will be the industry profit?

Equilibrium price: $_____; quantity: _____; firm profit:

$_____; industry profit: $_____.

h) Is the industry now in long-run equilibrium? Why or why not?

_____

Need a Hand?

a) Since marginal cost is the cost of each additional unit produced, to find each new total cost we need to add the marginal cost to the existing total cost. The 1st unit costs $4, so add this to the initial total cost of $6 (which must be fixed cost) to get $10. The marginal cost of the 2nd unit is $2, so add this to the total cost of $10, giving $12. Continue on down the column. Since the fixed cost (the cost at zero output) is equal to an unchanging $6, to find the total variable cost subtract $6 from the total cost at each level of output. The average (total) cost is the total cost divided by the quantity of output, and the average variable cost is equal to the total variable cost divided by the quantity of output. The completed table is as follows:

TABLE W8.4 (completed Table W8.2)

Quantity	Total Cost ($)	Total Variable Cost ($)	Marginal Cost ($)	Average Cost ($)	Average Variable Cost ($)
0	6	—	—	—	—
1	10	4	4	10	4
2	12	6	2	6	3
3	16	10	4	5.33	3.33
4	22	16	6	5.5	4
5	30	24	8	6	4.8
6	40	34	10	6.67	5.67
7	52	46	12	7.3	6.6

FIGURE W8.4 (completed Figure W8.3)

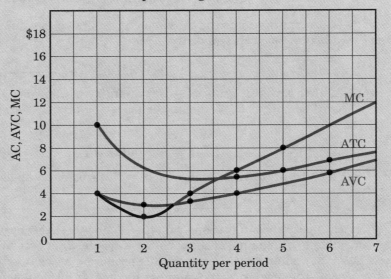

b) Before starting the calculations, it is worth establishing some benchmarks from the cost data. Looking at the table, we need to figure out, first, the break-even price. This is the value of the minimum average (total) cost. The lowest average cost that Farmer Blue can produce at is $5.33. This means that if the price is above this, then she can make an economic profit; if it is below this, she will make an economic loss. Next we need to find the shutdown price. This is the value of the lowest average *variable* cost. Looking down that column in the table we see that it is $3. This means that if the price is above $3, Farmer Blue will produce (even though it might entail an economic loss); below $3, it is better for her to shut down temporarily.

Given this information, we know that at a price of $2, Farmer Blue will not produce at all. Therefore, the output will be zero and the loss will be equal to the fixed costs of $6. At a price of $4, she will produce but at a loss. At prices of

$6, $8 and $10, she will produce at a profit. To identify the output levels at which she will produce, given various prices, we need to find the output where the marginal cost equals price. At a price of $4, the output will be 3; when the price is $6, MC = P at an output of 4; at a price of $8, output will be 5; finally, at a price of $10, output will be 6.

To find the total profit or loss for each price and output, we can either work in totals or averages. For instance, at a price of $4, we have established that Farmer Blue will produce 3. Her total revenue, therefore, is 3 times $4, or $12. The total cost at an output of 3, according to the table, is $16. The difference between the two represents her total loss of $4. In terms of averages, let's look at her profit if the price is $6. At that price, she will produce 4 units. The *average* cost at that output is $5.50. The difference between the two of $0.50 represents her *average* profit. $0.50 times the output of 4 gives a total profit of $2. Columns 2 and 3 are completed in Table W8.5.

TABLE W8.5 (completed Table W8.3)

(1) Price	(2) Output	(3) Profit (+)/ Loss (–)	(4) Total Quantity Supplied 1	(5) Total Quantity Demanded	(6) Total Quantity Supplied 2
$ 2	0	–6	0	800	0
4	3	–4	300	700	450
6	4	+2	400	600	600
8	5	+10	500	500	750
10	6	+20	600	400	900

c) Now we know the supply of Farmer Blue in column 2. To find the total supply, given that there are a total of 100 farmers, we multiply column 2 by 100. This is the industry supply in column 4.

d) To find the market equilibrium, we need to know the price at which the quantity demanded equals the quantity supplied. Looking down columns 4 and 5, we see that they are equal at a **price of $8** and a **quantity traded of 500**.

e) Column 2 already told us how much Farmer Blue would produce at each price. At a price of $8, she will **produce 5 units**. Her profit, as shown in column 3 is **$10**. Since there are a total of 100 firms in the industry, each making a profit of $10, the total industry profit is $10 times 100 or **$1,000**.

f) Since the average firm in the barley industry is making economic (above normal) profit, then firms **will enter** the industry.

g) The quantity supplied will increase by 50% at each price level. To find the new supply, multiply Farmer Blue's output by 150. This is done in column 6 above. The new supply is now equal to the demand at the lower **price of $6**. A glance at columns 2 and 3 shows that at this price Farmer Blue will produce an **output of 4** and make a **profit of $2**. The industry profit is now equal to $2 times the number of firms (now 150) giving **$300**.

h) **No**, this is not yet long-run equilibrium since there are still economic profits being made. Firms will continue to enter, and the price and profit will continue to fall until the economic profit is eliminated.

More of the Same

Table W8.6 contains the cost data for a purely competitive seller.

TABLE W8.6

Quantity	Total Cost ($)	Total Variable Cost ($)	Marginal Cost ($)	Average Cost ($)	Average Variable Cost ($)
0	50	—	—	—	—
1	90	_____	_____	_____	_____
2	120	_____	_____	_____	_____
3	140	_____	_____	_____	_____
4	170	_____	_____	_____	_____
5	210	_____	_____	_____	_____
6	260	_____	_____	_____	_____
7	320	_____	_____	_____	_____
8	400	_____	_____	_____	_____

a) Complete Table W8.6 and graph the MC, AC and AVC curves on Figure W8.5.

FIGURE W8.5

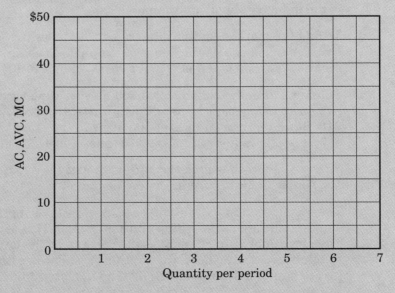

b) Given the prices shown in column 1 of Table W8.7 on the next page, complete columns 2 and 3 indicating how much the firm would produce, and what profit or loss it would make. (Partial units cannot be produced.)

TABLE W8.7

(1) Price	(2) Output	(3) Profit (+)/ Loss (−)	(4) Total Quantity Supplied 1	(5) Total Quantity Demanded	(6) Total Quantity Supplied 2
$25	_____	_____	_____	900	_____
35	_____	_____	_____	800	_____
45	_____	_____	_____	700	_____
55	_____	_____	_____	600	_____
65	_____	_____	_____	500	_____

c) Suppose that there are a total of 200 firms, including and identical to this one, in the market. Show the total supply in column 4.

d) If the market demand for this product is as shown in column 5, what will be the equilibrium price and quantity traded in the market?

e) At the equilibrium price, what quantity will this firm produce and what will be its profit or loss? Indicate the price and quantity on your graph. What will be the industry profit or loss?

f) As a result of your answer in e), will firms enter or leave this industry? Explain.

g) Suppose that in the long run, the number of firms changes by 60. Show the new totals in column 6 of the table. As a result, what will be the new equilibrium price, what quantity will this firm produce and what will be its profit? Again, indicate the new price and quantity on your graph. What will be the industry profit?

Other Problems

1. Figure W8.6 shows the TC and TVC curves of a perfectly competitive firm.

FIGURE W8.6

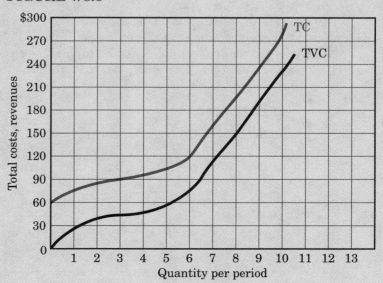

a) If the price is $30, draw in the total revenue curve and label it TR_1. At this price, what is the break-even output(s), the profit-maximizing output, and the level of profits at that output?

Break-even output: _____; profit-maximizing output: _____;

profit: $_____.

b) Draw a total revenue curve, labelled TR_2, which results in the firm, at best, breaking even. What is the value of the corresponding break-even price?

Price: $_____.

c) Draw a total revenue curve, labelled TR_3, which results in the firm, at best, just remaining in operation. What is the value of the corresponding shut-down price?

Price: $_____.

2. Table W8.8 shows the cost data for a perfectly competitive firm.

TABLE W8.8

Quantity of Output	Total Cost	Marginal Cost
0	$100	
1	_____	$40
2	_____	30
3	_____	20
4	_____	30
5	_____	40
6	_____	50
7	_____	60
8	_____	70

a) What is the amount of the shutdown loss, i.e., what loss will the firm incur if it doesn't produce at all?

b) Given that a firm should continue to produce as long as the price exceeds the marginal cost, how much will the firm produce and what will be its profit or loss at the prices in Table W8.9?

TABLE W8.9

Price ($)	Quantity of Output	Profit (+)/Loss (−) ($)
25	_____	_____
35	_____	_____
45	_____	_____
55	_____	_____
65	_____	_____

3. Table W8.10 presents the cost data for three firms which, we assume for simplicity's sake, are the only firms in a competitive industry.

TABLE W8.10

Quantity Output	FIRM 1 Marginal Cost	FIRM 2 Marginal Cost	FIRM 3 Marginal Cost
1	$30	$20	$25
2	25	15	20
3	30	10	15
4	35	15	10
5	40	20	5
6	45	25	10
7	50	30	15
8	55	35	20
9	60	40	25
10	65	45	30
11	70	50	35
12	75	55	40
Minimum average variable cost	30	12	10
Total fixed cost	30	45	60

a) In Figure W8.7 graph the supply curves for the three firms and the resulting market supply curve.

FIGURE W8.7

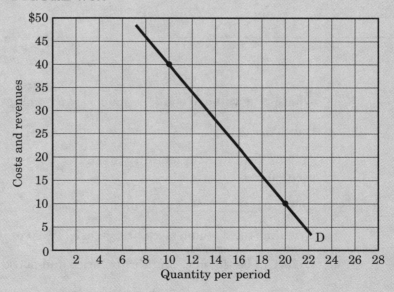

b) Given the demand curve shown, what will be the equilibrium price and output in the market?

Price: $_____; quantity traded: $_____.

c) At this price, how much will each firm produce and what will be the profit or loss of each? (Fill in your answers in Table W8.11)

TABLE W8.11

	FIRM 1	FIRM 2	FIRM 3
Output	_____	_____	_____
Profit (+)/loss (−)	_____	_____	_____

4. In Figure W8.8, part A shows the market demand and supply in a competitive market, and part B shows the cost curves of a representative firm in that industry.

FIGURE W8.8

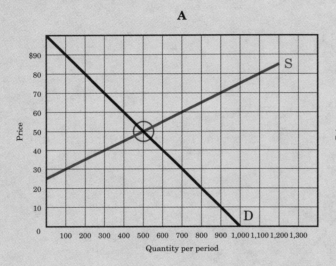

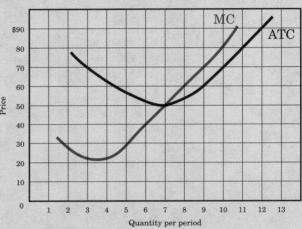

a) What is the value of equilibrium price and quantity in the market?

Price: _____; quantity traded: _____.

b) At equilibrium, what quantity is the firm producing, and what is its total profit or loss?

Quantity: _____; profit (+)/loss (−): _____.

Suppose that the demand were to increase by 600 units.

c) What will be the new equilibrium price and market quantity?

Price: _____; quantity traded: _____.

d) At this new equilibrium, what quantity is the firm producing, and what is its total profit or loss?

Quantity: _____; profit (+)/loss (−): _____.

Unanswered Questions

Short Essays

1. A competitive producer either would not, or could not, sell at a price which differs from that of the other producers. Discuss.

2. Explain why the supply curve of the competitive producer is the same as part of its marginal cost curve.

3. Why do the costs of production in certain industries increase as the industry expands whereas in other industries they fall.

4. Why, in competitive industries, are economic profits equal to zero in the long run?

5. Explain the effect on the price, profits, and number of firms in a competitive market that results from a decrease in the demand for a product.

Analytical Questions

1. For each of the following cases, a) – g), you are given certain cost and price data for a number of competitive firms at their present output levels. Indicate, based on this information, whether each firm should, in the short run:
   i)   produce more.
   ii) produce less.
   iii) shut down.
   iv) cannot determine from this information.

   (In all cases the marginal cost is increasing.)

   a) Average variable cost exceeds price.
   b) Price equals marginal cost.
   c) Price exceeds both marginal cost and average total cost.
   d) Marginal cost exceeds price, and price exceeds average variable cost.
   e) Total cost exceeds total revenue.
   f) Total variable cost exceeds total revenue.
   g) Total fixed cost exceeds total revenue.

2. Strong competition requires weak competitors. Discuss this statement.

3. Does the total revenue of a competitive firm need to exceed the total variable costs in order for it to produce in the short run? Does the total revenue of a competitive firm need to exceed the total fixed costs in order for it to produce in the short run?

4. Explain what will happen to the output and price of a decreasing cost industry if there is a fall in demand.

5. Suppose that the price of a product is equal to both a certain firm's average total cost and its marginal cost. Does it follow that the firm will be making economic profits? Will it be making normal profits? Explain.

6. If the market is in equilibrium, does this mean that the firms in the industry are making economic profits? Does it mean they are breaking even?

7. It is suggested that, given the demand and costs of production for a product, there is a "right" number of firms for each industry. Can there be such a thing as "too many" or, alternatively, "too few" firms in an industry?

Numerical Questions

1. Figure W8.9 shows the average and marginal costs of a competitive firm.

FIGURE W8.9

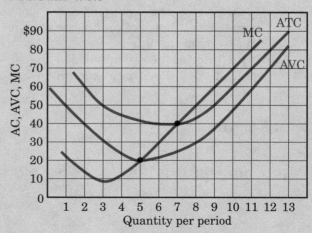

a) If the price is $60, draw in the marginal revenue curve and label it MR$_1$. At this price, what is the break-even output(s), the profit-maximizing output, and the level of *total* profits at that output?

b) Draw a marginal revenue curve, labelled MR$_2$, which ensures that, at best, the firm breaks even. What is the value of the corresponding break-even price?

c) Draw a marginal revenue curve, labelled MR₃, which ensures that, at best, the firm just remains in operation. What is the value of the corresponding shut-down price?

2. Table W8.12 cost data is for a competitive producer:

TABLE W8.12

Quantity of Output	Total Cost
0	$120
1	280
2	370
3	440
4	480
5	500
6	540
7	700
8	960

a) What is the value of the break-even price?
b) What is the value of the shutdown price?
c) If the price of the product is $100, what quantity will the firm produce and what will be its profit or loss?
d) If the price of the product is $160, what quantity will the firm produce and what will be its profit or loss?

3. Figure W8.10 depicts the average and marginal costs of a perfectly competitive firm.

FIGURE W8.10

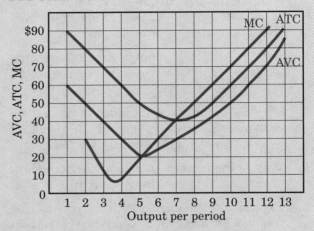

Which of the parts (I, II or III) of Table W8.13 below is the appropriate supply curve for this firm? Explain.

4. Suppose that the total fixed cost for a particular competitive firm is $80. The marginal cost of the first unit produced is $40 and decreases by $5 for each of the next 3 units produced; thereafter, marginal cost increases by $5 for each additional unit.

a) What is the value of the shutdown price and the break-even price?
b) If the price is $55, what is the firm's profit-maximizing output and the firm's total profit or loss?

TABLE W8.13

	(I)		(II)		(III)
Price	Quantity Supplied	Price	Quantity Supplied	Price	Quantity Supplied
$10	0	$10	0	$10	0
20	5	20	0	20	0
30	6	30	0	30	0
40	7	40	7	40	0
50	8	50	8	50	8
60	9	60	9	60	9
70	10	70	10	70	10

CHAPTER NINE

■■■■■■■■

An Evaluation of Competitive Markets

What's ahead . . . This chapter examines the successes and the failures of competitive markets and how, with such markets, the producer is, to use the words of Adam Smith, "led by an invisible hand to promote an end which was no part of his intention."[1] Out of this comes the concept of efficiency, which we define and explain. We look at some of the other benefits of competition and then examine various situations in which competitive markets fail. Finally, we look at the reasons for the failure and explore some of the ways that these problems can be addressed either through government intervention or by helping the market to find its own solutions.

We saw in Chapter 8 how competitive firms respond to changes in the price of what they sell and to the changes in profitability that result. Each change causes an adjustment by the firm and in the whole industry as well. This chapter will continue to examine this theme of adjustment and will appraise the results of such adjustment.

Adam Smith popularized the compelling and (at that time) original idea that a society and an economy functions best if government leaves it alone. The pursuit of self-interest, it seemed to Smith, would lead people, as if directed by an *invisible hand*, to create a harmony of interests. Further, it should be remembered that, in Smith's time, interference by governments in the lives of ordinary people was often arbitrary and despotic. Both of these points led Smith, along with other writers at the time, to suggest that the amount of both political and economic interference by the government should be limited in its extent. In other words he advocated the doctrine of **laissez-faire**.

laissez-faire: the economic doctrine that holds that an economy works best with the minimum amount of government intervention.

For Smith, political and economic liberty went hand in hand. He was arguing that people should be left free to decide their own economic actions, to work wherever, and in whatever firm or location, they wish, and to produce, sell and buy whatever products they desire. However, he tried to explain that not only was such a doctrine morally correct, but just as importantly, for our purposes, that it was also an economically sound doctrine. An economy works best, he felt, if it is left unplanned, uncoordinated and undirected. Interference by the government is undesirable because, for instance, if the government tries to direct you to purchase certain types of goods which it feels you want, then you would probably resent its interest in your

---

[1] Adam Smith, *Wealth of Nations* (Edwin Cannan Edition, 1877), p. 354.

welfare since you know, better than any government, what you want. Such interference is also unnecessary because you certainly don't need any government to persuade you to buy more of a product if it becomes cheaper since you will probably do it anyway. Similarly, an entrepreneur does not need to be told that it's a good idea to open a business in a profitable industry rather than in a loss industry; he already knows this. The market works perfectly well, Smith would have suggested, without a manager or a controller or a planning committee to direct it.

Such a doctrine of laissez-faire raises several questions, however. Will the pursuit of self-interest result in the best of all economies? Will it help to generate a good society? Might not the result be a society of greedy and selfish individuals who are unconcerned about their neighbours, a society in which one person's gain is at the expense of another's suffering? And is it possible that the result of an unplanned economy may be either chaos and anarchy, or at the very least, the production of unnecessary or resource-depleting products?

The major thrust of this chapter is to look at these questions to see how effective a perfectly competitive economy is, how well it reacts to economic changes, and how desirable are the resulting changes.

Smith's vision of laissez-faire was framed within the context of perfectly competitive markets. Thus, what we need to first look at is how other changes are accommodated by a perfectly competitive market. We begin by looking at probably the most fundamental cause of change in a modern economy — technological improvement.

Technological Improvement and Perfect Competition

If an industry, or an economy, is to grow and prosper there must exist an atmosphere which encourages and stimulates innovation and helps in its introduction. We will be discussing the importance of research and development in more detail in a later chapter. For now, let's trace how perfect competition accommodates technological change.

Suppose that Bobby Brewer discovers an improved brewing method which speeds up the fermentation process by 50%; so beer can now be produced more quickly and, therefore, more cheaply. The result for Bobby will be higher profits. Will the other brewers (assuming there are no patent laws) be inclined to introduce this new process? Some will, and some won't. Irrespective of this, as word of the new process spreads, it's likely that a number of new brewers will be attracted by the prospects of economic profits to join the industry. The whole industry will start to grow. However, the result of this influx of new brewers is a long-run increase in supply and a resulting decline in price. But what will happen to the older breweries which refused to introduce Bobby's new technology? Faced with a fall in the price, they will be forced to introduce it; if not, their accumulating losses will force their exit from the industry. Eventually, only those firms which use the new process will survive, but even they, in the long run, will end up making only normal profits. Producers in competitive markets are forced to be innovative then, since if they are not, competition from new, more progressive, firms will force them to change or go the way of the dodo. This aspect of perfect competition is often referred to as its dynamic efficiency.

The Size of the Firm and Perfect Competition

In Chapter 8, we observed that in the short run an increase in demand increases both the price and the profitability of the representative firm. This will stimulate firms to increase production. However, their ability to produce more depends on how close the firm is to its physical capacity and how high the resulting average costs of production are. If the firm believes that the industry is likely to remain a high-demand and high-profit industry, it will be encouraged to grow in size. The bigger the firm (at least up to a point as we saw in Chapter 7), the lower will be the average costs of production. If there are no barriers to the firm's growth, then it will continue to grow as long as economies of scale are obtainable. (However, since we are looking at a competitive industry, such growth is limited by diseconomies of scale setting in relatively quickly.) This idea is illustrated in Figure 9.1.

FIGURE 9.1 Long-Run Equilibrium for the Competitive Firm

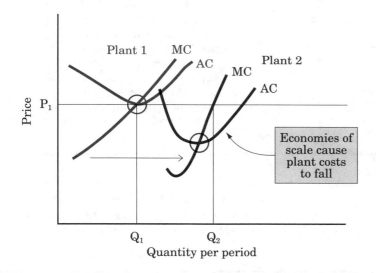

Suppose that the firm is operating out of Plant 1, and the present market price is P_1. The profit-maximizing output in this case will be quantity Q_1, where in fact the firm is just breaking even. However, since there are economies of scale to be obtained in this industry, it will pay the firm to move to a bigger plant such as Plant 2 and increase its level of production to Q_2 which is the profit-maximizing output for that plant.

If the firm is presently operating out of Plant 1, the best it can do is break even by producing an output of Q_1. It is not worth trying to produce a higher output than this since the average costs will be higher, and the result will be a loss. If there are economies of scale to be obtained in this industry, however, it will pay the firm to increase the size of its operations in the long run. For instance, if it were to operate out of Plant 2 it could make much greater economic profits since the average costs of production will be lower. In Plant 2, profit maximization occurs at an output of Q_2. In time then, firms will tend to grow in size if there are economies of scale to be enjoyed. (Conversely, they would be advised to downsize if they are experiencing diseconomies of scale.)

QUESTION 9.1
Exactly why should a firm downsize if it is suffering diseconomies of scale?

Unfortunately from the producer's point of view, what is true for our firm above will also be true for all firms in this industry: they will all be encouraged to grow in size. The effect on the market would be the same as if new firms entered the industry, i.e., the capacity of the industry will expand which means that the supply increases and this will result in a reduction in the price. The result of this expansion is illustrated in Figure 9.2.

FIGURE 9.2 Plant Growth and its Effect on the Market

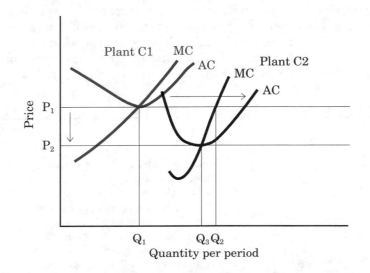

The existence of economies of scale will encourage firms to grow in size. Assume that, at present, the firm is operating out of Plant C1 and is breaking even at an output of Q_1. However, in the long run, it will wish to move into a bigger plant, say Plant C2, where by increasing the output to Q_2 it can now enjoy economic profits *if* the price stays the same. The problem is that if all firms do the same, then the market supply will increase causing the price eventually to drop to P_2 where the firm is back again making only normal profits, i.e., breaking even.

Suppose that the price of the product is initially at P_1 and the size of the average firm is such that its short-run cost curve is C1 in Figure 9.2. In the short-run the firm is making only normal profits, i.e., is breaking even. However, there is the prospect of higher profits to be made through growth because of

FIGURE 9.3 Price and Long-Run Equilibrium

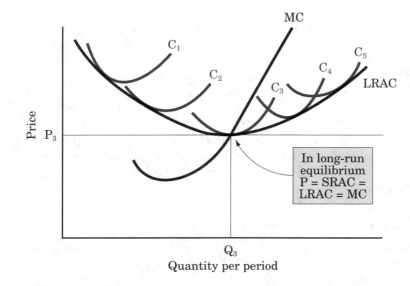

In long-run equilibrium
P = SRAC =
LRAC = MC

Over a period of time, competitive firms will tend to grow in size if there are economies of scale to be obtained. However, this causes the price to drop and to squeeze economic profits out. When the average firm in this industry has grown to size C_3 it will have no further incentive to grow since plants bigger than C_3 will experience diseconomies of scale. For plant size C_3, the optimum output will be Q_3.

the economies of scale which can be obtained. This will cause the representative firm to move into bigger plants such as Plant C2 *and* will cause the price to drop as the industry supply increases. In time, the eventual price of the product will drop to price P_2 in Figure 9.2. *In the long run, competitive firms will not make economic profits.* This is illustrated in Figure 9.3.

The lure of economic profits will cause firms to continue to grow as long as economies of scale are present. The force of competition, however, means that this growth will result in a drop in price. The two forces combined will result in the average firm producing an output of Q_3 in a plant of size C_3 in Figure 9.3 with the price level settling at P_3. This leads to a very important conclusion: *in the long run, in perfectly competitive markets, the price will be equal to both the long- and short-run average costs and also to the marginal cost.*

We need now to look at the implications of this important conclusion.

Productive and Allocative Efficiency

Concentrating on the average costs for a moment, we can see that in the long run the firm is forced to produce where:

$$P = SRAC = LRAC$$

productive efficiency: production of an output at the lowest possible cost.

This illustrates the concept of **productive efficiency**. This means that a product is being produced as cheaply as possible and, what is more, customers are the main beneficiary of this because, as there are no economic profits being made, they are paying a price equal to the lowest possible costs of production.

Productive efficiency is one way in which economists try to evaluate markets. They ask the question: does this particular system produce goods and services at their lowest costs, and does the price of the product reflect those costs? You can see from our analysis so far that, in the long run, a perfectly competitive market passes this test with flying colours.

It should be noted that in the long run, firms are forced, through competition, to be productively efficient. If a firm wishes to survive under these conditions it is left with little choice other than to be productively efficient. Competition forces the average firm to choose the most productively efficient plant size in that particular industry (C_3 in Figure 9.3), and competition forces them to produce the best output (i.e, the lowest cost output) in the plant (i.e., output Q_3). So not only is the firm producing out of the lowest cost plant, but in that plant is producing the lowest cost output.

allocative efficiency: the production of that combination of products which best satisfies consumers' demands.

But producing products at their lowest costs is not much use if nobody wants to buy those products, or customers are buying them reluctantly because no alternatives are available. There is a second, equally important, test of how well a market performs and that is to ask if consumers, given their tastes and incomes, are getting the products that they want. In other words, is the best possible bundle of goods being produced? Conversely, could the total welfare of people be increased by perhaps producing more of one product rather than another? This is known as the test of **allocative efficiency** and refers to the way that resources are allocated which in turn determines what and how many products are produced in an economy. The test of allocative efficiency takes into account the fact that resources are limited and that wants are unlimited. Society would like to ensure that these scarce resources are allocated to various industries in a way that the output of those industries yields the greatest satisfaction to consumers. In a sense this implies that we weigh the cost of using the resources against the satisfaction which their products yield. This means that the marginal utility from consumption should in some sense be measured against the marginal cost from production. We saw in Chapter 5 that consumers are purchasing their best bundle of goods when the MU per dollar spent is equal for all products, i.e., that:

$$\frac{MU_A}{P_A} = \frac{MU_B}{P_B} = \frac{MU_Z}{P_Z}$$

You recall that this is the optimal purchasing rule. We also know that, in order to maximize profits, perfectly competitive firms will produce an output where the price is equal to marginal cost:

$$P = MC$$

If all producers produce where P = MC, then the optimal purchasing rule can be rewritten (substituting MC for P) as:

For maximum utility:

$$\frac{MU_A}{MC_A} = \frac{MU_B}{MC_B} = \frac{MU_Z}{MC_Z}$$

Allocative efficiency implies then not only the maximization of consumers' utility but also the maximization of producers' profits.

Or put another way: allocative efficiency exists when the set of prices and quantities prevailing are those at which *consumers and producers preferences coincide*. The idea of allocative efficiency balances the tastes and incomes of consumers against the quantity and quality of a country's resources and its technology. The condition that the MU/MC of each product should be equal takes into consideration both the demand (MU) and the supply (MC). Essentially then, what allocative efficiency means is nothing more nor less than that at the prices prevailing for each product, the demand should equal the supply.

What perfect markets do is to adjust production and consumption between different products until no further gain could accrue to either producers or consumers from any other combination of goods. This is the essence of allocative efficiency and is a major characteristic of perfectly competitive markets. All the adjustments necessary to achieve allocative efficiency occur automatically through changes in price and profits. There is no need for government intervention of any kind. This is the strength of the market that led Adam Smith to advocate the doctrine of laissez faire.

Other Benefits of Competitive Markets

Productive and allocative efficiency are the two main standards by which economists try to evaluate markets, but they are not the only benefits which result from competition. As we have previously mentioned, another advantage which the market system (whether competitive or not) has over a planned economy is that *the system is costless*. The market system controls and coordinates itself; it does not require the costly presence of an army of bureaucrats and officials to organize it. In a planned economy, on the other hand, a whole host of officials have to establish the prices and quantities of all products and resources produced. The costs of government administration are very high in modern societies, and the bigger and more complex the society, the higher are these costs commensurately.

A final benefit of the market system is definitely open to discussion. Many people would suggest that the idea of freedom is meaningless unless people are guaranteed *economic freedom*. This means that people should have the right, free from government direction, to determine for themselves how to use their own private resources. Adam Smith wrote thus:

> Every man, as long as he does not violate the laws of justice, is left perfectly free to pursue his own interest in his own way, and to bring both his own industry and his own capital into competition with those of any other man, or order of men.[1]

This theme has been taken up in modern days by, among many others, Milton Friedman, the famous economist of the monetarist school. Friedman argues that freedom is impossible in a socialist state because the state, or officers of the state, direct people as to where and how they are to employ their industry (labour) and capital. Since everyone becomes an employee of the state, then the state and not the individual has the power to determine how this labour will be used. In addition, socialist states usually forbid the private ownership of capital so the individual has no control over how the country's capital will be used. And, for Friedman, while capitalism does not guarantee freedom, it is a necessary condition for it. He would suggest, then, that all free states are capitalistic though not all capitalist states are free.

BOX 9A
1. What is meant by the term *laissez-faire*?
2. Explain how competition forces firms to be innovative.
3. To increase profits, a firm may be forced to grow; but if all firms grow, none of them will increase profits. Explain.
4. What is meant by the term *productive efficiency*? If a firm is productively efficient, what condition must be true?
5. What is meant by the term *allocative efficiency*? What condition must exist in order for there to be allocative efficiency in a market?
6. What are the four main benefits of competitive markets?

Market Failures

Despite the advantages of the market system (and the closer it is to a perfect market, the better), it has been criticized over the years on many of grounds. The topic which will take up the remainder of the chapter will be

---

[1] Adam Smith, *Wealth of Nations* (Edwin Cannan Edition, 1877), p. 651.

market failures: the defects in competitive markets which prevent them from achieving productive or allocative efficiencies.

these criticisms, called **market failures**. There are five major criticisms of competitive markets. First, the market is no guarantor of fairness, and *income and wealth inequalities* often seem endemic to competitive markets. Secondly, *competitive markets are often unstable* and periodically seem to move without warning from an expansionary boom to a recessionary slump. Thirdly, competitive markets seem to contain the seeds of their own destruction because they easily admit *forces which work to destroy competition*. Fourthly, competitive markets do not guarantee the production of a number of important goods and services known as *public goods*. Finally, competitive markets often encourage the overproduction of undesirable, and underproduction of desirable, products because the marketplace has difficulty in integrating what are known as *externalities*. We will look at each of these in turn and try to understand why governments feel the need to interfere in the economy in an attempt to correct these deficiencies.

Income and Wealth Inequalities

The questions of fairness and freedom are particularly pertinent when trying to evaluate how well a particular economic system performs. Critics of competitive markets point out that allocative efficiency is not the same thing as fairness and that just because perfectly competitive markets guarantee allocative efficiency does not mean that the result will be a fair system. Allocative efficiency, as we have seen, means that resources are allocated in the most efficient manner *given the tastes and income distribution of that society*. But the competitive market system is unconcerned with what that income distribution is. In other words, if the income distribution were to change, the competitive market system would automatically adjust the allocation of resources so as to make the new allocation also efficient. For every different distribution of income (including extreme distributions where a major portion of the total income goes to a few very rich members of that society), there will be a different allocation of resources, each efficient in an allocative sense. But the system itself has nothing to say about which income distribution is better than any other. Since competition is blind, it is unconcerned at the fate of the participants.

An important aspect of the concept of fairness is that the rewards should be commensurate with the amount of effort expended. In many respects, competitive markets do reward greater effort with greater incomes. However, the competitive market system does not always guarantee that this will be so. In particular, many people earn great rewards without putting forth any effort because they are owners of resources. Wealth is not evenly distributed in competitive societies and is handed down from generation to generation with the result that the incomes which flow from this wealth are sometimes the result of parentage rather than effort. In short, competitive markets do nothing to correct the serious imbalances in wealth and income and indeed may cause even greater inequalities. As a result, critics point out that you cannot have political freedom without economic freedom. They would suggest therefore that one of the prime functions of a government is to correct the economic inequalities which competitive markets help to perpetuate. Poverty, they would argue, is not a disease of the individual, but of society.

Another cause of the maldistribution of income occurs when people possess no marketable resources, and without government intervention, would be left destitute by the competitive market. This is the case where people do not have even their own labour efforts to sell, perhaps because they are mentally ill or physically infirm, are too young or old, or in circumstances where they need to look after family members full-time. The market would normally fail to provide such people with any income.

The question of income distribution is a highly charged and emotional one that the market simply doesn't address. Some would argue, therefore, that this is a severe failure.

Instability of Competitive Markets

Since the dawn of the industrial age, observers have noticed that, despite a general upward trend, competitive economies do not grow at a steady pace. Instead they seem prone to go through business cycles of booms and slumps. A period of rapid economic growth and full employment eventually comes to an end, followed by a period of low or even negative growth and high unemployment. Such fluctuations are often unpredictable and still not fully understood. They also can, and do, cause great distress for some and, for this reason, governments have found themselves forced to intervene in an attempt to manage the economy to try to prevent or to minimize these fluctuations. Such intervention has often been criticized, but the truth remains that the competitive market by itself fails to prevent such harmful booms and recessions. (The attempts of government policy to manage the economy makes up part of the subject of macroeconomics.)

The Forces of Uncompetition

Writing in an era of small independent businesses at the end of the eighteenth century, Adam Smith looked at the possibility of monopolies flourishing in the future and dismissed the idea. But since the competitive market is based on the idea of economic freedom, this must include the freedom of firms to grow or to buy out other firms and in doing so, destroy competition. Smith, who was adamantly opposed to monopolies, remained largely unconcerned about the prospect of their flourishing in the future since, he reasoned, if a large firm tried to exert its growing power over the market by increasing the price of its products, then it would leave itself open to undercutting by the smaller firms. In this way, large firms would enjoy no extra advantage.

However, in many industries, it turns out that large firms do have one great advantage over small firms and that is the benefit they can get from economies of scale which we looked at in Chapter 7. In the automobile, oil-refining and hydroelectric industries, for instance, the benefits can be enormous. The twentieth century has seen a tremendous increase in the number of very big firms such that many industries these days are dominated by one or a few giant companies. The next three chapters will look in some detail at the implications of these uncompetitive markets, but we might note in advance that the further away a particular market deviates from our ideal model of a perfectly competitive market, the fewer will be the benefits from society's point of view. As we shall see, uncompetitive markets in varying degrees are productively and allocatively inefficient; they do not produce goods and services at the lowest possible cost and, almost always, charge a price that is higher than both the average and marginal costs of production.

Provision of Public Goods

public good: products which are collectively consumed so that private firms would be incapable of producing them at a profit and which therefore must be provided by the government.

private good: products which can be consumed separately by each individual and are normally provided by private firms.

non-excludability: a feature of certain products which means that it is impossible to exclude non-purchasers from enjoying the benefits of the product.

Many goods and services that we consume in Canada these days are provided by various different levels of government. Some of these products could just as well be provided by the private market, and in many other countries they are. So why do governments in general feel that they should be responsible for the provision of any goods and services? In most cases the provision requires the imposition of taxes, which all of us must pay regardless of whether or not we are consumers of these government-provided services. In this sense, the provision of public goods represents a retreat from the idea of personal freedom since it means, for instance, that I do not have the freedom to choose what I want to buy or not buy. There are however a number of compelling reasons why, throughout history, governments have felt it desirable to provide certain products. The most obvious case is where private firms would not be able to make a profit from the sale of certain products. To understand why this should be so, we need to look in a bit more detail at what exactly economists mean by a public good.

First let us contrast a **public good** and a **private good**. It's true to say that public goods must be provided by the government, but not all goods provided by the government are public goods — some in fact are private goods! Let's clear this up by defining our terms. Private goods, which include all the products supplied by private firms from Cokes to Sony TVs, from Volvos to Labatt's Blue are distinguished from public goods on three grounds. Private goods are said to be excludable, divisible and depletable, whereas public goods are non-excludable, non-divisible and non-depletable. Let us look at these three characteristics one at a time.

When you or I buy a private good we expect to have exclusive enjoyment of that product, to dispose of it as we wish. On the other hand, if we are not interested in buying the product, then of course we shall not expect to enjoy its benefits. The trouble is, with certain types of products it is impossible (or difficult without great cost) to prevent people who have not paid for the product from enjoying the benefits of it. If people can get the benefit whether or not they make a purchase, then few people will bother to buy it, and firms could not make a profit from its production. A classic example of a good which has this characteristic of **non-excludability** is a lighthouse. Imagine a small fishing village where the fishers are often coming to grief because of the hidden presence of a reef just offshore. Someone, quite rightly, decides that the construction of a lighthouse would provide sufficient warning. A lighthouse company constructs the needed lighthouse and charges a fee to all the fishers who are going to use its services. But you can easily see that in this situation, there will be no need for the fishers to pay such a fee since it will be very difficult for the lighthouse company to exclude non-subscribers from looking at the lighthouse. That being so, the lighthouse company will soon go out of business, and the only way that a future lighthouse could be built is by the government financing it out of tax revenues. A lighthouse is a public good, therefore, because it has, by its nature, the characteristic of non-excludability.

Some products, while not being excludable, are also public goods by dint of being non-divisible. This means that, for some goods, it is very difficult, if not impossible, to sell them in clearly definable units. By contrast, for a private good, you are able to buy as much or as little as you want, one bottle of pop, or a six-pack or a case. It would be very difficult for buyers (and for the seller) if you needed to structure some kind of cooperative effort with two thousand other people in order to buy a particular product. Yet, the nature of certain products is such that, since they are simply not divisible into small units, this type of cooperation is exactly what is required in order to make a purchase. An example of **non-divisibility** is military defence (which is also non-excludable, by the way). It's difficult to see how people could "buy" as much or as little military defence as they felt they personally needed. The same is true of a number of other "products" such as the court system, policing, public health and so on. For this reason, they are, by definition, public goods and must be financed out of the public purse.

non-divisibility: a feature of certain products which means that they can only be bought collectively and not by single individuals.

The final characteristic of some public goods is that they are non-depletable. Private goods, in contrast, are depletable which means that the production of more goods involves the depletion of more resources. This would be true of most physical products such as beer or new housing construction but is also true of services such as hairdressing or life insurance where more clients means more labour expended. However, with certain products, servicing one client or servicing one thousand clients still costs the same. Think, for instance, of swamp clearance. The clearing of a swamp costs, let's say, $5 million and will benefit a nearby town. However, whether this town has a population of 500 or 500,000 is irrelevant; the cost remains $5 million. In other words, the clearance costs are fixed costs and there are no variable costs. In this situation, the marginal cost of the activity is zero. For allocative efficiency, the price of such goods should be equal to the marginal cost. In other words it should be a free good. If a private company wants to make a profit from clearing the swamp, it is difficult to know what price it should charge to its "clients." The snow clearance of public highways is another service which has to be financed by the government (or done on a strictly volunteer basis) since it too exhibits the characteristic of **non-depletability**.

non-depletability: a feature of certain products where additional people are able to receive benefits without it costing the use of more resources.

If any product is non-excludable, or non-divisible or non-depletable then it is, by definition, a public good. Certain products possess all three dimensions: the provision of a military, for instance, meets all three criteria. In summary, a private firm will only produce a product if it is profitable and will not produce it unless it is excludable, divisible and depletable and all public goods must be provided by some means other than by the market.

Quasi-Public Goods

In the modern age, and indeed throughout history, governments have produced a number of goods and services which by our criteria are not strictly public goods. For example, education does not need to be a public good. Indeed, most countries have a private-school sector, since it is easy to exclude non-subscribers. In addition, people can buy as much or as little education as they wish, and the cost of education does increase with more students. Education is an excludable, divisible and depletable product. The same is true of private health services (treatment by doctors and hospitals), postal delivery and the provision of social infrastructure such as highways and harbours. Although all of these services could be produced by the private sector, for a number of reasons they are often provided by the government. Such goods are not public goods as defined by economists. If they are, nonetheless, provided by the government, they are known as **quasi-public goods** (i.e., they "look like" public goods). There are three main reasons why governments decide to provide these quasi-public goods.

quasi-public goods: products which, although not strictly public goods, are often provided by the government either because they involve such extensive effects on the public or for other reasons.

First, in some cases the costs (to the firm and to consumers) of collecting revenues in a private market might be prohibitive. This is the case with highways for example. Although a toll charge could be imposed on major highways, it would become a Kafkaesque nightmare if such tolls were introduced on all urban and suburban streets. To prevent this possibility, the provision and maintenance of roads is usually financed from property or gasoline taxes.

A second reason for the provision of quasi-public goods by the government are situations where it is felt that competition is inefficient since it might involve wasteful duplication. This is particularly true where large economies of scale are involved. Rather than allow a number of competing electricity distribution and transportation systems, for instance, a government might take responsibility for providing such services.

The final, and probably most important, reason why governments provide such services as health and education is that these and other quasi-public goods are important not only to the people who currently use the services but to society as a whole. These services involve what are known as external costs and benefits, a subject to which we now turn.

Externalities

externalities: benefits or costs of a product experienced by people who neither produce nor consume that product.

The fifth failure of competitive markets is its inability to take into account external costs and benefits, collectively known as **externalities.** We mentioned in our discussion of public goods that in the provision of certain goods it is impossible to prevent non-payers from enjoying a benefit. In actuality, with many products it is impossible to ensure that only the users of a product enjoy the benefits and pay the costs. With some products the degree of external benefits or external costs are so small that they can be ignored. For instance, if I were to spend money on having my front yard landscaped, I would enjoy a benefit not only in terms of greater aesthetic enjoyment but also because the value of my property would be enhanced. But so too would my neighbours who would similarly enjoy an increase in property values. My neighbours would therefore enjoy an external benefit. However, this is usually a "free" benefit, unless I go from door to door asking for contributions — not a good idea in my neighbourhood at least! With some products though, the external benefits or costs are so great that the market totally distorts the allocation of resources. Let us first take a look at the problem of external costs.

External Costs

When you pay for a product, it is assumed that you are paying for the full costs of producing that product. Often however, this is not the case and other people are forced to also pay a cost. Suppose that fishers cast their nets and earn their livelihoods downstream from a pulp mill. Lack of government intervention, however, would allow the mill to maximize its profits by discharging its effluent by the cheapest method possible, i.e., by simply dumping it into a nearby river. This has enormous implications for the fishers (not to mention the fish). In days gone by, the amount of external costs was limited and generally acceptable. The increase in population and incomes in this century has increased the value that people place on such things as clean air, clean water, public parks and gardens. At the same time, technological development has increased the amount of environmental damage that has been incurred as well as increased our knowledge of such damage. There are any number of examples of external costs besides the obvious ones of water and air pollution. Noise pollution is experienced by anyone living near a major airport or near the lines of an urban railroad. Aesthetic pollution is suffered by anyone whose scenic views from home or office are suddenly destroyed by a new monster home or skyscraper. It is also experienced by drivers confronted by huge ugly billboards on their daily commutes. It is now acknowledged that these external social costs are as important as the private costs of production. The competitive market however does not include these social costs, with the result that too much of certain products are being produced at too low a price. In a sense consumers of these polluting products are enjoying a benefit partly at the cost of other members of society. The present task of policy-makers, given the failure of competitive markets to do so, is to find a way of integrating these costs into the production process — which is what economists term integrating external costs (or internalizing social costs).

Integrating External Costs: Legislative Controls

One method of curtailing the production of pollutants is by way of *legislative controls*. The government could decree quotas on the levels of production or on the level of pollutants; it could set up pollution emission standards and fine or prosecute offending producers who exceed the limits; or it might decree that certain types of anti-pollution devices be installed at the polluters' expense. Each of these methods have been tried with varying degrees of success. Sometimes the offences are difficult to detect or to prove or to prosecute. And, in some cases, they may even discriminate against firms who have been conscientious in their practices. For instance, a decree that all steel mills reduce the volume of their emissions 20% by 1998 on the surface seems equitable since it applies to all mills. However it does not take into account the present levels of emissions. An environmentally conscious mill which has already spent a fortune on reducing emissions is treated the same as one who may have done nothing at all to reduce the level of pollutants. To further reduce emissions by 20% for the conscientious mill is going to be considerably more expensive than for the mill who has done nothing.

There are, however, other economic methods available to a government.

Integrating External Costs: Taxation

A second method of integrating the costs of pollution into the pricing decision is by *imposing taxes on the polluter*. This could be done by way of an excise tax, or general "pollution tax," the level of which varies with the amount of pollution. Suppose that the marginal costs of production in a particular industry are as shown in Figure 9.4 on the next page. The curve is the total marginal cost curve of the industry (which is the same thing as the supply curve) and is labelled MPC which stands for marginal (private) costs. These costs are the internal costs of producing the product (which up to now we have simply called marginal costs) and do not therefore include any external costs.

marginal social costs: the additional costs to both the producer (internal costs) and to society (external costs) of producing additional quantities of a product.

Suppose that we were able to measure the costs which this industry imposes on the rest of society in the form of air and water pollution, and these costs equal the amount *ec* in Figure 9.4. If we add both the marginal private costs *and* the external costs *ec*, the total costs to society are represented by the higher curve labelled MSC or **marginal social costs**. These are the true costs of production — the direct production costs and the costs

FIGURE 9.4 Marginal Private Costs and Marginal Social Costs

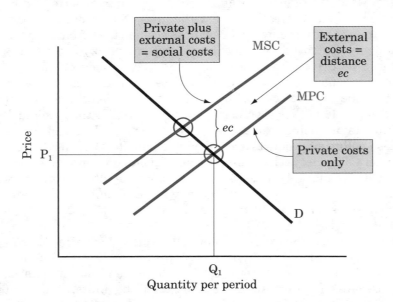

Marginal private costs are simply what we have so far referred to as the marginal costs of the firm. The total MPCs of all the firms in the industry are shown in this graph and are identical to the supply curve of the industry. However, the costs to society include not only these costs but also the external costs labelled *ec*. Adding these costs to the marginal private costs gives us the curve labelled marginal social costs (MSC) which therefore includes all costs, both private and external.

of the associated pollution. If the firms do not have to worry about these external costs, the resulting price is too low and the production level is too high from society's point of view. One way to force them to recognize these costs would be to impose an excise tax equal to the external costs. This is illustrated in Figure 9.5 below.

FIGURE 9.5 Taxing a Polluting Industry

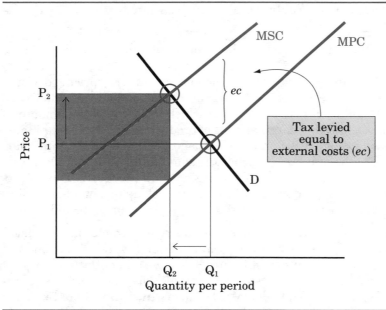

Because the market ignores external costs, the product is sold where the supply (MPC) is equal to the demand, i.e., at price P_1 and quantity Q_1. However, if the government imposes a pollution tax of *ec*, which is equal to these external costs, then the new supply curve would be synonymous with the MSC curve and the new price would be P_2 and the new quantity Q_2.

The effect of the tax will be to increase the price from P_1 to P_2 and reduce production from Q_1 to Q_2. The amount of these changes will depend on the elasticities of demand and supply which will also determine how much of the tax is paid by consumers of this product in the form of higher prices and how much by producers in the form of lower profits. However the tax is split, those people most directly involved with the product are being forced to pay the true cost. In addition, the government will be deriving a tax revenue equal to the rectangular shaded area which it could use to clean up some of the effects of pollution or help those suffering as a result.

Integrating External Costs: Marketing Pollution Rights

There is a third way in which the costs of pollution could be integrated into the market process and that is by what economists call the marketing of pollution rights.

Suppose that a particular lake is the central dumping ground for a number of industries and firms and the government is concerned about the amount of effluents being discharged into the lake. As a result, it decides to employ a research team to determine the maximum amount of pollution which this lake could safely endure without serious environmental damage. The scientists come up with a conservative figure of 200 tons a year. Given this "supply" of allowable effluents, the government decides to sell this quantity of rights to anybody wishing to purchase a licence to pollute. The price of these licences will depend on the demand for the right to pollute and the supply allowed by government as shown in Figure 9.6.

FIGURE 9.6 Demand and supply of Pollution Rights

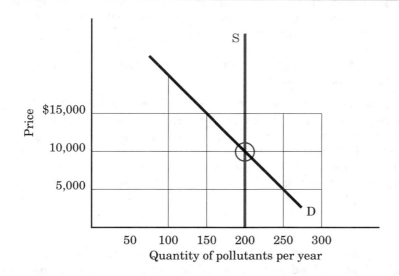

The lower the price of a pollution licence (i.e., the right to discharge a ton of effluence into the lake each year), the greater will be the number of firms wishing to buy them. In other words, the demand curve is downward-sloping. The supply of such licences, however, is a fixed amount of 200 tons per year (the maximum amount that research suggests the lake can tolerate). The market price, therefore, will be where the demand and supply are equal, i.e., at a price per licence of $10,000.

Given the demand and supply, the market price of the pollution licences is $10,000 a ton. Purchase of such a licence will allow the holder to discharge 1 ton of pollutants into the lake each year. Those firms who find this figure exorbitant will be forced to find other ways of controlling or disposing of their waste.

More significantly, this could also mean that environmental groups, wishing to keep the level of pollution down to a lower level, would be able to purchase the licences and not use the right to discharge, so preventing others from making use of them. In essence, the market is, in this way, providing private groups an additional avenue to the decision-making process which means that such groups don't have to win political elections in order to bring about change. In addition, the government may change the 200-ton acceptable limit from year to year as circumstances dictate. Additionally, the revenue from the licences could be used to finance other schemes to reduce or eliminate pollution.

QUESTION 9.2
What would happen if, in Figure 9.6, the government were to incorrectly estimate the demand and only charge $5,000 for a licence?

External Benefits

An external benefit occurs whenever non-users enjoy a benefit as a result of the production or consumption of a product. A new bridge, for instance may lower the prices of products for both users and non-users of the bridge. Another example occurs with inoculation against infectious diseases. The benefits of inoculation accrue to both those inoculated and also to those not inoculated since it lessens the chances of that disease being transmitted. Perhaps the biggest benefits of all come in the areas of health and education. Needless to say, each of us derives a personal benefit from being healthy but we also benefit from the fact that other people are healthy too. The benefits range from the decreased possibility of my also becoming ill to the increased productivity and decreased tax liability of a healthy labour force. The external benefits of an educated citizenry are also wide-ranging and include higher productivity and, often, lower levels of crime, poverty, and social unrest.

As with external costs, competitive markets do not account for these external benefits since the demand represents only the private individual benefits derived from consumption. The result is that, in a sense, products with extensive external benefits are underpriced and underproduced. Often governments feel the need to intervene to encourage the production of such products. We will look at three ways in which the government attempts to integrate these benefits into the provision of goods and services.

Integrating External Benefits: Provision of Quasi-Public Goods

It would be wrong to suggest that the prime reason why most governments provide public education and public medical care is because they recognize the extent of external benefits. In many cases the government has not so much granted, as the people over the centuries have demanded, fought and often rebelled for the basic "right" to free and public education and medical care. Such services have usually been regarded as necessities, more so than, say, food or housing or clothes. To a certain extent, how well a person is dressed, fed, or accommodated is usually regarded as a matter of private concern whereas the health and education of people are regarded as being of public concern.

The governments of many countries, in response to the experiences of the Great Depression of the 1930s and to fulfil the desire to create a "great new society" after World War II, increased the provision of government services and products. As the public sector increased appreciably, it often extended access from areas of basic coverage so that public education began to include post-secondary education; health service coverage extended to dental, chiropractic and psychiatric medicine; transportation began to include not only the building and maintenance of highways and harbours but also the provision of airports, airlines, interurban bus and railroad companies; communication started to include not just postal services but also telephone, radio and television services. In addition to this, in many countries a number of other industries including the hydroelectric and mining industries were nationalized, and in other countries, governments started competing with private industry in the provision of gasoline, concert theatres and racehorse tracks. This massive proliferation in public services led to a reaction in the 1980s and to a movement toward "privatization." The balance these days between the provision of public and private goods varies considerably from country to country and is in a state of flux generally as countries search for the ideal mixture.

Integrating External Benefits: Providing Subsidies

The direct provision of goods and services is not the only way that the government can encourage the production of certain products; it could do this instead by offering subsidies to private firms. A subsidy is merely a reverse tax in which the government pays the producer a certain amount for each unit produced. As an example, suppose that the government is convinced that the provision of day-care services involves not only benefits for the children and parents who use them but also external benefits to the rest of society. This is because the government believes, let's say, that the lack of sufficient day-care is acting as a barrier to entry for many women wishing to return to the labour market after the early years of raising children. The result is that society is being denied their skills and productivity. In Figure 9.7, the demand curve represents the benefits which the users of the day-care derives from day-care services and is labelled MPB, or marginal

FIGURE 9.7 Marginal Private Benefits and Marginal Social Benefits

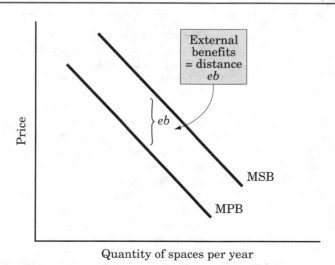

External benefits = distance *eb*

The demand curve for a product is a representation of the benefits which people derive from it and an indicator of how much they would be prepared to pay for various quantities. In other words, the demand is identical to the marginal private benefits. The MPB curve shown here for day-care services is the market benefits of all patrons. However, non-users of day-cares also enjoy benefits and this is shown as the amount *eb*. The total of the private and external benefits gives us the marginal social benefits (MSB) curve shown here.

marginal social benefits: the additional benefits to both the consumer (internal benefits) and to society (external benefits) of additional quantities of a product.

private benefits. In addition to this the government has determined that the external benefit is equal to an amount eb for each child. The total benefits, both private and external, are shown as the higher curve labelled MSB or **marginal social benefits**.

In Figure 9.8 below, the supply curve (representing the marginal social costs) has been added to the graph. Without a subsidy, the equilibrium price would be $500 per month and the number of spaces available equal to 50,000. If we included the external benefits in the marginal social benefit curve, the total number of spaces available would increase to 60,000.

FIGURE 9.8 Integrating External Benefits

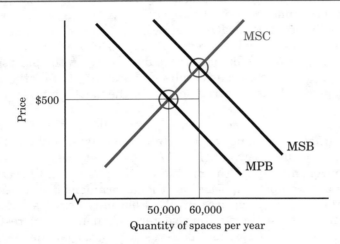

If the external benefits of day-cares could be integrated into the market, the resulting curve would be the MSB curve. Given the supply curve, MSC, the equilibrium quantity would increase from the present 50,000 to 60,000 places.

One way in which these external benefits can be integrated into the market is by the offer of a subsidy per child to day-care operators. The introduction of such a subsidy would be represented by a rightward shift in the supply curve as shown in Figure 9.9. This would have the desired effect of

FIGURE 9.9 Subsidizing Day-Care Operators

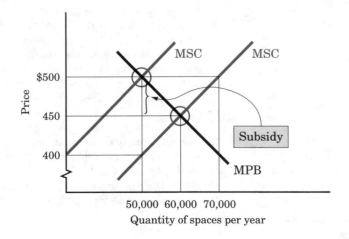

One way in which the government could increase the number of day-care places from 50,000 to 60,000 would be to grant a subsidy to day-care operators sufficient to induce them to build extensions to their premises and to employ additional staff. In this graph, the subsidy amounts to $100 per month for each day-care place. The result of the subsidy will be to increase the number of places and also reduce the day-care fee from $500 to $450 per month.

increasing the number of spaces to 60,000. It would also lead to a decrease in the monthly day-care charge to $450.

The problem with subsidizing suppliers in this way is that it does not correctly address the fact that because the market ignores externalities, both the price and the quantity supplied are too low. Certainly, in our example, a subsidy will increase the amount of day-care spaces, but the result of the subsidy was to make the price even more artificially low. To overcome this problem, some economists suggest that the subsidy should be given, not to the day-cares, but to the parents of children of day-care age. The result would be not only an increase in the number of day-care spaces but also an increase in the day-care fee. Usually this subsidy is not given in the form of cash but in coupon funds. This leads us to a more controversial way, in general, of integrating external benefits into the market.

Study Guide

QUESTION 9.3
In Figure 9.9, how many spaces would day-care operators offer at $500 per month? Why does the monthly fee drop to $450 after the subsidy?

QUESTION 9.4
Suppose that a subsidy equal to the estimated external benefits was given to parents of day-care children in the form of a cash payment. Diagrammatically, which curve would be affected, in what direction, and what effect would it have on the price and quantity?

Integrating External Benefits: Marketing Benefit Rights

An alternative way of integrating external benefits into the provision of goods and services is to use a method advocated by Milton Friedman some years ago. His suggestion was that, in the area of public education, the government should divide up the amount presently allocated to public education by the number of students presently attending. This amount per student would be given back to the parents in the form of an educational chit which they could then use to pay for their children's education at any privately run school of their choosing. If the government wanted to integrate external as well as private benefits into the scheme they would have to estimate the marginal social benefits as in Figure 9.10 on page 304.

If they wished, the government could estimate different marginal social benefits for each level of education — primary, secondary, post-secondary. Assuming competitive markets with a private-school system, the marginal private benefit curve is identical to the demand curve for secondary education. Adding to this the external benefits of secondary education gives us the marginal social benefits.

Suppose that presently the secondary school population in a particular city is 100,000 students. At that level of attendance, Figure 9.10 shows that the marginal private benefits per student are $4,000 per student per annum. In addition, the external benefits are estimated at $1,000 per student for a total marginal social benefit of $5,000. The total benefits derived from education in this particular city are 100,000 times $5,000, which equals

FIGURE 9.10 Marginal Social Benefits of Secondary Education

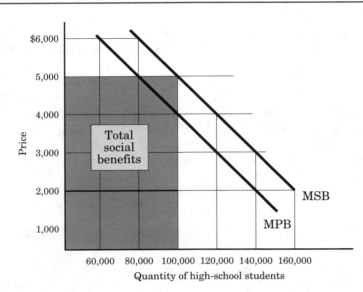

The marginal private benefits from secondary education have been estimated at, say, $4,000 per student at the present level of enrollment in this particular school district which has a secondary-school population of 100,000 students. In addition, external benefits of another $1,000 have been estimated giving a marginal social benefit per student of $5,000. The shaded area shows the total social benefits which equals $5,000 times 100,000 or $500 million.

$500 million. If the authorities wish to integrate external benefits into the provision of education, then the chit should have a value of $5,000 per child in this city. Parents would be provided with one chit per child to be spent at whichever school they choose. Marketizing the economic benefits of education in this way means that every child is guaranteed an education, but also that parents would have the freedom to choose the kind of education they want for their children. It also implies that entrepreneurs would have the right to set up private, independent schools. The choice of schools available would not only include different locations, but also differences in curriculum, facilities, quality of teaching and so on. Each school would be paid with educational chits which it would cash in with the city education board. Poor quality schools would be unable to attract sufficient students to be profitable and would be forced out of business. It could also mean that a "premium" school would be able to charge "premium" prices, i.e., you would tender the education chit plus say, an extra $1,000 cash per year for your child.

QUESTION 9.5

According to Figure 9.10, not all parents (or students) in this school district feel that the marginal private benefits of secondary education are worth only $4,000 per annum. Of the 100,000 households, how many feel that it is worth more than $5,000? How many feel that it is worth less than $5,000?

Understandably, you may have a number of objections to this particular scheme. The main point of the exercise is to make you aware that there are a number of ways that externalities can be integrated into the provision and pricing of most goods and services. In all cases, however, it does involve the government directing the market in some way so as to encourage the production of those things that society deems important and to discourage the production of those thought to be undesirable.

BOX 9B

1. What is meant by the term *market failure*?
2. Give, and briefly explain, five different market failures.
3. What is one of the major explanations for the inequalities in the amount of income and wealth in a society?
4. In what way are competitive markets said to be unstable?
5. Adam Smith felt that monopolies are unlikely to be successful. Why did he think that?
6. What are three ways in which a *public good* is distinguished from a *private good*? Explain each briefly.
7. What is a *quasi-public good*? Give three explanations of why governments provide quasi-public goods.
8. Explain, and give examples of, *externalities*.
9. Explain three ways in which external costs might be integrated into the provision of privately produced goods and services.
10. What effect does a pollution tax have on the price and quantity produced? Who pays for the pollution tax?
11. Explain three ways in which external benefits might be integrated into the provision of privately produced goods and services.

Chapter Highlights

This chapter looks at the benefits and costs to society of competitive markets and discusses some ways that can be used to either keep markets competitive or to correct their deficiencies. It begins by explaining how competitive markets are successful both in stimulating and in adjusting to technological change. It shows how competition forces firms to produce the best size of output for a given size of plant, and in addition, ensures that eventually firms are operating in the best size of plant.

The chapter then develops and explains the important ideas of productive and allocative efficiency. It shows that, in the long run, firms in competitive markets will make only normal profits and will also produce at the lowest possible cost, both of which will benefit society. This is the idea behind productive efficiency. Allocative efficiency is described as the production of that particular bundle of goods which maximizes both producers' profits and consumers' utility. It explains why this result is obtained when the demand and supply are in equilibrium in every market, and why this outcome occurs in a perfectly competitive world. It then mentions some other benefits of competition, such as the low cost of operating such markets and the level of freedom that they foster.

Next, the chapter looks at some of the ways in which markets perform badly or not at all. The first of these market failures arises because a perfectly competitive market does not guarantee that the results are fair, nor will it prevent big disparities in incomes and wealth. Secondly, the chapter mentions how competitive markets might be unstable and therefore unable to guarantee smooth and uninterrupted economic growth. Third, it explains that there is nothing in the nature of competitive markets to keep them competitive, with the result that big corporations come to dominate most markets. Fourth, it shows why the competitive market is unable to produce certain types of goods, so that often the government is forced to produce these public goods. It also mentions other reasons why governments produce many other goods, known as quasi-public goods, which could be produced by the private market. The final market failure results from the fact that in the marketplace private producers and consumers are not required to consider the effects of their action on outsiders. The result is the production of externalities which means that private and public desires do not coincide.

The last part of the chapter examines the way in which the government policy can encourage producers and consumers to recognize and take account of external costs and benefits. It mentions how external costs like pollution could be integrated into the market through legislative controls, through taxation or through the marketing of pollution rights. Finally it considers the ways in which external benefits might be integrated into the market by way of the direct provision of certain goods by the government, through the payment of subsidies or by marketing benefit rights.

New Glossary Terms

Workbook

Study Tips

1.   Some students confuse the concept of excludability with that of externalities. To sort out this difference, it is important to realize that the production of most products involves both private costs and external costs. The private costs are included in the price of the product and are paid for by the purchaser. The external costs are paid for (though not in money terms) by others who have no part in the production and consumption of the product. Also, most products involve both private and external benefits. The private benefits are the reward of consuming the product, and external benefits are the indirect benefits that non-buyers often receive. It is almost impossible at times to prevent external costs and benefits from occurring but the chapter analyzes a number of ways in which such externalities can be accounted for and integrated into the market. With certain products, however, it is impossible to prevent some people from enjoying external benefits but, additionally, it is impossible to prevent others from enjoying *private* benefits for free. It is this last aspect which defines the term non-excludability. So for most products, though you can't prevent people enjoying an external benefit you can, at least, prevent them from enjoying a private benefit (unless they pay for the product). With true public goods this is not true: you can't prevent them from enjoying either.

2.   Another possible point of confusion for students is in regard to the three criteria for a public good. A good is a public good and, therefore, must be provided by the government (if it is to be provided at all) if it is non-excludable *or* if it is non-divisible *or* if it is non-depletable. In other words, if a good fails any one of the three tests, it cannot be a private good. You should make sure that you know the definitions of non-excludabilty, non-divisibility and non-depletability.

3.   You should realize that since external costs and benefits are not usually bought and sold in the marketplace, then their value is merely an estimate. It is very difficult to put an *exact* valuation on the cost of noise pollution or on the societal benefits from having an educated populace. That doesn't mean that they are unimportant but on the other hand don't be mislead into thinking that a precise figure can be attached to them.

4.   Taxes and subsidies are often used by governments to adjust prices and outputs of privately produced goods. Remember that if the seller is responsible for paying the tax the supply curve will shift left; if the buyer is responsible for paying, the demand curve will shift left. If the subsidy is given to the seller to encourage more production, it will shift the supply curve right; if the subsidy is given to the buyer to encourage greater consumption, it will shift the demand curve right.

Are You Sure?

Indicate whether the following statements are true or false. If false, indicate why they are false.

1.   A market is productively efficient if the price of a product equals its average cost.
T or **F**   If false: _____

_____

_____

2.   When a competitive market is in long-run equilibrium, the firms will be making economic profits but not normal profits.
T or **F**   If false: _____

_____

_____

3.   The provision of private goods is an example of a market failure.
T or **F**   If false: _____

_____

_____

4.   Long-run equilibrium in competitive markets implies that P = MC = AC.
T or **F**   If false: _____

_____

_____

5.   By non-excludability, economists mean the inability of some firms to prevent certain people from buying a product.
T or **F**   If false: _____

_____

_____

6.   An externality is a benefit or cost experienced by people who neither produce nor consume that product.
T or **F**   If false: _____

_____

_____

7.   A subsidy granted to a polluting firm would be one way of integrating external costs.
T or **F**   If false: _____

_____

_____

8.   Marginal social benefits are the total of both marginal private benefits and marginal external benefits.
T or **F**   If false: _____

_____

_____

9.   By introducing a pollution licence fee for a lake the government allows the polluters to decide for themselves the acceptable level of pollution.
T or **F**   If false: _____

_____

_____

10. If external benefits are not integrated into the market, then insufficient quantities of a product will be produced.
T or **F**   If false: _____

_____

_____

Translations

Describe Figure W9.1, explaining what each curve means. In addition, explain the reason for, and effect of, taxing this product. Then explain the reason for, and effect of, subsidizing the product.

FIGURE W9.1

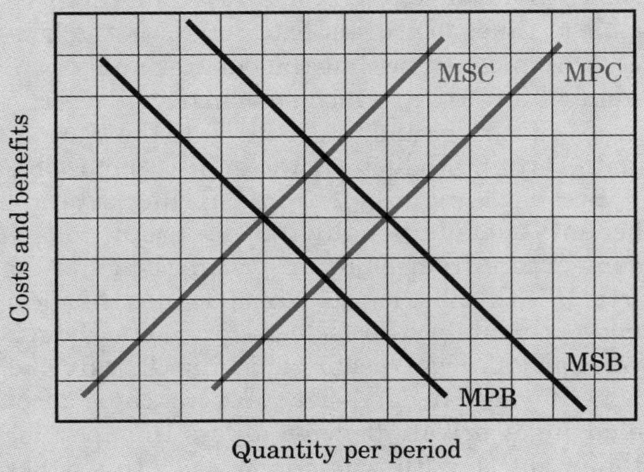

Answer

_____

_____

_____

_____

Choose the Best

1. When does allocative efficiency occur?
   a) When the price of the product is equal to its average cost.
   b) When the price of the product is equal to its marginal cost.

2. What does the doctrine of laissez-faire mean?
   a) That the government works best with limited market interference.
   b) That the market works best with limited government interference.

3. If the price of a product is less than its marginal costs, then:
   a) Society would prefer more of this product being produced.
   b) Society would prefer less of this product being produced.

4. Which of the following statements is correct regarding marginal social costs?
   a) They include only the private costs of production.
   b) They include only the external costs of production.
   c) They include both the private and the external costs of production.

5. Which of the following is an example of a public good?
   a) A prescription drug.
   b) Post-secondary education.
   c) A lighthouse.

6. What is a quasi-public good?
   a) A public good which also has many characteristics of a private good.
   b) A private good whose production involves extensive externalities so that a government feels obliged to provide it.
   c) A public good which is sold privately to individuals.

7. What does the long-run equilibrium of a perfectly competitive market suggest?
   a) That the price is equal to the lowest SRAC but not necessarily the lowest LRAC.
   b) That the price is equal to the lowest LRAC but not necessarily the lowest SRAC.
   c) That the price is equal to both the lowest SRAC and the lowest LRAC.

8. All of the following, *except one*, are features of a private good. Which is the exception?

   a) Private goods can be produced by private firms at a profit.
   b) Private goods are products which could not be produced by the government.
   c) Private goods can be consumed separately by each individual.
   d) Private goods are normally produced by private firms.

9. All of the following, *except one*, are features of a public good. Which is the exception?
   a) Public goods are products which are collectively consumed.
   b) Public goods do not usually cause external costs.
   c) Public goods are provided by the government.
   d) Public goods could not be produced by private firms at a profit.

10. What does the term market failure mean?
    a) The inability of markets to ensure that people get what they want.
    b) The inability of markets to ensure that productive or allocative efficiency is attained.
    c) The inability of the government to ensure that productive or allocative efficiency is attained.
    d) The inability of the government to ensure that people get what they want.

11. Why does the market fail to produce public goods?
    a) Because normally there is no demand for such goods.
    b) Because it is impossible for the producer to exclude non-buyers from enjoying the benefit.
    c) Because such products usually entail large spillover costs.
    d) Because their production normally leads to increased income inequality.

Table W9.1 at the top of the next page shows the ridership on a particular toll highway.

12. Refer to Table W9.1 to answer this question. If the toll is presently $1, by *how much* must the government increase the toll if it wants to reduce traffic by 50%?

TABLE W9.1

Toll Charge	Number of Vehicles per Hour
$1	4,000
2	3,000
3	2,500
4	2,200
5	2,000
6	1,800
7	1,600

a) $2.
b) $3.
c) $4.
d) $5.

13. All of the following, *except one*, are characteristics of a public good. Which is the exception?
    a) It is non-extendable.
    b) It is non-divisible.
    c) It is non-depletable.
    d) It is non-excludable.

14. All of the following, *except one*, are benefits of competitive markets. Which is the exception?
    a) Competitive markets promote personal economic freedom.
    b) Competitive markets eliminate externalities.
    c) Competitive markets are productively efficient.
    d) Competitive markets are costless to implement.
    e) Competitive markets are allocatively efficient.

15. All of the following, *except one*, are examples of market failures. Which is the exception?
    a) Competitive markets do not guarantee an equitable distribution of incomes and wealth.
    b) Competitive markets do not guarantee that the economy will be stable.
    c) Competitive markets do not guarantee that the demand for all products is met.
    d) Competitive markets do not guarantee that individuals get the type of jobs they would like.
    e) Competitive markets do not take externalities into consideration.

Refer to Figure W9.2 to answer questions 16 and 17.

FIGURE W9.2

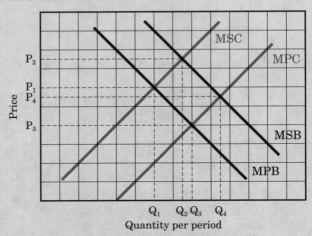

16. Refer to Figure W9.2 to answer this question. Which of the following statements is correct regarding an unregulated competitive market?
    a) It would underproduce by producing quantity Q_1.
    b) It would underproduce by producing quantity Q_2.
    c) It would overproduce by producing quantity Q_2.
    d) It would overproduce by producing quantity Q_3.
    e) It would underproduce by producing quantity Q_4.

17. Refer to Figure W9.2 to answer this question. Which of the following statements is correct regarding an unregulated competitive market?
    a) Its price of P_1 would be lower than a price which included all externalities.
    b) Its price of P_1 would be higher than a price which included all externalities.
    c) Its price of P_2 would be higher than a price which included all externalities.
    d) Its price of P_3 would be lower than a price which included all externalities.
    e) Its price of P_4 would be lower than a price which included all externalities.

Figure W9.3 shows the demand and supply of a product in a competitive market.

FIGURE W9.3

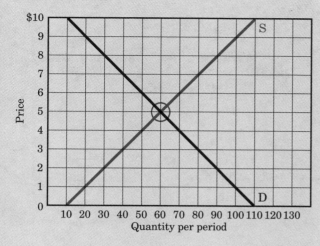

18. Refer to Figure W9.3 to answer the question. Suppose that this graph represents a polluting industry and the government wishes to decrease its output by 10 units. Which of the following will produce this result?
    a) The imposition of an excise tax of $2.
    b) The imposition of an excise tax of $1.
    c) The granting of a subsidy of $2 to producers.
    d) The granting of a subsidy of $1 to producers.
    e) The granting of a subsidy of $2 to consumers.

19. Refer to Figure W9.3 to answer the question. Suppose that this graph represents an industry with big external benefits and the government wishes to increase its output by 10 units and lower its price. Which of the following will produce this result?
    a) The imposition of an excise tax of $2.
    b) The imposition of an excise tax of $1.
    c) The granting of a subsidy of $2 to producers.
    d) The granting of a subsidy of $1 to producers.
    e) The granting of a subsidy of $2 to consumers.

20. Refer to Figure W9.3 to answer the question. Suppose that this graph represents an industry with big external benefits and the government wishes to increase its output by 10 units and raise its price. Which of the following will produce this result?
    a) The imposition of an excise tax of $2.
    b) The imposition of an excise tax of $1.
    c) The granting of a subsidy of $2 to producers.
    d) The granting of a subsidy of $1 to producers.
    e) The granting of a subsidy of $2 to consumers.

What's Wrong?

Can you spot the four errors in the following passage? (Ignore grammatical mistakes!)

The major problem with external costs is the fact that they result in the overproduction of certain products. It also means that the price is higher than it should be from society's point of view. If we add the external costs to the private costs of production we derive what are called the marginal social costs. One way of ensuring that these external costs are integrated is for the government to give a subsidy to a firm so as to encourage it to produce less. Alternatively, the government could introduce a market for pollution rights. With this method, the firm would be allowed to pollute as much as it wished as long as it is willing to pay for it. Finally, a government could, itself, take over the firm or industry itself by privatizing it.

Key Problem

The airport in Nearvana is privately owned, and services many different types of aircraft and airlines, for which it charges landing and take off fees. Over the years, the demand for the use of the runway has increased and so have the fees. The airport owners have categorized the users into two major groups, the "commercials" (which includes international and major domestic airlines offering scheduled flights), and the "privates" (which includes the charter airlines as well as personal plane owners). The airport is presently operating from 8 a.m. to 8 p.m. and has a capacity of 20 landings/takeoff time slots per hour. It has estimated the demands for the two groups as shown in Table W9.2.

TABLE W9.2

Airport Landing Fee	Commercials: Quantity Demanded per Day	Privates: Quantity Demanded per Day	Total Both Groups: Quantity Demanded per Day
$ 100	800	600	_____
200	620	420	_____
300	500	300	_____
400	400	200	_____
500	350	120	_____
600	320	70	_____
700	290	60	_____
800	260	50	_____
900	230	45	_____
1,000	200	40	_____
1,100	190	35	_____
1,200	180	30	_____
1,300	175	25	_____

a) Complete the table above. What is the airport's present fee and how many time slots are being purchased by each group?

Fee: $_____;

Number of time slots: Commercial users: _____;

Private users: _____.

Because of protests from the private users, and in order to generate extra revenue, the airport authorities have decided to open 24 hours a day. Since the nighttime demand is considerably less than daytime demand (in fact, a survey suggests that the nighttime demand by commercials is only 20% of its daytime demand, whereas, for privates it is 80%), the airport has decided to charge a lower fee for the 8 p.m.–8 a.m. user.

b) Complete the nighttime demand in Table W9.3 below.

TABLE W9.3

Airport Landing Fee	Commercials: Quantity Demanded per Night	Privates: Quantity Demanded per Night	Total Both Groups: Quantity Demanded per Night
$ 100	_____	_____	_____
200	_____	_____	_____
300	_____	_____	_____
400	_____	_____	_____
500	_____	_____	_____

TABLE W9.3 *(continued)*

Airport Landing Fee	Commercials: Quantity Demanded per Night	Privates: Quantity Demanded per Night	Total Both Groups: Quantity Demanded per Night
600	_____	_____	_____
700	_____	_____	_____
800	_____	_____	_____
900	_____	_____	_____
1,000	_____	_____	_____
1,100	_____	_____	_____
1,200	_____	_____	_____
1,300	_____	_____	_____

c)   In Figure W9.4, graph the total nighttime demand and supply. (The latter is the same 240 time slots as in the daytime.)

FIGURE W9.4

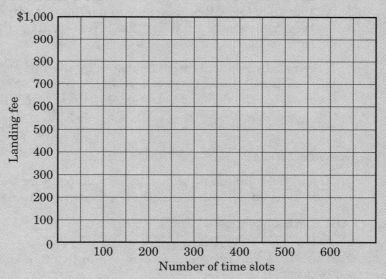

d)   What will the airport's new nighttime fee be and how many time slots are being purchased by each group?

Fee: $ _____;

Number of time slots: Commercial users: _____;

Private users: _____.

Soon after the inauguration of the nighttime flights, local residents become increasingly vocal in showing their displeasure with the external cost of noise which they are forced to endure. Their lobbying of the Nearvana government is successful and so the government decides to impose a $100 tax on all nighttime landings and take-offs, the tax to be incorporated into the airport fee.

e) Show the effect of the tax in Figure W9.4 above. What will be the immediate impact on the landing fee?

After-tax fee: $_____.

f) Will there be a surplus or a shortage as a result? _____.

g) What will eventually happen to the price? _____.

h) Who will eventually pay the landing tax? _____.

Noting the effects of this tax, a newly elected government in Nearvana decides to repeal it and instead impose a price floor on the nighttime flight with the aim of reducing usage by 50%.

i) What should the price floor be to achieve this reduction and what will be the resulting surplus or shortage of landing opportunities as a result?

Price floor: $_____; surplus/shortage: _____ of quantity: _____.

The following year sees another new government come to power in Nearvana (an annual occurrence) which is committed to finding a market solution for the airport problem. It decides to dismantle the price floor and instead announces to all interested parties, including local residents, community groups and the noise-abatement society that they too will now be able to purchase landing fees. Once they have paid the fee they will own the time slot that it represents and can therefore prevent any airline from using it.

j) If the nearby residents wish to ensure totally flightless nights for themselves, how much will it cost them to buy all the time slots? (To keep things simple, assume that the demand is the same as in Figure W9.4).

Total cost of time slots: $_____.

Need a Hand?

a) To find the total quantity demanded, add together the quantities of the commercial users, column 2, and that of the private users, column 3.

TABLE W9.4 (completed Table W9.2)

Airport Landing Fee	Commercials: Quantity Demanded per Day	Privates: Quantity Demanded per Day	Total Both Groups: Quantity Demanded per Day
$ 100	800	600	1,400
200	620	420	1,040
300	500	300	800
400	400	200	600
500	350	120	470
600	320	70	390
700	290	60	350
800	260	50	310
900	230	45	275
1,000	200	40	240
1,100	190	35	225
1,200	180	30	210
1,300	175	25	200

Since there are only 20 time slots per hour, and the airport is operating for 12 hours, the supply of time slots is a fixed 240 (12 × 20) per day. Equilibrium therefore occurs where the quantity demanded is also 240 and this is at a fee of **$1,000**. At this fee, column 2 tells us that the quantity demanded is **200 by the commercials** and **40 by the privates**.

b) To find out the nighttime demand of the commercials, we need to multiply column 2 in the last table by 1/5 (20%). To find the demand for the privates we multiply column 3 of the last table by 4/5 (80%). As before, we add together the quantities demanded by the commercials and by the privates to get column 4 in Table W9.5.

Since the number of nighttime hours is the same as the daytime hours, then the number of night time slots is the same 240. This is a fixed amount and therefore plots as a perfectly inelastic supply curve as shown in Figure W9.5.

TABLE W9.5 (completed Table W9.3)

Airport Landing Fee	Commercials: Quantity Demanded per Night	Privates: Quantity Demanded per Night	Total Both Groups: Quantity Demanded per Night
$ 100	160	480	640
200	124	336	460
300	100	240	340
400	80	160	240
500	70	96	166
600	64	56	120
700	58	48	106
800	52	40	92
900	46	36	82
1,000	40	32	72
1,100	38	28	66
1,200	36	24	60
1,300	35	20	55

c)   **FIGURE W9.5** (completed Figure W9.4)

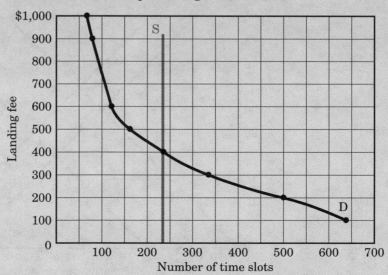

d) Equilibrium is where the supply of 240 is equal to the quantity demanded. This occurs at a fee of **$400**. Checking with the graph or the table, we see that at this fee, the quantity demanded by the **commercials is 80**, and by the **privates is 160**.

e) In general, a tax imposed on a product is shown as a decrease in the supply, i.e., a leftward shift in the supply curve (it doesn't affect the demand curve). But here we have a vertical supply curve and a shift in it in essence shifts the curve up on itself at the same output level. In other words, there will still be 240 time slots available whatever the price and whatever the tax. However, the landing fee will initially increase by $100 from $400 up to **$500**.

f) $500 is not an equilibrium price since, at this price, the quantity demanded (166) is less than the quantity supplied, which means there is a **surplus** of 74 time slots.

g) As a result, the airport authorities will be forced to **reduce the price until it returns to $400**.

h) **The airport authorities** will end up paying the whole tax themselves, since the fee returns to its previous $400, but the airport will have to send $100 of this to the tax department.

i) The new government wishes to effect a 50% reduction in nighttime usage. It therefore wants to reduce the quantity demanded from 240 to 120. A glance back at Table W9.5 shows that a quantity demanded of 120 will occur at a price of **$600**. This, therefore, should be the amount of the government's price floor. At this price the constant supply of 240 exceeds the quantity demanded. The **surplus** is equal to the difference of **120**.

j) In order for the nearby residents to get totally flightless nights they will have to purchase all 240 time slots at the equilibrium price of $400 each. The total cost, therefore, is 240 × $400 or **$96,000** per night.

Other Problems

1. Figure W9.6 shows the demand and supply of a certain product.

FIGURE W9.6

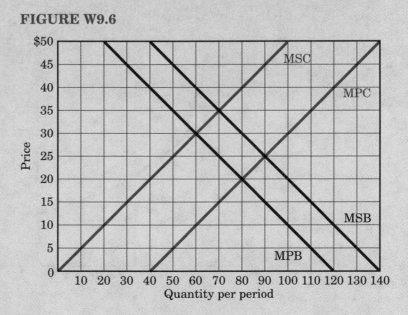

a) In an unregulated market, what would be the equilibrium price and quantity?

Price: $_____; quantity: _____.

b) If this product were taxed an amount equal to the external costs, what would be the equilibrium price and quantity?

Price: $_____; quantity: _____.

c) Alternatively, if this product were subsidized an amount equal to the external benefits, what would be the equilibrium price and quantity?

Price: $_____; quantity: _____.

d) Finally, if this product were both taxed and subsidized an amount equal to the external costs and benefits, what would be the equilibrium price and quantity?

Price: $_____; quantity: _____.

2. Figure W9.7 shows the daily demand for entry into the downtown core of a major city by commuter vehicles and by shoppers' vehicles in terms of how much they would be willing to pay by way of a traffic tax.

FIGURE W9.7

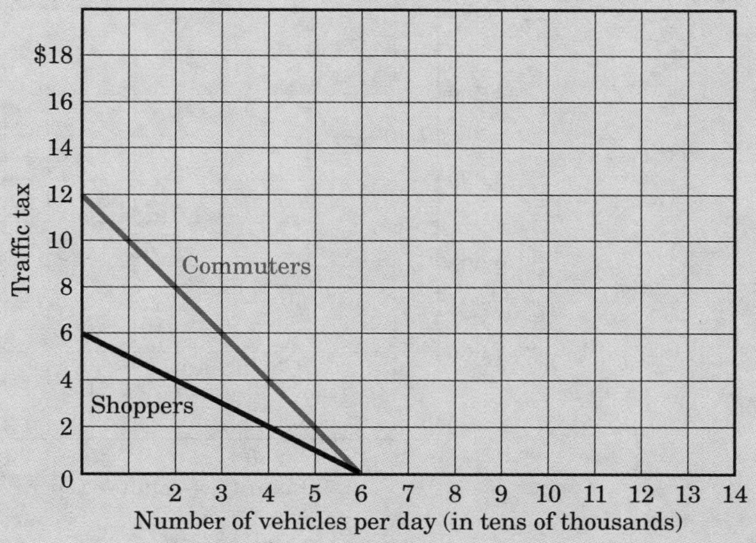

a) Draw the total demand curve. Assuming that there is no charge for entry, what is the total quantity of vehicles entering the downtown?

Number of vehicles: _____

b) Suppose that the government, in an effort to reduce the number of vehicles by 50%, decides to charge a traffic tax (the same tax for both commuters and shoppers) for entry into the downtown area . What will be the amount of the tax, and how many of each group will enter the downtown?

Tax: $_____; number of commuter vehicles: _____;

number of shoppers' vehicles: _____.

c) Assume that the government, alternatively, decides to have a two-tax system but still wishes to reduce the traffic by 50% of the no-fee entry level. If it decides to charge shoppers $3, how much will it have to charge commuters?

Commuter tax: $_____.

3. Table W9.6 shows the demand for pollution rights to emit hydrocarbons in a particular industrial park.

TABLE W9.6

Price per Pollution Right	Quantity of Pollution (tons)
$4,500	100
4,000	200
3,500	300
3,000	400
2,500	500
2,000	600
1,500	700

On Figure W9.8, draw the demand curve for pollution rights and label it D_1.

FIGURE W9.8

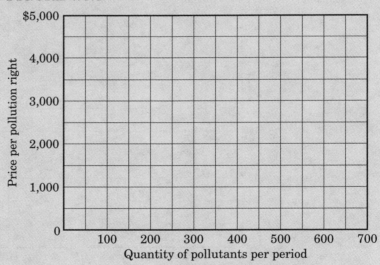

a) If no fee for a pollution right were charged, what quantity of pollutants would be discharged into the atmosphere, assuming a straight-line demand curve?

_____ tons.

b) Suppose the government were to set a fee of $3,000 per pollution right. Show this fee on your graph. What quantity of pollutants would now be dumped? What is the total revenue received by the government?

_____ tons   Government revenue: $_____.

c) Suppose that a new technology allows for a significant reduction in hydro-carbons at a relatively low cost so that the demand for pollution rights in the industrial park were to drop by 200 tons. Show the new demand on your graph, labelled D2. Assuming that the government holds the pollution fee at $3,000, what quantity of pollutants would now be dumped and what would be the total revenue received by the government?

_____ tons   Government revenue: $_____.

d) After the change in demand in c), what would happen if instead of maintaining the fee of $3,000, the government wants to maintain the same level of pollutants as in b). What fee would it have to charge, and what would be its new revenue?

Fee: $_____   Government revenue: $_____.

Unanswered Questions

Short Essays

1. Distinguish between allocative efficiency and productive efficiency.

2. Explain why competitive markets ensure that, in the long-run, prices and outputs are both productively and allocatively efficient.

3. What are the main benefits of a competitive market economy?

4. What is meant by the term market failure? Give examples of four such failures.

5. Explain the main differences between public goods and private goods.

6. If the production of a certain good involves extensive external costs, explain what methods could be used to reduce such costs.

7. If the production of a certain good involves extensive external benefits, explain what methods could be used to encourage its production.

Analytical Questions

1. Although market failures can be addressed in many cases by market solutions, it still requires the government to introduce such solutions. Discuss this statement.

2. In what ways are competitive markets part of the problem of income and wealth inequalities, and in what ways are they part of the solution?

3. The elasticity of demand for private long-term care facilities in Hither is far greater than it is in Yon. In which country will a sub-

sidy given to prospective patients have more impact on the amount of spaces available?

4. In order for an industry to achieve productive and allocative efficiency, three conditions must be fulfilled: a) the firms must be producing at capacity; b) the firms must be producing out of plants of minimum efficient scale; c) the firms must be making only normal profits. Explain, using a graph.

Numerical Questions

1. Table W9.7 shows the market for private long-term care facilities in Hither and in Yon.

TABLE W9.7

Monthly Fee	Quantity of Spaces Demanded: Hither and Yon	Quantity of Spaces Supplied: Hither	Quantity of Spaces Supplied: Yon
$1,000	2,000	500	0
1,200	1,800	600	200
1,400	1,600	700	400
1,600	1,400	800	600
1,800	1,200	900	800
2,000	1,000	1,000	1,000
2,200	800	1,100	1,200
2,400	600	1,200	1,400
2,600	400	1,300	1,600

a) Graph the demand and supply in each country. What is the present equilibrium fee and number of available spaces used in each country?

b) If the demand were to increase by 300 in each country, what would be the new equilibrium fees and quantity in each country?

What explains the different effects in the two countries?

c) From the initial situation in a), suppose that the governments in each country wished to increase the quantity of spaces available in long-term care facilities by 200. They have decided to give subsidies to long-term care residents to encourage this increase. How much subsidy must they give in each country? Explain the difference in the two countries.

2. Given the data for long-term care spaces in Hither and Yon as shown in Table W9.7 (from question 1), suppose that the government wished to increase the number of spaces available by 200. What subsidy would have to be paid to the long-term care operators in each country to produce such an increase?

3. Figure W9.9 shows the market for polio vaccinations in Nania. The present equilibrium price is $16 per vaccination and the quantity (in thousands of vaccinations) is 60.

FIGURE W9.9

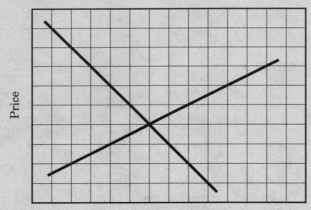

Quantity per period

If the marginal external benefit is estimated at an additional $12 per vaccination, what is the optimal price and quantity from society's point of view?

4. The government of Nearvana has decided to sell pollution rights to discharge pollutants into its largest freshwater lake. Each right is a right to discharge one ton of pollutants. It has determined that the lake will support a maximum of 40 tons of pollutants per year and has decided to sell the rights using a Dutch auction. This means that the auction starts at a very high price which is successively reduced until the price reaches a level which will result in all 40 tons of pollution rights being sold. The results of the bidding are shown in Table W9.8.

a) What will the price of pollution rights be as a result of this auction?

b) Suppose that bidder E happened to be an environmentalist group. If this group had not participated in the auction, what would the price of pollution rights have been, and what difference would there have been in the amount of pollutants discharged into the lake?

TABLE W9.8

Price Per Pollution Right	Bidder A	Bidder B	Bidder C	Bidder D	Bidder E
$6,000	2				
5,500	4	6			
5,000	6	6	1	1	1
4,500	8	7	2	2	2
4,000	10	7	4	3	3
3,500	12	9	6	3	4
3,000	14	10	8	3	5
2,500	16	11	9	4	6
2,000	18	12	10	4	7

CHAPTER TEN

■ ■ ■ ■ ■ ■ ■

Monopoly

W hat's ahead . . . The chapter looks at what is meant by monopoly and what conditions lead to their creation. We focus on how a monopoly goes about determining the price and output which will ensure the greatest profit. We next compare a monopoly market and a perfectly competitive market to find out which is better and why. In doing this, we also mention some of the social costs and benefits that may result from monopolies. Finally, the chapter looks at various ways in which governments have tried to deal with monopolies either through taxation, price setting or outright government purchase.

monopoly: a market in which a single firm (the monopolist) is the sole producer.

From the competitive world of the last two chapters we now turn to look at its opposite: **monopoly**. A firm is a monopolist if it is the sole producer of a product for which there are no close substitutes. The firm more than dominates the industry; the firm *is* the industry. There is no competition for the monopolist, which leaves it in a very powerful position. The study of monopoly then is a study in power. People have always been suspicious of monopolies because of the distinct possibility that the monopolist might use its power to exploit its customers, suppliers and employees. While self-interest might not lead to exploitation in competitive markets, because competition itself provides a check and balance on the behaviour of competitors, this constraint is largely absent in monopoly markets.

In a market economy, the private ownership of resources allows a degree of freedom to their owners and gives them licence to exercise very wide discretion, without public input, in the use of those resources. After all, as members of the public we do not get to vote for the presidents and executives of firms. However most people do not feel disenfranchised because of this since they can at least vote with their money. We cast votes for the products we like when we buy them. If we do not like a certain product, the "democracy of the marketplace" will mean that the product will not be successful. In addition, we do not feel uncomfortable by the lack of accountability since most firms represent such a small portion of the industry or the whole economy that any damage they might do is limited. However, none of this is true with monopolies which replace the democracy of the competitive market with the despotism of the sole producer. As a result of this, most countries including Canada, have acted to curtail the power of monopolies in various ways which we will look at later in the chapter.

Identifying what is, and what is not, a monopoly may not be quite as straight-forward as it sounds. Certainly the monopolist is the sole producer of a product in the market. But what is a product? What is the market? And if there are no close substitutes, what exactly is a substitute, and how close is close? For instance, we need to drink to stay alive and there are certainly no substitutes for drinkable liquids. Drinkable liquids, however, is a product group, not a product. Pop is a subgroup of drinkable liquids and colas is a subgroup of pop. And Pepsi is just one type of cola. As we saw when we looked at elasticity of demand in Chapter 4, the wider you define the product, the more inelastic will be the demand. The demand for colas in general will be more inelastic than the demand for any particular brand of cola. (Whether a product has close substitutes or not can be measured in terms of the cross-elasticity of demand for that product.) In general we can say that the demand for the monopoly's product will tend to be fairly inelastic. As for the definition of the market, if a particular small town has only one gas station and the next town is 50 miles away, to all intents and purposes, that gas station is a monopolist. But of course in the whole of the province or the country, that gas station is one of thousands or tens of thousands of gas stations. The wider the market, in the sense of accessibility for consumers, the less likely a single firm will be able to dominate. With easier and cheaper transport and communications these days we are able to buy from firms around the world, which means that a Canadian monopolist has to compete with foreign firms. Its power in the domestic market, therefore, is considerably reduced.

Nonetheless, given the above cautions, most people would agree that Manitoba Hydro, Rogers Cablevision and the Montreal Subway System are examples of monopolies.

Barriers to Entry

barriers to entry: obstacles which make it difficult for new participants to enter a market.

How do monopolies come into existence in the first place and how are they able to keep out-competing firms? The answer lies in the concept of **barriers to entry** which shelter the monopoly from new competitors in the market. There are a number of different barriers that we will categorize under three headings: *technical barriers, legal barriers, and economic barriers.*

Technical barriers are those that make it difficult for other firms to duplicate a monopolist's production methods because the monopolist is the sole owner of a resource or technique. For instance, the International Nickel Company (INCO) once controlled most of the world's supply of nickel, the De Beers Company of Kimberly, South Africa owns or controls the majority of the world's diamond mines. Sole ownership of a resource confers a monopoly status on the producer. Similarly, a firm is a monopolist if it is the sole owner of the technical knowledge necessary to produce the product. IBM, for instance, had a monopoly on computer expertise for many years before other companies caught up.

Legal barriers prevent, by force of law, other firms from competing in a particular industry. In certain instances this is designed to grant a monopoly to the production of a good or service as is the case with many crown corporations in Canada such as Canada Post or provincial government liquor boards. Other types of legal restriction are designed to give protection from competition for private firms and may take the form of a government licence (to fish commercially for salmon for example) or of a patent or copyright where the originator of the idea is given a monopoly for a number of years.

Data

Economic barriers are present whenever there are extensive start-up costs for new firms. It is difficult to compete internationally with the major automobile firms unless you are ready to invest billions of dollars. It should be noted that this investment needs to encompass not only the fixed costs of the factory buildings and assembly line but also the cost of a distribution network and marketing plan, and sufficient funds to hire the highly paid design engineers and executives who are able to put all this together. The bigger this initial investment, the more difficult it is for new entrants to join the industry. Automobile firms tend to be large because of extensive economies of scale, which allows big firms to produce at much lower unit costs than small firms. The existence of the huge corporations and international conglomerates that we see these days is the result, in many cases, of the drive for higher profits through growth. Sometimes the growth has been "organic," but more often than not, it has been the result of mergers and acquisitions.

natural monopoly: a market (usually with large economies of scale) where a single producer is able to produce at a lower cost than competing firms could.

In some industries, in order to make a profit, the firm will need to be very big to obtain economies of scale. The required size may be so big that the market can only support a single firm. Monopolies which come into existence in markets where *competing firms simply would not be profitable* are known as **natural monopolies**. This situation is illustrated in Figure 10.1 on the next page.

Suppose the graph illustrates the demand and costs for an urban rail system in a particular city. Because of the very high costs of the railbed and all the rolling stock, the system needs to operate with at least 100,000 users

FIGURE 10.1 Natural Monopoly

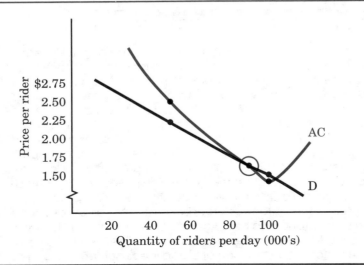

The graph shows that extensive economies of scale result in the break-even level of ridership occurring at 90,000 riders. If the rail fare is set at $1.50, then the quantity demanded will be 100,000 and a single transit company could make a profit since, at this level of ridership, the average cost is approximately $1.40. If the market were shared between two different rail companies, each serving, say, 50,000 riders, then the average cost would be $2.50 — well above a $1.50 fare. This would result in both companies experiencing losses.

a day in order to reduce the average cost enough for the system to be profitable. With 100,000 users it can charge a price of $1.50 per ride and since this is above the average cost of $1.40, the system will be profitable. However, given the size of this particular market, it would be impossible for it to support two competing systems. If each system had a ridership of 50,000, the average costs would be $2.50 per ride, well above the $1.50 that the 100,000 users would be prepared to pay. Because two firms could not make a profit in this market, we have a natural monopoly. Natural monopolies occur whenever start-up costs in an industry are so high that the market can only support one profitable firm. A small city in Canada simply could not support more than one competing urban rail system whereas Tokyo possesses a number of competing rail companies, some privately and one publicly owned. In most small urban markets (and in a number of large ones) such industries as water, electric and natural gas supply, urban bus and rail transportation, and telecommunications tend to be natural monopolies. Since they are also extremely important to a community, they may become publicly owned and are often referred to as **public utilities**. How best to regulate public monopolies is a problem of government policy, a topic we will take up in Chapter 14. The main focus of this chapter will be on the operation and control of privately owned monopolies.

public utilities: goods or services which are regarded as essential and which therefore are usually provided by the government.

QUESTION 10.1

In Figure 10.1, suppose there are two competing rail companies, each capturing 50% of the market. What would happen if they both charged a fare of $1.50? What would be the total profit or loss of each firm?

Total, Average and Marginal Revenues

The sole producer of a product is in a very powerful position. That does not mean, however, that it has unlimited power over the market. To a certain extent, the consumer is still sovereign and makes the ultimate decision of whether or not that product will be bought. Nonetheless, the monopolist, unlike the competitive producer, is a *price maker* rather than a *price taker*, which means that it is able to set the price at whatever level it chooses rather than having to accept the market-determined price. Even so, consumers will decide how much they will buy at that price. Alternatively, the monopolist could determine the size of production and leave it to the market to determine the price at which that output can be sold. Therefore, the monopolist can determine either the price *or* the quantity sold; what it cannot do is to determine *both* the price and quantity sold.

All this can be expressed another way: since the monopolist and the industry are one and the same, it faces the market demand for the product, and that demand is represented by a downward-sloping demand curve. From the consumers' point of view this means that if the price drops, they will buy more. From the monopolist's perspective, it means that in order to sell more, the monopolist must lower the price. A monopolist cannot sell all it wants at any given price; it is forced to decrease the price in order to sell more. This has important implications in terms of the monopolist's revenues.

Suppose that, through mergers and acquisitions, a monopoly brewer emerged in Canada calling itself Beavertail Brewers. The first two columns of Table 10.1 shows the quantities (in, say, hundreds of thousands of cases per day) that would be sold at various prices of Beavertail Beer, i.e., this is the demand for Beavertail Beer.

TABLE 10.1 Total, Average and Marginal Revenues of the Monopolist

Quantity (000,000)	Price (per case)	Total Revenue (TR)	Average Revenue (AR)	Marginal Revenue (MR)
5	$20	$100	$20	—
6	19	114	19	$14
7	18	126	18	12
8	17	136	17	10
9	16	144	16	8
10	15	150	15	6
11	14	154	14	4
12	13	156	13	2
13	12	156	12	0
14	11	154	11	–2

The terms total, average and marginal revenues were introduced in Chapter 8. Note that, as with the competitive firm, the average revenue is the same thing as the price. Notice also that the total revenue increases with quantity sold but only up to a point, that point being a quantity of 12. If Beavertail wishes to increase the number of cases sold to 13, it must drop the price to $12; it will have no effect, however, on the total revenue. The company's total revenue will remain at $156. And should the monopolist wish to increase output and sales to 14, then the price will have to come down to $11 with the result that total revenue will start to fall. Unlike a competitive firm then, the monopolist is faced with a maximum sales revenue.

Table 10.1 also shows that for the monopolist the marginal revenue is not equal to the average revenue. The extra (marginal) sales revenue that the monopolist receives for selling one more unit is not equal to the price. The reason for this is that when the monopolist sells one more unit it *gains revenue* equal to the price at which it sells that unit, but *it loses revenue* because it is forced to drop the price not only on the additional unit sold but on *every* unit it sells. Suppose for instance that the brewery is presently selling 9 (hundred thousand cases per week) beer at a price of $16 per case for a total revenue of $144. If it reduces the price to $15, it will be able to sell one more unit and will therefore gain revenue equal to $1 \times \$15 = \$15$. However, it will lose revenue because it is dropping the price by $1 on the previous 9 it was selling, i.e., it will lose revenue equal to $\$1 \times 9$ units $= \$9$. It gains $15 but loses $9, so that its net gain is only $6, which is its marginal revenue. Because the demand curve is downward-sloping, the extra amount of revenue the monopolist gains from an additional sale will always be less than the price. *In summary, in order to increase its sales, a monopolist is forced to reduce its price not just on the last units sold, but on the whole of its output.* These points are illustrated in Figure 10.2.

FIGURE 10.2 Total, Average and Marginal Revenues

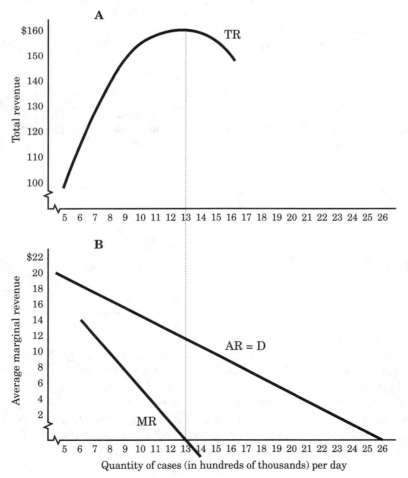

Up to a point, the total revenue of the monopolist increases as more units are sold. However, the rate of increase (i.e., the slope of the TR curve) declines throughout. The total revenue reaches a maximum at an output of 12. The 13th unit adds no additional revenue so that the total revenue remains the same. After that, as more units are sold, the total revenue starts to decline.

The average revenue received by the firm is the same thing as the price, since all units are sold at the same price. The average revenue curve is identical to the demand curve, which means that additional units can only be sold if the price is lowered. The marginal revenue represents the additional revenue derived from selling more units. In this graph, the price must drop by $1 in order to increase sales by one unit, i.e., the slope has a value of 1. (Note also that the MR curve drops twice as steeply as the AR curve so that it intersects the horizontal axis at exactly half the distance between the origin and the AR curve).

Quantity of cases (in hundreds of thousands) per day

Up to an output of 12, the total revenue curve is upward-sloping but the slope gets smaller and smaller with increasing output. The slope measures the rate at which total revenue changes, which is the same thing as the marginal revenue. In other words, as the bottom graph shows, the marginal revenue decreases as the output increases. Notice that the total revenue curve rises to a maximum at an output of 12 (and 13), and thereafter declines. On the bottom graph note that the average revenue curve is the same thing as the demand curve. The marginal revenue curve is consistently below the average revenue curve and is twice as steep; every time the average revenue (price) drops by $1, the marginal revenue drops by $2. As long as the marginal revenue is positive, even though it is falling, then total revenue must be increasing. When it becomes negative, after an output of 13, the total revenue must be falling. Total revenue must be at a maximum, then, when the marginal revenue is neither positive nor negative, i.e., when it is zero.

This monopolist will never produce an output greater than 13 units since a higher output will increase the total costs but will lower total revenue. Graphically in Figure 10.2 this means that the monopolist will produce an output of less than 13 or, in other words, on the upper portion of the demand curve. *Since the top portion of any demand curve is elastic it means that this monopolist, and all monopolists, will produce only where the demand is elastic.* However, to analyze the behaviour of monopolists a bit more thoroughly, we need to know exactly at what output a monopolist will produce. To do this we need to know not only the revenue but also the costs and therefore profitability of the monopolist.

QUESTION 10.2

Suppose a monopolist was charging a price of $50 for his product and was selling 1,500 units. He has now lowered his price to $45 and is selling 1,700 units. What is his marginal revenue? What is the price elasticity of demand over this price range?

BOX 10.2

One of the interesting aspects of monopoly and of other forms of imperfect competition is the fact that, in order to increase sales, a firm is forced to drop the price of its products. And it must normally drop the price, not just on additional units sold, but on the whole of its output. The way of avoiding this, as we saw in Chapter 5, is by practising price discrimination. If the monopolist, for example, could somehow divide up and segregate the market so that it could charge every single customer the maximum price that each is prepared to pay, it would be practising perfect price discrimination. In practice, such perfection is impossible. However, any method which allows the firm to charge different prices to different groups *for reasons not associated with costs* will generate a higher sales revenue for the firm. As a result, both its output and its profits will be greater.

BOX 10.2 *(continued)*

The practice of price discrimination requires not only that the seller is able to identify and separate groups which have different elasticities of demand, but also that there be no possibility of resale of the product in question. There are numerous examples of price discrimination practised by monopoly and other imperfectly competitive firms. Telephone and air-line companies both realize that business people generally have a more inelastic demand for their services than do more casual users. As a result, telephone rates are generally higher during business hours on weekdays than at "off-peak" periods. Similarly, airlines charge more for business-people booking last-minute who wish to travel on weekdays than for vacationers who book in advance and are willing to travel on weekends. Electricity companies also discriminate between their customers, charg-ing higher rates to day-time users whose demand is inelastic than to night-time users. In addition, they often discriminate between house-holds and corporate users, charging the former higher rates than the lat-ter since corporate users often have a choice of buying their own gen-erators if necessary, whereas this is not possible for most households.

Profit-Maximizing Output for the Monopolist

The cost structure for the monopolist is no different from that of the com-petitive producer. In the short run, it similarly enjoys the advantages of the division of labour as it produces more and later faces diminishing returns as it is constrained by the size of operations. In Table 10.2 we have added the total costs of Beavertail Breweries to the total revenue data from Table 10.1 to calculate the total profits at the various output levels.

TABLE 10.2 Calculating Total Profits of the Monopolist

Quantity (cases per day)	Price (= AR)	Total Revenue (TR)	Total Costs (TC)	Total Profit (Tπ)
5	$20	$100	$100	$ 0
6	19	114	107	7
7	18	126	112	14
8	17	136	115	21
9	16	144	119	25
10	15	150	125	25
11	14	154	134	20
12	13	156	148	8
13	12	156	167	−11
14	11	154	192	−38

Given the data in Table 10.2, the profit-maximizing output for Beavertail is either an output of 9 or 10. (For technical reasons we will explain in a moment the "correct" answer is an output of 10.) The price at this output level would be $15 per case, which will give the monopolist a total profit of $25. These points are shown on the graph in Figure 10.3.

Break-even outputs are at 5 and between 12 and 13. The maximum profit point is at an output level of 10 where the distance between the two total

FIGURE 10.3 Total Costs, Revenues and Profits for the Monopolist

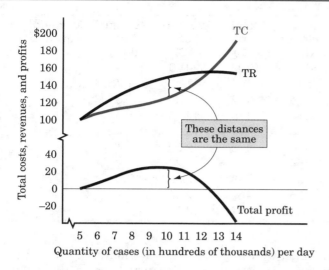

Break-even occurs where the TR and TC curves intersect, i.e., at outputs of 5 and approximately 12 1/2. Between those two outputs, TR is greater than TC and therefore any output will be profitable. Maximum profits occur at outputs of 9 and 10. At these outputs, the distance between the two curves is greatest. The total profit curve shows explicitly the amount of economic profit at each output and confirms these statements.

curves is at its greatest. Additionally, the maximum profit point is shown explicitly on the total profit curve where it occurs at the highest point.

QUESTION 10.3

Complete the following table for a monopolist, indicating the break-even outputs and the profit-maximizing output:

Quantity	Price (= AR)	Total Revenue (TR)	Total Costs (TC)	Total Profit (TΠ)
20	$100	2000	$2,060	-60
21	98	2058	2,080	-22
22	96	2112	2,112	0
23	94	2162	2,142	20
24	92	2208	2,177	31
25	90	2250	2,216	34
26	88	2280	2,257	23
27	86	2322	2,322	0
28	84	2352	2,417	-65
29	82	2378	2,530	-152

Now we need to look at things using the perspective of the average and marginal revenues and costs. This view is not quite so straightforward but it does reveal some interesting aspects. Table 10.3 on the next page shows the average and marginal costs for Beavertail Breweries as well as repeating the revenue data used earlier.

TABLE 10.3 Calculating Total Profits of the Monopolist Using the Marginal Approach

Quantity	Price (= AR)	Total Revenue (TR)	Total Costs (TC)	Average Cost (AC)	Marginal Cost (MC)	Marginal Revenue (MR)	Total Profit (Tπ)
5	$20	$100	$100	$20.00	—	—	$ 0
6	19	114	107	17.80	7	14	7
7	18	126	112	16.00	5	12	14
8	17	136	115	14.40	3	10	21
9	16	144	119	13.20	4	8	25
10	15	150	125	12.50	**6**	**6**	**25**
11	14	154	134	12.20	9	4	20
12	13	156	148	12.30	14	2	8
13	12	156	167	12.80	19	0	−11
14	11	154	192	13.70	25	−2	−38

The two columns on which we will concentrate are marginal cost and marginal revenue. The rule for profit maximization, which was developed in the context of perfect competition in Chapter 8, applies regardless of the type of market we are looking at. To make maximum profits (or to minimize losses) a firm should produce where the marginal revenue equals the marginal cost. Looking at those two columns confirms that profit maximization occurs at an output of 10 since at this output both the marginal revenue and marginal cost are equal to $6. (This is why we prefer to identify the output level of 10 rather than 9 as the profit-maximizing output although both produce the same total profits). The important difference between a monopoly and a perfectly competitive market is that in a monopoly market the marginal revenue is not the same thing as the price (or average revenue). Indeed, as we have seen, at an output of 10 units, the price will be $15 — far greater than the marginal revenue of $6. Figure 10.4 below plots the various average and marginal curves.

FIGURE 10.4 Average and Marginal Costs and Revenues for the Monopolist

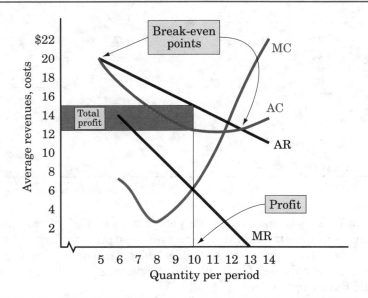

Break-even occurs where TR = TC. This must also be where AR = AC, i.e., at outputs of 5 and approximately 12 1/2. Every output between those two points is profitable. Maximum profit occurs where the MC and MR curves intersect. This is at an output of 10, where MC = MR = $6. This output would be sold at a price of $15, i.e., where the vertical line from the output of 10 meets the demand curve.

The break-even points occur where total revenue and costs are the same. This is also where the average revenue equals average costs. As we saw before, these points are at an output of 5 and between 12 and 13. At any outputs between the break-even points, the monopolist will make a profit. Profit maximization occurs where the marginal cost curve intersects the marginal revenue curve, and this is at an output of 10. At that output, the average cost of producing a case of beer is $12.50 and the selling price is $15 so that Beavertail Breweries are making an economic profit of $2.50 per case. Since they are selling 10 cases, we can confirm that the total profit is $25.

Note that, unlike a perfectly competitive industry, there is no supply and no supply curve for the monopolist. This is because there is no unique relationship between the price and the quantity. Looking at Table 10.3, you can see it doesn't make sense to ask how much this monopolist would produce at $18 since, given its cost and demand, an output level of 7 at a price of $18 is a combination that the monopolist would never choose. For each demand faced by the monopolist there is only a single price and a single quantity that is appropriate.

Study Guide

QUESTION 10.4
From Table 10.3, calculate the marginal profit at each output level and confirm that the profit-maximizing output does occur at 10.

QUESTION 10.5
Using the data below, complete the table and:
A) show that at break-even, the average revenue (= price) is equal to the average costs;
B) find the profit-maximizing output and price.

Quanity	Price	Total Revenue (TR)	Total Costs (TC)	Average Costs (AC)	Marginal Costs (MC)	Marginal Revenue (MR)
20	$100	$2,000	$2,067	103.40	-	-61
21	98	2,058	2,087	99.40	20	-21
22	96	2,112	2,112	96.00	25	0
23	94	2,162	2,142	93.13	30	10
24	92	2,208	2,177	90.70	35	31
25	90	2,250	2,216	88.64	39	34
26	88	2,288	2,257	86.80	41	31
27	86	2,322	2,322	86	55	0
28	84	2,352	2,417	86.30	95	-65
29	82	2,378	2,530	91.20	113	-162

We should mention that being a monopolist does not guarantee that profits will be made. If you return to Table 10.3, and assume that average costs were increased by $10 at every output level, you can see that no output would be profitable. This is in contrast to the fact that many people have the mistaken impression that, almost by definition, monopolists must be profitable. Though many are profitable, monopolists can and do make losses from time to time. This is illustrated in Figure 10.5.

FIGURE 10.5 Minimizing Losses for the Monopolist

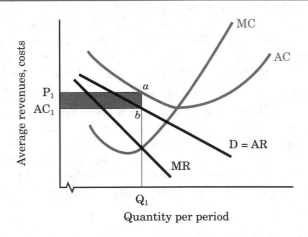

For this monopolist, its present AC curve is higher than the demand curve irrespective of what output it produces. Its best option will be to minimize its losses by producing where its marginal revenue equals its marginal costs, i.e., where the two curves intersect at a quantity of Q_1. It would charge a price of P_1 and would incur an economic loss denoted by the shaded area, P_1abAC_1.

Suppose that, as in Figure 10.5, the once profitable monopolist now faces a reduced demand for its product. The demand is so low that the demand curve is below the average cost curve at every output. Assuming that it is still able to cover its variable costs, the monopolist will still produce in the short run. Its loss-minimizing output will be where its marginal cost equals its marginal revenue. This occurs at an output of Q_1. The maximum price it can charge for this output is P_1, generating a total loss for the monopolist depicted by the shaded area, P_1abAC_1. Needless to say, this monopolist like any other firm will not be able to incur losses indefinitely. If conditions do not improve in the long run, it will be forced out of business.

What's So Bad about Monopoly?

Let's return our focus to a profitable Beavertail. If this was an example of a competitive firm we would need now to analyze what is likely to happen in the long run in response to the existence of economic profits. As we saw in Chapter 8, the effect would be to attract many new firms into the industry so that eventually economic profits would be competed away. However since this is a monopoly market, there is no competition, and because of this, *a profitable monopolist can continue to make economic profits indefinitely*.

Furthermore, the monopolist is reasonably secure, protected as it is by various barriers to entry. Of course, like any firm, monopolists might incur losses which could not be sustained indefinitely and would eventually force the monopolist out of business. However, monopoly profits do not lead to any change except to make the monopoly owners richer. Because of this the *monopolist is both productively and allocatively inefficient*.

Remember from Chapter 9, productive efficiency implies that the producer is producing the product at the lowest possible cost. This is not true for the monopolist. A glance back at Figure 10.4 shows that Beavertail Brewers, like all monopolists, will produce at less than capacity and therefore at a higher than minimum average cost. Consumers are having to pay a higher price than would be the case in a competitive industry both because the average cost is higher than it need be and also because the monopolist is making economic profits. And it is not only the consumers who lose out, but society as a whole, since the *existence of monopolies may lead to a more unequal distribution of income and wealth*. This must be so since with competitive industries, the (lower) profits are being spread among many producing firms whereas with a monopoly the (higher) profits may be concentrated in the hands of only a few owners.

In addition, Figure 10.4 shows that at the profit-maximizing output (where MC = MR), the price is above the marginal cost. This means that the monopoly is also allocatively inefficient and consumers' desire for this product at the margin, as measured by the price, is higher than its cost. In other words, consumers would prefer that more of this beer is produced and that its price be lower. Such results would be achieved in the long run *if* this market was competitive.

BOX 10A
1. Define the term *monopoly*.
2. Explain why the definition of monopoly hinges on the definitions of product and market.
3. What is meant by *barriers to entry*? What are the three types of barriers? Give examples of each.
4. What is a *natural monopoly*? Give examples.
5. Explain why the average revenue of the monopolist is not the same thing as the marginal revenue.
6. In terms of both totals and averages/marginals, define and explain how the profit-maximizing output is obtained for the monopolist.
7. Explain why monopolies are productively and allocatively inefficient.

Monopoly and Perfect Competition Contrasted

We can show the comparison between a perfectly competitive industry and a monopoly graphically. Suppose that Figure 10.6 on the next page illustrates a perfectly competitive mushroom industry which consists of 100 small mushroom growers all producing identical mushrooms. The supply curve represents the total supply of mushrooms from these growers, and the demand curve is the total market demand from millions of mushroom eaters.

The competitive price of mushrooms, as shown in Figure 10.6, is $4 per kilo and the total production is 200,00 kilos per month.

Suppose now that a monopolist were to buy out all the mushroom growers in the area. Having consolidated all the farms into one big combine, the monopolist sets out to maximize profits. How does it do this? The answer is by finding the output at which the marginal cost is equal to the marginal revenue. This will be the profit-maximizing point. Graphically, the supply curve of the perfectly competitive industry, you may remember, is synonymous with its marginal cost curve. The marginal revenue curve is reasonably straightforward to derive since the demand curve is the same thing as the average revenue curve. Given the straight-line demand curve in Figure 10.6, the marginal revenue can be drawn as a curve falling twice as steeply.

FIGURE 10.6 Monopoly and Perfect Competition Contrasted

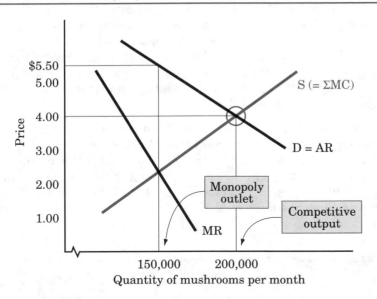

The competitive market's equilibrium occurs where the demand and supply are equal. This occurs at a price of $4, and an output of 200,000 kilos. This would be the price for each mushroom grower who would collectively produce 200,000 kilos. If, on the other hand, this were a monopoly industry, then the monopolist would produce where the MR equals MC. (The MR curve is twice as steep as the demand curve; the MC curve is the same thing as the supply curve.) The profit-maximizing output for the monopolist, then, is at an output of 150,000 kilos which could be sold at a price of $5.50 per kilo.

The intersection of the marginal cost and revenue occurs at an output of 150,000 kilos. To find out the maximum price at which this quantity could be sold, we graphically extend the output up to the demand curve which establishes that this quantity could be sold at a price of $5.50 per kilo.

In simple terms, the monopolist can make maximum profits by restricting the output, thereby pushing up the price of the product. In summary, the monopolist will make greater profits than will a competitive industry. In addition, if production costs are similar, the price will be higher and the output lower. No wonder then that governments have often interceded in the market and have often outlawed private monopolies or broken up existing ones. However, a history of anti-monopoly legislation and its enforcement in North America over the past century shows a singular lack of consistency. In certain periods, even the slightest suggestions that some firms were seeking to merge or were thought to be behaving in an uncompetitive way has been greeted by a chorus of protests and has prompted vigorous action by legislators. In other periods, trusts, monopolies and mergers have been greeted with benign indifference by governments. Why this ambivalence from governments, allowing for the fact that there may be other political considerations at work? One major explanation is that many people — and that includes economists — are not convinced that monopolies are necessarily bad. They point out that monopolies possess a number of advantages over competitive markets. So let us take a look at some of these benefits.

QUESTION 10.6

In Figure 10.6, what would be the total revenue earned by the perfectly competitive industry? What would be the total revenue earned by the monopolist industry? Then why isn't the monopolist charging the same price as the competitive industry?

QUESTION 10.7

Complete the following table of revenue and costs for an industry.

Output	Price (= AR)	Total Revenue	Marginal Revenue	Total Costs	Average Costs	Marginal Costs	Total Profit
10	$30	___	___	$258	___	___	___
11	29	___	___	268	___	___	___
12	28	___	___	280.3	___	___	___
13	27	___	___	293	___	___	___
14	26	___	___	306	___	___	___
15	25	___	___	319.5	___	___	___
16	24	___	___	334	___	___	___
17	23	___	___	350	___	___	___
18	22	___	___	368	___	___	___
19	21	___	___	389	___	___	___
20	20	___	___	414	___	___	___
21	19	___	___	444	___	___	___
22	18	___	___	482	___	___	___

A) Suppose that the data depicts a monopoly industry. What will be the monopoly price, output and profits?
B) Suppose, instead, that the data depicts a perfectly competitive industry. What will be the competitive price, output and profits? (*Hint:* Remember that the MC of an industry is the same as its supply.)
C) What general conclusions can you come to as a result of your answers?

In Defence of Monopoly

We can focus on one of the possible benefits of monopoly by returning to our illustration of the mushroom industry and the effects of its becoming monopolized. Some would argue that the conclusions made earlier are not valid since, if a competitive industry were monopolized, then the costs of production would likely change. A monopolist is unlikely to preserve one hundred separate mushroom farms, each one a replica of the others, with a duplication of many functions. More likely, the monopolist would rationalize the industry in an attempt to achieve *economies of scale*. It certainly would not require a hundred managers, a hundred accountants, a hundred crating machines and so on. As mentioned earlier, when economies of scale are so extensive in relation to the market demand, then a natural monopoly will be the result. If it is true that costs are less under monopoly, then graphically, this would mean that the whole average cost curve will be lower, resulting in a correspondingly lower price and a higher output than is shown in Figure 10.6. In fact, if costs were significantly lower, the profit-maximizing price could be lower and the output higher than under perfect competition.

A second suggested benefit of being big (and many monopolies are very big) is one that accrues to both the monopolist and to society as a whole and occurs because of *research and development*. A number of economists, including Joseph Schumpeter and John Kenneth Galbraith, have written extensively on the advantages which big firms have when it comes to research and development. Small competitive firms simply do not have the capability for extensive research and development, the scale and costs of which tend to be prohibitive. There are many examples of innovations which have been brought about by big businesses this century. As just one example, AT & T (American Telephone and Telegraph) in the United States, which at the time was a monopolist, has been given the major credit for the development of transistors and of lasers, both of which have been major technological breakthroughs. Against this, critics suggest that while big firms may have the *ability* to do research and development, they do not always have the *desire*; in fact the bigger and more dominant, the greedier and more complacent they may become. As a result, instead of using their energies and resources to improve technology, they are diverting them to creating bigger barriers to entry in an effort to keep out competition.

A final possible advantage which large corporations, like monopolies, may have over smaller firms is that they can *offer better salaries and conditions to their employees* and as a result attract a higher quality of staff. In addition, perhaps because their size makes them so conspicuous or because they have the finances to do so, big corporations often have better labour practices and are more consumer-aware than their smaller cousins.

Many observers, recognizing these benefits of monopoly, suggest that the government should take a laissez-faire attitude toward monopolies. There are, they suggest, other ways of curbing any possible excesses of the monopolist. Monopolists are not all-powerful since they will always be at the mercy of their consumers who may simply choose not to buy the product. The fear of the possible public scrutiny of their operations and the surrounding bad publicity that will accompany it often serve as a sufficient brake on any possible abuses. In addition, while the monopoly, by definition, does not have to worry about any present competition, it does have to worry about possible future competition. In other words, the barriers to entry are seldom totally insurmountable and the attraction of high profits may be a sufficient incentive to newcomers to try to overcome these barriers.

Controlling the Monopolist

In the past however, governments have seldom been persuaded that public scrutiny or the threat of competition are, by themselves, sufficient to redress the possible damage that can be caused by monopoly. They therefore feel impelled to take more direct action. We will consider three possible courses of direct action: taxation, price setting and nationalization.

What a government is often trying to do in regulating monopoly is to bring about a more competitive result. This means that, ideally, the aim of policy is to force the monopolist to reduce its price and profits, and to increase its output. As we shall see, the specific measures that are often attempted have varying degrees of success. Let's look at the first of these measures: the taxation of the monopolist.

FIGURE 10.7 Profit Tax Levied on a Monopolist

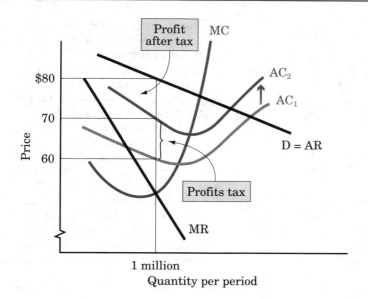

Before the imposition of the profits tax, the monopolist was maximizing its profits where MC = MR, producing an output of 1 million units at a selling price of $80. The effect of a fixed tax of $10 million will be to increase the average costs of the monopolist which increases from $60 to $70 at the 1 million level of output. However, this tax has no effect on the MC. As a result, the monopolist will continue to produce 1 million units at a price of $80. However, its profits will decline by the $10 million tax.

Taxing the Monopolist

There are two major types of tax that could be levied on the monopolist: a profits tax and a monopoly sales tax. We will look at both. Suppose, for instance, as in Figure 10.7, the government allows the monopoly to exist and to control its own affairs in return for the payment of an annual lump-sum profits tax of $10 million. What effect will this have on the monopolist? In particular, will the monopolist end up paying this tax, or will it simply pass this tax on to its customers? Let us look at the results graphically.

Suppose that before the imposition of the tax, the monopolist was producing a profit-maximizing output of 1 million units which were being sold at $80 per unit. What effect will the lump-sum tax have on output and price? The important point to bear in mind is that the monopolist must pay this $10 million tax regardless of the level of profits or output. In other words, the tax represents a fixed cost to the monopolist and will increase the average costs of production while leaving the marginal cost unaffected. In the above figure, the average cost curve will shift up to reflect this new tax: by $20 at the 500,000 level of output, by $10 at the present 1 million output and so on. However, since the variable costs are unaffected by this tax, then the marginal cost curve does not change. The profit-maximizing output remains unaffected then. Given the new costs, the best output level is still 1 million and the best price is still $80 per unit. The only thing that has been affected is the profitability of the monopolist.

Since the output and price levels are unaffected by a lump-sum profit tax, such a policy is not a particularly effective policy though it does at least return some of the excess profits to society.

Instead of a profits tax, a government might decide to introduce a *monopoly sales tax* specific to the monopolist's output. What effect, if any, will this tax have on the monopolist and will the tax be passed on to the consumer?

FIGURE 10.8 The Effect of A Monopoly Sales Tax on a Monopolist

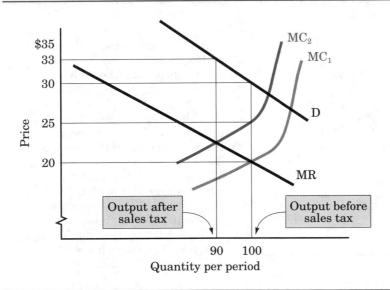

Prior to the tax, maximum profit was obtained by the monopolist producing an output where the marginal cost equals the marginal revenue, i.e., where the MC and MR curves intersect — at an output of 100. This gives a selling price of $30. Imposing a $5 per unit sales tax means that the MC increases by $5 at every output level. This is shown by an upward shift in the MC curve from MC_1 to MC_2. The new profit-maximizing equilibrium now occurs where the MC_2 curve intersects the MR curve, i.e., at an output of 90. The resulting price at which this output can be sold is $33.

Since a monopoly sales tax is a tax on each unit sold, unlike the lump-sum profits tax, it will affect the marginal cost as shown in Figure 10.8.

The average cost curve has been omitted in the graph since we don't need it in order to bring out the main points. Prior to the tax, the output level is 100, the marginal cost and revenue equal $20, and the price is $30. Suppose that the government now imposes a monopoly sales tax of $5 per unit. The result will be that the marginal cost curve will shift upwards by $5 at every level of output, from MC_1 to MC_2. So, the new profit-maximizing output is reduced to 90 and the new price will be $33. Part of the new tax of $5 does pass on to the customer since the price has increased by $3. The other $2 is absorbed by the monopolist. The extent to which the monopolist is able to shift the tax onto the consumer depends in good part on the price elasticity of demand. In most cases the cost is shared between the producer and consumer, and as a result, the total profit of the monopolist will be reduced. However, this type of tax is an abysmal failure in the attempt to get the price reduced and the output increased since it has exactly the opposite effect.

Government Price Setting

For the reasons we have discussed, governments, particularly in Canada, have seldom used taxation to control monopolists. Instead they usually prefer the more direct method of *price setting*. Governments, in theory, have the power to force the monopolist to sell at any price as long as this does not impose losses on the monopolist. However, some prices are better than others. From society's point of view, the most allocatively efficient solution would be to force the monopolist to charge a price which is equal to the marginal cost of production. This is known as the **socially optimum price** and is illustrated in Figure 10.9.

socially optimum price: the price which produces the best allocation of products (and therefore resources) from society's point of view, i.e., P = MC.

Without government regulation, the monopolist would produce the quantity Q_{UM} (unregulated monopolist) at a price P_{UM}. Suppose now that the government decides to regulate the monopolist and forces it to charge a price equal

FIGURE 10.9 The Socially Optimum and Fair-Return Prices

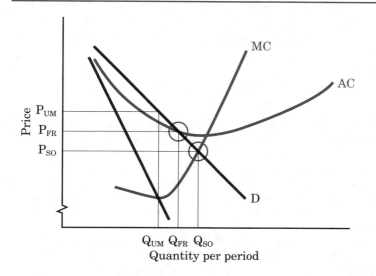

With no interference by the government, the monopolist would maximize profits where MC = MR. This occurs at the output marked Q_{UM} and at a price of P_{UM}. The socially optimum price is where the price is equal to the MC. This occurs where the MC curve intersects the demand curve, producing a socially optimum output of Q_{SO} and a price of P_{SO}. In the situation depicted here, however, this price is below the AC so that the monopolist would be forced to incur a loss. As a result, the government might instead impose a fair-return price where the price is equal to the AC. This occurs where the AC intersects the demand curve and produces the output Q_{FR} and a price of P_{FR}.

to its marginal cost. If you think of the demand curve as being the price curve, then it is easy to find the socially optimum price since it is located where the MC curve cuts the demand curve. (You might recall from an earlier discussion that if this were a perfectly competitive industry, then the marginal cost is the same as the supply, so that the socially optimum position is the equivalent to the equilibrium between demand and supply.) The socially optimum price therefore is P_{SO} and at this price the quantity purchased will be Q_{SO}. This regulated price will have the desired effect of reducing the price (and profits) of the monopolist and inducing an increase in output.

Wherever possible the socially optimum price is the best. In certain circumstances, however, the imposition of such a price might result in the monopolist operating at a loss. This is particularly true where, as in Figure 10.9, the costs of production are high relative to the demand at the relevant price. A price of P_{SO} in the above example is below the average costs of production regardless of what output is produced. In circumstances like this, the government will need to ensure that the monopolist is able to earn a reasonable profit. And what is a reasonable profit? Presumably, it is an amount sufficient to keep the company in business and to prevent owners looking for other avenues for their financial investment. This is what economists mean by normal profits, and if you remember, normal profits are regarded as a cost of production and are therefore included in the average cost shown in Figure 10.9. A **fair-return price** in other words, is a price that allows the monopolist to earn a normal profit and no more. This means that the price should be set equal to average costs. To find it in Figure 10.9, we need to locate the point at which the AC curve cuts the demand curve. This occurs at a price of P_{FR}, and at this price, the quantity purchased is equal to an output of Q_{FR}. You can see that the fair-return price tends to be something of a compromise between the unregulated monopolist's position and the socially optimum position. In many cases, however, a government may have no choice but to compromise.

fair-return price: a price which guarantees that the firm will earn normal profits only, i.e., where P = AC.

One issue associated with guaranteeing a fair return for the monopolist is what is called the extravagance problem. Since the return is based on average costs, it may be to the advantage of the monopolist to pad its costs by spending extravagant amounts on facilities, amenities and salaries.

BOX 10.3

Since there are potentially both benefits and costs of monopolies, governments have often differed in their approach to them. Canada, unlike, for example, the United States, has tended to look at monopolists not so much as problems in themselves but as part of a wider problem of restrictive practices where firms often combine to restrain competition. As such, the first anti-combination legislation was passed in Canada in 1889 and sought to prevent the formation of monopolies or near-monopolies, but also forbade collusion by firms to raise prices or restrict supplies to other firms, or to do anything which would "unduly lessen competition." Over the years, this legislation has been revised and updated, the last revision coming in the form of the 1986 Competition Act. This act forbids things which would lessen competition but does not automatically outlaw mergers or monopolies but forbids only the "abuse of dominant position." In fact, it explicitly recognizes that some mergers may be warranted as being in the public interest if, for example, this would allow Canadian firms to better compete in world markets.

QUESTION 10.8

The following table gives the cost and demand data for a monopolist.

Output	Price	Marginal Revenue	Average Cost	Marginal Cost
0	$175	—	—	—
1	160	$160	$240	$100
2	145	130	150	60
3	130	100	116.7	50
4	115	70	105	70
5	100	40	100	80
6	85	10	97.5	85
7	70	–20	96.40	90
8	55	–50	96	93
9	40	–80	95.9	95

What would be the price, output and profit of the monopolist if it were:
A) unregulated?
B) regulated and required to charge a socially optimum price?
C) regulated and required to charge a fair-return price?

Nationalization   A final way in which governments attempt to deal with monopolies is to remove them from private ownership by nationalization. This means that the state acquires the monopoly reluctantly (sometimes) or eagerly (often) either by compulsory and uncompensated acquisition (seldom) or by a buyout of the owners (usually). The state then operates the enterprise (as a Crown corporation in Canada) on whatever terms it sees fit. It may or may not operate the enterprise to make a profit; it may or may not charge the socially optimum price. There is no guarantee however that simply because the monopoly is operated by the state it is likely to be any more efficient or socially responsible than when it was privately owned.

BOX 10.4

In efforts to ensure that certain monopoly and oligopoly industries act in the public industry, some countries have taken the extreme measure of taking over the industry completely (either with, or without, compensation). Supposedly, the government can then appoint its own managers who will therefore have full knowledge about the costs of production and can ensure that "fair" prices and a "proper" level of production is maintained. In the U.K. after the World War II, a number of industries such as coal mining, steel, and railways were nationalized by the then-ruling Labour government and run by government-appointed boards. In contrast, in the United States, these and other industries were left in private hands but regulated by government-appointed bodies. In Canada, as might be expected, some firms and whole industries have been nationalized, while some are still privately owned but regulated and others private and unregulated. The nationalized firms (called crown corporations in Canada) include federally controlled corporations like CBC and Canada Post, and until recently, Canadian National (CN), Air Canada and PetroCanada. In addition, most provinces also have crown corporations producing electricity, while at the municipal level, urban transit, the water system and garbage collection are usually public enterprises.

BOX 10B

1. Contrast monopoly and perfect competition in terms of the profit-maximizing price and output.
2. Explain three major benefits which a monopoly market might have over a perfectly competitive one.
3. What are the three major ways in which the government attempts to control monopoly?
4. Why would a lump-sum profit tax have no impact on either the price or output produced by the monopolist?
5. To what extent will an excise tax be passed on to the customer by a monopolist?
6. What is the *socially optimum* price? Is it higher or lower than the unregulated monopolist's price?
7. What is the *fair-return* price? Is it higher or lower than the unregulated monopolist's price? From society's point of view, which is preferable?

Chapter Highlights

The chapter begins by defining a monopoly as being the sole supplier of a product in a market and then explains how this definition depends on what exactly is meant by the terms "product" and "market." Next it explains how barriers to entry help to create and perpetuate monopolies. These barriers may be in the form of technical, legal or economic barriers and serve to keep out competitive rivals. A particular type of monopoly, known as a natural monopoly, is defined and it is explained that such monopolies arise whenever economies of scale are large in relation to the size of the market.

The next section explains how, and under what circumstances, monopolies maximize their profits. It first explains why the marginal revenue of the monopolist is less than the price because the monopolist has to reduce the price on the whole of its output in order to increase its sales. The profit maximizing output is then explained in terms of total revenue and costs and then from the viewpoint of average and marginal revenue and costs. This latter approach shows that the monopolist's profits are maximized where marginal revenue is equal to marginal costs. The chapter then explains why this results in the monopolist being both productively inefficient, selling at a price above average costs, and allocatively inefficient since it charges a price higher than its marginal costs. For comparison, the monopoly position is contrasted with that of a perfectly competitive industry. Next, it is explained why, given the same costs, a monopoly will produce a lower output and charge a higher price than a competitive industry. The final part of this section then offers a defence of monopoly and explains why the costs of production might be lower, and research and development more extensive than in competitive markets.

The final section of the chapter looks at three general ways in which monopolies have, or might be, controlled. It looks first at the imposition of a monopoly profits tax and of a monopoly sales tax. Next, it shows that both types of tax will reduce the profits of the monopolist, but that a profits tax leaves the monopolist's price and output unchanged, while a sales tax increases the price and lowers output. It is then explained why neither outcome is desirable from society's point of view. Then, the section investigates the effect of the government imposing a price on the monopolist and explains how it would determine this price. The idea of a socially optimum price is introduced and is defined as a price set by the government equal to the monopolist's marginal cost. It shows why this is the best price from society's point of view but why the imposition of such a price might cause eventual bankruptcy for the monopoly. The chapter continues by looking at the possibility of the government introducing instead a fair-return price on the monopolist, which will allow it to make a normal profit. Finally, the chapter looks at the third way in which governments can exercise control which is by the state directly acquiring or nationalizing the monopoly.

New Glossary Terms

Workbook

Study Tips

1. Students initially have problems understanding why the marginal revenue is less than the price. The best way to understand the difference is to make up a few tables for yourself with quantities increasing by 1 unit and price decreasing by any constant amount. Work out the total and marginal revenues and think out what is happening. Now put it into words. If you are able to do this, then you understand the concept.

2. Figure 10.4 is probably the most complicated single graph that you have so far encountered. It is also very important that you are able to draw it for yourself and understand what it says. It's probably a good idea to first draw a smooth, saucer-shaped average cost curve with a clearly identifiable lowest point. Now draw the marginal cost curve intersecting this lowest point. Next put on the demand curve so that it intersects the average cost curve to the right of the lowest point. Finally, draw in the marginal revenue curve. Strictly, this is supposed to be twice as steep as the demand curve and should cut the horizontal axis at the halfway point between the origin and the demand curve. But don't worry if it's not exact and you find you have to cheat a little. Once you have located the intersection between the marginal cost and revenue curves, draw a vertical line down to the quantity axis to get the profit-maximizing output. Then continue this vertical line upward until you hit the demand curve. Go across to the price axis to get the profit-maximizing price.

3. The other difficult graph to draw in this chapter is Figure 10.9, which shows the effect of government price setting. Since you want to set up a situation where the socially optimum price involves a loss for the monopolist, proceed as you would for the normal monopoly diagram. However, when you come to draw in the demand curve make sure that it intersects the average cost curve to the *left* of the latter's lowest point.

Are You Sure?

Indicate whether the following statements are true or false. If false, indicate why they are false.

1. A monopolist is free to charge any price it wishes for its product.
T or **F**   If false: _____

_____

_____

2. A patent is an example of a barrier to entry.
T or **F**   If false: _____

_____

_____

3. The marginal revenue of the monopolist may be equal to, greater than, or less than its average revenue.
T or **F**   If false: _____

_____

_____

4. A natural monopoly exists when a single producer is able to produce at a lower cost than competing firms could.
T or **F**   If false: _____

_____

_____

5. At the profit-maximizing output of the monopolist, the price will be equal to the marginal cost.
T or **F**   If false: _____

_____

_____

6. A monopolist will only be able to make a profit if, at some output level, the average revenue exceeds the average cost.
T or **F**   If false: _____

_____

_____

7. A lump-sum profit tax imposed on a monopolist will cause the monopolist to increase the price and reduce output in order to maximize its profits.
T or **F**   If false: _____

_____

_____

8. A fair-return price is a price set equal to a firm's lowest average cost.
T or **F**   If false: _____

_____

_____

9. A socially optimum price is a price set equal to a firm's marginal cost.
T or **F**   If false: _____

_____

_____

10. A monopolist will break even if it is producing an output where the average revenue is equal to the average cost.
T or **F**   If false: _____

_____

_____

Translations

Tom, a steel drum manufacturer (the only one in Nania), can sell a single drum for $30. However, for every extra drum he wants to sell, he is forced to reduce the price (for all his customers) by $2. The total fixed costs in his workshop are $15 and the first drum produced costs $25. For each extra drum thereafter, the cost drops by $5 until the fifth drum. After that, the cost of each extra drum increases by $5. Draw the AR, MR, ATC and MC curves in Figure W10.1 and identify the profit-maximizing output and the amount of profits.

FIGURE W10.1

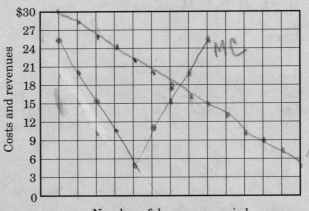

Number of drums per period

Choose the Best

1. Given that a monopolist faces a downward-sloping demand curve, which of the following statements is true?
   a) Its average revenue is equal to the price.
   b) Its average revenue is equal to its marginal revenue.

2. Sole ownership of a particular resource is an example of what?
   a) It is an example of a natural monopoly.
   b) It is an example of a barrier to entry.

3. Which of the following is true?
   a) A monopolist cannot make economic losses in the short run.
   b) A monopolist cannot make economic losses in the long run.

4. All of the following, *except one*, are true statements about a natural monopoly. Which one is the exception?
   a) It is able to produce at a lower cost than competing firms could.
   b) It faces decreasing returns to scale and a declining LRAC over the relevant range of demand.
   c) The demand for its product is perfectly elastic.

5. Which of the following statements regarding the definition of a monopoly market is *incorrect*?

a) Whether a certain market is regarded as a monopoly depends upon the definition of the demand.
b) Whether a certain market is regarded as a monopoly depends upon the definition of the market.
c) Whether a certain market is regarded as a monopoly depends upon the definition of the product.

6. Under what circumstances will a monopolist be forced to shut down?
a) If the average revenue exceeds the average costs of production.
b) If the average revenue exceeds the average variable costs of production.
c) If the average variable costs of production exceeds the average revenue.

7. What will be the effect of a sales tax imposed on a monopolist's product?
a) It will lead to an increase in the price and a reduction in the output.
b) It will lead to an increase in the price but will have no effect on the output.
c) It will have no impact on the price nor on the output.

8. All of the following statements, *except one*, are true. Which is the exception?
a) A monopolist is able to control the price of the product but not also the quantity purchased.
b) A monopolist is able to control the quantity purchased of the product but not also the price.
c) A monopolist can control both the price and the quantity purchased.

9. Which of the following statements is true regarding the marginal revenue curve of the monopolist?
a) It is twice as steep as the average revenue curve.
b) It is equal to the price.
c) It is a horizontal line.
d) It is the same as its average revenue curve.

10. All of the following, *except one*, are examples of barriers to entry. Which is the exception?
a) Economies of scale.
b) Minimum wage legislation.

c) Copyrights.
d) Government licences.

11. Which of the following is a correct statement of the socially optimum price?
a) It is a price equal to the average cost.
b) It is a price equal to the marginal cost.
c) It is a price equal to the *lowest* average cost.
d) It is a price equal to the marginal revenue.

12. All, *except one*, of the following statements regarding the profit-maximizing output of the monopolist are correct. Which is false?
a) At that output, the marginal cost will be equal to the price.
b) At that output, marginal profit is zero.
c) At that output, the difference between the total revenue and the total cost will be at a maximum.
d) At that output, marginal cost will equal marginal revenue.

13. Suppose that a perfectly competitive industry is monopolized. If the costs of production remain unchanged, then which of the following statements is correct?
a) Both the price and the output of the perfectly competitive industry will be higher than the monopoly industry.
b) Both the price and the output of the perfectly competitive industry will be lower than the monopoly industry.
c) The perfectly competitive price will be higher and the output will be lower.
d) The perfectly competitive price will be lower and the output will be higher.

Table W10.1 outlines the cost and revenue data for a monopolist.

TABLE W10.1

Quantity Demanded	Price	Total cost
0		$ 40
1	$45	58
2	40	73
3	35	87
4	30	100
5	25	118
6	20	143

14. Refer to Table W10.1 to answer this question. What are the profit-maximizing level of output and price respectively?
    a) 3 and $35.
    b) 4 and $30.
    c) 5 and $25.
    d) 5 and $30.
    e) 6 and $20.

15. Refer to Table W10.1 to answer this question. What is the level of profits at the profit-maximizing output?
    a) 0.
    b) $7.
    c) $15.
    d) $20.
    e) $120.

Refer to Figure W10.2 to answer questions 16 and 17.

FIGURE W10.2

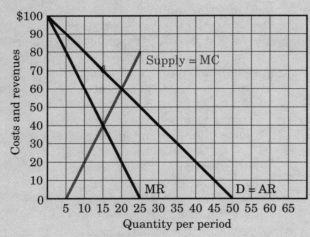

16. Refer to Figure W10.2 to answer this question. Suppose this graph depicts a perfectly competitive industry. What will be the equilibrium price and output respectively?
    a) $40 and 15.
    b) $40 and 30.
    c) $60 and 20.
    d) $60 and 25.
    e) $70 and 15.

17. Refer to Figure W10.2 to answer this question. Suppose this graph depicts a monopoly industry. What will be the profit-maximizing price and output respectively?

a) $40 and 15.
b) $40 and 30.
c) $60 and 20.
d) $60 and 25.
e) $70 and 15.

Figure W10.3 depicts the cost and revenue curves for a monopolist. Use it to answer questions 18, 19 and 20.

FIGURE W10.3

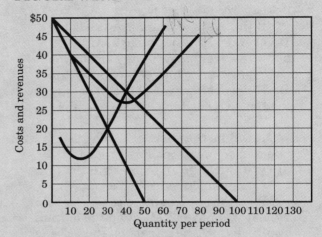

18. Refer to Figure W10.3 to answer this question. What are the profit-maximizing level of output and price respectively?
    a) 30 and $20.
    b) 30 and $35.
    c) 35 and $27.50.
    d) 40 and $30.
    e) 42 and $28.

19. Refer to Figure W10.3 to answer this question. At the profit-maximizing level of output, what is the amount of total costs?
    a) $20.
    b) $600.
    c) $900.
    d) $1,200.
    e) Cannot be determined from this information.

20. Refer to Figure W10.3 to answer this question. What is the level of profits at the profit-maximizing output?
    a) 0.
    b) $20.
    c) $150.

d) $450.
e) $600.

What's Wrong?

Can you spot the five errors in the following passage? (ignore grammatical mistakes!)

Compared to a competitive industry, a monopolist will, given the same costs of production, charge a higher price and produce a greater quantity. In addition, the monopolist is able to make economic profits in the short run, and, like a competitive firm, it will also be able to do so in the long run. Because of this, governments may well intervene. The intervention can take many forms. For instance, the government might levy a tax on the firm in order, among other things, to reduce its profits. However, a monopoly sales tax generally does not affect the price or output of the monopolist. Another method of intervention is in the form of price setting. If the price that the monopolist is forced to charge is equal to its average variable costs, this is known as a fair-return price. If the price is set equal to the monopolist's marginal cost, it is known as an equitable price.

Key Problem

Corona is a military dictatorship whose most important industry is the production of (empty) metal beer kegs. The industry is perfectly competitive and has the following costs and demand as shown in Table W10.2 (all units, apart from the price are in thousands per week):

TABLE W10.2

Price ($)	Quantity Demanded	TR ($)	MR ($)	MC ($)	TC ($)	Tπ ($)	ATC ($)
30	0	0	—	—	28	-28	—
28	1	28	28	20	48	-20	48
26	2	52	24	11	59	-7	29.9
24	3	72	20	8	67	5	22.3
22	4	88	16	16	83	5	20.75
20	5	100	12	17	100	0	20
18	6	108	8	18	118	-10	19.7
16	7	112	4	20	138	-26	19.7
14	8	112	0	25	163	-51	20.4
12	9	108	-4	30	193	-85	21.4

a) Complete the table and, in Figure W10.4 on the next page, draw in the demand and supply curves for the industry. (Recall that the supply curve for a perfectly competitive industry is the same as its MC curve.)

b) What are the equilibrium values of price, quantity traded and total profit (or loss) in the industry? Label the competitive equilibrium as E_1 on the graph.

Price: $___18___; quantity: ___6___; profit/loss $___10___.

Suppose that the sister-in-law of Corona's president is given the metal keg industry as a birthday present. Irina immediately amalgamates all the firms into one large monopoly.

FIGURE W10.4

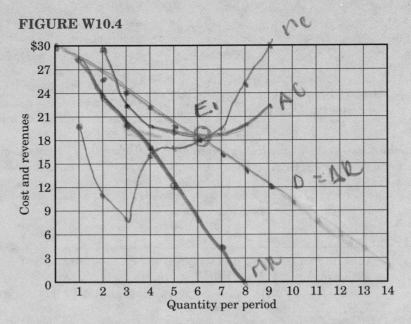

c) Assuming that she wishes to maximize her profits from the industry, what price and quantity will Irina produce and what will be her total profits? (*Hint:* Draw in the ATC and the MR on your graph in Figure W10.4).

Price: $_____4_____; quantity: ____16_____; profit/loss $_____5_____.

The following year, the president becomes concerned with the big profits being made by Irina and informs her that, if she wishes to remain in business, she has a choice. She can either pay a weekly tax of $5,000 to the government or not pay a tax but have the government determine what price she will be allowed to charge. If she chooses the latter option, then the government will require her to either charge a price equal to her average cost or a price equal to her marginal cost.

d) Locate the two price choices available to Irina and identify them on Figure W10.4.

e) Summarize the results of the three options in Table W10.3.

TABLE W10.3

	Price ($)	Quantity Traded	Profit/Loss ($)
1. Tax of $5,000	_____	_____	_____
2. P = AC	_____	_____	_____
3. P = MC	_____	_____	_____

Given the three options, which is the best one from Irina's point of view? From the governments's? From the people of Corona's?

Irina's choice: _____

Government's choice: _____

Coronan's choice: _____

Need a Hand?

a) First work out the total revenue (TR) by multiplying the price by the quantity demanded (column 1 times column 2). The marginal revenue (MR) is the difference in total revenue from one output level to the next, i.e., TR at quantity of 1 is $28, at quantity 2 it is $52; therefore the marginal revenue of the 2nd unit is the difference between $52 and $28, or $24. Similarly, marginal cost (MC) is the difference in total cost (TC) from one output level to the next. Total profit (Tπ) is the difference between total revenue and total cost at each level of output. Average total cost (ATC) is equal to TC divided by quantity of output. The completed table is as follows:

TABLE W10.4 (completed Table W10.2)

Price ($)	Quantity Demanded	TR ($)	MR ($)	MC ($)	TC ($)	Tπ ($)	ATC ($)
30	0	0			28	−28	
28	1	28	28	20	48	−20	48.0
26	2	52	24	11	59	−7	29.5
24	3	72	20	8	67	+5	22.3
22	4	88	16	16	83	+5	20.75
20	5	100	12	17	100	0	20.0
18	6	108	8	18	118	−10	19.7
16	7	112	4	20	138	−26	19.7
14	8	112	0	25	163	−51	20.4
12	9	108	−4	30	193	−85	21.4

Since the marginal cost of the industry is synonymous with its supply curve, you need to relate it with the quantities to plot it. In this case, for both the demand and supply curves, begin with the quantities on the horizontal axis and plot the dollar price and marginal cost, e.g., at a quantity of 1, the price is $28 and the marginal cost (supply) is $20; at a quantity of 2, the price is $26, the marginal cost (supply) is $11, and so on. This gives:

FIGURE W10.5 (completed Figure W10.4)

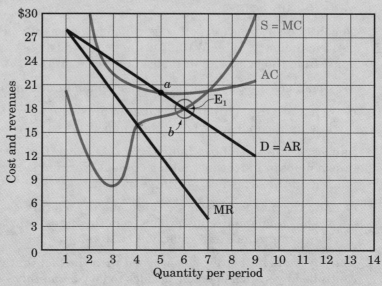

b) From the graph in Figure W10.5, or looking at Table W10.4, you can see that the price is equal to MC at a **quantity of 6. Price (equals the marginal cost) of $18**. At this level of output, there is a **loss of $10**.

c) To maximize profits, a monopolist will produce that output where marginal revenue is equal to marginal cost. The two curves intersect, which is confirmed in Table W10.4, at an **output of 4.** This quantity will be sold at a **price of $22.** The table shows that at this output, **total profit is equal to 5.**

d) See Figure W10.5. To locate a price equal to average cost, find where the demand curve intersects the average cost curve. This is identified as point *a* on the graph. To locate a price equal to marginal cost, find where the demand curve intersects the marginal cost curve. This is identified as point *b* on the graph.

e) A tax of $5,000 is a fixed cost to Irina. Therefore it will have no effect on the marginal costs. It will increase the total costs and reduce profits by $5,000 at every output level. The best output level is the same as before; she would simply be making $5,000 less profit at this output, i.e., reducing it to zero. You have already located the P = AC level on the graph. Figure W10.5 shows that the price and average cost are equal at an output of 5. The P = MC level you have previously identified as the perfectly competitive solution. The results are summarized below.

TABLE W10.5 (completed Table W10.3)

	Price	Quantity Traded	Profit/Loss
1. Tax of $5,000	$22	4	$ 0
2. P = AC	20	5	0
3. P = MC	18	6	−10

Irina's choice: Either option 1 or 2 (probably 2, since she might object paying a tax to the government. This latter is the fair return price, guaranteeing Irina normal profits only.)

Government's choice: If their sole interest is in raising revenue, then option 1.

Coronan's choice: Option 3, which is the socially optimal price giving the lowest price and the highest quantity.

More of the Same

Nopoli's major export is golf bags which are presently produced in a perfectly competitive industry. Table W10.6 outlines the industry's costs and demand (all units, apart from the price, are in thousands per month).

a) Complete the table and graph the demand and supply curves for the industry.

b) What are the equilibrium values of price, quantity traded and total profit (or loss) in the industry? Label the competitive equilibrium with an *a* on your graph.

Suppose that the golf bag industry is taken over by Norman Greg (known as the brown dolphin in Nopoli's golfing circles). Norm immediately sets about amalgamating all the firms into one large monopoly.

c) Add the marginal revenue curve and the average cost curve to your graph. If he wishes to maximize his profits from the industry, what price and quantity will Norman produce and what will his total profits be?

The government, however, concerned with the fact that its major export industry is controlled by a single person, decides to levy a monthly tax of $6,000 on Norm's firm.

TABLE W10.6

Price ($)	Quantity Demanded	TR ($)	MR ($)	MC ($)	TC ($)	Tπ ($)	ATC ($)
50	0	—	—	—	64	____	—
48	1	____	____	____	97	____	____
46	2	____	____	____	124	____	____
44	3	____	____	____	148	____	____
42	4	____	____	____	168	____	____
40	5	____	____	____	192	____	____
38	6	____	____	____	220	____	____
36	7	____	____	____	252	____	____
34	8	____	____	____	286	____	____
32	9	____	____	____	326	____	____
30	10	____	____	____	376	____	____

d) What will be the new price, quantity and profits of the firm as a result of the imposition of the tax?

e) Suppose, alternatively, that the government decides to impose a socially optimum price on the firm. What will be the new price, quantity and profits of the firm as a result?

f) What if, instead, the government decides to impose a fair-return price on the firm. What will be the new price, quantity and profits of the firm now?

Other Problems

1. a) Complete the following table of costs and revenues of a monopolist, assuming the demand curve is a straight line.

TABLE W10.7

Quantity per Period	Price	TR	MR	MC	TC	ATC
0	—	—	—	—	25	—
1	____	____	____	____	____	60
2	____	____	46	30	____	____
3	____	____	____	____	115	____
4	____	____	____	____	135	____
5	____	210	____	____	____	32
6	____	____	____	30	____	____
7	38	____	____	____	225	____
8	____	____	____	40	____	____
9	____	____	18	____	310	____
10	____	____	____	____	____	36

b) What are the values of the profit-maximizing output?

Price: $_____; output: _____ units; total profit/loss $_____.

c) At what output will sales revenue be maximized and what will be the value of sales revenue?

Output: _____ units; total revenue: $_____.

2. Figure W10.6 shows the demand for a monopolist's product.

FIGURE W10.6

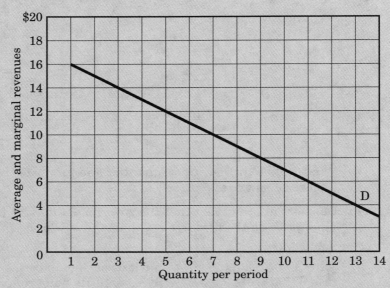

a) From this information, complete Table W10.8 and add the MR curve to Figure W10.6.

TABLE W10.8

Quantity Demanded	Price = AR ($)	TR ($)	MR ($)
1	____	____	____
2	____	____	____
3	____	____	____
4	____	____	____
5	____	____	____
6	____	____	____
7	____	____	____
8	____	____	____
9	____	____	____
10	____	____	____
11	____	____	____
12	____	____	____

b) At what output level is total revenue maximized? What is the marginal revenue at this output?

Output of: _____ units; marginal revenue: $_____.

c) What is the elasticity of demand between outputs of 8 and 9?

Elasticity: _____.

d) What is the maximum output that this monopolist would produce?

Output of: _____ units.

e) Is the demand elastic or inelastic for outputs less than this maximum?

_____

f) What general rule can you derive from these observations?

_____

3. Figure W10.7 shows the cost and revenue information for a monopolist.

FIGURE W10.7

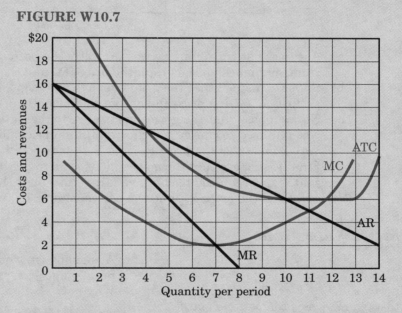

What are the levels of (1) price; (2) output; (3) total (sales) revenue; and (4) total profits if the monopolist were to produce at the positions a) through d) in Table W10.9?

TABLE W10.9

	(1) Price ($)	(2) Output	(3) Total revenue ($)	(4) Total profits ($)
a) Sales revenue maximization	_____	_____	_____	_____
b) Profit maximization	_____	_____	_____	_____
c) Socially optimum price	_____	_____	_____	_____
d) Fair-return price	_____	_____	_____	_____

4. Figure W10.8 depicts the cost and revenue curves for a particular industry.

FIGURE W10.8

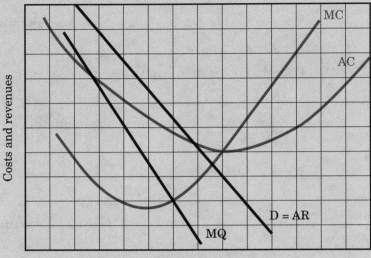

Quantity per period

a) Assume that this industry was perfectly competitive. Identify the equilibrium, and mark on the graph the price (P_c) and the quantity (Q_c).

b) Suppose instead that the graph depicts a monopolistic industry. Identify the profit-maximizing price and output and label them on the graph, P_M and Q_M.

c) Now suppose that the government were to regulate this monopoly so that it was required to charge a socially optimum price. Identify this on Figure W10.8 and label the price P_{SO} and the corresponding quantity Q_{SO}.

d) Finally, suppose that the government were to regulate this monopoly so that it was required to charge a fair-return price. Identify this on the graph and label the price P_{FR} and the corresponding quantity Q_{FR}.

Unanswered Questions

Short Essays

1. Explain why a monopoly market is not as beneficial to consumers as a competitive market.

2. What are some of the advantages which a monopoly industry might have over a competitive industry?

3. Explain why the marginal revenue of the monopolist is always less than the average revenue.

4. Explain, with examples, the meaning of barriers to entry. In what way do they lead to the creation of monopolies?

5. What methods are available for a government wishing to regulate a monopoly? How successful are such methods likely to be?

Analytical Questions

1. A monopolist would never produce in the price range where the demand was inelastic. Why not?

2. There is no such thing as the supply curve for a monopolist because there is no unique relationship between the price of the product and the quantity produced. Explain.

3. Suppose that the average variable costs for a monopolist remained constant regardless of how much it produced. What would then determine the profit-maximizing output of the monopolist?

4. Suppose that a monopolist could practise perfect price discrimination and charge each separate consumer the maximum that each was prepared to pay. Draw the monopolist's

new demand and marginal revenue curves. How do they compare with those for the non-discriminating monopolist? (*Hint:* Try using some actual numbers.)

5. What are the implications of a government forcing a monopolist to charge a price equal not just to its average costs but to its *minimum* average costs?

Numerical Questions

1. Presently, Clay Monopoly is considering whether it is worthwhile producing an additional 10 units of his terra cotta pots which will cost him an additional $80. At present, he is selling 120 pots a week at $18 each. In order to increase his sales by 10 units, however, he would need to reduce the price of all his pots to $17. What would you recommend?

2. Table W10.10 outlines the cost and revenue data for Mo the monopolist.

TABLE W10.10

Quantity per Period	Price	Total Costs
0	$21	18
1	20	40
2	19	50
3	18	58
4	17	62
5	16	70
6	15	80
7	14	91
8	13	105
9	12	123
10	11	148

a) Graph Mo's demand, MR and MC curves. What is Mo's profit-maximizing price and output and what will be the amount of his profits?

b) Suppose that the demand for Mo's products increased by 3 units at every price level. Graph Mo's new demand and MR curves. What will be Mo's new profit-maximizing price and output and what will be the amount of his profits?

3. Figure W10.9 shows the demand and marginal cost curves for Meanie the monopolist.

Draw in Meanie's marginal revenue curve and identify the following points:
a) the profit-maximizing output and price;
b) the sales-maximization output and price.

FIGURE W10.9

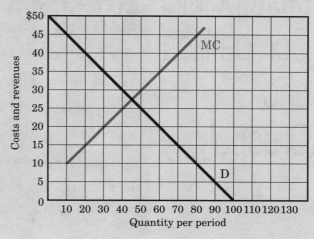

4. Unisel is the sole automobile manufacturer in Concordia, which prohibits the importation of cars. Figure W10.10 depicts the demand and the costs for Unisel.

FIGURE W10.10

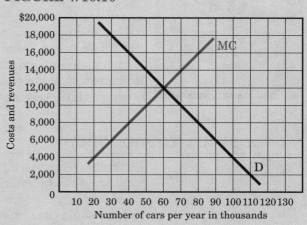

a) What is Unisel's profit-maximizing output and price?

b) Suppose that the government of Concordia imposes a price ceiling of $10,000 per car. What is Unisel's profit-maximizing output now?

c) What would be the output if this were a perfectly competitive market?

CHAPTER ELEVEN

■ ■ ■ ■ ■ ■ ■ ▶

Monopolistic Competition and Oligopoly

W *hat's ahead . . . This chapter looks at the behaviour of firms in the context of two market structures referred to as oligopoly and monopolistic competition. We explore the conditions for equilibrium in both structures and evaluate how these market structures compare with that of perfect competition. In the case of the monopolistically competitive firm, a distinction between the short run and the long run is important. In the case of the oligopoly firm we emphasize the important characteristic of interdependence between firms. Finally we look at the phenomenon of advertising and the assumption, found throughout the analysis of the firm, of profit maximization.*

So far we have examined the two market structures of monopoly and perfect competition. Lying between these two models are two others, monopolistic competition and oligopoly, both of which embrace some aspects of the first two. The term imperfect competition is sometimes used to refer jointly to these two market structures.

monopolistic competition: a market structure in which there are many firms who sell a differentiated product and have some control over the price of the products they sell.

There are few examples of a pure monopoly, and, as we saw, the model of perfect competition is more of an abstraction (albeit a very useful abstraction) than it is a description of our present world. In contrast, the models of monopolistic competition and oligopoly do describe much of modern capitalism reasonably well and are, therefore, more realistic. We will look at **monopolistic competition** first.

Monopolistic Competition

Examples of monopolistically competitive industries abound: almost all retailing, from ladies' clothes stores to gasoline retailing; almost all the services that are provided directly to the retail consumer — travel agents, hairdressing, shoe repair and tax accounting; almost all the services aimed at the home owner — roofers, plumbers, carpet layers and painters; most of the growing cottage industry sector, from software designers to authors and proofreaders; and some manufacturing markets such as the textile, footwear, and furniture industries.

Characteristics of Monopolistically Competitive Industries

There are four characteristics of a monopolistically competitive industry. The first characteristic is that the industry is made up of *many relatively small firms* that act independently of each other. Across any metropolitan area are dozens of dry cleaning shops, travel agencies, and plumbers, each of which tries to distinguish itself from its competition. Similarly, across the whole economy are dozens of T-shirt or chair manufacturers acting in the same way.

Second, there is *freedom of entry* into the industry for new firms. This is analogous to the perfect competition model. Free entry does not mean that entry requires no money. What it does mean is that there are no significant barriers to entry, as discussed in the previous chapter.

Third, firms within a monopolistically competitive industry have *some control over the price* of the products they sell. This is unlike the firms within a perfectly competitive industry. Despite such control, there often is very little price competition between firms. Instead, competition centres on attempts by individual firms to differentiate the products they sell.

The fourth characteristic of a monopolistically competitive industry is the fact that firms sell a differentiated product. **Product differentiation** involves the attempt by the seller to offer a product that is *seen* by the consumer as different and presumably better than the others on the market. There are several ways that this may be done. First there is the possibility that the product is actually better — at least in the eyes of many consumers. If, for example, a large number of people feel that a haircut by Hai is the best that they have ever had, then Hai has succeeded in differentiating his product. Second, we need to recognize that unique packaging, brand names and recognizable logos are all forms of product differentiation. There may, in fact, be no difference, between two brands of motor oil, but if people think there is a difference then product differentiation has occurred. Third, in the case of retail outlets, location and service can often be a significant way in which a firm can differentiate itself. This would explain, for example, why some convenience stores do a brisk business while others do not. Fourth, when firms redevelop their product by introducing a new and improved version, they are attempting to differentiate it, in the eyes of the consumer, even more than before. The final way that firms attempt to differentiate their products is through advertising. We will return to this last topic in some detail at the end of this chapter after we have discussed oligopoly firms, whom we shall see are also big advertisers.

product differentiation: the attempt by a firm to differentiate its product from that of its competitors.

The Short-Run Equilibrium for the Firm

The costs of production between firms in a monopolistically competitive industry tend to be very similar — the cost of running one hair cutting salon isn't much different from the cost of another. On the other hand, the presence of non-price competition and product differentiation does result in the possibility that the demand faced by one firm can be quite different from that facing another. This is why our analysis of this type of market structure focuses on the role of the demand faced by the individual firm. Usually, the individual firm faces a highly elastic demand curve, although it is not perfectly elastic as in the case of the perfectly competitive model.

To launch the analysis of the monopolistically competitive model, let's imagine a trendy restaurant that is currently doing well. Could this firm be making economic profits? Figure 11.1 on the next page will illustrate an answer.

In this figure, we have an elastic demand curve (D_1) that the restaurant faces along with its associated marginal revenue curve (MR_1). This demand curve for a representative firm is more elastic than the market demand

FIGURE 11.1 The Monopolistically Competitive Firm in Short-Run Equilibrium

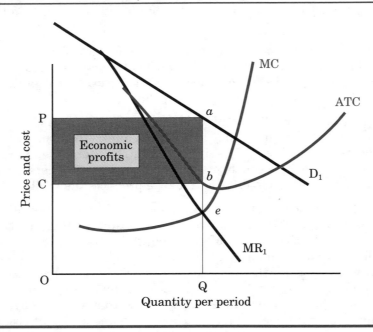

D_1 is an elastic demand curve with its associated marginal revenue curve MR_1. ATC and MC are the normal U-shaped cost curves. The area in the box OQaP represents total revenue. Similarly, box OQbC represents total costs. If we subtract costs from revenue we get economic profits which is represented by box CbaP.

curve for the whole industry, because it is so easy for customers to stop coming to this establishment and go to a competitor instead. In fact, the firm's elasticity of demand will depend on the amount of competition as well as the degree of product differentiation that it has achieved.

Also on the graph is the average cost curve (ATC) and its associated marginal costs curve (MC). These two curves are the same as those developed in the chapter on short-run costs.

Next, recall the two basic questions that any firm must answer: what is the right output level at which to operate and what is the right price to charge? The answer to the first question is: that output level which maximizes total profits, which in Figure 11.1 is quantity Q. This is where the marginal cost equals marginal revenue (point *e*). The right price is the highest price that can be charged and still sell the optimum quantity — in this case price P.

Remember that total revenue equals price times quantity. This is represented on the graph by the box OQaP. Similarly, average total cost times quantity equals total costs, and this is represented by box OQbC. Total revenue less total cost is total profit and the graphical representation of this is box CbaP. These are economic profits since normal profits are incorporated in our definition of costs.

We now come to the crucial point in understanding how monopolistically competitive industries function. What will be the response of outsiders not yet in the industry to the fact that this restaurant is making economic profits? The answer is that some of these outsiders will want their share of these profits and will enter the industry as new firms. And what will be the effect of this entry? You may recall that entry by new firms into an industry will increase *market* supply and this will result in a lower equilibrium price. In other words, increased competition will cause a drop in price.

This entry will effect our restaurant and the first indication of this effect is that the restaurant will notice that business just isn't as good as it used to be. In graphical terms, the demand curve that the restaurant faces (the one in Figure 11.1) shifts back to the left and it also becomes more elastic. The reason for this is simply the fact that the restaurant in question must now share the market with new competitors. Figure 11.2 illustrates the eventual result of this entry.

FIGURE 11.2 The Monopolistically Competitive Firm in Long-Run Equilibrium

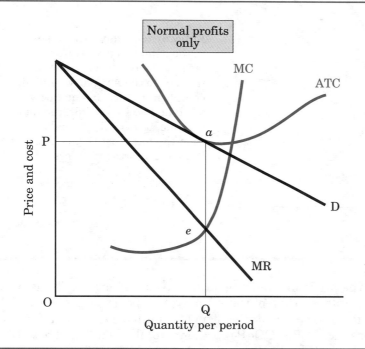

The equilibrium price and quantity are P and Q. Further, since the demand curve and the average total cost curve are tangent to each other at point *a*, the area in the box OQ*a*P represents both total revenue and total cost. This is the case of zero economic profit.

Again, the firm's best output level is where marginal cost equals marginal revenue (point *e*) which occurs at quantity Q. The best price is the highest that can be charged which ensures maximum profits. This is price P. The crucial thing to notice about the graph above is that the demand curve faced by the restaurant has shifted back to the left (because of the entry of new firms) and has become more elastic so that it is now tangent to the average total costs curve at point *a*. Given this point of tangency between the ATC curve and the demand curve (which is also the average revenue curve) the box OQ*a*P represents both the restaurant's total revenue and its total cost. Therefore economic profits are zero. Another way of stating this is that the firm is making only normal profits.

How can we be sure that economic profits will end up at zero in the long-run equilibrium? Well, as long as even some economic profits continue to be made by the representative firm, then more entry will occur and this additional entry will mean that the demand curve faced by that representative firm will continue to shift back until it is eventually tangent to the average total costs curve and economics profits are eliminated. In short, the existence of economic profit triggers a reaction that continues until that profit disappears.

Can too many firms enter the industry? To answer this question, let's look at the effects of too many firms trying to jump into a previously profitable industry at the same time. Figure 11.3 will help to explain the effects.

FIGURE 11.3 The Effect of Too Much Entry

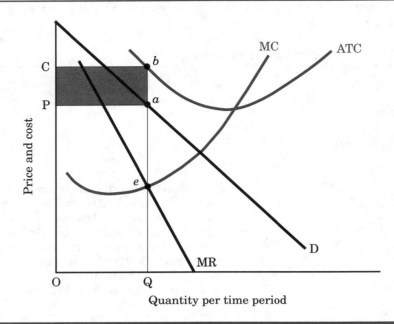

Entry by too many firms results in the demand curve shifting so far to the left that it can not be tangent to the ATC curve. Again, equilibrium price and quantity are P and Q. As a result, the total revenue, box OQaP, is smaller than the total cost OQbC. Thus, box PabC represents a loss.

Quantity Q is the profit-maximizing output level and price P is the maximum price possible at that output. Entry has been so great that the demand curve for the representative firm has shifted so far to the left that an economic loss occurs. Box OQaP represents total revenue and box OQbC is total cost with box PabC representing the size of the loss.

Can this be long-run equilibrium? The answer is no, since in the long run a firm must earn at least normal profits in order to remain viable. What will happen here is that some firms will exit from the industry. This means that each remaining firm will experience a slight increase in demand as represented by its demand curve shifting somewhat to the right. This will result, once again, in the normal profit we saw in Figure 11.2.

We are now ready for the main conclusion from our analysis of the monopolistically competitive industry model: in the long run the representative firm makes only normal profits.

Another way of saying the same thing is that there are no (economic) profits to be made in, say, the dry cleaning business or in shoe repair, or in the hardware retailing business or in textile manufacturing. Think of it this way: if there were economic profits to be made in doing something as simple as running a dry cleaning shop, wouldn't some of you start doing that? And if enough of you did open your own shop what would happen to those economic profits? They would surely disappear.

Now, this last point should not be interpreted to mean that there are *no* monopolistically competitive firms that make economic profits in the long run. We are probably all aware of some travel agent or gas station or convenience store that seems, even in the long run, to be so busy that they must be making an economic profit. Such exceptional firms do exist, and usually the reason for their success can be summed up in two words: product differentiation (whether caused by location, service or some other reason). However, for every one of these kind of success stories, there are three or four other stories of firms who, over the previous years, have entered the same industry, hung on until the owner's money was gone, and then went out of business. If we subtract these firms' losses from the profits of the successful firms, we would more closely approximate zero economic profits in the long run in the *whole industry*.

QUESTION 11.1

What would be the effect on any individual restaurant's demand curve if thousands of new restaurants entered the industry and product differentiation was impossible?

QUESTION 11.2

Assume that a representative firm in monopolistic competition is experiencing economic losses. What series of events will occur to return this firm to its long-run equilibrium?

Excess Capacity   You may recall from Chapter 6 that economic efficiency is achieved by the firm when output is produced at minimum average cost. This is an automatic result for the representative firm in perfect competition because the firm's demand is perfectly elastic. However, the monopolistically competitive firm faces less than perfectly elastic demand. The result is that the point of tangency between the demand curve and the average total costs curve cannot be at the latter's minimum point. Figure 11.4 illustrates this point.

FIGURE 11.4 Excess Capacity

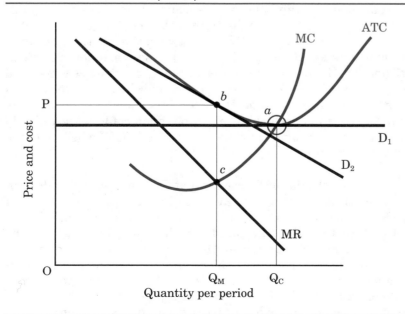

The long-run equilibrium for a perfectly competitive firm with a perfectly elastic demand curve, D_1, is at point a. This is the point of minimum average total cost. The long-run equilibrium for a monopolistically competitive firm with a downward-sloping demand curve, D_2, is not at the point of minimum average total cost as can be seen by point b. The difference in the two outputs $Q_C - Q_M$ is referred to as excess capacity.

In Figure 11.4, the perfectly elastic demand curve, D_1, is tangent to the average cost curve at point a which is its minimum point and as you may recall is referred to as capacity output. This is the long-run output of the competitive firm. Demand curve D_2 is the demand curve of the monopolistically competitive firm. Since it is not perfectly elastic, the point of tangency with the average total cost curve must be to the left of, and above, its minimum — such as at point b.

The conclusion from this analysis is that monopolistically competitive firms, unlike firms in perfect competition, do not produce at capacity and consequently do not achieve productive efficiency because the long-run equilibrium price does not equal minimum average total cost. This difference between output Q_M, which is produced, and Q_C, which would be produced given production efficiency, is excess capacity.

In addition, the price that the monopolistically competitive firm will charge is $Q_M b$ (equal to OP) which is greater than marginal cost ($Q_M c$). Since this price exceeds marginal cost we can also conclude that the firm does not achieve allocative efficiency as defined in Chapter 9.

This is the same excess capacity concept that was discussed in earlier chapters. At the root of this excess capacity is product differentiation. Each firm's attempt to differentiate itself, or its product, from all the others in the market results in the overall market being fragmented. Excess capacity is the result.

The market has been so fragmented that the representative firm in each industry finds its profit-maximizing output to be one at which average total costs are not at the minimum. This means, in effect, that the total output of a monopolistically competitive market could be produced by a fewer number of firms and at a lower cost. Examples of excess capacity are seen in the large number of hairdressing salons, gas stations and travel agencies that dominate the urban landscape.

Does this then mean that public policy should somehow restrain firms from fragmenting the market by attempting to differentiate themselves? The answer to this is almost certainly no, because, apart from its being very difficult to do, there are benefits from differentiation. The most important is that consumers have a wide choice of different variations of the same general product which makes it more likely that diverse consumer tastes will be fully satisfied. There are many gasoline stations, convenience stores and shoe styles available to choose from in our economy. Most people see this as a strength of the market system. However, this wide choice does come with a cost to the consumer which is that production could be technically more efficient if each firm could raise its output to the level where average total costs are at a minimum.

Franchise Phenomenon   It should be clear from the discussion so far that there are no economic profits in a monopolistically competitive industry in the long run because of easy entry of new firms into the industry. We can turn this observation around and deduce that if entry could somehow be blocked, then the chances for most firms to experience economic profits would be greatly enhanced. How would it be possible to block entry, i.e., to make a monopolistically competitive industry less competitive? The question again raises the phenomenon of product differentiation. If a product could be successfully differentiated to redefine what constitutes an industry then it might

Study Guide

QUESTION 11.3

Given the following data:

Quantity	MC	AC	MR
140	$ 80	$99.57	$86
160	84	97.62	84
180	89	96.67	82
200	95	96.50	80
220	102	97.00	78
240	111	98.08	76

A) What output will this firm produce?

B) How much excess capacity exists at this output level?

be possible to partially block entry into it. This is the explanation for the enormous growth in nation-wide groupings of franchised firms. We find such groupings in the fast-food industry, real estate agencies, auto repair specialists and convenience stores, among others. There are several potential advantages to such groupings including bulk purchasing, national advertising and, in particular, brand identification. In addition, it allows for individuals to own their own business without having to accumulate the large sum of money it would take to get started on their own. If such brand identification becomes strong enough that going out for a hamburger is redefined as going out to MacDonald's, then the meaning of the term industry is changed. This means that entry can be controlled, since each franchise holder has a contractual commitment from the franchiser that entry into his territory is blocked. Now, of course, there is no guarantee that a rival grouping will not enter the same territory but, nonetheless, entry by a new firm selling the same differentiated product is controlled. Proof that even this limited blocking of entry is valuable is found in the fact that the price to purchase an established franchise firm is often quite high.

Professional associations also try to redefine the industry in which their members practice. They do this by trying to create the perception in the public's mind that members of the association are better qualified to do a certain kind of work than are non-members. If hiring an accountant is redefined, through advertising, to hiring a Certified General Accountant, then the demand for CGAs will increase. If, in addition, the association is able to limit the number of new certifications that it issues (restrict entry), then those who already hold certification will benefit in the form of higher fees.

Blocked Entry through Government Policy

There are examples where entry into a monopolistically competitive industry is blocked by government law or regulation. For example, there are several things required to enter the taxi cab business in the City of Vancouver. One would, of course, need a special driver's licence, a car, a kilometrage meter and a sign. But that is not all. One would also have to obtain a taxi licence. But this is unlike any ordinary business licence, because the City of Vancouver limits the quantity issued. Therefore, often the only way to buy a licence is to purchase one from an existing holder. This, of course, can be done, but the price is rather steep — approximately $125,000 (in the spring of 1994). How can the holders of existing licences get away with such a price? The answer is because entry is blocked by the policy of the city government to allow no net increase in the total number of cabs. Government-regulated quotas on such agricultural products as chickens, cheese and milk have the same effect — the existing holders of such quotas can sell their quota for a (sometimes high) price. If entry ceased to be blocked by a change in government policy, then the price of an existing licence or quota would immediately drop to zero.

In summary, a purely monopolistically competitive industry will experience zero economic profits in the long run. Free entry by new firms ensures this. If successful product differentiation and a redefinition of what is an industry is successful then what was free entry becomes controlled entry and economic profits could exist in the long run. Similarly, if government pursues a policy of limiting entry by new firms into a particular industry, then long-run economic profits are likely.

BOX 11A
1. What are the four characteristics of a monopolistically competitive industry?
2. In the short run, is it possible for a monopolistically competitive firm to make economic profits?
3. What reaction will be triggered if the average firm in a monopolistically competitive firm is making economic profits?
4. What can be said about a firm's average total cost if it is experiencing excess capacity?
5. If entry into a monopolistically competitive industry can be, at least partially, blocked, then the possibility of firms' making economic profits is increased. True or false?

Oligopoly

oligopoly: an industry dominated by a few large firms.

Let us now turn to the last of our four market models, **oligopoly**. An oligopoly is characterized first of all by the fact that the industry is made up of a *few large firms*. That is to say, the concentration ratio discussed in Chapter 7 is high in an oligopoly industry.

The few firms in such an industry may produce a standardized product, such as steel pipe, or a differentiated product such as a Ford automobile. Examples of oligopolistic industries include tobacco, breweries, automobiles, major appliances, petroleum products, batteries, steel, lumber and pulp. Individual oligopolistic firms are generally large enough to be commonly known by most people. They include all the "Generals" — General Motors, General Foods, General Tire, General Electric, General Paint, etc., plus a host of other household names from Phillips to Nikon to Alcan.

New firms do occasionally enter an oligopoly industry. Yet, *entry is difficult* — much more so, for example, than in a monopolistically competitive industry. Let's examine why this is so. Notice that the firms mentioned above concentrate on the production of a physical product such as a car, a tire, a TV set or a box of cereal. This is no coincidence since the production of almost any physical product involves economies of scale, and such economies result in falling average cost as output is increased. Thus, at the

BOX 11.1

Below is some data on selected industries in Canada that are highly concentrated. The figures indicate the percentage of total industry output produced by the largest four firms within the industry.

Industry	Percentage
Tobacco products	99.4
Breweries	97.7
Motor vehicles	95.1
Asphalt roofing	86.1
Major appliances	85.0
Cement	81.7
Distilleries	77.0
Petroleum products	64.0
Steel pipe and tubes	63.7

Source: Statistics Canada, *Industrial Organization and Concentration in the Manufacturing, Mining and Logging Industries,* 1985 (Ottawa, June 1989).

early stages of a new industry, those firms that are first able to increase their output levels will gain a tremendous advantage over their rivals who lag behind. This leads to the dominance of an industry by the few firms who grew fastest in the beginning. Thus, once the industry has experienced its early stages of existence, barriers to entry become more significant.

The third characteristic of an oligopoly industry is that they, like firms in monopolistic competition, engage in a great deal of *non-price competition*. This is especially so when product differentiation is present. Such non-price competition can take the form of advertising, competing in terms of standards of product quality, or guarantees, or various other kinds of sales promotion activities.

mutual interdependence:
the condition where Firm A will not take action without considering the reactions of rival firms.

The fourth characteristic is the ability of the firm to have significant *control over the price* that it charges for its product. However, in addition to the effect of consumer demand in determining the price, the oligopolist's control is also circumscribed by a phenomena called **mutual interdependence** which is the fifth characteristic of this market structure. Mutual interdependence exists when one firm, contemplating a course of action, must consider the reaction of rival firms. It is this phenomena of mutual interdependence that, more than any other characteristic, distinguishes oligopoly from the other types of market structures. For example, let's imagine a typical oligopolistic industry where a large percentage of the total output is produced by only two firms (the soft drink industry in North America is similar to this situation). Each firm is large and powerful and would, presumably, be able to set the price of its own product. Yet, any pricing decision that either firm might decide on could generate a response from the rival firm. Thus, the power of firm A is very much constrained by the anticipated reaction of Firm B. Such interdependence plays a crucial role in any oligopoly environment.

The idea of firm interdependence can be traced back to the work of the French mathematician Antoine Cournot in the first half of the nineteenth century. Much can be gained by working through his duopoly (two firms only) model.

We begin the discussion of the Cournot model by imagining an isolated village in a remote, mountainous region of ancient Persia. The village sheikh has recently given exceptional service to the empire's sultan, who responds by granting the sheikh ownership of his local village's only water well which, up to now, has been treated as a common property resource.

The shiekh wasn't at all sure what to do with his new endowment so he travelled to the capital city to seek the advice of a famous seer. Upon hearing of the sheikh's situation, the seer told of several other sheikh's who have recently reported that village wells had ran dry as a result of overuse. Thus, the seer's advice to our sheikh was to take on the role of stewardship of the well and to reduce the rate of water usage by one-half.

The sheikh thanked the seer for his wise counsel, returned to the village, and spent the next week observing how many jugs of water were taken from the well each day. This number turned out to be a daily average of 1,200 jugs. The following day, the sheikh assigned some of his guards to surround the well and to allow only 600 jugs to be drawn. Such action created immediate chaos. Some villagers who arrived early in the day got three jugs, others only two or one and still others, who arrived late, got none. Some of this latter group, all of whom were angry, attempted to bribe the guards by offering to *pay* for a jug of water rather than go home empty handed.

This phenomenon, which was quite novel to our well-intentioned sheikh, gave him an idea. He thought that all the people should start to pay for the water since it was a precious resource that needed to be conserved. Further, the sheikh had a vague sense (he had not heard of the theory of marginal utility) that each person would pay according to how much he or she valued water.

The price bidding began the very next day as another 600 jugs of water were made available but confusion continued for a few days with the individual bids ranging from a low of 10 shekels (again by those who arrived early) to a high of 50 shekels by the rich rug merchant who obtained the last jug sold that particular day.

But things soon settled down and a market-determined equilibrium price of 33 shekels was established and the 600 jugs a day supply was carefully counted out each morning. The villagers were, at first, not happy about having to pay for water that was previously free. Nonetheless, the sheikh did manage to convince everyone that water needed to be rationed to ensure its continued supply and that price was the only fair way to accomplish this rationing.

The sheikh's daughter, Mahak, who loved to dabble in theoretical mathematics and abstract thought, concluded that what had recently transpired in the village could be illustrated by a graph such as the one in Figure 11.5.

Mahak, being quite intrigued with her graph went on to discover that there was a marginal revenue curve associated with the demand curve which fell at a rate twice that of the demand curve. Further, she realized that marginal revenue was exactly zero with the 600th jug sold. Quick calculations revealed that, since marginal revenue was zero, total revenue gained from the sale of water had been maximized. This made Mahak very happy since all of the income from the sale of water was going into a fund to build a

FIGURE 11.5 The Demand Curve for Water

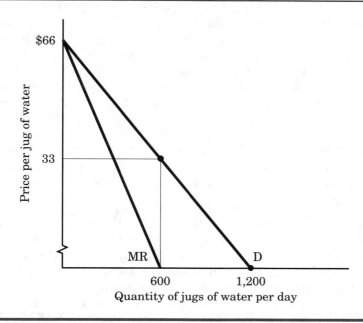

When water was free (price = 0) the villagers drew 1,200 jugs a day. The sheikh's rationing of water at a quantity of 600 jugs, which is both where MR = 0 and where total revenue is maximized, resulted in a market-determined price of 33 shekels.

school for the village children. Knowledge of this also convinced all the other villagers of the wisdom of a market-determined price as a means of rationing a precious resource.

What Mahak overlooked was that 600 jugs a day at 33 shekels was also a monopolists profit-maximizing output and price since the marginal revenue of zero *also equalled* the zero marginal cost of production. (We are assuming that the costs of the guards are a fixed cost.) Furthermore, the elasticity of demand at this point on the demand curve is at unity, exactly, since total revenue is being maximized. (Mahak missed this last point too.)

Our story could end here but, alas, one day a village shepherd was digging some large stones out of the ground to give his sheep better access to a nearby mountain trail when he discovered a bountiful spring of fresh water.

Omar was, at first, not sure what to do with his new found fortune. He decided to also hire some guards and, not wanting to upstage the sheikh, put up for sale only one-half the sheikh's quantity. Thus, 300 jugs of Omar's water went on sale the next morning at the same price of 33 shekels. Word about Omar's water quickly spread but he only sold a few jugs and the sheikh found that his sales fell by exactly the same number of jugs that Omar had sold.

Disorder once again returned the following day as, again, 900 jugs were offered for sale (600 and 300) and both Omar and the sheikh, not wanting to again be left with unsold water at the end of the day, began to offer jugs at a lower price. Some villagers reported being able to buy a jug for as low a price as 10 shekels, others paid as much as 28 shekels.

But the market forces are strong, so calm returned within a few days as an equilibrium price of 14 shekels was established.

At this point, Mahak informed her father that total revenue from the daily sales had dropped from its previous level of 19,800 (600 × 33) to only 8,400 (600 × 14) shekels. This angered the sheikh who became determined to get his total revenue back up. Mahak explained to her father that the easy way to do this was to *reduce* the quantity of water offered for sale. She knew (from Figure 11.5) that the total market size was 1,200 and that Omar was offering 300. She assumed that Omar would not change his output. Therefore, the remaining market size was equal to 1,200 − 300 = 900 and she knew that her father's sales revenue would be maximized by producing 450, which is one-half of the 900. She advised him that 450 would be the optimum quantity to put up for sale. This resulted in a total quantity supplied of 750 jugs (300 by Omar and 450 by the sheikh) which quickly resulted in an equilibrium price of 20 shekels (the villagers were catching on to the price fluctuations).

It was now Omar's turn to appraise the effects of the sheikh's action of cutting his supply from 600 to 450. We will assume that Omar made the same assumption that Mahak made in advising her father, i.e., the other player in this game will continue to supply the quantity of water currently being supplied. The sheikh was currently supplying a quantity of 450 jugs and so the remaining size of market was the original 1,200 less 450 or 750. One-half of 750 is 375. So this was what Omar put onto the market. This 375 plus the sheikh's 450 is a total of 825 which was greater than the previous total of 750 and this caused the market clearing price to drop to 17 shekels. Day by day this process continued with both the sheikh and Omar continuing to assume that the other would continue to produce the same quantity. Table 11.1 below illustrates the dynamics of this market.

TABLE 11.1 The Quantity Adjustment Dynamics of the Cournot Model

Sheikh Supplies	Omar Supplies	Total Supply	Market Clearing Price
600	0	600	33
600	300	900	14
450	300	750	20
450	375	825	17
413	375	788	18
413	394	807	17.5
404	394	798	18
404	399	803	18
402	399	801	18
402	400	801	18
400	400	800	18

The Cournot model always finds its long-run equilibrium at a combined supply of two-thirds of the total market size which in this case is two-thirds of 1,200 or 800.

Once again, this solution necessitates that each of the two players, the sheikh and Omar, react to each in a particular way. The sheikh recognizes his interdependence with Omar by continuing to adjust his quantity supplied but only in the sense that he assumes Omar will continue to supply the quantity currently being supplied. Omar reacts to the sheikh in the same way.

The end of the story is that each ended up producing one-third of the total market and Mahak eventually married Omar and they consolidated their holdings and cohabited in a non-codependent relationship.

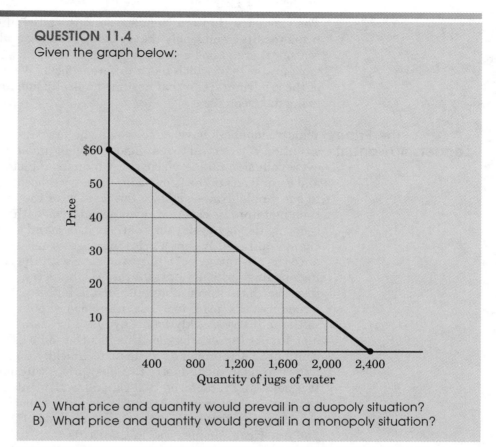

QUESTION 11.4
Given the graph below:

A) What price and quantity would prevail in a duopoly situation?
B) What price and quantity would prevail in a monopoly situation?

QUESTION 11.5
A) If after Omar and Mahak had married, they decided to maximize the total revenue from both wells combined, how much water would they put up for sale each day?
B) What would happen if, instead, *many* shepherd's had Omar's luck and discovered hundreds of new springs?

Let's now update this story by discussing four contemporary variants of oligopoly theory. In doing so we will refer back to the simple, yet powerful, Cournot model.

Collusion or Non-collusion

In today's world, the small number of firms in an oligopoly industry and the phenomena of mutual interdependence between firms raises the question of whether firms might collude with each other. Collusion means a secret agreement or understanding between firms for the purposes of setting prices and/or dividing up the market. In the story we just finished, Omar and the sheikh did not collude.

Such collusion is illegal in North America but there are definite benefits to the firms who collude which make such action tempting despite its illegality. Collusion between firms reduces the intensity of competition between them and thereby enhances their profitability and greatly reduces the risks and uncertainty that they face. In addition, colluding firms are better able to block any possible entry by a new firm.

The existence of interdependence and the possibility of collusion between firms results in oligopoly theory being complex and rather messy. For this reason, there is not a single oligopoly model but, rather, several possible variants, each of which has a different focus. We are going to look at four of these variants: two that assume non-collusion and two that assume collusion between firms.

The Price Leadership Variant

What economists have come to call the practice of *price leadership* is the situation where rival firms engage in what amounts to price fixing without overt collusion taking place. Here, industrial history and a process of trial and error leads to the firms in an industry conceding the role of price leader to one single firm — usually the largest, or the most efficient. The leader then monitors its cost and revenue patterns with the long view in mind — ignoring the day-to-day fluctuations in demand and costs. When conditions change sufficiently that a price increase seems urgent, the leader will balance the advantages of a large increase with the risks of creating a tempting opening for a new entrant into the industry. Having decided on a price increase that is profitable but not too high to risk new entry, the leader announces this price increase in some very public way and the rival firms in the industry quickly follow by also increasing their prices by a similar amount. As far as prices go, this has the same effect as would overt collusion but is accomplished without technically doing anything illegal. This allows firms in the industry to adjust prices without triggering a price war. It is generally recognized that Canadian Cement Ltd. was a price leader in the 1940s; Canadian General Electric was a price leader in light blubs in the 1950s; and, in their respective industries, U.S. Steel was in the 1960s and American Airlines was in the 1970s.

In the Cournot model story above, neither the sheikh nor Omar was willing to acknowledge the other as the industry leader. Had either one done so, a stable equilibrium would have been reached much quicker.

The Kinked Demand Curve Variant

Staying with the Cournot model story for a moment, once a stable equilibrium with both the sheikh and Omar supplying 400 jugs of water a day was reached you can imagine that neither would be anxious to "rock the boat" with any kind of deliberate change. The *kinked demand curve* variant is helpful in understanding this situation. If one were to observe, in a particular industry, that all the rival firms were charging the same (or very similar) price, would this necessarily imply that this must be an industry in which the price leadership model is operating or that the firms were colluding? The answer is that it may be neither. There is a third explanation which involves an understanding of the kinked demand curve. The basic proposition of this model is that any one interdependent firm, say Wonder Inc., will reason that if it increases the price of its product, rival firms will see this as a golden opportunity to gain market share at the expense of Wonder by simply *not* increasing their price. Thus, in effect, the demand curve that Wonder faces for all prices above the prevailing price is quite elastic, and we know that increasing the price of a product which has an elastic demand is not advantageous to the firm since its total revenue would fall. At the same time, Wonder Inc. reasons that if it were to lower its price, then its rivals may well interpret this as a very aggressive move on Wonder's part to attempt to steal customers from them. They would have no option, Wonder reasons, but to match the lower price and, thus, the overall distribution of market share between firms wouldn't change. This means that Wonder's lower price would attract very few new customers. Thus, in effect, the demand curve that Wonder faces for all prices below the prevailing price in inelastic. And, of course, lowering the price of a product with inelastic demand is also not advantageous since this too would decrease total revenue.

This leads us to the conclusion that the demand curve faced by Wonder Inc., given its view of the way that rivals would react to any price change it might initiate, is kinked at the prevailing price. This is illustrated in Figure 11.6 below.

FIGURE 11.6 The Kinked Demand Curve

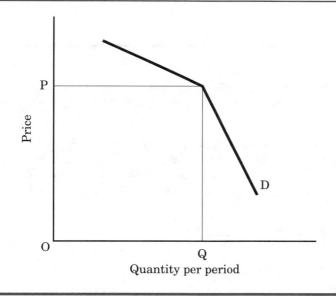

Wonder Inc. thinks that any price decrease that it might initiate will be matched by its rivals, which will result in inelastic demand below the prevailing price. Further, it thinks that if it raises the price of its product its rivals will not raise their prices, which will result in elastic demand above the prevailing price. Thus, Wonder Inc. views its demand curve as kinked at the prevailing price.

Given this then, it's a case of "damned if you do, and damned if you don't." The best action that Wonder Inc. could take is no action at all. This explains why oligopoly prices tend to be fairly rigid. What is of additional interest about the kinked demand curve is that the marginal revenue curve associated with this peculiar demand curve has a discontinuity in it. Figure 11.7 at the top of the next page will help sort this out. In the figure we have labelled the inelastic portion of the kinked demand curve D_1 and extended it in a straight line upwards on the graph. Similarly, we have labelled the elastic portion D_2 and extended it down to the right. Now, associated with both D_1 and D_2 are the appropriate marginal revenue curves which are labelled MR_1 and MR_2. Next, we drop a line directly down from the point P, which represents the prevailing price level, to the horizontal axis. The portion of MR_2 which is associated with the elastic demand curve above the prevailing price is represented by ab on MR_2. Similarly, the portion of MR_1 that is associated with the inelastic demand curve below the prevailing price

FIGURE 11.7 The Kinked Demand Curve and Marginal Revenue Curve

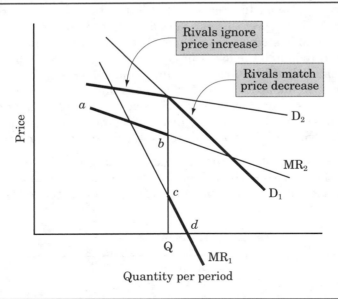

The elastic portion of the kinked demand curve is extended down to form D_2. The inelastic portion is extended up to form D_1. The associated marginal revenue curves, MR_2 and MR_1 are then added such that ab on MR_2 is the marginal revenue curve associated with the elastic portion of the kinked demand curve. Similarly, cd is the marginal revenue curve associated with the inelastic portion of the kinked demand curve. The vertical bc represents a discontinuity in the whole marginal revenue curve that is associated with the kink in the demand curve.

level is represented by cd on MR_1. The marginal revenue curve associated with the kinked demand curve D_1D_2 is therefore $abcd$. The result is that we have a discontinuity in the marginal revenue curve as represented by bc.

It turns out that this discontinuity in the marginal revenue curve could be of some significance. Figure 11.8 below illustrates this. In the figure we have labelled the relevant portion of the demand curves and the marginal revenue curves D_K and MR_K and added the marginal cost curve (MC_1) for

FIGURE 11.8 The Kinked Demand Curve with Associated Cost Curves

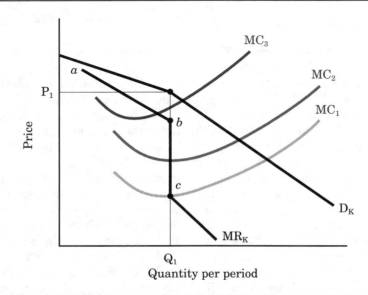

The discontinuity in the marginal revenue curve is the result of the kink in the demand curve. MC_1 is the original marginal cost curve. Quantity Q_1 is the profit-maximizing output which results in price P_1. An increase in marginal cost to MC_2 results in no change in equilibrium price or quantity. Only if the marginal cost rises to MC_3 will the firm lower its output and raise its price.

Wonder Inc. The intersection of MC_1 with *abcd* is consistent with the prevailing price of P_1 and quantity Q_1. Next, observe what happens if Wonder Inc.'s marginal cost rises to MC_2. Wonder's profit-maximizing price and quantity remain P_1 and Q_1.

Now, in normal circumstances an increase in a firm's cost of production will be (at least partially) passed on to the customer in the form of a higher price. But this does not happen here, because the firm is afraid of the loss of business from increases in its price and will be forced, reluctantly, to absorb the higher costs. In fact, the average cost of production must increase up to MC_3 before the firm will finally increase its price. This means that it is common to observe very stable prices in oligopoly industries despite changing demand and cost conditions. For example, prices of some cars or of fridges can remain unchanged for months, if not years, at a time.

One rather serious qualification about the kinked demand theory needs to be added before we leave it. If you go back and quickly reread this section you will notice that nowhere in the analysis did we explain how the prevailing price of *P1* originally got established! Thus, while it is a rather neat and logical explanation for price rigidity, but it cannot explain how that price came about in the first place.

QUESTION 11.6
Given the following graph:

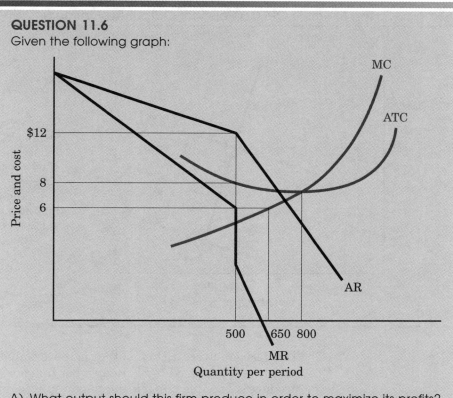

A) What output should this firm produce in order to maximize its profits?
B) What price should this firm charge?
C) What is the firm's total revenue at the profit-maximizing output?
D) What is the firm's total cost at the profit-maximizing output?

The Cartel Variant

Our third variant assumes the presence of collusion which, as we mention above, is illegal in Canada and the United States. However, in some parts of the world such collusion is not illegal and, in fact, is openly practised. Whether the collusion is out in the open or secret, the term *cartel* is used to describe the collusive cooperation of different firms.

The classic example of an openly practised cartel arrangement is that of the Organization of Petroleum Exporting Countries, OPEC, which came into existence in 1961. Within a few years it controlled over 85% of the world's oil exports, but it did not draw much worldwide attention until 1973 when the member countries decided to intensify their cooperation by restricting their (combined) output, thereby decreasing the market supply of oil. This was accomplished by setting a total output target and then assigning each member a quota based on that (restricted) quantity. This had a dramatic effect on world markets and some straightforward elasticity analysis will help us understand why. Prior to this point in OPEC's history, the demand faced by any of the twelve individual member countries was undoubtedly elastic. However, the world demand for oil is inelastic and once the member countries agreed to act in concert, the group organization created a near monopoly on oil exports. Thus OPEC, as an organization, faced a highly *inelastic demand*. Figure 11.9 shows the effect of OPEC's policy of restricting the output of oil.

FIGURE 11.9 The Effect of OPEC's Policy of Output Restriction

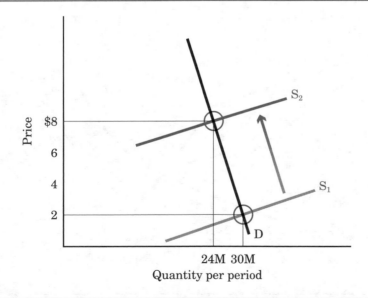

The twelve members of OPEC were able, by forming a cartel, to reduce the world's supply curve of oil which resulted in the supply curve shifting to the left. Since the world demand for oil is inelastic, this resulted in a dramatic increase in the price of oil.

The decision to restrict oil output is represented by a shift to the left in the supply curve from S1 to S2. Remember that our definition of supply is what producers are able and *willing* to put onto the market at various different prices. What we are saying here is that the OPEC producers were, at each and every price, only willing to put onto the market less than before. The inelastic demand curve in Figure 11.9 above means that a relatively modest 20% restriction in quantity (from 30 million barrels a day to 24 million) caused a dramatic 400% increase in price (from $2 a barrel to $8). Notice what happened to OPEC's revenues — they rose from $60 million a day ($30 million × 2) to $192 million day ($24 million × $8). Each of the twelve member nations were selling less oil than they had before but were, combined, receiving over three times the previous revenue. This was the beginning of a very significant shift in the wealth of the world's economies, and it all came about through former rivals acting cooperatively and treating the market as if they were a monopoly. How long could this last? Seemingly, as long as each of the twelve stuck to their assigned quotas and *trusted* that others were doing the same.

However, like most things, OPEC's oil export stranglehold on the world markets changed. On the supply side of things, the high price of oil (it peaked at about $35 a barrel in the early 1980s) brought new productive capacity onto the market by countries not in OPEC who were keen to enter the market at these high prices. In addition, the world's demand for oil was reduced as a result of conservation efforts that often involved new technology, and by some success in developing alternate sources of energy. All of this caused the world price of oil to start to drop. Then, when the worldwide recession of 1981–83 hit, the price of oil began to plummet and the OPEC countries found that cutting their quotas again and again did not stop the trend towards much lower prices. Oil revenues to the OPEC twelve fell dramatically and this was quite a shock given that these countries had come to assume that they would enjoy fantastic revenues forever and had begun to spend accordingly. In the face of falling revenues and growing excess capacity, various members of OPEC began to cheat. They started to sell their quota at the official (agreed-upon) price and then also try to sell additional quantities under the table at a reduced price. The net effect of this was a further increase in the world's supply of oil and even greater downward pressure on the price. By 1985, OPEC officially abandoned its system of quotas, and the most significant cartel of the century was reduced to a paper tiger. In summary we can say that cartels work to the advantage of their members if there is no cheating between the participants.

The Game Theory Variant Returning to the Cournot model story, the sheikh and Omar recognized their mutual interdependence in a very particular way — each making his decision based on the assumption that the other would maintain output at its present level. We call this *first-level mutual interdependence*.

The interesting question now is what would happen if the parties involved engaged in *second-level mutual interdependence*? What this means is as follows: rather than the sheikh, for instance, assuming that Omar's production would remain constant, what if the sheikh tried to predict what Omar's reaction would likely be as a result of taking some action?

A branch of mathematics called "game theory" can be used to examine this more sophisticated level of mutual interdependence. For simplicity, we will suppose that a certain industry consists of just two firms. Let's assume that these firms have made a secret agreement to collude and each, as a result, has reduced its level of production so as to drive up the price of the product. Let's start with the agreement in place with the price above its preagreement level.

Figure 11.10 on the next page is the profit pay-off matrix, as it is called, for the two firms, Deception Inc. and Deceit Unlimited. As long as each holds to the agreed-upon reduced output level they will both make $120 million in profits, as indicated by cell A.

However, there is unlikely to be absolute trust between these two firms because of the rewards that can be obtained by each firm from cheating and the constant threat that the rival firm might cheat. Each has the option to either cheat on the production quota by increasing its own output or to not cheat by sticking to the agreed-upon output level. Let's look at the thinking each firm will engage in. Deception's thinking will be as follows: "If Deceit cheats and increases output, and I do not, he gets all the advantages of my continuing to restrict output." This would raise Deceit's profits to $160 and lower Deception's to $40 as illustrated by cell C. Deception's thinking continues: "On the other hand, if Deceit does not cheat and I do, then I get all the advantages of his restriction on output, and I do not have to pay the price of restricting my own output." This would raise Deception's profits to $160 and lower Deceit's to $40 as in cell B.

FIGURE 11.10 Game Theory Pay-Off Matrix

	Deception Inc.	
	Doesn't Cheat	**Does Cheat**
Doesn't Cheat	A) Deception's Profit $120 Deceit's Profit $120	B) Deception's Profit $160 Deceit's Profit $40
Does Cheat	C) Deception's Profit $40 Deceit's Profit $160	D) Deception's Profit $60 Deceit's Profit $60

(Left axis label: **Deceit Unlimited**)

Deception has to make a decision about how to act. If it decides not to cheat, and Deceit also sticks to the agreement, the outcome represented by cell A will prevail. On the other hand, if Deceit doesn't stick to the agreement, the outcome would be represented by cell C. Thus, a decision on Deception's part to not cheat is rational only if there is *absolute* conviction that Deceit will do the same. In the absence of such absolute trust, the rational thing for Deception to do is to cheat. Meanwhile, of course, Deceit Unlimited is going through the exact same thinking process and will arrive at the exact same conclusion. The net result is that this situation will end up with both firms cheating and the agreement between them breaking down, and they will be back where they started. This is illustrated by cell D. In this case they both lose since the profits of each is reduced to $60.

This analysis has lead some economists to conclude that the likelihood of cheating is probably a more effective barrier to collusion than all the anti-combine ("anti-trust" in the U.S.) laws that Parliament has passed.

Price Wars What is normally described as a "price war" is not an uncommon occurrence in an oligopolistic industry. We now have some understanding of the various ways that such phenomena could occur. In the context of game theory it is likely that if collusion between firms broke down, one of the first signs of breakdown would be all-out price competition that took on the characteristics of a war. Similarly, if tacit collusion in the form of the price leadership model came unglued, say by an aggressive young firm challenging the established leader, then we would expect vigorous price cutting by one firm followed by retaliation by other firms. And finally, price wars can sometimes be traced to established firms taking evasive action to ward off the possible entry of a new firm.

What is significant to note in this whole discussion is that the whole concept of a price war makes sense only in an oligopoly industry where firms are interdependent and each firm does have the option and the ability to change its price — albeit usually with serious consequences.

QUESTION 11.7
Assume that two firms dominate the running shoe industry. One of these firms hires a high-profile sports figure to endorse its product by appearing in its advertising.
A) What would you expect the other firm to do in response and why?
B) After the second firm has reacted in the way you said it would above, what do you think the relative share of the market that each firm enjoyed would be?
C) Given your answer in B) above, what might these two firms be tempted to try to do?

This completes our discussion of the four variants of oligopoly theory. It is not nearly as concise and neat as the theory of monopoly or perfect competition. This is an inevitable result of the complication of mutual interdependence.

Oligopolies and Efficiency From an overall economic point of view, how do oligopolies measure up — are they an efficient form of market structure? The typical oligopoly firm possesses a degree of market power which means that its demand curve is downward-sloping. Thus it will not operate on the minimum point of its average cost curve. This means that it will not achieve economic efficiency. Furthermore, it will charge a price that exceeds average total cost and thus will not achieve productive efficiency either. Next, recognize that an oligopoly firm will charge a price higher than its marginal costs. Thus, it will also not achieve allocative efficiency. When we compare these results with that of the firm in perfect competition we see that oligopolies do not stack up very well at all.

Some people have even gone as far as to argue that monopolies are preferable to oligopolies. At least it is politically feasible to regulate monopolies, whereas oligopoly industries, which often produce very similar outcomes to those in a monopoly industry, go unregulated.

On the other hand it has been argued that oligopolies operate in an environment that is very conducive to the vital research and technological change that our economy needs in order to remain competitive by world standards. John Kenneth Galbraith is a leading proponent of this view and points out that modern research is very expensive. For this reason large oligopoly firms are the most likely firms to be able to finance research. In addition, the barriers to entry that they enjoy give them some assurance that they will be able to recover the cost of research before the new technology or new product is imitated by others.

If this view is correct, this will mean that an oligopoly industry, over the long haul, will foster technological change and improvement. This would reduce its average cost, with the result that prices would fall, and output levels would rise. However, many suggest that oligopoly industries, because they are protected by barriers to entry, may well become greedy and complacent and lose their competitive edge. In addition, they often spend their time and energy in non-price competition like advertising (thereby creating even higher barriers to entry), rather than in initiating research and development.

Once again, you can see a sharp point of debate within the discipline: oligopolies are too powerful and produce inefficiently, versus the view that oligopolies are at the cutting edge of new technology development and, in the long run, push the average costs of production down.

There is another area of controversy within economics related to the study of imperfect competition to which we now turn.

Advertising Advertising by rival firms can be thought of as a very expensive and very important form of non-price competition. The word "advertising" conjures up in most people's minds images of expensive television commercials which only very large firms can afford. However, advertising comes in other forms as well — from flyers delivered directly to households or signs in a mall. One way that smaller monopolistically competitive firms attempt to differentiate themselves from their rivals is to use the this type of advertising. Larger oligopoly firms, on the other hand, can afford national television exposure.

There is debate within the discipline of economics over the benefits of advertising to society as a whole. We will try to sort through the highlights of this debate by presenting the in-favour view which focuses on the positive aspects of advertising and the contrary view which is much more critical of advertising as a method of competition.

The in-favour view points out that advertising provides the consumer with vital information about the availability, quality and location of products that helps to greatly cut down on the consumers' search time in acquiring products. For instance, it would be very time-consuming if, because of the lack of advertising, you could only obtain information about buying a used car by driving from lot to lot.

A second argument put forward by the in-favour view is that advertising increases the degree of competition in the market since new firms are better able to enter an industry when they can announce their entry through advertising. For example, you can imagine the near impossibility for a firm like Hyundai to break into the North American car market without the benefits of national advertising. An extension of this argument is that the development and introduction of new products is also greatly enhanced by the presence of advertising. Further, the point is sometimes made that advertising creates an atmosphere which encourages new product development so that technological change is encouraged.

The third argument in the in-favour view is that advertising can actually lower the price of many products that are extensively advertised. There are two reasons for this. The first is that increased competition, mentioned above, would be expected to heighten consumer knowledge about prices and thereby lower profit margins for the representative firm, and this would be to the benefit of the consumer by forcing down prices. In addition, it has been argued that advertising enables a firm to expand its size and thereby enjoy economies of scale in production, which lower average costs, and thus, ultimately, lead to a lower price for the final product.

Lastly, another benefit credited to oligopolistic advertising is the increased availability of magazines and television shows financed by sponsors' ads. Whether this improves our overall standard of living is a value judgement best left to the reader.

In summary, the in-favour view is that advertising is beneficial in that it provides the consumer with vital information, enhances competition between firms and lowers the prices of products.

In rather dramatic contrast, the contrary view argues that advertising is wasteful because even if all advertising were eliminated tomorrow, total consumption expenditures in the economy would not decline. Expenditure patterns may well change as fewer products that were highly advertised are brought, but more of other products would be brought so that total consumer spending would be little affected. This argument continues by stating that the billions of dollars spent on trying to *persuade* consumers to buy a certain brand of product could then be spent in much more socially desirable ways. This argument discounts the informational value of advertising by pointing out that most advertising (TV in particular) is aimed at persuasion, and its effectiveness is cancelled out by a rival firm's large expenditures with the same goal in mind. For instance, millions of dollars are spent by both Proctor and Gamble and by its rival Johnson and Johnson as they go head to head in the shampoo wars on television. It might be questioned, after all is said and done, whether the consumer is any better off as a result.

Proponents of the contrary view also challenge the idea that advertising increases competition by arguing that it is just as likely that huge advertising budgets used to promote brand loyalty in a product can create a barrier to entry that could, in fact, encourage the emergence of monopoly tendencies. As an example, think of some brand names commonly used in the generic sense: a Hoover is a vacuum cleaner; Kleenex is really facial tissue; a Band Aid is an adhesive dressing; Saran Wrap is quite ordinary plastic sheeting; and Scotch tape is just one of many types of adhesive tape. Because of this brand identification with a product, it is very difficult for new firms to enter these markets.

Finally, the contrary view holds that expenditures on advertising must raise the price of products. Someone pays for the billions of dollars spent every year on advertising and that someone must be either the producer of the product or the consumer of it. If the producer in fact ended up paying, it would seem logical for them to not advertise. But, the argument goes, they don't pay and thus the consumer does and it is very unlikely that any-one's hair is any cleaner or more beautiful because of advertising — but the shampoo is probably more expensive than it would otherwise be.

In summary, the contrary view is that advertising is mostly persuasive, wasteful, encourages concentration within industries and raises prices to the detriment of consumers.

As you can see, there are valid points on both sides, and empirical studies have not succeeded in putting an end to this argument. One clear observation remains however, which is that huge expenditures on advertising continue to be made every year, especially by large firms who are locked in direct competition with one another. Suppose that in the following example, there are two large competing firms who dominate an industry. One big question that faces both firms is how much to spend on advertising. To a large extent the answer to this question depends on how much the rival firm spends. Figure 11.11 below shows the pay-off matrix (total profits) that each firm can expect under the four possible conditions of each firm spending a little or spending a lot on advertising.

FIGURE 11.11 Rival Firm's Advertising Strategies

	Western's Advertising Strategy	
	Small budget	**Large budget**
Small budget	A) Western's Profits $500 Eastern's Profits $500	B) Western's Profits $800 Eastern's Profits $150
Large budget	C) Western's Profits $150 Eastern's Profits $800	D) Western's Profits $300 Eastern's Profits $300

(left axis label: **Eastern's Advertising Strategy**)

If both firms — Western and Eastern — were to choose the strategy of a small advertising budget, the result would be represented by cell A above in which each firm receives $500 million in profits per year. There is, however, an enormous risk involved if either firm chooses this strategy, as can seen by examining the results in cells B and C. The fact is that if either firm chooses a small budget strategy and its rival chooses a large budget strategy, then its profits will suffer a significant decline while its rival's profits will increase. For example, if Western goes with a small bud-get and Eastern goes with a large budget, then Eastern's profits will rise to $800 million, while Western's profits will fall to $150 million (cell C).

The reason for this is not hard to understand. If Western greatly increases the advertising expenditure on its product while Eastern does not, then Western will gain market share at its rival's expense. In effect, the demand for Western's product will increase while Eastern's demand will decrease, with the result that profits will rise in the one case and fall in the other. Cell B illustrates the opposite behaviour by the two firms. Each firm, being aware of the possible disaster that could result from choosing a small budget strategy, reasons that it has no choice but to go with a large budget strategy and the result of this reasoning is represented in cell D where each firm ends up with $300 million profit. And, as we have seen, trust is often conspicuously absent in oligopoly industries. This helps to explain the large expenditures on advertising in today's market economy. Now, you may well ask: Wouldn't it be advantageous for the two firms to get together and agree with each other not to use the large budget strategy? On the surface the answer to this question would seem to be yes but for this solution (represented by cell A) to persist, as we have seen, both firms must trust each other.

Profit Maximization

John Kenneth Galbraith's work is also at the centre of another, much more profound, point of debate within the discipline. All four market models — from perfect competition to oligopoly — contain an underlying assumption which we need to examine. This is the assumption that the firm behaves in a way that maximize its profits. If the demand changes or if costs change or if taxes change, then the firm will adjust its output level and (if it can) its price level in response, so as to continue making maximum profits. This assumption is what underlies the concept of firm equilibrium and is at the heart of microeconomics. This can be seen by the following quote from the University of Chicago's George Stigler:

> [Profit maximization is] the strongest, the most universal, and the most persistent of the forces governing entrepreneurial behaviour.[1]

Galbraith challenged this fundamental assumption in his work *The New Industrial State* (1967). In this book, Galbraith pointed out that a characteristic feature of the large multinational corporation of today is that management and ownership have become divorced. Ownership of publicly traded companies is typically very diverse and unknown to the hired managers that make up the decision-making corps whom Galbraith calls the technostructure. Galbraith goes on to say:

> So long as earnings are above a certain minimum it would be agreed that management has little to fear from the stockholders. Yet [the discipline of economics assumes that] it is for these stockholders, remote, powerless and unknown, that management seeks to maximize profits.[2]

Most would find, argues Galbraith, that the proposition that individual managers seek to maximize their own return — to make as much income for themselves as is possible — is reasonable and sound. For management to maximize the profits of the corporation, they would have show great

---

[1] George J. Stigler, *The Theory of Price*, revised edition (New York: MacMillan, 1952), p. 149.
[2] John Kenneth Galbraith, *The New Industrial State* (Boston: Houghton Mifflin Co., 1967), p. 115

restraint in what they pay themselves. In effect they would have to forego personal reward to enhance it for others. Galbraith says:

> Accordingly, if the traditional commitment to profit maximization is to be upheld, they [the managers] must be willing to do for others, specifically the stockholders, what they are forbidden to do for themselves.[1]

If the behaviour of today's modern corporations is not driven by profit maximization, how might one understand their behaviour? Galbraith sees the *multiple* goals of today's corporations as including the earning of sufficient profits to keep the stockholders happy as well as other goals such as obtaining autonomy of decision making, developing state-of-the-art technology, achieving high rates of growth, and even social goals such as the design and manufacture of a superior space vehicle which would greatly enhance the company's image and give the corporation's management a great sense of pride. There need not be a particular hierarchy in such a list of possible goals since one corporation's ranking of goals may not be the same as another corporation's. The point is that modern management is often motivated to pursue a number of goals rather than the single one of attempting to maximize profit.

Again, we do not feel any particular ability, or see any particular need, to try to resolve this issue. We do, however, find it important and interesting that something as fundamental as the assumption of profit maximization has not gone without challenge. This is evidence that the discipline of economics is alive and its ideas continue to be debated and developed.

QUESTION 11.8
A) Explain how one might argue that the existence of oligopolies means *higher* prices for consumers.
B) Explain how one might argue that the existence of oligopolies means *lower* prices for consumers.

BOX 11B
1. List four characteristics of an oligopoly industry.
2. What is meant by mutual interdependence?
3. Explain how the demand curve for an oligopoly firm might be kinked.
4. What is the main deficiency of the kinked demand curve variant of oligopoly theory?
5. What is a cartel?
6. On what aspect of interfirm behaviour does game theory focus?
7. In what way does the in-favour view argue that advertising is beneficial to consumers?
8. What might be some of the goals of the technostructure?

---

[1] Ibid., p. 117.

Chapter Highlights

The chapter begins by identifying the characteristics of the market structure called monopolistic competition, which is an industry made up of many firms into which there is freedom of entry. The firms have some control over price and engage in product differentiation. Next, the short-run equilibrium position for a typical firm within this market structure is contrasted with the long-run situation. The important result is that entry by new firms in the long run will drive economic profits for the typical firm down to zero. From this analysis we conclude that monopolistically competitive firms experience excess capacity and, therefore, do not achieve either productive or allocative efficiency. Discussion of the franchise phenomenon and blocked entry by government policy is done to highlight the important role of freedom of entry.

The chapter then turns to a discussion of the theory of oligopoly industries. Five characteristics of oligopoly are discussed. The fact that an oligopoly is an industry dominated by a few large firms into which entry is difficult is examined, as well as the fact that the firms have control over the price of the product which they sell and engage in non-price competition. Most importantly, mutual interdependence exists between firms. Then the chapter moves into a story built around what is known as the Cournot model of duopoly, which is a special form of oligopoly. The conclusion of this story is that this particular kind of mutual interdependence leads to an output that is larger than we would expect in the situation of a monopoly.

This story is used to set up a discussion of the four variants of oligopoly theory that are variations on the theme of interdependence between firms. The possibility of collusion among firms is also examined.

Discussion of each of the four variants — price leadership; the kinked demand curve; cartels, and game theory then follows.

We then conclude that oligopolies fail to achieve either productive or allocative efficiency because they maximize profits at an output that is not at minimum average total cost and charge a price that exceeds the marginal cost of production.

The chapter closes with a discussion of the role of advertising, by looking at arguments that favour the practice and some that do not, and with a discussion of the assumption that firms are profit maximizers.

New Glossary Terms

Workbook

Study Tips

1. Students often relate well to this chapter because it is able to explain some observations that they make about the real world. If this is your reaction, this will be an enjoyable chapter and don't think that you must be missing something because "it seems so obvious."

2. The following is to help you to keep in mind three important concepts that are used in this chapter to evaluate industry performance:

> *Economic efficiency* occurs when the firm is producing at an output which results in minimum (short-run) ATC.
>
> *Production (or productive) efficiency* occurs when the firm is producing at an output which results in minimum ATC and is charging a price equal to ATC.
>
> *Allocative efficiency* occurs when the firm is charging a price equal to MC.

3. The chapter's Figure 11.2 is key to your understanding of firm equilibrium under conditions of monopolistic competition. In stark contrast, oligopoly theory comes in four variants and Figure 11.10 is key to understanding but one of those, the game theory variant.

4. Key problem I (like the one in Chapter 9) asks you to use knowledge from earlier chapters as well as this one to find solutions. This is done in order to emphasize that the quantity produced and the price of any product depends on the type of market structure in which that production takes place.

5. When you are asked to sketch the long-run equilibrium of a monopolistically competitive firm you need to ensure that the demand curve is just tangent to the ATC curve and that this point of tangency is at the same output level where MR = MC. Therefore, leave the drawing of the marginal revenue curve until last.

Are You Sure?

Indicate whether the following statements are true or false. If false, indicate why they are false.

1. One characteristic of monopolistic competition is the existence of many firms operating in the same industry.
T or **F**   If false: _____

_____

_____

2. Monopolistically competitive firms typically make economic profits in the long run.
T or **F**   If false: _____

_____

_____

3. Productive efficiency occurs when firms charge a price which is equal to ATC.
T or **F**   If false: _____

_____

_____

4. The franchise system attempts to limit the entry of new firms into an existing industry.
T or **F**   If false: _____

_____

_____

5. Mutual interdependence is a significant characteristic of a monopolistically competitive industry.
T or **F**   If false: _____

_____

_____

6. Both firms in the Cournot model of duopoly assume that the rival firm will continue to produce the same output that it is currently producing.

T or F   If false: _____

_____

_____

7. Allocative efficiency is absent if price exceeds marginal cost.
T or F   If false: _____

_____

_____

8. Both the kinked demand curve and the game theory variants of oligopoly theory assume that firms collude with each other.
T or F   If false: _____

_____

_____

9. Galbraith argues that oligopoly firms can be efficient because of the research they engage in and the technological change that they foster.
T or F   If false: _____

_____

_____

10. The assumption that firms attempt to maximize revenues underlies much of the analysis in microeconomics.
T or F   If false: _____

_____

_____

Translations

On the grid in Figure W11.1, draw a demand curve for Firm A that indicates a current price of $12 and an output of 300, and reflects the fact that this firm thinks rivals will match any price decrease and ignore any price increase. Then sketch in the associated marginal rev-

enue curve. Finally sketch in two marginal costs curves, MC_1 and a lower MC_2, so that the same output would be produced regardless of which of the two curves was being referred to.

FIGURE W11.1

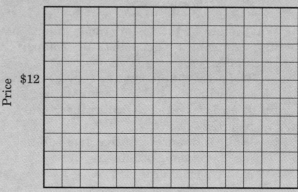

Quantity of output per period

Choose the Best

1. In which of the following two market structures is entry easiest?
    a) Monopolistic competition.
    b) Oligopoly.

2. What does product differentiation mean?
    a) It is the attempt by the firm to offer a product that is different from that of its rivals.
    b) It is the attempt by the firm to offer a product that is seen to be different from that of its rivals.

3. What price does a monopolistically competitive firm charge?
    a) A price that is equal to marginal cost.
    b) A price that is greater than marginal cost.

4. What is the level of economic profits earned by a firm operating in the short run under conditions of monopolistic competition?
    a) It is positive.
    b) It is likely to be positive but could be negative.
    c) It is zero.

5. What will be the effect of entry by new firms into a monopolistically competitive industry?
   a) It will shift the firm's demand curve up.
   b) It will shift the market's demand curve up.
   c) It will shift the market's supply curve to the right.

6. What might be the result of many new firms entering a monopolistically competitive industry?
   a) The price charged by the representative firm will be equal to marginal cost.
   b) The representative firm will certainly incur losses.
   c) While the representative firm will not make economic profits, it will be able to make normal profits.

7. What is meant by the term "allocative efficiency"?
   a) When a firm is producing an output that equals minimum ATC.
   b) When a firm is producing an output and charging a price that equals minimum ATC.
   c) When a firm is charging a price equal to MC.

8. Which of the following would measure excess capacity?
   a) The difference between what is being produced and the level of production that minimizes long-run average costs.
   b) The difference between what is being produced and the level of production that minimizes short-run average cost.
   c) The difference between what is being produced and the level of production that minimizes short-run marginal cost.
   d) The difference between the levels of production that minimize short-run average cost and those which achieve economic capacity.

9. All *except one* of the following are oligopoly industries. Which is the exception?
   a) The manufacture of automobiles.
   b) The manufacture of cigarettes.
   c) The provision of accounting services.

   d) The provision of long-distance telephone services.

10. Which of the following statements is correct about price and quantity when comparing a monopoly situation and the Cournot duopoly situation?
    a) Both price and quantity would be higher in the monopoly situation than in the duopoly situation.
    b) Both price and quantity would be lower in the monopoly situation than in the duopoly situation.
    c) The price would be lower and the quantity would be higher in the monopoly situation than in the duopoly situation.
    d) The price would be higher and the quantity would be lower in the monopoly situation than in the duopoly situation.

11. All *except one* of the following statements about the kinked demand curve theory of oligopoly are correct. Which one is the exception?
    a) It explains why the price charged by rival firms are often similar.
    b) It explains why rival firms that charge similar prices may not be in collusion.
    c) It explains why the prices charged by rival firms sometimes go for months, or even years, without changing.
    d) It explains, particularly well, how the prevailing price in the industry first got established.

12. If we assume that the price leadership variant of oligopoly theory is operating effectively in a particular industry, what prevents the leader from announcing a dramatic increase in the price of the product sold?
    a) The fear that the ATC of the firms within the industry would decrease.
    b) The fear that new firms would be tempted to enter the industry.
    c) The fear that one of the other firms would break ranks and increase their price even more.
    d) The fear that such action would provide proof that the firms are engaged in overt collusion.

13. All of the following statements *except one* are correct concerning the cartel variant of oligopoly theory. Which one is the exception?
    a) An effective cartel restricts the supply of the product being sold.
    b) The individual members of the cartel must agree to and respect quotas on their output.
    c) The primary threat to the success of a cartel is government regulation.
    d) The output and the price of the cartel will be similar to that of a monopoly.

14. All of the following statements *except one* are correct about the game theory variant of oligopoly theory. Which one is the exception?
    a) Game theory analysis has lead some economists to conclude that the likelihood of cheating is a more effective barrier to collusion than government legislation.
    b) Game theory analysis involves a more sophisticated level of mutual interdependence than found in the Cournot model.
    c) The origin of game theory analysis is closely related to mathematics.
    d) It is rational for each firm to trust the other.
    e) Game theory analysis is able to predict a likely outcome of the actions of two firms.

15. All of the following *except one* could be an explanation of a price war between firms. Which one is the exception?
    a) A breakdown in the collusive agreement between firms.
    b) The intense competition that one finds in a perfectly competitive industry.
    c) An aggressive young firm challenging the established price leadership of a rival firm.
    d) The action taken by established firms to ward off the possible entry of a new firm.

16. Which of the following statements is correct about oligopoly firms?
    a) They typically achieve economic efficiency.
    b) They may or may not charge a price higher than marginal cost.

c) They maximize profits by equating marginal revenue and marginal cost.
d) They operate in an intensely competitive atmosphere in which the market dictates price.
e) They produce an output which puts them on the rising portion of the ATC curve.

17. All of the following statements, *except one*, are valid arguments for the existence of large profits and barriers to entry in an oligopoly industry. Which statement is not valid?
    a) The barriers to entry are needed to provide the assurance that large sums spent on research can be recovered in future sales.
    b) The barriers to entry and the large profits allow for the introduction of various kinds of non-price competition.
    c) The large profits are needed to finance the development of new technology.
    d) The barriers to entry help maintain large-size firms within the industry which enhances the ability of these firms to capture economies of scale.
    e) The barriers to entry increase the prospect of downward shifts in the short-run average cost curves.

18. All *except one* of the following statements are valid arguments in favour of advertising. Which one is the exception?
    a) Advertising provides consumers with information.
    b) Advertising reduces the search time needed by consumers to acquire products.
    c) Advertising increases the barriers to entry into an industry and thereby enhances competition.
    d) Advertising can lower the prices of products by reducing the firms average cost through increased output levels.
    e) Advertising increases the availability of radio and television program choices for the consumer.

19. Most economic theory is based on the assumption that firm's have one goal. Which one of the following is that goal?
    a) Profit maximization.

b) Continued growth of the corporation's sales and size of operations.
c) The achievement of management autonomy in decision making.
d) Development of state-of-the art technology.
e) Enhancement of the company's image and the management's pride.

20. All of the following statements *except one* are correct about a firm operating under conditions of either monopolistic competition or oligopoly. Which one is the exception?
a) It faces a downward-sloping demand curve.
b) It charges a price that is above marginal cost in both the short run and the long run.
c) It charges a price that is equal to average cost in both the short run and the long run.

d) It fails to achieve economic efficiency.
e) It fails to achieve productive efficiency.

What's Wrong?

Can you spot the four errors in the following passage? (Ignore grammatical mistakes!)

Both the market structures of monopolistic competition and oligopoly assume that the firm has at least some control over price. In both cases it is assumed that entry by new firms is easy. One point on which they do differ is that profits are possible in the long run in the case of monopolistic competition whereas they are not in the case of oligopoly. It is also true that product differentiation plays a bigger role in oligopoly than it does in monopolistic competition. One of the interesting aspects of comparing these two market structures is how game theory can so easily be applied to both and how firms are unable to achieve economic efficiency in either.

Key Problem I

Figure W11.2 shows the demand and the marginal cost curves for Firm S which is the only producer of vegetable juicers in the country of Asu.

FIGURE W11.2

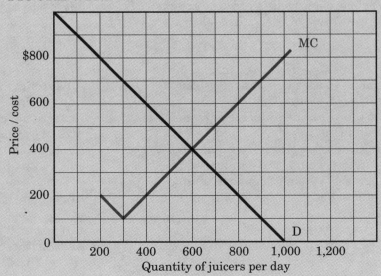

a) How many juicers will Firm S produce each day and what price will it charge? (*Hint:* Remember the profit-maximizing criteria involves marginal revenue.)

Quantity: _____; price: _____.

Figure W11.3 shows the demand and marginal cost curve for Firm D which is the only producer of vegetable juicers in the country of Adanac.

FIGURE W11.3

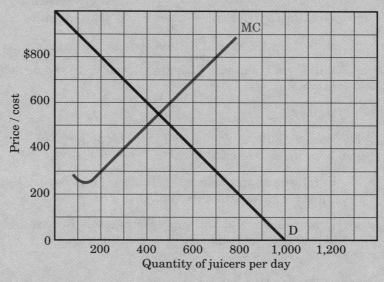

b) How many juicers (per day) will Firm D produce and what price will it charge?

Quantity: _____; price: _____.

c) Next, a political event of some significance occurs — the countries of Asu and Adanac form a single country. Fill in the demand column in Table W11.1 to reflect the market demand faced by both firms in their new country, Adsu. (Ignore the supply column for now.)

TABLE W11.1

Price	Demand	Supply
$200	_____	_____
300	_____	_____
400	_____	_____
500	_____	_____
600	_____	_____
700	_____	_____
800	_____	_____
900	_____	_____

It quickly becomes evident that Firm S is the dominant firm in the new country. As a result, Firm D is forced to match Firm S's price. Also assume that S continues to produce the same output and charge the same price that it did before the countries joined together.

d) What price will Firm D charge and what quantity will it produce?

Price: _____; quantity: _____.

e) Will Firm D's profits be higher, lower or the same as they were before the political union?

Higher: _____; lower: _____; the same: _____.

Next, assume that Firms S and D decide to form an (illegal) cartel and act as a single profit-maximizing firm.

f) Fill in the supply column in Table W11.1 above. (*Hint:* Each firm is willing to supply a particular output at each price.)

g) Draw the demand and supply curves for the cartel on the grid in Figure W11.4 below. Then add the marginal revenue curve.

FIGURE W11.4

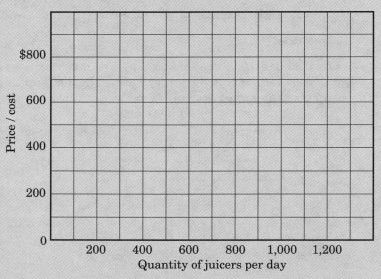

h) What quantity will the cartel produce and what price will it charge?

Quantity: _____; price: _____.

i) Will the cartel's profits be higher, lower or the same as the profits of *both* firms under the price leadership situation?

Higher: _____; lower: _____; the same: _____.

j) Based on the supply and demand curves in Figure W11.4, what would be the price and output if this market were perfectly competitive?

Price: _____; output: _____.

Need a Hand?

a) The key here is to remember that the marginal revenue curve falls twice as fast as the (straight-line) demand curve and draw this on the graph in Figure W11.2. Once this is done and the point where MR = MC is found, one can read the answers of **400** for quantity of **$600** for price directly from the graph.

b) As in a) you need to sketch the marginal revenue curve, find the point where MR = MC and then read the answers **300** for quantity and **$700** for price.

c) Find the quantity demanded in each firm's case in Figures W11.2 and W11.3. Adding the two figures for each price gives the following market demand.

TABLE W11.2

Price	Demand
$200	1,600
300	1,400
400	1,200
500	1,000
600	800
700	600
800	400
900	200

d) We can assume that Firm D will match the **$600** price charged by Firm S. Therefore, D's demand curve is, in effect, horizontal at the price of $600. Its best output under these conditions is where price (which also equals marginal revenue) equals marginal cost and this is at an output of 500. However, the market demand at the $600 price is only 800 units per day. So if S is producing and selling 400, then D must be producing and selling only **400**.

e) Firm D's profits must be lower because its output is higher than it was (400 not 300) so its marginal cost must be higher and its price is lower ($600 and not $700). In addition, we know that it was previously producing its profit-maximizing combination of P = $300 and Q = 700. Any combination other than this must be less profitable.

f) Here again you can read the quantity supplied by each firm at different prices from the graphs in Figures W11.2 and W11.3. For example, at the price of $400, Firm S is willing to supply 600 units and Firm D 300 units, for a total supply of 900. Doing this for each price results in the following.

TABLE W11.3

Price	Supply
$200	400
300	700
400	900
500	1,100
600	1,300
700	1,500
800	1,700
900	1,900

g)   **FIGURE W11.5** (completed Figure W11.4)

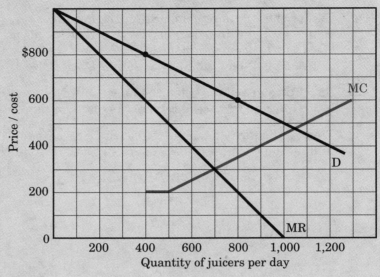

h)   MC = MR at a quantity of **700** and a price of **$650**.

i)   The cartel's profits must be **higher** than the sum of the profits of the two firms under the price leadership model because *both* firms will be producing at their profit-maximizing output.

j)   A perfectly competitive market would dictate a price and quantity where market supply (the sum of the firms MC curves) equals market demand and this would be **$475** and **1,050**.

More of the Same

On the graph in Figure W11.6, you will find the demand and the marginal cost curves for Firm H which is the only producer of fruit juicers in the country of Hither.

FIGURE W11.6

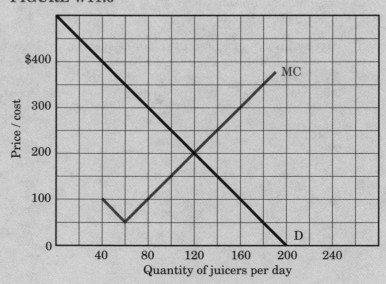

a) How many juicers will Firm H produce each day and what price will it charge?

On the graph in Figure W11.7 you will find the demand and the marginal cost curve for Firm Y which is the only producer of fruit juicers in the country of Yon.

FIGURE W11.7

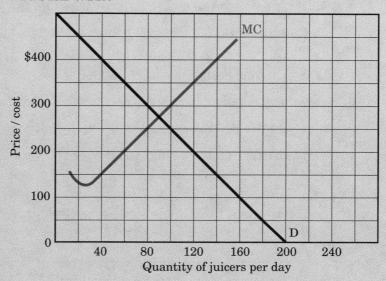

b) How many juicers (per day) will Firm Y produce and what price will it charge?

c) These two countries also form a political union. Fill in the demand column on Table W11.4 which is the market demand facing both firms in their new country (Yither?) Ignore the supply column for now.

TABLE W11.4

Price	Demand	Supply
$ 50	_____	_____
100	_____	_____
150	_____	_____
200	_____	_____
250	_____	_____
300	_____	_____
350	_____	_____
400	_____	_____

Assume that it quickly becomes evident that Firm H is the dominant firm and Firm Y is forced to match Firm H's price. You may assume that Firm H continues to produce the same output and charge the same price as it did before the countries formed a union.

d) Given this information, what price will Firm Y charge and what quantity will it produce?

e) Will Firm Y's profits be higher, lower or the same as they were before the merger?

Assume that Firms H and Y decide to form a cartel and act as a single profit-maximizing firm.

f) Fill in the supply column in Table W11.4 above.

g) Draw the demand and the supply curves for the cartel.

h) What quantity will the cartel produce and what price will it charge?

i) Will the cartel's profits be higher, lower or the same as the profits of both firms under the price leadership situation?

j) Based on the supply and demand curves in your graph in g), what would be the price and output if this market was perfectly competitive?

Key Problem II

The graph in Figure W11.8 is for a representative firm in the womens' garment industry, which is monopolistically competitive.

FIGURE W11.8

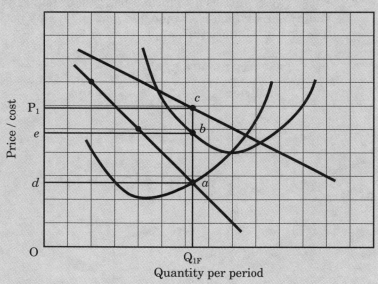

a) Label the four curves in Figure W11.8 above.

b) What area in Figure W11.8 represents:

Total cost: _____; total revenue: _____; economic profit: _____.

The graph in Figure W11.9 below represents the market supply and demand for the womens' garment industry.

FIGURE W11.9

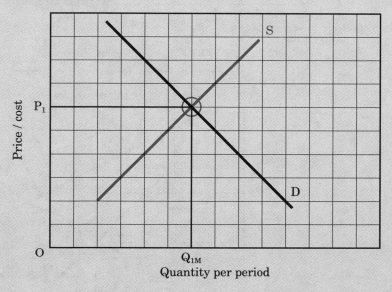

c) On the Figure W11.9, sketch in the effect of entry by new firms into this industry and label the new price and quantity traded as P_2 and Q_{2M}.

d) Using the average/marginal cost curves in Figure W11.10 (which are the same as in Figure W11.8 above), sketch in the firm's new demand and marginal revenue curves that would be consistent with zero economic profits. Label the equilibrium price and quantity traded as P_2 and Q_{2F}.

FIGURE W11.10

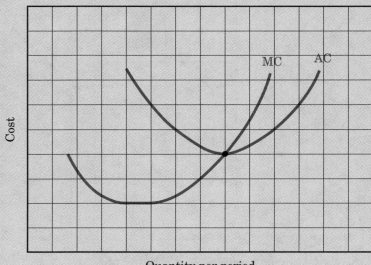

e)   Indicate, with Q_C, the capacity output for the firm.

f)   What is the amount of this firm's excess capacity?

Answer: _____.

Need a Hand?

a)   **FIGURE W11.11** (completed Figure W 11.8)

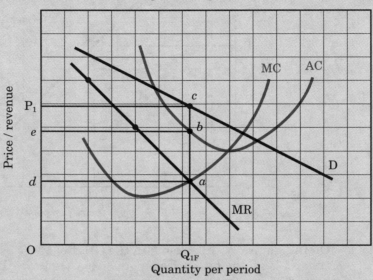

b)   Total cost is the area OQ*be* while total revenue is OQ*c*P and economic profits *ebc*P.

c)   **FIGURE W11.12** (completed Figure W 11.9)

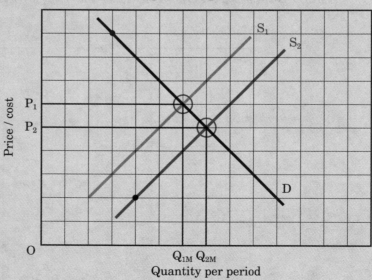

d) and e)   See Figure W11.13. Remember that the MR curve drops twice as quickly
as the AR (demand) curve. The demand curve has shifted to the left until it is
just tangent to the AC curve. The new price is at this point of tangency.

f) Excess capacity is the difference between the quantity at the lowest average cost, Q, and the actual (profit maximizing) output, Q_{2F}.

FIGURE W11.13 (completed Figure W11.10)

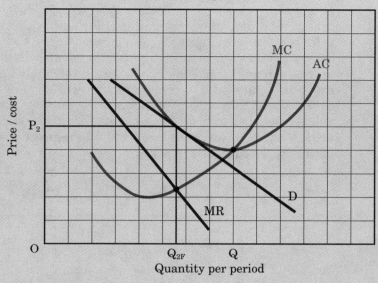

Other Problems

1. The graph in Figure W11.14 is that of a representative firm in the dry-cleaning industry.

FIGURE W11.14

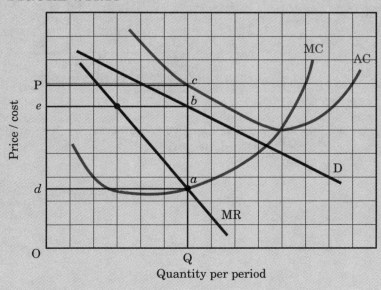

a) Identify the firm's total revenue, total cost and its losses.

TR: _____ ; TC: _____ ; total loss: _____ .

b) If this firm made a rational decision to continue to produce, despite the losses, average variable cost at output Q must be below what level?

AVC must be less than _____.

2. Aruna owns a small firm, Pottery Plus, that produces terra cotta pots which are sold in the Edmonton area. Pottery Plus has two rival firms and the current price that each firm charges for a dozen 6" pots is $12. Aruna is convinced that she dare not raise her price because her rivals will not and that she dare not decrease price because her rivals will simply match her lower price. On the graph in Figure W11.15 below, sketch in the demand and marginal revenue curves that fits Aruna's perception of the market (Aruna is currently producing 8 dozen pots per period). Next, sketch in two marginal cost curves, MCI and MCII that are at different levels but still indicate that Aruna is maximizing profits at the current $12 price.

FIGURE W11.15

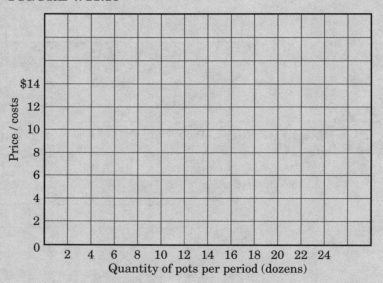

Quantity of pots per period (dozens)

3. Table W11.5 is the demand faced by Firm I, a monopolist, who enjoys zero variable cost in its production:

TABLE W11.5

Price	Demand
$5	30
4	60
3	90
2	120
1	150
0	180

a) What is the price the monopolist will charge and what quantity of output will she produce?

Price: _____; quantity: _____.

b) Suppose that Firm II, which also has zero variable cost, enters this industry and assumes that Firm I will continue to produce its current output. What output will Firm II choose to produce and what will be the new price that will prevail?

Firm II's output: _____; new price: _____.

c) If Firm I responds to Firm II's action assuming that Firm II will continue to produce at its current output, and then II responds again to I, etc., what will be the ultimate price and quantity for the each of the two firms?

Price: _____; quantity: _____.

4. Assume that the only two firms in an industry, firms X and Z, have agreed to restrict their output to 300 units per day (for each firm) and charge a price of $1,200 per unit.

a) Fill in the pay-off matrix in Figure W11.16 assuming that any possible increase in output, contemplated by either firm, is from 300 to 500.

FIGURE W11.16

Firm X

	Does not increase output	**Increases output**
Firm Z — **Does not increase output**	X's Qu: _____ Z's Qu: ____	X's Qu: _____ Z's Qu: ____
Firm Z — **Increases output**	X's Qu: _____ Z's Qu: ____	X's Qu: _____ Z's Qu: ____

b) Explain what quantity you think both firms will end up producing and why.

Unanswered Questions

Short Essays

1. Describe the four characteristics of monopolistic competition and of oligopoly. What are the main points of difference between the two?

2. Describe the five characteristics of oligopoly and explain which one distinguishes this market structure from that of the other three structures.

3. While there are social advantages to advertising, some economists remain critical of its practice. Explain.

4. What are three ways in which oligopolies are not efficient?

5. What other goals, besides profit maximization, might be important to a firm?

Analytical Questions

1. In long-run equilibrium, a monopolistically competitive firm's ATC equals price. Given this, why hasn't it achieved productive efficiency? How is excess capacity related to your answer?

2. How would your analysis of a monopolistically competitive industry be altered if the government were to block the entry of new firms?

3. The assumption underlying the interdependence between firms in the kinked demand curve variant of oligopoly theory is both similar and different from that in the Cournot model. Explain.

4. Use game theory analysis to explain why an agreement between two firms to restrict output will likely be violated.

5. Productive efficiency is nearly impossible to achieve. Explain.

Numerical Questions

1. Table W11.6 contains some revenue and cost data for the Rising Moon T-shirt company (quantities for packets of a dozen shirts).

TABLE W11.6

Price	Quantity Demanded	Total Revenue	Marginal Revenue	Marginal Cost	Total Cost
—	0	—	—	—	$ 28
——	1	——	64	——	60
——	2	——	60	——	90
——	3	——	56	——	122
——	4	——	52	——	156
——	5	——	48	——	192
——	6	——	44	——	230
——	7	——	40	——	270
——	8	——	36	——	312
——	9	——	32	——	356
——	10	——	28	——	402

a) Fill in the Marginal Cost, Total Revenue and Price columns.
b) What price will the firm charge and what output will it produce?
c) What is the firm's profit or loss?

Assume that entry into the industry results in this firm's demand decreasing by 3 at every price. Construct new TR and MR columns.

d) What price will the firm now charge and what output will it produce?
e) What is the firm's new profit or loss?

2. Suppose that there are (only) two identical firms in an industry, Hickory Dick and Hickory Dock, and that there is no collusion between them. Currently, neither firm is spending anything on advertising and each is making a profit of $15 million a year. If Dick advertises and Dock does not, Dick will increase its profits to $22 million and Dock will suffer a loss of $2 million. The opposite will be true if Dock advertises and Dick does not. If both advertise, each will have profits of $6 million.
a) Construct a pay-off matrix illustrating these circumstances.
b) Explain what you think will be the outcome of these circumstances.

3. A zero variable cost monopolist is currently maximizing profits by producing an output of 36. What output would you expect to be eventually produced by each firm if a second zero-variable-cost firm appeared on the scene?

4. Assume that an oligopoly industry is composed of three identical-cost firms who share the market equally. Table W11.7 contains the cost data for one of the firms along with its demand.

TABLE W11.7

Price	Quantity Demanded	Total Revenue	Marginal Revenue	Total Cost	Marginal Cost
$70	0	—	—	$ 0	—
65	1	____	____	15	____
60	2	____	____	25	____
55	3	____	____	40	____
50	4	____	____	60	____
45	5	____	____	85	____
40	6	____	____	115	____
35	7	____	____	155	____
30	8	____	____	205	____

a) Complete Table W11.7.
b) What price would this firm charge in order to maximize profits?
c) What would be the total output produced in the industry?
d) What would be the total industry's profit/loss?

CHAPTER TWELVE

■ ■ ■ ■ ■ ■ ■

The Factors of Production

W *hat's ahead . . . In this chapter we shift our focus from the structure of the market for goods and services to that of the market for the factors of production. The key concept here is the productivity of those factors under consideration, be they labour, land or capital. You will learn that it is both productivity and the prices of the output produced that lies behind the demand for any factor. We also examine the supply of each of the factors putting particular emphasis on the supply of labour and we explain the reasons behind different wage rates.*

---

product market: the market for consumer goods and services.

Our discussion of supply and demand in Chapters 2 through 5, as well as the market structure discussion in Chapters 8 through 11 were focused on the **product market**, e.g., the demand for orange juice and gasoline; the supply of automobiles by oligopoly firms; or of shoes from a monopolistically competitive firm.

factor market: the market for the factors of production.

We now want to shift the focus to the **factor market** and look at the supply of and demand for the factors of production — labour, natural resources (land), capital and entrepreneurial ability — as well as at some of the more interesting issues that arise from this discussion.

The Demand for Labour

To ask what determines the demand for labour is equivalent to asking: what does an employer consider in deciding whether or not to hire one more employee or one more hour of labour? The discussion in Chapter 6 on marginal productivity is key to formulating an answer. What the employer has to balance in her mind in making such a decision is the benefit derived from one more hour of labour, which is called the marginal product of labour, with the cost of employing that person, which is called the wage rate. If the benefit appears to outweigh the cost, then the additional hour will be bought. If, however, the cost outweighs the benefit, no new work will be created.

Actually, this cost/benefit comparison is a little more complicated because productivity is measured in physical units (of output), i.e., marginal product, while cost is in money units. To emphasize this point, economists often use the term marginal physical product (MPP) which is defined in the same way as was the marginal product earlier. We, therefore, need to convert marginal product into money terms. This is done by multiplying marginal

marginal revenue product: the increase in a firm's total revenue which results from the use of one more unit of input.

product (or marginal physical product) by the price the employer receives from the sale of each unit of output. This gives us what is termed the **marginal revenue product** which is formally defined as the change in total revenue as a result of using one more unit of input — in this case, one more hour of labour. We can envision the employer balancing the cost of one more hour of hired employment, which is the wage rate, with the marginal revenue product of the person supplying that extra hour.

Table 12.1 will help clarify this.

TABLE 12.1 Marginal Revenue Product of Labour Data

Hours of Labour	Total Product	Hourly Marginal Product of Labour	Unit Price of Product	Total Revenue	Hourly Marginal Revenue Product of Labour
0	0	—	$1.50	0	—
1	8	8	"	$ 12.00	$12.00
2	20	12	"	30.00	18.00
3	45	25	"	67.50	37.50
4	75	30	"	112.50	45.00
5	100	25	"	150.00	37.50
6	120	20	"	180.00	30.00
7	130	10	"	195.00	15.00
8	135	5	"	202.50	7.50
9	135	0	"	202.50	0
10	130	−5	"	195.00	−7.50

The first three columns in the above table are from Table 6.3 in Chapter 6 and need no comment. Column four indicates that the per unit price of the product is $1.50 and, further, that this price does not change as more and more output is produced and sold; e.g., we are assuming that the producer is selling its output in a perfectly competitive environment. The figures in the Total Revenue column are obtained by multiplying the total product by the $1.50 price per unit. The marginal revenue product of labour figures can be obtained by simply determining the change in total revenue or, as indicated above, by multiplying the marginal product by price.

Having identified the marginal revenue product of labour, we will now ask the question: in our hypothetical example, how many hours of labour would an employer hire if the wage rate is, for example, $10 per hour? The answer can be read directly from Table 12.1. Seven hours of labour would be hired. The reason is that each of the seven hours hired add more to total revenue — have a marginal revenue product — that exceeds the $10 wage rate. The eighth hour of labour would not be hired because its marginal revenue product ($7.50) is less than the hourly wage of $10.

We are now in a position to make a significant generalization. An employer, operating under conditions of a perfectly competitive labour market, will hire up to the point at which the marginal revenue product of labour equals the wage rate. This can be expressed as:

$$MRP_L = W$$

In fact we can generalize by saying that *any* factor (under the same market conditions) will be bought up to the point where its MRP (of capital, of land) just equals its price. If the marginal revenue product of capital, for example, is $600 per unit and its price is $550, it will be bought. If, however, its marginal revenue product is only $500, it will not be bought. Generally then, so long as the marginal benefit (MRP) of employing/purchasing the additional factor unit exceeds the marginal cost (price) of hiring/purchasing it, the firm should employ it.

Now let's return to the data in Table 12.1 and ask: how many hours of labour would be hired if the wage rate was exactly $12? Well, the MRP_L is equal to $12 when one hour of labour is hired — is this the right answer? No it isn't because this would violate the assumption that all firms act in a way that will maximize their profits. Failing to hire hours two through seven, all of which have a marginal revenue product in excess of $12, would be acting in a way that did not maximize profits. What we are saying here is that labour will be hired up to the point of equality between the marginal revenue product of labour and the wage rate *as long as MRP_L is declining* (and as long as the firm's total wage bill is less than its total revenue). This point is illustrated in Figure 12.1.

FIGURE 12.1 The Firm's Marginal Revenue Product of Labour

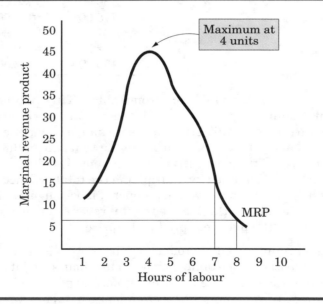

The downward portion of the firm's MRP_L curve represents its demand curve for labour. For instance, when the wage rate is $15, seven hours of labour will be hired. At a wage rate of $7.50, eight hours of labour would be hired.

In Figure 12.1 we graph the marginal revenue product data from Table 12.1. If the wage rate was, say, $15, the firm would hire seven hours of labour. An eighth hour of labour would be hired only if the wage rate dropped to $7.50. In general, the demand by firms for *any* factor depends on that factor's marginal revenue product which is illustrated by the downward-sloping portion of its MRP curve.

The above illustration of the firm's demand for labour assumed that the firm was selling its output in a perfectly competitive product market. Would our analysis change if we dropped this assumption in favour of, say, an oligopolistic product market? The only change would be that the marginal revenue product of labour would decline faster. This is because using more of any factor always increases output and this increase in output would mean the firm would be forced to decrease price in order to sell the increased quantities. That is to say that the marginal revenue for competitive firms is constant and equal to price, whereas for imperfectly competitive firms it declines with output driving marginal revenue product down faster.

The Supply of Labour

labour force: the total number of people over fifteen who are willing and able to be employed.

labour force supply: the total hours that those in the labour force are willing to work.

An economy's **labour force** is, simply, the number of people over the age of 15 who are willing and able to work for paid employment. The total amount of hours that these people are willing to work is the **labour force supply**.

We know that the labour force supply tends to expand as the wage rate increases. There are two explanations for this. First, as the wage rate increases, the rate at which the population is willing to participate in the labour force increases because the higher wage rate makes employment more attractive, e.g., younger people enter the labour force sooner, older workers tend not to retire as quickly and others who were previously not participating in the labour force are more likely to enter it.

How would those who are already in the labour force respond to a higher wage rate? Wouldn't everyone be willing to work more hours through taking on overtime work or a second job? Some would and some would not. The reason for this is that it involves more than just the maximization of income. For instance, either of your authors could work weekends at MacDonalds and increase his income. Why don't we? The answer involves what economists call the income effect of higher earnings and the substitution effect of substituting leisure time for work time. If an individual values leisure highly, the substitution effect may well outweigh the income effect so that he would be unwilling to work more hours, even at a higher wage rate. Others, however, may well put the income effect over the substitution effect and be quite willing to work more hours in response to a higher wage.

The net effect of both explanations is that economists know that the supply curve for labour is upward-sloping but it is relatively inelastic so that, say, a 10% rise in the wage rate will result in something less than a 10% increase in the quantity of labour supplied. This is illustrated in Figure 12.2 on page 406.

Theoretically, if we were to imagine a very high wage rate such that a majority of people weighed the substitution effect of more leisure over the income effect of more earnings, then the labour force supply curve would start to bend back to the left as it continued to rise. However, we will ignore this possibility.

An increase in the wage from W_1 to W_2 would result in an increase in the quantity of hours that the population was willing to work as indicated in the movement up on the labour force supply curve, S1, from point *a* to point *b*.

FIGURE 12.2 The Labour Force Supply Curve

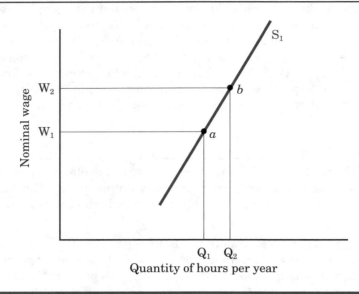

An increase in the wage rate from W_1 to W_2 results in the quantity of labour supplied rising from Q_1 to Q_2, i.e., from point *a* to *b*. This indicates that the supply of labour curve is upward-sloping with a reasonably steep slope.

Figure 12.2 illustrates the *market* supply of labour curve. We know from our earlier discussion that a single firm's demand for labour curve is determined by that firm's marginal revenue product. Just as we did in Chapter 2, we could sum each firm's demand for labour to obtain a *market* demand for labour curve. When we put the market demand for labour curve together with market supply of labour curve, as we do in Figure 12.3, we get the equilibrium wage, W_1, for labour.

Market Equilibrium   Given the market demand for labour, D_1 and the market supply of labour, S_1, we obtain the equilibrium wage rate, W_1, and the equilibrium quantity of hours, Q_1, that are bought and sold.

FIGURE 12.3 The Market Equilibrium Wage Rate

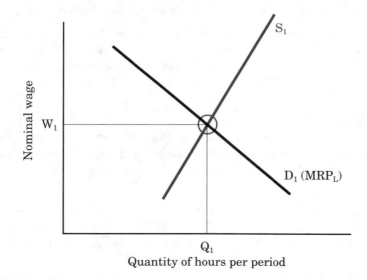

Given the upward-sloping supply of labour curve and the downward-sloping demand for labour curve, the equilibrium wage rate is W_1 and the equilibrium quantity is Q_1.

Now, we ask the very important question: what determines the wage rate for labour? We get the rather conventional answer: the supply of and demand for labour. We do not mean to imply that this general answer has universal application. There are, after all, many wage rates for labour — not just one and as we will soon see, labour markets are not always competitive. However, we have uncovered something significant. There are both supply and demand elements lying behind every wage rate.

If the labour market is competitive, the market-determined wage rate will be the wage rate applicable to each individual firm. As a result, the firm is able to hire as much labour as it wishes up to the point where the wage rate equals the marginal revenue product of labour. Graphically this is illustrated in Figure 12.4.

FIGURE 12.4 The Firm's Equilibrium Quantity of Labour in a Competitive Labour Market

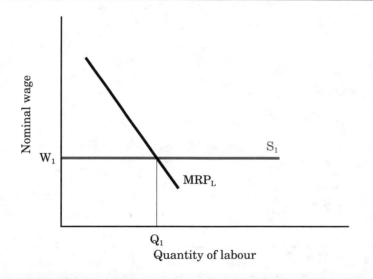

In a competitive labour market, the wage rate is determined by the forces of market supply and demand. Given this market-determined wage rate, W_1, the individual firm faces a perfectly elastic supply of labour curve, S_1. The quantity of labour this firm would hire is determined by the intersection of the firm's marginal revenue product for labour curve with the perfectly elastic supply curve, resulting in quantity Q_1 being hired.

In a competitive labour market, the market supply and demand for labour determines the market wage rate of W_1. The individual firm operating within this market faces a perfectly elastic supply curve for labour, S_1, at this market wage rate. The quantity of labour that this firm will hire is determined by the equality of its marginal revenue product for labour and the market wage rate. This quantity, Q_1, is illustrated in Figure 12.4 by the intersection of the supply curve and the MRP_L curve.

The Case of a Monopsony

monopsony: a market structure in which there is only one buyer.

The next question we need to ask is: what if the firm is operating in a **monopsony** labour market, i.e., what if the firm is the only buyer of labour? Imagine a firm that was the only employer of some highly specialized labour. Here the firm would face an upward-sloping supply of labour curve just as we saw for the *entire market* in a competitive labour market since the supply curve that the firm faces is the market supply curve. Recall that the firm operating within a competitive labour market can hire *additional* labour at the going market wage rate. A firm operating in a monopsony labour market would have to pay a higher wage rate in order to obtain additional labour since its labour supply curve is upward sloping. And here's the rub, it would have to pay all the previous labour that it has already hired that higher wage rate as well. The net result is that a firm operating in a monopsony labour market faces an escalating total wage bill as a result of hiring additional labour compared to the firm which operates in a competitive labour market.

QUESTION 12.1

A) Given the following data, and assuming that the output of the firm can be sold for $3 per unit, fill in the table below:

Hours of Labour (thousands per week)	Total Product (thousands of units)	Total Revenue (thousands of dollars)	Marginal Revenue Product of Labour (per hour)
0	0	—	—
1	80	240	240
2	180	540	300
3	260	780	240
4	320	960	180
5	360	1080	120
6	380	1140	60
7	390	1170	30
8	395	1185	15
9	398	1194	9
10	400	1200	6

B) If the firm can hire all the labour it wants for $9 an hour, how many hours per week will it hire and what output will it produce?

The Supply of Labour over Time

The size of Canada's labour force has grown considerably over the last 30 years as can be seen in Table 12.2 below.

TABLE 12.2 Canada's Labour Force for Selected Years

1966	7,493,000
1976	10,530,000
1986	13,378,000
1995	14,832,000

Source: Statistics Canada, *Historical Labour Force Statistics* (Ottawa, 1995).

There are two distinct explanations of this growth in Canada's labour force. The first is the growth in population. This influence was most significant in the late 1960s and 1970s reflecting the high birth rate in the years immediately following World War II. In addition, Canada has experienced a great deal of immigration over the last few decades. As a result of these factors, Canada's population has grown from just over 16 million in 1956 to nearly 30 million in 1996.

The second reason for the very strong growth in the labour force supply is an increase in the rate at which the population participates in the labour force. Since 1950, the percentage of the female population in the labour force supply has steadily grown from under 30% to approximately 60% by the early 1990s, while the male participation rate has declined, in the same period, only slightly from nearly 80% to about 75%.

In explaining the cause of the growth in the labour force, we raise the question of exactly how to define the labour force supply. Since we earlier defined the supply as total hours worked, rather than the number of individuals working, then the average number of hours per week worked is relevant. It is interesting to note that the average hours per week worked has been increasing in the last few years, reversing a downward trend of many decades.

The Demand for Labour over Time

We have established the importance of the marginal revenue product of labour in determining the demand for labour. Our discussion so far has assumed that technology and the size of the economy's capital stock remains unchanged. Yet, of course, technology improves and the capital stock grows over time. The effect of this can be seen in the growth of labour productivity which has the effect of shifting each firm's MRP_L curve out to the right. Table 12.3 gives some data on recent growth in productivity in Canada.

TABLE 12.3 Average Annual Percentage Change in Labour Productivity in Canada

1962–73	1.9%
1974–79	0.9%
1980–90	0.7%

Source: P. Someshwar Rao and Tony Lempriere, Canada Communication Group, *Canada's Productivity Performance* (Ottawa, 1992).

As you can see from this data, the average annual increase in labour productivity in Canada slowed considerably through the 1970s and 1980s. There are, however, some indications that this figure might be higher for the 1990s.

In addition to increases in productivity, the long-term-demand for labour has grown because of the overall growth in the economy's total output. The value of *real* output has grown from $104.8 billion in 1950 to $598 billion in 1994 (in constant 1986$). Both of these effects increase the market demand for labour and shift the demand for labour curve to the right.

We can put these trends together in Figure 12.5 (see page 410) where what we see is a shift to the right (D_1 to D_2) in the demand for labour curve because of increases in overall labour productivity and in the economy's total output. As mentioned earlier, the labour force supply has also grown because of increases in population and in the labour force participation rate and this has shifted the labour force supply curve to the right (S_1 to S_2).

FIGURE 12.5 The Long Run Trend in Labour Force Supply and Demand

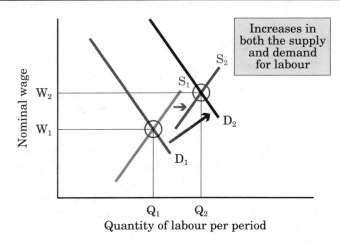

Increases in labour productivity and the growth in overall output cause the demand for labour curve to shift to the right as illustrated by D_1 to D_2. The supply of labour curve has also been shifting to the right as illustrated by S_1 to S_2. Since the long-run trend in wages is up, the shifts in the demand curve must have been greater than the shifts in the supply curve.

QUESTION 12.2

The economy's supply and demand for labour is as follows:

Wage Rate	Supply of Labour (billions of hours)	Demand for Labour (billions of hours)
$12	12	16
14	13	15
16	14	14
18	15	13
20	16	12

and data for Firm B is as follows:

Hours of Labour Used	MRP_L
200	$18
240	16
260	14
300	12
340	10

A) How many hours of labour will Firm B hire?
B) If the supply of labour increased by two billion at every wage rate, what effect would this have on the quantity of hours that Firm B hires?

real wage: the purchasing power, given a set of prices, of the nominal wage.

Productivity and the Real Wage

nominal wage: the wage rate expressed as a dollar and cents figure.

To extend the discussion of the importance of productivity let's ask the question: what was Robinson Crusoe's real wage? By **real wage** we mean the purchasing power of any given wage. In contrast, the **nominal wage** is the dollar and cent figure received from work. That is to say:

$$\text{real wage} = \frac{\text{nominal wage}}{\text{price level}}$$

Returning to the question above, Robbie's real wage is whatever he is able to produce for himself. If he produces nothing, his real wage would be nothing. If he produced this month more than he had produced the previous month, his real wage would have risen.

What is true for Robinson Crusoe, who lived alone on a uninhabited island (this is before Friday appears in the story), is also true for a whole economy. Given the labour force supply, the real wage for Canadians depends on how much is produced by Canadians and, generally speaking, the more Canada produces, the higher will be Canadians' real wage. This inevitable relationship between productivity and the real wage is illustrated in Figure 12.6.

FIGURE 12.6 Trend in Business-Sector Real Hourly Compensation and Productivity, Canada, 1946–91

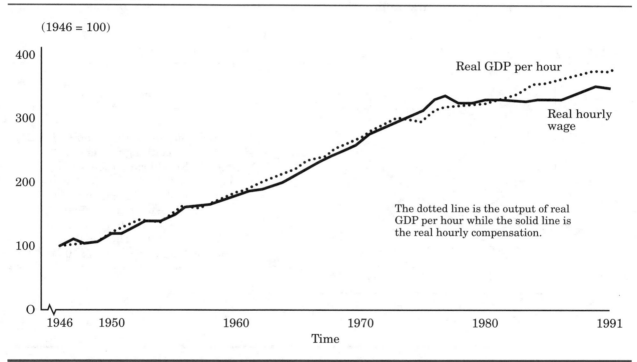

(1946 = 100)

Real GDP per hour

Real hourly wage

The dotted line is the output of real GDP per hour while the solid line is the real hourly compensation.

Time

What is really being said here is that an economy's real output and real income are the same thing. Thus, the real income (real wage rate) per worker can only increase at about the same rate as output per worker.

In summary, there are both supply and demand elements involved in determining how much labour is paid. Further, there are distinct long-run trends of growth in both the labour supply and demand. Finally, the average real wage for labour for the whole economy has increased and this increase is closely related to increases in labour productivity.

Having established these quite general, but important, points we now need to examine some explanations of why wage rates for specific groups of individuals differ. In other words, we need to examine what explains the wage rate differentials between pipefitters and nurses, or between medical doctors and helicopter pilots.

The Influences of Trade Unions and Professional Associations

Many individuals who earn a living by selling their labour belong, in association with their fellow workers, to a trade union such as the Canadian Autoworkers' Union or to a professional association such as the Nova Scotia Medical Association. From an economist's point of view, the broad objectives of such groups are to: (a) increase the work available to their members; (b) increase the compensation received by their members; and (c) improve the working conditions of their members. If such unions and associations have any influence on how labour markets perform, then their existence forces our analysis out of the context of perfectly competitive markets.

There are three basic approaches that organizations use to achieve the objectives of increased work and increased compensation. Figure 12.7 looks at the first approach, which is to increase the demand for the type of work their members perform.

FIGURE 12.7 The Effects on Wage Compensation of an Increase in Demand for Clothing Makers

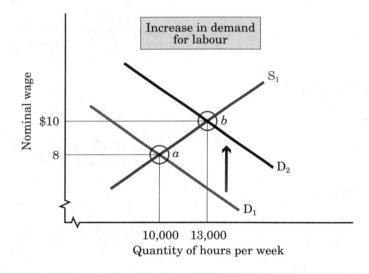

The non-unionized demand and supply for clothing makers is D_1 and S_1. Equilibrium occurs at an equilibrium wage of $8 and quantity of 10,000. Effective unionization could result in the demand for labour shifting to the right as illustrated by D_2. This would increase the wage rate to $10 and the quantity to 13,000.

Figure 12.7 could refer to any specific type of work such as that of medical practitioner, gas-line plumber or tailor. Let's choose the latter for our illustration. D_1 and S_1 are the demand for and the supply of labour in a non-unionized environment. This yields a wage of $8 and an equilibrium quantity of 10,000 hours per week.

Now, if the clothing workers become unionized, and their union is able to increase the demand for this type of work, what happens is that the demand curve shifts out as illustrated by D_2. This results in the wage rate increasing to $10 and the equilibrium quantity increasing to 13,000 hours. This is obviously to the advantage of the organization and to its members.

How might the organization achieve this increase in demand for its members? One way is by the union spending its own funds to advertise the employer's product. An ad campaign to encourage people to buy only those clothes with a union-made label would increase the demand for union-made clothing and thus increase the demand for the union members that make it. Another example would be a "Hire a CGA" campaign which is paid for by the organization aiming to increase the demand for its members.

Some organizations may not be able to use the above method to increase the demand for their members but instead may be able to restrict the supply of those who are qualified to do the work. Figure 12.8 illustrates this situation.

FIGURE 12.8 The Effects on Wage Compensation of Supply Restriction

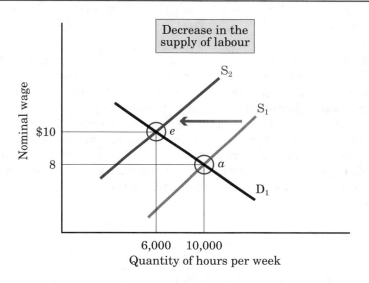

Restricting the supply of labour shifts the supply curve from S_1 to S_2. As a result the wage rate rises to $10, but equilibrium quantity declines to 6,000.

The effect of restricting the supply of labour as illustrated by the shift from S_1 to S_2 is to cause the wage rate to rise from the non-unionized $8 an hour to $10 an hour. However, in this case the equilibrium quantity declines from the original 10,000 hours per week to only 6,000. This approach is not as desirable to the organization and its members as was the one of increasing the demand which raised both the equilibrium wage rate and quantity hired.

How might an organization restrict the supply of labour? One way is for the organization to successfully lobby for the passage of laws that restrict who can perform a certain task — e.g., only those who are certified as brokers can legally sell stock, or only licensed pipefitters can work on gas plumbing. The most effective way an organization can restrict the supply of labour occurs when it can gain control of the certification (or licensing) process itself. Examples of this are the medical associations which control the licensing of new M.D.s or the Bar Associations which do the same with new lawyers or universities whose professors control how many students successfully complete graduate studies.

We should also point out that any organization that can both increase the demand for its members *and* restrict the supply of them will succeed in raising the wage rate even higher than the $10 used in our example.

QUESTION 12.3

A) Draw supply and demand for labour curves for an entire economy and label them S_1 and D_1.

B) Indicate the equilibrium wage as W_1 and the equilibrium quantity as Q_1.

C) Increase the demand for labour by drawing in D_2 and restrict the supply of labour by drawing in S_2.

D) Will the new wage rate, W_2, be higher or lower then W_1?

E) Will the new quantity, Q_2, be higher or lower than Q_1?

F) Give two reasons for the increase in the demand for labour and for the decrease in the supply of labour referred to in C) above.

Many individuals who sell their labour to an employer do common work that can not be easily licensed or certified, and so the methods discussed above are not open to the organizations that represent them. Is there any other way that these organizations might increase the wage rate of those they represent? The answer is yes, and here we find the situation that most students probably think of when the word union is used. Many (but not all) trade unions are well enough organized to have sufficient bargaining power to *simply impose* a wage rate in negotiating contracts of employment that is above what would otherwise be market equilibrium. Figure 12.9 illustrates this case.

FIGURE 12.9 A Negotiated Wage Rate Above Equilibrium

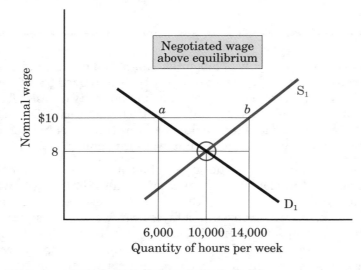

A union may succeed in obtaining a $10 wage rate in contract negotiations, but the consequences of an imposed wage settlement above equilibrium is that the quantity of hours supplied exceeds the quantity demanded by the horizontal distance *ab* which, in this case, is 8,000 hours per week.

As in the previous figure, Figure 12.9 illustrates a market equilibrium wage rate of $8 an hour and a quantity of 10,000. If, through bargaining power, the union negotiates a contractual wage rate of $10 an hour we would have the situation as shown here. Note that the quantity of labour demanded has declined to 6,000 hours per week at point *a* while the quantity supplied has increased to 14,000 at point *b*. The result is that 8,000 more hours per week are supplied than are demanded. This is the distance *ab* in Figure 12.9. This is essentially the phenomenon that we have when an outsider looks enviously at a job that someone else has and says to himself that he really wished he had a job like that.

How successful are such attempts to raise the wage rate above what would be market equilibrium? We do have studies that attempt to measure the effect of trade unions on wage rates and the consensus seems to be that union organizations do increase the wage rate by anywhere from 10% to as much as 30%. It is interesting to note, however, that this same evidence seems to conclude that the total payment going to labour (as opposed to going to the factors, land or capital) does not change despite the influences of organizations aimed at increasing the wage of their members. This implies that to the extent that such organizations are successful, it is at the expense of labour who have no organization to represent them.

QUESTION 12A

1. What is another term for marginal product?
2. What is *MRP*?
3. What is the demand curve for the factor, labour?
4. What effect would an increase in the wage rate have on the quantity of labour supplied?
5. How can a union increase the demand for it members' services? How can it decrease the supply of such services?
6. Distinguish between the *real wage* and the *nominal wage*.
7. What is the consequence of a negotiated wage rate that is above the market equilibrium wage?

Explanations of Wage Differentials

Conceptually, if all people and all jobs were the same, and we had a competitive labour market with no trade unions or professional associations, we would have only a single equilibrium wage rate. People are not the same, however, and this results in differences in the supply of different kinds of labour. Similarly, all jobs are not the same, and this results in differences in the demand for different types of labour. Further, as we just saw, trade unions and professional associations do alter wage compensation in different occupations. The result is that we have many different wage rates. Let's take a closer look at the wage differentials that exist in our economy.

human capital: the accumulation of all skills and knowledge acquired by individuals.

The accumulation of skills and knowledge that each individual has acquired is known as **human capital**. All individuals have some human capital — the ability to read, write, count and perceive — but it is obvious that some people possess much more than others either because of natural gift or because of much greater investment efforts such as many years of formal education. Usually, a greater level of human capital means a more productive individual and we have already established that higher productivity means a higher wage.

BOX 12.1

It has long be established by economic research that individuals with more formal education enjoy, on average, higher earning capacity throughout their lives. The data below illustrates this point. The dollar figures are average incomes for males in the age category of 45 to 54 years old.

Level of Formal Education	Median Annual Income
Elementary school only	$31,308
Some high school	36,502
High school graduation	40,278
Some post-secondary	53,763
Post-secondary degree	60,691

Source: Statistics Canada. *Earnings of Men and Women, 1993.* (Ottawa, 1994).

Next, we should recognize that some jobs involve considerable risks which are absent in other jobs, and we usually find a higher wage being paid as compensation for such risks. Examples here would be power-line construction jobs or the work of deep sea divers, which pay commensurately higher than equivalent low-risk jobs.

Third, some jobs have unpleasant characteristics that must be compensated for in order to get enough people to do them. This is why we often find a higher wage rate being paid, for example, for the night shift or for dirty, exposed work such as that on an oil exploration rig, especially if that rig is 200 kilometres northeast of Aklavik.

Fourth, some jobs have very attractive non-pecuniary benefits that result in the wage rate being lower that it would otherwise be. These benefits range from lots of time off (e.g., school teachers) to flexible working hours (e.g., a self-employed writer) to the opportunity to be creative (e.g., a landscape architect).

As a fifth explanation we need to mention the aspect of luck in all this. Some people seem to have just lucked into a job that they really love and as a result they do the job very well and get better compensation for doing so than others who do the same work — imagine the really happy gardener or hairdresser.

Finally we need to mention the fact that discrimination exists in the labour market which results in some jobs being difficult to obtain by members of certain groups, such as women or visible minorities. This restricts the supply of labour into these kind of jobs which raises the wage rate paid in them. In addition, the supply of labour into jobs traditionally held predominately by women (day-care workers) or visible minorities (janitorial work) and requiring relatively low skills is greater than it might otherwise be, with the result that wage rates are lower.

This is not an exhaustive list of the reasons for wage differentials, but the point is made that people are different, and jobs are different, so wage rates differ despite the impersonal forces of supply and demand which underlie every wage rate.

BOX 12.2

Many people have observed that the price of tickets to a concert or to the theatre have become almost prohibitive. There is an explanation for this. Live performances require direct contact between those who consume the service and those who provide it. In contrast, the consumer (buyer) of, say, a VCR has no idea who worked on it or how much labour time went into its production, i.e., there is no contact between producer and consumer.

Next, consider that technological change which saves labour time in producing the VCR does not mean a reduction in product quality. On the other hand, few such innovations are possible in providing live theatre or musical performances and, therefore, it is difficult to increase the productivity of a live performer.

The possible increases in labour productivity in manufacturing that come from technological change increase the wage rates paid throughout that sector. When wages for common labour in manufacturing rise, musicians and actors expect to receive an increase too. Such increased labour costs must be paid for from increased ticket prices since it cannot come from increased productivity.

This general point, that the service sector faces raising (real) cost of production, can be extended to include most public services as well. Firefighters, teachers and social service workers are some examples.

The Concept of Economic Rent

economic rent: the return to a factor of production that has a perfectly inelastic supply.

The original concept of economic rent is rooted in the work of the nineteenth century classical economist David Ricardo. Ricardo assumed a single use for land: agriculture. Since the quantity of land is fixed, he went on to argue that it was perfectly inelastic in supply. Therefore, Ricardo saw the price of land as being purely demand-driven. If land is in high demand, its price will be high, as was the case in Ricardo's England. However, if the demand for land is low, as it was in nineteenth-century North America, its price is very low (in many cases it was free). Whatever the price of land might be, this is the price that the owners of land earn. Ricardo called this return to land which has a perfectly inelastic supply **economic rent**. This point is illustrated in Figure 12.10.

FIGURE 12.10 The Concept of Economic Rent as Applied to Land

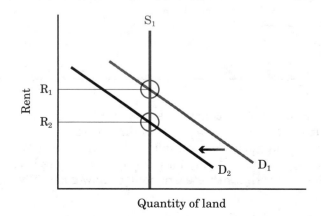

If we assume that land has only one use, then its supply is perfectly inelastic, as illustrated by S_1. Given this, the price of land, or the rent that it receives, is purely demand driven. If demand is high, as in D_1, then rent is R_1. Low demand, as illustrated by D_2, results in the lower rent of R2.

If we suppose that the supply of land is perfectly inelastic, its price is demand-driven. Even if the price of land is zero, its supply is the same. Because land has this unique aspect, Ricardo considered the return to land, the economic rent, a surplus.

We know today, however, that land has alternate uses besides agriculture. The larger the number of alternative uses that land might have, the less inelastic the supply curve. Because the supply curve of any factor is less than perfectly inelastic, we need to distinguish between rent and **transfer earnings** when discussing the return to the factor. Transfer earnings are defined as the necessary payment that a factor of production must earn in order to remain in its present use. Let's now turn to an example of another factor of production that has a very inelastic supply.

> **transfer earnings:**
> a necessary payment that a factor of production must earn in order for it to remain in its present use.

Economic Rent and Professional Athletes

We are all aware of the fact that there are many well-paid professional athletes who love the game so much that they would continue to play even if they received only a fraction of what they are currently getting. The wage rate that would be necessary to ensure that they continued to play is their transfer earnings. The difference between the transfer-earnings wage and the actual wage received is the economic rent. Figure 12.11 will help us understand this concept better.

FIGURE 12.11 Economic Rent and Transfer Earnings

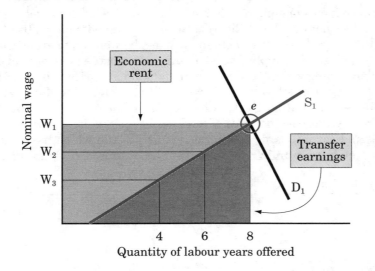

At wage rate W3, our athlete will play for only four years. At wage rate W_2, he will play for six years. The dark-shaded area is the pay that is necessary to induce him to commit to the full eight years. Given the wage rate W_1, the entire rectangle is what he actually receives. Therefore, the light-shaded area is his economic rent.

To really understand this concept of economic rent, we need to view the supply curve, S_1 in Figure 12.11, as showing the minimum price at which a given quantity is willingly supplied. For example, if the wage rate is W_3, our hypothetical professional athlete will play for a total of four years because he loves to play. Yet, he knows that athletes, no matter how good they may be, age very quickly in the world of professional sports. Therefore, he is not willing to play more than four years because the current wage is not sufficient for him to postpone getting on with his life any longer. To get him to agree to play for a fifth and a sixth year, a higher wage rate, W_2 for example, would have to be offered. Similarly, he will willingly play for eight years only if the wage offered is again increased, this time to W_1. The dark-shaded area under the supply curve, therefore, is the transfer earnings necessary to induce our athlete to play for the full eight years. On the other hand, if our athlete is paid wage rate W_1 for each of the eight years, his total pay is the entire rectangle. Thus, the light-shaded area represents his total pay less his transfer earnings, i.e., his economic rent. This economic rent is a real bonus for him; it is the pay he receives over and above what he would have been willing to accept in order to continue doing what he is already doing.

Next, look back at Figure 12.11 and imagine, first, a supply curve that is drawn with much greater elasticity and, second, one that is drawn with even greater inelasticity. It should be clear to you that the more inelastic the supply curve, the greater the economic rent that any particular wage rate will generate. Now, ask: what is likely to be the elasticity of supply of good athletes for any professional sport? The answer is, of course, that it is *very* inelastic.

The demand for several kinds of professional athletes has increased dramatically in the last several years due to the expansion of the number of teams in all four major leagues and to the fact that most leagues have enjoyed rapidly escalating revenue from television contracts. If you combine this increase in demand with the inelastic supply we have just mentioned, you get a good explanation for the great increases in the wages paid to professional sportsmen and women.

What we are really saying here is that the high pay many athletes today enjoy is *demand-driven*. To clinch this point, let us point out that the world's very best squash players are paid only about $150,000 a year. Is this because there are so many of them, or because they really aren't as skilful as a football linebacker, or that they don't really work as hard as a baseball outfielder? The answer to all these questions is, of course, no. So why does Joe Carter, a baseball outfielder, get paid 20 times more than Jansher Khan, one of the world's best squash players? The answer is because the ticket sales and television contract revenue earned by a baseball team are so enormous that the demand for good baseball players is much greater than the demand for good squash players. This demand-side phenomenon explains Wayne Gretzky's tens of millions of dollars; and the concept of economic rent explains the sense, shared by many, that maybe he doesn't deserve all of it. In addition, both Gretzky and Carter have a union representing their interests while Janshar Khan does not.

As we all know, the very high salaries of athletes in major sports have led to the attempt by team owners to impose salary caps (maximums) in one form or another on individual players. What this boils down to is a question of who (the team owner or the athlete) is entitled to what percentage of the economic rent that exists?

The Natural Resource Market

Natural resources are both renewable (trees and wild fish) and nonrenewable (minerals). The use of one more unit of a nonrenewable resource reduces, forever, the supply with which nature has endowed this planet. For this reason, nonrenewable resources are a topic of particular interest to both economists and the public in general. As an example, oil is non-renewable. Does this mean that the supply curve of the world's oil is perfectly inelastic as illustrated by S_1 in Figure 12.12?

FIGURE 12.12 The World's Supply of Oil

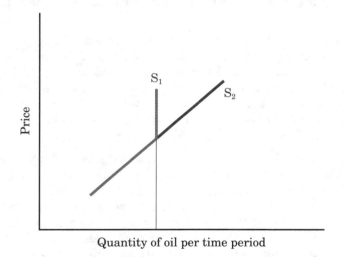

Given the fact that not all of the oil in the world has been discovered and the fact that not all the discovered oil is for sale at the present price, the supply curve for oil is upward-sloping as illustrated by S_2. Only in the very long run can we think of the supply curve of oil as being perfectly inelastic as in the curve S_1.

Given that there is only so much oil on our planet, some people assume that a perfectly inelastic supply curve, such as S_1 in Figure 12.12, represents the circumstances facing humankind. In some grand sense, over the very long run, this is valid. However, it must be recognized that not all the oil has been discovered. Furthermore, much of the oil that has been discovered is not for sale at current prices. Therefore, the present supply curve of oil is much more like S_2 and represents not so much the total quantity that exists, but the amount being made available for sale.

Given that in the very long run there is only a finite amount of oil available, we need to ask if the price system, involving supply and demand, leads to an overly rapid exploitation of oil. Or is it possible that the future will prove our current rate of use to be too conservative?

This is a highly politicized question but economists do have something to say about it. Let's try to follow an argument that can get rather complex. The current value of oil to consumers is the amount they are willing to pay for one more barrel. Let's assume this figure is $20. Further, let's assume this is also the current market price for oil. An additional barrel extracted and sold now will yield $20 in revenue which can be held and earn interest which we will assume to be 5%, so that we would have a value of $21 in a year from now. Alternatively, we could leave the barrel of oil in the ground in order to extract and sell it one year from now. Which is better, to extract and sell it now or in one year from now? The answer depends on what the price of the barrel of oil turns out to be in one year. If, one year from now, its price is $21.50 we will realize that we should have left it in the ground. If, however, the price turns out to be $20.50 then we will realize that we should have extracted and sold it a year ago.

Understanding the little conundrum above leads us to a very useable conclusion:

> The rate of extraction of oil should be such that the price of oil rises at the same rate as the current interest rate.

To nail this down, again assume that the present rate of interest is 5% and that it remains unchanged so that extracting a barrel of oil today and selling it for $20 would give us (approximately) $25.50 in five years. If, five years from now, the price of a barrel of oil is also exactly $25.50, then our rate of extraction is exactly correct. On the other hand, if the price of oil turns out to be only $24.00, then we have been extracting oil far too fast. Similarly, if the price of oil turns out to be $27.00, then we have been conserving oil too much. Interesting, isn't it?

Let us hasten to say that we are not proposing this idea as the complete solution to the complex question of how quickly we should use up non-renewable resources. We do, however, wish to emphasize the point that economists do have some ideas in this area.

Common Property Resources

There is also an interesting question concerning (some) renewable resources that are called **common property resources**. This term means that no one individual or firm (or government for that matter) owns the resource. Wild fish in the ocean are the classic example of a common property resource.

common property resource: a resource which is not owned by an individual or a firm.

As we saw in the case of non-renewable resources such as oil, the question here is: what is the correct rate of exploitation of a common property resource? If this question is not addressed and answered by some regulatory body, we can be certain that the resource will be overextracted and, possibility, destroyed. Consider the cod stocks in the Grand Banks off the coast of Newfoundland. From a social point of view, these fish should be harvested at a rate that does not exceed their natural rate of reproduction. This will ensure that there are fish to catch next year and 10 years from now and 100 years from now. However, from an individual fisher's point of view, the more fish he can catch now the greater his income. But isn't a sound conservation policy to that individual's long-term benefit? Yes, but *only if all* other fishers don't do what each and every one is strongly tempted to do — fish intensely before the stocks are all gone. You can see the need for the social regulation of a common property resource. Given the state of the east coast cod fisheries in the mid 1990s, one can conclude that such regulation was not done well.

Let's now leave the natural resource market and turn to the capital goods market.

The Capital Goods Market

In a sense, the market for capital goods — be they machines used in a factory, or a computer system for an office, or a simple carpenter's tool — is very similar to the market for any *product* as discussed in Chapter 2. There is a quite conventional demand for and supply of capital goods as illustrated in Figure 12.13.

FIGURE 12.13 The Market for Capital Goods

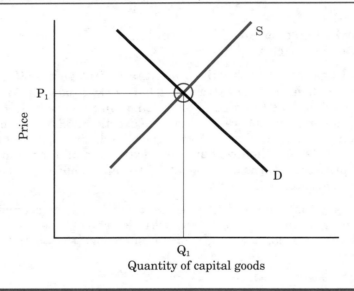

The equilibrium price for capital goods occurs at the intersection of the supply and demand curves, i.e., at a price of P_1 and a quantity of Q_1.

In the figure, the interaction of the demand for and the supply of capital goods yields an equilibrium price and quantity of P_1 and Q_1. We don't have anything more to say about the supply of capital goods than we have already said in reference to the supply of any particular product such as orange juice — as the price increases, the quantity supplied rises.

It is the demand for capital goods that is more interesting. First, we need to point out that the demand for capital goods is in fact derived from the marginal revenue product of capital, just as the demand for labour depended on its marginal revenue product. In this case the MRP of capital is the additional benefit accruing to the firm from the employment of the last unit of capital and is equal to the marginal physical product it produces multiplied by the price. Second, we need to recognize that the purchase of capital goods almost always needs to be financed with borrowed money. Even large firms are not able to lay out several hundred thousands of dollars in cash for a new computer system. Instead, they arrange for a loan to finance the purchase, which is then paid back over time. They must, of course, pay interest on this loan, and it is because of this that the demand for capital goods is (inversely) related to the cost of financing capital purchases, which is the interest rate. In other words, the higher the interest rate the lower will be the amount of borrowed funds and, therefore, the lower the amount of spending on capital goods. What factors determine the rate of interest is a matter for discussion in a macroeconomics course.

The demand side of the capital goods market is also interesting because a change in technology can certainly affect the demand for such goods. Significant improvements in technology can render existing capital goods obsolete and require that they be replaced by the newer versions. This increases the demand for new capital goods, and would be illustrated by a rightward shift in its demand curve.

Just as technological change increases the marginal revenue product of labour, it also increases the marginal revenue product of capital and this can result in (the newer) capital goods being more productive *relative to* labour. Firms will then be very tempted to substitute the now more productive capital for labour, which has become relatively less productive and, therefore, relatively more expensive. In other words, when deciding on amounts of substitutable factors, like capital and labour, a firm would take into account both productivity and the price of the factors. Thus, if

$$\frac{MP_K}{P_K} > \frac{MP_L}{P_L}$$

it would be profitable to substitute capital for labour.

Such substitution of capital for labour is something that we witness almost every day. One of your authors, as a teenager, used to work after school unloading cases of beer from railway cars — one case at a time. Today, one person, using a forklift, does the work that half a dozen kids used to do. As another example, think of the labour that is saved at a grocery supermarket because of the use of the conveyor belt and the bar-code reader. A third example is the use of computerized testbanks in economics courses which have replaced student graders.

factor substitution effect: the phenomenon of one factor replacing another factor as a result of technological change.

The phenomenon of capital being substituted for labour raises the question of whether or not such automation destroys jobs and is therefore something that society needs to be concerned about. There is a lot of misconception about this issue that can be easily cleared up. There is no question that automation does indeed eliminate certain types of jobs — the days of young people unloading beer cars are gone. Economists call this the **factor substitution effect** of technological change. If technological change leading to the substitution of capital for labour was the whole story, we would have to wonder how it is that anyone is still working given the fact that our economy has experienced over 200 years of dramatic changes in technology.

factor output effect: the phenomenon of rising total output leading to an increased demand for labour.

Yet the substitution effect is not the whole story. Capital substitution increases labour's productivity (the labour that was not replaced by capital) and thus lowers the cost of production. This, in turn, lowers the price of the final products being produced which increases both the quantity demanded for those products and, thus, total output. This increase of total output increases the demand for labour and thus the **output effect** of technological change *creates* jobs. Given the fact that there are more people working in our society today than ever before, the output effect of technological change must have been stronger than the substitution effect over the last two centuries or so.

QUESTION 12.5

Given its current output, a firm is experiencing a marginal product of capital of 60 and a marginal product of labour of 10. If the price of capital is $100 a unit, and the price of labour is $25 a unit, how should this firm substitute factors?

Entrepreneurial Talent

The fourth of our four factors of production is enterprise or entrepreneurial talent. No economist explored the role of entrepreneurial talent in the market economy more than Joseph Schumpeter who taught at Harvard University in the first half of the twentieth century. Schumpeter saw the entrepreneur as an innovating doer who bridged the gap between a mere idea and a productive application. Eccentric minds invented, and common businesspeople managed, but it was the risk-taking entrepreneur who had the vision and the chutzpa to take truly new and revolutionary *action*. The entrepreneur, in Schumpeter's eyes, is the engine of economic growth and development in a capitalist economy.

From the time of Adam Smith, economists have argued that competition within a capitalist economy would tend to result in (economic) profits being competed down to zero — a process we explored in the context of both the perfectly competitive and monopolistically competitive market models. What then explained the continued existence of profits nearly two centuries after capitalism took root in the western European and North American economies?

Surely, Schumpeter argued, it was the innovations of the entrepreneur that were the source of profits within capitalism. New innovation created unique situations where economic profits could be made. In time, the swarm of imitators of the innovation would become established and such profits would be driven to zero. However, in a dynamic and growing economy, another wave of innovation would have already occurred and new profit opportunities would continuously be created.

While entrepreneurs create profits, they are often not long the beneficiaries of them. As John Kenneth Galbraith points out in *The New Industrial State*, the risk-taking entrepreneur sometimes loses control of his growing business to the impersonal forces of what he calls the technostructure, which is at the heart of the modern transnational corporation. When this happens, more conservative and more bureaucratic managers take over from the risk-taking entrepreneur.

Before we leave this topic we should point out that there is an alternative explanation for profits and that is simply the existence of oligopoly and monopoly influences that inhibit the natural tendency for profits to be competed away. This explanation, while valid, just doesn't have the same zing to it as Schumpeter's.

Review

QUESTION 12B

1. List four explanations of wage differentials.
2. Define *transfer earnings.*
3. What is *economic rent?*
4. What economic variable is relevant when considering the right rate of extraction of a non-renewable resource?
5. What is a *common property resource?*
6. What is the price of finance?
7. What is the factor *substitution effect?*
8. What is the factor *output effect?*
9. What, according to Schumpeter, might prevent profits from being driven to zero in a competitive world?

Chapter Highlights

The chapter begins by making a distinction between the product market and the factor market. Analysis of the factor market begins with a definition and illustration of marginal revenue product in context of the labour market. This leads to the conclusion that the firm's demand for labour is determined by labour's marginal revenue product.

The chapter then turns to a discussion of labour supply in the context of the whole market by explaining the reasons behind the upward-sloping supply of labour curve. It is then pointed out that a market demand for labour can be obtained by summing each firm's labour demand. Next, the market demand for labour and the market supply of labour are put together graphically to obtain an equilibrium market wage rate. Then the text explains that for a firm in a competitive factor market, the wage rate is a given and the firm will maximize profits by equating this given wage rate with its marginal revenue product.

The chapter then moves out of the context of a competitive labour market by mentioning the idea of a monopsony market structure in which there is a single buyer of labour.

Next is a brief look at two reasons that explain the rapid growth in Canada's labour supply over the last 40 years and at the increase in labour productivity and total output that have led to the growth in labour demand.

The discussion makes the important point that the real wage experienced by the workers of any economy is determined by the growth in labour productivity. We then move into a discussion of the effects of trade unions and professional associations on equilibrium wage rates and the quantity of labour hired. Next, the topic of wage rate differentials is addressed and six factors, ranging from investment in human capital to discrimination in the labour market, are explored in order to explain such differentials.

The chapter then turns to the concept of economic rent as originally seen by David Ricardo and as applied to today's professional athletes. A brief discussion of the natural resource market follows with the focus being what economists have to say about how quickly a society should extract non-renewable resources such as oil, and common property resources such as wild fish.

A brief look at the factor, capital, is next and here the focus is on the effects of the substitution of capital for labour and its effect on employment. The conclusion reached is that the substitution effect of capital replacing labour (commonly referred to as technological change) does eliminate specific jobs but the output effect of such replacement creates more jobs overall. The chapter closes with a brief discussion of the fourth factor of production, entrepreneurial talent, and the cause of profits in a dynamic, growing economy.

New Glossary Terms

Workbook

Study Tips

1.   This chapter is about the demand and supply of factors, not products. In short we have shifted our focus from the product market to the factor market. Most of the chapter assumes a perfectly competitive factor market. This concept means that a firm can buy all it wants of a particular factor, say labour, at the going wage rate; i.e., the firm's hiring practices will not drive the wage rate up. Another way of looking at this is that the price of a factor remains constant for sellers and individual buyers do not affect the price. This is analogous to the perfectly competitive product market we studied in Chapter 8 in which the price of the product remains constant for sellers and individual sellers do not affect the price.

2.   You may recall that in Chapter 6 we stressed the importance of the relationship between the costs of production and productivity of inputs. Productivity plays a key role in this chapter also in that it determines, in the long run, the real return received by the factor; e.g., the real wage of labour is determined by labour's productivity.

3.   Students tend to confuse the effect of a change in the price of a competitive firm's product with the effect of a change in the price of a factor it is hiring. The former shifts the firm's factor demand curve, while the latter results in a movement along the demand curve for the factor.

4.   Even though it may seem like a small point, make sure you understand the distinction between the real wage and the nominal wage. This will be essential when you take on the study of macroeconomics.

5.   You should not assume that the concept of economic "rent" applies only to land. Under the right conditions any factor can receive economic rent.

6.   The calculation of the MRP of any factor can be done in one of two ways. The first is by multiplying the MP of the factor times the price of the product sold. The second way is to simply determine the change in total revenue resulting from the use of one unit of the factor in question.

Are You Sure?

Indicate whether the following statements are true or false. If false, indicate why they are false.

1.   While supply and demand analysis can be used to analyze the product market, it cannot be used to analyze the factor market.
T or **F**   If false: _____

_____

_____

2.   Marginal revenue product is the increase in a firm's total revenue which results from the use of one more unit of input.
T or **F**   If false: _____

_____

_____

3.   An employer operating under conditions of a perfectly competitive labour market will hire labour up to the point where the marginal product of labour equals the wage rate.
T or **F**   If false: _____

_____

_____

4.   If the product market is imperfectly competitive rather than perfectly competitive, the marginal revenue product curve declines faster.
T or **F**   If false: _____

_____

_____

5.   The fact that neither of the authors work weekends at MacDonalds demonstrates that

they both value an extra hour of leisure over the added hourly income that they could earn.
T or **F**   If false: _____

_____

_____

6.   Canada's labour force has doubled over the last 30 years.
T or **F**   If false: _____

_____

_____

7.   The typical range for the annual increase in labour productivity in Canada over the last 30 years has been between 3% and 5%.
T or **F**   If false: _____

_____

_____

8.   The real wage is defined as the nominal wage divided by labour productivity.
T or **F**   If false: _____

_____

_____

9.   Often, trade unions have the same effect as do professional associations on the labour market.
T or **F**   If false: _____

_____

_____

10. Some form of regulation is needed to ensure that a common property resource is not overextracted.
T or **F**   If false: _____

_____

_____

Translations

FIGURE W12.1

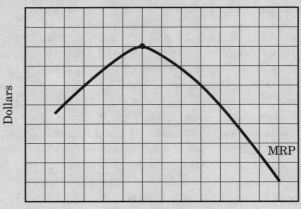

Describe the meaning of the graph in Figure W12.1 above. In doing so, make reference to marginal product, the law of diminishing returns and marginal cost. You may assume that this firm operates in both a competitive factor and product market.

_____

_____

_____

_____

_____

Choose the Best

1. The argument that technological change creates jobs assumes that:
   a)   The factor substitution effect outweighs the factor output effect.
   b)   The factor output effect outweighs the factor substitution effect.

2. Which of the following is assumed in Ricardo's concept of economic rent?
   a)   A perfectly inelastic supply curve.
   b)   A perfectly inelastic demand curve.

3. The world's supply of oil is:
   a)   Perfectly inelastic at all prices.

b) Elastic at prices up to a certain level and then becomes perfectly inelastic.

4. Which of the following statements best describes Schumpeter's view of profits?
   a) Profits come in a steady stream in a capitalist economy as long as full employment is achieved.
   b) Economic profits are zero in a capitalist economy in the long run.
   c) The source of profits, whatever level they may be, is the entrepreneur.

5. What is the most likely consequence if a monopsonist hires more labour?
   a) A decrease in the wage rate.
   b) An increase in the wage rate.
   c) A wage rate that neither increases nor decreases.

6. What is the most likely effect of an increase in the demand for a particular type of labour?
   a) The wage rate for that type of labour will rise and the quantity hired will decrease.
   b) The wage rate for that type of labour will rise and the quantity hired will also increase.
   c) The wage rate for that type of labour will rise but the quantity hired will remain unchanged.

7. Which of the following would be most advantageous to a trade union or professional association?
   a) The supply of labour is restricted.
   b) The demand for labour is decreased.
   c) The supply of labour increases by more than the demand increases.
   d) The demand for labour increases by more than the supply increases.

8. The average wage rate in Canada has increased over the last 30 years. Which of the following is the most likely explanation?
   a) The demand for labour has decreased.
   b) The supply of labour has decreased.
   c) The demand for labour has increased more than the supply of labour has decreased.

d) The demand for labour has increased more than the supply of labour has increased.

9. All *except one* of the following statements are correct concerning the explanation of wage rate differentials. Which is the exception?
   a) All individuals possess the same amount of human capital.
   b) Different jobs involve different degrees of risk.
   c) Some jobs have unpleasant characteristics that are absent in other jobs.
   d) Some jobs have very attractive non-pecuniary benefits.

10. All *except one* of the following statements are correct concerning the labour market for high-profile professional athletes. Which is the exception?
    a) The supply is inelastic.
    b) The wage rate is demand-driven.
    c) There is an element of economic rent in their pay.
    d) There is no transfer earnings involved in their pay.

11. What do most economists think is the socially optimum extraction rate of a natural resource such as oil?
    a) One that equals the MRP of the resource.
    b) A rate that ensures the price of oil increases at the same rate as the interest rate.
    c) One that is less than the rate of discovery of new sources.
    d) One that is less than 2% of known reserves so as to guarantee at least 50 years' supply at all times.

12. If the MP_K/P_K is greater than the MP_L/P_L, which of the following is correct?
    a) The firm should substitute labour for capital.
    b) The firm should substitute capital for labour.
    c) The firm should raise the wage rate of its labour.
    d) The firm should decrease its output.

13. Suppose that the MRP_L for a competitive firm is currently $50 and the hourly cost of labour is $40. Which of the following is the correct action for the firm?
    a) Since the firm must be profitable, it need not do anything.
    b) The firm should hire more labour.
    c) The firm should substitute labour for capital.
    d) The firm should raise the wage rate of its labour.

14. At what point will a competitive firm stop hiring additional labour?
    a) When its total product is maximized.
    b) When the marginal product of labour is maximized.
    c) When the marginal revenue product of labour is maximized.
    d) When the marginal revenue product of labour is just equal to the wage rate.

15. Which of the following would cause a shift to the right in the demand curve of a factor?
    a) A decrease in the price of that factor.
    b) An increase in the price of a substitute factor.
    c) A decrease in the price of the product produced by the factor.
    d) An increase in the marginal product of a substitute factor.

16. If most people's desire for leisure increases, which one of the following statements is correct ?
    a) The wage rate would fall and the quantity of products produced would rise.
    b) Both the wage rate and the quantity of products produced would fall.
    c) The wage rate would fall and the demand for labour would increase.
    d) The wage rate would rise and the quantity of products produced would fall.
    e) Both the wage rate and the quantity of products produced would rise.

17. All *except one* of the following statements concerning the concept of economic rent are correct. Which is the exception?
    a) The more inelastic the supply of a factor, the more economic rent that factor earns.

b) A factor that has a perfectly inelastic supply will earn no transfer earnings.
c) It is possible for a factor to receive both economic rent and transfer earnings.
d) If we assume that land has only one use, such as agriculture, then all of its return is economic rent.
e) The higher the transfer earnings of a factor, the higher its economic rent will be.

18. When is the marginal revenue product of a factor at a maximum?
    a) When its marginal product is at a maximum.
    b) When the firm's total product is at a maximum.
    c) When its marginal product is at a minimum.
    d) When both its marginal product and the firm's total product are at a maximum.
    e) When average product is at its maximum.

19. If a firm is operating in a monopsony market, which of the following statements is correct?
    a) The firm can hire additional labour at the same wage rate it is currently paying.
    b) The firm would hire more labour in the monopsony situation than in the competitive situation.
    c) The firm faces an upward-sloping supply of labour curve.
    d) The MRP_L declines faster in the case of the monopsony situation than in the competitive one.
    e) The firm's demand for labour curve is downward-sloping in the situation of the monopsony market and horizontal in the case of the competitive one.

20. All *except one* of the following statements are correct when a trade union successfully imposes a wage rate above equilibrium. Which one is the exception?
    a) There will be more workers willing to work than are hired.
    b) The firm's total wage bill will definitely be higher.
    c) The average firm is not operating in a competitive factor market.

d) The quantity of workers hired will be less after the imposition of the higher wage than it was before.

e) Neither the demand for nor the supply of labour has changed.

What's Wrong?

Can you spot the four errors in the following passage? (Ignore grammatical mistakes!)

The MRP_L is determined by multiplying the AP_L by the price of the product sold. Putting the MRP_L on a graph enables us to visualize the firm's supply curve of labour. The supply curve of labour, for a firm operating in a monopsony market structure, is horizontal. The intersection of the supply and demand curves for the firm would determine the quantity of labour a firm should hire. If the price of labour decreased, then the firm's demand curve for labour would shift to the right.

Key Problem

Heavenly Bubbles is a small soap company whose main product is hand soap which sells in a competitive market for $2 a bar. The bars are produced at autonomous workstations which feature a specially designed machine. The output per hour of each workstation varies with the amount of labour used as the data in Table W12.1 indicates. Labour costs $16 per hour.

TABLE W12.1

Quantity of Labour	Output per Hour	Marginal Product	Total Revenue	Marginal Revenue Product
0	0	—	—	—
1	24	_____	_____	_____
2	44	_____	_____	_____
3	60	_____	_____	_____
4	72	_____	_____	_____
5	80	_____	_____	_____
6	84	_____	_____	_____

a) Fill in the marginal product, total revenue and marginal revenue product columns in Table W12.1.

b) How many workers should the firm assign to each workstation?

Number of workers: _____.

c) Assuming the firm has 6 workstations, construct the firm's demand for labour curve (and label it D_1) on the graph in Figure W12.2 on page 432. Indicate, with the letter a, the total amount of labour that the firm will hire at a wage rate of $16.

d) Now, assume that there is an increase in employment taxes (the employers share of UIC and Workers' Compensation) which raises the cost of labour to $24 an hour. Now, how many workers per hour should the firm assign to each workstation and how many should it hire in total?

Number of workers: _____; number of workers in total: _____.

e) On the graph in Figure W12.2 indicate, with the letter *b*, the effect of this increase in the cost of labour.

f) Suppose the price of each bar of soap rises to $3. Indicate the effect of this on the graph in Figure W12.2.

FIGURE W12.2

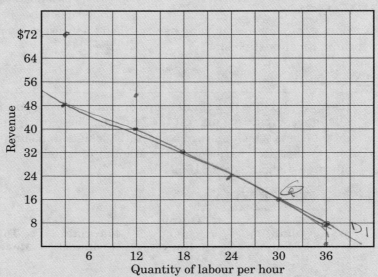

g) Assuming that the cost of labour remains at the $24 an hour level, how much labour per hour will the firm now hire? Label it *c* on the graph.

Number of workers: _____.

h) Suppose that there is a 25% increase in labour productivity over that in Table W12.1. If the price of soap is $2, fill in Table W12.2.

TABLE W12.2

Quantity of Labour	Output per Hour	Marginal Product	Total Revenue	Marginal Revenue Product
0	_____	—	—	—
1	_____	_____	_____	_____
2	_____	_____	_____	_____
3	_____	_____	_____	_____
4	_____	_____	_____	_____
5	_____	_____	_____	_____
6	_____	_____	_____	_____

i) On the graph in Figure W12.2, draw in the demand for labour curve that reflects the increase in productivity and label it D_3.

j) Compare the changes in d), f) and h).

_____

_____

_____

_____

_____

Need a Hand?

a)   **TABLE W12.3** (completed Table W12.1)

Quantity of Labour	Output	Marginal Product	Total Revenue	Marginal Revenue Product
0	0	—	—	—
1	24	24	$ 48	$48
2	44	20	88	40
3	60	16	120	32
4	72	12	144	24
5	80	8	160	16
6	84	4	168	8

b) With the cost of labour of $16 an hour the firm should assign **5** workers to each workstation because the hourly marginal revenue product of the 5th worker is also $16.

c), e) and i).

FIGURE W12.3 (completed Figure W12.2)

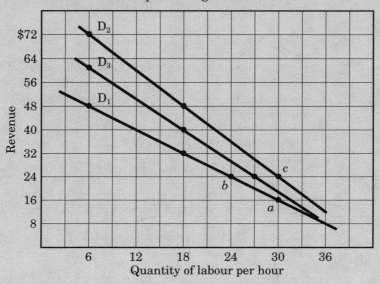

d) With the increase in the cost of labour to $24, the firm should reduce the number of workers at each workstation to **4** since the hourly marginal revenue product of the 4th worker is also $24. Since there are 6 workstations, the total quantity of labour hired would be **24**.

f) The increase in the price of soap shifts the demand curve for labour to the right. We have labelled the new demand curve D_2 on Figure W12.3.

g) With the increase in the price of soap and the resulting shift to the right in the demand curve for labour, the firm will again hire 5 workers per station even at the higher wage rate of $24 since the (new) hourly marginal revenue product of the 5th worker is $24. Since there are six workstations, the total workers hired per hour would be **30**.

h) The effect of the increase in labour productivity is given in Table W12.4.

TABLE W12.4 (completed Table W12.2)

Quantity of Labour	Output per Hour	Marginal Product	Total Revenue	Marginal Revenue Product
0	0	—	—	—
1	30	30	$ 60	$60
2	55	25	110	50
3	75	20	150	40
4	90	15	180	30
5	100	10	200	20
6	105	5	210	10

i) See Figure W12.3 on page 433.

j) The change that occurred in d) was a movement along the demand curve D_1 which was caused by an increase in the price of labour. The change in both f) and i) are shifts in the demand curve. The D_1 to D_2 shift is caused by an increase in the price of the soap being produced and, the D_1 to D_3 shift is caused by an increase in the productivity of labour.

More of the Same

Rainbow Sky is a small company that sells packages of scented incense in a competitive market. The daily output of each worker is given in Table W12.5 opposite. The firm sells the incense for $2.50 a packet and labour costs $30 a day.

a) Fill in the marginal product, total revenue and marginal revenue product columns in Table W12.5.

b) How many workers per day should the firm hire?

c) On a graph construct the firm's demand for labour curve (label it D1). Indicate, with the letter A, the total amount of labour that the firm will hire.

d) Now assume that wages decrease to $25 per day. How many workers per day will Rainbow Sky hire now?

e) On your graph, indicate with the letter B the effect of this decrease in wages.

TABLE W12.5

Quantity of Labour	Output per Day	Marginal Product	Total Revenue	Marginal Revenue Product
0	—	—	—	—
1	22	____	____	____
2	40	____	____	____
3	56	____	____	____
4	70	____	____	____
5	82	____	____	____
6	92	____	____	____

f) Next, assume that the price at which Rainbow Sky can sell its product decreases to $2. Draw in a new demand curve for labour and label it D_2.

g) Assuming that the cost of labour remains at the $25 a day level, how much labour per day will the firm now hire?

h) Now assume a 25% decrease in labour productivity, along with the original $2.50 price for incense, and construct a new demand for labour curve and label it D_3 on your graph.

i) Does your graph verify that an increase in the cost of labour is a movement on the demand curve for labour while both a decrease in the price of the incense and in the productivity of labour will shift it?

Other Problems

1. The demand for film animators is illustrated in Figure W12.4.

FIGURE W12.4

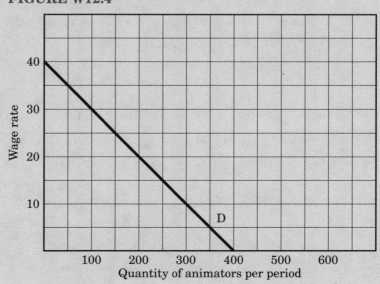

a) Draw in a supply curve that comes out the origin of the graph showing that the quantity increases by 100 for each $10 increase in the wage rate.

b) What are the total earnings per period of the animators as a group?

Answer: _____.

c) How much of the earnings in b) are transfer earnings and how much is economic rent?

Transfer earnings: _____; economic rent: _____.

d) If the supply of animators increased, would the total earnings for the group increase or decrease?

Increase: _____; decrease: _____.

2. Some data for the country of Valhalla is presented in Table W12.6.

TABLE W12.6

Wage	Demand for Labour I	Supply of Labour	Demand for Labour II
$12	600	0	900
14	500	200	800
16	400	400	700
18	300	600	600
20	200	800	500
22	100	1,000	400

a) Assuming Demand I, if the firm Odin is operating in a perfectly competitive labour market what will it have to pay for labour?

Answer: _____.

b) If, instead, Odin was a monopsonist, would it hire more or less labour and would the wage rate be higher or lower?

Quantity hired: _____; wage rate: _____.

Now assume that the demand for labour increased as illustrated by Demand II in the table above.

c) Given the same conditions as in a) above, what is your answer now?

Answer: _____.

3. Table W12.7 lists some productivity data for the firm Omir in the country of Hanu.

TABLE W12.7

Units	$MP_K 1$	MP_L	$MP_K 2$
1	23	11	50
2	21	10	45
3	18	8	38
4	14	6	30
5	10	3	11
6	5	0	10

a) Assume that both the price of capital and labour is $1 per unit. If the present MP of capital is the column MP_K1, what is the right capital to labour ratio for Omir to use?

Ratio: _____.

b) Assume that the price of capital remains at $1 but the price of labour increases to $2. Now what is the right ratio of capital to labour for Omir to use?

Ratio: _____.

c) Assume, again, that the price of both capital and labour is $1 a unit. If the present MP of capital is MP_K2, what is the right capital/labour ratio to use?

Ratio: _____.

4. In the land of Nod there are only two industries, A and B. The demand for labour in these two industries is illustrated on the graphs in Figure W12.5 below.

FIGURE W12.5

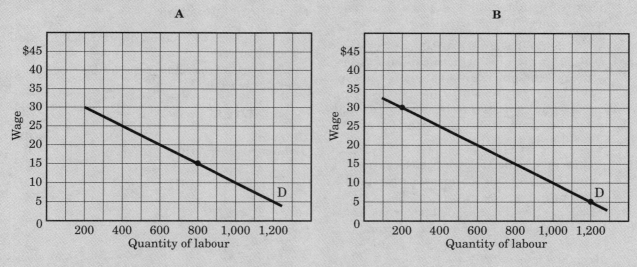

Nod is populated with 1,200 workers, each with identical productivity, of whom half are female and half are male. For many years now, 16.67% of the female workers and 50% of the male workers have worked in Industry A while the rest have worked in Industry B.

a) How many workers will there be in each industry?

Industry A _____; Industry B _____.

b) What will be the wage rate in the two industries?

Industry A _____; Industry B _____.

c) What do you think would be the effects on both the number of workers and the wage rate in each industry if there were no barriers of entry of any kind — physical, psychological, cultural, traditional, legal, etc. — into either industry for either males or females?

Effect on the number of workers: _____.

Effect on the wage rates: _____.

Unanswered Questions

Short Essays

1. Describe three ways in which a union might be able to increase the wage rate received by its members. Make reference to the quantity of members that would be hired in each of the three instances.

2. What does Schumpeter see as the key to economic growth in a capitalist economy? Do you think that Schumpeter's idea is likely to become more or less relevant in the next 20 years?

3. While the use of a common property resource must be regulated, that of a non-renewable resource need not be. Discuss.

4. An individual worker's productivity is increased by giving her more capital to work with. Yet, the process of increasing the capital/labour ratio results in labour being replaced by capital. Surely, this means that as labour's productivity increases, fewer people will have jobs. Discuss.

5. Comment on the following observation: "I know of an economics professor who spent 9 years in university to prepare for his profession, and now earns $60,000 a year. I also know a stockbroker who did not attend college or university who is making over $60,000. Obviously, the professor is underpaid or the stockbroker is overpaid."

Analytical Questions

1. Use the theory of marginal productivity and the concept of the real wage to discuss whether you think Robinson Crusoe's standard of living increased or decreased as a result of Friday coming onto the scene.

2. Discuss the following statement: "The Canadian Medical Association is perhaps the most powerful union in the country."

3. The price of a ticket for a good seat at a professional hockey game in some cities in Canada is now over $80. The long-run consequences of this will be that the pay earned by professional hockey players will surely fall. Discuss.

4. The government of Canada subsidized the oil industry to the tune of billions of dollars in the 70s in order to encourage the exploration of oil in the arctic and off the coast of Newfoundland. Oil was found, lots of it, in fact. Why aren't we extracting any of it?

5. Any of the owners of a major sports team in North America could pay their players considerably less and still get them to play. Discuss.

Numerical Questions

1. In Table W12.8 below is data for a small company, Soft Pine, that makes wooden stir sticks. The marginal product figures are for kilos per day.

TABLE W12.8

Units of Labour	MPL	MRP$_L$ A	MRP$_L$ B
1	12	_____	_____
2	9	_____	_____
3	8	_____	_____
4	7	_____	_____
5	6	_____	_____
6	5	_____	_____

a) Fill in column 3 in the table above assuming that Soft Pine sells its product in a competitive market for $30 a kilo. Then fill in column 4 assuming the price of sticks increases to $36.

b) If labour costs $180 a day, how much labour will Soft Pine hire in each of the two situations, A and B?

c) On a graph, sketch in the two demand curves and indicate the quantity of labour hired.

2. Assume that the current equilibrium price for a barrel of oil is $18 and the interest rate is 6%.
   a) What does the price of oil need to be two years from now to justify extracting it now?
   b) What if oil producers think that the price of a barrel of oil in two years will be more than this figure?

3. Table W12.9 lists some data for the economy of Onlyoneland in which all labour is homogeneous.

TABLE W12.9

Wage Rate	Supply Labour I (millions of workers)	Demand for Labour I (millions of workers)	Supply of Labour II	Demand for Labour II
$ 6	12	16	_____	_____
7	13	15	_____	_____
8	14	14	_____	_____
9	15	13	_____	_____
10	16	12	_____	_____

Table W12.10 lists data for the firm Oneofmany which operates in a competitive labour market.

TABLE W12.10

Hours of Labour Used	MRP$_L$
2,000	12
3,000	10
4,000	8
5,000	6
6,000	4

a) Given Supply I and Demand I, how many workers will Oneofmany hire and what wage will it pay?
b) Now fill in columns 4 and 5 in Table W12.9 assuming that both the supply of and the demand for labour increases by 2 million at each wage rate.
c) What will be the quantity of labour hired by Oneofmany and the wage rate it pays after this change?

4. On a graph, draw a supply and demand curve for a factor which illustrates all of the earnings of a factor as economic rent.

CHAPTER THIRTEEN

International Trade

What's ahead . . . We start by looking at the reasons why individuals and countries trade with each other, and discover that the reason in both cases is because of differences of endowment: some are endowed with attributes not available to others but often lack those things possessed by others. These differences lead to cost advantages which some producers enjoy over others and is at the heart of Ricardo's theory of comparative advantage which we investigate in the first part of the chapter. We then look at the concept of the terms of trade and show how this determines who gets what share of the increased production that results from trade. Finally the chapter looks at some of the arguments against free trade and ends by an investigation of how and why trade has often been restricted and impeded.

People have traded in one form or another since the dawn of time, and most of the great nations of history have also been famous traders: the Phoenicians and the Greeks; medieval Venice and Elizabethan England; the American Colonies and modern Japan. While it seems obvious that there are benefits to be obtained from trading, there has always been the underlying suspicion that someone also loses as a result. For many, what is meant by a great trading nation is one which consistently, and through shrewd practice, always manages to come out on top during trade negotiations. This "beggar thy neighbour" attitude was the cause of no great concern for writers immediately preceding Adam Smith, who thought it was part of the natural state of affairs that there are always winners and losers when it comes to trade. It was the job of policy-makers they felt to ensure that their own country was always on the winning side.

It took the mind of Adam Smith, however, to see that whenever two people enter into a voluntary agreement to trade, both parties must gain as a result. If you trade a textbook in exchange for your friend's new CD of Guns 'n Butter, then you obviously want that CD more than the textbook, and your friend must want the textbook more than the CD. Trade is to the advantage of both of you, otherwise it would not take place. When we look at international trade between nations, all we are doing is simply looking at this single transaction multiplied a billionfold. It is not really nations who trade, but individual people and firms who buy from other foreign individuals and firms. In many ways the reason you trade with a friend is the same reason you buy products from a Toronto brewery or from a Winnipeg car dealer or from a Tokyo fishing rod manufacturer: you hope to gain something as a result, and what you give up in return (usually money) is of less value to you than the thing you obtain in return.

All of which begs the question of why you personally (or a whole nation for that matter) would want to buy something rather than make it at home. In other words, why are people not self-sufficient? Why do they not produce everything that they personally consume? Well, Adam Smith had an answer for this (as for most things):

> It is the maxim of every prudent master of a family, never to make at home what it will cost him more to make than to buy.[1]

There, in essence, is the main argument for trade: why make something yourself if you can buy it cheaper elsewhere? If it takes Akio three hours to make a certain product, but he can buy it elsewhere from the income he gets from one hour's work in his regular job, then why would he bother? It would pay him to do his own job for three hours; he could afford to buy three units of the product. Not to mention the fact that there are many things (actually, most things) that Akio is incapable of making, or could make only after extensive training and with the help of very expensive equipment.

Specialization and Trade

Specialization is the cornerstone of trade. As we have seen in earlier chapters, there are big advantages to be gained from specialization. From an individual's point of view, each of us is better suited to one thing than another. Rather than trying to grow all our own food, make our own clothes, brew our own beer and so on, it makes more sense to specialize in our own occupation and with the proceeds obtain those things which other people could make better and cheaper. Similarly, as we saw in Chapter 6, firms will be far more productive if they specialize in the production process, i.e., make use of the division of labour. As we shall see in this chapter, there are also great benefits to be enjoyed by countries which similarly specialize rather than try to be self-sufficient.

It follows that the result of more specialization is more trading. Specialization and trade go hand in hand. Modern nations, firms and individuals have become increasingly specialized, and with this has come a huge increase in the volume of trade, domestically and internationally. But is there a limit to specialization? From a technical point of view, Smith thought not; but he did believe that specialization would be limited by the size of the market. The smaller the market, the less output and therefore the less opportunity or need for extensive specialization. The bigger the size of the market, the more specialization that can take place and the lower will be the cost of producing goods. The prime driving force behind the expansion of markets is that it enables firms to produce in higher volumes and at a lower cost. All things being equal (including demand), it is the cost of production and therefore the price of the product which induces trade. If you can produce a product cheaper than I can, then it will make no sense for me to try to produce it myself. And why are you able to produce certain products

---

[1] Adam Smith, *Wealth of Nations* (Edwin Cannan Edition, 1877), p. 354.

cheaper than I can? The answer presumably is that you possess certain advantages over me. Let us look at these advantages.

Factor Endowment

One person has an advantage in production over others if he or she is endowed with certain natural or acquired skills or has more or better equipment or other resources. There are many explanations of why some people are better gardeners or truck drivers or hockey players than others. So too with countries. A country will have a great advantage in producing and trading pineapples for instance if it possesses the right type of soil and climate. But the same country may well be at a disadvantage in growing coniferous trees. Another country has an advantage in producing electronic equipment if it has the right capital, the technical expertise and a well-educated labour force. It may not however be able to compete with other countries in raising sheep. All people are different. Although some are graced with certain advantages over others they are often handicapped in other areas. So too with countries; they are well endowed in certain areas, they are impoverished in others. Japan has a well-educated and motivated work force, possesses great technical expertise and is highly capitalized, yet it is very poorly provided with arable land and possesses very few mineral resources.

It is often suggested that the prime reason a country trades is in order to buy those resources which it does not naturally possess. While there is a great deal of truth in this, it often obscures the main motivation. Canada, for instance, is not endowed with a warm and sunny climate throughout the year and is unable to produce bananas commercially. Through the use of geodesic domes with artificial light and heating, it could grow its own bananas, but the cost would be enormous. The reason it does not grow bananas is not because it cannot, but because it is cheaper to buy them from countries who possess the necessary resources at lower cost. Most countries then can often overcome a resource deficiency by using different methods or other resources, but it would not make sense if this production method results in products which are more expensive than those obtainable from abroad.

Theory of Absolute Advantage

A country will tend to gravitate to producing in those areas where, because of its own factor endowments, it possesses a cost advantage over other producing countries: Canada produces wheat, lumber and minerals; Colombia produces coffee; Malaysia produces rubber; Japan produces electronic equipment, and so on. This is no more nor less than what Adam Smith proposed when he put forward his *theory of absolute advantage*. Nations, like firms and individuals, should specialize in producing goods and services for which they have an advantage, and trade with other countries for goods and services in which they do not enjoy an advantage. Let us work through a simple example of this theory. We will concentrate on just two countries and suppose that they produce just two products. We will assume that the average cost of producing each product remains constant. In addition, to begin with, we will further assume that each country is self-sufficient and no trade is taking place. Table 13.1 shows the productivity per worker (i.e., average product) of producing wheat and beans in Canada and Mexico.

TABLE 13.1 Output per Worker by Country and Industry

| | Number of Bushels per day | |
	Wheat	Beans
Canada	3	2
Mexico	1	4

We can see at a glance in Table 13.1 that Canada is more productive than Mexico at producing wheat whereas Mexico is more productive than Canada at producing beans. Let us examine the possibility of gains if both countries were to specialize, Canada in wheat and Mexico in beans. Since the table is in output per worker, let's move a single worker in Canada out of the bean industry and over to the wheat industry. In Mexico, the transfer is in the opposite direction: one worker goes from the wheat industry to the bean industry. Table 13.1 has already shown us what each country will gain and what it will lose. Canada would gain an additional 3 bushels of wheat, since that is the average productivity in that industry, but would lose 2 bushels of beans. In Mexico, the gain would be 4 bushels of beans at a loss of 1 bushel of wheat. (To keep things simple here we are assuming that the average and marginal products are equal, i.e., each worker in Canada, for instance, produces three bushels of wheat regardless of the number of workers employed.) The movement of workers is summarized in Table 13.2.

TABLE 13.2 Gain/Loss of Output

| | Number of Bushels per Day | |
	Wheat	Beans
Canada	+3	−2
Mexico	−1	+4
Total	+2	+2

It is possible then, with just the transfer of one worker in each country for there to be a net increase in the production of both products. These are what are known as the *gains from trade*. Strictly speaking, they are the gains

Study Guide

QUESTION 13.1

Suppose that the productivity per worker in the beer and in the wine industries of Freedonia and Libraland are as follows:

| | Output in Hundreds of Litres | |
	Beer	Wine
Freedonia	4	1
Libraland	3	4

A) Which country should specialize in which product?
B) Suppose that a single worker in each country is transferred from the less to the more productive industry. What will the total gains from specialization be?

from specialization. It would seem to be the case from this example that if more workers were to shift industries in this manner, then the gain would be commensurately higher. Presumably, the greater the specialization, the bigger the gains. Note that if a country is not to end up consuming just a single product, it will be forced to trade.

Theory of Comparative Advantage

The eminent economist David Ricardo, following in the footsteps of Adam Smith, agreed in principle with his mentor and added a subtle but important refinement to Smith's theory of trade. To see the effect of his modification, let's change our example to that of theoretical trade between the United States and the Philippines, but keep the same two products, wheat and beans. The output per worker in each country is shown in Table 13.3

TABLE 13.3 Output per Worker by Country and Industry

| | Number of Bushels per Day | |
	Wheat	Beans
United States	6	4
Philippines	1	2

If we compare the United State's productivity in wheat, you can see from the table that it is six times as great as the Philippines; similarly, it is twice as productive as the Philippines in producing beans. If we were to follow Smith's dictum, then presumably the U.S. should produce both products itself. After all, how can it possibly be of any advantage to the U.S. to trade with the Philippines, since it could produce both products cheaper? The nub of Ricardo's idea is that it is not *absolute* but **comparative advantage** that provides the mutual gains from trade. Let us see exactly what this means through an example.

comparative advantage: the advantage which comes from producing something at a lower opportunity cost than others are able.

Suppose that you happened to be the absolutely best lawyer in your town. Not only that, but you are also its greatest secretary. Given this, why would you bother to hire a secretary to do your clerical work since you are faster, and by all measurement, more efficient than anyone you could possibly hire? The answer is that you would still hire a secretary since you couldn't afford not to. The reason for this is because you are so productive. Your high productivity is both a blessing and a curse. It is a blessing because you earn a great deal as a lawyer; it is a curse because you sacrifice a great deal not being a secretary. In other words your opportunity costs of being a lawyer is the lost salary of not being a secretary. Your opportunity cost of being a secretary is your lost earnings as a lawyer. But because you can earn *comparatively* more as a lawyer than as a secretary, you would be advised to concentrate on that career and hire someone (admittedly less productive than yourself) to act as your secretary.

What Ricardo did with his idea of comparative advantage was, in a sense, to direct attention away from making comparisons between countries and instead focus attention on the comparison between products. In Table 13.3, for instance, what is the cost for the U.S. in producing wheat? One way to answer this would be to express it in dollars and cents. Knowing that the value of money varies over time, and it is often misleading to translate one currency into another, Ricardo was at pains to express costs in more fundamental terms. One way of doing this would be to express costs in terms of the number of hours it takes to produce something. For example, if in our example, the average worker in the U.S. can produce 4 bushels of beans in an average eight-hour day, then the cost of 1 bushel of beans would be 8/4, or 2 hours. In comparison, the cost of one bushel of beans in the Philippines would be 8/2, or 4 hours. So, it is twice as expensive in the Philippines. However, a better and more illuminating way of measuring costs is in terms of opportunity costs. And this is the method Ricardo chose.

You will remember that the opportunity cost of producing one thing can be measured in terms of another thing that had to be sacrificed in order to get it. As far as the U.S. and the Philippines are concerned, the cost of producing more wheat is the sacrifice of beans, and the cost of increased bean production is the loss of wheat. Let us work out these costs then for each country. The cost of employing a worker in the wheat industry is what that worker could have produced in the bean industry, assuming that the country is fully employed. In other words, for every 6 bushels of wheat that an American worker produces, the country sacrifices 4 bushels of beans. In per unit terms, since 6 bushels of wheat costs 4 bushels of beans, then 1 wheat costs 4/6 or 0.67 beans. Likewise, since the production of 4 bushels of beans costs 6 bushels of wheat, then 1 bean costs 6/4 or 1.5 wheat. In the Philippines, the cost of 1 wheat is 2 beans and the cost of 1 bean equals 1/2 wheat. Let us summarize these figures in Table 13.4.

TABLE 13.4 Opportunity Costs of Production

| | Cost of Producing one Unit | |
	Wheat	**Beans**
United States	0.67 beans	1.5 wheat
Philippines	2 beans	0.5 wheat

You can perhaps understand now the significance of comparative costs. As we saw earlier, in absolute terms, whether this is measured in hours or dollars, beans are very cheap to produce in the United States. But in comparative terms they are very *expensive*. Why is that? Because to produce beans, the U.S. has to make a big sacrifice in the product in which it is even more productive: wheat. Similarly, although beans in absolute terms are very expensive in the Philippines, in comparative terms they are cheap, since to produce them the Philippines doesn't have to make much sacrifice in wheat production because productivity in the wheat industry is so low.

In this example then, as Table 13.4 suggests, the U.S. should specialize in producing the product in which it has the comparative advantage, i.e., wheat; and the Philippines should specialize in beans where it has the comparative advantage.

Let us extract some further insights by showing the production possibilities of the two countries on the assumption that the size of the labour force in the U.S. is 100 million and that of the Philippines is 80 million and that unit costs are constant. Their respective production possibilities are shown in Table 13.5 on the next page.

TABLE 13.5 Production Possibilities

	United States: Output in Millions of Bushels per Day				
	A	**B**	**C**	**D**	**E**
Wheat	600	450	300	150	0
Beans	0	100	200	300	400

	Philippines: Output in Millions of Bushels per Day				
	A	**B**	**C**	**D**	**E**
Wheat	80	60	40	20	0
Beans	0	40	80	120	160

Suppose that initially the countries are self-sufficient and both are producing combinations B. Before specialization and trade, therefore, their joint totals are as shown in Table 13.6.

TABLE 13.6 Output before Specialization and Trade

	Total Output in Millions of Bushels per Day	
	Wheat	**Beans**
United States	450	100
Philippines	60	40
Total	510	140

If the two countries now specialize, the U.S. producing wheat and the Philippines producing beans, their output levels would be as shown in Table 13.7.

TABLE 13.7 Output after Specialization and Trade

	Total Output in Millions of Bushels per Day	
	Wheat	**Beans**
United States	600	0
Philippines	0	160
Total	600	160

You can see by comparing the before and after positions that production of both products is now higher. Table 13.8 outlines the gains from trade.

TABLE 13.8 Gains from Specialization and Trade

Total Output in Millions of Bushels per Day	
Wheat	**Beans**
+90	+20

Before we try to figure out which country will get this increased production, let us look at the production possibilities graphically. Figure 13.1 opposite shows the production possibilities of each country on the same graph.

As we saw in Chapter 1, the slope of the production curve measures the cost of production. In Figure 13.1 this is the cost of beans measured in wheat. The slope of the U.S. production possibilities curve is 3/2 reflecting the fact that beans are relatively expensive at 1.5 wheat per unit of beans. The Philippines' production possibilities curve in contrast is much flatter. Its

FIGURE 13.1 U.S. and Philippines' Production Possibilities Curves

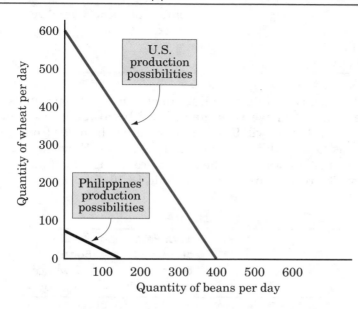

The slope of the production possibilities curve measures the average cost of production of the product shown on the horizontal axis, i.e., beans. In this figure, the slope of the U.S. production possibilities curve is equal to 3/2 (wheat production drops by 3 for every increase of 2 beans), i.e., the cost of 1 bean in the U.S. is 1 1/2 wheat. In contrast, the cost of beans in the Philippines is cheap since it sacrifices only 1/2 wheat for each 1 bean produced, i.e., the slope of the Philippines' production possibilities curve is 1/2.

slope is 1/2 which means, as we have seen, that the cost of beans is only 0.5 wheat per unit of beans.

This shows that it is possible for both countries to gain from trade, but the remaining questions are: Will they? How will the increased production be shared? Will it be shared equally or will one country receive more than the other? Before addressing these questions, however, let us confirm the lesson that we have learned: it is the differences in *comparative* costs that is the basis of trade between nations.

Study Guide

QUESTION 13.2

Suppose that the labour force in Freedonia is 10 million, of whom 6 million are presently producing apples, one of the two crops which it produces, the other being pears. In contrast, Libraland's labour force is 16 million, one-half of whom are producing apples, and the rest, pears. The labour productivity in the two countries is as follows:

Output per Worker (number of bushels per day)

	Apples	Pears
Freedonia	5	2
Libraland	1	3

Assuming constant costs, draw the production possibilities curves of the two countries on the same graph. Mark on it the present production combinations and the quantities that each would produce were they to specialize according to their absolute advantages.

The last example, using the same two products, looks at the theoretical trade between Canada and the U.S. The output per worker in each country is shown in Table 13.9 on the next page.

TABLE 13.9 Output per Worker by Country and Industry

| | Number of Bushels per Day | |
	Wheat	Beans
Canada	3	2
United States	6	4

Clearly, the U.S. has an absolute advantage in producing both products, but as we shall see, it does *not* have a **comparative advantage** in either product and for this reason there will be no profit or gain to be made from trade. To see this, let us look at things in comparative terms. From the data in Table 13.9, we can easily work out the cost of producing wheat and beans in each country. The results are shown in Table 13.10.

TABLE 13.10 Opportunity Costs of Production

| | Cost of Producing one Unit | |
	Wheat	Beans
Canada	0.67 beans	1.5 wheat
United States	0.67 beans	1.5 wheat

Although the U.S. is more productive in both products, since it is equally more productive in each product, it really has no comparative advantage. This can be seen by looking, as we did earlier, at what happens when we shift workers from one industry to another. To prove that there are no benefits to be had from specialization and trade in this instance, we need to show that the output of one industry increases without a compensating loss in the other industry. So, this time let's shift *two* workers from the bean to the wheat industry in Canada and one worker from the wheat to the bean industry in the U.S. The results will be as in Table 13.11.

TABLE 13.11 Gain/Loss of Output

| | Number of Bushels per Day | |
	Wheat	Beans
Canada	+6	–4
United States	–6	+4
Total	0	0

In other words, since comparative costs are identical in the two countries (although the absolute costs are very different), there are no gains that can be made from trade. We could similarly suggest that, since the U.S. in this example is so much more productive than Canada, when it switches workers over to the bean industry it gains a great amount of beans; unfortunately, since it is also extremely productive in the wheat industry, it loses a great deal of wheat. Similarly, Canada does not have a comparative advantage in either product.

What emerges from our Canada/United States example is that as long as there are differences in comparative costs between countries, regardless of the differences in absolute costs, there is the basis for mutually beneficial trade.

Let us now see how these gains from trade will be divided up between the countries.

QUESTION 13.3
From the data contained in Table 13.9, graph the production possibilities curves of the two countries assuming that the labour force in Canada is 10 million and in the United States it is 100 million. What do the slopes of the curves suggest?

BOX 13A
1. Why are trade and specialization interdependent?
2. Is there a limit to specialization?
3. What is meant by the term *factor endowment*?
4. What is the theory of absolute advantage? Who introduced it?
5. What is the theory of comparative advantage? Who introduced it?

Terms of Trade

terms of trade: the average price of a country's exports compared with the price of its imports.

The **terms of trade** refers to the price at which a country sells its exports compared with the price at which it buys its imports. In reality, the price of any product is determined by a whole host of factors which we collectively gather under the headings of demand or supply. If the worldwide demand for softwood lumber were to increase, for example, it would increase the price of Canadian exports with the result that the terms of trade would be said to have moved in Canada's favour. The result would be the same if Canadian prices remain the same but the price of imports drops. In either case, the sale of our exports would enable us to purchase more imports. On the other hand, the terms of trade would shift against Canada if Canadian export prices dropped, and/or the price of imported goods rose.

In our United States/Philippines example the simple answer to which country gains most from trade is that it all depends upon the terms of trade. But let us look at what would be acceptable prices from the two countries' point of view. Remember that the U.S. is the wheat producer and exporter. A glance back at Table 13.4 shows that it costs the U.S. 0.67 beans to produce 1 unit of wheat. What price would it be willing to sell its wheat for? Presumably for as high a price as it can get but certainly not for less than 0.67 beans. What about the Philippines: how much would it be willing to pay for wheat? Remember, Table 13.4 tells us that the Philippines can itself produce 1 unit of wheat at a cost of 2 beans each. It certainly would not pay any higher than this price. It would be happy to buy it for less, and the lower, the better. You can see that as long as the price is above the U.S. minimum and below the Philippines' maximum, both countries would be willing to trade. In other words, trade is possible if the price of one unit of wheat is anywhere between 0.67 and 2 units of beans. We could have just as easily expressed things in terms of beans, and a glance back at Table 13.4 shows that feasible terms of trade would be anywhere between 0.5 wheat to 1.5 wheat for 1 bushel of beans. Where the actual terms of trade end up will depend on the strength of demand in the two countries for these products.

Let us suggest possible terms of trade and work out the consequences. Suppose, for simplicity's sake, that the terms end up at one bushel of wheat for one bushel of beans. Suppose further that the Philippines is quite happy consuming the 40 million bushels of beans that it was producing before it decided to specialize, as shown in Table 13.5. However it is now producing solely beans and will have therefore 160 − 40 = 120 million bushels of beans available for export which it sells to the U.S. at a rate of 1 bean for 1 wheat. It will receive back 120 million bushels of wheat and will finish up with 40 million bushels of beans and 120 million bushels of wheat. Because of trade, it will have gained an additional 60 million bushels of wheat compared with its self-sufficient totals shown in combination B of Table 13.5. The U.S. will also gain. It was the sole producer of wheat, and of the total of 600 million bushels produced, it has sold 120 million bushels to the Philippines in exchange for 120 million bushels of beans. It will end up with 480 million bushels of wheat and 120 million bushels of beans which is 30 million bushels of wheat and 20 million bushels of beans more than when it was producing both products as shown in combination B.

QUESTION 13.4
Suppose that the average productivity in Freedonia and Libraland are as follows:

	Output per Worker (no. of bushels per worker)	
	Apples	Pears
Freedonia	6	3
Libraland	3	2

Assuming that the two countries wish to trade, would terms of trade of 1 pear = 2.5 apples be feasible? What about 1 pear = 1 apple? 1 pear = 1.75 apples?

Terms of Trade and Gains from Trade, Graphically

Let us look at each country's trading picture separately. Figure 13.2 shows the production possibilities curve for the United States. Before it decided to trade, this was also its consumption possibilities curve since it could obviously not consume more than it produced. The slope of the curve is 1.5, which is the cost of 1 bean (i.e., equals 1.5 wheat). The curve to the right is its trading possibilities curve which shows how much the U.S. could obtain through a combination of producing and trading. Note that the slope of the trading possibilities curve is equal to 1, which is the new, lower cost of beans which the U.S. can now obtain from the Philippines. You can see from this graph that the U.S., at one extreme, could produce the same maximum quantity of 600 million bushels of wheat as before and keep all of it. However, before trade, the maximum amount of beans available was 400. Now, if it wished, the U.S. could produce 600 million bushels of wheat and trade *all* of it and receive in exchange 600 million bushels of beans. More likely, of course, it will opt to have a combination of both products such as 480 million bushels of wheat and 120 million bushels of beans as in our numerical example above.

FIGURE 13.2 U.S. Production and Trading Possibilities Curves

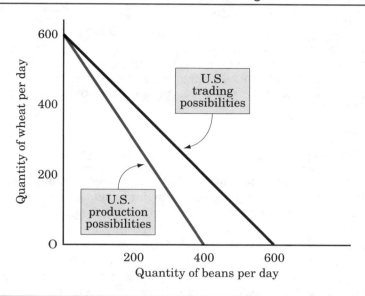

The slope of the production possibilities curve shows the cost of producing beans in the United States and is equal to 1.5 wheat per bean. The slope of the trading possibilities curve shows the cost of buying beans internationally, i.e., it is the terms of trade and equals 1 wheat per bean. The previous maximum obtainable quantity of beans was 400 million bushels when the United States was self-sufficient. Its new maximum, as a result of trading, is now 600 million bushels since it could produce, if it wished, a maximum amount of 600 million bushels of wheat and trade the total output and receive 600 million bushels of beans in exchange.

Figure 13.3 shows the position from the Philippines' point of view. The inside curve is its production possibilities curve representing the maximum of both products that could be produced when the country is self-sufficient. The slope of the curve represents the cost of 1 bushel of beans and is equal to 0.5 (bushels of wheat). The outer curve is the trading possibilities curve based on the terms of trade: 1 bean = 1 wheat. You can see that trading allows the Philippines also to enjoy increased consumption. After specialization, the maximum amount of beans remains unchanged at 160 million bushels. However the maximum amount of wheat has increased from 80 (if produced in the Philippines) to 160 (by trading away all its 160 million bushels of beans for this quantity of wheat).

FIGURE 13.3 Philippines' Production and Trading Possibilities Curves

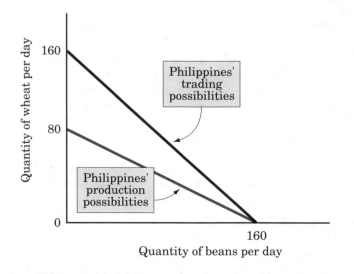

Since the Philippines is specializing in the production of beans, the trading possibilities curve is to the right of the production possibilities curve. In other words, irrespective of whether it trades or not, the cost of beans remains the same; the cost of wheat however is now lower as a result of trade since it can now obtain wheat at a cost of 1 bean per 1 wheat, whereas producing its own wheat costs 2 beans per 1 wheat.

QUESTION 13.5
From the data contained in Figure 13.2, how many beans can the United States obtain if it is self-sufficient and is producing 420 million bushels of wheat? If, instead, it specializes in wheat production and can trade at terms of 1 wheat = 1 bean, how many beans could it have to accompany its 420 million bushels of wheat? What if the terms were 1 wheat = 2 beans?

The Benefits of Free Trade and Some Important Qualifications

Ricardo's theory of comparative advantage, which we have been looking at, is very important since it clearly highlights the major benefits of trade. Free and unrestricted trade allows nations and individuals the opportunity to sell in world markets and this will, as a result, enable them to specialize in the products in which they enjoy an advantage over others. The result will be that products will be produced and sold at a *lower price and in higher volumes*, which translates into higher incomes and standards of living for all. In addition, the *variety of products* available when the world becomes one big market would presumably increase. A final benefit of free trade is the fact that it is more difficult to be a world monopolist than it is to be a monopolist in the home market. In other words, it is often suggested that free trade *increases competition*.

These are indeed powerful arguments in favour of free trade, but before we leave the topic let us look at some of the qualifications which need to be introduced. First, free trade is never free as there will always be transport, insurance and other freight charges which must be added to the cost of production and which will usually reduce the trading advantage of foreign sellers. (However, in a country as extensive as Canada, it is often cheaper to transport products from American states bordering the country than it is to transport them from one end of the country to the other.) In addition, selling in a foreign country is always going to be more difficult (and usually, therefore, more expensive) than selling in the domestic market because of the differences in language, culture, taxation, regulations and so on. Besides cost differences, the analysis we have presented so far has assumed constant costs. This leads to the result in our examples that countries should specialize in, perhaps, a single product and produce that product to a maximum. However, as we learned in Chapter 1, if any country tries to concentrate on a single product, its production is subject to the law of increasing costs. This means that one country only enjoys a cost advantage over others *up to a point*. As it tries to push production levels higher, its cost will start to increase so that it no longer enjoys a competitive advantage. This is the reason why few countries specialize entirely, and also why many countries both produce *and* import the same product. The presence of increasing costs will also lessen the advantages which one country enjoys over another in trade.

Even allowing for these caveats, it is still true that there are a number of benefits that can be obtained from trade. This leads us to ask: why then does free trade tend to be the exception rather than the rule throughout history? Why does the question of free trade still divide countries and lead to such acrimonious debate? To understand part of the reason, let us look at the consequences of trying to restrict trade.

Trade Restrictions

Let us set up a scenario where, initially, we have two self-sufficient countries, France and Germany in our example, each producing wine. The demand and supply conditions in the two countries will be very different, of course, with both the demand and supply being greater in France than in Germany as is shown in Table 13.12.

TABLE 13.12 The Market for Wine in France and Germany (in millions of litres per month)

	France			Germany	
Price (per litre)	Demand	Supply	Price (per litre)	Demand	Supply
$3	24	13	$3	12	2
4	19	14	4	11	3
5	**15**	**15**	5	10	4
6	12	16	6	9	5
7	10	17	7	8	6
8	9	18	8	7	7

The equilibrium price in France is $5 per litre and the equilibrium quantity is 15. In Germany, the equilibrium price and quantities are $8 and 7 respectively. These are shown in Figure 13.4.

FIGURE 13.4 Demand and Supply of Wine in France and Germany

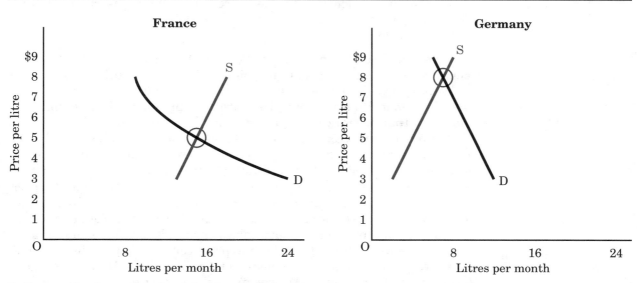

In France, the demand and supply of wine are both higher than in Germany. The consequence is a greater quantity of wine traded in France at 15 million litres compared to 7 million in Germany. The price of wine, however, is lower in France than in Germany.

Now suppose that the two countries decide to engage in free trade. To keep things simple, let's assume that there are no transport costs. If free trade is now introduced, what will be the price of wine in the two countries? Well, we know that at $5 per litre, the French winemakers were making a profit so they should have no difficulty in competing with the German producers and presumably could easily undercut the German price of $8. Since we've assumed there are no transport costs, then the price in the two countries should be the same. To find this price all we need to do is look at the combined market of France and Germany. In other words, we need simply to add the demands and supplies of the two countries, as shown in Table 13.13.

TABLE 13.13 Deriving the Total Market Demand and Supply of Wine for France and Germany (in millions of litres per month)

Price (per litre)	France Demand	France Supply	Germany Demand	Germany Supply	Total Market Demand	Total Market Supply
$3	24	13	12	2	36	15
4	19	14	11	3	30	17
5	15	15	10	4	25	19
6	12	16	9	5	**21**	**21**
7	10	17	8	6	18	23
8	9	18	7	7	16	25

The total market demand is obtained by adding together the French demand and the German demand at each price. For instance, at $3 per litre, the quantity demanded in France is 24 and in Germany it is 12, giving a total for the two countries of 36. Similarly, the quantity supplied at $3 is 13 in France and 2 in Germany giving a total market supply of 15. This is done for all prices. The new market price (let's call it the world price) then, will be $6 per litre, and at that price a total of 21 million litres will be produced and sold.

Now let us look at the effect in each market. French winemakers are delighted at the situation since they are getting a higher price now that free trade has opened up a new market in Germany and their volume of business is higher. French winemakers are now producing 16 million litres. Note also that in France the quantities produced (16) exceeds the demand from French consumers (12). What happens to the surplus of 4 million litres? The answer is that it is being exported to Germany. And what is the situation in that country? Well certainly, German consumers are delighted since the new world price of $6 is lower than the previous domestic price $8. But we can imagine that the German winemakers are far from happy. The new lower world price has caused a number of producers to cut back production, and presumably there are some producers forced out of business. At the world price of $6, German producers are only producing 5 million litres, below the German demand of 9 million litres. How is this shortage going to be made up? Answer: from the import of French wine. This simply means that the French exports of 4 million litres equals the German import of 4 million litres. These points are illustrated in Figure 13.5.

FIGURE 13.5 Demand and Supply of Wine in France and Germany with Free Trade

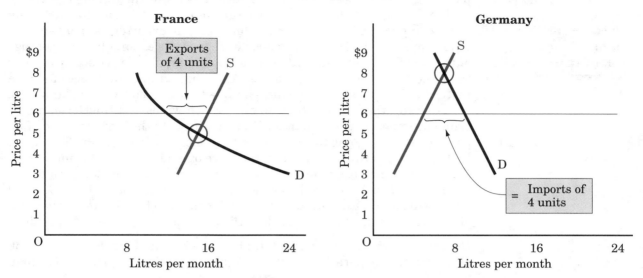

The new world price of wine is above the previous French price but below the previous German price. The result is a surplus of wine in France of 4 million litres but a shortage in Germany of 4 million litres.

QUESTION 13.6
In Table 13.13, if the demand for wine in Germany increased by 5 (million litres) at every price, how much wine would now be produced in Germany, and how much would be imported from France?

So who are the losers and who are the gainers as a result of markets being opened up? The answer in our example is that both German consumers and French wine producers gain and French consumers and German producers lose. Free trade has cost French consumers $1 a litre and it has cost German winemakers $2 per litre. Previously these winemakers were selling 7 million litres at $8 per litre for a total revenue of $56 million. Now, they are selling only 5 million litres for $6 per litre, for a total revenue of $30 million. In total then, these producers, of whom there may be less than 100, have collectively lost $30 million in revenue. It is easy to see why these producers may not be in favour of free trade! In fact, it would pay them to lobby their own parliament and to launch publicity campaigns in an attempt to keep out "cheap" French wines. As long as their efforts do not cost more than $30 million, they will be ahead of the game.

protectionism: the economic policy of protecting domestic producers by restricting the importation of foreign products.

It is easy to see why powerful lobby and special interest groups have been very vocal throughout history trying to persuade parliament and the public that it is in the country's interest to ban or curtail foreign imports. This **protectionism** can take many forms which we need to look at.

Imposition of Quotas

quota: a limit imposed on the production or sale of a product.

The most obvious restriction on imports is to ban them either entirely or partially, and this is exactly what is meant by a **quota**. A quota can take a variety of forms ranging from, as we said, a total restriction to a maximum limit being placed on each individual foreign exporter, or perhaps the requirement that each foreign exporter reduces its exports by a percentage of the previous year's sales. The essence of a quota is to reduce or restrict the importation of certain products. And what will be the effect of such a restriction? Suppose in our wine example that German winemakers were successful in their efforts to keep out French wines and the German government imposed a total ban on French wines. At the current price of $6 per litre, there is going to be an immediate shortage in Germany. The result of the shortage will be to push up the price of wine. It will continue to rise, encouraging increased German production until the price returns to the pre-free trade price of $8. In France, the immediate effect of the German quota will be to cause a surplus of French wine which will depress the price of French wine until it too is back at the pre-free trade price of $5 per litre.

Usually, quotas do not imply a total ban on imports. Therefore, let us look at the effect in general of a quota in Figure 13.6, which depicts the German wine market.

FIGURE 13.6 The Effects of the Imposition of a Quota

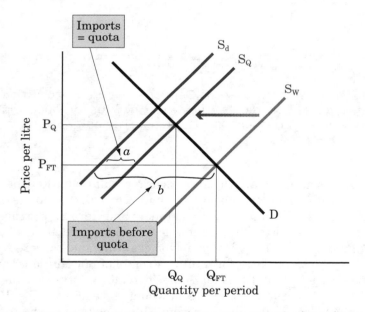

D is the demand for wine in Germany and, assuming free trade, the supply of wine from both domestic German producers and from foreign producers is shown by S_w. The resulting price is P_{FT} and the quantity is Q_{FT}. If a quota is imposed and this reduced the quantity imported into Germany to the amount a, then the new supply is shown by the curve S_Q. The result is a reduction in the quantity to Q_Q, and an increase in the price to P_Q.

The domestic supply of wine is shown as S_d, the world supply is S_w. If Germany was open to free trade then the market price of wine in Germany would be P_{FT} and the quantity traded would be Q_{FT}, of which foreign imports would account for the quantity shown as b, the remaining demand being met by German winemakers. Suppose that the German government now restricts the quantity of foreign wine entering Germany by imposing a quota represented by the amount a in Figure 13.6. The new reduced world supply is now shown as the supply curve S_Q. As a result of this reduction, the price of wine increases to P_Q and the quantity drops to Q_Q. From this, it can be seen that the losers are going to be German consumers (who are paying a higher price and are having less quantity and variety of wines) and foreign winemakers whose exports are being restricted. The winners will be German winemakers who are producing more wine and receiving a higher price.

The Imposition of a Tariff

tariff: a tax (or duty) levied on imports.

A second way of restricting imports is by the use of a **tariff** which is a tax on imports. It is a more frequently chosen method than quotas, because governments can derive considerable revenue from tariffs. The effects of a tariff are much the same as a quota in that, in both cases, the price of the product will increase. With a quota, however, the domestic producers get the whole benefit of the higher price, while with a tariff, the benefit is shared between the domestic producers and the government. An additional benefit of a tariff over a quota is that a quota tends to treat foreign producers indiscriminately since each and every producer is treated the same while with a tariff, only the more efficient producers will continue to export since only they will be able to continue to make a profit. A tariff discriminates against the less efficient producers and from an efficiency point of view, therefore, is superior to a quota. These points are illustrated in Figure 13.7.

FIGURE 13.7 The Effects of the Imposition of a Tariff

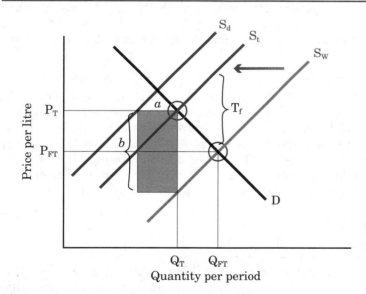

With free trade, the initial demand and supply are D and S_W, giving an equilibrium quantity of Q_{FT} and a price of P_{FT}. The imposition of a tariff equal to T_f reduces the supply of foreign wines, shown as a leftward shift of the supply curve to S_t. The result will be a higher price of P_T and a lower quantity Q_T. Additionally, the government will receive part of the proceeds from the sale of foreign wines equal to the distance a which represents the amount of imports at price, P_T times the amount of the tariff T_f, which is equal to the vertical distance b. The tax revenue is equal to the shaded rectangle.

In Figure 13.7, suppose again that we are describing the German wine market and, as in Figure 13.6, the initial free trade position, given the demand as D and the total supply as S_W, is a quantity Q_{FT} and a price P_{FT}. The German government now imposes a tariff equal to the amount T_f. The new supply is given as S_t which causes an eventual drop in output to Q_t and an increase in price to P_T. The result is very similar to that produced by a quota. Again, it is German consumers and foreign producers who lose out, and German producers who gain. There is a difference, however. Although the price of P_T is the same for both German and foreign wines, it is only the foreign wine that is subject to the tariff; German winemakers receive the whole of the price P_T. The other gainers in this scenario will be the German government who will receive tax revenue equal to the shaded rectangle in Figure 13.7.

Other Trade Restrictions

exchange controls: restrictions imposed by a government limiting the amount of foreign currencies that can be obtained.

Besides the two popular protectionist measures of tariffs and quotas, there are a number of other methods available that deserve mention. **Exchange controls** are similar to quotas, but instead of a restriction being placed on the importation of a good, the restriction is placed on the availability of foreign currencies (i.e., foreign exchange). The effect is the same because since foreigners wish to be paid in their own currencies, if an importer is unable to get his hands on the appropriate currency, he will not be able to buy the foreign goods. The controls might be across the board restrictions or on particular currencies or on particular products or industries. The effect in all cases will be to increase the domestic price of the products affected which will help the domestic producer at the expense of the domestic consumer. Another more subtle but often equally effective way of cutting imports is by way of *restrictions and regulations*. A government might make trade so difficult or time-consuming for the importer that the amount of trade is significantly reduced. For instance, the Customs Department of a particular country might tie the importer up with red tape by requiring that all imports must be accompanied by 10 different forms (all in triplicate) obtainable from 10 different government departments. Or perhaps the product must comply to certain very unrealistic standards of safety, or packaging, or hygiene standards which are not required for domestically produced items.

voluntary export restrictions (V.E.R.s): an agreement by an exporting country to restrict the amount of its exports to another country.

A more recent type of trade restriction is known as **voluntary export restrictions (V.E.R.s)**. Rather than imposing, say, tariffs and quotas, the importing country requests that the exporting country itself voluntarily restrict the amount being exported. In this way, the exporting country is given the power to administer the quotas, which will also prevent the importing country from receiving tariff revenue on the imports. Since the restrictions are voluntary, the exporting country does not have to comply. However, since the importing country has other weapons at its disposal, then...

Free Trade and Protectionism

In this chapter we have tried to avoid making an outright declaration in favour of free trade though the flavour of the chapter would suggest that there are many benefits to be derived from trade, and probably the majority of economists feel that the freer the trade, the better. But even a notable free-trader like the astute Adam Smith recognized that there may be occasions when a degree of protectionism in the way of tariffs and quotas might be called for. He suggested, for instance, that a country's strategic industries should be offered protection so that, for instance, the country does not become dependent on foreign manufacturers for the production of military hardware. The problem with this idea, however, is that most industries would claim that they are of "strategic importance" to a nation and therefore deserve similar protection from foreign competition. Also, the idea of hindering the production of military goods has appeal to many.

In addition, Smith suggests that in order for there to be a level playing field for both domestic and foreign producers, if the produce of domestic industry is being taxed, then foreign imports should be taxed by a similar amount. He also felt that if a foreign country is placing tariffs and quotas on your country's exports, then you should do likewise to their exports, but not, it should be noted, just for retaliation, but to help the foreign country to recognize the folly of its actions and to persuade it to restore free trade. Finally, Smith was prescient enough to realize that if a country has had a long history of protectionism, then the sudden arrival of free trade is likely to cause dramatic shifts of labour and capital away from industries which can no longer compete to those industries which find themselves in the ascendancy. This dislocation may cause a great deal of suffering in the short term so Smith felt that a wise government would introduce free trade gradually and would try to mitigate the suffering. This caveat is of particular importance in terms of the North America Free Trade discussions. Although many feel that there will be great long-term benefits for all the participating countries, it is equally certain that in the sort term there will be a great deal of suffering experienced by those industries, firms and individuals who, through no fault of their own, find themselves unable to compete. Some type of government assistance may be needed to help in the adjustment process.

Finally, it ought to be mentioned that some economists feel that certain "infant" industries should be given a helping hand by the government until they are sufficiently mature to compete with foreign competition. This argument is the strongest when the government feels that undue reliance on the exportation of a few staple products leaves the country in a vulnerable position should a future change in demand or technology occur. In order to diversify the economy and develop other industries, many feel that these "infants" should be sheltered from competition. However, the trouble is, these infant industries often never grow up! In addition, even if there are persuasive arguments in favour of protecting or assisting certain industries it may be better for the government to give this aid in the form of direct subsidies rather than by interfering with normal trading patterns through the imposition of tariffs and quotas.

Review

BOX 13B
1. What is meant by *terms of trade*? Explain.
2. In general, what could cause the terms of trade to move in Canada's favour?
3. What does the slope of the production possibilities curve indicate? What does the slope of the trading possibilities curve indicate?
4. Give three major advantages of free trade.
5. What does *protectionism* mean? Mention five ways in which governments control trade.
6. Who is helped and who is hurt by the imposition of quotas and tariffs?
7. Explain some of the reasons why Adam Smith felt that domestic industries might need protection.

Chapter Highlights

The chapter begins by addressing the fundamental question of why countries wish to trade with each other. It answers this by explaining that countries trade for the same reason that individuals trade: because it is to their advantage to do so. The advantage is the result of differences between people and between countries. The key to explaining trade is that countries tend to specialize in producing those products in which they have an advantage because of differences in factor endowment.

The chapter then goes on to give a theoretical explanation of why it is to the advantage of all countries to specialize. It looks first at Adam Smith's theory of absolute advantage which simply suggests that a nation should specialize in what it does best because it will be able to produce in greater quantities and at lower costs than other nations. Next, it introduces Ricardo's very important refinement of Smith's idea: the theory of comparative advantage. It explains why it is to the advantage of all countries to trade. It shows why this is so even for a country which can produce all products cheaper than any other. It shows by way of production possibilities, why it is differences in comparative costs of production that lies at the heart of trade.

The next section explains how the gains from trade are distributed between nations and explains the concept of the terms of trade which measures the relative price of a country's exports compared to the price of its imports.

The first part of the chapter concludes by summarizing the main benefits to be derived from trade: that products will be produced in higher volumes and at lower costs; that trade will lead to a greater number of products being available; and that it helps to promote competition.

The second half of the chapter begins by looking at the reasons why many countries prefer to protect their own domestic industries by restricting foreign imports. It explains why domestic producers gain and domestic consumers and foreign producers lose as a result. It shows that protectionism leads to higher prices and a decrease in the volumes produced.

The chapter ends by examining the five ways by which trade is restricted. It looks at the first two methods — quotas and tariffs — in some detail and explains, using graphs, how they operate and what are the results. It then describes the other three methods, exchange controls, restrictions and regulations and voluntary export restrictions before concluding with some arguments that have been used in support of protectionism.

New Glossary Terms

Workbook

Study Tips

1. Most of the arguments in favour of free trade are based on Ricardo's theory of comparative advantage. It is important that you fully understand the basic idea of opportunity costs which lies behind this theory. A good way to test yourself is to make up your own figures for a two-country, two-product world, draw the corresponding production possibilities curves and work out which country has an advantage in which product and why.

2. Some students have difficulty understanding that if we are dealing with only two products, then if a country has a comparative advantage at producing one product, it must have a comparative disadvantage in the other product. Make sure you understand why.

3. To get an understanding of the terms of trade, again try to make up some numbers for yourself and plot them on a production possibilities diagram. For instance, start off with a country which could produce 30 units of wool or 20 computers and has an advantage in wool production. If it could trade at 1 wool = 1/2 computer, what combinations could it have? Try 1 wool = 1 computer, 1 wool = 2, 3, 5 computers and so on. Draw each resulting trading possibilities curve. Note that both the trading and production possibilities curves reflect opportunity costs. In the first case it shows what must be given up in trading; and in the second what must be given up in production.

4. To understand the idea behind world markets, note as in Figure 13.5, that what one country is exporting, another country must be importing. This means that if one country produces a surplus, then the other country must be experiencing a shortage. In the exporting country, the world price must be higher than the domestic price. In the importing country, the world price must be lower than the domestic price.

5. You will get a good grip on the effects of tariffs and quotas by drawing a simple demand and supply curve and noting first, the effect of a price set above market equilibrium (which is what a tariff produces) and second, a quantity below market equilibrium (which is what a quota produces). This approach suggests that the effect of both tariffs and quotas is to produce higher prices and lower quantities.

Are You Sure?

Indicate whether the following statements are true or false. If false, indicate why they are false.

1. A country has a comparative advantage over another only if it is able to produce all products cheaper.
T or **F**   If false: _____

_____

_____

2. David Ricardo first introduced the theory of comparative advantage.
T or **F**   If false: _____

_____

_____

3. If a country chooses to specialize its production, it is forced to trade.
T or **F**   If false: _____

_____

_____

4. If a country is able to produce all products cheaper than any other country, then there is no advantage in trade.
T or **F**   If false: _____

_____

_____

5. The terms of trade relate to the laws and conditions which govern trade.

T or **F**   If false: _____

_____

_____

6. If the price of both a country's exports and imports decrease, then the terms of trade will move in its favour.

T or **F**   If false: _____

_____

_____

7. If a country's trading possibilities curve lies to the right of its production possibilities curve, there are no gains from trade.

T or **F**   If false: _____

_____

_____

8. Protectionism is the economic policy of protecting domestic producers by restricting the exportation of products.

T or **F**   If false: _____

_____

_____

9. A tariff is a tax on exports; a quota is a tax on imports.

T or **F**   If false: _____

_____

_____

10. Domestic producers gain and domestic consumers lose as a result of the imposition of tariffs and quotas.

T or **F**   If false: _____

_____

_____

Translations

Latalia has a labour force of 12 million, one-third of whom work in the wool industry, the remainder being employed in rice farming. The labour productivity in the wool industry is 40 kilos per worker per year, and in rice farming is 100 kilos per worker per year. Latalia has discovered that the international terms of trade are 2 kilos of rice per kilo of wool. It is presently happy with its consumption of rice but would like to obtain more wool.

FIGURE W13.1

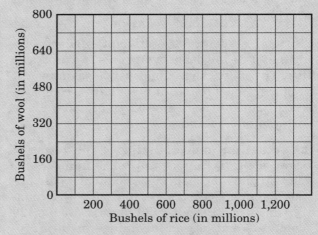

Assuming constant per unit costs, on the graph in Figure W13.1, draw a production and a trading possibilities curve for Latalia. Explain what product it should specialize in and show the gains, if any, it could receive from trade.

Explanation:

_____

_____

_____

_____

_____

Choose the Best

1. To what does the term "gains from trade" refer?
    a) The surplus of exports over imports.
    b) The increase in output resulting from international trade.

2. What is a tariff?
   a) It is a tax imposed on an import.
   b) It is a tax imposed on an export.

3. Who was the originator of the theory of absolute advantage?
   a) Adam Smith.
   b) David Ricardo.

4. What is the definition of "the terms of trade"?
   a) It is the average price of a country's imports divided by the average price of its exports.
   b) It is the average price of a country's exports divided by the average price of its imports.
   c) They are the rules and regulations governing international trade.

5. What does it mean if the opportunity costs differ between two countries?
   a) Then comparative costs must be the same.
   b) There can be no gains from trade.
   c) It is possible for both countries to gain from specialization and trade.

6. On what basis are the gains from trade divided between countries?
   a) According to the terms of trade.
   b) According to international trade agreements.
   c) According to the quantity of resources possessed by each.

7. Under what circumstances will there be no opportunity for mutually advantageous trade between two countries?
   a) When the terms of trade are the same.
   b) When comparative costs are the same.
   c) When comparative costs are different.

8. Suppose that originally the average price of Happy Island's imports was 120, and the average price of its exports was 180. Now, the price of its imports drop to 100, and the price of its exports drop to 160. What effect will this have on Happy Island's terms of trade?
   a) There will be no change in the terms of trade.
   b) The terms of trade have moved in Happy Island's favour.

   c) The terms of trade have moved against Happy Island.

9. Suppose that the cost of producing 1 unit of wine in Happy Island is 2 units of rice and in Silly Island, 1 wine costs 4 rice. What does this mean for the two countries?
   a) Happy Island should specialize in and export rice to Silly Island.
   b) Happy Island should specialize in and export wine to Silly Island.
   c) Happy Island should specialize in rice but export wine to Silly Island.
   d) Happy Island should specialize in wine but export rice to Silly Island.

10. Suppose that the cost of producing 1 unit of wine in Happy Island is 2 units of rice; in Silly Island 1 wine costs 4 rice. What might be possible terms of trade between the two countries?
    a) 1 rice = 3/8 wine.
    b) 1 rice = 3 wine.
    c) 1 rice = 6 wine.
    d) 1 wine = 1 rice.

11. All the following, *except one*, are forms of protectionism. Which is the exception?
    a) Import subsidies.
    b) Tariffs.
    c) Exchange controls.
    d) Quotas.

Figure W13.2 shows the market for cloth in Smith Island. Refer to it to answer questions 12, 13, and 14.

FIGURE W13.2

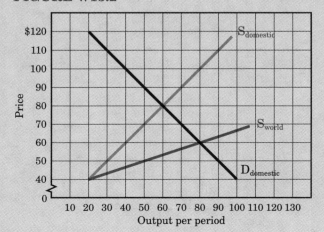

12. Refer to Figure W13.2 to answer this question. What is the world (free trade) price of cloth?
    a) $40.
    b) $50.
    c) $60.
    d) $80.

13. Refer to Figure W13.2 to answer this question. How much is Smith Island producing at the world (free trade) price of cloth?
    a) 0 units.
    b) 20 units.
    c) 40 units.
    d) 80 units.

14. Refer to Figure W13.2 to answer this question. At the world (free trade) price of cloth, how much is Smith Island trading?
    a) It is importing 30 units.
    b) It is importing 40 units.
    c) It is exporting 30 units.
    d) It is exporting 40 units.

15. What is the difference between a tariff and a quota?
    a) A tariff causes an increase in the price, whereas a quota does not affect the price.
    b) Both a tariff and a quota will affect the price but a tariff has no effect on the quantity, whereas a quota will lead to a reduction.
    c) Both a tariff and a quota will affect the price but a tariff has no effect on the quantity, whereas a quota will lead to an increase.
    d) A quota affects all foreign producers equally, whereas a tariff does not.
    e) A tariff affects all foreign producers equally, whereas a quota does not.

Refer to Figure W13.3 to answer questions 16, 17, 18 and 19.

16. Refer to Figure W13.3 to answer this question. What is the opportunity cost of producing 1 apple in Harmony and in Tranquillity?
    a) 2 pears in Harmony and 3 pears in Tranquillity.
    b) 1/2 pear in Harmony and 1/3 pear in Tranquillity.

FIGURE W13.3

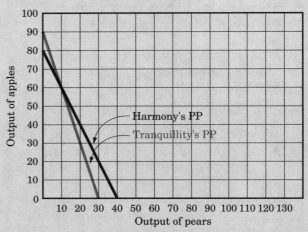

    c) 2 pears in Harmony and 1/3 pear in Tranquillity.
    d) 1/2 pear in Harmony and 3 pears in Tranquillity.
    e) 3 pears in Harmony and 2 pears in Tranquillity.

17. Refer to Figure W13.3 to answer this question. What do the comparative opportunity costs in the two countries suggest?
    a) That there are no advantages to be gained from trade.
    b) That Harmony should specialize in apples but export pears.
    c) That Tranquillity should specialize in apples but export pears.
    d) That Harmony should specialize in pears but export apples.
    e) That Harmony should specialize in pears and Tranquillity should specialize in apples.

18. Refer to Figure W13.3 to answer this question. Suppose that both Harmony and Tranquillity are presently producing 20 pears, what will be the total gains from trade for the two countries?
    a) 20 apples and 0 pears.
    b) 30 apples and 10 pears.
    c) 20 apples and 10 pears.
    d) 20 apples and 30 pears.
    e) 0 apples and 20 pears.

19. Refer to Figure W13.3 to answer this question. What could be possible terms of trade between the two countries?

a) 1 apple = 0.25 pears.
b) 1 apple = 2.5 pears.
c) 1 apple = 3 pears.
d) 1 pear = 0.5 apples.
e) 1 pear = 2.5 apple.

Table W13.1 shows the output of kumquats per month. Refer to this table to answer question 20.

TABLE W13.1

Price (per kilo)	Smithland Demand	Smithland Supply	Imports into Smithland Supply
$3	100	40	30
4	90	50	40
5	80	60	50
6	70	70	60

20. Refer to Table W13.1 to answer this question. What is the world (free trade) price and what quantity of this product is being consumed domestically?

a) $4 and 50 kilos consumed.
b) $4 and 90 kilos consumed.
c) $5 and 80 kilos consumed.
d) $6 and 70 kilos consumed.
e) $6 and 130 kilos consumed.

What's Wrong?

Can you spot the six errors in the following passage? (Ignore grammatical mistakes!)

The chapter then goes on to give a theoretical explanation of why it is to the advantage of all countries to become self-sufficient. It looks first at Alfred Marshall's theory of absolute advantage which simply suggests that a nation should specialize at what it does best because it will be able to sell those products at much higher prices than can other nations. Next, it introduces Adam Smith's very important refinement of Marshall's idea: the theory of comparative advantage. It explains why it is to the advantage of all countries to trade. It shows by way of the terms of trade possibilities curve why it is differences in wage rates which lie at the heart of trade.

Key Problem I

Suppose that Peaceland and Prosperity have the output figures shown in Table W13.2.

TABLE W13.2

Country	Average Product per Worker Wheat	Wine
Peaceland	4 bushels	2 barrels
Prosperity	4 bushels	3 barrels

Assuming that the costs remain constant and average and marginal products are equal:

a) What is the opportunity cost of producing 1 bushel of wheat in Peaceland? _____

b) What is the opportunity cost of producing 1 barrel of wine in Peaceland? _____

c) What is the opportunity cost of producing 1 bushel of wheat in Prosperity? _____

d) What is the opportunity cost of producing 1 barrel of wine in Prosperity? _____

e) In what product does Peaceland have a comparative advantage? _____

f) In what product does Prosperity have a comparative advantage? _____

Suppose that the labour force in Peaceland is 10 million, and it is 20 million in Prosperity.

g)   Fill in the missing production possibilities data for both countries in Table W13.3.

TABLE W13.3

Peaceland's Production Possibilities (in millions of units)

	A	B	C	D	E
Wheat	40	30	20	10	0
Wine	____	____	____	____	____

Prosperity's Production Possibilities (in millions of units)

	A	B	C	D	E
Wheat	____	____	____	____	____
Wine	0	15	30	45	60

Suppose that both countries are presently producing combinations D.

h)   Show the joint totals below:

Total output in millions of units:

	Wheat	Wine
Peaceland		
Prosperity	_____	_____
Total: both countries		

Now suppose that each country specializes in the product in which it has a comparative advantage.

i)   Show the new totals below:

Total output in millions of units:

	Wheat	Wine
Peaceland		
Prosperity	_____	_____
Total: both countries		

j)   As a result, the joint gain from trade is equal to:

_____ wheat   _____ wine.

Suppose that the two countries establish the terms of trade at 1 wine = 1.5 wheat, and Prosperity decides to export 15 wine to Peaceland.

k)   As a result the two countries will gain as follows:

Gains for each country in millions of units:

	Wheat	Wine
Peaceland		
Prosperity	_____	_____
Total: both countries		

Need a Hand?

a) and b)   A worker in Peaceland can produce either 4 bushels of wheat or 2 barrels of wine. The opportunity cost of 4 wheat is therefore 2 wine. The cost of **1 unit of wheat = 2/4 or 1/2 wine.** To find the cost of 1 unit of wine, simply take the reciprocal of the wheat cost (i.e., just invert the number). This gives a **cost of 1 wine = 2 wheat.**

c) and d)   In Prosperity, a worker can produce either 4 wheat or 3 wine. The opportunity cost of 4 wheat is therefore 3 wine. **The cost of 1 unit of wheat = 3/4 wine.** Again, to find the cost of 1 unit of wine take the reciprocal of the wheat cost. This gives a cost of **1 wine = 4/3 or 1 1/3 wheat.**

e)   Peaceland can produce wheat cheaper than can Prosperity. Therefore, **Peaceland should specialize in wheat**.

f)   Prosperity can produce wine cheaper than can Peaceland. Therefore, **Prosperity should specialize in wine**.

g)   To figure out the production possibilities data for Peaceland, start at combination E where no wheat is produced. All the labour (10 million) must be employed producing wine, and since each worker can produce 2 units of wine, total output = 10×2, or 20 million units. Moving to combination D, which represents an additional 10 units of wheat, you know that each unit of wheat costs 1/2 wine. Therefore an additional 10 units of wheat will cost $10 \times 1/2$ or 5 wine, so that production of wine drops to 15. In general, moving from right to left on the production possibilities table, implies that each extra 10 wheat costs 5 wine.

Do a similar exercise with Prosperity's production possibilities data and note that since 1 wine costs 1 1/3 wheat, that each additional 15 wine costs $15 \times 1\,1/3$ or 20, wheat.

This gives us Table W13.4.

TABLE W13.4 (completed Table W13.3)

Peaceland's Production Possibilities (in millions of units)

	A	B	C	D	E
Wheat	40	30	20	10	0
Wine	0	5	10	15	20

Prosperity's Production Possibilities (in millions of units)

	A	B	C	D	E
Wheat	80	60	40	20	0
Wine	0	15	30	45	60

h) This requires that you copy combinations D from the two production possibilities tables above and total them:

Total output in millions of units:

	Wheat	Wine
Peaceland	10	15
Prosperity	20	45
Total: both countries	30	60

i) Since you've already decided that Peaceland will specialize in the production of wheat, the production possibilities table above shows the country's maximum wheat production (combination A). Similarly, Prosperity will specialize in wine production and its maximum is shown as combination E in its PP table. This gives us:

Total Output in millions of units:

	Wheat	Wine
Peaceland	40	0
Prosperity	0	60
Total: both countries	40	60

j) This requires you to simply subtract the pre-trade totals, shown in h) from these new totals resulting from specialization, which gives:

 __10__ wheat __0__ wine

k) As a result of specialization, Prosperity is producing 60 wine. If it trades away 15, it will be left with 45 wine (the same as it had before it specialized). If it can receive 1.5 wheat for each wine, it will receive 15×1.5 or 22.5 wheat in return. Peaceland, in return will receive these 15 wine and pay 22.5 wheat. Since it produced 40 wheat, it will be left with $40 - 22.5$, or 17.5 wheat. This is summarized below:

Gains for each country in millions of units:

	Wheat	Wine
Peaceland	7.5	0
Prosperity	2.5	0
Total: both countries	10	0

More of the Same

Suppose that Hopeland and Faithland have the output figures contained on Table W13.5, shown in terms of productivity per worker.

TABLE W13.5

	Average Product per Worker	
Country	**Wheat**	**Wine**
Hopeland	3 bushels	1 barrels
Faithland	1 bushels	2 barrels

Assuming that the costs remain constant and that average product is constant:

a) What is the opportunity cost of producing wheat and wine in Hopeland and Faithland?

b) In which product does each country have a comparative advantage?

Suppose that the labour force in Hopeland is 20 million, and it is 10 million in Faithland.

c) Show the production possibilities data for both countries in a table.

Assume that both countries are presently producing 5 million wine.

d) What are their present joint output totals?

Now suppose that each country specializes in that product in which it has a comparative advantage.

e) What will be the new output totals, and what will be the gains from trade?

Suppose that the two countries establish the terms of trade at 1 wine = 2 wheat, and Hopeland decides to trade 15 wheat to Faithland.

f) As a result, what will be the consumption totals for the two countries?

Key Problem II

Table W13.6 shows the (hypothetical) market for wool in Australia and New Zealand

TABLE W13.6

Totals in Millions of Metric Tons

Price (per ton)	Australia		New Zealand		Total Market	
	Demand	Supply	Demand	Supply	Demand	Supply
$1,700	100	25	35	20	_____	_____
1,800	90	30	30	30	_____	_____
1,900	80	35	25	40	_____	_____
2,000	70	40	20	50	_____	_____
2,100	60	45	15	60	_____	_____
2,200	50	50	10	70	_____	_____

a) Table W13.7 show the equilibrium domestic prices and outputs in the two countries if they were self-sufficient:

TABLE W13.7

	Price	Output
Australia	_____	_____
New Zealand	_____	_____

b) Suppose the two countries are now open to free trade. By completing the Total Market column in Table W13.6 find out the new world (free trade) price, and the quantities produced and exported or imported in each country:

New world price: _____.

	Quantity Produced	Quantity Exported	Quantity Imported
Australia	_____	_____	_____
New Zealand	_____	_____	_____

c) Now, suppose that the Australian government decides to put a quota on the import of wool and restricts the quantity to 15 (million) metric tons. What will be the new price in Australia and how much will Australian producers now be willing to produce?

New price: _____ Domestic output: _____.

d) Remembering that total imports must equal total exports, what will be the new price and quantity produced in New Zealand as a result of the Australian quota?

New price: _____ Domestic output: _____.

Need a Hand?

a) Look at each market separately. In Australia, the only price where the quantities demanded and supplied are equal is at $2,200. In New Zealand, it is at $1,800. The equilibrium quantities are as shown in Table W13.8.

TABLE W13.8 (completed Table W13.7)

	Price	Output
Australia	$2,200	50
New Zealand	$1,800	30

b) To get the market demand, add the Australian demand (column 2) and the New Zealand demand (column 4). To get the market supply, add the two supplies, columns 3 and 5, as shown in Table W13.9.

TABLE W13.9 (completed Table W13.6)

Totals in Millions of Metric Tons

Price (per litre)	Australia Demand	Australia Supply	New Zealand Demand	New Zealand Supply	Total Market Demand	Total Market Supply
$1,700	100	25	35	20	135	45
1,800	90	30	30	30	120	60
1,900	80	35	25	40	105	75
2,000	70	40	20	50	**90**	**90**
2,100	60	45	15	60	75	105
2,200	50	50	10	70	60	120

Equilibrium is where the total market demand is equal to the total market supply, i.e.:

New world price: __$2,000__ .

Now that you know the world price, look back at the effects in each market. In Australia, at a price of $2,000, the quantity demanded (70) exceeds the quantity produced by Australian producers (40). There is a shortage of 30, which is the amount which will be imported. In contrast, at a price of $2,000 in New Zealand, the quantity supplied (50) exceeds the quantity demanded (20) by 30. This surplus will therefore be exported to Australia. Summarized:

	Quantity Produced	Quantity Exported	Quantity Imported
Australia	__40__	__0__	__30__
New Zealand	__50__	__30__	__0__

c) With a quota of 15 in place (irrespective of the price), the new quantities available in Australia will be the amounts brought on the market produced by Australian producers as shown by its supply schedule plus 15. To get the new supply in Australia, add 15 to each quantity supplied domestically, as shown in Table W13.10.

TABLE W13.10

Price (per litre)	Australia Demand	Australia Supply
$1,700	100	25 + 15 = 40
1,800	90	30 + 15 = 45
1,900	80	35 + 15 = 50
2,000	70	40 + 15 = 55
2,100	60	45 + 15 = 60
2,200	50	50 + 15 = 65

The new equilibrium in Australia, therefore, will be:

New price: __$2,100__   Domestic output: __45__ .

(and 15 will be imported).

d) Since 15 are imported into Australia, you need to look at the market in New Zealand to find a price which results in a surplus of 15 (the amount which will be exported). This happens at a price of $1,900 where the quantity demanded is 25 and the quantity supplied is 40, i.e.:

New price: __$1,900__   Domestic output: __40__ .

More of the Same

Table W13.11 shows the market for kumquats in Hopeland and Faithland

TABLE W13.11

| | Totals in Millions of Kilos | | | | | |
| | Hopeland | | Faithland | | Total Market | |
Price (per kilo)	Demand	Supply	Demand	Supply	Demand	Supply
$4	32	32	24	8	_____	_____
5	30	34	23	11	_____	_____
6	28	36	22	14	_____	_____
7	26	38	21	17	_____	_____
8	24	40	20	20	_____	_____
9	22	42	19	23	_____	_____

a) What are the domestic prices and outputs in the two countries if they were self-sufficient?

b) Suppose the two countries now engage in free trade. What will be the new world (free trade) price, and the quantities produced and exported, or imported, in each country?

c) Now, suppose that the Faithland government decides to put a quota on imports of kumquats and restricts the quantity to 4 (million) metric tons. What will be the new price in Faithland and how much will Faithland producers produce?

d) Remembering that total imports must equal total exports, what will be the new price and quantity produced in Hopeland as a result of the Faithland quota?

Other Problems

1. The following shows the maximum output levels for Here and There:

	Cloth		Computers
Here	100	or	50
There	60	or	120

a) What is the cost of a unit of cloth and a computer in Here?

1 unit of cloth: _____ ; 1 computer: _____ .

b) What is the cost of a unit of cloth and a unit of computers in There?

1 unit of cloth: _____; 1 computer: _____.

c) In what product does each country have a comparative advantage?

Here: _____; There: _____.

d) What would be feasible terms of trade between the two countries?

1 unit of cloth: _____; 1 computer: _____.

2. Table W13.12 shows the production possibilities for Canada and Japan. Prior to specialization and trade, Canada is producing combination D, and Japan is producing combination B.

TABLE W13.12

Product	Canada's Production Possibilities					
	A	**B**	**C**	**D**	**E**	**F**
Compact Disc Players	10	8	6	4	2	0
Wheat	0	4	8	12	16	20

Product	Japan's Production Possibilities					
	A	**B**	**C**	**D**	**E**	**F**
Compact Disc Players	30	24	18	12	6	0
Wheat	0	6	12	18	24	30

a) On the graph (Figure W13.4), draw the production possibilities curve for each country, and mark their present output positions.

b) Suppose that the two countries specialize and trade on the basis of 1 CD player = 1.5 wheat. Draw the corresponding trading possibilities curves.

FIGURE W13.4

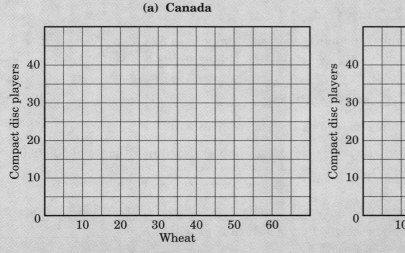

(a) Canada

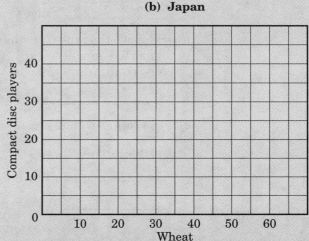

(b) Japan

3. The following incomplete table (Table W13.13) shows the productivity levels of producing beer and sardines in Canada and Mexico.

TABLE W13.13

Production per Worker (average product)	Beer	Sardines
Canada	6	4
Mexico	3	?

In order for there to be no advantage to be gained from trade, what does the Mexican productivity per worker in the sardine industry need to be?

4. Suppose the Canadian demand and the Japanese supply of cars to Canada is as shown in Table W13.14. (Quantities in thousands)

TABLE W13.14

Price	Quantity Demanded	Quantity Supplied (before tariff)	Quantity Supplied (after tariff)
$12,000	180	60	_____
13,000	160	80	_____
14,000	140	100	_____
15,000	120	120	_____
16,000	100	140	_____
17,000	80	160	_____
18,000	60	180	_____
19,000	40	200	_____

a) The present equilibrium price is $_____ and quantity is

   _____ (thousand).

b) Suppose that the Canadian government imposes a $2,000 per car tariff on imported Japanese cars. Show the new supply in the last column above. The new equilibrium price is:

   $_____ and quantity is _____ (thousand).

c) The total revenue received by the government will be $_____.

d) Assume, instead, that the government imposes an import quota of 100,000 cars. The new equilibrium price is $_____ and quantity is

   _____ (thousand).

e) The total revenue received by the government will be $_____.

Unanswered Questions

Short Essays

1. Explain the difference between Adam Smith's and Ricardo's theories of trade.

2. Explain what is meant by comparative costs and why there are no advantages to trade if nations have identical comparative costs.

3. Explain Adam Smith's dictum that the division of labour is limited by the extent of the market.

4. What are "terms of trade" and how can they be measured for nations which generally trade in more than two products?

5. Explain the main advantages to be derived from free trade.

6. Discuss the main arguments against free trade.

7. What are the main methods used by governments to protect domestic industries? Which do you think are the more successful methods?

8. Who gets helped and who gets hurt by the imposition of a tariff?

9. In what way does a tariff differ from a quota? Which is preferable, and why?

Analytical Questions

1. If comparative costs is the basis for trade, why are third world countries, which have very low wage rates, not the world's greatest trading nations?

2. If third world countries are unable to compete in world markets, why are so many North American corporations locating plants in these countries?

3. The analysis in this chapter suggests that if a country produces only two products, and if it has a comparative advantage in one, it must have a comparative disadvantage in the other. How is this affected if a country produces three, or four, or a thousand products?

4. To what extent are the conclusions from the theory of comparative advantage affected if

unit costs increase, rather than remain constant, as output increases?

5. Why do some countries enjoy a cost advantage over others in the production of certain products? To what extent do these advantages remain constant? How may they disappear over time?

6. In what way is a direct subsidy from the government preferable to a tariff or quota as a way of assisting an infant industry?

Numerical Questions

1. Table W13.15 shows the production possibilities curves for Concordia and Harmonia.

TABLE W13.15

Concordia's Production Possibilities

Product	A	B	C	D	E
Pork	4	3	2	1	0
Beans	0	5	10	15	20

Harmonia's Production Possibilities

Product	A	B	C	D	E
Pork	8	6	4	2	0
Beans	0	6	12	18	24

a) What are the costs of the two products in each country?
b) What products should each country specialize in and export?
c) If, prior to specialization and trade, Concordia produced combination C and Harmonia produced combination B, what would be the total gains from trade for the two countries?
d) What would be feasible terms of trade between the two countries?

2. Given the production possibilities in question 1, suppose that before trading Concordia experienced a doubling of productivity in the pork industry but continued to produce 15 beans. From this initial position, answer the following questions:
a) What are the costs of the two products in each country?
b) What products should each country specialize in and export?

c) If, prior to specialization and trade, Concordia produced combination D and Harmonia produced combination B, what would be the total gains from trade for the two countries?

d) What would be feasible terms of trade between the two countries?

3. Figure W13.5 shows the production possibilities for the countries of Kinell and Bugudifican.

a) What are the costs for the two products in each country?

b) What products should they each specialize in and export?

FIGURE W13.5

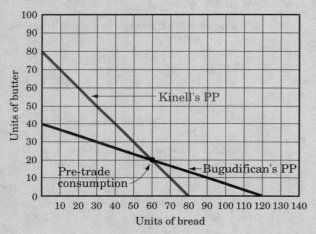

c) Suppose that terms of trade are established at 1 unit of butter = 2 units of bread. Show the trading possibilities curve for each country.

d) Assuming that each country is happy consuming the same quantity of its specialized product as it did before trade, show the amount of the imported product which is now available to it.

4. Suppose three countries have the productivity figures shown in Table W13.16.

TABLE W13.16

Productivity per Worker	Wheat	Beans
Alpha	1	2
Beta	4	2
Gamma	2	2

a) Which country can produce wheat comparatively cheaper? Which country can produce beans comparatively cheaper?

b) Suppose that the international terms of trade were 1 wheat = 3/4 beans. Which countries would export wheat? Which countries would import wheat?

c) Suppose instead that the international terms of trade were 1 wheat = 1 1/2 beans. Which countries would export wheat? Which countries would import wheat?

5. Table W13.17 shows the (hypothetical) annual demand and supply of cellular phones in Canada (in tens of thousands annually), where D is the quantity demanded by Canadian consumers, S_C is the quantity supplied by Canadian manufacturers, and S_J is the quantity supplied to the Canadian market by Japanese manufacturers:

TABLE W13.17

Price	D	S_C	S_J
$ 200	28	4	0
300	26	6	2
400	24	8	4
500	22	10	6
600	20	12	8
700	18	14	10
800	16	16	12
1,000	14	18	14

a) Add a final column showing the total quantity supplied in the Canadian market, labelled S_T. Graph D, S_C, and S_T.

b) If Japanese exports were totally banned, what would be the price and quantity of cellular phones in Canada?

c) If Canada was open to Japanese imports, what would be the price and quantity of cellular phones in Canada as a result?

d) Suppose that the Canadian government were to impose a quota on Japanese imports limiting them to 4 (tens of thousands) per year, what would be the price and quantity of cellular phones in Canada now?

e) To produce the same result as in d), alternatively what amount of tariff would the Canadian government have to impose on Japanese imports?

CHAPTER FOURTEEN

Towards a Political Economy

W hat's ahead . . . This chapter looks at six ways in which government intervention can fail and then examines some failures of the discipline of economics itself. Next, the role of positive economics is questioned. Finally, the subject of power is discussed and we look into the future to ask if we are witnessing the rise of a new powerful class of individuals.

The study of economics is the study of how an economy produces wealth. Wealth comes in the form of commodities, or goods and services, which are intended to satisfy the vast and varied wants and needs of individuals. If the economy is successful, the citizens of the society served by it enjoy a high standard of living. If the economy's output of goods and services grows over time, that economy is healthy and vibrant, and the promise of the good life creates a sense of optimism and excitement within people. Such growth requires that the economy's productive resources be effectively mobilized and efficiently combined. It requires, among other things, the use of appropriate technology and a smoothly working price system to allocate resources in the way required to maximize their effectiveness. The result is a growing **gross domestic product (GDP)**.

gross domestic product: the market value of all goods and services produced in the whole economy per year.

Canada and the United States have been particularly successful at obtaining strong growth in GDP. The result has been a rising standard of living. For example, Canada's GDP (in constant 1986 dollars) grew from approximately $44 billion in 1926 to over $609 billion in 1994. Canada's income per capita (in 1981 dollars) grew from approximately $6,000 in 1960 to over $20,000 in 1994. Many other statistics could be marshalled to verify this upward trend in our *material* well being. As a result, Canadians today enjoy one of the highest standards of living in the whole history of humankind. Those who are 30 years old are *twice* as well off compared to the averages that existed when they were born, for those approaching the age of 60, four times better off. We live in a rich society with a powerful economy and we enjoy an abundance of goods and services. We are truly affluent.

If this fantastic increase in our material wealth was an accurate reflection of our *total* well-being, one would think that our society would be filled with happy people who experience contentment and satisfaction in their daily lives. As you look around, is this what you see?

It seems instead that many (most?) people in our society are not happy or content. Further, we see a great deal of conflict and physical violence that seem to be growing rather than abating. The percentage of our population experiencing some form of addiction (to alcohol, drugs, gambling, etc.) is increasing. Young people in this age of affluence seem to be, strangely, very anxious and uneasy about their future. In addition, we face a growing list of social problems that are becoming more serious. For example, despite society's increase in wealth, real poverty remains among a small but persistent percentage of the population (many of whom are children). Just how serious the threat of an environmental collapse is remains a point of social debate, but the fact that we do face environmental problems is beyond debate. Furthermore, despite the growth in our economy and the increased tax revenues that have been generated by this growth, our governments seem incapable of keeping spending within revenues. Many people in our society seem to be very confused by the whole concept of responsibility. Almost daily we hear of acts of extreme transgression against others that go virtually unpunished because the perpetrators "are not responsible for their actions." In addition, special interest groups abound and each group has some new grievance that, they would have us believe, society as a whole is responsible for redressing.

For generations we have focused on a rising level of GDP as the primary goal of our economy and we have achieved that goal to a greater extent than anyone could have predicted. Yet, paradoxically, achieving this goal (to an extent that can only be described as remarkable) has not given us the pay-off that most assumed it would. People in our society are richer, but many are not more content nor happy. Quite the opposite, there is a sense of restlessness and discontent. How can this be?

No one has *the* answer to this question but this is no reason to ignore it. The difficulty in writing (and teaching) about this kind of thing is that there is a very strong tendency for the topic to become loose and unstructured and therefore degenerate into a very opinionated polemic. We want to try to avoid this.

In this chapter we will first take a rather conventional look at our expectations concerning the way government intervenes in the economy and the ways in which this intervention might fail. We do this because we feel that, in many cases, such intervention has not lived up to its promise and has therefore contributed to a general malaise in the population. We will then examine aspects of the discipline of economics itself and look at why it is often unable to even address some of the real problems of society, let alone offer solutions. One of the fundamental aspects that the discipline doesn't address is power. Therefore we will also look at the question of economic power and, finally, look at how this may be in the process of transformation.

Government Failures

Throughout the first 13 chapters of this book, we have pointed out various ways in which markets can fail. Classic examples of market failures are its inability to account for the real cost of externalities such as pollution, and its inability to quickly reallocate resources to meet emergencies such as war or natural disasters. In these and other cases, there is a natural expectation that the government should step in and respond. We usually accept this intervention without thinking. There is, however, a danger in doing this.

Government intervention by way of regulation or policy aimed at achieving some greater good is also subject to different kinds of failure. We will identify six possible ways in which intervention could fail.

The Cost of Intervention May Exceed the Benefits

First, government intervention usually involves a cost, and that cost might well exceed the benefits gained by the intervention. For example, automobile emissions that cause pollution are a market failure. If the government set emissions standards below the unregulated level, the benefit would be cleaner air. However, such standards would also increase the per unit cost of producing an automobile since more sophisticated exhaust systems and cleaner burning engines would have to be developed. These increased production costs would be reflected in higher automobile prices. But do the benefits to society exceed the cost to car owners? For instance, it may well be that the benefits of reducing these emissions by 50% exceed the costs of doing so. However, to reduce emissions to, say, 10% of the unregulated level may well involve costs that greatly exceed the resulting benefits. Thus, while it may make sense to use government policy to reduce emissions, it is possible for such a policy to go too far.

As another example, consider the case of a city health department officer banning the sale of Chinese-style barbecue pork because of the (remote) possibility that it could be a source of food poisoning. This actually happened in Vancouer in the late 1970s. The benefit here is the perception, on the part of some, that the civic authorities are really doing their job of ensuring that food being sold in the city is safe. The cost was that a concentrated segment of the population became very angry at what they saw as an arbitrary and bureaucratic fiat. They argued that they were being denied a cultural delicacy that has, over a period of 4,000 years, proved itself as safe as it was delicious. (In the end, the city health officer resigned and barbecue pork once again hung in the widows of dozens of shops.)

Intervention Itself May Fail

There is the possibility that government intervention to correct a market failure simply might not work. For example, 40 to 50 years ago a trend towards government regulation of various oligopoly and monopoly industries gained significant momentum. This intervention was justified on the basis that the lack of competition in many concentrated industries was a market failure in the sense that the consumer was at the mercy of powerful transnational corporations that would often put their interests above those of the general public. As a result, many countries, including Canada, set up regulatory bodies in a number of industries to set prices and dictate quantity. Then, about 15 or 20 years ago these policies of government regulation began to be reversed and "deregulation" became one of the buzzwords of the day. Essentially what happened is that, in many cases, the outcomes of regulation, in terms of availability of the product and the price of the product, were probably no better (and maybe worse) than having no regulation at all. A dramatic example can be found in the airline industry in the United States A post hoc measure of the costs of regulation can be seen in the results that followed deregulation in the 80s. New airlines emerged, fares plummeted and passenger miles travelled increased to previously unheard of levels.

There are, at least, two reasons for such failure. First, it is now clear that regulatory bodies all too often fall under the influence of the industry that is being regulated. As a result, these bodies cease to keep the interest of the consumer paramount. Second, it is often not clear just how keeping the interest of the consumer paramount should be achieved. On one hand, large regulated firms that face little competition should be able to achieve economies of scale and thus reduce the cost of production and the price of the product. On the other hand, the lack of competition could also mean that these large firms become complacent about costs and become as a result bureaucratic and inefficient. Thus, regulatory bodies are often uncertain of their roles — whether they are to assist an industry or, simply, to prosecute perceived infractions of the regulatory rules, or both.

Difficulty in Identifying the Problem or the Solution

It is sometimes very difficult to identify just what is the real cause of the problem that warrants intervention. A classic example is the perennial Canadian problem of regional disparities. Ever since Confederation, certain regions of the country have lagged behind other regions in terms of per capita incomes, job opportunities and public infrastructure. Is the underlying cause of Canada's poor regions a lack of natural resources? Or is it inadequate local markets? Or a lack of entrepreneurial talent? Does government policy to try to address this problem help narrow the disparities or might it, in the light of decades of apparent failure, now be perpetuating it?

Another related difficulty is trying to identify the kind of intervention which is appropriate in dealing with a problem. For instance, consider the case of insider-trading on a public stock market, a practice which reaps enormous profits for a few to the detriment of many. This could be viewed as a market failure but just what kind of intervention is needed, and might be effective to prevent this kind of activity, is not clear.

Special Interests versus the Interests of Society as a Whole

One problem endemic to government intervention arises from the fact that such intervention often results in a reallocation of the economy's productive resources. This makes it attractive for special interest groups to try to persuade governments to intervene in a particular way that will benefit that group. Such lobbying (which some economists call rent seeking) involves corporations, industry associations, trade unions, and professional associations using political pressure to gain favourable regulations, direct subsidies, profitable contracts or other special treatment. There are many examples of the success of such special interest groups. Over the years, the Canadian aircraft industry has received large subsidies from the federal government. Farmers the world over have been able to gain direct subsidies from governments as well as the protection of marketing boards. This is at the expense of the taxpayer and consumer and drives up the price of food. In an earlier chapter we mentioned the benefit received by taxi-cab-license holders as a result of local government policy of restricting the number of licences.

In a more general sense, whenever intervention results in a small group of people making *large* gains at the expense of a large number of people who will *each* (not in total) experience small losses, then such intervention is not likely to benefit the society as a whole. As an example consider the Canadian textile and footwear industry which has enjoyed tariff protection from the federal government for over 100 years. A tariff on shoes imported into Canada reduces the competition this industry faces. As a result, the relatively few people who own resources used in this industry gain from the fact that all footwear in this country is priced higher than would be the case if there were no tariffs. And who pays these higher prices? Everyone living in the country. Thus, owners in this industry enjoy higher profits, and there are more shoe-industry wage earners than would otherwise be the case. In the meantime, 28 million Canadians each spend $50 to $100 more a year on shoes as a result.

Given the fact that small groups of potential beneficiaries are usually well informed and very vocal and the fact that the large group who stand to lose are generally unorganized and not well informed, one can understand how this potential problem with intervention often occurs.

Rent control is another example. There is no question that rent controls benefit existing tenants, and tenants as a group are quite aware of this and thus put pressure on governments to impose controls. What is not so obvious is that rent controls work to the detriment of *future potential* tenants who may not be able to find a place to rent because controls have discouraged the construction of new rental-housing stock. Surely our concept of a democratic government includes the basic proposition that governments should act in the interest of *all* the people and this would include both current and future tenants.

Finally, we all know that it takes money for a political party to win an election and form a government. Because money talks in politics, we often see governments take actions that confer benefits on specific groups of industries. It has been estimated, for example, that the quotas that the U.S. imposed on Japanese automobiles in the 1980s added $300 million per year to the U.S. automobile industry while costing U.S. consumers over $2 billion *per year*. There are various possibilities as to why these quotas were imposed, including: the fact that the governing party truly thought that this intervention was in the best interest of Americans; perhaps the automobile lobby was especially effective in having this measure imposed; or it may be within the realm of possibility that the industry was a big contributor to the governing party.

Another classic example of intervention that benefitted a particular industry is the use of plastic pipe for plumbing, which is cheaper and easier to use than copper pipe. Yet it took years to cut through the red tape of outmoded building code regulations before plastic pipe was allowed on the market. This, of course, was to the benefit of the copper industry. This kind of government action, or in this case inaction, leads us to our next problem.

Bureaucracy A potential failure, inherent in government as an institution, is the sometimes limited incentive for government agencies (and the people who work within them) to be cost-conscious. Bureaucratic inefficiencies within private-sector firms will lead to the decline and probable demise of those firms while the same kind of inefficiencies in the public sector often carry no such consequences. On the contrary, senior government bureaucrats are seldom rewarded for cutting costs. As a matter of fact, if an official were to reduce expenditures below the allocated budget, the reward is more likely to be a smaller budget and less administrative influence in the following year than praise for managerial competence. Let us hasten to add that this is not to imply that the individuals involved in government work are lazy or incompetent. It is the nature of the institution of government itself that we are commenting on. Bureaucracy in government is increased by the fact that competing interests sometimes put pressure on government for a particular decision. As a result, in order to be even-handed, the government is often required to conduct public hearings and publish the findings of this process. This can be very slow and cumbersome adding to the perception of bureaucratic inefficiency.

Myopic Intervention

Finally, because governments face reelection every few years, they are often attracted to projects which reap immediate rewards and shy away from projects that involve large *short-run* costs but promise even larger *long-run* benefits. Government expenditures on various kinds of health programs are a classic example. Expenditures on the universal, government-funded medical plan in this country is the largest single type of government spending and is growing at a very significant rate. Nearly all of this expenditure is on allopathic treatment which is used only after the disease is well advanced. If one takes a long view on rising health care costs, it could be argued that significant funds should also be spent (shifted from conventional-treatment expenditure?) on a wide variety of preventive measures aimed at greatly reducing the incidence of disease in the future. Here the short-run costs are very high, but the long-term pay-offs would most likely be even higher. Yet, if a government initiated such a policy it would be long gone before the pay-off really kicked in.

The Failure of Economics

Having looked at the score sheet of government, we need to examine another failure. What we want to consider is not the exclusive failure of governments but the collective failure of society to clearly define and agree on the primary economic goals which it wants governments to pursue. Here economics has often hurt more than it has helped in defining these goals since it has usually placed undue emphasis on a few simple, measurable goals and has managed to convince society that these are the most important goals to be achieved.

The task of defining individual and societal goals is indeed a difficult one since it involves the fundamental question of the purpose of our own existence and raises the question of what we are trying to achieve in life. Many people believe that economics has often muddied the process of goal defining because it has clearly given itself the mission of examining how societies and individuals go about satisfying human wants without first trying to determine what those wants are. Of course, this is not true of the whole profession, but practitioners of the discipline do tend to get hooked on the idea that satisfying (or maximizing) material wants is the only object of life. After all, what significant contribution has economics offered on the perennial topics of the human search for love, truth or beauty? Of course, you might also suggest the same is true of accounting or geography. But remember that economics is all about our attempts to satisfy wants. However, it takes it for granted that this is done merely through the increased production of goods and services. Perhaps we have forgotten that the purchase of goods and services is not an end in itself but merely a means to an end. The discipline needs to do more to spell out why the purchase of goods and services will satisfy human wants, and which wants are satisfied as a result.

This historical overemphasis on material goods in the discipline of economics is evidenced by the fact that only in comparatively recent literature do we find mainstream economists beginning to regard the desire for clean air, clean water, open spaces, and leisure as part of the domain of economics. If we consider our love of beauty in all forms, our passionate desire for freedom and friendship, the desire for a safe environment, our need for stimulating work, and our search for spiritual values, we must concede to the conclusion that human wants are far more extensive and complex than can be summed up in the phrase "material wants."

It would be unfair to suggest that all economists have a totally materialistic view of human happiness. For example, a number of economists have criticized the use of GDP figures as a measure of a country's welfare, and have suggested that a more all-embracing index should be constructed and used. What should be included in this index is the moot point. Some suggest that it should include not just market-produced products but things like housework and voluntary work (not to mention activities in the underground economy). But does this mean that the more housework we do, the better off we are? And what about the value of leisure? Shouldn't the amount of leisure we have be an important ingredient of our welfare? But then we need to put a value on it. Shall we judge its value in terms of opportunity cost? For instance, should it have a value equal to the work foregone? But if we measure it that way, doesn't it mean that if we take more leisure and work less, then the value of goods and services produced will decrease but the value of the leisure enjoyed increase, leaving the total unchanged? And what else can we throw into this new index of welfare? Unemployment rates? Infant mortality rates? Literacy levels? Or a personal freedom rating? All of these certainly have an impact on human welfare, but it is difficult to see how we could come up with a single number to indicate this. And even if we could, would we know what to do with such an index?

The question here seems to be: why, if we recognize the many human wants that motivate us, do we give overriding precedence to things economic? It is not just economists who do this. Many people are persuaded that the only criterion for judging whether or not some project should be undertaken is in terms of "the bottom line." It seems not to matter if the project will enhance the beauty of our environment or create greater harmony or respect among people; it must pay its way. It is in this way that economists and accountants have been demonstrably successful in persuading the public that material costs and benefits are the only relevant yardstick to judge by. One of the reasons of course is that material goods and services are reasonably easy to quantify and measure. Because of this, they are amenable to all sorts of fascinating (to the economist) mathematical manipulations. The data is easy to graph, to table and to algebratize! This means to some people that it is more exact and definite and therefore more trustworthy than ephemeral input like the amount of clean air, open space, and friendly smiles we receive.

What makes this matter of satisfying human wants even more complicated is that economists are unable to deal with broad collective wants. Generally, the emphasis is on the individual or single decision-maker like the "consumer," the "firm" or the "government." It must drive sociologists to distraction to realize how naive is economics when it comes to its treatment of group and social dynamics. To economists it is generally the individual who receives pleasure from the private consumption of goods and services. But if this is the case, what happens if having bought a product, I give it to a friend as a gift? Within the framework of consumer behaviour, economists would suggest that I receive utility from someone else's pleasure and this is entirely rational. But what if my wife gives a gift to my son? Now, since I didn't purchase the gift, the utility which I derive from my son's pleasure simply cannot be integrated into my utility "nest." Yet it seems apparent that much of our behaviour is based on how we act and react toward others. People surely have shared utility functions and yet the discipline denies this point outright. We are motivated by greed and jealousy, by love and friendship, by fear and hate, and other powerful emotions all of which require a social context. The individual consumption of goods and services simply does not address these aspects of human existence.

The fact that our own happiness is contingent on the happiness of others is something that has been demonstrated by income surveys time and again. Such surveys suggest that people in higher income groups tend to be happier than those in lower income groups. But it is not true that people in rich countries are any happier than people living in poor countries. And despite the fact that the average Canadian is much richer than, say, 40 years ago, that average person is no happier. All of this seems to suggest that happiness is not determined by absolute levels of income but by income relative to that of others. If we accept this, then we come to the perverse conclusion that if my income rises relative to the rest of the community, then I may well be happier; but if they also get a pay increase, then my happiness is unaffected. There are many complexities here that the discipline of economics seems unable to deal with.

Finally, even if we could clearly define what things are to be included in the term "human wants" and even if we knew exactly what will satisfy them, we must still recognize that the task is further complicated by the fact that our wants do not remain constant. Many observers have noted that a driving force of large firms today is not only to produce goods and services in order to satisfy consumer demand, but to help create that demand. Galbraith has suggested that the act of producing automatically creates wants. The job of modern advertising, he argues, is often to impress upon the consumer that he has a desperate need for a certain product that until last month, perhaps, he had never heard of. After all, if human wants are constant and therefore capable of satisfaction, what were the wants of the average Canadian in say 1920? An exercise bike? A new microwave? Perhaps, a big screen TV for the entertainment room? Of course not. These things did not exist and so no one wanted them. So how can we have any idea of what wants will exist in the year 2020, or 2050? The point is that material wants are always changing and can therefore never be satisfied. Perhaps for this reason it might be better if we were to try to find out what are the *human wants* that *material wants* are trying to satisfy. In other words, perhaps it will be more instructive to regard the satisfaction of certain material wants as being a means to an end, and not the end itself.

Normative and Positive Economics

In Chapter 1 we made a distinction between the terms "positive" and "normative." Positive statements are regarded as assertions (or statements of fact) about the world that can be tested by empirical data. Normative statements on the other hand are based on value systems and cannot be tested by empirical data. "Children like candy" is a positive statement, whereas "Children should not be given candy" is a normative statement. It is often suggested that normative statements have no place in economics since, as a science, economic theory is based solely on positive statements. Along with this is the suggestion that since economics is a positive science, it must be dealing with fundamental truths which are independent of time and place. This means that the law of diminishing returns, for instance, is not a law which is merely applicable to French agricultural production of the eighteenth century, but a law which pertains to all productive effort anywhere and anytime in the world. In this sense it is a natural law like the law of gravity. As a positive science, economics, while admitting a kinship to the other social sciences such as sociology and political theory, is regarded by many of its practitioners as being a discipline which can make valid and predictable statements about the world without the need to borrow from the other social sciences. They believe that it is not necessary (and may, in fact, be an impediment) for economists to lean on history or psychology or political theory to help explain the workings of an economy. Economics is autonomous and independent of those disciplines. Furthermore, they would suggest that while individual economists will have opinions on a range of topics, these should in no way interfere with the advancement of theorizing within the discipline or the conclusions which will follow from it.

This view of economics is a far cry from those of earlier economists like Adam Smith, John Stuart Mill or Karl Marx. For them, economics was, by its nature, tied to politics and history, and economists were enjoined to enter the fray. The idea of economics as a pure and positive science is a twentieth century idea and is very closely allied to the rise of logical positivism in philosophy. Logical positivism held that all statements and theories which are not verifiable are nothing but "meaningless noise," and for that reason are worthy of no further investigation — at least, not by scientific thinkers. As far as devotees of logical positivism are concerned (and they are the dominant force in philosophy), discussions of such things as ethics or morality or religion or metaphysics are unproductive and pointless. This is because any statement that could be made about these topics would either be incapable of verification or would be merely tautological. "God is an omniscient and benevolent creator" can not be verified. "Helping one another is a good thing to do" depends on an arbitrary definition of what constitutes goodness and defining goodness in a particular way results in the statement being true by definition. As far as logical positivists are concerned, the process of scientific theory starts with the empirical investigation of the world through sense perception and the formulation of hypotheses. These are then put through logical analysis so as to produce theories which can be verified through observation or experimentation. If tests succeed in verifying a theory, then it should be accepted; if not, it should be discarded. Sound economic theories are developed in the same way according to those economists who are only willing to recognize the validity of positive statements. The key word in all scientific theorizing is verifiable. Only statements which are verifiable have any meaning. Some statements may be difficult to verify immediately but as long as it is possible to verify them at some time in the future, then they are scientific (positive) statements.

Economics over the last 50 years or so has borrowed the language and methodology of logical positivism in an attempt to become more "scientific." Questions of improvement or goodness have, as a result, been expunged from the discipline as being merely expressions of value judgements. Truth is acceptable only if it meets the test of being verifiable. The result of this is that economics has often failed to address some very fundamental aspects of life. In addition, it has severely narrowed the range of "acceptable" topics and of acceptable investigative methods. In essence it has played safe and, as a result, has been reluctant to chart new and possibly dangerous waters. As a result it is in great danger of being regarded as boring, predictable — and the worst sin of all — irrelevant. The tragedy of all this is that the perceived solid foundation of "positive" economics is not all that solid. Let us look at some of the reasons why.

On the surface, the idea that economics should confine itself to observable data from the real world seems reasonable enough. However, this is impossible methodologically, as well as in practice, because the question arises: which data? After all, data doesn't just sit up and beg for attention. What data is relevant and what is not relevant requires a value judgement. If it is relevant because it is important, then who is judging the question of importance and on what basis? What we are saying here is that economists make value judgements when they make the initial decision on what is worthy of study. If an economist makes the assertion that, for instance, economics is concerned with the allocation of scarce resources, one is immediately entitled to ask why. If the answer is that this is an important topic, then a value judgement has already been made. Not that there is anything wrong with this, but it is dishonest to suggest that no judgement is involved. Next comes the question of verification. Consider the following statement: Positive economics requires that the discipline deals only with statements of fact, i.e., statements which are verifiable. Now this statement itself, like all others, is either a positive or a normative statement. If it is a positive one, then how could one possibly go about verifying it? And if it is a normative statement, i.e., that the discipline *should* only deal with verifiable statements, then it is merely a value judgement on the part of the writer and, some would have us believe, should therefore be ignored.

Finally, if economics is to deal only with verifiable statements, then it presumably includes statements which have not yet been verified but which are capable of verification. This would include a statement like: XYZ drug will reduce the levels of cholesterol in the heart. But it would also include statements like: Robots will replace all human effort in the production of goods by the year 2025; or the banking system will totally collapse in the next ten years; or, to be consistent but silly, the end of the world is nigh. Such silliness is permissible if the only criteria for allowable statements are that they be analytically consistent and empirically verifiable.

prescriptive statement: a statement which gives directions or injunction.

Part of the reason many economists feel the discipline should focus solely on the investigation of positive statements is based on the mistaken impression that since normative statements relate to value judgements, they are merely expressions of personal opinion. However, as Homa Katouzian points out in his insightful book *Ideology and Method in Economics* (to which these comments owe a big debt), there is a big difference between *moral or ethical statements* and *policy judgements* or **prescriptive statements.** There is a big difference for example between the statements that income should (or should not) be more equally distributed, and the statement that a more equal (or unequal) distribution of incomes will increase incentives to work and ultimately increase levels of production. The first statement is one of personal belief while the second one is a policy judgement. Trying to eliminate not only value judgements but also policy judgements just because normative thinking is involved serves only to emasculate the discipline. Smith, Ricardo, Mill, Keynes and other economic greats all introduced prescriptive theories, i.e., ideas to promote and achieve private and public goals, and were not afraid to offer specific remedies in line with those theories. Further, positive economists also make prescriptive statements although they may not always recognize it. For instance, by suggesting that economics should be concerned with the efficient allocation of scarce resources because that will ensure the greatest production of goods and services from limited resources, they forget to add the prescriptive proviso: *assuming that this is a desirable thing to do*. The subject matter of economics, therefore, should not be limited to an investigation of the mobilization and allocation of scarce resources but should explicitly look at other important social objectives, such as, in Katouzian's words:

> A decent (yes, decent) minimum standard of living; a fair (yes, fair) distribution of income; an agreeable (yes, agreeable) condition for daily labour; a healthy (yes, healthy) environment for living....[1]

Does this mean then that all statements in economics should be given equal attention and importance and that we discard the idea of trying to verify statements? And if it does, are we not in danger of allowing people to make outrageous or false statements, or just as bad, of permitting economics to be "just a matter of opinion"? Not at all. If anything, it means that its practitioners become more honest and more scrupulous in the presentation of their ideas since they would not be allowed to hide behind the defence of objectivity.

In addition, the test of the validity of any theory is that it be open to criticism and that its predictions be consistent with all possible events.

Katouzian suggests that economics should be reinvigorated by a change in emphasis. This certainly does not mean a shift from the scientific to the nonscientific but from a change in its methodological approach. He suggests that economics should:

(i) place a high priority on the understanding and solution of important and real economic problems in contrast to minute puzzles, etc.

(ii) recognize the importance of other, "non-economic," social facts, categories and theories, in their analysis of specific economic problems; and make an earnest effort to allow for such "variables" in their analysis and solutions.

(iii) use *any* set of techniques (including mathematics which are appropriate for the problem in hand; but never allow *any* set of techniques to dominate, much less determine, the choice of problem.

---

[1] Homa Katouzian, *Ideology and Method in Economics* (New York: University Press), p. 147.

(iv) always maintain the history of (the relevant) ideas and events as a background to their study.[2]

The study of political economy should, therefore, go far broader and much deeper than the current preoccupations of positive economics. For example, one important error of omission that the discipline currently commits is due to its refusal to recognize the role of power in any of its many forms.

Economics and Political Power

It is surprising that few economics textbooks mention the subject of power. It seems that it is regarded as either an irrelevant topic or, even worse, the object of taboo. Often the only power groups that seem to exist in modern economic discussions are the faceless and anonymous groups of consumers, producers and government. And the interaction among them seems both polite and baroque. Their rival claims seem to be easily moderated through changes in prices or profits or the sedate arrival and departure of new players in the game. It all seems so well-mannered and orderly that it can be easily described in terms of game theory. Love and hate, life and death, greed and envy, struggle and survival would seem out of place in such courtly surroundings and one is hesitant to mention that such things do exist in the world. The discipline was not always like this. Malthus, Ricardo, Veblen and Marx all agreed that the economic world and the behaviour of people was incomprehensible without an understanding of the power structure of society.

The exorcism of power from economics is an important exclusion for a discipline which places the market at centre stage. (Robert Heilbroner notes in his review of *The New Palgrave: A Dictionary of Economics* that in a collection of over 4,000 pages and 2,000 entries, there is no entry for power.) Market behaviour involves a voluntary exchange between people, and perfectly competitive markets imply a total absence of power. The only decision to be made by the participants is whether, and to what extent, to participate in the exchange. No one supposedly acts out of fear or coercion or through persuasion or inducement: no one is forced to work, or to buy or to produce. The players in the game, it seems, are not only faceless, they are also anaemic and totally impotent. But the history of our planet and our species is a history of power struggles and of our attempts to control our environment, each other, and ourselves.

The power which individuals or groups exercise over others is not gained solely by appropriation; it is often conferred. For a minority to exercise power over a majority requires that the majority confer this power on the minority. A leader can only govern if the governed agree to be governed. Of course, in most instances, this agreement is seldom declared but usually becomes institutionalized through tradition and ceremony so that it forms a bond stronger and more powerful than control by the whip or through the barrel of a gun. The slave owners of Ancient Egypt and Greece exercised power over a population which far exceeded their own numbers. The only way in which they could have continued to exercise this life and death con-

---

[2] Ibid.

trol was if the slaves acquiesced. Power always requires a hierarchical structure and an acceptance of the prescribed social and political role of each person in this structure.

The basis from which power is derived can vary, but one of the most important is through ownership of productive resources. Those who own resources are usually powerful; those who do not are usually powerless. In ancient societies, slaves were the most important productive resource. As a result, a wealthy and powerful individual was someone who owned many slaves and the more slaves, the wealthier and more powerful he became. But as slavery was slowly eradicated in Europe (as it entered the Middle Ages) and as economies became increasingly agrarian, the power of land (and of agricultural production) became paramount. The owners of land, which included kings, baronial lords, and the Catholic Church became the powerful groups with landless peasants occupying the bottom of the power pyramid. But times and technology change and so does the valuation of what constitutes an economy's most powerful resource. As Europe embarked on a period of exploration and trade during the mercantilist period of the sixteenth and seventeenth centuries, money became the new symbol of wealth, and a power shift took place away from landowners to the rising class of traders and merchants. The landowners still exercised some power, but they were now forced to share it with this emerging merchant class. It was also during the mercantilist period that a new focus of power emerged: parliamentary government. Initially the rival parties in parliament were merely the agents of the two major classes of landowners and merchants (with the clergy often holding the balance of power). It did not take long before the parliamentarians started to act autonomously and began to wield power of their own.

The Industrial Revolution saw the rise of the factory and the market system. Manufacturing became the new source of wealth and power and created a new class of industrialists to challenge the status quo of the merchants and landowners. The rising industrialist also demanded representation in parliament. This period of change also saw the creation of an increasingly powerful group of industrial workers organized into trade unions. The struggle for power thus became both more intense and more extensive as the western economies entered the twentieth century, particularly with the rise of totalitarian governments in the 1920s and later.

What we have witnessed historically is a shifting of the power base from one era to the next. Often these shifts have involved violent revolution and war, because power is seldom acceded peacefully. The result of each power struggle has been the emergence of a new dominant power. The power to control is usually the result of the ownership to a title or the ownership of wealth. In addition, what is regarded as the major source of wealth has changed over the centuries. Pharaohs in Ancient Egypt had power as a result of the ownership of a hereditary title; baronial lords as owners of land; merchants owned gold and silver; and industrialists owned the capital necessary to manufacture goods. As technology changes, productive resources, wealth and power all change as a result. This does not mean that the old power base evaporates however. Instead, as each shift occurred, power became more diffuse and more complex and what we may well be witnessing as we enter the third millennium is the rise of another power base.

The Social Transformation

Historians may well look back on the end of the twentieth century as the beginning of a social change of profound magnitude. Borrowing on the work of Peter Drucker, let's try to summarize some of what is happening.

At the beginning of this century, farmers made up the largest single category of workers in the labour force in every country in the world. The second largest employment group in most industrial countries was that of live-in servants, while industrial workers formed barely 10% to 15% of the work force. At this time the industrial worker typically had no pension plan to participate in; no paid vacation; no overtime pay; received no premium for shift work; had no health insurance; no unemployment insurance and no job security.

The blossoming of industrial capitalism in the first half of this century resulted in industrial workers becoming the largest single category of workers in the developed countries of the world. In addition, these industrial workers were highly visible, and they worked in concentrated groups so that they were relatively easy to organize. As a result, by 1950, the industrial worker had gained all of the above benefits plus a *lot of political power*. No class in history has risen as fast as the industrial worker in the first half of this century. In the same 50-year period, the number of farmers, expressed as a percentage of the labour force, declined by something like 80% and household servants virtually disappeared. Both groups slipped into the class of industrial worker with relative ease.

Yet, in the 1990s, in North America, the industrial workers and their unions are in full retreat. They make up barely 20% of the labour force and estimates are that this percentage will fall to under 12% by the year 2010. Unlike the domestic servant, the industrial worker will not disappear in the future, but like the farmer, they will become merely auxiliary to the total productive capacity of the economy.

knowledge worker: those who must continuously learn and use theoretical and analytical knowledge in their work.

Is there a new class on the horizon that will become a new centre of power and influence? Drucker believes there is. He calls this rising class the **knowledge worker.** The skills possessed by knowledge workers include the ability to acquire and apply theoretical and analytical knowledge and, above all, the habit of continuous learning. It is estimated that by the year 2000, fully one-third of the labour force will fall into the category of knowledge workers. This figure is almost as large as industrial workers as a group ever achieved.

In short, the industrial worker is being replaced by the knowledge-based technologist who is as likely to work with theoretical concepts as with her hands. Examples of workers in this group are computer software programmers, lab technicians, paralegal workers, music therapists, animators and engineer-design technicians.

The economies of the world which will (very soon) have a comparative advantage in the world's marketplace will be those that are best able to train the greatest number of knowledge workers and can widely employ knowledge-based concepts such as computer-aided inventory control, just-in-time delivery systems, computer-aided design methods and flexible-production processes that are able to target niche markets.

Entry into knowledge work is through education and not by apprenticeship. What is regarded as knowledge in the new knowledge society is determined by its successful application to the process of identifying and solving problems of design, production and marketing. It will involve educated people whose knowledge is effective only when it is highly specialized. Thus, the educational institutions of society will be the key to the success or failure of the economy as a whole. Above all, the definition of an educated person will be one who has learned how to learn. More and more, we will see that, in the knowledge society, it is the team and not the individual who performs. Most knowledge workers will be affiliated with an organization even though they may not be employees of that organization. This is because a group effort, working within the structure of an organization, is needed to convert specialized knowledge into performance.

Increasingly, the knowledge worker will own the primary tool of production — knowledge — but also increasingly she will have to coordinate this highly specialized knowledge with others in order to put it to work.

One of the more significant points in this great transformation is that displaced industrial workers cannot simply move into knowledge work in the way that farmers and servants moved into industrial work. Because of this we are facing a social conflict of potentially enormous proportions. Those in the knowledge sector of the economy will probably never be a majority but they will probably be the ones with high incomes, creative work challenges and wide job opportunities. Neither the non-knowledge-service workers nor the (now much smaller) industrial and agricultural workers will enjoy such circumstances.

Just who falls into one group and not the other will depend far less on birth and social class than ever before in history. In the age of industrial capitalism, capital was the most important factor of production, and capital could be accumulated and monopolized. In the emerging information age, knowledge is the most important factor of production, and it is more widely accessible and is much more difficult to monopolize. Therefore, it may well be that the knowledge society will be far more competitive than any preceding it.

To summarize, our society has experienced the rise and the fall of the industrial class as the largest group of workers within the short span of one century. It is now experiencing the beginnings of a significant social and economic transformation where power is once again shifting.

One of the important outcomes of all this is that the old communities of the agricultural/industrial age — the family, the parish, the village — have either disappeared or have become stunted. The new unit of social integration in our daily lives is the work-based organization needed to coordinate the efforts of the highly specialized knowledge worker. But these organizations are not organic. They are, instead, a creation of our new technology. In addition, as an individual's abilities grow and as opportunities continually change, we will see the typical person in the span of a career living in several locations, doing several different types of jobs and working intimately with several different groups of people.

What all this adds up to is that people are losing their sense of community — their roots are being cut out from under them. This contributes to our society's growing list of social problems: high divorce rates, widespread drug addition, crime, and violence as well as a general sense of restlessness on the part of a majority of the population.

The knowledge society will make it possible for many more people to be successful, in the way that we normally define that term. It is also likely that many more people will face failures in their lives. We currently tend to view such individual failures as some kind of failure *of society* with the result that our concept of individual responsibility is becoming very muddled. Most people feel that it is the responsibility of government to address such failures.

As a result, governments everywhere have already become huge welfare bureaucracies and the bulk of their budgets are expenditures on various kinds of entitlements to individual members of society. This phenomena will probably intensify. In a sense, because our *traditional* sense of community has broken down, we are turning to government to try to fill this void.

Yet, it may well be that the class which is growing in size and gaining more in power, that of the knowledge worker, is coming to realize that large-scale government intervention just isn't working. As a result, there may be a growing sense that government, as an institution, is more prone to failure than it is to success.

If this sense prevails, we will still be left with the question: who takes care of the social challenges of individual failures? The answer might lie in the emergence of a new sector within our society that we shall call the *community sector*. The function of the community sector will be to provide the institutions aimed at helping people cope with the changing world and care for individuals who have experienced failure. Above all, its work will include helping human beings change in ways that make our society a better place to live. Governments will continue in the role of policy-maker, standard-setter and paymaster but the actual work in this new community sector will often be done on a voluntary basis. Many people today have a degree of social consciousness that results in their caring about the social problems faced by our society but are at a loss as to what they might be able to do. They want to help, but feel that the efforts of a single individual no longer matter in the face of the complex, political, bureaucratic institutions of today. On the contrary, it is possible that an individual working in the community sector *can* make a difference.

Some have already found that volunteering in a hospice program or an environmental organization or a youth sports club can be very satisfying. A startling fact recently appearing in the media is that, in the United States in 1993 fully one-half of the adult population were engaged in some kind of volunteer work at an average of 4.2 hours a week. Why might this be? It may well be that this kind of activity gives one a sense of community that many have almost lost. As this sense of contribution and community is regained, we may become happier as individuals and more productive as citizens. We may begin to regain a sense of priority that shifts our emphasis from material well-being to a definition of well-being that is broader in scope and more profound.

When all this happens we may begin to realize that we have looked to government for the wrong things — that we have misunderstood the role of government. The result of this misunderstanding is that we have set up our governments to try to do things that they simply cannot do — give us a sense of caring and community — and as a result our governments have failed us.

Just what role will the business sector likely play in a world that might see governments pull back from an active interventionist role? How might the business sector and the new community sector interact? These are intriguing questions but well worth keeping in mind as we watch the new century unfold.

As you can see, as we look forward into the very near future, there are many more questions than there are answers. Yet many of the changes that are beginning to emerge have the potential for enormous good. If this potential is to be realized, we as a society will have to learn quickly and, above all, begin to take responsibility for our own thoughts and actions. As the range and scope of this chapter indicates, economics is a fascinating discipline, one that is well worth a student's serious consideration as a career choice. So much is to be done within the discipline. Perhaps you will be among those who agree to accept the challenge.

BOX 14A
1. What is the conventional meaning of a *high standard of living*?
2. Can intervention by government produce benefits but still fail?
3. Give an example of how the interest of a specific group might differ from the interest of society as a whole.
4. What is the difference between intervention failing because a problem is difficult to identify and it failing because the government's vision is myopic?
5. Why is it difficult to define and agree on the economic goals which society wants to pursue?
6. What is meant by a *shared utility function*?
7. Is the law of diminishing returns a positive or a normative concept?
8. Define the term *prescriptive statement*.
9. What was the power base of the slave owner, the medieval lord and the industrialist?
10. Define the term *knowledge worker*.
11. What class of worker rose and fell very quickly within the twentieth century?

Chapter Highlights

The chapter begins with a rather conventional look at our expectations concerning the way in which government intervenes in the economy and the ways this intervention might fail. Such failure can come in six forms: the cost of intervention may exceed the benefits; the intervention might simply fail to achieve its goal; the problem at which the intervention is aimed may not be clearly defined; the intervention may benefit some at the expense of others; the intervention may be ineffective because of bureaucratic inefficiency; and the intervention may be myopic in the sense of weighing short-run costs more heavily than larger long-run benefits.

Next, the chapter discusses the difficulty involved in defining social goals and how the discipline of economics may have muddled this process by over-emphasizing measurable, material goals at the expense of more abstract but valuable ones. It is pointed out that the discipline does seem to see the satisfaction of material wants as an end in itself rather than as a means to more significant ends.

The chapter then discusses the normative (assertions that cannot be tested with data) and positive (involving references to fact) approaches to posing economic questions and pursuing answers. Underlying this discussion is the question of whether economics is, or should be, a science or whether the political economy approach that was popular in the nineteenth century should once again be embraced.

The section goes on to suggest that the latter approach would allow economists, among other things, to include things like power in their analysis. The strictly scientific approach makes doing this nearly impossible. The text then discusses the fact that those who have held power in society have changed through time in step with the changing technology and with the changing importance of various factors of production. When slaves were the key factor, slave owners held power. Then it was land owners whose power gave way to the owners of capital.

The chapter ends with a brief look at the future and at the possibility that the current changes in our society will lead to yet another significant shift in who holds power — those who posses knowledge.

New Glossary Terms

Workbook

Study Tips

1. You will not find a chapter like this one in any other principles textbook. Here we have "cut loose" from the traditional confines of the standard approach in order to raise questions that we think all students should spend a little time thinking about. We ask that you, also, cut loose a little in reading the chapter by not expecting "right answers" and that you not be hesitant in disagreeing with some of what is said.

2. There are two sections in the chapter that you should treat very much like the previous chapters since they are fairly conventional topics. They are the discussion of the five ways in which government can fail and the section on normative versus positive economics.

3. If you enjoyed reading this chapter and thinking about the questions that are raised in it, then you should probably seriously consider majoring in economics!

Are You Sure?

Indicate whether the following statements are true or false. If false, indicate why they are false.

1. Gross domestic product is the market value of all goods and services produced in the whole economy per year.
T or **F**   If false: _____

_____

_____

2. Canada's income per capita (in constant 1980 dollars) has approximately doubled in the last 30 years.
T or **F**   If false: _____

_____

_____

3. One form of government failure is that the costs of government intervention in the economy may exceed the benefits.
T or **F**   If false: _____

_____

_____

4. The discipline of economics treats the purchase of goods and services as a means to an end.
T or **F**   If false: _____

_____

_____

5. Income surveys seem to indicate that an individual's happiness is determined by absolute levels of income.
T or **F**   If false: _____

_____

_____

6. The idea that economics is a positive science is a twentieth century idea and is very closely allied to the rise of logical positivism in philosophy.
T or **F**   If false: _____

_____

_____

7. A prescriptive statement is one that can be verified with empirical data.
T or **F**   If false: _____

_____

_____

8. Earlier economists such as Veblen, Ricardo, Malthus and Marx all agreed that the eco-

nomic world and the behaviour of people were incomprehensible without an understanding of power within society.

T or **F**   If false: _____

_____

_____

9.   While knowledge workers may one day become the centre of power, they will always be a very small percentage of the labour force.

T or **F**   If false: _____

_____

_____

10. In terms of economic power and influence, agricultural workers, as a class in North America, rose and fell very quickly during the twentieth century.

T or **F**   If false: _____

_____

_____

Translations

The following paragraph might have been written by an economist who believed that the positive approach was the correct one to use in economics. Use your judgement to revise, amend or otherwise convert the paragraph such that it might have been written by another economist who believed in a political-economy-type approach to the discipline.

Economics is a positive science that can make valid and widely applicable statements about the world without the need to borrow from other disciplines. Sound economic theory is built by starting with empirical observations, which, through logical analysis, produce theories which can be verified by testing those theories with objective data. Such testing of theories is very important since only verifiable statements have meaning. The training of economists, therefore, needs to emphasize statistical data-gathering, logical deduction and mathematical techniques of testing theory.

_____

_____

_____

_____

_____

_____

_____

_____

_____

Choose the Best

1. In which situation is government intervention *not* likely to benefit society as a whole?
   a) Whenever a small group of people stand to make large gains at the expense of a large number of people who will each experience small losses.
   b) Whenever a large group of people stand to make large gains at the expense of a small number of people who will each experience small losses.

2. Which of the following would be an example of myopic intervention?
   a) The spending of billions of dollars on disease treatment but only millions on disease prevention.
   b) The Ministry of Education decides to put computer on every student's desk.

3. Which of the following statements is a prescriptive statement?
   a) Income should be more equally distributed.
   b) A more equal distribution of income will decrease the incentive to work.

4. Two of the following statements help explain why many economists now believe that attempts to regulate oligopoly industries often fail. Which one does *not*?

a) Regulatory bodies often fall under the influence of the industry that is being regulated.

b) Regulatory bodies are often uncertain as to whether their role is to enforce rules or assist the industry or both.

c) Regulatory bodies seem incapable of enforcing their rulings.

5. Which one of the following is an example of a serious shortcoming in economics?
   a) It ignores the fact that people have shared utility functions.
   b) It fails to recognize external costs of production.
   c) It assumes that all markets are perfectly competitive.

6. It is often suggested that economics ignores the topic of power. Which of the following statements confirms this?
   a) Consumer behaviour can be explained in terms of the voluntary exchange that takes place between people.
   b) People often act out of fear or as a result of coercion.
   c) The history of humankind is a history of our attempts to control our environment, each other and ourselves.

7. The source of power has shifted throughout the history of humankind. Which of the following is the correct sequence?
   a) Slaves, land, money, capital and technology.
   b) Slaves, land, capital, money and technology.
   c) Money, slaves, land, capital and technology.

8. All of the following statements, *except one*, are feasible explanations of regional disparities in Canada. Which one is the exception?
   a) Canada's poor regions lack natural resources.
   b) Canada's poor regions suffer from inadequately sized markets.
   c) Canada's poor regions rely primarily on agriculture.
   d) Canada's poor regions lack entrepreneurial talent.

9. All of the following, *except one*, are examples of favoured treatment being given to special interest groups. Which one is the exception?
   a) Government subsidies to farmers.
   b) Government expenditures on infectious-disease control.
   c) A tariff on footwear.
   d) Rent controls.

10. All *except one* of the following statements are positive statements. Which one is the exception?
    a) Economies of scale occur only in the long run.
    b) The price of air fares in Canada today is high relative to other goods.
    c) While the quantity of cigarette smoking will rise as the price decreases, the rise will be modest.
    d) We need a new index to measure the economy's well-being.

11. Katouzian argues that the emphasis in economics should change from positive economics to political economy. All of the following statements, *except one*, agree with this idea.
    a) Economics should recognize the importance of other non-economic social facts and data.
    b) Economics should use a wide variety of techniques, including mathematics, in its inquiry without letting any one technique dominate.
    c) Economics should place a high priority on addressing real problems and not minute puzzles.
    d) Economics should confine itself to those propositions that are verifiable.

12. All of the following, *except one*, is a broad social trend that has occurred in the United States in the twentieth century. Which one is the exception?
    a) Farmers made up the largest single category of workers in the labour force at the beginning of the twentieth century.
    b) Industrial workers made up only 10% to 15% of workers at the beginning of the twentieth century.

c) Industrial workers make up the largest category of workers at the end of the twentieth century.

d) The knowledge worker is the fastest growing category of workers at the end of the twentieth century.

13. Which of the following is most likely to give an economy an advantage over others in the twenty-first century?
   a) Abundant natural resources.
   b) A high capital/labour ratio.
   c) Extensive training facilities for knowledge workers.
   d) A stable political environment.

14. Though difficult to measure, all of the following, *except one*, could legitimately be included in a broad index used to measure the well-being of a society's population. Which one is the exception?
   a) Unemployment rates.
   b) A value for leisure measured in terms of the opportunity cost of the work given up.
   c) Literacy rates.
   d) A measurement of personal freedom.
   e) Infant mortality rates.

15. All of the following, *except one*, are likely to be major problems in the first half of the twentieth century. Which one is the exception?
   a) Finding an answer to the question of who takes care of the social challenges which result from individual failures.
   b) Preventing the GDP of our economy from falling.
   c) Redefining the roles of government and personal responsibility.
   d) Inventing new ways of generating a sense of community.
   e) Redefining our definition of social well-being.

What's Wrong?

Can you spot the four errors in the following passage? (Ignore grammatical mistakes!)

There are many ways in which government intervention can fail. First, intervention involves a cost and that cost might be below the benefits gained from it. Second, it is sometimes difficult to identify the real cause of the problem that warrants intervention. Environmental pollution is an example here. Third, the fact that intervention often results in a reallocation of resources makes it attractive for special interest groups to try to persuade governments to intervene in a way that will benefit society as a whole. Finally, governments often shy away from projects that involve small short-run costs but promise long-run benefits.

Other Problems

1. Which of the following statements are positive and which are normative?

   a) Canada's GDP (in constant dollars) grew from approximately $44 billion dollars in 1926 to over $609 billion in 1994.

      Answer: _____.

   b) Crime rates are correlated with poverty.

      Answer: _____.

   c) The government should provide free education for all.

      Answer: _____.

   d) Positive economics requires that the discipline deal only with statements of fact.

      Answer: _____.

e) Industrial workers are becoming a less numerous group in society.

Answer: _____.

2. Which of the following statements are legitimate topics of discussion according to a positive economist, or to a political economist, or to both?

a) With the help of computers, the discipline of economics has advanced to the point that few mysteries remain about the behavior of the firm.

Answer: _____.

b) If the conclusions of a theory cannot be verified by appealing to empirical data, then the theory is not a valid topic within economics.

Answer: _____.

c) Deregulation of the airlines in the U.S. in the 80s caused fares to plummet, passenger miles travelled to increase and new companies to emerge.

Answer: _____.

d) An analysis of power has had a significant impact on economics.

Answer: _____.

e) AIDS is a terrible disease and no effort should be spared in coming to grips with it.

Answer: _____.

3. What is the source of power for each of the following individuals?

a) Conrad Black:

b) Jean Chrétien:

c) Saddam Hussein:

d) Madonna:

e) The Queen of England:

f) Gary Bettman:

4. Consider the following three statements:

If investment in Canada had been higher, then unemployment would have been lower.

If the government had encouraged investment in Canada, then unemployment would have been lower.

The government should have encouraged more investment in Canada.

Clearly, the first is a positive statement and the third is a normative statement. What is the second?

Answer: _____.

Unanswered Questions

Short Essays

1. Give three examples in which special interest groups have successfully lobbied governments to act in a way that benefits them at the expense of society as a whole.

2. Explain why governments are often myopic in their decision-making.

3. In our society, do you think that material wants are over-emphasized to the exclusion of other wants?

4. What things would you take into consideration if you were asked to invent an index of well-being for our society?

5. Explain why you agree or disagree with Drucker's prediction that the knowledge worker will become the most powerful group of workers in the future.

Analytical Questions

1. Comment on the following: "There is no such thing as a positive statement."

2. If Drucker's view of the immediate future proves more or less accurate, do you think that the world's economies will become more or less competitive? Explain your answer.

3. Explain how you think a redefinition of personal responsibility might impact on the perceived role of government.

4. Assume that your pay increased significantly at a time of a booming economy when many other people's pay was also increasing. Next, assume that your pay increased (by the same amount as in the first instance) at a time of recession in which many other people's income was not increasing or was even falling. Do you think that the increase in pay in the first instance would be as satisfying as in the second? Why?

5. Do you see the power of the big transnational corporations increasing or decreasing in the next 50 years? How will the growth of knowledge workers affect this?

GLOSSARY

■ ■ ■ ■ ■ ■ ■ ■ ────────────────────────────

absolute advantage: the advantage which comes from producing something at lower cost than others are able to do.

aggregate demand: the aggregate quantity of goods and services demanded by all buyers at various different prices.

aggregate expenditures: total spending in the economy, divided into the four components: C, I, G, and (X–IM).

aggregate supply: the aggregate quantity of goods and services produced by all sellers at various different price levels.

allocative efficiency: the production of the combination of products which best satisfies consumers' demands.

anti-dumping regulation: a law or regulation found in most countries that prohibits the importation of any good at a price below the cost of production.

arbitrage: the process of buying a commodity in one market, where the price is low, and selling it in a second market where the price is higher.

asset demand for money: the desire by people to use money as a store of wealth, i.e., to hold money as an asset.

assets: the part of a company's balance sheet that represents what it owns or what is owed to it.

autonomous consumption: the portion of consumer spending which is independent of the level of income.

autonomous dissavings: the amount of depleted past savings when income is zero.

average fixed cost: total fixed cost divided by the quantity of output.

average product: total product (or total output) divided by the quantity of inputs used to produce that total.

average profit: the profit per unit produced, i.e., the total profit divided by the output.

average propensity to consume: the ratio of the level of consumption to the corresponding level of income.

average propensity to save: the rates of the level of savings related to a given level of income.

average revenue: the amount of revenue received per unit sold. It will always equal the price of the product.

average total cost: total cost divided by quantity of output.

average variable cost: total variable cost divided by total output.

balance of payments: an accounting of a country's international transactions which involves the payment and receipts of foreign currencies.

balance of trade: the value of a country's exports of goods and services less the value of its imports.

balanced budget: the equality of net tax revenues and government spending on goods and services.

balanced budget philosophy: the belief that a government's budget should be balanced each budget period.

bank rate: the rate of interest payable by the chartered banks on loans from the Bank of Canada.

barriers to entry: obstacles which make it difficult for new participants to enter a market.

black market: an illegal market where products are bought and sold at a price above the government-imposed price ceiling.

break-even income: the level of income where consumption is equal to income (and where savings is zero).

break-even output: the level of output at which the sales revenue of the firm just covers the fixed and variable costs including normal profit.

break-even price: the price at which the firm makes only normal profits, i.e., makes zero economic profits.

budget deficit: government spending on goods and services in excess of net tax revenues.

budget surplus: net tax revenue in excess of government spending on goods and services.

business cycle: recurrent fluctuations in the economy's GDP and employment levels.

capacity output: that output where average total cost is at a minimum.

capital: all human-made resources which can be used to produce other goods and services.

capital account: a subcategory of the balance of payments that reflects changes in ownership of assets associated with foreign investment.

capital goods: those things such as buildings, tools, equipment and machinery that are used to aid in the production of other goods.

change in demand: a change in the quantities demanded at every price, caused by a change in the determinants of demand.

change in supply: a change in the quantities supplied at every price, caused by a change in the determinants of supply.

change in the quantity demanded: the change in the quantity which results from a price change. It results in a movement along a demand curve.

change in the quantity supplied: the change in the amounts that will be produced as a result of a price change. This is shown as a movement along a supply curve.

commodity money: a type of money which can also function, and is useful, as a commodity.

common property resource: a resource which is not owned by an individual, firm or government.

comparative advantage: the advantage which comes from producing something at a lower opportunity cost than others are able to.

complementary products: products which tend to be purchased jointly and whose demands, therefore, are directly related.

concentration ratio: a measurement of what percentage of an industry's total sales is controlled by a few large firms.

constant returns to scale: the situation where a firm's output increases in proportion to the increase in its inputs.

consumer goods: goods used directly by consumers to satisfy their wants and needs.

consumer price index: an index of the changes in the prices of goods and services based on the cost of those same items in a base period.

consumer surplus: the difference between the consumer's evaluation of a product and the price which is paid for it.

consumption: the expenditure by households on goods and services.

consumption function: the relationship between income and consumption stated in mathematical form.

contractionary fiscal policy: a reduction in government spending or an increase in taxes aimed at reducing aggregate demand.

contractionary monetary policy: a policy in which the amount of money in the economy is decreased and credit becomes harder to obtain and more expensive.

cost-push inflation: inflation that is caused by an increase in the costs of production or in profit levels with the effect being on the supply side.

counter-cyclical fiscal policy: action by the government that tends to push the economy in a direction opposite to the way it is leaning.

cross-elasticity of demand: the responsiveness of the change in the quantity demanded of product A to a change in the price of product B.

crowding-out effect: the idea that any stimulation to aggregate demand that increases GDP will also increase interest rates which will, in turn, reduce the expansion of aggregate demand.

currency appreciation: a rise in the exchange rate of one currency for another.

currency depreciation: the fall in the exchange rate of one currency for another.

current account: a subcategory of the balance of payments that shows the income or expenditures related to exports and imports.

cyclically adjusted budget: a concept that calculates what the current budget balance would be if the economy was at full employment.

cyclically balanced budget philosophy: the idea that the government should aim to balance its budget over the life of the business cycle.

cyclical unemployment: unemployment that occurs as a result of the recession phase of the business cycle.

decreasing returns to scale: the situation where an increase in inputs of X% results in output increasing by less than X%.

demand: the quantities which consumers are willing and able to buy per period of time at various prices.

demand management: the use of fiscal and monetary policies in order to affect aggregate demand.

demand schedule: a table showing the various quantities demanded.

demand-pull inflation: inflation that occurs when the total demand for goods and services exceeds the economy's capacity to produce those goods.

depreciation: the annual cost of any asset which has a life of more than one year.

devaluation: the refixing of an exchange rate by government at a lower level.

direct investment: the purchase of real assets.

dirty float: an exchange rate that is not officially fixed by government but is managed by ongoing central bank intervention in the market.

discouraged worker: an individual who wants work but is no longer actively seeking it because of the conviction that no opportunities exist.

diseconomies of scale: bureaucratic inefficiencies in management that lead to increases in long-run average costs.

disposable income: the personal after-tax income of people.

division of labour: the dividing of the production process into a series of specialized tasks, each one by a different worker.

dumping: the sale of a product abroad for a lower price than is being charged in the domestic market or for a price below the cost of production.

economic capacity: the output which results in minimum average total costs.

economic growth: an increase in an economy's real GDP per capita or an increase in the economy's capacity to produce.

economic profits: revenue over and above all costs.

economic rent: the return to a factor of production that has perfectly inelastic supply.

economies of scale: cost advantages that are achieved as a result of large-scale operations.

elastic demand: quantity demanded that is quite responsive to a change in price.

elasticity coefficient: a number that measures the responsiveness of quantity demanded to a change in price.

employed: those who are in the labour force and hold paid employment.

enterprise: the human resource which manages, innovates and takes risks.

equation of exchange: a formula which states that the quantity of money times the velocity of money is equal to nominal GDP (price times real GDP).

equilibrium: a state of balance of equal forces with no tendency to change.

equilibrium income: the income at which the value of production and expenditures are equal.

equilibrium price: the price at which the quantity demanded equals the quantity supplied such that there is neither a surplus nor a shortage.

equilibrium quantity: the quantity which prevails at the equilibrium price.

excess capacity: the situation where a firm produces an output which is less than that which achieves minimum average total costs.

excess reserves: the reserves in excess of what the bank wants to hold as its target reserves.

exchange controls: restriction imposed by a government limiting the amount of foreign currencies which can be obtained.

exchange rate: the rate at which one currency converts into another.

expansionary fiscal policy: an increase in government spending or a reduction in taxes in order to stimulate aggregate demand.

expansionary monetary policy: a policy which aims to increase the amount of money in the economy and make credit cheaper and more easily available.

expenditure gap: the amount of the change in aggregate expenditures necessary to move the economy to full-employment GDP.

explicit costs: costs that are actually paid out in money.

exports: goods and services produced in one country and sold in another country.

externalities: benefits or costs of a product experienced by people who neither produce nor consume that product.

factor market: the market for the factors of production.

factors of production: the productive resources that are available to an economy and are categorized as land, labour, capital and enterprise.

factor output effect: the phenomenon of rising total output leading to an increase in demand for labour.

factor substitution effect: the phenomenon of one factor replacing another factor as a result of technological change.

fair-return price: a price which guarantees the firm will earn normal profits only, i.e., where P = AC.

financial security: any claim on assets which usually takes the form of a bond or certificate of deposit or similar financial instrument.

fiscal policy: spending and taxation policy used by the federal government to stabilize the economy.

fixed cost: those costs that do not vary with the level of output.

fixed exchange rate: a rate of currency exchange which is pegged by government and therefore prevented from rising or falling.

flexible exchange rate: a rate of currency exchange which is determined by the market forces of supply and demand and is not interfered with by government action.

foreign-trade effect: the effect which a change in prices has upon exports and imports.

fractional reserve system: a banking system whereby banks keep only a small fraction of their total deposits on reserve in the form of cash.

frictional unemployment: that part of total unemployment caused by the fact that it takes time for people to find their first job or to move between jobs.

full employment: the situation where there is only frictional and structural unemployment, i.e., where cyclical unemployment is zero.

GDP deflator: a price index based on a representative bundle of GDP goods and services.

GDP gap: the difference between potential GDP and actual GDP.

gross domestic product (GDP): the market value of all goods and services produced in the whole economy per year.

gross national product (GNP): the total market value of all final goods and services produced by the citizens of a country regardless of the location of production.

human capital: the accumulation of all skills and knowledge acquired by individuals.

implicit costs: an opportunity cost that does not require an actual expenditure of cash.

imports: goods and services bought from other countries and which reflect a leakage from the circular flow of income.

income: the earnings of factors of production expressed as an amount per period of time.

income effect: the effect which a price change has on real income, and therefore on the quantity demanded of a product.

income elasticity: the responsiveness of quantity demanded to a given change in income.

incomes policy: a policy concerned with controlling inflation by directly controlling prices and wages.

increasing returns to scale: the circumstances under which an increase in inputs of X% results in output increasing by more than X%.

induced consumption: that portion of consumer spending which is independent of the level of income.

inelastic demand: quantity demanded that is not very responsive to a change in price.

inferior products: those products whose demands will decrease as a result of an increase in income and will increase as a result of a decrease in income.

inflation: a persistent rise in the general level of prices.

inflationary gap: the amount by which actual GDP exceeds full-employment GDP.

injection: is any spending flow which is not dependent on the current level of income.

interest: a payment made for the use of funds (borrowed to purchase capital goods).

interest rate effect: the effect which a change in prices, and therefore interest rates, has upon investment, e.g., high prices cause high interest rates which leads to lower investment.

investment: spending on capital goods.

knowledge worker: those who must continuously learn and use theoretical and analytical knowledge in their work.

labour: any human physical or mental effort that can be used to produce goods and services.

labour force: the total number of people over 15 years of age who are willing and able to be employed.

labour force population: the total population of the country less those under 15 years of age, inmates of institutions, those in the armed forces, and residents of Indian reserves or the territories.

labour force supply: the total hours that those in the labour force are willing to work.

labour productivity: a measure of the amount of output produced per unit of labour input.

Laffer Curve: the graphical representation of the idea that, in terms of tax revenue, there is an optimal tax rate; above or below this rate, tax revenue would be less.

laissez-faire: the belief that an economy works best with limited government interference.

land: any natural resource that can be used to produce goods and services.

law of diminishing marginal utility: the amount of additional utility decreases as successive units of a product are consumed.

law of diminishing returns: as more of a variable input is added to a fixed input in the production process, the resulting increase in output will at some point, being to diminish.

law of increasing costs: as the production level of any particular item increases, its per unit cost of production rises.

leakage: income received within the circular flow which does not flow directly back.

liabilities: the part of a company's balance sheet that represents what it owes to others.

loanable funds: that portion of savings which is available for loan through financial intermediaries.

long run: the period of time in which all inputs are variable.

long-run aggregate supply: the aggregate quantity of goods and services produced after all prices and wages have adjusted, i.e., the full-employment level of GDP.

long-run average cost curve: the per unit costs of production in the long run.

M1: currency in circulation plus demand deposits.

M2: M1 plus notice deposits and non-personal term deposits.

M3: M2 plus certificates of deposit.

macroeconomic equilibrium: a situation where the quantity of real GDP demanded equals the quantity of real GDP supplied.

macroeconomics: the study of the economy as a whole including the topics of unemployment, inflation, interest rate policy and the spending/taxation policies of the government.

margin(al): the extra or additional unit.

marginal costs: the increase in total variable costs as a result of producing one more unit of output.

marginal leakage rate: the ratio of change in leakages that results from a change in income.

marginal product: the increase in total product as result of adding one more unit of input.

marginal profit: the additional economic profit from the production and sale of an extra unit of output.

marginal propensity to consume: the ratio of the change in consumption that results from a change in income.

marginal propensity to expand: the ratio of the change in expenditures that results from a change in income.

marginal propensity to import: the ratio of the change in imports that results from a change in income.

marginal propensity to save: the ratio of the change in savings that results from a change in income.

marginal revenue: the extra revenue derived from the sale of one more unit.

marginal revenue product: the increase in a firm's total revenue which results from the use of one more unit of input.

marginal social benefits: the additional benefits to both the consumer (internal benefits) and to society (external benefits) of producing additional quantities of a product.

marginal social costs: the additional costs to both the producer (internal costs) and to society (external costs) of producing additional quantities of a product.

marginal tax rate: the ratio of the change in taxation as a result of a change in income.

marginal utility: the amount of additional utility derived from the consumption of an extra unit of a product.

market: a mechanism to bring buyers and sellers together and to assist them in negotiating the exchange of products.

market demand: the total demand for a product by all consumers.

market failures: the defects in competitive markets which prevent them from achieving productive or allocative efficiencies.

market supply: the total supply of a product offered by all producers.

medium of exchange: something that is accepted as payment for goods and services.

microeconomics: the study of the specific parts that make up the economy such as the supply and demand of products and resources, costs and market structures.

minimum efficient scale: the smallest level of output at which a firm is able to minimize long-run average cost.

minimum wage: the lowest rate of pay per hour for workers as laid down by government.

monetarism: an economic school of thought which believes that cyclical fluctuations of GDP and inflation are usually caused by changes in the money supply.

monetary policy: economic policy designed to change or influence the economy through changes in the money supply or rate of interest.

monetizing the debt: the action by government of borrowing from the central bank to finance increased spending.

money: anything which is widely accepted as a medium of exchange and therefore can be used to buy goods or to settle debts.

money multiplier: the increase in total deposits that would occur in the whole banking system as a result of a new deposit in a single bank.

monopolistic competition: a market structure in which there are many firms who sell a differentiated product and have some control over the price of the products they sell.

monopoly: a market where a single firm (the monopolist) is the sole producer.

monopsony: a market structure in which there is only one buyer.

multiplier: the ratio of the change in income resulting from a change in autonomous expenditures.

mutual interdependence: the condition where Firm A will not take action without considering how Firm B will react.

national debt: the sum of the federal government's budget deficits less surpluses.

national income (Y): total earning of all the factors of production.

national income equilibrium: that level of income where total leakages from the circular flow equals total injections.

natural monopoly: a market (usually with large economies of scale) where a single producer is able to produce at a lower cost than could competing firms.

natural rate of unemployment: the unemployment rate at full employment.

near-banks: financial institutions like credit unions or trust companies which share many of the functions of chartered banks but which are not defined as banks under the Bank Charter Act. (Also known as non-bank financial intermediaries.)

net domestic income: incomes earned in Canada (equals the sum of wages, profits, interest, farm, and self-employed income).

net exports: total exports minus total imports of goods and services which can be written as (X–M) or as Xn.

net national product: gross national product less capital consumption (or depreciation).

net tax revenue: total tax revenue received by government less transfer payments.

net worth: the total assets less total liabilities of a company — also called equity.

nominal GDP: the value of GDP in terms of prices prevailing at the time of measurement.

nominal income: the present-dollar value of a person's income.

nominal wage: the wage rate expressed as a dollar and cents figure.

non-depletability: a feature of certain products where additional people are able to receive benefits without it costing the use of more resources.

non-divisibility: a feature of certain products which means that they can only be bought collectively and not by single individuals.

non-excludability: a feature of certain products which means that it is impossible to exclude people from enjoying the benefits of the product.

normal products: those products whose demand will increase as a result of an increase in income and will decrease as a result of a decrease in income.

normal profits: when revenue is just equal to all costs — explicit and implicit.

Okun's Law: the observation that every 1% of cyclical unemployment causes an economy's GDP to be 2.5% below its potential.

oligopoly: an industry made up of a few large firms who produce a significant amount of the industry's total output.

open economy: an economy whose borders are open to international trade.

open-market operations: the buying and selling of securities by the Bank of Canada in the open (to the public) market.

opportunity cost: that which must be given up as a result of making a particular choice

optimal purchasing rule: in order to maximize utility, a consumer should purchase each product which has greatest marginal utility per dollar.

paradigm shift: a significant change in pattern or in the model that one is looking at.

participation rate: the percentage of those in the labour force population that are actually in the labour force.

perfect competition: a market in which all buyers and sellers are price takers.

personal income: incomes paid to individuals before the deduction of personal income taxes.

planned investment: the amount of intended investment spending by firms.

portfolio investment: the purchase of shares or bonds.

prescriptive statement: a statement which gives directions or injunction.

price ceiling: a government regulation stipulating the maximum price which can be charged for a product.

price control: government regulation to set either a maximum or minimum price for a product.

price discrimination: the selling of an identical product at a different price to different customers for reasons other than cost.

price elasticity of demand: the responsiveness of quantity demanded to a change in price.

price floor: a government regulation stipulating the minimum price which can be charged for a product.

private good: products which can be consumed separately by each individual and are normally provided by private firms.

pro-cyclical policy: action by the government that tends to push the economy in the same direction that it is leaning.

producers' preference: an allocation system where sellers are allowed to determine the method of allocation on the basis of their own preferences.

product differentiation: the attempts by firms to make their own product appear different from that of their rivals.

production possibilities curve: a graphical representation of various combinations of maximum output that can be produced.

productive efficiency: production of an output at the lowest possible cost.

product market: the market for consumer goods and services.

profits: the return made from the use of the factor, enterprise.

propensity to consume: the level of consumption related to a given level of income.

propensity to save: the level of savings related to a given level of income.

protectionism: the economic policy of protecting domestic producers by restricting the importation of foreign products.

public good: products which are collectively consumed so that private firms would be incapable of producing them at a profit and which therefore must be provided by the government.

public utilities: goods or services which are regarded as essential and which therefore are usually provided by the government.

purchasing power parity theory: a theory that suggests that exchange rates will change so as to equate the purchasing power of each currency.

quasi-public goods: products which, although not strictly public goods, are often provided by the government either because they involve such extensive effects on the public or for other reasons.

quota: a limit imposed on the production or sale of a product.

rationing: a method of allocating products which are in short supply by the use of ration coupons issued by the government guaranteeing a certain quantity per family.

real-balances effect: the effect which a change in the value of real balances has on consumption spending (the value of real balances is affected by changing price levels).

real GDP: the value of GDP measured in terms of prices prevailing in a given base year.

real income: income measured in terms of the amount of goods and services which it will buy. Real income will increase if either actual income increases or prices fall.

real interest rate: the rate of interest measured in constant dollars.

real wage: the purchasing power, given a set of prices, of the nominal wage.

recessionary gap: the difference in GDP between actual income and potential income when the economy's actual is below its potential.

rent: a payment made for the use of land.

rent control: a government regulation making it illegal to rent accommodation above a stipulated level.

reserve ratio: the percentage of a bank's deposits that is in the form of cash.

savings: that portion of income which is not spent on consumption.

savings function: the relationship between income and savings stated in mathematical form.

Say's Law: the proposition that "supply creates its own demand," i.e., that production (supply) creates sufficient income and spending (demand) to purchase the production. Attributed to French economist Jean-Baptiste Say.

short run: any period of time in which at least one input in the production process is fixed.

short-run aggregate supply: the quantity of goods and services produced at various different price levels assuming that factor prices remain constant.

shutdown price: the level of price which is just sufficient to cover a firm's variable costs.

socially optimum price: the price which produces the best allocation of products (and therefore resources) from society's point of view, i.e., $P = MC$.

spread: the difference between the rate of interest a bank charges borrowers and the rate it pays savers.

stagflation: the simultaneous occurrence of both high inflation and unemployment.

store of wealth: the function of money that allows people to hold and accumulate wealth.

structural unemployment: that part of total unemployment that results from structural changes in an economy's industries.

subsidy: a payment by government for the purpose of increasing some particular activity or increasing the output of a particular good, which may be a lump-sum grant or may be dependent on the amount produced.

substitute products: those products which consumers see as interchangeable one for the other.

substitution effect: the substitution of one product for another as a result of a change in their relative prices.

sunk costs: the historical costs of buying plant, machinery and equipment that is unrecoverable.

supply: the quantities which producers are willing and able to sell per period of time at different prices.

supply elasticity: the change in the quantity supplied of a product as a result of a change in price.

supply schedule: a table showing the various quantities supplied per period of time at different prices.

symbolic analyst: individuals who use symbolic knowledge to identify problems, create solutions and then broker those solutions in a systematic form.

symbolic knowledge: knowledge that encompasses data and information which is then systematically improved and refined into a form that has direct application to defining problems or creating solutions.

target reserve ratio: the portion of deposits that a bank wants to hold in cash.

tariff: a tax (or duty) levied on imports.

terms of trade: the average price of a country's exports compared with the price of its imports.

total cost: the sum of both total variable cost and total fixed cost.

total product: the total output of any productive process.

total revenue: the total amount of money a firm receives from its sales; formally, it is price multiplied by the quantity of the product sold.

total variable costs: the total costs that vary with the level of output.

transactions demand for money: the desire of people to hold money as a medium of exchange, i.e., to effect transactions.

transfer earnings: a necessary payment that a factor of production must earn in order for it to remain in its present use.

transfer payments: one-way transactions where payment is made, but no good or service flows back in return.

transmission process: the Keynesian view of how changes in money affect (transmit to) the real variables in the economy.

unemployed: those who are in the labour force and are actively seeking employment but do not hold paid employment.

unemployment: a situation where some persons over the age of 15 are actively seeking work but do not have employment.

unemployment rate: the percentage of those who are in the labour force but do not hold paid employment.

unitary elasticity: where the elasticity coefficient is equal to 1 which is the midpoint on any straight-line demand curve.

unit of account: the function of money that allows us to easily determine the relative value of products.

unplanned investment: the amount of unintended investment by firms in the way of a build-up or run-down of inventories.

utility: the satisfaction or pleasure derived form the consumption of a product.

value of production: the total receipts of all producers.

velocity of money: the number of times that the average unit of currency is spent (or turned over) buying final goods or services.

voluntary export restrictions (V.E.R.s): an agreement by an exporting country to restrict the amount of exports to another country.

wage: a payment made for the use of labour.

wealth: the sum of all valuable assets less liabilities.

wealth effect: the effect of a change in wealth on consumption spending (a direct relationship between the two).

INDEX

■ ■ ■ ■ ■ ■ ■ ■ ■━━━━━━━━━━━━━━━━━━━━━━

STUDENT REPLY CARD

In order to improve future editions, we are seeking your comments on
Principles of Microeconomics
by John Sayre and Alan Morris. After you have read this text, please answer the
following questions and return this form via Business Reply Mail. *Your opinions
matter! Thank you in advance for your feedback!*

Name of your college or university:——————————————

Major program of study:—————————————————

Course title:—————————————————————

Were you required to buy this book?   ——— yes ——— no

Did you buy this book new or used?   ——— new ——— used ($ ———)

Do you plan to keep or sell this book?   ——— keep ——— sell

Is the order of topic coverage consistent with what was taught in your course?

Are there chapters or sections of this text that were not assigned for your course?
Please specify:

Were there topics covered in your course that are not included in this text?
Please specify:

What did you like most about this text?

What did you like least?

If you would like to say more, we'd love to hear from you. Please write to us at the
address shown on the reverse of this card.